QUANTITATIVE HISTORY

Selected readings in the quantitative
analysis of historical data

QUANTITATIVE HISTORY

Selected readings in the quantitative analysis of historical data

Edited by

DON KARL ROWNEY

and

JAMES Q. GRAHAM, JR.

Both of Bowling Green State University

1969
THE
DORSEY
PRESS   Homewood, Illinois
Irwin-Dorsey·Limited, Georgetown, Ontario

© THE DORSEY PRESS, 1969

All rights reserved. No part of this publication may be reproduced, stored in a retrieval system, or transmitted, in any form or by any means, electronic, mechanical, photocopying, recording, or otherwise, without the prior written permission of the publisher.

First Printing, September, 1969

Library of Congress Catalog Card No. 76-90239

Printed in the United States of America

Preface

THE QUANTITATIVE MOOD IN HISTORY

Historians are always absorbed in discovering what history is all about. This question may be counted on to generate discussion among historians under almost any circumstances. In the past such discussions have been constructive. While maintaining and enlarging their own particular view of the world, historians have likewise gradually discarded previously accepted postulates. Of course this process of self-examination, experimentation, addition, and rejection is typically attended by cries of anguish and even recrimination. One commentator, for example, has condemned recent experimentation as "whoring after false gods."[1] In spite of such reactions, however, most historians consider the process of examination to be characteristic as well as necessary, and as providing what Arthur Schlesinger, Jr., has called "a wholly salutary shock to a somewhat uncritical and even complacent discipline."[2] It is the editors' hope that the present volume of essays will make a constructive contribution to the examination of history by historians. With this in mind, the following prefatory remarks have been designed to clarify some of the points at issue in the "debate" on quantitative history as well as to explain more fully what this book proposes to do.

Too often the real merits of the case for or against quantitative history have been obscured by ancient specters which continually intrude upon the controversy. G. R. Elton, for example, affirms that history is "ideographic" (particularizing) rather than "nomothetic," and that, hence, the search for valid generalization through statistical technique is foredoomed to failure.[3] He further asserts, however, that history can properly function as a descriptive and analytical science "producing a series of experimental truths."[4] Regardless of what logic is made from this argument, the sort of generalization Elton apparently wanted to protect history from was the all-encompassing systems associated with Spengler, Toynbee, and the economic determinists. This concern may have been legitimate 20 years and more ago: Henry Thomas Buckle wanted historians to study the regularities of human behavior in order to discover "the

---

[1]G. R. Elton, *The Practice of History* (New York: Thomas Y. Crowell Co., 1967), p. 8.
[2]Arthur Schlesinger, Jr., "The Humanist Looks at Empirical Social Research," *American Sociological Review,* XXVII (December, 1962), p. 768.
[3]Elton, *op. cit.,* pp. 26-27.
[4]*Ibid.,* p. 27.

fixed and universal laws" governing the science of man.[5] It may become the issue again in the future if history is indeed in "the chrysalid stage of proto-science," as Louis Mink has suggested.[6] At the moment, however, we would be content to focus on a much more homespun issue: Will history find the "Common Frontiers of the Social Sciences" a dreary and enervating battleground or a rich deposit of insights and methods to be profitably mined by historians?

In one sense, the question of whether or not history will find the techniques and models of social science to be useful has already been vigorously answered in the affirmative. We hope that the contents of this volume will illustrate the point. That historians have always used many different explanatory techniques for various purposes is surely obvious. One might even say that history's "mixed inheritance," the refusal of practicing historians to be bound to one kind of technique or to be restricted to one kind of evidence, has been one of the chief reasons why history continues to flourish as an intellectual discipline. Though this is anything but a new idea, its statement may require some underlining. In 1912, James Harvey Robinson assessed history's chances of "getting ahead and doing good" as being

> ... dependent upon its refraining from setting itself off as a separate discipline and undertaking to defend itself from the encroachments of seemingly hostile sciences which now and then appear within its territory. To do this is to misapprehend the conditions of scientific advance. No set of investigators can any longer claim exclusive jurisdiction in even the tiniest scientific field, and nothing indeed would be more fatal to them than the successful defense of any such claim. The bounds of all departments of human research and speculation are inherently provisional, indefinite, and fluctuating; moreover, the lines of demarcation are hopelessly interlaced, for real men and the real universe in which they live are so intricate as to defy all attempts even of the most patient and subtle German to establish satisfactorily and permanently the *Begriff und Wesen* of any artificially delimited set of natural phenomena, whether words, thought, deeds, forces, animals, plants, or stars. Each so-called science or discipline is ever and always dependent on other sciences and disciplines. It draws its life from them, and to them it owes, consciously or unconsciously, a great part of its chances of progress.[7]

Among the more intriguing features of the debate on quantitative history is the extent to which opponents of quantification appear to be convinced that the resources of history, in both method and material, are already fixed and known beyond reasonable doubt. According to this view, the task of apprentice

---

[5]Henry Thomas Buckle, *History of Civilization in England* (3rd ed.; London: Parker, Son, and Bourn, 1861), p. 6.

[6]Louis Mink, "The Autonomy of Historical Understanding," *History and Theory,* V (1966), p. 29.

[7]James Harvey Robinson, *The New History: Essays Illustrating the Modern Historical Outlook* (New York: Macmillan Co., 1912), p. 73. Quoted by permission of the Macmillan Company, Publishers.

historians is largely limited to following the well-established paths of the masters who have preceded them. This habit of mind, to quote Robinson again, "stands in the way of the proper development of historical study," because "it is the business of the historian to find out anything about mankind in the past which he believes to be interesting or important and about which there are sources of information."[8] Far from restricting themselves to a limited view of history, historians who use quantitative methods have been noteworthy for their willingness to extend the boundaries not only of historical method but of historical subject matter also.[9] If they do nothing else, the essays in this volume should serve to underline this fact.

What then is quantification all about? To answer this question is not an easy task, because, to some extent, quantification is a movement lacking agreed-upon boundaries or precise forms. As a movement it is diffuse, never having formulated a manifesto or platform of grievances. Moreover, the quantifiers themselves do not constitute a "younger generation" of historians any more than they reflect a particular interest in a specific area or period of history. Their common interest in analytic technique and quantitative historical data may well be the only band of unity among so disparate a group.

The most common meaning attached to quantification in history is that which identifies it as a set of devices for counting the incidence of many types of phenomena—from the opinions of Little Orphan Annie to the socioeconomic structure of Constantinople—and for comparing the quantities so obtained. Whatever additional implications quantification may have, this is probably the aspect of it most congenial to historians because it answers the traditional questions of how many, what kind, and who. Lee Benson has been most tireless in reminding historians that virtually everyone in the profession is, or ought to be, a quantifier in at least this basic sense.

> . . . any statement containing some form of measurement logically can be viewed as quantitative in nature. When historians cite "typical" newspaper editorials and the beliefs of "representative men," or when they use terms such as "significant," "widespread," "growing," "intense," in effect they are making quantitative statements.[10]

In this context, then, the issue of quantification is simply the extent to which historians are willing to substitute relatively precise quantitative statements for the imprecise ones they are in the habit of making.

From this vantage point, it is not difficult to see why some historians, more clearly identified as "quantifiers," should believe in the advantages of seeking out quantitative information and asking mainly quantitative questions about it.

---

[8]*Ibid.,* pp. 71-72.

[9]Leonard Krieger, "The Horizons of History," *American Historical Review,* LXIII (October, 1957), pp. 62-74.

[10]Lee Benson, "Research Problems in American Political Historiography," in *Common Frontiers of the Social Sciences,* edited by Mirra Komarovsky (Glencoe, Ill.: The Free Press, 1957), p. 117.

While this is clearly not characteristic even of all the historians represented in this book, many have certainly arrived at this point. For one thing, such an approach to history satisfies the desire of many historians to concentrate on the numerous details of a given historical problem. It is a paradox of some magnitude that those historians who use quantitative methods should be criticized by those who do not on the basis that the "individual" is lost in statistics: an individual detail—whether it is part of what we know of a person or an event—is frequently represented more exactly and uniformly in quantitative history than it is in the nonquantitative varieties of the discipline. For example, the vote of a single congressman on a specific question may, in fact, be more carefully accounted for by statistical methods than by any approach which deals with politics at the level of concepts—"Jacksonian" or "Populist," for example—or of personalities, such as "hardliners" or "liberals." It need hardly be explained that all such terms, if conscientiously analyzed, would reveal the subsumption of huge clusters of facts which are far more thoroughly lost or blurred than they would be in a statistical analysis. Quantitative historians, moreover, may well have benefited the entire profession by calling attention to the immense collections of numerical and statistical data generated daily for the past several decades by modern bureaucracies, modern legislative assemblies, modern economic enterprises, and, most recently, by professional polling organizations. In each case, the advantages of being familiar with the analytic techniques capable of making the most of these funds of information about the modern world are obvious. Equally obvious are the disadvantages of being unable to deal with these resources in a profession so inclined to accept generalizations about a given society, administration, or institution. Finally, it seems necessary only to mention the influence which electronic computers and other data-handling machines have had on the development of quantitative history. History is not the first academic discipline to have been changed by the presence of data-processing equipment on the university campus.

Quantification may also imply a rather marked empirical orientation on the part of the quantifier. This may be expressed as a theoretical commitment to the validity of operationalizing every research problem, considering most forms of information to be numbered events (observations) in one or more sequences or classes dependent upon or independent of other sequences. It is an attempt, in Paul Lazarsfeld's words, "to translate ideas into empirical operations and to look for the regular relations between the variates so created."[11] It is here that the most elaborate methods of empirical conceptualization and statistical analysis play a crucial role. It is this area which, in recent decades, has revolutionized other social sciences. It is also this area where most historians, because they lack sympathy with the methods and theoretical assumptions involved, feel themselves on alien, even treacherous, ground. ". . . the finest historians will not be

---

[11]Paul F. Lazarsfeld, "Notes on the History of Quantification in Sociology—Trends, Sources and Problems," in *Quantification: A History of the Meaning of Measurement in the Natural and Social Sciences,* edited by Harry Woolf (Indianapolis: Bobbs-Merrill Co., 1961), pp. 202-3.

those who succumb to the dehumanizing methods of the social sciences, *whatever their uses and values, which I hasten to acknowledge.*"[12] This remark of Carl Bridenbaugh's is by no means unique in its expression of disquiet and ambiguity felt by historians concerning the social sciences. However, if we recall that any of these operations, however sophisticated and rationalistic in their use of mathematics, are still only strategies for research and need never be regarded as its boundaries, then we will see the situation in clearer perspective. Crude empiricism, if uninformed by a substantial grasp of the problems of the research area, is not likely to be productive of anything but meaningless numbers. Quantification of any kind, in short, must not diminish the scholar's control over his material. On the contrary, the scholar needs to have the distinct sense that his control has been increased before any quantitative procedure will warrant confidence. Moreover, these procedures should serve to make the relationship between research hypotheses and the subject investigated more rigorous and explicit in all its dimensions. The search for "regular relations between the variates" may thus be useful not only in providing relatively precise confirmation for relations that the historian suspected, but also in discovering others which had not occurred to him. Quantification adds a new dimension of inquiry to the understanding derived from the scholar's familiarity with his field as well as a set of tools by which historical research is broadened and deepened.

It is this last point—the possibility of extending the range of research questions that a historian can ask of his material—which is probably more fundamental to the quantitative mood in history than either the involvement with statistics or the fascination with computers. Fortunately, this broader interest is by no means confined to quantitative historians; it is, and has been, a characteristic of historical study in general. History has been written anew each generation. This is done not only because the perspective of time rearranges the importance of particular events by diminishing the partisanship attached to a given interpretation, but also because the theoretical framework through which the events are viewed changes through time. Eclecticism of this sort is regarded by some as a major weakness, vitiating history's claim to be considered an independent discipline. Insofar as historians have adopted explanatory techniques uncritically or have made connections between events without rigorously examining the assumptions on which the connections were made, the criticism is justified. However, the appearance of many books and journals such as *History and Theory, Comparative Studies in History and Society,* the *Historical Methods Newsletter,* and the *Journal of Social History* all indicate a growing interest in questions of method, theory, and interdisciplinary analysis. Moreover, the recent report of the Social Science Research Council's Committee on Historical Analysis, *Generalization in the Writing of History,* in which Louis Gottschalk summed up the views of the committee as calling upon historians to become more conscious of their methodology, may well serve as the manifesto of yet

---

[12]Carl Bridenbaugh, "The Great Mutation," *American Historical Review,* LXVIII (January, 1963), p. 326. [Italics ours. Eds.]

another "new history."[13] Depending on one's perspective, the quantitative mood in history can be seen either as the advance guard of a movement toward greater methodological sophistication or as an attempt to transform history into a social science. In either case, it behooves historians to find out more about it. The editors have come forward with this collection of articles as an auxiliary in this task.

The purpose which dictated the structure of this volume was that of providing historians with a sampling of the best and most recent work being done in quantitative history. This is in no sense a complete collection. Because of the very real limitations of space we have not been able to publish many excellent essays which have made substantial contributions to research in quantitative history. In some cases we can console ourselves with the fact that the authors of these pieces are so well known and their works reprinted so extensively elsewhere that their views are part of the general literature of the profession. The nine essays written by nonhistorians were included because they represented an innovative approach to historical data or because they featured a theoretical discussion which, we felt, was of considerable significance to historians. We deliberately chose not to concentrate on one set of quantitative techniques or upon one area or time period. By emphasizing the range and flexibility of quantitative history, we hoped to maximize cross-fertilization and to encourage as much general discussion and speculation as possible. Of course, by choosing the more comprehensive approach, we intended to illustrate the wide range of historical documents which can be quantitatively analyzed. We were, after all, choosing essays to suit various needs—so the student could have an overview and, as importantly, so the practicing historian, familiar enough with all the literature in his own field, could get some idea of the variety of uses for quantitative techniques. Except for the introductory section, we have preferred articles which deal with specific, substantive problems, rather than ones which deal with sophisticated problems of method and theory. Additionally, we have preferred an article by a historian to a similar one by a nonhistorian on the assumption that the historian's language as well as his approach would be more familiar to an audience of historians.

One of the many problems facing the editors of any book of readings is that of the relevance to current research of the material chosen. It is not an act of modesty but one of simple truth to point out that we lay no claims to expertise in many of the subject areas from which we have chosen articles; we would be equally presumptuous to make claims in the area of statistics. Since this book is not designed as a primer on quantitative techniques, but rather to provide examples of the use of some of these techniques, we hope that our lack of all-encompassing expertise will not prove to have been an insurmountable obstacle.

The editors wish to thank many kind individuals who encouraged or

---

[13]Louis Gottschalk (ed.), *Generalization in the Writing of History* (Chicago: The University of Chicago Press, 1963), p. 209.

contributed directly to this volume. Principally, however, we must name Mrs. Phyllis Wulff, Mrs. Joanne Limbach, and Mr. Gerald Nye. In addition, we wish to thank the Institute for Research on Social Behavior and the Faculty Leaves and Research Committee of Bowling Green State University.

Helsinki, Finland   D.K.R.
Bowling Green, Ohio   J.Q.G.
August, 1969

Table of contents

PART I.   Varieties of quantitative history

1. Quantification in history, *William O. Aydelotte*   3
2. An approach to the scientific study of past public opinion, *Lee Benson*   23
3. Public opinion research: a contribution to historical method, *Robert A. Kann*   64
4. On making historical techniques more specific: "real types" constructed with a Computer, *G. G. S. Murphy and M. G. Mueller*   81
5. Notes on the historical study of social mobility, *Stephan Thernstrom* .   99
6. United States: the 'new' political history, *Alan G. Bogue*   109

PART II.   Bureaucrats, deputies, and decision makers:
studies in elite history

1. Class, corruption and politics in the French Chamber of Deputies, 1846-1848, *Patrick L.-R. Higonnet and Trevor B. Higonnet*   129
2. Bureaucratic development and the structure of decision-making in the Meiji Period: the case of the Genrō, *Bernard S. Silberman*   148
3. The introduction of industrialists into the British peerage: a study in adaptation of a social institution, *Ralph E. Pumphrey*   164

PART III.   Social history and social change

1. The analysis of a counter-revolution, *Charles Tilly*   181
2. Aspects of mobility in pre-industrial Japanese cities, *Robert J. Smith* .   209
3. Patterns of industrial strike activity in France during the July Monarchy, *Peter N. Stearns*   217
4. Social mobility in England, 1500-1700, *Lawrence Stone*   238

PART IV.   Historical demography

1. A quantitative approach to Medieval population change, *J. C. Russell* .   275
2. Families in colonial Bristol, Rhode Island: an exercise in historical demography, *John Demos*   293

3. Population movements and political changes in nineteenth century
    France, *G. de Bertier de Sauvigny*   308

PART V.   *"Cliometrics," the new economic history*

1. The new economic history, its findings and methods, *R. W. Fogel* . . .   320
2. A quantitative approach to the study of the effects of British imperial
    policy upon colonial welfare: some preliminary findings, *Robert Paul
    Thomas*   336
3. Inequality and instability: the relation of land tenure to politics,
    Bruce M. Russett   356

PART VI.   *Voters and publics: studies in legislative
and electoral history*

1. New perspectives on Jacksonian politics, *Richard P. McCormick*   372
2. Was 1928 a critical election in California? *John L. Shover*   385
3. The simulmatics project *Ithiel de Sola Pool and Robert Abelson*   399
4. Voting patterns in the British House of Commons in the 1840s
    William O. Aydelotte   415
5. Party loyalty in the progressive years: the Senate, 1909-1915, *Jerome
    M. Clubb and Howard W. Allen*   443
6. Sub-group formation in the Constitutional Convention, *S. Sidney
    Ulmer*   457

Bibliography

Bibliography   473

Index

Index   483

PART I

Varieties of quantitative history

1. Quantification in history*

WILLIAM O. AYDELOTTE†

Over the past generation a number of historians have recognized that counting, when circumstances permit it, may assist in the explanation of a limited class of historical problems. The historical monographs in which quantitative methods have been used are already sufficiently numerous so that a review of them would require an article by itself. The purpose here is not to survey this literature but, instead, to raise several general questions related to it. Professional opinion regarding the value of quantification for history has been rather less than unanimous, and discussion of the subject has occasionally been acrimonious. There have also been a few misunderstandings. I wish to consider here what is involved in trying to apply quantitative methods to history, what kinds of results may be expected, and what difficulties lie in the way. Though I shall say something about the advantages of quantification, I am also, in a sense, concerned to speak against it and to make clear the problems it presents. My own approach to the subject is conservative and skeptical, and at times I feel that the current fad for quantification has been pushed too far. In any case, the exploration of the limitations of a method is an effective device for revealing its characteristic features.

The principal value of quantification for the study of history, stated in the simplest terms, is that it provides a means of verifying general statements. Some historians, of course, disclaim any intention of making such statements and insist that the business of a historian is not to generalize but to tell a story. Such a view can hardly be seriously entertained as a description of the objectives of all historians, for it manifestly does not apply to the work of a number of eminent

* Reprinted from the *American Historical Review*, LXXI (April, 1966), pp. 803-25, by permission of the author.

† A professor at the University of Iowa, Mr. Aydelotte is interested primarily in modern British history. He has written, among other things, "Voting Patterns in the British House of Commons in the 1840s," *Comparative Studies in Society and History*, V (Jan. 1963). [Editors Note: Mr. Aydelotte, who received his Ph.D. from the University of Cambridge, England in 1934, has also authored numerous articles on the theory of history and on British political history in the mid-19th century.]

members of the profession. One might question, indeed, whether any historian can avoid generalizing altogether.[1] It is an idle task, however, to attempt a formal prescription of a historian's duties. If some wish to emphasize narrative more than others, there is no reason why they should not. History is what historians do, and they do different things. It would be presumptuous to dismiss any of their objectives as being in some fashion improper. The day of a single methodology in history, if it ever existed, is at any rate now gone. In a discipline where there are at present so much upheaval, reassessment of methods and values, and introduction of new approaches, it seems better to say that anything historians do is useful if it can be shown to be useful.

For historians who do wish to generalize, however, quantitative methods can offer certain advantages. Generalizations are implicitly quantitative in character, even though this may not always be clearly brought out. As Lee Benson says, historians who use words like "typical," "representative," "significant," "widespread," "growing," or "intense" are making quantitative statements whether or not they present figures to justify their assertions. Unfortunately, not all historians seem to realize the need to check general statements. Benson complains, in the same passage, of "the impressionistic approach long dominant in American historiography,"[2] and I have occasionally been bothered by this kind of thing in my own field. Historians justly pride themselves on their techniques of verification, which have become in some areas highly sophisticated. It seems fair to say, however, that these techniques have more often been applied to individual bits of information than to broader statements. Some writers, after a precise description of a few cases, will proceed to generalize blithely about the motives of large groups of men even though the evidence to support their views is often not presented and, indeed, would be hard to come by, for the motives of most men are obscure and not easy to discern. To an uncritical audience several concrete illustrations may carry more conviction than a statistical table. Yet to support an argument by only a few examples, though it may be a persuasive rhetorical device, is not logically adequate. There are exceptions to most historical generalizations, and, if the citation of occasional instances were accepted as proof, it would be possible to prove almost anything.

Quantitative methods, the numerical summary of comparable data, make it possible, in some cases, to avoid these pitfalls. The condensation of data by such means, when it is clearly legitimate, constitutes a saving of time and a convenience in that it makes the information easier to describe and to handle. It also helps to ensure a greater degree of accuracy. Memory is selective, and general impressions are notoriously untrustworthy. When the data are so numerous that they cannot all be kept clearly in mind at once, the investigator is

---

[1] The eleven contributors to a recent volume of essays on this subject, as the editor states in his summary: "all agree that the historian willy-nilly uses generalizations at different levels and of different kinds." (*Generalization in the Writing of History*, ed. Louis Gottschalk [Chicago, 1963], 208; see also, on this point, Alfred Cobban, *The Social Interpretation of the French Revolution* [Cambridge, Eng., 1964], 5-7.)

[2] Lee Benson, "Research Problems in American Political Historiography," in *Common Frontiers of the Social Sciences,* ed. Mirra Komarovsky (Glencoe, Ill., 1957), 117.

likely to remember best the cases that fit his own preconceptions or his pet hypotheses. An orderly presentation of the evidence in quantitative form helps the student to escape the tricks that his memory plays upon him. Quantitative analyses are, of course, gratuitous when the number of cases is small, when the student is concerned with only a few men or, perhaps, one man, and when the general tenor of the materials can be immediately grasped. As the data become more numerous, however, a systematic arrangement of them becomes the more desirable. There are, indeed, some questions, of which examples will be given presently, which could hardly be attacked without the use of methods of this kind.

A quantitative presentation of the available information can help to direct the student's attention to the questions most worth investigating. Since it brings the whole of the evidence, on the point it covers, into intelligible focus, the general character of the findings can be more readily perceived and relationships and differences emerge that could not so easily have been observed without this reduction of the data. Such an analysis reveals what events or issues were of special interest, in the sense of involving change through time or departure from the norm, and hence might particularly repay investigation. It can, in this manner, help in defining or restating the historical problem to be studied.

Beyond this, a quantitative analysis offers a systematic means of testing hypotheses. It establishes how many examples there are to support each side of the argument and thus reveals not only the main features of the evidence but also, more important, the exceptions to them, the nuances, the degree to which the emerging generalizations need to be qualified. Measurement locates the defect in the original hypothesis and registers "the departure from theory with an authority and finesse that no qualitative technique can duplicate." A quantitative discrepancy between theory and observation is obtrusive. "No crisis is . . . so hard to suppress as one that derives from a quantitative anomaly that has resisted all the usual efforts at reconciliation."[3]

The general overview of the whole evidence obtained by quantitative means can also be a powerful stimulus toward the reformulation of one's ideas. When anomalies occur, the student can direct his attention to the cases that do not fit the original theory, try to find out why they are exceptional, and, by rearrangements of the data, test alternative hypotheses that may account for a larger proportion of the evidence. Such manipulations of the data would take an immense amount of time to do by hand, but, ordinarily, they can readily be performed by machines. I advise my students, if they are working with fifty cases or more, to punch the information. This is easily done, and, once it is done, there is no great difficulty about trying additional correlations. By the same token a quantitative analysis can even, in some cases, point the way to the formulation of new hypotheses that will make the findings more intelligible.

The case for quantification might be made in still a different way by saying

3 Thomas S. Kuhn, "The Function of Measurement in Modern Physical Science," in *Quantification: A History of the Meaning of Measurement in the Natural and Social Sciences,* ed. Harry Woolf (Indianapolis, 1961), 50, 52.

that it is a method of reasoning, one that involves number. As one of my colleagues at the University of Iowa has put it, quantification adds, to whatever factual or historical premises may have been established, the premises of mathematics as well. "Arithmetic is a vast treasure house of additional premises, or, what amounts to the same thing, of patterns of deductive inference. Quantification is the key to the treasure."[4]

The advantages of this approach have been appreciated by a number of present-day historians. G. Kitson Clark suggests as appropriate advice to someone who wishes to generalize about a group or a class: "do not guess, try to count, and if you can not count admit that you are guessing."[5] Lawrence Stone writes: "Owing to the obstinate perversity of human nature, it would no doubt be possible in England of 1958 to find, if one tried, declining manual labourers and rising landed gentry. To have any validity at all, conclusions about social movements must have a statistical basis."[6]

Applications of quantitative techniques to historical materials have, in some cases, materially advanced the discussion of major problems. Monographs on the composition of the British House of Commons which are now fairly numerous and cover a span of six centuries, have brought to light significant continuities and changes in the social structure of the British political elite. Crane Brinton, in his well-known quantitative study of the members of the Jacobin Clubs, reached the conclusion that the Jacobins represented "a complete cross-section of their community" and that: "The Jacobins of 1794 were not a class, and their enemies the 'aristocrats' were not a class; the Terror was not chiefly then a phase of the class-struggle, but even more a civil war, a religious war."[7] Donald Greer, on the basis of a quantitative analysis of the victims of the Terror, argued that the lower classes, by the definitions he used, supplied 70 per cent of the victims and the upper classes less than 30 per cent and that: "The split in society was perpendicular, not horizontal. The Terror was an intra-class, not an inter-class, war."[8] From the researches of Brinton, Greer, and others, crude class theories about the French Revolution have received a setback. Revisions have also been made in accepted views about American history. Richard P. McCormick published in the *American Historical Review* a set of tables, drawn from readily available election statistics, on the basis of which he was able to show that the great popular turnout of 1824 was a myth and that: "In the 1824 election not a single one of the eighteen states in which the electors were chosen by popular vote attained the percentage of voter participation that had been reached before 1824." His finding contradicts the assertion he quotes from a standard text that, in the period before 1824, "only small numbers of citizens seem to have

---

[4] Gustav Bergmann, *Philosophy of Science* (Madison, Wis., 1957), 69.

[5] G. Kitson Clark, *The Making of Victorian England* (London, 1962), 14.

[6] Lawrence Stone, letter to editor, *Encounter,* XI (July 1958), 73.

[7] Clarence Crane Brinton, *The Jacobins: An Essay in the New History* (New York, 1930), 70-72.

[8] Donald Greer, *The Incidence of the Terror during the French Revolution: A Statistical Interpretation* (Cambridge, Mass., 1935), 97-98.

bothered to go to the polls." It contrasts also with Charles and Mary Beard's colorful statement that, by 1824, "the roaring flood of the new democracy was now foaming perilously near the crest . . ." and with Arthur M. Schlesinger, Jr.'s reference to the "immense popular vote" received by Jackson in 1824.[9] Albert Ludwig Kohlmeier, using statistical data on canal and riverboat traffic, was able to show when and how rapidly the trade of the Old Northwest shifted away from the South and to the Northeast.[10] Stephan Thernstrom, by a quantitative analysis based largely on census records, exploded various familiar hypotheses about social mobility in a Massachusetts town in the later nineteenth century. [11] Quantitative presentations have formed the basis for substantial generalizations by an impressive group of additional historians including Thomas B. Alexander, Bernard and Lotte Bailyn, Allan G. Bogue, Jean Delumeau, Robert W. Fogel, Frank L. Owsley, Lawrence Stone, Charles Tilly, Sylvia L. Thrupp, and Sam B. Warner, Jr.[12] This list of examples could be considerably extended.

These results have often been achieved by fairly simple methods; for much historical research the quantitative procedures required are not complex. Historians do not ordinarily need to deal with problems of statistical inference in which an attempt is made to ascertain the characteristics of a large population by inspection of relatively small samples. Their work is usually limited to the easier task of descriptive statistics in which the object is to portray the characteristics of a group, all members of which have been studied, and to correlate some of these characteristics with each other. The computations needed for this are not ambitious. All that is generally required are a few totals, a few percentages, and a few correlations in which the relationship between certain variables is examined while other variables are controlled. This is a simple

---

[9] Richard P. McCormick, "New Perspectives on Jacksonian Politics," *American Historical Review,* LXV (Jan. 1960), 288-301, esp. 289-91; Richard Hofstadter *et al., The American Republic* (2 vols., New York, 1959), I, 391; Charles A. and Mary R. Beard, *The Rise of American Civilization* (new ed., 2 vols., New York, 1931), I, 550; Arthur M. Schlesinger, Jr., *The Age of Jackson* (Boston, 1945), 36.

[10] Albert Ludwig Kohlmeier. *The Old North-West as the Keystone of the Arch of American Federal Union: A Study in Commerce and Politics* (Bloomington, Ind., 1938).

[11] Stephan Thernstrom, *Poverty and Progress: Social Mobility in a Nineteenth Century City* (Cambridge, Mass., 1964).

[12] Thomas B. Alexander *et al.,* "Who Were the Alabama Whigs?" *Alabama Review,* XVI (No. 1, 1963), 5-19; Thomas B. Alexander and Peggy J. Duckworth, "Alabama Black Belt Whigs during Secession: A New Viewpoint," *ibid.,* XVII (No. 3, 1964), 181-97; Bernard and Lotte Bailyn, *Massachusetts Shipping, 1697-1714: A Statistical Study* (Cambridge, Mass., 1959); Allan G. Bogue, *From Prairie to Corn Belt: Farming on the Illinois and Iowa Prairies in the Nineteenth Century* (Chicago, 1963); Jean Delumeau, *L'alun de Rome,* xve-xixe *siècle* (Paris, 1962, and *Le mouvement du port de Saint-Malo à la fin du* xviie *siècle 1681-1700* (Rennes, 1962); Robert William Fogel, *Railroads and American Economic Growth: Essays in Econometric History* (Baltimore, 1964); Frank Lawrence Owsley, *Plain Folk of the Old South* (Baton Rouge, La., 1949); Lawrence Stone, "The Educational Revolution in England, 1560-1640," *Past and Present* XXVIII (July 1964), 41-80, and *The Crisis of the Aristocracy, 1558-1641,* (Oxford, Eng., 1965); Charles Tilly, *The Vendée* (Cambridge, Mass., 1964); Sylvia L. Thrupp, *The Merchant Class of Medieval London, 1300-1500* (Chicago, 1948); Sam B. Warner, Jr., *Streetcar Suburbs: The Process of Growth in Boston, 1870-1900* (Cambridge, Mass., 1962).

matter mathematically, although the research may be laborious, and it is simple mechanically as well. Even so modest a use of quantitative methods can sometimes produce results of great interest and can be used to test historical generalizations of some scope on which there has heretofore been scholarly disagreement. Since only a limited amount of such research has been done, much gold is still near the surface. It may turn out, however, that richer veins lie deeper. Though it has proved extremely useful to classify, arrange, and summarize the available information, it may be even more rewarding—to judge from some of the ventures that have already been made—to attempt more complex methods of descriptive statistical analysis by the use, for example, of mathematical models or of scaling techniques.[13]

Although substantial and interesting work has been done along these lines, much more could be attempted. Historians who have used quantitative methods have been timid in their application of them and have come nowhere near exploiting their full potentialities. Also, many historians who deal with problems for which such methods might be helpful have not tried to use them at all. Economic history is, perhaps, an exception. This field is naturally suited to quantitative research since many of the original data come in quantified form, the problems and hypotheses tend to assume a quantified shape, and, in the field of economics, theoretical analysis is more advanced. In political and social history, however, opportunities have been missed. Though the area of historical research to which these methods can be applied may be limited, it has certainly not yet been fully explored.

Furthermore, much hostility to quantitative methods still remains among some members of the historical profession. Despite what might seem the obvious advantages of these methods for certain kinds of problems, despite their notably successful application in many historical projects, and despite their long acceptance as a matter of course in several related disciplines, some historians still object to them vociferously and consider them altogether inappropriate for historical research. Questions have been raised regarding: (1) the value of the work that has been done; (2) the feasibility of this approach in view of the admittedly limited materials available to historians; (3) the reliability of the results obtained by these techniques; and (4) the usefulness or significance of the results. These objections are not wholly without foundation. It would be pointless to deny either the limitations of the method or the lapses of some of its practitioners. To concede this, however, is not to tell the whole story.

(1) Certainly the ventures of historians into this kind of research have not

13 On the use of models, see the review of the work of Harold Hotelling and others and the further discussion of this problem in Donald E. Stokes, "Spatial Models of Party Competition," *American Political Science Review,* LVII (June 1963), 368-77. On scaling techniques, see Duncan MacRae, Jr., *Dimensions of Congressional Voting: A Statistical Study of the House of Representatives in the Eighty-first Congress* (Berkeley, Calif., 1958), and "Intraparty Divisions and Cabinet Coalitions in the Fourth French Republic," *Comparative Studies in Society and History,* V (Jan. 1963), 164-211; William O. Aydelotte, "Voting Patterns in the British House of Commons in the 1840s," *ibid.,* 134-63.

been uniformly fortunate. Some of these studies, far from revolutionizing historical thought, have themselves not stood the test of time and have been shown to contain imperfections of method, which, to some extent, vitiate their conclusions. It would be unfair to mention individual monographs without a more extended discussion of their arguments than is possible in this paper. I shall have occasion to describe some of the statistical solecisms committed by a few workers in my own field in separate articles on special topics. In general, it has been contended, sometimes plausibly, that a number of the pioneers in quantitative historical research overlooked certain elementary precautions. They did not, it is said, always appreciate or remember that a sample that is small and, hence, biased or unrepresentative may distort the results, that percentages should be figured in terms of what is hypothesized to be the independent variable, that a conscientious search should be made for all possible relevant variables (though it is unlikely that they can all be found), that failure to make such a search may produce spurious correlations, or that refinements of technique cannot compensate for the inaccuracy or incompleteness of the original data. Doubtless the application of quantitative techniques to history has not paid off as well as might have been expected because of the statistical naïveté of a few of those who first tried it. To say this, however, is not to disparage quantitative methods. On the contrary, these are exactly the errors that an experienced statistician would not commit, and they arise not from an overemphasis but from an underemphasis on accepted statistical procedures. It may not be unreasonable to expect that simple technical errors of this kind will occur less frequently in the future as a new generation of historians becomes more alert to what is needed for this type of work.

(2) A more serious objection is that quantitative techniques may not be feasible at all in history, or can be used only within narrow limits, because of the complexity of historical materials and the restrictions on historical knowledge. It is difficult to get accurate information, for the sources may prove inconsistent or unreliable. Also the task of correctly recording so great a mass of data is more arduous than is likely to be believed by anyone who has not tried it; the natural proclivity of almost all men to error, to incorrect observation, has been repeatedly shown by experiment. Beyond this, however, there are formidable problems of taxonomy. A given body of data can generally be classified in any of many different ways, and skill and experience are needed to choose the categories that will prove most useful. Unfortunately it may not become apparent which these are until one is well into the research and it is too late to change. It is also no easy matter to make the categories precise and clearly distinguishable from one another. The existing vocabulary of social history is inexact, and many of the terms in common usage are too vague to permit unequivocal classification of the data. To give one example, problems of this kind have, according to a recent review article, bedeviled research on the supposed conflict of the aristocracy and the bourgeoisie during the French Revolution. The ambiguities in the definitions of these terms have had the result that:

the central doctrine of the class struggle between bourgeois and aristocrats can now only be accepted as an act of faith; for no two people can agree on who the bourgeois and the aristocrats were; no one can formulate (and few even try to formulate) a criterion for distinguishing between them that can be followed consistently, and every argument is thus liable to be at variance with easily ascertainable facts.[14]

Similar problems arise, of course, in the social history of other countries. If a historian tries to distribute a group of men among conventional categories of this kind, borderline cases may necessitate so many subjective judgments that the resulting classifications will not be worth much. No amount of *expertise* in the manipulation of the figures will make adequate correction for imprecision in the original data or for categories that do not adequately measure what it is claimed that they measure. A quantitative approach does not of itself ensure accuracy. Jeremy Bentham's "felicific calculus" was set forth in quantitative terms, but it is not generally regarded as a precise conceptual scheme. There is a danger, in this kind of work, of a spurious precision—giving the results, to several decimal places, of calculations based on incorrect original assumptions. If the classifications used at the start are worthless, the computations based upon them will be equally so, no matter how many times they are passed through the computer, and the situation will develop which is known in the trade as "GIGO": "garbage in and garbage out."

Furthermore, historical information is restricted. Historians who seek to use quantitative methods are, in comparison to those working with contemporary affairs, at a disadvantage. It is difficult—and the difficulty generally increases with the remoteness of the period studied—to obtain relevant data for a large enough sample of the group or "population" under consideration to make a quantitative presentation useful and effective. It is feasible, for example, to study the composition of the British House of Commons in recent centuries, though the task becomes harder as one goes back in time, but it might be less rewarding to attempt an analysis of the personnel of Justinian's army.

Even some of the historians who have made conspicuously successful use of these methods complain frequently about the inadequacy of the sources with which they had to work. Brinton found the membership lists of the Jacobin Clubs incomplete, a problem heightened by the considerable turnover in membership, while the occupations of some Jacobins were not listed and the occupations of others were described in ambiguous terms. He insists that part of his information does not "have even the relative accuracy possible in a study of contemporary demography."[15] Greer speaks of "the impossibility of deter-

---

14 Betty Behrens, " 'Straight History' and 'History in Depth': The Experience of Writers on Eighteenth-Century France," *Historical Journal*, VIII (No. 1, 1965), 125; see Greer's comments on the ambiguities of his own categories, in *Incidence of the Terror*, 88-96; for a more extended discussion of these problems, see Cobban, *Social Interpretation of the French Revolution*, Chaps. III, VI, VIII-XIV.

15 Brinton, *Jacobins*, 48-51, 57-58.

mining with any degree of exactitude the total death roll of the Terror." [16]
Owsley found that the tax lists for many large areas of the South had not
survived, while the census reports, besides being less accurate as a rule than the
tax lists, were seriously incomplete except for the latter part of the ante bellum
period.[17] Warner found rich statistical materials surviving for nineteenth-century
Boston, but noted that city, state, and federal counts did not agree with each
other and added the warning that: "The presence of substantial errors in the
census requires the local historian to use census data with the same sophistication he would use any other source. The past tendency to check writings of
individuals against other sources but to accept statistics as prima facie fact must
be abandoned."[18]

Even in cases of groups for which quantitative methods can to some extent be
used, it is not always possible to employ tests of sufficient refinement to verify
what appear to be the most significant hypotheses. Benson, in his discussion of
Beard's interpretation of the battle over the Constitution, has suggested that "we
are likely to progress further if we group men, not according to their 'economic
interests,' " but according to various other things including, for example, "their
values, their beliefs, their symbols, their sense of identity."[19] Yet it may not be
easy to obtain this kind of information for all or most members of a population
of any size removed at some distance in time. It could, perhaps, be found for a
few individuals on whom detailed information can be gathered from their
correspondence and papers, but in statistics arguing from a few not necessarily
representative examples is the great heresy. Doubtless more can be done than has
always been realized, and, in another book, Benson has applied imagination and
ingenuity to available materials, to draw impressive and persuasive inferences on
some of these difficult matters.[20] It can scarcely be denied, however, that these
are obdurate questions, and anyone who tries to solve them has his work cut out
for him; ingenuity can carry only a limited distance. For many groups in the past
the kind of information needed to make such tests, much of it at least, has long
since disappeared and is now irretrievable.

Clearly, formal statistical presentations are feasible only for a limited range of
historical problems. The available information may be insufficient or may
contain ambiguities that make it difficult to summarize in intelligible categories.
Nothing is to be gained by pretending otherwise or by attempting to force the
use of these methods beyond where evidence will carry. Frank Knight once
observed that the dictum attributed to Lord Kelvin—"If you cannot measure,
your knowledge is meagre and unsatisfactory"—has in practice been translated

---

[16] Greer, *Incidence of the Terror,* 37.

[17] Owsley, *Plain Folk of the Old South,* 150-51.

[18] Warner, *Streetcar Suburbs,* 173-74.

[19] Lee Benson, *Turner and Beard: American Historical Writing Reconsidered* (Glencoe,
Ill., 1960), 169-70.

[20] *Id., The Concept of Jacksonian Democracy: New York as a Test Case* (Princeton,
N.J., 1961), Chaps. XII-XIV.

into the injunction: "If you cannot measure, measure anyhow."[21] This, of course, would be a counsel of darkness. Whether quantitative methods will be helpful on a given problem is a matter not of rule but of the strategy of research.

Though these difficulties are substantial, it would be a gross distortion to regard them as insuperable. Taxonomic problems vary in incidence, and it is mistaken to suppose that all subjects are equally difficult to quantify. Social categories may be tricky, but other kinds of information, such as votes in a legislative body, can be tabulated with some assurance. Economic and demographic data have been handled quantitatively with success for some time.

Even in the study of social history it has sometimes proved possible, as it has in scientific investigation,[22] to advance the argument by jettisoning subjective definitions and adopting objective ones, by disregarding earlier concepts that were too vaguely defined to admit of measurement, and by concentrating instead on categories that could be unmistakably specified—not "aristocrats," but peers and their sons; not "gentry," but men included by John Burke in his reference work *The Landed Gentry of Great Britain and Ireland;* not "businessmen," but men engaged in certain ways in certain types of business. Whether these more sharply defined categories correspond accurately to the old categories is a question that cannot be answered since the old ones are so indefinite that they cannot be said to correspond accurately to anything. One cannot, by using the new categories, effectively test propositions couched in terms of the old ones. Such propositions cannot, indeed, be tested at all, for an imprecise or slipshod formulation is impregnable; a statement that has no exact meaning cannot be disproved. What is feasible, however, is to study a group or an entity that might be conjectured to correspond somewhat to the old and loosely defined concept but that at least has the virtue that it can be identified. The investigator must, of course, assume the burden of showing that his new categories are viable and useful. The great step forward is to take the objective or unequivocal definition as the norm, as describing the entity that will be subjected to analysis, and to demote the subjective or vague concept to a subordinate position, to appreciate that, though it may serve as a useful starting point in the formulation of an operational definition, it may also contain variables that are difficult to measure or even to identify and that it cannot, therefore, be handled in any conclusive fashion. By this procedure one at least knows where one stands, and the problems of social measurement may become less intractable.

Nor is the argument about limitations on historical knowledge really convincing. No doubt much valuable information has been lost. It is clear

---

21 Kuhn, "Measurement," 31, 34; remarks by Frank H. Knight in *Eleven Twenty-Six: A Decade of Social Science Research,* ed. Louis Wirth (Chicago, 1940), 169. The quotation ascribed to Kelvin appears on the facade of the Social Science Building at the University of Chicago. Kuhn has been unable to find these exact words in Kelvin's writings, though Kelvin expressed the idea more than once in slightly different language.

22 See the discussion of the development of the concept "degree of heat" in Kuhn, "Measurement," 58-59.

enough, however, that historical materials that lend themselves to quantitative research, even if they do not cover everything, are enormously abundant. Some great storehouses of information such as census records and tax records are still relatively unused, except by a few pioneers. Other rich sources such as recorded votes in legislative bodies have been used only in a desultory and sporadic fashion, and much more could be done with them. Ample materials exist for collective biographies of groups of prominent individuals, and in some cases obscure ones too; for the economic and demographic characterization of constituencies; and for ascertaining the relationship of the facts unearthed in such investigations to political choice.[23] Evidence is particularly rich for serial and political history, two areas in which quantitative methods have not been extensively attempted.

Furthermore, it has proved possible, again and again, to describe in quantitative terms things that were formerly thought to fall beyond the reach of this net. Matters that seemed to an earlier generation unquantifiable can sometimes be caught and measured by a change in approach or by reaching a clearer perspective concerning what it may be most profitable to measure. This applies, for example, to the study of attitudes, a field in which notable advances have been made over the last several decades. David Hume, speaking through the mouth of Philo, a man of "careless scepticism," argued that "controversies concerning the degrees of any quality or circumstance" can never "reach a reasonable certainty or precision." Thus, he says, it is impossible to settle how great a general Hannibal was or "what epithet of praise Livy or Thucydides is entitled to . . . because the degrees of these qualities are not, like quantity or number, susceptible of any exact mensuration, which may be the standard in the controversy."[24] Even if we cannot measure qualities of excellence, however, we can perfectly well measure opinions about them, which are all we have to go on anyway, and this is done all the time with questionnaires. Similarly, ways have been found to measure degrees of liberalism and conservatism by indexes in which men have come to place some reliance, or degrees of attachment to a particular cause or principle, or degrees of interest or apathy regarding political questions, or even degrees of patient welfare in a hospital. It has been possible to do this last by a set of objective tests that fit into a cumulative scale and that have turned out to be reliable and consistent.[25]

Recent quantitative research in history contains several examples of a tour de force of this kind, attempts—fairly convincing attempts—to measure what previously seemed impossible to measure. One is the effort of Alfred H. Conrad

[23] An extended account of the work that has been done and that might be attempted along this line in American history has been given by Samuel P. Hays in "New Possibilities for American Political History: The Social Analysis of Political Life," a paper presented at the Annual Meeting of the American Historical Association in December 1964; see also *id.*, "Archival Sources for American Political History," *American Archivist,* XXVIII (Jan. 1965), 17-30.

[24] David Hume, *Dialogues concerning Natural Religion* (London, 1779), Pt. XII.

[25] Myrtle Kitchell Aydelotte, *An Investigation of the Relation between Nursing Activity and Patient Welfare* (Iowa City, Iowa, 1960), 41-123.

and John R. Meyer to appraise the profitability of slavery and the efficiency of the slave labor market in the American South before the Civil War. It would be difficult to summarize here their complex and rather technical analysis, but it is interesting that their conclusions tell strongly against the long-standing though not wholly unchallenged view that the system of slavery was being undermined because of its unprofitability and because of the impossibility of maintaining and allocating a slave labor force. They found, on the contrary, that "slavery was apparently about as remunerative as alternative employments to which slave capital might have been put" and that: "Slavery was profitable to the whole South, the continuing demand for labor in the Cotton Belt ensuring returns to the breeding operation on the less productive land in the seaboard and border states."[26] Another example is the attempt by McCormick to describe, for the period in which he does research, the relation between the economic status of members of the electorate and their political choice. This topic, though important, is difficult for historians to study since the rich and poor in an electorate are generally buried in the anonymity of mass figures, and it is now virtually impossible to distinguish who voted for whom. McCormick, however, in attacking the problem, was able to take advantage of the dual franchise existing in North Carolina in the years 1836-1856, when only adult freemen who owned fifty acres of land within the county could vote for a member of the state senate while all freemen, including the above, who had paid county or state taxes, could vote for governor. By comparing county by county, the size of the vote cast for governor with the comparable vote for state senators it was possible to determine the proportion of the electorate that could not meet the fifty-acre requirement. Then, by examining the distribution of each class of the electorate between the two major parties, McCormick was able to reach some conclusions on the relation of economic status to party affiliation. His finding, one of considerable interest, was that "the economic distinction implicit in the dual suffrage system had no substantial significance as a factor in determining party alignments in these North Carolina elections."[27]

In any case, the complexity and the limited scope of historical information are not arguments against quantification in particular. These limitations exist no matter what techniques are used. They arise from the insufficiency of the evidence and not from the peculiarities of the method. The obstacles to quantitative generalizations apply with equal force to nonquantitative ones, and what cannot be done with statistics cannot be done without them, either. No serious student of methodology would contend that a disciplined approach can overcome the inherent frailties in the data. But it hardly follows that, when the

[26] Alfred H. Conrad and John R. Meyer, *The Economics of Slavery and Other Studies in Econometric History* (Chicago, 1964), 66, 82.

[27] Richard P. McCormick, "Suffrage Classes and Party Alignments: A Study in Voter Behavior," *Mississippi Valley Historical Review,* XLVI (Dec. 1959), 398-403; for a review of other attempts to measure what cannot be measured directly and a discussion of the problems involved, see Robert William Fogel, "Reappraisals in American Economic History–Discussion," *American Economic Review,* LIV (May 1964), 377-89.

sources are suspect or the facts incomplete, an impressionistic, subjective approach can surmount these difficulties. Problems due to inadequacy of the data may be brought out more sharply and may become more apparent in a formal and systematic investigation, but they cannot in any circumstances be evaded.

(3) The objection is also sometimes made that the general conclusions of a quantitative investigation are not proved by the figures. This is, of course, true, and no one who knows anything about statistical theory would argue otherwise. To expect finality for the broader conclusions of a quantitative investigation is to misconstrue the nature of the approach. On this point some misunderstanding apparently exists for, in everyday speech, reckless claims are sometimes made as to what "statistics prove." Actually the range of statistical proof is limited. A statistical table is nothing more than a convenient arrangement of the evidence, and it proves only what it contains: that there was, for example, a relationship or, more usual, a partial relationship between two variables. Theories that attempt to account for such a relationship, in the sense of fitting the findings into a wider conceptual scheme, are not proved by the figures. They are merely propositions that appear to explain what is known in a plausible fashion and that do not conflict with any relevant evidence that can, after a conscientious search, be uncovered. This is not to say that they are nonsense, for they may be supported by persuasive arguments. Yet since, notoriously, different arguments have proved persuasive to different audiences, the broader inferences from a quantitative investigation can scarcely be accepted as final. Thus it is possible, if the information is available, to establish how people voted, but it is much more difficult to say why they voted as they did. There might, of course, even be some difference of opinion on how they voted: for example, the accuracy of the records or of the tabulations made from them might be challenged. Yet such a disagreement is clearly on a lower level than a disagreement about men's motives, and there is a greater likelihood that it could be resolved through collecting and arranging the relevant data by acceptable procedures. In regard to more general explanatory propositions, however, a statistical inquiry, like any other method of verification, can only disprove. If the hypothesis does not fit the evidence, it may be rejected; in this sense a quantitative finding can indeed be conclusive. "Once we recognize that the Jacksonians won either by narrow majorities before 1837 or by narrow pluralities after that date, or frequently failed to win by any margin, it will surely become apparent that there is no basis for explanations that tell why they were the 'popular party.' "[28] The absence of unfavorable findings does not, however, prove an explanatory generalization for there may be some other explanation, and it is also possible that adverse evidence may be discovered later. Strictly speaking, a generalization of this kind is never proved and remains on probation indefinitely.[29]

---

[28] Benson, *Concept of Jacksonian Democracy*, 289-90.

[29] For a further discussion of this point, see W. I. B. Beveridge, *The Art of Scientific Investigation* (rev. ed., New York, 1957), 115-22.

Hence there is always, in quantitative research of any scope, a gap between observation and theory. To bridge this gap it may be necessary to resort to assumptions that are not demonstrated by the evidence. Some recent presentations of this kind depend not only on the figures but also on the use of hypotheses that are designed to show either what the figures measure or what their relevance is to certain general questions. The gap cannot always be bridged. Interesting findings may be obtained that are difficult to explain in the sense of devising an acceptable theory that will account for them. An example from my own research is a cumulative scale, derived through Louis Guttman's technique of scalogram analysis, that ties together votes in the House of Commons on a number of different subjects in a way consistent with the hypothesis that they all measure a single variable. Yet the nature of this variable, this larger issue that subsumes many smaller ones, has proved difficult to determine. Though the existence of the scale can be demonstrated with about as much certainty as can ever be obtained in historical research, the characterization of it can be, for the present, only tentative and hypothetical.[30] Comparable dilemmas have sometimes been encountered in other fields.[31]

The hypotheses used to connect observation and theory are, no matter how plausible they at first appear, always open to challenge. The broader conclusions of a quantitative presentation may be vulnerable regardless of the accuracy of the mathematics or the reliability of the original data, and questions may be raised about them that cannot be answered by a resort to numbers. A critic may accept the findings, but then point out that the conclusions based upon them follow only if certain assumptions are made, and go on to question these assumptions. Some of the large modern quantitative studies have been criticized exactly on this ground: that the chain of argument, the series of connecting hypotheses, was too long and too tenuous to make the conclusions convincing.[32]

By the same token, a quantitative investigation may not and often will not settle an argument. It may settle certain disputed points about the evidence. The discussion of larger questions of historical interpretation, however, concerns not merely what the facts were but also what may be inferred from them, and on this level controversy may continue.[33] A quantitative finding may be open to

---

30 Aydelotte, "Voting Patterns," 148-51.

31 "In spite of the great social and scientific usefulness of psychological tests it must be acknowledged that for the most part we have had very inadequate ideas as to what it is that they actually measure." (Joy Paul Guilford, *Psychometric Methods* [2nd ed., New York, 1954], 470.)

32 Nathan Glazer, " 'The American Soldier' as Science: Can Sociology Fulfil Its Ambitions?" *Commentary*, VIII (Nov. 1949), 487-96; C. Wright Mills, *The Sociological Imagination* (New York, 1959), 72.

33 Greer based his conclusions on a calculation of what percentage each social or occupational group constituted of the total number of victims of the Terror. If he had argued from percentages figured in the other direction—designed to show what proportion of each of the various divisions of French society was executed in the Terror—the picture would have looked somewhat different. This is because, as Greer points out, the "proportional incidence" of the Terror was "almost directly inverse to its absolute

more than one interpretation: in some cases it can be used to support either of two alternative and mutually exclusive theoretical schemes.[34] It can also happen that quantitative results that appear to disprove an accepted theory will simply be "explained away." This procedure can be quite legitimate, since it may prove possible to achieve a reformulation of the earlier view, which preserves some of the original insights, but does not conflict with the new evidence. If contradictory findings continue to accumulate, however, it may eventually be more satisfactory to abandon the earlier position altogether.

Quantitative procedures by no means preclude, nor indeed can they possibly eliminate, the use of value judgments, speculations, intelligent guesses, or "the imagination and intuitive feel which the historian, and for that matter the social scientist, should bring to his subject."[35] What is gained by attempting such exactitude as the circumstances allow is not finality but reasonable credibility, not the elimination of subjective factors but the minimizing of their role. No greater claim than this would be asserted by responsible social scientists or statisticians.

These points, though they are elementary, are not always understood or remembered. Quantitative findings are impressive in appearance and may, by their psychological impact, numb or blunt the critical abilities of the reader. It does occasionally seem to happen that a statistical presentation wins acceptance not through intellectual persuasion but through a kind of hypnosis. There is, however, no magic about quantitative evidence. It may be more conveniently arranged and, on the points it covers, more complete than other forms of documentation. Its significance, however, depends on what can be inferred from it, and such inferences, like all other inferences, may be fallible.

This disadvantage is not, of course, peculiar to quantitative procedures. On the contrary, quantitative evidence stands, in this respect, on a level with all other kinds of evidence, and arguing from it is subject to the same rules and the

---

incidence"; in proportion to their numbers, "the nobles, the clergy, and the rich suffered far more than the lower classes." (Greer, *Incidence of the Terror*, 105-109.) This aspect of the findings has been made the ground for a sharp critique of Greer's book by Richard Louie who argues that Greer's own data contradict his principal conclusion and show "with 95 per cent confidence that the Terror was an 'inter-class war.' " (Richard Louie, "The Incidence of the Terror: A Critique of a Statistical Interpretation," *French Historical Studies*, III [Spring 1964], 379-89.) Neither way of presenting the figures is "right" in any ultimate sense; it is a matter of what question one wishes to answer and what features of the evidence it is most useful, for this purpose, to bring out.

[34] In case this appears puzzling, it may be helpful to summarize the hypothetical illustration given by Hans Zeisel. If Company A increases its sales volume in a year from one to two million dollars and Company B, a bigger outfit to begin with, increases its sales in the same period from four to seven million dollars, then one could argue either that Company B did better since its net increase was three times that of A, or that Company B did better since its net increase was three times that of A, or that Company A did better since it increased its sales 100 per cent in comparison to B's 75 per cent. Which alternative is preferred depends not on the figures but on what causal assumptions are implied in making the comparison and on what kinds of questions the investigator wishes to test. (Hans Zeisel, *Say It with Figures* [4th ed., New York, 1957], 8-13.)

[35] James Cornford, "The Transformation of Conservatism in the Late Nineteenth Century," *Victorian Studies*, VII (Sept. 1963), 40.

same hazards. The danger of false reasoning from good evidence occurs in any kind of research. It is not only in the field of statistics that men may agree on the facts but disagree on the inferences to be drawn from them.

(4) Questions have been raised not merely regarding the feasibility and reliability of quantitative research in history but also regarding its usefulness. It is sometimes argued that quantitative findings, even if they can be trusted, tend to be trivial, inconsequential, and uninteresting. This is because any system of classification, such as is needed for such work, uses only a small part of the available information and leaves out the full richness of reality. Hence the ordinary statistical categories are too crude and threadbare to explain the complicated events with which history is concerned. The problems in which historians are most interested are so complex that they elude these methods. One critic holds that: "almost all important questions are important precisely because they are not susceptible to quantitative answers."[36]

It is true, of course, that any quantitative procedure involves using only selected classes of data. It is seldom possible to include everything, or to come anywhere near this. Hence, statistical tables, though they seem impressive, may also present an appearance of bleakness or barrenness which can act as an impediment to thought. Often they will not stimulate the imagination as the detailed recital of an individual case will do. Indeed, it is useful, when one comes to an impasse in interpreting the figures, to turn to the consideration of individuals about whom much is known. Such individuals may not be representative, and one cannot generalize from them to the whole group; a study of them may, however, yield suggestions or leads, fresh hypotheses that can be tested, which will make the evidence as a whole more intelligible. It is always necessary, when working with the figures, to remember that they do not tell the whole story, that many elements of the situation are not reflected in them, and that what they do not cover may turn out to be more important than what they include. To interpret the quantitative evidence it is generally necessary to have recourse to the more conventional sources of historical information: memoirs and biographies, congressional debates, private papers, and the like.

The charge that quantification abstracts and uses only limited parts of the available information, however, is not an objection to this method specifically. On the contrary, any generalization abstracts. A generalization is a comparison of a number of cases, not in terms of all the attributes of each, but in terms of certain selected attributes in respect to which the cases are comparable. This problem is not peculiar to quantification; it arises in any research in which a conscientious effort is made to substantiate general statements.

The objection that the findings of quantitative studies are not significant sometimes takes other forms. It has been alleged, for example, that this kind of research is destructive and not constructive and that: "the recent use of quantitative methods to test historical generalization has resulted in the wholesale destruction of categories that previously held sway in the historian's

---

36 Arthur M. Schlesinger, Jr., "The Humanist Looks at Empirical Social Research," *American Sociological Review*, XXVII (Dec. 1962), 770.

vocabulary without supplanting them with new generalizations of comparable significance."[37] As an objection to quantification, however, this argument has no weight for it applies equally to any form of verification. All verification is in this sense negative. The argument fails to distinguish between the two quite different activities involved in research: getting ideas and testing them. Quantitative inquiries are generally directed to testing hypotheses formulated in advance. It has frequently been observed that, in work of this kind, a flat-footed empiricism is not likely to rise above a fairly low conceptual level and that systematic thought will progress more rapidly when it is directed by some adequate general hypothesis. The point should not be pushed too far for it occasionally happens that important relationships are not anticipated, but emerge as windfalls after the inquiry is completed. Also, in an area in which little work has been done, the original investigations must often be to some extent exploratory. It would be pedantic to insist on a full-fledged hypothesis in every case.[38] Nevertheless, the criticism that quantitative methods destroy and do not create is clearly based on a mistaken notion of the usual role of hypothesis in research. Hypotheses and generalizations are not simple inductions that emerge of their own accord from the evidence; they have, as is now better understood, different and more complex origins.[39]

Nor does a negative finding necessarily represent a dead end. If a generalization is wrong, it is useful to have it disproved; the disproof constitutes an advance in knowledge. As J. H. Hexter observes: "it may be worth saying that violent destruction is not necessarily of itself worthless and futile. Even though it leaves doubts about the right road for London it helps if someone rips up, however violently, a 'To London' sign on the Dover cliffs pointing south."[40] A negative finding can be, in some cases, as valuable as a positive finding, depending on what theoretical inferences follow from it. Furthermore, to blame the quantitative method for disproving bad hypotheses is to blame the doctor instead of the disease. What is at fault is the mistaken opinion, not the technique that reveals when we have gone astray. The remedy is not to abandon the technique but to try to develop a new theory that fits the evidence better.

It is also sometimes argued that quantitative methods only prove the obvious, that they merely demonstrate, by an unnecessarily cumbersome apparatus, what everyone already knew.[41] It is admitted that they can occasionally be used to disprove certain crude generalizations that still appear in the textbooks. Yet, it is

---

37 Richard Hofstadter, "History and the Social Sciences," in *Varieties of History: From Voltaire to the Present,* ed. Fritz Stern (New York, 1956), 415, n. 14.

38 Patricia L. Kendall and Paul F. Lazarsfeld, "Problems of Survey Analysis," in *Continuities in Social Research: Studies in the Scope and Method of "The American Soldier,"* ed. Robert K. Merton and Paul F. Lazarsfeld (Glencoe, Ill., 1950), 133, 137-42, 161; L. H. C. Tippett, *Statistics* (London, 1943), 139-40.

39 I have discussed this point at greater length in "Notes on the Problem of Historical Generalization," in *Generalization in the Writing of History,* ed. Gottschalk, 163-72.

40 J. H. Hexter, "Storm over the Gentry," in *Reappraisals in History,* ed. *id.* (Evanston, Ill., 1961), 138.

41 Mills, *Sociological Imagination,* 53-55, 75.

said, the crudity of such generalizations is already widely appreciated, and, on the whole, they are not accepted by sophisticated historians. In other words, quantitative techniques are useful only when historians have made fools of themselves. Their function is to clear away rubbish. However, if there is no rubbish, if scholarship in a field has been reasonably careful and responsible, a quantitative analysis is unlikely to reveal anything that is not already fairly well understood.

This criticism, also, is not well taken. Even if research merely confirms in a more conclusive fashion what some people already believe, it is good to have this additional assurance and to establish this belief on a more solid foundation. Also, on many questions that can be studied by quantitative methods, the answer is by no means a matter of course. More often there is evidence pointing in both directions, and both sides of the argument have been supported with some plausibility by different individuals. In such cases, it is useful to establish which of two contradictory statements comes closer to describing the total evidence and just how close it comes. It might be added that, in disputes of this kind, either answer will be "obvious" in the sense of being already familiar, even though the two alternative answers exclude each other. Furthermore, the results of quantitative investigations have frequently told directly against interpretations that had been widely accepted. Several examples have already been given; another is Fogel's attempt to appraise the role of the railroads in American economic growth, which resulted in the conclusions, disheartening to some enthusiasts, that even in the absence of railroads the prairies would have been settled and exploited, that the combination of wagon and water transportation could have provided a relatively good substitute for the railroad, and that "no single innovation was vital for economic growth during the nineteenth century."[42]

Whether the results of a quantitative investigation are important or trivial is and can only be a matter of opinion. The presumption of significance is based not on a demonstration of fact but on a judgment of value. This applies, incidentally, even to the so-called "tests of significance" commonly used in statistics. Properly speaking, they are evaluations of probability, and, while probability can be mathematically determined, the degree of it that will be regarded as acceptable in any study is a question not of mathematics but of the investigator's preference. A quantitative study, it might be said, is significant if the investigator thinks it is and can persuade others to share his view. Speaking simply on this basis, it seems difficult to support the assertion that the topics open to quantitative investigation are of no consequence. Far from this being the case, an intelligent use of the method opens up a host of new, potentially interesting questions that could be approached in no other way. Some of these possibilities and some of the studies conducted along these lines have already been discussed. Perhaps it is enough to say here that the substantive weight of the findings of the limited number of historians who have attempted

[42] Fogel, *Railroads and American Economic Growth,* 219, 234.

quantitative research is already impressive enough to render the accusation of triviality something less than plausible.

It seems reasonable to argue, furthermore, that the significance of a project of research does not depend on whether it is quantitative or not. Quantitative presentations vary greatly in value. They may be significant or trivial, interesting or uninteresting, and it is incorrect to suppose that they are all on the same level in these respects. What gives them such worth as they may have are the importance of the problem, the abundance, reliability, and relevance of the available evidence, and, above all, the intelligence with which the work is executed.

In fact, what is most needed in research of this kind is not the automatic application of certain techniques but, rather, qualities of logic and imagination. The main problems here, as in all research, are not technical and mechanical but intellectual and analytical. It is not easy to make the figures "talk" or to show their bearing on significant problems, and nothing is drearier than a presentation that merely summarizes the evidence. I am disturbed by students who want to do quantitative research and who seem to expect that this will solve their problems and that the application of a method will save them the trouble of thinking. This expectation is erroneous. Quantitative techniques, though they may play a crucial role in demolishing previous theories, are usually not adequate, by themselves, to establish general alternative hypotheses. They are nothing more than a means of deploying the evidence, although they perform this limited service wonderfully well. Once this subordinate and ancillary work has been done, however, the basic problems of historical interpretation still remain to be dealt with; they are not to be resolved by a gimmick. The greatest hazard in quantitative research is not that of neglecting techniques but that of becoming too much absorbed in them. This danger is particularly threatening now because of the rapid development of mechanical facilities for the processing of data. It is only too easy to become absorbed in the gadgets and to forget the ideas. The refinement and sophistication of methods, though desirable in themselves, can become a kind of escapism, an evasion or postponement of the intellectual tasks that must ultimately be faced.

In general, the discussion of quantification in history has involved much talking at cross-purposes. Many of the common objections to this approach seem to arise from a misconception of its function. They appear to assume that claims have been made for it that no responsible statistician would make. No one well versed in this line of work would argue that all historical materials can be quantified, that the figures provide any final demonstration of the broader inferences derived from them, or that the figures tell the whole story. Such assertions are clearly improper. If they are not made, however, as by informed workers in this line they are not, much of the current offensive against quantitative techniques fails. The central point around which discussion of the subject has in part revolved is not an intellectual issue but a problem of communication.

The use of quantitative methods for history presents substantial difficulties not always appreciated by enthusiasts or neophytes. Those who have employed them are likely to be less starry-eyed about their possibilities than those who have merely commended them without trying them. Indeed, quantitative projects may be more glamorous in the planning stage than they are after the results have been gathered; the findings sometimes turn out to be flatter and less revolutionary than had been hoped.

Though the difficulties are real enough, however, it is not clear that they constitute objections specifically to a quantitative approach, or that they can be resolved by dispensing with it. The standard objections are misconceived or placed out of context when presented as grounds for rejecting these methods altogether. Properly understood, these reservations serve not to discredit quantification but to mark the boundaries of what it can accomplish. Indeed, the apparent disadvantages of quantitative research, the impediments to generalization that it presents, are actually advantages for they call attention to limits in knowledge or to flaws in reasoning that might not otherwise be perceived or fully appreciated. When all reservations have been made, quantification has still shown itself, in the light of the considerable experience we now have, to be a powerful tool in historical analysis. It helps to make the work both easier and more reliable, and, in some cases, it provides a means of dealing with questions that could not be attacked in any other way. Those wrestling with problems for which this approach is appropriate can ill afford to dispense with it. In the general intellectual twilight in which historians are condemned to spend their lives, even some small effort to render the darkness less opaque may be advantageous.

2. An approach to the scientific study of past public opinion*

LEE BENSON †

Lacking relevant opinion surveys or polls, can contemporary researchers study past public opinion scientifically? Yes. Has past public opinion been studied scientifically? No. If I answer "No" to the second question, how can I responsibly answer "Yes" to the first? That is *the* question this essay tries to answer. A final question-answer set completes our agenda: Should social scientists other than historians seriously concern themselves with the study of past public opinion? Yes.[1]

I. DEFINING CONCEPTS

Some definitions may help to minimize communication difficulties. They are presented here, it cannot be overemphasized, as working "specifications of meaning," not as definitive statements.[2]

A. Public opinion

"VOX POPULI may be Vox Dei, but very little attention shows that there has never been agreement as to what Vox means or as to what Populus means."

---

* Lee Benson, "An Approach to the Scientific Study of Past Public Opinion," *Public Opinion Quarterly*, XXXI (Winter, 1967, 1968), pp. 522-567. Reprinted by permission of author and copyright holder.

† Lee Benson received his Ph.D. from Cornell University. He is Professor of History, University of Pennsylvania. Among his publications are: *Merchants, Farmers and Railroads: Railroad Regulation and New York Politics, 1850-1887*, 1955 (1969); *Turner and Beard, American Historical Writing Reconsidered*, 1960; *The Concept of Jacksonian Democracy: New York as a Test Case*, 1961 (1964).

1 During the 1950's, Paul Lazarsfeld stimulated my interest in the problems considered in this essay. He bears no responsibility, of course, for the particular solutions proposed here. I am glad to have this opportunity, however, to acknowledge my intellectual indebtedness to him.

2 In this connection, see Abraham Kaplan, *The Conduct of Inquiry*, San Francisco, Chandler, 1964, pp. 71-78.

Coined many years ago by Henry Maine,[3] that epigram wittily suggests the confusion still beclouding the concept of public opinion. The confusion stems partly from the concept's moral implications. Particularly in societies boasting democratic forms of government, it seems mandatory that the will of the people prevail. The claim that public opinion supports one side has considerable potency, and the question of "who" constitutes the public represents, therefore, more than a scholastic exercise in concept clarification. Not surprisingly, political theorists, statesmen, and assorted pundits have displayed marked ingenuity in answering it according to different predispositions and interests.[4]

In similar fashion, the concepts moral connotations have provoked other difficult questions: What is meant by "opinion"? When is "opinion" simply the product of habit rather than thought? When is it a "real opinion" instead of a "mere prejudice or meaningless impression"? About what subjects is the "public" capable of having opinions worth consideration by public officials? What degree of coercion by government, or by other agencies or agents, makes it invalid to speak of the existence of public opinion? Under what conditions, and in respect to what type of issue, should a minority submit to majority opinion?

The last question suggests another possible source of conceptual confusion. "Public opinion" sometimes is equated with consensus. Does "public opinion" imply unanimity, near-unanimity, or numerical majority? Does it refer to the "effective" rather than the numerical majority? Differences on these and similar questions have confused the concept and provoked heated but unilluminating controversies.

The final source of confusion considered here illustrates the validity of Gresham's Law, whether applied to the minting of currency or of concepts. Pollsters have become so ubiquitous, man-in-the-street interviews so commonplace, that the concept of "public opinion" has lost its original meaning. Instead of referring only to political issues of consequence to governments, "public opinion" now connotes views on questions of such different mettle as: Do Europeans make better lovers than Americans? Should teenagers "go steady"? Should the United States halt the bombing of North Vietnam?

As Harwood L. Childs persuasively argues, despite numerous attempts, no *intrinsic* reasons can be found to restrict the term "public opinion" to opinions

3 As quoted in A. Lawrence Lowell, *Public Opinion and Popular Government,* New York, Longmans, 1914, p. 3.

4 Excellent historical reviews of the public opinion concept that deal with this question, and with other questions posed below, are presented in Paul A. Palmer, "The Concept of Public Opinion in Political Theory," in Bernard Berelson and Morris Janowitz, eds., *Reader in Public Opinion and Communication,* Glencoe, Ill., Free Press, 1953 ed., pp. 3-13; Hans Speier, "Historical Development of Public Opinion," *American Journal of Sociology,* Vol. 55, January 1950, pp. 376-388; Paul F. Lazarsfeld, "Public Opinion and the Classical Tradition," *Public Opinion Quarterly,* Vol. 21, 1957, pp. 39-53; Harwood L. Childs, *Public Opinion: Nature, Formation, and Role,* Princeton, N.J., Van Nostrand, 1965, pp. 12-41. See also George Carslake Thompson "The Evaluation of Public Opinion," in Berelson and Janowitz, eds., *op. cit.,* pp. 14-20; A. V. Dicey, *Lectures on the Relation Between Law and Public Opinion in England During the Nineteenth Century,* 2nd ed., London, 1914, pp. 1-47; Lowell, *op. cit.,* pp. 3-54; James Bryce, *Modern Democracies,* New York, 1921, Vol. 1, pp. 151-162.

of a certain type held by individuals of a certain type.[5] But scientific disciplines, and fields of specialization within a discipline, seem to progress most rapidly when, at any given time, they abstract from "total reality" a limited range of phenomena for intensive study. As noted in more detail below, historians have not yet generally even *begun* to try to develop scientific procedures to study past public opinion. It seems good strategy, therefore, to begin that job by sharply restricting attention to one type of opinion—and one that historians are likely to find *relatively* easy and congenial to study systematically. At any rate, that is the strategy advocated by, and adopted in, this essay. For our purposes, "public opinion" is *arbitrarily* defined to refer only to opinions on "political issues." It has neither moral, majoritarian, nor effective connotations, and does not imply legitimate, correct, or informed opinion, which should prevail.

In the sense of "who," the "public" is defined as referring to all inhabitants of a specified political entity having the right, *or claiming the right,* explicitly or implicitly, to influence government actions, directly or indirectly. (The famous "strong-minded" women of the pre-Civil War period had no right to vote, but few American historians would deny that they exercised more influence than many men legally entitled to participate in the decision-making process.) In the sense of "what," "public" refers to government "actions" of concern to members of the political entity and about which they hold opinions—including no opinions. "Actions" are broadly defined to encompass the laws, policies, rulings, personnel, and structure of government. "Opinion" is taken to mean the *position* or *stand*—favorable, unfavorable, undecided, and variations thereof—held by individuals (or groups) on proposed, future, present, or past government actions. It refers either to action on a specific issue or to some over-all course of action on related issues. Clearly, therefore, as defined here, government action forms the core of the public opinion concept.[6] But conceptual clarification also requires us to distinguish explicitly between "opinions" and "attitudes."

As defined here, an opinion always connotes a *position* on some specific government action or general course of action; an attitude represents a persistent, general *orientation* toward some individuals, groups, institutions, or processes, but it does not necessarily result in a specific position on specified public issues.[7] A substantive example may highlight the distinction. Americans' positions during the 1840's relevant to government actions to abolish, restrict, or foster slavery are, according to our definition, viewed as their *opinions* on issues relating to the institution. Their evaluations of slavery as "good or bad," "moral or immoral," are viewed as their *attitudes* toward the institution. (At the boundary line between opinions and attitudes, blurring occurs, of course, but that familiar classification problem need not detain us.)

---

[5] Childs, *op. cit.,* pp. 14-26.

[6] I have freely adapted the definition of public opinion suggested by Speier, *op. cit.,* p. 376.

[7] Once again, I have freely adapted a definition offered elsewhere. See Theodore M. Newcomb, Ralph H. Turner, Philip E. Converse, *Social Psychology,* Holt, Rinehart and Winston, New York, 1965, pp. 47-114.

Distinguishing between opinions and attitudes is more than a semantic exercise. The claim that a large majority of Northerners had antislavery attitudes during the 1840's, for example, may well be credible. But it may also provide little credible information about the distribution of Northern opinion on specific public issues related to slavery and may, in fact, encourage a highly distorted description. It is easily conceivable that men had similar *attitudes* toward slavery and directly contradictory opinions on, for example, the annexation of Texas. They may have disagreed on the consequences of that action, they may have differed in their views on the powers of the Federal government or the importance of national unity, they may have differed in their political or economic interests, and so on. Equating an antislavery or proslavery attitude with an opinion for or against annexation, therefore, confuses very different things. To say that is not to deny that attitudes may *help* to shape opinions and that both may be used as indicators of each other. The argument is that the complex interrelationships between opinions and attitudes can perhaps be uncovered and disentangled after painstaking investigation; they cannot be automatically assumed, a priori, to take a particular form. This problem will be further discussed below. But it seems worth emphasizing at the outset that, in my judgment, failure to distinguish sharply between opinions and attitudes hampers public opinion research in general and research on past public opinion in particular.

B. Historical study of public opinion

As defined here, "historical" study of public opinion connotes more than the study of past phenomena, it connotes research carried out by procedures that secure data by means other than personal interviews, mail questionnaires, or direct observation. Put another way, the concept, "the historical study of public opinion," for our purposes, means the use of procedures to secure data from *documents* (broadly defined) that the researcher *locates and selects but does not create, directly or indirectly.* By selecting documents and, so to speak, "interrogating" their authors, historical researchers *generate* data designed to answer questions about past public opinion.

Contemporary opinion researchers also generate data, but they do so by conducting more or less structured interviews with respondents selected according to some specified sampling criteria. When they use documents not created by researchers for that purpose as data sources, they are, according to our definition, engaged in the historical study of public opinion. In short, it is not the "distance" from the present that determines if a study is historical in character, it is the procedures used to generate data about some dimension of public opinion. Can historical procedures be scientific, however, or must that term be restricted to procedures that, to quote Daniel Lerner, yield "largely quantified data accumulated by structured observation in empirical situations approximating (with specified deviations) the model of controlled experiment"?[8]

_____

[8] As quoted in Allen H. Barton and Paul F. Lazarsfeld, "Some Functions of Qualitative

C. Scientific historical study of public opinion

Is history art or science? An old question, much chewed over, never resolved—never to be resolved because it is a badly formulated old question. A better question, I think, is: Can past human behavior, e.g. past public opinion, be described and explained "scientifically," as well as "artistically"? That question poses a prior one: What is science? More precisely: What do we mean by "science"?

In my judgment, Ernest Nagel's definition of science can help us develop a fruitful approach to the study of past public opinion. According to his liberal definition, the enterprise has two main dimensions, goals and means. The main goal, or "the distinctive aim of the scientific enterprise is to provide systematic and responsibly supported explanations [of phenomena]." The main means to achieve that goal is the practice of scientific method: more specifically, "the persistent critique of arguments, in the light of tried canons for judging the reliability of the procedures by which evidential data are obtained, and for assessing the probative force of the evidence on which conclusions are based."[9]

As Joseph Strayer has noted, historians have "been talking about the importance of public opinion for several generations, longer perhaps than any other professional group."[10] It seems indisputable, however, that they have not yet developed "tried canons for judging the reliability of the procedures by which evidential data [relevant to public opinion] are obtained," nor "tried canons . . . for assessing the probative force of the evidence on which conclusions are based."[11] Why not?

One answer may be that such canons or principles cannot be developed, given the nature of public opinion and the kinds of documents available for historical research. That may turn out to be the right answer. At present, however, no warrant exists for it other than as a hypothesis that, ultimately, may or may not be confirmed. A more optimistic, and in my judgment a more compelling, answer is that "tried canons" for research on historical public opinion have not been developed because historians have not systematically tried to develop them.[12] Instead, historians studying public opinion have strongly tended to rely

---

Analysis in Social Research," *Frankfurter Bertrage Zur Soziologie,* Band 1, 1955, p. 321. This important methodological essay is particularly relevant to historical research and is conveniently reprinted as "S-336," in the Bobbs-Merrill Reprint Series in the Social Sciences.

9 Ernest Nagel, *The Structure of Science,* New York, Harcourt, Brace & World, 1961, pp. 1-15.

10 Joseph Strayer, "The Historian's Concept of Public Opinion," in Mirra Komarovsky, ed., *Common Frontiers of the Social Sciences,* Glencoe, Ill., Free Press, 1957, p. 263.

11 *Ibid.*

12 See the stimulating critiques in Ernest R. May, "An American Tradition in Foreign Policy: The Role of Public Opinion," in William H. Nelson, ed., *Theory and Practice in American Politics,* Chicago, University of Chicago Press, 1964, pp. 101-122; Robert A. Kann, "Public Opinion Research: A Contribution to Historical Method," *Political Science Quarterly,* Vol. 73, September 1958, pp. 374-396. Though focused on foreign policy, May's essay provides an excellent overview of the American literature relevant to the study of

upon "historical method" to perform tasks for which it was not designed and for which, as it now stands, it is grossly inadequate.

My basic assumptions are that historical method, as developed to date, cannot satisfy the demands made upon it by researchers interested in mass behavior, and that a serious methodological gap therefore exists in historiography that will require large-scale, sustained efforts to close. Widespread recognition of the gap, I further assume, must precede its eventual elimination—an assumption consonant with my fond hope that this paper will be viewed as an essay in constructive criticism.

As is well known, modern historical method was founded in Germany during the early nineteenth century. Trained in philology, Barthold Niebuhr, Leopold von Ranke, and others then brilliantly applied that discipline's critical method to ancient, medieval, and early modern documents. As a result, "scientific history" came into being—a term that primarily meant the critical study of primary sources, not science in Nagel's sense. Essentially, the rules laid down by the founding fathers of the discipline focused attention upon the authentication of documents and the evaluation of testimony that credibly could be extracted from different kinds of authentic documents. A quotation from the preface of one of Ranke's major works illustrates the point:

The basis of the present work, the sources of its material, are memoirs, diaries, letters, diplomatic reports, and original narratives of eyewitnesses; other writings were used only if they were immediately derived from the above mentioned or seemed to equal them because of some original information.[13]

Later scholars added important refinements to the rules laid down by Niebuhr, von Ranke, and other pioneers but did not greatly extend the boundaries originally mapped out for the "new science." And it is equally well known that historical method in the United States today differs little from that taught in European universities during the late nineteenth century.

Though the *methods* taught today in seminars and described in manuals essentially remain unaltered, historians' *interests* have shifted radically. Since Western historians no longer focus primarily upon ancient, medieval, and early modern events, research necessarily is not confined to the activities of relatively homogeneous, small, elite groups in a highly stratified society. In particular, American historians largely concern themselves with mass behavior in a dynamic, pluralistic, mass society. Thus a serious gap between historiographic theory and

public opinion. For a comprehensive bibliographic guide to the literature, see the chapter notes and supplementary reading suggestions in Childs, *op. cit.*

May has carried further his study of the impact of public opinion upon American foreign policy in his "American Imperialism: A Reinterpretation," in Donald Fleming and Bernard Bailyn, eds., *Perspectives in American History,* Cambridge, Mass., Harvard University Press, 1967, Vol. I, pp. 123-286. It appeared too late for consideration in this essay. Another essay in the same volume, Donald Fleming, "Attitude: The History of a Concept," *ibid.,* pp. 287-365, also appears to warrant intensive study.

[13] As quoted in Fritz Stern, ed., *The Varieties of History,* New York, Meridian, 1956, p. 57.

practice has resulted; the traditional rules of historical method were not devised by scholars dealing with mass behavior and have not been amended in any systematic form by later scholars concerned with such phenomena. It follows, therefore, that historical method, as developed to date, can have only limited value as a guide to researchers trying to study public opinion in a mass society.

Instead of directing criticism against the general principles of historical method, the purpose here is to call attention to the necessity of extending them. For example, one will search in vain through the manuals of historical method for observations that offer anything but elementary guidance to researchers engaged in studying public opinion. Moreover, the task of prying out useful procedures from specialized studies is greatly complicated by the tendency of historians to avoid making them explicit. In sum, good ground is believed to exist for the assumption that historical method, as now codified, is inadequate to the demands made upon it by scholars interested in an aspect of mass behavior such as public opinion. A recent statement on the advantages of codifying the research procedures employed in different disciplines is put so cogently as only to require repetition.

The advancement of research procedure in social science as elsewhere depends on making explicit what researchers actually do, and systematically analyzing it in the light of logic and of substantive knowledge. Such a 'codification' of procedures points out dangers, indicates neglected possibilities, and suggests improvements. It makes possible the generalization of methodological knowledge—its transfer from one specific project or subject to others, from one researcher to the scientific community. Finally, it makes possible a more systematic training of students, in place of simply exposing them to concrete cases of research in the hope that they will somehow absorb the right lessons.[14]

As discussed in Section V below, an implicit pattern can be seen in the procedures American historians have spontaneously and intuitively developed to study past public opinion. Those procedures, used painstakingly and imaginatively, as the three articles in this issue by Helbich, Lancaster, and Maxwell on public opinion and the Versailles Treaty concretely suggest, can yield data that significantly improve our understanding of the role public opinion played in past governmental decisions. In my judgment, however, if we hope to make major advances in the historical study of public opinion, we must sharply reverse our priorities and concentrate primarily upon methodological rather than substantive problems.

Codification of *existing* procedures, although helpful, will not get us very far. Until we consciously try to develop a general analytic model, or system of analysis, and seriously engage in theory construction and concept and index formation, we are not likely to develop a genuinely scientific study of past public opinion. Bluntly stated, we historians need to move beyond that "brute empiricism" which relies upon "saturation" in primary sources unguided by

---

14 Barton and Lazarsfeld, *op. cit.,* in Bobbs-Merrill Reprints "S-336," p. 321.

canons for generating data and for making inferences from the data generated. Before sketching an approach that at least points in that direction, it seems useful to suggest that non-historians also have a vital stake, and should therefore participate vitally, in the enterprise.

II. SOCIAL SCIENTISTS AND THE HISTORICAL STUDY OF PUBLIC OPINIONS

Bernard Berelson and Morris Janowitz, in the second edition (1965) of their *Reader in Public Opinion and Communication,* optimistically observed that significant progress had been made in developing a "generally accepted theory of public opinion" since the first edition appeared fifteen years earlier. "It is still true," they conceded, however, "that there is no generally accepted theory of public opinion, nor does it appear likely that one will emerge in the immediate future." Lack of long-term trend data, they suggested, seriously retards theoretical progress:

The main contribution of opinion polling to the understanding of opinion formation is through the accumulation of trend data over time. After public opinion polling had provided a body of answers to standardized opinion questions, it became possible to chart trends in the gross development of opinions and relate them to external political and military events. Unfortunately, the number of such long-term bodies of data is limited because survey organizations have generally not accepted responsibility for this task.[15]

Almost a decade earlier, in the twentieth-anniversary issue of this journal, Herbert Hyman had similarly pointed to the "deficiencies of discontinuous data" as:

perhaps the most crucial deficiency for the growth of a theory. The absence of data which provides a sound description of even the *lack* of public opinion on a problem, at a time when it is not under discussion, means that there is no basis for developing adequate theory as to the formation of public opinion. Similarly, the waning of an issue has generally meant the neglect of it by survey research. Thus, no theory can really be built as to either the formation or decline of public opinion. . . . Obviously, what would be desirable would be to extend public opinion research from the *ad hoc* description of whatever part of the current social world is hot to the systematic description of both the hot and the cold. With such an extension, theory could develop in a number of fruitful directions. Taking any point in time, the *structures* of public thinking, the *mental organizations* of public attitudes, would be better understood by seeing the connections between different bodies of opinion. And if these same areas were dealt with over long spans of time, providing trend data, a theory of public opinion formation and opinion change would be well on its way to formulation. As a result of the rise of panels, part of that theory is now available, but only that part which deals with the flux of opinion over short ranges of time in

---

[15] Berelson and Janowitz, *op. cit.,* 2nd ed., New York, Free Press of Glencoe, 1965, Vol. 1, pp. 65-66.

relation to very specific stimuli or psychological factors. By contrast, long term trends in the systematic description of public opinion would enable us to relate opinion processes to much more macroscopic determinants: for example, law, social change, demographic processes, and the like. And such trend data in juxtaposition with political analysis would lead not merely to theories of opinion formation, but also to theories about the *consequences* of popular opinion for political actions.[16]

Paul Lazarsfeld, probably more than any other individual, has focused attention on the value of long-term trend studies for opinion research. Beginning at least as early as his 1950 presidential address to the American Association for Public Opinion Research, he repeatedly called for such studies, and urged establishment of a " 'commission for the utilization of polls in the service of future historiography,' whose specific task it would be to furnish us [pollsters] with appropriate ideas [on significant questions to ask] ."[17] But, as the recent observation by Berelson and Janowitz suggests, the programatic statements of Lazarsfeld and Hyman have had relatively little effect. Historians certainly have not joined with pollsters in the service of future historiography and survey organizations have generally not accepted responsibility for the task of developing long-term bodies of data.

The situation may change to some extent, of course. But it seems reasonable to believe that the Lazarsfeld-Hyman-Berelson-Janowitz statements, by restricting attention to public opinion research carried out by survey methods, do not go far enough. That is, serious deficiencies in long-term trend data, in my judgment, must continue to exist and handicap theory construction if public opinion research continues to depend exclusively, or primarily, upon *non-historical sources of data.*

For one thing, macroscopic social and cultural changes tend to take a very long time indeed to develop and make their consequences felt. Only extraordinarily long-lived and patient pollsters or survey organizations, therefore, might be expected to devote the resources needed to measure continuously the impact of macroscopic changes on opinion formation, and, in turn, the impact of opinion change over time on government policies. For another, lacking the perspective gained by "20-20 hindsight," it is doubtful that any group could identify in advance most of the issues that, in time, would come to be recognized as important. And it is even more doubtful that significant opinion-forming events (broadly defined) could be recognized, as it were, on the spot, and surveys quickly organized and conducted to secure *valid* retrospective before-and-after data. Moreover, even under the best circumstances, contemporary researchers surely find it difficult to secure valid data about the impact of public opinion on government action. Not only are contemporary researchers unlikely to have continuous access to decision makers and get truthful answers

16 Herbert H. Hyman, "Toward a Theory of Public Opinion," *Public Opinion Quarterly,* Vol. 21, 1957, pp. 56-57.

17 See Lazarsfeld's essay in the "Debate" on history and public opinion research, "The Historian and the Pollster," in Komarovsky, ed., *op. cit.,* pp. 242-268.

to probing questions, but government officials and political influentials are highly unlikely, *retrospectively,* to provide comprehensive, candid, accurate answers—even if they really tried hard to do so. In respect to this dimension of public opinion research, non-historians could profit from the emphasis historians place upon the painstaking procedures needed to extract reliable and valid data from primary sources.

Other difficulties could be sketched but would only belabor the main argument: If we need many "long-term bodies of data" to develop a powerful general theory of public opinion, heavy, although certainly not exclusive, reliance will have to be placed upon historical studies. The argument should not be caricatured as maintaining that historical procedures can be developed to secure all the types of data that can be secured by contemporary opinion research. Under the best of foreseeable circumstances, serious gaps will remain, e.g. historical data about the influence of primary groups and personality traits upon opinion formation. But historical study of public opinion can be significantly improved and its improvement would contribute significantly to the general study of public opinion. If that argument has merit, it follows that all social scientists interested in public opinion have a vital stake in developing the scientific character of its historical study.

III. THE CONCEPT OF PUBLIC OPINION: MAIN DIMENSIONS AND SUBCATEGORIES

Non-historians may find it surprising, but the three main dimensions of the concept of public opinion were clearly identified by a historian over two thousand years ago. Thucydides, in his classic *History of the Peloponnesian War,* organized his book around three closely related but different themes, the *distribution* of public opinion, the processes of opinion *formation,* and the *impact* of opinion upon government decisions.[18] Unfortunately, historians did not exploit the lead Thucydides provided and did not go on to develop a classification system for the different phenomena subsumed under the over-all concept, "public opinion." As a result, the historical study of public opinion has been seriously handicapped by lack of a good classification system to (1) distinguish among different types of phenomena; (2) provide a logical framework for ordering data; (3) suggest the need to devise different procedures to study different phenomena; (4) help bring complex relationships into focus; and (5) illuminate uniformities and differences. On the assumption that a good classification system is indispensable to fruitful research dealing with complex phenomena, it seems useful to try to develop one based upon Thucydides' dimensions as, in effect, elaborated by modern opinion researchers.[19]

[18] See the discussion of Thucydides in Lee Benson, "Causation and the American Civil War," *History and Theory,* Vol. 1, No. 2, 1961, pp. 167-168.

[19] They differ somewhat in emphasis, but see the classification systems in, V. O. Key, *Public Opinion and American Democracy,* New York, Knopf, 1961; Robert E. Lane and David O. Sears, *Public Opinion,* Englewood Cliffs, N. J., Prentice-Hall, 1964; Childs, *op. cit.*

A. Distribution of opinion

"Spartans, those of you who think that the treaty [with Athens] has been broken and that the Athenians are aggressors, get up and stand on one side. Those who do not think so, stand on the other side," and he pointed out to them where they were to stand. They then rose to their feet and separated into two divisions. The great majority were of the opinion that the treaty had been broken.[20]

That is how Thucydides described the decision taken at the climactic meeting of the Spartan Assembly that declared war on Athens in 431 B.C. As the quotation indicates, he provided some explicit information about what we can call the "direction of opinion" but none about the "quality of opinion." Those two categories constitute the main subdivisions of the proposed classification system's first dimension, "distribution of opinion." In turn, each can usefully be subdivided to permit more precise categories for differentiating, ordering, and relating phenomena.

1. Direction of opinion. What do we want to know about the direction of public opinion on an issue over time and place? At least two very different things: (a) the quantitative *divisions* of opinion among the public; (b) the *attributes*, or *characteristics*, of the individuals who held different positions on the issue. We can combine them, of course, to make statements about the distribution of opinions among members of specified groups, or the group characteristics of the individuals holding a specified position. But the two categories are significantly different, a simple observation that forcefully points up the limitations of the information Thucydides provided, as well as the desirability of developing a good classification system for research on public opinion, past or present.

We know from Thucydides—assuming his account to be accurate—that "the great majority [of the Spartans] were of the opinion that the treaty had been broken." But we know nothing else about them. For example, we do not know how, if in any way other than their different positions on the issue, they differed from the small minority of Spartans who believed that the treaty had *not* been broken. As a result, although this essay is not the appropriate place to do so, I think it could be shown that Thucydides' explanation of the Peloponnesian War can neither be confirmed nor disconfirmed. The relevant point is to observe that systematic research requires us to get data about both the quantitative divisions of opinion *and* the attributes of the members of a public who hold different positions. This observation gives us two categories, "Positions" and "Attributes," under the more general heading, "Direction of opinion."

a. Positions. For each of the different possible positions on a specific issue, we want to know the distribution of opinion of the members of the groups we designate as constituting "the public." Such information would permit us to

---

20 Thucydides, *History of the Peloponnesian War*, Rex Warner translation, Great Britain, Penguin Books, 1956, Book I, p. 61.

identify who held what position, to state the distribution of opinion *within* a specified group, and to compare the distributions *between* different groups. Giving the "Ayes and Nays," as, in effect, Thucydides did, is the simplest form of stating divisions of opinion. Though numerous positions might be created, the range of useful variations on the "aye-nay" formula is narrow; it is hard to go much beyond some variant of "Favorable, Neutral, Undecided, No Opinion, Unfavorable." In short, when the qualitative content of opinion is ignored and each head is counted as an equal unit, there are not many ways to count heads on an issue.

  b. Attributes. We can identify only a limited number of different positions on an issue, but, at least in theory, no limit exists to the number of attributes or characteristics we can use to stratify (or divide) a public into different groups. In practice, particularly in historical research, the range of choice tends to be much more restricted. For example, we might wish to group individuals according to personality type because we believe that significant relationships exist between personality type and opinion formation. Obviously, we cannot do so "historically," except perhaps with individual members of elite groups for whom we happen to have the requisite personal documents. Such limitations upon some aspects of historical opinion research need only induce caution, however, not paralysis.

  It seems unlikely that personality characteristics are the only, or even the most significant, attributes relevant to opinion formation. Moreover, it seems reasonable to assume that significant relationships exist between some types of group membership (i.e. "interacting" rather than "categorical" groups) and personality characteristics. As John J. Honigman, a specialist on culture and personality, observes, "the members of any enduring group tend to manifest certain relatively common personality characteristics." That proposition, by enabling historians to treat personality, in effect, as only *one* "intervening variable" between group membership and opinion formation, puts our inability to secure data about individual personalities in much less alarming perspective— particularly if we sensibly restrict our claims about public opinion to those dimensions for which we can secure empirical data, do not pretend to offer exhaustive reconstructions and explanations, and do not feel compelled to imply perfect confidence in our claims. Nevertheless, given the past tendency of historians to ignore personality characteristics in opinion research, it seems useful to emphasize that we do not exhaust the range of possible determinants when we group men according to "external" attributes.[21]

  To help overcome the "deficiencies of discontinuous data" pointed to by Hyman, it clearly would be highly desirable for studies of past (and present)

---

[21] For a somewhat less optimistic view of the problems personality variables pose for historical opinion research, see May, *loc. cit.* On the relationships between personality and culture, see John J. Honigmann, *Culture and Personality,* New York, Harper & Row, 1954, pp. 195-225; and, a particularly relevant essay for historians, Anthony F. C. Wallace, "The Psychic Unity of Human Groups," in Bert Kaplan, ed., *Studying Personality Cross-culturally,* New York, Harper & Row, 1961, pp. 128-163.

opinion to use *comparable* (not necessarily identical) attributes to stratify the publics studied. But the choice of attributes inevitably is influenced by the specific issue(s) involved, the source materials available, the degree of precision desired, and the hypotheses being tested. Only a specialist in Greek history, therefore, could identify the attributes that Thucydides, ideally, would have used to study the relationships between public opinion and the coming of the Peloponnesian War. It is possible, nevertheless, to identify four *types* of attributes generally relevant to opinion studies. Because the papers in this issue that deal with public opinion and ratification of the Versailles Treaty provide concrete examples of how they are used in substantive research, the attributes will be identified in American terms. With appropriate changes in terms, however, the typology seems widely applicable.

Place is the type of attribute perhaps most commonly used to divide "a public" into "publics." That is, researchers can try to ascertain the quantitative divisions of opinion on specified issues at specified times among Americans as a group, or among the inhabitants of different sections, states, localities, and the like.

"Political role" identifies another type of attribute. "Formal political roles" permit researchers to distinguish members of the electorate, voters from eligible nonvoters, *et al.* "Informal roles" in principle—that is, if the requisite data can be obtained—permit researchers to distinguish the members of a political system according to party or faction, "liberal" or "conservative" attitudes, differential power to influence decisions (e.g. "elites" and "masses"), or other attributes that seem theoretically relevant.

Demographic attributes can be used to stratify "the public" into a very large number of smaller "publics." Relevant demographic attributes vary according to time, place, issue, *and theory,* but the standard divisions are some variant and combination of economic, ethnic, religious, urban-rural, educational, age, and sex differences.

Formal voluntary association is the last type of attribute identified in the typology sketched here. To some extent, these attributes overlap with demographic ones, but the difference is that they connote "voluntary" membership (or nonmembership) in formal *organizations* (e.g. Chambers of Commerce, trade-unions, farmers' organizations, veterans' organizations, religious organizations, ethnic societies) rather than "categorical" membership in some group identified by a demographic attribute.

In principle, of course, the four types of attributes can be combined into an extraordinarily large number of subdivisions among "the American public." In practice, limitations of resources and data sharply restrict the ability of researchers to deal with all publics that might be theoretically relevant. This observation again need induce only caution, not paralysis. To know what theoretically ought to be done, even if historians cannot do it, is useful—and chastening. But inability to do *everything* worth doing is not equivalent to inability to do *anything.*

2. *Quality of opinion.* Attention thus far has been restricted to *quantitative*

divisions of opinion among the members of different groups. Two assumptions, however, seem reasonable: heads do not count equally in determining the impact of public opinion on government actions; the *qualities* of men's opinions form a significant component of their relative will and power to influence government actions. If we accept those assumptions, it seems useful to create subdivisions under the general category, "Quality of opinion."

a. State (or crystallization) of opinion. At any given time, have the members of a group crystallized their positions on a given issue or are opinions in a formative state? The two main states have been termed "latent" and "manifest." That historians feel both compelled and able to distinguish between these states is nicely illustrated in the paper by James L. Lancaster on "The Protestant Churches and the Fight for Ratification of the Versailles Treaty," in this issue. In effect, one of his basic themes is the transition of opinion from a latent to a manifest state. For example, he emphasizes that specified types of Protestant leaders, those of "liberal theological persuasion," were overwhelmingly sympathetic to the general idea of a league of nations but not necessarily favorable to "whatever specific plan emerged from Versailles." He then advances and supports the claim that three specific events helped to crystallize their latent support into manifest support: "the release of the text of the Covenant, the speeches made by . . . President [Wilson] on its behalf, and the debate in Boston on March 19, 1919, between President A. Lawrence Lowell of Harvard University and Senator Henry Cabot Lodge" (p. 6).

b. Saliency of opinion. For the members of specified groups, how "salient" (important) is a given public issue *compared* either to other public issues or to other "issues" affecting their lives? That question points up the need to study opinion on an issue not in isolation from opinions on other issues, but as one strand of an interrelated web of opinion. Men may share the same position on an issue but vary enormously in the importance they attach to it. Historians, therefore, must grapple with the problem of ascertaining the relative saliency of an issue to different groups at the same time, or to the same group at different times.[22] That dictum can also be illustrated by Lancaster's paper.

In effect, Lancaster explains the tremendous *activity* certain Protestant leaders engaged in to secure ratification of Wilson's plan by noting its extraordinary *saliency* for them. For one minister, "the League [of Nations] was the practical application to the whole world of Christ's teachings concerning individuals"; for another, it was "cementing the nations of earth so that the Kingdom of God may come" (p. 602).

c. Intensity of opinion. How convinced are men that their position on an issue is the right position? That is, in addition to wanting to know something about the saliency of an issue to members of a group, we want to know something about the relative intensity (or strength) of their convictions concerning the positions they favor. Depending upon the data available and the

---

[22] In this connection, see the chapter, "Texas Annexation and New York Public Opinion," in Lee Benson, *The Concept of Jacksonian Democracy: New York as a Test Case,* Princeton, N.J., Princeton University Press, 1961, 254-269.

precision desired, we can try to group men in categories ranging from some variant of "strongly favorable" to "strongly unfavorable."

d. Duration of opinion. One determinant of the strength of an opinion, it seems reasonable to postulate, is how long an individual holds it. To treat "duration" separately from "strength," however, is not to engage in conspicuous creation of categories. Duration is by no means the only determinant of strength of conviction. Moreover, if we treat determinants separately, we improve our ability to measure and explain their relative contributions to the strength of opinion. Still another consideration is that when we deal with opinion formation, we particularly need to secure data about the durability of opinions.

e. Knowledgeability of opinion. As conceived here, no more legitimacy is attributed to "informed" than to "uninformed" opinion. But the assumption seems reasonable that informed opinions tend to be stronger and more durable than uninformed ones, and that government officials take those qualities into account when considering opinion distribution on an issue. The "Knowledge-ability" category is therefore included in the classification system, although I cheerfully concede that it may be difficult to secure relevant historical data.

B. Formation of opinion

The papers in this issue focused on the Versailles Treaty provide answers to a wide variety of questions related to opinion formation. To order such questions systematically and comprehensively, the dimension can conveniently be sub-divided into five categories: (1) Formative agents, (2) Agents' motives, (3) Agents' actions, (4) Impact of agents' actions, and (5) Explanation of impact of agents' actions. Those categories, although interrelated, are analytically distinct. To secure historical data about the different types of phenomena assigned to them requires, therefore, different procedures and, in Nagel's terms, different "tried canons" for judging both the reliability of the procedures and "the probative force of the evidence on which conclusions are based."

1. Formative agents. "Every factor that makes the individual what he is attitudinally enters into the formation of political opinion."[23] That all-encompassing proposition may be true, almost by definition, but it gives little guidance to researchers trying to develop an operational strategy for the study of opinion formation. Rather than begin by trying to identify either the diverse environments in which members of the public form their opinions or their even more diverse predispositions, historians might better begin by trying to identify the relatively small number of individuals or groups actively working to form opinions on specific issues. The basic assumption here is that public opinion on an issue (broadly defined) does not evolve spontaneously but strongly tends to be "made" by the conscious actions of a relatively small number of "formative agents." Once we explicitly identify the issues that concern us in our research, it seems reasonable to assume—and the three papers support the assumption—that

---

[23] That sentence begins the section on "Formation," in Key, *op. cit.,* p. 291.

we can systematically identify the "leading agents" if we consciously try to do so and saturate ourselves in the historical situation. And once we systematically identify the leading agents, it can be further assumed, we place ourselves in a better position to try to reconstruct and explain the complex processes of opinion formation.

No implication is intended that formative agents either act with perfect knowledge and rationality or achieve the precise results they want or expect. On the contrary, I assume that all agents fall considerably short of perfection, that they display wide variations in knowledge and rationality, and that their actions frequently "boomerang." Moreover, I assume that the actual distribution of opinion on any given issue at any given time represents the outcome of conflicting actions whose impact could, at best, have been predicted only within wide limits—if for no other reason than the occurrence of uncontrollable changes in the general historical situation. But my operative assumption is that if we with *conscious agents acting purposively,* we stand on solid theoretical ground and can conduct research according to a workable design.

Granted that assumption, it seems useful to try to develop a standard typology of formative agents. Among other advantages, its development and adoption would tend to produce comparable, cumulative studies and thereby contribute to both theoretical and substantive progress. The typology sketched below obviously is neither elegant nor exhaustive. It represents a beginning rather than an end; its deficiencies, I trust, will stimulate other researchers to repair them rather than to dismiss the enterprise as hopeless.

a. Government officials. Of the different types of formative agents, government officials head the list. We can safely assume that, to some extent, they always consciously try to form public opinion on all "major" issues because we can safely assume that, to some extent, public opinion always affects their operations. Depending upon the subject, officials can be differentiated according to position, level, branch, unit of government, etc. A less obvious but significant differentiation is between "official role" and "nonofficial role." That is, in addition to opinion-making power derived from their government positions, officials may also have influence on various groups, organizations, or individuals, and they may use their influence to help shape public opinion. To cite only one possible reason for making the distinction: It may help us to understand why different men occupying the same position, or similar positions, differ markedly in their ability to influence the distribution of opinion.

b. Political leaders. In this context, "political leaders" connotes men who either do not hold public office or who function as officeholders in one type of nonofficial role. Like government officials, political leaders have a vital stake in the distribution of public opinion and can reasonably be assumed, therefore, to act constantly to shape it. Distinctions between government officials and political leaders may not be universally applicable, but the latter term is not restricted to the modern era. In any era, I assume, a relatively small group of men lead "parties," "factions," "cliques," "circles," and variants thereof.

c. Mass media directors. This term is restricted to the modern era. It designates men who own, operate, or significantly influence the mass media used to communicate information and views. Actually, sharp distinctions between "information" and "views" tend to be somewhat misleading. As George Gerbner suggests, the best proposition to adopt in studying opinion formation is, "all news are views."[24] But it is important to recognize that the opinion-forming power of any communication medium varies widely over time, place, and type of issue, an observation particularly relevant to the problem considered in Section V below of constructing *indicators* of opinion distribution.

d. Leaders of nonpolitical formal organizations. We might extend Gerbner's proposition to claim that, at least in the United States, all major formal organizations (e.g. National Council of Churches, National Association of Manufactures, AFL-CIO) are political organizations. To do so, however, would be to engage in reductionism and obliterate the boundaries between a political system and its environment. A more reasonable position is to assume that the leaders of all major organizations *consciously* act to form public opinion at some times, on some issues. Depending upon the issue and situation, therefore, we could estimate the likelihood that the leaders of specified organizations acted to form opinion, and design our research operations accordingly. To illustrate the point concretely Lancaster's paper can again be cited, although the other two papers, by Maxwell and Helbich, also provide striking examples.

Given the long history of participation by American Protestant organizations in the "crusade for peace," dating from 1815, and the specific work of the Federal Council of Churches of Christ in America during 1917-1918, Lancaster "naturally" (my term) focuses on that organization's efforts to gain support for the League of Nations. Accordingly, he finds (pp. 598-599):

The Executive Committee of the Federal Council of Churches issued on December 12, 1918, a ringing endorsement of President Wilson's plan for a league of nations. Acting on the recommendation of its Commission on International Justice and Goodwill, the committee challenged its affiliates to strengthen the President's position in Paris and at home. . . . The Federal Council asked local churches to provide suitable courses of study on the League of Nations and directed its Commission on Inter-Church Federations to secure expressions of approval of the League by public vote in local congregations. Sunday, January 12, 1919, was designated a day of prayer for the establishment of a league of nations.

In similar fashion, his paper, essentially a study of opinion formation, focuses on the activities of other religious organizations that, given their nature and history, might have been expected to support or oppose Wilson's plan.

e. Pressure-group leaders. To a considerable extent, the analytic distinction between "pressure-group leaders" and "leaders of nonpolitical formal organizations" is arbitrary and not easily applied in practice. The main criterion suggested for assigning organizations to different categories is neither their size

---

[24] George Gerbner, "Ideological Perspectives and Political Tendencies in News Reporting," *Journalism Quarterly,* Vol. 41, Autumn 1964, p. 495.

nor power but the range of issues likely to concern their leaders and members. The National Council of Churches and the American Medical Association, for example, both function today as pressure groups. But the activities of the latter are far more circumscribed—if less circumspect—than those of the former. I would therefore classify the AMA leaders, in their opinion-making roles, as "pressure-group leaders," the leaders of the National Churches of Christ as "leaders of nonpolitical formal organizations." Since one aim of the classification system proposed here is to help provide operational guidelines for opinion researchers, it seems useful to create categories that distinguish between men who lead such different kinds of pressure groups.

f. Influentials. "Influentials" is the label for the final type of formative agent considered here. Following Robert Merton, they can be further subdivided into "cosmopolitan" and "local" influentials.[25] The characteristic that differentiates them from other opinion leaders (who, of course, can also be viewed as "influentials"), is that their power derives from their personal qualities rather than their control of governmental or organizational resources.

Walter Lippmann serves as a convenient example. Hundreds of other individuals also write columns designed to influence public opinion, and many of them are more widely syndicated. It seems safe to say, however, both that he is the most influential publicist in the United States today and that his influence derives from his reputation and persuasiveness rather than from his relationships to the media that present his views.

In short, the "influentials" assigned to this category influence public opinion through their control of personal rather than corporate resources.

2. Agents' motives. As the three papers below by Helbich, Lancaster, and Maxwell concretely suggest, different agents, impelled by different motives, can try to move public opinion in the same direction. The "liberal" editors of the *Nation* and the "hyphenated" leaders of Irish-American groups, for example, both worked to defeat ratification of the Versailles Treaty. But their motives differed significantly. To ignore this dimension would make any study of their activities seriously incomplete. Questions about *why* men wanted to form public opinion in specified ways force historians (and other researchers), of course, to explore motivational thickets abounding in thorns and pitfalls. Their exploration can be avoided, however, only by sharply reducing a study's explanatory power and theoretical interest.

3. Agents' actions. It is relatively easier to reconstruct the actions agents take to form opinion than to reconstruct their motives for wanting to do so. But some difficult questions need to be answered about phenomena assigned to this category: In addition to *overt* actions to form opinion, what *covert* actions did specified agents take? Which groups constituted the main targets for specified activities by specified agents? Which groups constituted the "real" targets as distinct from the "nominal" targets? (For example, in the current controversy

25 Robert K. Merton, *Social Theory and Social Structure,* rev. and enlarged ed., Glencoe, Ill., Free Press, 1957, pp. 387-420.

over "open housing," do the groups opposed to "fair housing laws" *nominally* address themselves to "property owners" but *really* aim at "whites," irrespective of their propertied status?).

4. Impact of agents' actions on specified groups. Apart from other considerations, we need answers to the questions posed immediately above if we are to assess the relative success of different agents. The main question posed here is really a composite question: In relation to specified issues, which agents influenced which groups how much? The groups influenced can be characterized as "nominal target," "real target," "unintended target" ("boomerang" or "windfall" effects). "How much" refers to both the direction and the quality of opinion.

5. Explanation of impact of agents' activities. After we have answered the questions posed immediately above, *and only then,* we can tackle the hard job of explaining the differential success achieved by different agents. In other words, we need to secure data that permit us to say who took what actions, which had what impact, on what groups, in relation to what issue, *before* we can hope to develop systematic and responsible explanations of opinion formation. We may not be able to do so in any event, of course, but, if we first secure the specified types of data, our chances improve considerably.

Six types of determinants can be identified as helping to explain the impact of agents' actions upon public opinion. Again the topology is neither elegant nor exhaustive. But the brief notes below at least provide a beginning.

a. Group receptivity. It seems reasonable to assume that the predispositions of the members of a group are the most important determinants of their response to the actions taken by different agents.

b. Group attitudes toward agents. Contemporary studies support the proposition that "who" says something to someone significantly influences the response to what is said.[26] No reason exists to assume that the proposition applies uniquely to the present.

c. Agents' resources. One obvious determinant of the differential success agents enjoy is the differences in the financial and organizational resources available to them.

d. Arguments used. I assume that, except in unusual cases, the arguments used by agents have *some* significant weight in determining the opinions members of a group form on an issue. Another assumption: Persuasive arguments need not be "rational"—whatever we mean by "rational"—but researchers can hope to identify at least some of the reasons arguments *seem* rational and persuasive to the groups influenced by them. Put another way, I assume that, to respond favorably (or unfavorably) to arguments, most individuals need to perceive them as rational (or irrational). If that assumption is accepted, historians need not try to demonstrate that arguments *were* rational,

[26] See M. Brewster Smith, "Opinions, Personality, and Political Behavior," *American Political Science Review,* Vol. 52, March 1958, pp. 1-17. This article seems particularly useful for historians since it provides, in reasonably clear terms, a review of the "major foray[s] by psychologists into the personal determinants of opinion...."

they need only (*sic*) try to explain why specified arguments *seemed* rational to specified groups.[27]

e. Agents' skill in presenting arguments. Except to make explicit the assumption that skill is a significant determinant of success in opinion formation, no comment seems necessary.

f. Historical situation. Here I refer to phenomena that occur independently of actions agents take to form public opinion. For example, Maxwell points to "events in Ireland" as one of three sets of factors helping "to provide the framework within which Irish-American opposition to the League of Nations was to emerge and grow" (p. 620). In effect, what might be called the "specific historical situation" relevant to a particular issue or group, and the "general historical situation" relevant to all issues and groups, strongly tend to *condition* responses to actions designed to form opinion.

C. Impact of public opinion on government decisions

That public opinion significantly influences public policy has long been assumed. In fact, that assumption probably serves as the main scholarly justification for opinion research in general and historical opinion research in particular. How much hard evidence exists to support it, however? Rather little, according to V. O. Key, Ernest May, and Harwood L. Childs. All three have specifically focused on that question and all three essentially agree.[28] To quote the most recent (1965) statement by Childs:

... notwithstanding the accumulation of much data regarding voting behavior in elections and referenda, mounting quantities of opinion survey data, and many specialized studies of pressure groups, the mass media, and other links between citizens and government, few of the many hypotheses and speculations on the influences of public opinion on government found *concrete, empirical verification*. Specifically, even though public opinion is expressed regarding a specific public policy, it is seldom known which officials or agencies were aware of this state of public opinion, and what, if anything, was done about this awareness. [Emphasis added.]

Agreeing with Key that "the sharp definition of the role of public opinion as it affects different kinds of policies under different types of situations presents an analytical problem of extraordinary difficulty," Childs observed that:

For more than twenty-five years polling agencies have been making nationwide surveys of public opinion, and a wealth of opinion data has been collected regarding the views of the American people on issues of domestic and foreign policy. The question arises to what extent, if at all, public opinion actually

---

[27] The perspective adopted here leads to a more optimistic and less relativistic position than the one suggested in May, *op. cit.,* pp. 103-108.

[28] Key, *op. cit.,* pp. 409-431; May, *op. cit.,* pp. 102-103, 113-122; Childs, *op. cit.,* pp. 291-319.

influences public policy. There has been much theoretical speculation regarding the answer but very few hard facts.[29]

Historians might be tempted to adopt a superior tone to "pollsters" on the ground that historical method, applied to manuscript and other primary sources, has yielded the hard data so elusive to researchers lacking access to such sources. Any historian yielding to that temptation, however, would find it a chastening experience to read May's devastating critique.

Relationships between public opinion and American foreign policy have long concerned historians, May observed, but we still have little credible knowledge about them. That embarrassing state of affairs, he suggested, and my researches on the historiography of the annexation of Texas and other pre-Civil War issues lead me to agree strongly, in large measure derives from the fact that historians have "scarcely . . . raised, let alone answered," the key questions. His concluding paragraph is particularly pertinent for our purposes:

Our chief reason for believing that public opinion has influenced and does influence foreign policy is our knowledge that American statesmen have traditionally thought themselves responsible to, and supported or constrained by, some sort of general will. The national tradition is to accept as true the definition attributed to William of Malmesbury: *vox populi, vox Dei.* American political leaders have hearkened to the voice of the people as their seventeenth-century forebears did to the voice of God. Perhaps scholars instead of listening for these voices themselves, ought to begin by inquiring what it is that these men thought they heard.[30]

In effect, May observed that historians have strongly tended to assume that something like one-to-one relationships exist among the *distribution* of opinion, the *perception* of opinion by government officials, and the *decisions made* by government officials. But it is very difficult, he suggests, for anyone, contemporary official or later historian, to ascertain the actual distribution of public opinion at any specified time on any specified issue. Historians therefore would be better advised to begin research by focusing on decision makers' perception of public opinion rather than by "listening for these voices themselves. . . ."

As indicated in Section IV below, I incline toward a different research strategy from the one advocated by May. But he has made a significant

---

29 *Ibid.,* pp. 291-292, 309-310. It should be noted, however, that Childs reports upon six case studies directed by him that were explicitly designed to secure some "hard facts" to answer the question "to what extent, if at all, public opinion actually influences public policy." As he summarizes those studies, they provide highly interesting and suggestive answers to the question. But it is not another incident in interdisciplinary warfare, I trust, to observe that historians would strongly tend to doubt that firm conclusions can be drawn from case studies not based on intensive examination of correspondence and other personal documents of the government officials involved. No implication is intended that Professor Childs presents the studies as conclusive; on the contrary, my point is to reinforce his observation about the difficulty of securing relevant and significant "hard facts."

30 May, *op. cit.,* p. 122.

contribution to historical opinion research, I believe, by forcefully directing attention to the problem of identifying the main categories of the dimension variously referred to by different authorities as "linkage," "influence," or "impact."

In the classification system suggested in the present essay, the "impact" dimension is subdivided into four main categories: (1) Communication of opinion to officials; (2) Impact of opinion on distribution of political power; (3) Officials' perception of opinion; and (4) Impact of perception on specified decisions.

1. Communication of opinion to officials. Although the term "communication" has some misleading connotations when used to identify the phenomena assigned to this category, I have thus far been unable to find or devise a better one. To minimize misconceptions arising from the term's connotations, it is useful to emphasize that the category contains data designed to answer three questions: (a) Who *initiates* the processes by which government officials ultimately receive "information" about the distribution of opinion on issues? (b) What are the sequences of *"steps"* by which information about specified issues reaches officials? (c) What *"media"* are used to convey information on specified issues to officials?

Data relevant to each of those questions, I believe, are best grouped in a separate subcategory. They are identified here only in broad terms since different studies will require different sets of more or less detailed subcategories.

a. Initiators of communication process. For reasons previously suggested, I assume that, generally speaking, government officials actively try to form public opinion. For the same reasons, I assume that officials actively seek information about the distribution of opinion on issues over time. It would severely distort reality, I believe, to depict public officials only, or even primarily, as passive recipients of information. On the contrary, American public officials have always used a wide variety of devices (e.g. consultation with "expert" observers, analysis of newspapers, commissioning of "surveys") in their hot pursuit of information about public opinion.

An astonishing variety of "nonofficials" also exercise initiative in communicating information about the distribution of opinion on an issue to relevant or potent officials. One main type of "initiator" can be characterized as "spokesman" (authorized or self-appointed) for specific groups; another main type can be labeled "middleman." The "middleman" category connotes some on-going institution such as, for example, newspapers which poll the "man on the street" and *publicly* report their "findings," organizations that purport to have studied the distribution of opinion on specific issues and *privately* report their "findings" to selected officials, and so forth.

What difference does it make who initiates the processes that culminate in officials having specific perceptions of opinion distribution on an issue? Hard data to answer that question are lacking, it must be confessed. But the assumption seems reasonable that official perceptions vary considerably depending upon who initiates the communication processes and who thereby helps to determine the selection of information communicated. Granted that assumption, it follows that researchers ought to try to identify "initiators" of information on specific issues.

b. Sequence of steps in communication process. In addition to variations in official perceptions depending upon variations in who initiates the process, I assume that perceptions will vary significantly, depending upon (1) which officials receive the information in what order, and (2) the number, kind, and sequence of steps in the communication process.[31] For example, spokesmen for a group may directly communicate their perception of its opinion to one official rather than another, they may communicate it to party leaders who in turn communicate their *perceptions* to one official rather than another, they may communicate it to specific mass media, and so forth.

No implication is intended that historians (or contemporary researchers) can reconstruct all the steps in any sequence of communication flows by which specific officials receive information about public opinion on a specific issue. But it seems axiomatic that historians ought to *try* to reconstruct such sequences if they hope to reconstruct official perceptions with any reasonable degree of precision and credibility, or hope to understand and explain how those perceptions came about. May's point, in effect, is that historians have not acted upon that axiom; my point is that, to do so effectively, they need to develop and use a classification system that explicitly indicates the kinds of data to secure relevant to officials' perception.

c. Media of communication. Marshall McLuhan's guru-like dictum about "the medium is the message" at best represents only a half-truth. But opinion researchers have long been aware that the type of media used to communicate information to officials does significantly influence their perceptions of the messages communicated. No need exists to present a long list of the different media that can be used in different sequences of steps in the communication process from public to official. Two points, however, seem worth making: (1) Not only the source of information about public opinion and the circumstances under which the information is received, but the form (or media) of communication must be taken into account when we try to reconstruct and explain how the voice of the people sounded to specified officials. (2) In addition to written and verbal forms of communication, various types of action, e.g. riots, demonstrations, meetings, serve the same function—and frequently speak louder, and more persuasively, than words.

2. *Impact of opinions on distribution of political power.* Voting can be regarded, of course, as simply another form of communication of information about public opinion to public officials. It is important and complex enough, however, to warrant separate treatment.

---

[31] For a stimulating analysis of the way information flows influence opinions and decisions, see Elihu Katz, "The Two-step Flow of Communication: An Up-to-date Report on an Hypothesis," *Public Opinion Quarterly,* Vol. 21, 1957, pp. 61-78. See also Key, *op. cit.,* pp. 411-431.

We need not assume perfect democracy in a political system to recognize that voting is a particularly potent form of communication. Its potency stems from its dual character. Voting may simultaneously function as a form of communication of opinion to public officials and an act which, in a formally democratic system, formally determines who the officials ultimately are to whom opinions are to be communicated. The problem, of course, is that opinions on any specified issue, or set of issues, do not *necessarily* play any significant role in determining voting behavior; they may, but then again they may not.

Put another way, we are entitled to assume that voting can function as a form of communication about public opinion. But how do we know when it actually does perform that function to any significant degree and how do we know what information it actually does convey? Those questions have long bedeviled politicians and researchers. Further discussion of them is best reserved for Section V, which deals with the general problem of constructing indicators and indexes of public opinion.

3. Officials' perception of public opinion. Truth in history is not only what happened but what men believed to have happened. Public officials may—and frequently do—misperceive public opinion. For our present purposes, that does not matter. What does matter is that the *reality,* not the *accuracy,* of their perceptions influences their actions—to the extent that they consciously allow public opinion to influence their actions. "Reality" here means what they "really" think they perceive, not what they *say* they perceive.

Which officials? What is perceived? Those are the two main questions relevant to this category.

Different officials, it is obvious enough, may have radically different perceptions of the distribution of public opinion on an issue, or set of issues. Researchers, equally obviously, must therefore specifically identify the officials about whose perceptions they make claims; if they cannot do so with some reasonable degree of specificity, they are not entitled to make claims about the impact of public opinion on public policy.

The problem of identifying what is perceived by specified officials is more complex. As indicated previously, the dimension "Distribution of opinion" contains numerous and radically different components. It is not very useful, therefore, to describe the perceptions of specific officials in vague terms, e.g. "public opinion favored (or opposed) Texas Annexation." Since it seems reasonable to assume that officials are influenced by perceptions of both the "direction" and "quality" of opinion, data are needed relevant to the different subcategories of those broad headings. Again, no counsel of perfection is being urged here. Such data may be impossible to get, even if one really tries hard to get them. The point is, one really ought to try hard—and to recognize the implications for one's study if one does not succeed.

4. Impact of officials' perception of public opinion on specified decisions. This category is the "pay-off" one for studies focused on the relationships between public opinion and public policy. In a sense, research carried out in respect to all other categories of the proposed classification system can be regarded as preliminary research to help answer two main types of questions:

a. *What kind* of impact did officials' perception of public opinion have on the *timing* (e.g. accelerate, delay) of specified decisions? On the direction (e.g. reinforce, or weaken, an official's adherence to his own preferred position)?

b. *How much* impact, i.e. how much "weight," did officials' perception of public opinion have on both the timing and direction of specified decisions?

Posing those questions gives rise to another: Can historians really be expected to answer them systematically with any reasonable degree of credibility? For reasons indicated previously, I do not think historians can *now* be expected to do so, but I do think that eventually they may be able to do so. Development and wide *use* of a classification system of the type sketched in this essay, I have tried to suggest, would contribute significantly to the coming of that happy day. But an even more important contribution, I suggest, would be development and wide use of a general research strategy and system of analysis for the historical study of public opinion. It is to that problem that attention can now be appropriately directed.

IV. A RESEARCH STRATEGY AND TENTATIVE SYSTEM OF ANALYSIS FOR THE HISTORICAL STUDY OF PUBLIC OPINION

A. A research strategy

The strategy advocated here assumes that historians who undertake opinion research should schedule their operations according to the classification system sketched above.[32] That is, researchers should, *in sequence,* try to (1) reconstruct the distribution of opinion on specified issues over time, (2) reconstruct and explain the formation of opinion, (3) reconstruct and explain the impact of opinion upon policy.

Like all research strategies, the one advocated here derives from a particular theoretical orientation that should be stated explicitly. No implication is intended, of course, that I have developed anything resembling a general theory capable of stating the conditions under which public opinion has varying degrees of impact upon specified types of public policies. My "theoretical orientation," if the term does not seem overblown, simply assumes that public officials strongly tend to play the most important roles both in consciously forming public opinion and in determining its impact upon government decisions. Given that orientation, the research strategy advocated here seems to follow logically.

How can we hope to find out who played significant roles in forming public opinion, or to explain their ability and desire to do so, if we do not *first*

---

[32] I make a sharp distinction between the operations involved in *conducting* research and those involved in *reporting* the results of research; my comments refer only to the former set of operations.

reconstruct the distribution of opinion over time? Similarly, how can we reconstruct and explain the impact of opinion on policy if we do not first reconstruct the distribution of opinion?

Granted that what "counts" in decision making is not the "real" distribution of opinion but officials' perception of the distribution of opinion. Surely, however, a systematic and responsible explanation requires us to make some estimates of the relationships between reality and officials' perception of reality. If officials misperceived the distribution of opinion and acted to some significant extent on their misperceptions, did those misperceptions derive from the officials' having already decided on the policies they wanted to follow, or from poor channels of communication, or both? And *before* we try to estimate the extent to which officials acted on what they thought they heard as "the voice of the people," shouldn't we try to find out whether they essentially were listening only to their own voices as echoed by people who, in effect, they had taught what to say?

Put another way, the research strategy advocated here derives from the following line of argument:

Verifying claims about popular support for, or opposition to, specified government actions is a crucial *preliminary* step in the verification of explanations that emphasize the impact of public opinion upon public decisions. No causal relationship *necessarily* exists between the distribution of public opinion and the occurrence of a particular decision, or set of decisions. If a researcher asserts that such a relationship exists, it therefore seems reasonable to ask him to justify his description of public opinion before evaluating his argument about its impact upon events. In short, it seems logical to evaluate the data and procedures used to *ascertain* public opinion on given issues before evaluating the data and procedures used to *assess* its effect. Paraphrasing Mrs. Glasse's celebrated advice on how to cook a hare, the recipe suggested here for assessing the causal role of public opinion begins, "First, catch your public opinion."[33]

B. A tentative system of analysis for historical opinion research

How can historians—or anyone doing historical research—proceed to "catch" public opinion? To begin with, I suggest, by recognizing the implications of an obvious "fact": the distribution of opinion on an issue changes constantly. It may not change much, it may fluctuate wildly. Over time, it changes. Indeed, measured finely enough, we can assume that opinion distribution changes daily. But no researcher, of course, is likely to want to try to "catch" it on a daily basis, except for extremely limited periods of time.

1. Selection of periods for measurement. From those elementary observa-

---

[33] It may be pedantic to note that the recipe was attributed to Mrs. Glasse erroneously; it actually appeared in a *Cook Book* published in 1747. See Kate Louise Roberts (reviser), *Hoyt's New Cyclopedia of Practical Quotation,* New York, 1922, p. 138. The recipe goes, "To make a ragoût, first catch your hare."

tions, a basic problem emerges for historical opinion researchers: Which "poll days" or "poll periods" should be chosen to measure trends in the distribution of opinion on an issue over time? Depending upon the general nature of the study and the specific claims made, the poll periods might vary in length from a single day, to a month, or, in unusual cases, to a year (if the study focused on long-lived, relatively unchanging issues such as "the tariff" prior to the Civil War). But, in systematic opinion research, some specific dates must be selected on which public opinion must be described as having had some specific distribution. Obviously, to perform the operations required to develop valid descriptions of opinion distribution over time, some principles of selection must be used to minimize distortions due to "accidental circumstances" affecting opinion at certain times. "Accidental circumstances," in this context, are those not covered by the principles of selection.

One solution to the problem of identifying *valid* poll periods, i.e. periods when a researcher can reasonably expect to measure what he says he is measuring, is to use a sampling formula designed to lessen the chances of "accidents" distorting opinion distribution. For example, beginning with a carefully selected date, "polls" might be taken every five or seven or eleven months, or any other interval that rotates the dates in different years. Such solutions undoubtedly tend to lessen distortion due to chance factors and increase reliability; i.e. different researchers using the same formula, and using the same procedures and sources with comparable skill, would get similar results. But to use such solutions we must pay a heavy price; we must sacrifice the flexibility that constitutes one of the great advantages historians enjoy over contemporary researchers.

As noted in the discussion of Hyman's incisive observations about the "deficiencies of discontinuous data" that retard theoretical development, contemporary researchers lack the "20-20 hindsight" enjoyed by historians. Unless they resort to retrospective interviews, of dubious validity even after short periods of time and ever more dubious thereafter, they are *"locked into"* the questions that happened to be asked about particular issues at particular times. In contrast, historical researchers, given the availability of relevant documents—a large "given," I concede—have unlimited flexibility to benefit from historical perspective and range over issues and events, as well as choose any poll periods they regard as best suited to test any theories or hypotheses they (or others) have formulated. (The "relevant document" problem is discussed in Section V below).

By unlimited flexibility to choose dates, I mean, of course, unlimited flexibility to choose poll periods *controlled by some objective criteria.* Put another way, systematic opinion research requires historians to develop a "chronicle of events," or "narrative framework," for the issue(s) studied that specialists would strongly tend to agree was based on reasonable, unarbitrary criteria.

Once historians have developed an objective narrative framework appropriate to their particular studies, they can systematically proceed to identify the poll dates (or periods) on which to measure opinion distribution. Having done so, they can try to carry out, in sequence, research designed to secure the data called for by a classification system of the type sketched above. (The question of whether we have, or can develop, methods capable of securing those data is also postponed until Section V below).

If the argument thus far is accepted, or merely granted for the sake of argument, it follows that development of an objective narrative framework is the indispensable first operation required by the proposed system of analysis for historical opinion research. Do we now know how to perform that operation?

2. *Constructing a narrative framework to catch public opinion.* My unpublished research on Texas Annexation has convinced me that it is possible to construct an objective narrative framework for historical opinion research; alas, I cannot yet cite published work to support the claim. What I can do now, however, in addition to emphasizing the importance of the problem, is to identify three main types of events (broadly defined) that can be combined to construct a narrative framework for any historical opinion study: (a) sequence of relevant government *decisions;* (b) actions (other than government decisions) taken by agents to form opinion; and (c) events contributing to significant changes in the historical situation. For convenience and clarity, my illustrations are all drawn from the Texas Annexation issue, but the typology and operations seem generally applicable.

a. Government decisions. On December 29, 1845, President James K. Polk signed the congressional resolution that formally made Texas the thirtieth state in the Union. To what extent, and in what ways, did public opinion influence the sequence of events that culminated in that decision? The volume of historiographic literature touching on that problem is large—and shallow. Its shallowness, I suggest, stems from the general lack of recognition among historians that to solve the problem we must begin by trying to construct a narrative framework. Failure to recognize the importance of that operation, I maintain, is primarily responsible for the failure to perform it. Put another way, the argument here is that if historians doing research on the Texas Annexation issue made a concerted and systematic attempt to construct such a framework, they would be able to achieve substantial agreement on its main parts and basic shape.

If we begin by explicitly designating Polk's action on December 29, 1845, as the decision that we ultimately have to explain, we can reasonably regard it as the terminal decision in a series of government decisions that began on February 22, 1819, with the signing of the "Transcontinental Treaty" between the United States and Spain. That treaty dealt with the southwestern boundaries of the United States, including its claims to Texas as far south as the Rio Grande. Just as it is reasonable and unarbitrary to designate the Transcontinental Treaty as the initial decision, it is possible to designate other actions, on various governmental levels, as constituting the sequence of "main decisions" between the initial and terminal decisions.

The argument can be summarized and extended as follows: Using reasonable criteria, we can identify a sequence of governmental decisions from February 22, 1819, to December 29, 1845, as "the decision to annex Texas." We can then go on to designate those decisions as major parts of an objective narrative framework for studies dealing with some aspect of public opinion and Texas Annexation. Their major role stems from their dual character; they are the decisions upon which public opinion may have had some impact and, once made, we can assume, they had some impact upon the formation of public opinion.

b. Agents' actions. Government decisions do not constitute the only parts of a narrative framework for historical opinion studies; actions taken by agents consciously trying to form opinion on an issue must also be included. We need not expect specialists unanimously to agree on all actions to be included. It seems reasonable, however, to expect that substantial agreement would be reached if an explicit, systematic, sustained attempt were made to identify the "main actions" agents took to form opinion on an issue.

Based upon a survey of the relevant secondary literature, I am confident that specialists on Texas Annexation would unanimously agree that its narrative framework should include, for example, the following actions: Senator Robert J. Walker's "immediate annexation" letter, published on February 3, 1844; Henry Clay's "anti-immediate annexation" letter, published on April 27, 1844; Martin Van Buren's "anti-immediate annexation" letter, also published on April 27, 1844; the Democratic national convention's nomination of Polk for President on an "immediate annexation" platform, May 29, 1844. In similar fashion, it seems reasonable to suggest, agreement could be reached to include many other "main actions" between 1819 and 1845.

Given the proverbially disputatious temperament of historians and the nature of the problem, some disagreements undoubtedly would persist on whether specific actions should be included in the narrative framework for a specific issue. But no need exists to belabor the point that such disagreements do not alter the basic argument made here, and that a variety of means could be used to handle the problem of what might be called "marginal actions." In general, if disagreement continued after direct and conscious confrontation of specialists, I would favor including "marginal" actions on the ground that an overly inclusive framework is preferable to an overly restrictive framework.

c. Events that change the historical situation. In relative terms, specialists trying to construct a common narrative framework for a specific issue would probably find it most difficult to agree on the type of event included in this category. Again it seems reasonable, however, to expect substantial agreement if attention is explicitly focused on the problem of deciding which events should be included and the grounds for inclusion (or exclusion) are made explicit.

For example, in respect to Texas Annexation, I think agreement could be secured among specialists that the narrative framework for the issue ought to include the 1835-1836 Congressional conflict over antislavery petitions and President Tyler's break with the Whig Party in August 1841. Neither set of events originated as conscious actions taken to influence public opinion on

Texas Annexation. But those events significantly contributed to changes in the historical situation that made it both necessary and possible for agents favorable to, and opposed to, Texas Annexation to take certain actions consciously designed to influence public opinion—actions that probably would *not* have been taken if the events specified had not occurred. Moreover, without now attempting to support the claim, I think it could be shown that the distribution of public opinion on Texas Annexation differed significantly before and after each set of events cited above.

In short, the argument here is that a narrative framework designed to facilitate systematic reconstruction and explanation of opinion distribution and formation should not be restricted to government decisions and agents' conscious actions. It should also include events that, in effect, conditioned "the climate of opinion" by producing changes in the historical situation relevant to specific issues.

V. OPERATIONS TO MEASURE THE DISTRIBUTION OF OPINION

According to the research strategy advocated here, after constructing a narrative framework relevant to some specified issue(s), researchers proceed to perform operations designed to secure, in sequence, the data called for by the three main categories of the classification system. Although my own work has not progressed to the point where I can try to deal systematically with all three categories, it seems useful to make a start on the operational problems they pose by restricting attention to the first category and trying to codify, on a fairly primitive level, the procedures historians have used to find out the distribution of opinion. The discussion that follows is based on an analysis of the historical literature specifically dealing with the Civil War but it holds, I believe, for American historiography in general.[34]

A definite pattern can be detected in the procedures historians have intuitively and implicitly developed to study the distribution of opinion relevant to the coming of the Civil War. In general terms, they have acted on the assumption that information about the distribution of opinion *can reasonably be inferred* from data found in contemporary documents not originally designed for that purpose. Put another way, historians have extracted related "facts" from a wide variety of sources and grouped them together to form *indicators* of public opinion.

For example, newspaper editorials dealing with a proposed law are frequently taken to reflect some aspect of public opinion regarding it, and historians use those editorials to buttress or justify their claims about public opinion. Instead of relying on a single indicator, however, historians have tended to combine several of them to form an index. Thus, if editorials are used as one indicator,

---

[34] Part of this study was reported in Lee Benson and Thomas J. Pressly, "Can Differences in Interpretations of the Causes of the American Civil War Be Resolved Objectively?" New York, Columbia University, Bureau of Applied Social Research, 1956, pp. 43-63, mimeographed.

the public speeches or private views of influential or "representative" men might be a second, mass meetings on the issue a third, and so on. Many different indicators have been devised and an even larger number of different indexes constructed. But the pattern invariably has been the same: (1) attempts are made to establish certain facts from source materials; (2) certain *inferences* are then drawn from those facts about the distribution of public opinion.

If some contemporary researchers believe that personal interviews are the only means by which reliable and valid information can be secured about public opinion, they would be impressed, perhaps appalled, by the astonishing variety of sources historians have ransacked in their search for opinion indicators. Unfortunately, the ingenuity displayed by historians in creating such indicators is matched by their casualness and reticence concerning their procedures. Only rarely does one find an explicit statement of the logical considerations dictating the choice of sources or justifying the inferences drawn from the factual data.

Such an individualistic, spontaneous approach to the creation and use of indicators might suggest that historians follow no rules in trying to reconstruct the distribution of public opinion on an issue. At first sight, the motto appears to be "anyone can play." Closer examination reveals that "historical opinion indicators" can be arranged into three distinct types and that some un-articulated, but loosely understood, rules govern their creation and use. The incomplete, tentative, and compressed classification system sketched below is designed to be suggestive, not exhaustive. Its purpose is simply to identify the main types of indicators created by American historians; no attempt will be made to discuss the considerations governing their formation and use. But one general point can be stressed. *Indicators are made, not found.* That is, a fact (or set of facts) extracted from historical documents does not constitute an indicator of public opinion. *It becomes an indicator only when an inference is drawn from it.* Granted this point, it will be unnecessary to distinguish hereafter between an indicator and the documents from which it is created.[35]

A. *Types of historical opinion indicators and rules to use them*

I. Actions or events
  A. Official government actions
    1. Legislative
      a. Laws
      b. Resolutions

---

35 In the classification scheme presented here, an effort has been made to demonstrate that distinctions can be drawn not only between types of indicators, but between the same indicators when different kinds of sources are used. As a result, the compressed classification scheme is not presented uniformly. In dealing with the problem of devising historical opinion indicators, I have benefited heavily from two articles by Paul F. Lazarsfeld and Allen H. Barton: "Qualitative Measurement in the Social Sciences: Classification, Typologies, and Indices," in Daniel Lerner and Harold D. Lasswell, eds. *The Policy Sciences,* Stanford, Calif., Stanford University Press, 1951, pp. 155-192, and Barton Lazarsfeld, *op. cit.,* pp. 321-361.

    c. Etc.
  2. Executive
    a. Actions on legislation
    b. Recommendations in prescribed or customary addresses
    c. Etc.
  3. Judicial
    a. Formal decisions
    b. Charges to juries
    c. Etc.
  4. Etc.
B. Official actions, nongovernmental institutions
  1. Resolutions or platforms adopted
  2. Literature published
  3. Etc.
C. Individual, customary, or prescribed actions
  1. Voting at elections for public office
  2. Voting at elections for private office
  3. Etc.
D. Individual, spontaneous, nonprescribed actions
  1. Demonstrations or riots not planned by existing organizations
  2. Acts of violence against officials
  3. Etc.
E. Etc.
II. Expert estimates of the distribution of public opinion
  A. Official estimates made in performance of duty
    1. Government officials in reports
    2. Nongovernment officials in reports to their organizations
    3. Etc.
  B. Estimates made for, or published in, mass media
    1. Newspaper surveys (as distinct from editorial expressions of opinion)
    2. Expert estimates reported in mass media
    3. Etc.
  C. Private estimates of knowledgeable individuals
    1. Politicians or "unbiased" observers
    2. Foreign travelers or visiting experts
    3. Etc.
  D. Etc.
III. Expressions of opinion (oral or written in origin)
  A. Influential men
    1. Private opinions (letters, diaries, etc.)
    2. Public opinions (speeches, publications, etc.)
  B. Representative men (merchants, farmers, workers, etc.)
    1. Private opinion (letters, diaries, etc.)
    2. Public opinions (petitions, letters to editor etc.)

C. Sensitive men (writers, artists, intellectuals, etc.)
1. Private opinion (letters, diaries, etc.)
2. Public opinions ("works of art," books, articles, etc.)
D. Mass media
1. Influential media (prestige papers, large circulation papers, etc.)
a. Newspaper editorials
b. Magazine editorials
c. Etc.
2. Representative media (class, section, ethnic group, etc.)
a. Newspaper editorials
b. Magazine editorials
c. Etc.
E. Etc.

One example may be enough to support the assertion that some informal rules govern historians engaged in studying the distribution of public opinion. Suppose the issue is repeal of the Fugitive Slave Act after 1850. Suppose the assumption is granted that newspaper editorials can be analyzed in such a way as to form a "good" indicator of opinion, i.e. that the opinions expressed in specific newspaper editorials varied as the opinions of specific groups varied. Let us further suppose that a historian relied heavily on newspaper editorials as an indicator of the distribution of "Northern" public opinion. Finally, let us suppose that the newspapers used consisted exclusively of the *New York Tribune* ("rabidly antislavery"), the *Liberator* (William Lloyd Garrison's abolitionist paper), and several semi-official organs of the Free Soil Party. Clearly, the indicator created could not be a *valid* one. At best, it did not measure "Northern" public opinion but only an extremely unrepresentative segment of it.

Though no explicit standard operating procedures have been agreed upon by historians, it is *taken for granted* that a representative, weighted sample of extant newspaper files should be used in creating an indicator.[36] And it would be possible to cite other informal "rules" that historians are supposed to observe while using newspaper editorials to construct an opinion indicator. In fact, those "rules" are so much taken for granted that they are sometimes ignored and violated by historians who probably would subscribe to them in theory.

This last observation enables us to answer, in general terms, the basic question posed by this section of the essay. A logical way for historians to try to reconstruct the distribution of public opinion is to do systematically, explicitly, and precisely what has tended to be done impressionistically, implicitly, and vaguely. For there can be little doubt that even impressionistic methods have enabled historians to secure a great deal of information about the distribution of

---

[36] Some interesting but general comments on newspaper editorials and public opinion are found in Lucy M. Salmon, *The Newspaper and the Historian*, New York, 1923, pp. 252-253, 270-286, 439-440, 470-471.

opinion over time and place.[37] The assumption seems logical, therefore, that an attack upon the problems that historians encounter in systematically creating and using opinion indicators is at least likely to yield modest returns. Couched in such general terms this answer does not get us very far, but it leads to consideration of other questions that may.

The methodological problems historians face in trying to reconstruct the distribution of public opinion can be identified broadly as follows: (1) What indicators are most appropriate for a particular study? (2) Given a number of appropriate indicators, how can they be combined in one index that maximizes their individual advantages and minimizes their disadvantages? (3) How does one actually go about creating and using opinion indicators and indexes? (4) What sampling principles can be devised to govern the selection of documents from which data can be extracted to form an indicator? A few general observations relevant to the first problem will be offered below; the other three are best treated specifically in relation to substantive events and will be dealt with in a future book, tentatively titled "New York Public Opinion and American Civil War Causation."

B. Choosing the "best indicator" for a study

Under ideal conditions historians might use all the indicators in the classification system sketched in the preceding section. If the requisite source materials were available, and if enough time and effort could be given to the task, every indicator probably would yield *some* information about public opinion. But since conditions never are ideal, historians always must choose among possible indicators. In effect, they must decide upon a hierarchical rank order of "best indicators" for the particular aspects of public opinion that concern them. An example might make the point more clearly than an abstract definition.

His terminology was different but James Bryce was essentially dealing with the problem of "best indicator" when he posed the question, "How is the drift of Public Opinion to be ascertained?" After analyzing the advantages and disadvantages of several different indicators, Bryce concluded, in his famous chapter on "Public Opinion":

The best way in which the tendencies at work in any community can be discovered and estimated is by moving freely about among all sorts and conditions of men and noting how they are affected by the news or the arguments brought from day to day to their knowledge. In every neighborhood there are unbiased persons with good opportunities for observing, and plenty of skill in "sizing up" the attitudes and proclivities of their fellow citizens. Such

---

[37] See the discussion in Henry David, "Opinion Research in the Service of the Historian," in Komarovsky, ed., *op. cit.,* pp. 270-271. But, in my opinion, that commentary exaggerates the methodological differences between historians and contemporary researchers engaged in studying public opinion. In this connection, see the two articles by Lazarsfeld and Barton cited in note 35.

men are invaluable guides. Talk is the best way of reaching the truth, because in talk one gets directly at the facts, whereas reading gives not so much the facts as what the writer believes, or wishes to have others believe. Whoever, having himself a considerable experience of politics, takes the trouble to investigate in this way will seldom go astray. There is a *flair* which long practice and "sympathetic touch" bestow. The trained observer learns how to profit by small indications, as an old seaman discerns, sooner than the landsman, the signs of coming storm.[38]

Translated into our terms, Bryce designates as the best indicator of opinion distribution some version of "private estimates of knowledgeable individuals." And examination of the literature dealing with causes of the Civil War demonstrates that historians have viewed private estimates of knowledgeable individuals as a good indicator of opinion. But the literature also demonstrates that historians have relied much more heavily upon an indicator that Bryce and other theorists tend to deprecate—voting for public office.[39] The literature, in fact, demonstrates that historians have depended much more heavily on voting than upon any other indicator for evidence to "prove" their claims about the distribution of public opinion in the pre-war period. To anyone familiar with the ruggedly individualistic traditions of American historiography, this similarity in research design appears highly suggestive. Together with other considerations, it tends to support the following conclusion: Given the American political system and the actual course of events, *as a general rule,* voting for public office provides the single best indicator of public opinion.

1. Advantages of voting behavior as an observable indicator of opinion distribution. An objection to this line of reasoning is immediately apparent. Because historians have taken voting to be the best indicator of opinion, it does not necessarily follow that they are correct. Consensus is not the only criterion of validity and reliability. But in this case consensus has resulted from the independent and continuous efforts of historians to reconstruct the distribution of opinion rather than from routine adherence to standard procedures. Unless convincing arguments to the contrary are presented, their collective experience supports the proposition that voting is the historian's best indicator of American opinion distribution.

"But," critics may immediately reply, "haven't leading theorists—Bryce, Lowell, Lippmann—presented just such convincing arguments, and don't they apply to the pre-Civil War period in the United States, as well as to other times and places?"[40]

Without analyzing the arguments of these men in detail, four points can be made in rebuttal. In the first place, they were not writing about historical studies

---

[38] Bryce, *op. cit.,* Vol. 1, pp. 155-160. The quotation is from p. 156.

[39] The reader can test the statement's accuracy by picking up at random works dealing with the coming of the Civil War and examining them in the light of this analysis. In addition to Bryce's criticisms of voting as an opinion indicator, see Lowell, *op. cit.,* pp. 24-25, 70-128; Walter Lippman, *Public Opinion,* New York, 1922, pp. 193-197.

[40] *Op. cit.*

and their judgments cannot be applied mechanically to historical source materials. Second, some of their criticisms demonstrate only that voting is not a perfect indicator, not that other indicators are relatively better. Third, to some extent their criticisms derive from moral judgments as to *what public opinion should be and how it should be formed;* such judgments are not applicable to the study of public opinion as defined here. Finally, their most telling points are directed against faulty and impressionistic use of election results as an opinion indicator, not against the potential value of voting records studied systematically.

That American voting behavior has been imperfectly studied as an indicator of opinion is readily conceded, and the present essay partially stems from a long-range, continuing research project which attempts to document that conclusion in detail. But the project has also led to the conclusion that systematic procedures can be devised to increase the value of voting records as an opinion indicator. In works already published, I have tried to support the conclusion in practice; here the aim is to suggest some general advantages they offer compared to other opinion indicators.[41]

Voting records have at least one unique advantage; they are the only documents left by the American public from which inferences can *directly* be drawn about mass opinions concerning public policies. All other documents from which indicators can be created require making two different types of inferences. Like voting records, other historical documents require drawing an inference from them about the distribution of opinion. But other documents require the additional inference that they actually reflect the views of the public *en masse,* not merely the views of the men responsible for the particular documents *selected* by historians as sources of opinion data.[42]

For example, when used as an indicator, newspaper editorials are assumed to reflect the opinions of "publics" that actually had no part in their composition or publication. The serious problems that arise in connection with that type of inference need little comment except to note that the problems would exist even if all relevant newspaper files were extant, equally accessible, and good sampling methods were used. But the hard job of finding out whose opinions are reflected in editorials—the publisher, the editor, the readers, the public in general—is complicated by the fact that extant files frequently are not a representative or adequate sample of the newspapers published at a given time and place. It seems

---

[41] The project was partially reported in Benson, "Research Problems," in Komarovsky, ed., *op. cit.,* pp. 113-181. A substantive demonstration of how voting behavior can be systematically used to reconstruct opinion distribution on an issue is presented in Benson, *Concept of Jacksonian Democracy,* pp. 254-269. But the major "demonstration" belongs to that familiar category of scholarship known as "research in progress." According to present plans, it will be reported in a book jointly written with Professor Joel Silbey, tentatively titled, "New York Public Opinion and American Civil War Causation: An Essay in the Logic and Practice of Historical Explanation."

[42] In a somewhat different context and formulation, the same point has been strongly emphasized by the Social Science Research Council's Committee on Historiography. See Thomas C. Cochran, "Methods: Theory and Practice," in *Bulletin 64, The Social Sciences in Historical Study,* New York, Social Science Research Council, 1954, pp. 158-164.

to be a law of history that the party which ultimately dominates a particular area gets its papers preserved more frequently, and in more accessible places, than the losing party. In contrast, both the winners and the losers—even the very minor parties—secure immortality (sic) in the voting records. The argument here is that voting records usually are more complete, detailed, and precise, and *comparatively* more easily worked, than the materials from which any other indicator can be formed—and that those advantages will increase enormously when a major project now well under way is completed.[43]

An analogy may suggest the serious disadvantages of other historical opinion indicators compared with those based upon voting for public office. Suppose contemporary researchers wish to reconstruct the distribution of public opinion on given issues. They first have to draw up a representative sample of the public. Failure to meet that requirement would open the study to serious criticism and probably invalidate it. Having drawn up their sample, they try to interview all its members. Some *reasonable* degree of incompleteness is not fatal; the operative word is "reasonable." But if the sample design was poorly drawn, or if the design was poorly executed, the study's findings would be given little credence.

Now let us suppose that contemporary researchers were forced to draw their sample of people to be interviewed from the same "elite" groups whose records constitute the historian's sources. (On any social level, the records of unusual or atypical individuals are the only ones available to historians.) And let us further suppose that interviews could be secured only with a small, unrepresentative fraction of the original sample. Under those conditions, historians undoubtedly would view contemporary findings about public opinion with even greater skepticism than they do at present. Yet those are the conditions under which historians ordinarily work when they use opinion indicators other than voting behavior. That historians have been able to obtain useful information by using such indicators testifies only to their ingenuity in overcoming difficulties and to the insights gained from "saturation" in source materials.

The difficulties suggested above apply most strongly to the type of indicator classified as "Expressions of opinion," but they are also encountered in using "Expert estimates." Bryce claimed that a talk with experts was the "best way" to learn the drift of opinion, but he was careful to emphasize the necessity of "moving freely about among all sorts and conditions of men. . . ." Historians do not have that freedom. Except in rare cases, the highly unrepresentative nature of "surviving" historical documents prevents historians from following Bryce's research design.[44]

---

43 Thanks to the joint efforts of the Inter-university Consortium for Political Research and the American Historical Association's Committee to Collect the Quantitative Data of History, the county voting and relevant demographic statistics from 1824 to date will be available in machine-readable form in the near future. When that day arrives, and when historians have acquired the methodological training needed to make good use of those data, I predict that major advances will be made in the use of voting behavior as an opinion indicator.

44 Historians may occasionally unearth a fairly complete file of documents written by government officials charged with the responsibility of reporting the distribution of public

For any period, the expert estimates available to historians were made by men who cannot be viewed as representative of all groups comprising the "American public." Historians have learned enough about their own "frames of reference," and other scholars enough about the "sociology of knowledge," to recognize that the truly "unbiased observer" is an extremely rare bird. When expert estimates are contradictory, as they frequently are, the differences tend to be closely associated with the different group characteristics of the men making the estimates.

Unless logical or factual flaws can be demonstrated in one set of conflicting estimates, the only way to decide between them is to check them all against other opinion indicators. But if those indicators also simply represent expressions of opinion, we run into the same problem of establishing their representative quality. In practice, historians implicitly try to find some act or event against which conflicting expert estimates can be checked. But this is a circular procedure, for it first must be established that the acts or events really do indicate something specific about public opinion. Carefully staged and costly "spontaneous demonstrations," for example, have been known to occur in places other than opera houses. Thus, *whenever possible*, it seems more logical to start with acts or events as indicators of public opinion, and to use "expert estimates" and "expressions of opinion" to supplement them. Additional arguments can be offered to support this line of reasoning.

2. Action the best test of opinion. Attention has been directed thus far to the advantages voting data have in respect to the representative quality of documents from which inferences can be drawn about past opinion. But such data also have advantages in respect to the validity of the inferences about public opinion that can reasonably be drawn from any document.

In the classification scheme outlined above in section V.A, it will be recalled, voting for public office is designated as an "Action or events" type of indicator. Simply on the face of it, the claim seems reasonable that, other things being equal, men's actions are better *tests* of their opinions than verbal or written expressions and better *measures* of opinion than expert estimates.[45] The key phrase is, of course, "other things being equal."

Things never are exactly equal. Judgments must always be made about the degree of inequality that permits meaningful comparisons, and borderline cases inevitably produce differences in judgment. But substantial agreement is not always difficult to achieve. If life, fortune, or liberty had to be risked to "express" an opinion through a public act such as voting or signing a petition, and a "private" written or verbal expression of opinion posed no such risk, hardly anyone would dispute the claim that things were not equal. When such

opinion. That excellent public opinion indicators can be created from such documents is demonstrated in Lynn M. Case, *French Opinion on War and Diplomacy during the Second Empire*, Philadelphia, University of Pennsylvania Press, 1954.

[45] See, in this connection, Strayer, *op. cit.*, pp. 264-265. But I have somewhat changed Strayer's emphasis upon action as a test of opinion and tried to suggest the conditions under which the assumption is likely to hold.

dangers are not attached to public acts, however, things frequently are equal *enough* to warrant the claim that action is a better test of opinion than written or verbal expression. Moreover, if acts do entail much heavier risks *and men do act,* more valid inferences can be drawn about the *saliency* and *intensity* of their opinions from their acts than from their verbal or written expressions.

Recognizing that many exceptions to the rule exist, and that it can never be automatically assumed to hold, the claim seems warranted that in American history the act of voting is the best single *test* of opinion. Under the American political system, even with nonsecret ballots, voting *ordinarily* does not entail a heavy risk, nor are extremely heavy external pressures (governmental or social) brought to bear upon men to vote a given ticket. Some social pressures undoubtedly are brought to bear upon voters almost everywhere and at all times; but those pressures usually do not prevent some reasonable degree of "free choice." Moreover, the fact that Americans are not completely free agents in their political behavior increases rather than decreases the value of voting as a test of opinion.

To change allegiance after long attachment to one party usually forces a voter to overcome considerable social pressures. Such pressures are especially heavy when voters change to a new party, or to a minor party challenging the *status quo* (however defined). Pronounced changes in an area's voting patterns, therefore, usually are excellent clues to the saliency and intensity of opinion and indicate that "something is up." But long periods of stability are also revealing, for they suggest the absence of intense discontent.

Skeptics may not be convinced that the American people exercise their theoretical power to control government actions; only uninformed cynics fail to recognize that they attach great importance to it. In theory, at least, the American political system is dominated by the voting process. The political realities may not strongly resemble the theory, but being a "good citizen" to an American means that *he is supposed to make his opinion count.* That supposition is so basic to the democratic ideology that not having the right to vote condemns one to inferior social status.

For the vast majority of Americans, it can be assumed, voting has been the only direct means used to make opinions count. Whether their opinions were worth counting, or whether they made them count for much, are irrelevant for our present purposes. What is relevant is that the record of American history convincingly demonstrates that the masses occasionally have exercised considerable control over government actions. Even the Supreme Court, the irreverent Mr. Dooley observed, follows the election returns.

Unlike verbal or written expressions of opinions or expert estimates, voting produces some direct consequences that can be credibly reconstructed, even if the consequences are only to continue the same administration in power by the same majority. Government officials may not want to heed public opinion. They are acutely aware, however, that it *can* make itself felt through the voting process. Failure to win newspaper approval, for example, need not affect an administration's actions; failure to win voters' approval on election day inevitably affects the administration's power to act. The direct link between voting and government action is summed up in the aphorism, "Before you can be a statesman, you gotta get elected—and re-elected."

Because voting for public office directly indicates the opinions of the masses, and because it has direct consequences that can be traced, we can say that American historians have acted reasonably in implicitly treating it as the single best indicator of public opinion in the pre-Civil War period. But the discussion cannot end here. In effect, historians have agreed that the act of voting is the best *test* of opinion but they have sharply disagreed about the opinions *indicated* by the election returns. This observation might lead to the paradoxical conclusion that although voting is the best test of opinion, Bryce and others are right that it is not a good indicator of opinion. That conclusion, however, does not necessarily follow.

Like all sensitive instruments, to produce accurate results opinion indicators formed from voting records must be carefully constructed and skillfully used. Disagreement among historians and contemporaries over the "meaning" of an election outcome only underscores the central propositions of this section: (1) opinion indicators are made, not found; (2) systematic procedures have to be developed to obtain reasonably accurate results from them. In short, voting records cannot be studied casually and impressionistically, for they do not automatically yield correct inferences about the distribution of opinion on specific issues. But a marked difference exists between using the results of one election as the basis of inferences about public opinion and using the entire range of voting behavior displayed in a number of successive elections. In other words, contradictory answers can be given to two questions which frequently are treated as the same but which are essentially different. What can be learned about the distribution of opinion on given issues from an election outcome? Frequently, very little or nothing. What can be learned from *the entire range of voting behavior in a number of elections?* If the data are studied systematically, almost invariably a good deal can be learned about the distribution of opinion and, under certain conditions, a great deal.[46]

It would only belabor the point to show in detail that similar observations can be made about all other types of documents used as sources of data to construct indicators of opinion distribution. The point is that they yield

---

[46] I have tried to demonstrate that argument concretely in my *Concept of Jacksonian Democracy*, pp. 254-269, and *passim*. The tendency of historians to focus attention upon election results rather than upon voting behavior patterns is cogently treated in Robert T. Bower, "Opinion Research and Historical Interpretation of Elections," *Public Opinion Quarterly*, Vol. 12, 1948, pp. 457-458. In this connection, see the incisive critique of historians' use of congressional voting as an indicator of public opinion in Joel Silbey, "The Civil War Synthesis in American Political History," *Civil War History*, Vol. 10, June 1964, pp. 130-140. And for an incisive critique of historians' use of legislative resolutions, as well a demonstration of how they can systematically be used as an indicator of public opinion, see an unpublished masters' thesis written under my direction by Madeleine S. Shapiro, "Michigan Public Opinion, the Mexican War, and the Wilmot Proviso: A Study of Legislative Resolutions as Opinion Indicators," Detroit, Wayne State University, 1964.

remarkably different results depending upon whether systematic or impressionistic procedures are used.

The basic argument can now be stated: To practice scientific method and develop good indicators of opinion distribution, historians must consciously and systematically tackle the hard job of developing valid and reliable procedures to "generate" specific types of data from specific types of documents. In similar fashion, historians must tackle the even harder job of developing principles, in Nagel's words, "tried canons," that permit them reasonably to judge the validity of inferences drawn from the data generated.

This essay can appropriately end with a restatement of its basic argument: Historians have not yet scientifically studied past public opinion, not because it is impossible to do so, but because they have not yet tried to do so. The approach sketched here, I trust, at least focuses attention upon the problem and suggests a specific course of action that might ultimately lead to its solution or, more precisely, might stimulate other researchers to propose courses of action that might ultimately lead to its solution.

3. Public opinion research: a contribution to historical method*

ROBERT A. KANN†§

I

The investigation and evaluation of the character and influence of public opinion represent one of the most crucial tasks of the historian. In more ways than one, what are perhaps the two most basic questions of any philosophy of history, the causation and predictability of historical events, are inextricably connected with this problem. It now seems appropriate that the historical method should take cognizance of the techniques of public opinion research, a discipline which has penetrated and permeated political science and social psychology, and more recently economics as well, to a degree hardly thought conceivable less than twenty years ago.

It is a most difficult logical problem to define public opinion correctly. In the specific context of this paper on historical method, it may be permissible to by-pass this question and to accept the simplest workable formulation of its meaning as a convenient starting point. James Bryce has provided us with such a formula. Public opinion is the "aggregate of the views men hold regarding matters that affect or interest the community."[1] In so far as the historian looks

---

* Reprinted from the *Political Science Quarterly,* LXXIII (September, 1968), pp. 374-96, by permission of the publisher.

† Robert A. Kann, professor of history, Rutgers University, received his Ph.D. from Columbia University and Dr. jur. from the University of Vienna. He is the author of *The Problem of Restoration: A Study in Comparative Political History* and *A Study in Austrian Intellectual History.*

§ I am indebted to my friend Mr. Paul K. Perry of Audience Research Institute, Princeton, N.J., for valuable advice in regard to technical questions of opinion research. The responsibility for any errors in this paper is, of course, mine.

[1] Quoted from George Gallup *A Guide to Public Opinion Polls* (Princeton, 1948), p. 84. The definition of Wilhelm Bauer is more specific but it is not essentially in disagreement with that of Bryce: "Public opinion represents the formulation of a certain group will. Without being rationally thought through in detail, it confers on the judgment and expression of will of most individuals a certain equal coloring." Wilhelm Bauer, *Die öffentliche Meinung in der Weltgeschichte* (Potsdam, 1930), p. 19. See, further, William

at the present as a continuous development of the past, it should be permissible, for our specific purpose, to extend this statement as follows: Public opinion is the aggregate of the views men have held regarding the evolution of their social institutions and the current matters that affect or interest the community.

In dealing with a discipline based on a tremendous body of research and a complex set of statistical rules two points should be made very clear at the outset.

The first is that this confrontation of historical method and public opinion research within the frame of this study cannot go beyond the analysis of the most elementary points of the new techniques of social measurements. Nothing would be more desirable than continued research into the finer points of this association as well as its extension into wider areas of social relations in general. One of the main objectives of this study would indeed be achieved if the suggestions sketched here were to be followed up with greater thoroughness by others.

The second is—it should be emphatically stated here—that no method of public opinion research or motivation research as applied to social measurements, market research, political forecasts or other social objectives, as the case may be, could ever be substituted for the individual evaluation and the individual judgment of the historian. Consequently the techniques of public opinion research can be applied only in a limited way to the recognition and evaluation of public opinion in the past. Their function would be merely to supplement and control historical research.

This, then, should be the third introductory point: Where established historical methods can conceivably be helped by support from those of other disciplines, it is important to learn to use them according to the rules of the game. As will be shown in the following, this does not mean the mechanical transfer of rules and principles from one discipline to another. It does mean, however, that they should be understood, practiced and adjusted to the specific requirements of historical problems.

II

The question with which this study is concerned has been raised in general, though not fully explored, several times.[2] The essence of previous comment may

---

Albig in his *Public Opinion* (New York, 1939), p. 3: "Public opinion results from the interaction of persons upon one another in any type of group."

See finally the illuminating paper by Paul F. Lazarsfeld, "Public Opinion and the Classical Tradition," *Public Opinion Quarterly,* vol. XXI, No. 1, Spring 1957, pp. 41-53, and the literature quoted there.

[2] For instance, papers read by Professors J. H. Hexter, Karl Polanyi and J. R. Strayer, at the Meeting of the American Association for Public Opinion Research, Princeton, N.J., 1951; and papers read by Professors Lee Benson and Paul F. Lazarsfeld at the meeting of the American Historical Association, New York, 1954; Robert T. Bower, "Opinion Research and Historical Interpretation of Elections," *Public Opinion Quarterly,* vol. XII, No. 3, Fall 1948, pp. 455-464.

be roughly stated as follows. Stress has been laid on the value, for current and future historical research, of data ascertained by methods of public opinion research—as for instance data collected by the American Institute of Public Opinion and by various government agencies. Moreover, the importance of such types of source material as the records of parliamentary elections, plebiscites and parliamentary roll calls has been emphasized.

These comments, however, do not bear directly on the problem raised here. In the first instance we are dealing with findings established only within the last two decades, that is, the very recent past since techniques of public opinion research have begun to be developed. Furthermore, in both cases we are dealing with data devised with the express purpose of measuring public opinion in however imperfect form.[3] It is quite obvious that the historian will avail himself of such records whenever the opportunity presents itself. There is no need here for specific techniques of public opinion research.

The necessity to adjust the modern devices of public opinion research to the needs of the historian arises, however, whenever he is faced by the far more intricate problem of gauging public opinion from sources not designed for that specific purpose. This will generally mean the sources of a more distant past. In a sense this difficulty exists, of course, even in regard to modern parliamentary elections, in so far as elections—unlike the rarer specimens of plebiscites and public referenda—do not measure the reactions of voters to specific issues, however important, but to a multitude of issues. To abstract the reaction of a voter to an individual issue from his reaction to the general ones would be then a real problem of modern techniques of public opinion research.[4] Still it would be relatively simpler than the afore-mentioned problem, the analysis of records

---

[3] Obviously—to note only two points—the vote in parliamentary elections is largely representative of the electorate only under conditions of universal, equal and secret franchise as well as an unrestricted freedom of choice for the voter. Condition two is naturally lacking in all contemporary dictatorial and pseudo-dictatorial régimes; condition one in practically all franchise laws before the twentieth century.

As to the representative character of parliamentary roll calls, it is equally obvious that the members of any legislature form a kind of élite and not an exact replica of the "statistical universe". Furthermore their freedom of voting even in many democratic countries is limited by rules of party caucuses, parliamentary clubs, etc. On the concept of the statistical universe see Mildred Parten, *Surveys, Polls and Samples* (New York, 1950), pp. 116-17. Also M. S. Heidingsfield and A. B. Blankenship, *Market and Marketing Analysis* (New York, 1947), pp. 137-37.

[4] In this respect a unique historical source in a class of its own is the famous *cahiers de doleances,* preceding the French Revolution of 1789, in which the representatives of the Estates to be assembled at Versailles in May 1789 record their instructions from the voters. In spite of obvious shortcomings in the electoral process, the following facts stand out. The *cahiers* are fairly representative, not of election results, but of genuine public opinion trends not necessarily tested in the elections. These instructions to the representatives do not deal with their general attitudes but with specific issues to be raised at the meeting of the Estates General. Thus answers to questions are given here which elections fail to provide. If we agree that this is one of the foremost tasks of public opinion research in the field of politics, one has to admit that the *cahiers* introduce a basic concept of public opinion research into the world of historical facts. On the nature of the *cahiers* see particularly Beatrice Hyslop, *A Guide to the General Cahiers* (New York, 1936).

drawn up originally for purposes not at all related to the measurement of public opinion.

III

At this point it may be convenient to trace the major steps in the conducting of an average public opinion survey. Next we shall formulate the basic differences between public opinion research where it is concerned with the present, or with predictions for the future, and where it is focused on the past. After this, we shall examine the various steps taken in the average survey in the light of the requirements of our specific problem and shall attempt to adapt them to these specific requirements.

The following may be considered as typical steps in a simple survey operation in public opinion research.

a) the clear formulation and definition of the given research problem which are also, or should be, the first steps in approaching a problem of historical research;

b) the planning of the survey operation, that is, of the particular techniques to be employed;

c) the drafting of the questionnaire;

d) the planning and setting up of the actual sample, the cross section of the population from which information is to be gathered;

e) the actual collection of the data;

f) and g)—here combined for the sake of convenience—the statistical tabulation, interpretation and presentation of the data to the public.

An outside observer, when asked for his opinion as to the basic differences between regular public opinion research and public opinion research concerned with the past, would in all likelihood point to two facts: The historian is exclusively concerned with the past, the public opinion researcher with the future. The historian interested in public opinion of the past has to deal with extremely imperfect records which are subject to the grace and caprice of historical providence, while the professional public opinion researcher deals with nearly perfect records, a complete statistical universe from which he elicits his samples and his subsequent prediction.

Actually this seemingly basic difference is one of degree rather than of kind. The public opinion researcher's objectives and predictions, it is true, are primarily concerned with the future. In the selection of his material, however, in setting up the statistical sample of the population and the estimated attitudes on which the questionnaires and the computation of future action are based, he deals with the past and, in the case of research concerned with general social problems of mores, he will have to cover the ground of an individual's accumulated experiences over a good number of years if he wants to do his job well.

The historian has to deal with far greater distances of time and, in all likelihood, with far more extensive physical and social changes in his data than does the average public opinion analyst of today. In kind, however, the problems of the historian are the same as those of his colleague in the field of social psychological measurement.

Seemingly more obvious is another distinction. One cannot confront bygone people with a questionnaire. Apart from such individual statements as diaries, letters, autobiographies, which do not belong in this context, of course it is true that dead ancestors cannot be interviewed either in depth or otherwise. Yet, in terms of public opinion research, this only means that they are not subject to one group of research techniques, those of direct or indirect questioning, the most common but by no means the only conceivable techniques at the disposal of the discipline of public opinion research.

It should be helpful to turn for a moment to a basic concept of law, more specifically of Roman law, namely, the concept of tacit expression of will or so-called concludent action. This means simply the conclusion of a legally valid transaction by an action the intent of which is so obvious that written or even oral confirmation can be dispensed with.[5] We might go further and refer to another principle of Roman as well as modern law. *Quis tacet consentire videtur.* He who keeps quiet is assumed to approve. As a rule anyone who does not challenge a statement is simply assumed to approve of it and is not required to confirm it.

What does this phenomenon of legally valid action or nonaction as opposed to oral or written statement signify? Very simply this. In many spheres, law and, to an even greater degree, social life do not measure the intention and opinion of people by words but by attitudes expressed in action or nonaction. The reasons for action or nonaction, as the case may be, may yet be measured, though written records may have been lost or, what is even more likely, may never have existed.

This procedure is easily applicable and has, in fact, been widely and increasingly applied to public opinion research. To take only one outstanding example: The English public opinion research project Mass Movement has, since 1938, published a series of extremely enlightening studies on public opinion research which were based on observations of attitudes by the staff members of the project to a far greater extent than on questionnaires and interviews.[6]

---

[5] "Informal juristic acts (and most juristic acts are informal) are those in which the will may be expressed in any form whatever by writing or speaking, by messenger, letter or otherwise, nay, even without any proper act of communication at all (by so called tacit expression of will) where the act is performed in such a way as to clearly imply an intention. All that is required in informal acts is that the will shall be expressed in some manner or other." Rudolf Sohm, *The Institutes: A Textbook of the History and System of Roman Private Law* (transl. from the German) (Oxford, 1901), p. 219. See also Ludwig Mitteis, Leopold Wenger, eds., *Institutionen* (Berlin, 1949), pp. 217-18.

[6] See for instance Charles Madge and Tom Harrisson, *Britain by Mass-Observation* (London, 1939); Mass-Observation, ed., *War Begins at Home* (London, 1940); *Us, Mass-Observation Weekly,* Intelligence Service, London, annual, 1940, a journal that made important contributions to the British war effort; Mass-Observation, ed., *The Pub and the People* (London, 1943); Mass-Observation, *The Press and Its Readers* (London, 1949);

The reasons for the application of techniques of mass observation[7] in themselves bear little relation to the contingencies which historians must face. They relate not to a lack of records to be obtained by the sample-interview technique but to their possible distortion. In other words, the public opinion researcher is haunted by various uncertain factors, some of which result from the inadequacy of verbal methods, such as loaded questions, the possible bias of the interviewer, the reluctance and probably just as often the lack of ability on the part of the interviewee to express his opinions, and so on. There is further the still controversial "bandwagon effect," that is, the possibility that reports which reveal verbal majority reaction to a controversial question may in themselves influence public opinion. Consideration of these problems had led increasingly to the change from direct to indirect methods of questioning, namely, to the observation of attitudes, particularly in the rapidly expanding field of motivation research. This means that the public opinion researcher may deduce with a high degree of probability from nonverbal or informal verbal reaction to a variety of different problems the attitude of an individual to a certain problem which the same person would be reluctant to reveal under direct questioning. The researcher may possibly even go further and, through the observation of attitudes, be able to abandon the recording of verbal statements altogether.

Here the historian enters the stage again. If he wants to supplement his findings by methods approximating those of modern public opinion research, he will be bound to do what the public opinion researcher may possibly do. Of course in dealing with the distant past he cannot make use of informal questioning, let alone of a formal questionnaire. He may, however, substitute for this procedure, or preferably combine with it, one of planned observation of group action or conclusive nonaction as found in or deduced from historical records. In this case the records will provide him with some evidence based not on directly or indirectly solicited statements but on concludent actions or nonactions substituted for verbal declarations made as intended response to questioning.

One field where this method had to be employed by scientific public opinion research is that of measurement of prejudices against racial, religious or ethnic minority groups which by direct questioning would never come fully into the

---

Mass-Observation, *The Journey Home* (London, 1944). The two last-mentioned reports were prepared for the Advertising Service Guild.

See, further, D. Willcox, "Mass-Observation", *American Journal of Sociology*, vol. 48, 1943, pp. 445-56; R. Robinson, "Progress in Mass Observation", *International Journal of Opinion and Attitude Research*, vol. 2, 1948, pp. 369-78.

The famous sociographic study, *Middletown,* by Robert S. and Helen M. Lynd (New York, 1929), may likewise be referred to in this context.

The most comprehensive study, as far as the principles of observational methods and the use of available data as source material are concerned, is probably Marie Jahoda, Morton Deutsch, S. W. Cook, *Research Methods in Social Relations with Especial Reference to Prejudice,* vol. I (New York, 1951) – see particularly chapters v and viii.

[7] Mass-Observation, *The Pub and the People,* pp. 10, 11. See also *idem, The Press and Its Readers,* p. 8; *Us,* annual, 1940, pp. 25, 46.

As to an outstanding example for the use of the indirect method, see Jahoda, Deutsch, Cook, *op. cit.*

open.[8] It is clear that the results of this method, in conjunction with the previous observations on the factor of attitudes established by concludent actions, are of particular importance for the historian in the wide problem of nationalism, perhaps beyond that in the history of ideas in general.

It is obvious that the historian who has to resort to such a method is at a considerable disadvantage as compared with the modern public opinion researcher who has the questionnaire method at his disposal. It is less obvious that along with the defects of the procedures of approximated public opinion research, as we may call them, there are also their virtues. They are twofold. The indirect method which is bound to encounter much greater difficulties in procuring a reasonably accurate sample is, on the other hand, far less impeded by the problems of semantics and of bias.[9] The historian is, after all, the drafter of the equivalent of the questionnaire, the computer of the sample, the tabulator and analyst of the result of the survey, all in one person. This may, though it will not necessarily, weaken certain control possibilities given to a research team. On the other hand, the concentration of all functions in one person plus the stress on a nonverbal method of approach largely eliminates subconscious and nonconscious ambiguities arising from problems of semantics as well as the frequent danger of interviewer bias in the selection of respondents. Thus, if one turns from the verbal method to that of observation by concludent action, the decisive problem is and remains that of the impartiality of the historian. This, however, is truly germane to the whole realm of historical research.

The very fact that the historian determines his own research problem, and combines in one person so many functions, simplifies the problem in another way as well. In dealing with the past he is free to synchronize the starting point of his investigation, the establishment of the sample and the study of the individual cases. In modern public opinion research, on the other hand, the most experienced expert may be thrown off balance by *imponderabilia,* such as the time lag between, for instance, the publication of a population census and the time of the actual survey, the turnout problem in elections and even more so in primaries, and other questions of a similar kind which relate in a way to the unpredictable presence or absence of respondents at a certain time.

IV

In the following an attempt will be made to sketch the various steps to be taken in historical investigation employing methods approximating those of public opinion research.

---

[8] Jahoda, Deutsch, Cook, *op. cit.,* and the recent studies of depth interviewing of Hungarian refugees. For instance, H. Gleitman and J. Greenbaum, *Inquiry into Political and Social Attitudes in Hungary,* Free Europe Committee (New York, 1957).

[9] The concept of bias in modern public opinion research is frequently not understood in the mere colloquial subjective sense of "a propensity or pre-possession; bent; prejudice" (Webster) whether conscious or subconscious, but in the wider meaning of error in general, namely, as "a systematic error in procedure resulting in distortion". Heidingsfield and

Of the six main stages listed at the beginning of the second section of this paper the first, the formulation of the research problem itself, may be restated as follows:

To ascertain in a given area, at a given time in the past, the trends of public opinion in regard to general or specific issues. The techniques of historical public opinion research are here merely to be considered (a) as a supplementary tool to control the historian's own judgment and (b) as a means to broaden and possibly deepen the use of source material acquired by other methods.

As to the second step, the planning of the particular techniques to be followed, we must reluctantly confine ourselves to the collection of data on the basis of concludent action by some kind of mass observation rather than through response to specific questions.

The next step then would be to draw up a substitute for the questionnaire. Here a distinction concerning the indirect method must be borne in mind. More often than not, the desired results will in themselves be of an indirect nature. This means that the data to be obtained should merely serve as supporting evidence in deducing a certain trend of public opinion. In other cases, however, the data to be found may be the direct objectives of the investigation. In many cases the research procedure may serve both ends.

A few examples will serve to illustrate the point. An investigation which proposes, for instance, to measure the trend of nationalism in Germany on the eve of the First or Second World War may be concerned with the following questions, among many others:

What kind of books did people read in public libraries?

How many of them were by foreign authors and of what countries?

What newspapers did readers prefer?

Prices and quality being equal, did people show a marked preference for consumer goods manufactured in Germany?

What kind of associations did they join?

An investigation of the state of national prosperity at that time would concern itself with the obvious data on production with particular regard to consumer goods, internal and external debt, mortgages, stock market movements, national income, foreign and domestic travel, tax arrears, and so on.

The investigation may be undertaken solely for the purpose of obtaining data which would shed light on a national trend, or simply of exploring this particular subject, or it may aim at achieving both objectives. From the few obvious examples selected from a practically endless series it appears that the research methods discussed in this paper lend themselves far more easily to the measurement of social, economic and intellectual trends than to the gauging of attitudes toward specific events, that is, to political history. This is hardly surprising. The prediction of such political events as a change of government, the outbreak of war or revolution, which are determined not only by many

---

Blankenship, *op. cit.,* p. 321. The concept of bias as referred to here is to be understood, however, in the general colloquial sense.

spontaneous, unpredictable factors but also quite frequently by a limited number of persons, usually in the higher echelons of government, lies for the most part outside the scope of political opinion research in a scientific sense. [10] The main objective is largely, and for the historian in his retrospective approach exclusively, not the answer to questions which have been answered by past events anyway. It is rather the measuring of gradually changing attitudes within the historical continuum of social life in the past. In this respect, the historian is still at a disadvantage as compared with the public opinion researcher *pro futuro* because of the greater scarcity of data available to him. On the other hand he is in a far better position in that his indirect questions can be geared to events in the past already known to him. The public opinion researcher concerned with the third-term issue in the early spring of 1940 was hardly in a position to foresee the sudden fall of France and the *Blitz* over England which proved to have important bearing on the outcome of the election he was attempting to predict. The historian who measures public opinion from the past is of course able, in the course of his investigation, to take into account the particular effect of these events on specific areas and groups of people.

As to the other items pertaining to the questionnaire, it has been noted that the historian does not have to worry about a number of problems which may haunt the drafter of the questionnaire and his agent, the interviewer. Errors in modern public opinion research arise, for instance, from the difficulty of creating rapport with the interviewee, of avoiding leading questions or a sequence of questions which might inadvertently give a clue to the answers to be expected and so on. Here it is particularly important to keep in mind that the historian wants to find out not only what the respondent thinks but how he arrives at his conclusions as well. [11] Therefore the question raised—not asked—should be as specific as possible, and the historian, who need not bother with the problem of warming-up questions, the possible resentment when questions are of a personal nature, and so on, is in a good position to conform to the requirements of the modern technique. Likewise by careful planning he can avoid the common error of raising a questions composed of "multiple elements," [12] the answer to which may be erroneously interpreted as applying to a single issue when in fact it responds to a variety of more or less hidden issues

---

[10] It is assumed here that the answer to such questions as "How many people will vote for candidate X in the presidential elections?" has only a short-living news value—apart from the technical insight to be gained by predicting the answer to a strictly verifiable question—since it will be answered by the elections anyway. While the question, "What type of man is likely to win an election under constantly changing conditions?", is of course not strictly verifiable, it penetrates actually far deeper into the core of the problem of public opinion research.

[11] Heidingsfield and Blankenship, *op. cit.,* pp. 109, 113. In our example, to measure the intent of nationalism qua foreign goods it would be of little use then to establish the volume of English manufactured goods in Germany in general at the time of the Boer War. The pertinent question would be to check, for instance, the sale of a widely known specific English article, say of a certain brand of cigarettes of undoubted previous snob appeal in a German "Middletown".

[12] *Ibid.,* pp. 116-17, 159-60.

and thus may throw the results entirely off balance. One answer to this by no means simple problem is "depth interviewing." This procedure attempts, by a whole chain of follow-up questions which are worked out in detail, to single out a specific issue. Thereby the pitfall of a hidden multiple causation result will be eliminated as far as possible. Thus it may be feasible "to approach the analysis of the individual on a historical basis."[13] It is obviously impossible to discuss here the theoretical and practical devices involved in this complex technique. Neither is it suggested, in view of the character and scantiness of the historian's records, that depth measurement could be applied by him within the full meaning of the concept. On the other hand, in regard to the specification of the question or rather the dissection of one question into several, some commonly admitted impediments—those of time, cost, and the training of special interviewers—do not exist for the historian. His material is restricted but it is not subject to the above limitations. Errors in the handling of the respondent's reaction, for instance, are easily corrected. The historian may well avail himself of these advantages.

The very core of public opinion research is the planning and setting up of the actual representative sample, the cross section of the population from which the pertinent information is to be obtained. In very general terms the sample should fill these requirements:

"An adequate sample should be a true miniature of the universe of total population which is to be sampled and should give proportionate representation to all the characteristics found in that universe which may affect the problem."[14] Regarding the relatively modest requirements about the size of the sample, the laws of probability first developed by Bernouilli in the early eighteenth century are still valid. Furthermore, "an adequate sample should be so designed as to meet reliability requirements set up by the sponsor,"[15] that is, in our case, the historian. The basic idea of such a sample is its "randomization"—"that sampling process which gives every unit of a population an equal chance of being selected."[16] This may refer to the statistical universe of the total population or to the particular stratum of the population with which the survey is concerned. In this latter respect we speak of "stratified sampling," that is, a grouping according to the characteristics of geography, occupation, age, sex, denomination, ecology, and so on. Thus in an election forecast the sample would be stratified in regard to that part of the population eligible to vote; in a survey concerned with the potential sales appeal of dishwashers to housewives the sample would, of course, be stratified on a much narrower basis.

From among a number of important distinctions in the matter of survey sample designs[17] which, however, go beyond the scope of this paper, two basic distinctions must be included: area sampling and purposive sampling. Area

---

13 *Ibid.,* p. 159. See also Parten, *op. cit.,* pp. 74, 183.

14 Parten, *op. cit.,* pp. 136-37.

15 Parten, *op. cit.,* pp. 106 *et seq.,* 219 *et seq.*

16 Heidingsfield and Blankenship, *op. cit.,* p. 155.

17 Parten, *op. cit.,* pp. 219 *et seq.;* A. B. Blankenship, ed., *How to Conduct Consumer and Opinion Research* (New York, 1946), pp. 25-26.

sampling may be defined as "a specialized random method of pre-selecting dwelling units for interviewing." Therewith "the areas in which the sampling is to be done are selected at random, usually making use of the principle of stratification." Random selection applies to the selection of households and individuals within the area as well.[18]

"Purposive sampling denotes the method of selecting a number of groups of units in such a way that the selected groups together yield as nearly as possible the same averages or proportions as the totality with respect to those characteristics which are already a matter of statistical knowledge."[19] One variety of purposive sampling is the method in which comparatively small areas are selected as representative of the population in respect to certain criteria and the interviewing of as many potential respondents as possible is done within a rather brief span of time. Here it is not randomization in general but a kind of integral randomization on the basis of a particularly representative expression of public opinion about certain issues which is the criterion of selection. As to this method, which, if applied at all, is primarily employed in election forecasts, one may well paraphrase a famous saying of George Orwell: All areas are equally representative but some areas are even more equally representative. Obviously the decisive factor here is the problem of area selection. Another variety of purposive sampling, sometimes called "quota" sampling, is designed "to obtain a total sample similar to the population." This means that, usually on the basis of a preëstablished census, "persons be selected from all major groups in the population in proportion to the numerical size of these groups."[20]

Stated in the simplest terms, sampling is merely a short cut to the polling of the entire population, the statistical universe, a process which if it could be applied ad libitum would make public opinion research superfluous. Yet, if for obvious reasons the single segment of the orange has been chosen instead of the whole fruit,[21] it is necessary in making a random selection to see "that every item in the total population is given an equal chance of being selected in the sample."[22] This is necessary in any general poll pertaining to the population as a whole and it applies as well to polls concerned with what is referred to as "specific population"—women, merchants, car owners, readers, farmers, and on.

As to the choice of basic methods, public opinion researchers are generally agreed that area sampling circumvents a major source of statistical error and possible interviewer bias, that is, in the composition of the various quotas of population strata within the sample and the subsequent selection of respondents

---

[18] Heidingsfield and Blankenship, *op. cit.,* p. 321; Gallup, *op. cit.,* pp. 26 *et seq.*

[19] Parten, *op. cit.,* pp. 236 *et seq.,* quoted from A. Jensen, "Report on the Representative Method in Statistics", *Bulletin,* Institute Internationale de Statistique, Rome, Pt. 1, 1928, pp. 359 *et seq.*

[20] Heidingsfield and Blankenship, *op. cit.,* p. 322; Gallup, *op. cit.,* pp. 27-28.

[21] Heidingsfield and Blankenship, *op. cit.,* p. 135.

[22] *Ibid.,* p. 137. For reasons of necessary simplification, the rather technical problem of what constitutes the population as a whole in relation to the problem—for instance, the inclusion of minors, institutionalized people, noncitizens, etc.—must be omitted here.

according to quota by the interviewers. Quota sampling, on the other hand, generally operates at lower cost and greater speed since it does not encounter some of the difficulties which arise in the setting up of a proper area sample, the frequent need for call backs in interviewing, and the like.[23] Finally, the first-noted variety of purposive sampling (the selection of small representative areas) is used as a rule only for very specific investigations or as experimental control procedure.

What does all this add up to in terms of the problems of the historian? First and foremost, the method of sampling itself is even more of a problem for the historian than for the public opinion researcher concerned with present and future. To modern public opinion research the sample is a miniature model of the statistical universe. The same may be true for the historian, but the sample may also mean something even more vital than the model in miniature. It may have to be considered not only the segment of the orange but the orange itself, that is, the whole available statistical universe. This would hold true whenever comprehensive records of the whole population or of the whole specific population are no longer available. In such cases, the selected area or a quota of the specific population by necessity has to combine the functions of statistical universe and sample, that is, of the model in miniature. It will be readily granted that this is not sampling in the technical sense of the term. However, methods which approximate those of modern techniques can be employed in historical public opinion research.

As to the chief methods of area sampling and purposive sampling, it will be realized that differences in time and cost are not pertinent to the problem of the historian who in general works with documentary records and not with respondents and interviewers scattered over the country. Both methods could be used by him, if otherwise applicable. The emphasis rests clearly on the "if." The establishment of a proper purposive sample will of course depend upon an essential basic premise, namely, the existence of a population census or its equivalent. Even if we confine our reflections to Western Civilization, it is fair to say that there were few truly workable population surveys prior to the middle of the nineteenth century, that is, if our requirements are a little more technical than those of William the Conqueror in his Domesday Book. But, granted that we are fortunate enough to be able to consult a general census or its equivalent, we have solved only the initial problem.

The main problem is naturally that of setting up a sample which will represent a true cross section of the whole population or the whole specific population. This is a formidable task, for it means that what must be done is "to divide the total population of the nation or of each state or city into component parts or strata and to make certain that each part is represented in the sample in proportion to its magnitude."[24] This in turn means that we should need not only a kind of general census but a fairly detailed one and, what appears to be even more difficult, fairly accurate regional information of a census character.

[23] Gallup, *op. cit.,* pp. 28 *et seq.*
[24] Gallup, *op. cit.,* pp. 27-28.

Such fortunate possibilities cannot be ruled out entirely. A historian, for instance, who proposes to assess the tax morale of the country within, say, the last fifty years might successfully check the files of the collectors of internal revenue across the nation and find out how many people were in arrears, how many penalties were imposed, how many letters to the editors of local newspapers were written on tax problems. Similar procedures might be followed in regard to reading habits, traffic problems and law enforcement problems in general. Information based not on specific statements but on what we have called concludent action may well be found everywhere.

Two reservations must be made, however. It is not likely, in this country, that information of sufficient detail could be found concerning the nation as a whole for a period further back than about two generations. If we go back further we may still be on fairly safe ground in New England and the Mid-Atlantic coastal section, but in the Southwest, West and Deep South institutions tend to be so much out of step with the above-mentioned industrialized areas that it would be difficult if not impossible to find a workable common denominator. In other words, the purposive sample could be successfully used by the historian even under relatively favorable conditions only where such standards of fair comparability—not necessarily equality—in regard to literacy, law and standards of living do exist. Thus the method will be applicable to the United States of the last generations; it might well be used in thoroughly industrialized nations such as the United Kingdom, also Germany, Switzerland or Belgium, or possibly in those of advanced agricultural development like Sweden, Denmark or Holland. It would hardly be applicable to Eastern Europe or Latin America. Either the range of comparable development between the urbanized-commercial-industrialized and the agricultural areas of the nation would be too wide or, if we have to deal with purely agricultural countries, the standards would in most cases be so low that it would be exceedingly difficult if not impossible to collect the necessary data. In the field of the struggle of conflicting nationalisms the methods might be used in the area of nineteenth-century Central Europe but not of Eastern Europe or the Middle East at that time.

How do these observations pertain to the area-sampling method? First and foremost, this method is far less dependent upon a census or its equivalent. Supposing we were to make a nationwide inquiry in some field of consumer taste and set up regional samples, as is indeed frequently done by county or municipality and township. We would still like to have some nationwide information about the number of counties, their population figures, composition of population—that is, roughly speaking a classification according to rural, mixed rural-industrial, and urban sections. Only then would we be able to set up a fair stratification by regions. Yet obviously, if we are concerned with regional samples on, say, the county level, this preliminary information need not be nearly as detailed as the breakdown in the quota sample where an elaborate knowledge of the social stratification of the general population is required. Apart from very backward areas, the historian would face far lesser difficulties. Still he would not be over the hump, since he would require considerable detailed information once he came to the actual investigation of individual households and household members. Here, a thorough knowledge of regional ecology would be necessary. Nevertheless, his task would not be nearly as difficult as that of the purposive sampling historian in a comparable investigation.

To clarify this we will go back to the example of the assessment of tax morale. The purposive (or quota) sampler would need a detailed statistical breakdown of the whole population by sex, family status, age, occupation, income, and would in addition be confronted with the much harder job of supplementing this with specific parallel information on the local level. Without this he could not check the records of the required quota of bachelors, married couples, couples with one to x children, professional people, farmers, sharecroppers, industrial laborers, merchants. The area-sampling historian, on the other hand, needs only a far more general, preliminary knowledge of the stratification of the area sample as such. All the specific information would come from a scrutiny of the individual household records. Beyond this he would not have to bother about the quota stratification of the population. What he does need, however, is a detailed city, township or county map to be able to check the individual fifth, tenth or xth household as the case may be. This may well be a rather large order, but the point is that if he has such information he will not be as easily and radically thrown off balance by the possible inadequacy of the sample as the quota sampler is. This holds true even for the general public opinion researcher; it is doubly true for the historian, the public opinion researcher concerned with the past, whose quota sample would be naturally far less reliable.

It will be readily admitted that the procuring of adequate nationwide regional ecological information is still not very likely. But it is less unlikely than the establishment of reliable quota samples. We might possibly be able to go somewhat further back into the past in our area-sampling research than in the quota-sampling investigation. Still, we will not be able to go very far in investigations pertaining to the whole nation. If we confine ourselves, however, to problems concerning the specific population in industrial or fully urbanized areas, the prospects are far brighter. Here we are likely to find much more easily the ecological information we need and correspondingly we will be able to extend our research further back into history. It is vital to recognize, however, that we must adjust our research objectives to the data available where we may have a chance of succeeding and not the other way around where in all likelihood we will fail.

The fact that sufficient ecological information in area sampling is not likely to be available for the distant past on a nationwide level brings us finally to the evaluation of the other kind of purposive sampling previously discussed,[25] that is, interviewing in one or a few most typically representative, carefully selected areas. Here major errors may still result from the selection of the area. The

---

[25] See note 19.

interviewing, however—in our case the search for concludent action—covers such a large section of the population, frequently as much as 25 per cent, that errors regarding questioning or our equivalent, the perusal of available records, will be held to a minimum. The "typicalness" of the area can be established on the basis of information as detailed as that supplied by a modern census. Obviously the difficulty here is that, although for many areas such detailed information is available, this very fact may make such an area appear nontypical in several respects.

The method is of particular interest for the historian, however. Preservation of records in history, particularly those of an archeological nature, may often be accidental. In most cases it is fair to say that this preservation has been due to some highly untypical facts. Troy was not a typical principality in Asia Minor, or Mycenae in Greece. Pompei certainly was not merely a Roman "Middletown." Neither can we consider Carcassonne or Williamsburg as ordinary French or American communities in medieval or early modern history. The very fact of historical preservation or excavation is usually directly related to nontypicality. The examples listed here are all extreme cases but it is probably fair to say that historical preservation is related in a kind of reverse proportion to the typicality of an area. From this it follows that it would be absurd to hope that a typical area from which nontypically detailed information can be obtained could ever form the basis of selected-area public opinion research by the historian.

Must we then conclude that purposive sampling could be disregarded by the historian? To answer in the affirmative is to imply that the very areas of which most has been known in the recent or distant past are to be eliminated from our investigation. If we are unwilling to accept this, we will again have to adjust our research objectives to the material at hand.

One thing should be clear from the start. If we make use of the untypical area, we must do so with the full recognition that it is untypical and that, most probably, we are not in a position to select a few distinct areas conspicuous for their typical behavior, such as certain counties in Ohio and Pennsylvania whose voting records for generations have consistently followed the national trend. We may as well face the fact that in all likelihood we simply do not have sufficient information to enable us to find areas which are particularly typical and of which, at the same time, much detailed information has been available through several generations.

Here the historian's task is to attempt to crystallize from the welter of nontypical information a few facts which might be typical. Using again an extreme example, it would be entirely misleading to take the standard of living of Pompei, that is, of a rather fashionable bathing resort at the time of the Flavian emperors, as representative of the standard of living in Roman cities of comparable size. Yet it would be entirely proper to take the proportion between men and women there or—a non-public-opinion example—the standards of engineering, as typical of the Roman civilization of the time. One would probably not be far off either in taking the designs of interior decorating in Pompei as typical of the color preferences of that time. It would be entirely erroneous to take reading habits in sixteenth-century Oxford as evidence of the literary tastes of the time, but it would be very informative in a historical study of general food and drink consumption and preferences in England to ascertain conditions in the town during that age. In all these cases it would be necessary only to look for the typical evidence entailed in an, on the whole, untypical example of general high informative value. The untypical information provided by such examples might be of the highest value in itself though it is beyond the topical limits of this paper.

To be sure, the use of special areas for historical public opinion research of this kind encounters a basic difficulty in so far as the historian is probably bound to select a non-typical area and adjust his investigation accordingly, while the modern public opinion researcher may be able—though with difficulty—to draw on a typical area. Still the historian would be bound by other rules of sampling, and some basic problems in the selection of a specific area for penetration in depth would be the same. What it adds up to is the necessity of combining various methods and techniques, including the important task of controlling the results previously ascertained. In this combining of various methods the historian would follow only procedures well established in public opinion research.

The subsequent steps to be taken by the historian differ in detail but not too much in essence from those of the modern public opinion researcher. The collection of data, that is, in public opinion research the process of actual interviewing, has no direct equivalent in the activities of the historian. Its parallel is the historian's perusal of available records. The minus in information resulting from the impossibility of using the direct questioning method is at least partly cancelled in our province by the fact that the subjective factor of bias on the conscious or subconscious level in formulating questions and selecting respondents by interviewers can be held at a minimum.[26]

Because of the relatively modest scope of historical public opinion inquiry by approximation, the subsequent complex and cumbersome process of tabulation of the ascertained data is reduced to a small-scale operation. It remains nonetheless a very important operation. In the first place the limitations of the historian's sources of information must be compensated as far as possible by strict adherence to standards of reasonable accuracy in the classification of data into proper, mutually exclusive categories as the preliminary step to a quantitative and qualitative analysis of the records. Secondly, the extremely important concept of weighted tabulations comes into play.

When disproportionate sampling has been employed or when the percentage of returns differs among the various groups in the sample population, it is necessary to adjust the tabulations in which the groups are combined, to get a balanced sample. This adjustment usually is made by multiplying the raw figures for each of the various groups by figures which will take care of their under- or over-representation in the total.[27]

26 Parten, *op. cit.*, pp. 136-37.
27 Parten, *op. cit.*, pp. 483-84.

Again, what may happen in the case of general public opinion sampling, because of the insufficiency and irregular appearance of available records of the past, will probably happen to the historian. His figures will require adjustment. Thus the command of a carefully worked out technique in this respect should prove not only helpful but indispensable.

The final and last step in public opinion research is the interpretation and presentation of the ascertained data. This kind of work constitutes the very core of the historian's professional duty and privileges. The difficulties to be encountered are not to be underestimated but they are thoroughly germane to his work. Here it seems appropriate to make a final comment. From the foregoing it may have appeared that the difference between modern public opinion research and its more or less feeble historical application rests essentially in the fact that the social psychologist or statistician of today operates with dynamic, living material and the historian with static, dead data. This, however, is true in only a literal sense. The more the historian exerts himself in his study of the past, the more genuinely representative primary sources he is capable of transmitting to posterity, and the better he is able to interpret them, the more dynamic, the more alive this past will become. His data are and should be subject to change by the discovery of further records and by more searching interpretation and thus may be made truer to life.

4. On making historical techniques more specific: "real types" constructed with a computer*

G. G. S. MURPHY AND M. G. MUELLER †

I. THE NOTION OF A "REAL TYPE"

In this paper we describe the exercise of attempting to construct a "real type" from actual statistical data by use of an IBM 7094 computer.[1] Programming a computer to perform such a task brings out sharply problems involved in using this kind of historical technique, for each thought-process involved has to be made explicit in some form so that it can be represented as instructions to the computer, and any ambiguity or need for an arbitrary decision is quickly revealed.

Our notion of a real type is that of a sentence which exactly describes neither a single society nor a class of societies but is *generally descriptive of a class of societies.* This may seem a strange usage, but we believe that if the practice of historians, of comparative political scientists, and of sociologists of history were analyzed, it would be found to be fairly common. When we say "x is an underdeveloped country" or "y is a parliamentary democracy," what we intend to say is that these countries generally conform to a set of features, although the conformance may not be perfect. An example from another discipline may help. Child psychologists who construct types of children of particular ages construct a real type, as it is understood here. For example, a four-year-old child may not display all the characteristics which Gesell asserts that such a child displays, but it will display some. We call them "real types" because they are constructed out

† George G. S. Murphy, associate professor of economics, University of California at Los Angeles, received his Ph.D. from the University of Washington. He is the author of *Soviet Mongolia: A Study of the Oldest Political Satellite.* M. G. Mueller, lecturer, University of Glasgow, received his Ph.D. from the University of Illinois. He is the editor of *Readings in Macroeconomics.*

[1] Our computer program is concerned with "real types," as used by Spiethoff, specifically his Type 1. See Arthur Spiethoff, "Pure Theory and Economic Gestalt Theory: Ideal Types and Real Types." *Enterprise and Secular Change,* ed. Frederic C. Lane and Jelle C. Riemersma (Homewood, Ill., 1953), 451.

of experience. They are not a model of society intended to have a regulative or prescriptive function. If we were to use a simpler notion of a "real type," a description true of all members of the described class, many of the difficulties which emerge in our analysis would be forestalled. However, given the fact that societies and individuals differ so much—a fact that quantitatively-oriented social scientists soon find out when they try to test any social theory—it is very unlikely that we would find many descriptions which classed a number of societies in this way, except for some very general features.

In performing this exercise, we are mainly interested in how the historian produces his results and not so much in how he presents them. The computer print-out, which is our final product, clearly would not be suitable for ordinary historical discourse. We assume that the results would be written up as skillfully as possible, but that this would not alter the substantive conclusions.

Finally, this paper is not some brief for the use of "real types." What we say is: "If you use this way of thinking, this seems to be what you are doing. Here are some of the problems in what you are doing."

II. ADAPTING THE "REAL TYPE" TO COMPUTER USE

Fortunately, a computer program already exists which essentially constructs a type along the lines we have indicated and which is easy to adapt for our own purpose.[2] We use this computer program to demonstrate the kind of intellectual processes which must have taken place in the emergence of the real types—"developed economy" and "underdeveloped economy."

III. DATA ARRAY

How does the historian or social scientist form the notion of such types? First, we must suppose that he knows a field of data or a data array. His familiarity with this leads him to see types of economic systems. In our simulation on the computer, we use a 45 x 216 data array. The first number refers to the number of variables, and the second refers to the number of geographic areas for which the United Nations and other statistical agencies have published values of the variables. The forty-five characteristics, together with the numbers by which they are identified in Tables 1 and 2, are given below. (The first three characteristics, which are based on logical dichotomization, have not been numbered; the others, which are derived by variable dichotomization, begin with 6. The numbers of those characteristics which turned out to be insignificant, and hence do not appear in the print-out, are italicized.)

---

2 This program is described in Arthur S. Banks and Robert B. Textor, *A Cross-Polity Survey* (Cambridge, Mass., 1963), 1-118. The major modifications were: 1) a simplification of the syntax of the language printed out by the computer, 2) introduction of an algorithm to increase the number of times the computer could compute Fisher's P, 3) increasing the computer's search for associations between the variables used, and 4) decreasing the number of variables involving judgment based on other than economic time-series.

Membership of an area group
Government stability
Membership of the communist bloc

(6) Population size
(7) Population density per square kilometer
(8) Agricultural population as a percent of total population
(9) Urban population as a percent of total population
(10) Persons under 15 years of age as a percent of total population
(11) Population between 15-64 years as a percent of total population
(12) Life expectancy at birth
(13) Crude birth rate
(14) Crude death rate
(15) Infant mortality rate
(16) Rate of natural growth of population
(17) Per capita daily calorie intake
(18) Percent of daily calorie requirements met
(19) Per capita daily protein intake
(20) Per capita daily fat intake
(21) Number of inhabitants per doctor
(22) Number of persons per hospital bed
(23) Number of deaths per 1,000 due to infectious and parasitic diseases
(24) Wheat yield per hectare
(25) Rice yield per hectare
(26) Percent of illiterates over age 15 to all persons over age 15
(27) Percent of persons between 5 and 14 registered as primary students
(28) Percent of persons between 15 and 19 registered as secondary students
(29) Number of persons over age 19 registered as students per 100,000 of population
(30) Number of pupils per teacher in primary schools
(31) Kilograms of newsprint consumption per capita per year
(32) Number of radio receivers per 1,000 of population
(33) Kilograms of energy consumption per capita per year
(34) Gross domestic product at factor cost in US dollars
(35) Money supply as a percent of GNP
(36) Government disposable income as a percent of GDP
(37) Imports as a percent of GNP
(38) Exports as a percent of GNP
(39) Food expenditure as a percent of GNP
(40) Growth of GDP
(41) Per capita GDP at factor cost in US dollars
(42) Growth of per capita GDP
(43) Agricultural output as a percent of GDP
(44) Manufacturing output as a percent of GDP
(45) Incremental capital-output ratio

(46)   Gross domestic savings as a percent of GDP
(47)   Gross domestic investment as a percent of GDP

It should be noted that even the production of the table—the act of statistical description—involves discovery and the use of judgment. We could describe a class of societies in an infinite number of ways, but of all possible data these seem to be interesting. This is to say that some notion of a type has already emerged. Each set of data collected suggests a new set. We have not investigated how this process—an important one in concept formation—takes place. However, it may well proceed in something like the way the program we have used proceeds—except that the end-result is not a data print-out, but, as it were, an instruction to look for more data. That this seems the correct way to view it follows from the fact that many of the variables discussed were only defined long after the distinction between "developed" and "underdeveloped" economies had been current.

Our selection of variables was arbitrary, except that we wished to use quantitative data as far as possible. There is no difficulty in adapting the program to take more kinds of data, or evaluations requiring an answer "True" or "False" rather than a number. But, of course, to make a real type one must start with some data. We compiled such data on the assumption that significant comparisons between countries can be based on them; this must be an assumption of anyone constructing a real type in this way. Some people may hold that the data do not really enable us to draw conclusions from them. For example, comparative statistics of gross national product or gross domestic product, which essentially sum up and compare the annual output of certain types of goods, assume that we can meaningfully compare the quite different outputs of, let us say, India with Canada. Primary schooling in America may be entirely different from primary schooling in the Congo—or perhaps of higher quality—but we maintain that we can learn something important from comparing the number in school to the number not receiving any organized instruction. Those who feel that quantitative data of this sort are worthless because subtler qualitative discriminations can and must be made will of course reject comparative analysis of this type.

IV. SELECTION OF COMPARED CLASSES

The computer sequentially considers each of the variables on our list. For example, it may take per capita income (or GDP). Let us call this the comparison variable. It prints out this comparison variable with a particular value of the variable (say $700) and separates countries with higher than $700 per capita income from those with lower. It lists the two subsets of countries under an appropriate heading. Essentially, it names classes of countries that we may call "developed countries" and "underdeveloped countries"—often also, and more accurately, referred to as "rich" and "poor" countries—in the way we name the class of under-achieving or over-achieving children, or the class of "mercantilist countries."

V. PREPARATION OF 2 X 2 TABLE AND DECISION TO RETAIN INFORMATION ABOUT IT

Next, the computer examines the two sets of countries now established on the basis of $700 per capita income and asks whether they have high or low values of one of the other variables, which we will call the matching variable. It thus, essentially, constructs a 2 x 2 table. For example, having grouped countries into developed and underdeveloped categories, it may further divide these two sets into those with a high value of the incremental capital-output ratio (ICOR) and those with a low value.

	Underdeveloped Countries	Developed Countries
High ICOR	*a*	*c*
Low ICOR	*b*	*d*

It finds values for *a, b, c, d* (which stand for the frequencies of class memberships) by simple enumeration. It next computes the probability of the table emerging by using Fisher's equation[3] and Armsen's decision rule for a two-tailed test of significance.[4] If the probability is less than .01 that the values in the table emerge by chance alone, assuming such values to be independently determined, then it prints out sentences which are descriptive of the table, and the probability value.[5]

VI. SYNTAX DECISIONS

Table 1 gives an example of the print-out. The sentences to the left each describe the two cells of the left column of each 2 x 2 table. The sentences to the right each describe the two cells of the right column. The syntax of the sentence depends on the entries in the cells of the column. First, the computer prints out the variable which is being matched against the comparison variable. In the example above, the development status is the comparison variable and ICOR is the matched variable. Next, it describes the table. The way it describes the table not only permits the reader to reconstruct the numerical entries but also gives additional information. Consider the example above. In the case *b* is greater than *a*, and *c* is greater than *d*, it prints out in the left column "Tends to

---

[3] R. A. Fisher, *Statistical Methods for Research Workers* (New York, 1950), 97.

[4] P. Armsen, "Tables for Significance Tests of 2 X 2 Contingency Tables," *Biometrika* 32 (1955), 494-511.

[5] The program also records a value of χ^2. The original Barnes and Textor program could not always calculate Fisher's P, as it involves rational expressions with factorial numbers, and they did not have an algorithm to reduce the expression. Hence, they used x^2 as a decision variable to help decide whether to store or suppress a given piece of information. The probability .01 says that the event under consideration would happen 1 out of 100 times by chance alone. Any lower probability is looked upon as a rather rare event and hence significant enough to be recorded.

be low" and in the right column "Tends to be high." In the reverse situation, the language statements would be reversed. In the case that either *a* equals *b*, or *c* equals *d*, then "No tendency" is printed out to describe the appropriate column. In the case that any cell has zero as an entry, then the entry "Always" will appear in the appropriate column. "Always High" or "Always Low" will appear as the situation demands. In the case that *a* is greater than *b*, and *c* is greater than *d*—so that, for example, irrespective of the development status, two sets of countries tend to show high values for a given variable—the computer determines in which set of countries the tendency is stronger. It does this by computing the relative percentages of countries displaying high values of the matched variables for the two subsets of, say, developed and underdeveloped countries. And, for that set with the higher percentage, it prints out "Tends more to be high" or "Tends more to be low," as the situation demands; similarly, for the set of countries with the lower percentage, it prints out "Tends less to be high" or "Tends less to be low."

VII. INCREASING SIZE OF MATCHING VARIABLES

After matching one variable with the comparison variable in this way, the computer proceeds to the next matching variable and follows the same procedure. However, to increase the number of possible comparisons,[6] the computer essentially shifts the value of the matching variable used to partition the set of countries. It does this by establishing the range of the matching variable and then by dividing the range into quartiles. The three quartile values are then used as the partitioning value each in turn. This permits three comparisons of a matching variable to be made with each comparison variable.

Each comparison generates two sentences which are descriptive of two real types. However, as already pointed out, not all sentences are printed out. The computer suppresses associations which are trivial—that is, those which seem likely to be the result of chance alone. Undoubtedly, historical intuitive processes suppress information also, although whether the criteria are as consistently applied as with the computer is a matter for speculation.

We are left with a set of sentences which describes the developed or underdeveloped countries. Up to this point, a person interested in the use of real types may have made no objections. He may have accepted the use of data,

---

[6] The number of possible 2 X 2 tables describing a given type with quantitative data is given by:

$$N = C^i (M - 1)$$

C^i is the number of variations of the *i*th matching variable, which itself is the number of intervals minus 1. *M* is the number of total variables, including the comparison variable. If we used real numbers as intervals instead of, for example, the quartiles we used, then the number of 2 X 2 tables is infinitely many. Hence, for our program to be useful it is essential to restrict the number of uses of a matching variable.

The formula above only holds for the use of all variables. The term C^i however, does not equal the number of intervals minus one in the case of non-quantitative data. For example, if we use geographic subsets, then for obvious reasons we will get a larger number of possible comparisons than the number of geographic subsets minus one.

accepted the need to make decisions on the basis of the data, and accepted the criteria used to make decisions. However, he might at this point end up disagreeing with the configuration of the data, with the expression that can be read on the face of the facts, so to speak, rather than with the facts themselves. What can we do in such a situation? We can go back to the original data field and introduce new data. We can then go through the whole process again. If the resulting configuration is still unsatisfactory and remains so with each successive configuration, then we must change the criteria used to suppress information. So long as these criteria are not intrinsically intuitive, *i.e.,* as each new case of a society is to be classed, we discover new variables of importance and make new criteria which work retroactively over the whole field of societies, then eventually it seems possible in principle to mechanize the processes involved. Undoubtedly, however, it is a feature of historical judgment that people do select different data fields and do select criteria differing both from other people's and from ones they have used at other times.

To continue: our computer program gives us the possibility of not only considering the real types we were originally interested in but a great number of other ones.

VIII. GENERATION OF OTHER TYPES

After matching all variables in this way against the comparison variable, the computer shifts the comparison variable to the next variable on the list and repeats the whole operation. It does this until all variables on the list have been used as a comparison variable. Thus, the computer exhausts the possibilities of creating real types. Naturally, the print-out which emerges is very lengthy.[7] The final procedure is to select interesting real types from the set of real types printed out.

IX. SELECTION OF INTERESTING TYPES

This final step is difficult to program on the computer. Suppose we have a large set of real types—e.g., "developed countries," "underdeveloped countries," "high food-consuming countries," "low food-consuming countries," "Soviet-bloc countries," "non-Soviet-bloc countries." What criteria can we use to select one or more from the set? Consideration of the matter suggests to us that the only criterion is the interest of the historian or social scientist.

The child psychologist looks at the real types of seven-year olds, nine-year olds, and so on. The psychologist looks at types of adults. Normally, this focus of interest depends on the pragmatic interest of the person involved. He may wish to predict or manipulate behavior. The historian may have such purpose or he may be guided purely by a descriptive interest. We ourselves give in Tables 1

---

[7] The description of any type will vary in length according to the value of P used to select or reject sentences. This value will also to some extent affect the number of real types printed.

TABLE 1

Real Types of "Developed" and "Underdeveloped" Economies

Comparison Variable::	[Per Cap GDP below 700 Dollars]	Comparison Variable:	[Per Cap GDP above 700 dollars]

25 COUNTRIES ABOVE

AUSTRALIA	AUSTRIA	WEST BERLIN	BELGIUM	CANADA	DENMARK	ENGLAND	FINLAND	FRANCE	E GERMANY
M GERMANY	ICELAND	IRELAND	ISRAEL	ITALY	LUXEMBOURG.	NETHERLANDS	NEW ZEALAND	NORWAY	PUERTO RICO
SWEDEN	SWITZERLAND	USSR	USA	VENEZUELA					

121 COUNTRIES BELOW

ADEN	AFGHANISTAN	ALBANIA	ALGERIA	ANGOLA	ARGENTINA	BARBADOS	BHUTAN	BOLIVIA	NO BORNEO
BRAZIL	BR GUIANA	BULGARIA	BURMA	BURUNDI	CAMBODIA	CAMEROON	CEN AFR REP	CEYLON	CHAD
CHILE	CHINA	COLOMBIA	CONGO BRAZ	CONGO LEOP	COSTA RICA	CUBA	CYPRUS	CZECH	DAHOMEY
DOMINICAN REP	ECUADOR	EL SALVADOR	ETHIOPIA	FIJI ILS	GABON	GAMBIA	GHANA	GREECE	GUADELOUPE
GUATEMALA	GUINEA	HAITI	HONDURAS	HONG KONG	HUNGARY	INDIA	INDONESIA	IRAN	IRAQ
IVORY COAST	JAMAICA	JAPAN	JORDAN	KENYA	NORTH KOREA	SOUTH KOREA	LAOS	LEBANON	LIBERIA
LIBYA	MADAGASCAR	MALAYA	MALI	MALTA / GOZO	MARTINIQUE	MAURITANIA	MAURITIUS	MEXICO	MOROCCO
MOZAMBIQUE	MUSCAT OMAN	NEPAL	NEW GUINEA	NICARAGUA	NIGER	NIGERIA	PAKISTAN	PANAMA	PAPUA
PARAGUAY	PERU	PHILIPPINES	POLAND	PORTUGAL	PORT GUINEA	PORT INDIA	PORT TIMOR	REUNION	RHODESIA N
RUMANIA	RWANDA	RYUKYU ILS	SAUDI ARABIA	SENEGAL	SIERRA LEONE	SINGAPORE	SOMALIA	SO AFRICA	SOUTH ARAB
SPAIN	SUDAN	SURINAM	SYRIA	TAIWAN	TANGANYIKA	THAILAND	TOGO	TRIN TOBAGO	TUNISIA
TURKEY	UGANDA	UAR	UPPER VOLTA	URUGUAY	N YIETNAM	S YIETNAM	W NEW GUINEA	YEMEN	YUGOSLAVIA
ZANZIBAR/PEM									

[Per Cap GDP below 700 dollars]	[Per Cap GDP above 700 dollars]
LOCATED IN WEST EUROPE	LOCATED IN WEST EUROPE
C.03 PERCENT	0.40 PERCENT
4 OF 121 COUNTRIES	10 OF 25 COUNTRIES
	P= 0.0000
	CHI=32.1783

TABLE 1 (continued)

[Per Cap GDP below 700 Dollars]	[Per Cap GDP above 700 Dollars]	
LOCATED IN WEST EUROPE, NORTH AMERICA, SCANDINAVIA AND AUSTRALASIA 0.05 PERCENT 6 OF 121 COUNTRIES	LOCATED IN WEST EUROPE, NORTH AMERICA, SCANDINAVIA AND AUSTRALASIA 0.76 PERCENT 19 OF 25 COUNTRIES	P= 0.0000 CHI=73.6863
LOCATED IN ASIA 0.22 PERCENT 27 OF 121 COUNTRIES	LOCATED IN ASIA 0. PERCENT 0 OF 25 COUNTRIES	P= 0.0045 CHI= 6.8442
LOCATED IN AFRICA 0.35 PERCENT 42 OF 121 COUNTRIES	LOCATED IN AFRICA 0. PERCENT 0 OF 25 COUNTRIES	P= 0.0001 CHI=12.1821
STABLE GOVERNMENT SINCE WORLD WAR 2 0.60 PERCENT 37 OF 62 COUNTRIES	STABLE GOVERNMENT SINCE WORLD WAR 2 0.96 PERCENT 22 OF 23 COUNTRIES	P= 0.0011 CHI=10.2261
8) POPULATION IN AGRICULTURE TENDS TO BE HIGH 30 OF 37 COUNTRIES(0.81) ARE ABOVE 28 PERCENT	8) POPULATION IN AGRICULTURE TENDS TO BE LOW 17 OF 21 COUNTRIES(0.81) ARE BELOW 28 PERCENT	P= 0.0000 CHI=21.2525
8) POPULATION IN AGRICULTURE TENDS TO BE HIGH 20 OF 37 COUNTRIES(0.54) ARE ABOVE 51 PERCENT	8) POPULATION IN AGRICULTURE ALWAYS LOW 21 OF 21 COUNTRIES(1.00) ARE BELOW 51 PERCENT	P= 0.0000 CHI=17.3257
9) POPULATION IN URBAN AREAS TENDS LESS TO BE HIGH 35 OF 54 COUNTRIES(0.65) ARE ABOVE 25 PERCENT	9) POPULATION IN URBAN AREAS TENDS MORE TO BE HIGH 14 OF 14 COUNTRIES(1.00) ARE ABOVE 25 PERCENT	P= 0.0071 CHI= 6.8360
9) POPULATION IN URBAN AREAS TENDS TO BE LOW 48 OF 54 COUNTRIES(0.89) ARE BELOW 50 PERCENT	9) POPULATION IN URBAN AREAS TENDS TO BE HIGH 10 OF 14 COUNTRIES(0.71) ARE ABOVE 50 PERCENT	P= 0.0000 CHI=22.4799

TABLE 1 (continued)

[Per Cap GDP below 700 Dollars]	[Per Cap GDP above 700 Dollars]	
10) POPULATION UNDER AGE 15 TENDS TO BE HIGH 32 PERCENT 66 OF 77 COUNTRIES(0.86) ARE ABOVE	POPULATION UNDER AGE 15 TENDS TO BE LOW 32 PERCENT 18 OF 25 COUNTRIES(0.72) ARE BELOW	P= 0.0000 CHI=30.8942
10) POPULATION UNDER AGE 15 TENDS LESS TO BE LOW 42 PERCENT 43 OF 77 COUNTRIES(0.56) ARE BELOW	POPULATION UNDER AGE 15 TENDS MORE TO BE LOW 42 PERCENT 23 OF 25 COUNTRIES(0.92) ARE BELOW	P= 0.0002 CHI=10.8029
11) POPULATION AGED 15-64 TENDS TO BE LOW 58 PERCENT 45 OF 69 COUNTRIES(0.65) ARE BELOW	POPULATION AGED 15-64 TENDS TO BE HIGH 58 PERCENT 21 OF 24 COUNTRIES(0.88) ARE ABOVE	P= 0.0000 CHI=19.8151
11) POPULATION AGED 15-64 TENDS MORE TO BE LOW 64 PERCENT 59 OF 69 COUNTRIES(0.86) ARE BELOW	POPULATION AGED 15-64 TENDS LESS TO BE LOW 64 PERCENT 13 OF 24 COUNTRIES(0.54) ARE BELOW	P= 0.0035 CHI=10.0047
12) LIFE EXPECTANCY AT BIRTH TENDS LESS TO BE HIGH 48 YEARS 34 OF 57 COUNTRIES(0.60) ARE ABOVE	LIFE EXPECTANCY AT BIRTH TENDS MORE TO BE HIGH 48 YEARS 24 OF 24 COUNTRIES(1.00) ARE ABOVE	P= 0.0001 CHI=13.5245
12) LIFE EXPECTANCY AT BIRTH TENDS TO BE LOW 59 YEARS 41 OF 57 COUNTRIES(0.72) ARE BELOW	LIFE EXPECTANCY AT BIRTH ALWAYS HIGH 59 YEARS 24 OF 24 COUNTRIES(1.00) ARE ABOVE	P= 0.0000 CHI=34.9579
13) BIRTH RATE TENDS TO BE HIGH 21 PER 1000 97 OF 108 COUNTRIES(0.90) ARE ABOVE	BIRTH RATE TENDS TO BE LOW 21 PER 1000 14 OF 25 COUNTRIES(0.56) ARE BELOW	P= 0.0000 CHI=27.9167
13) BIRTH RATE TENDS TO BE HIGH 34 PER 1000 73 OF 108 COUNTRIES(0.68) ARE ABOVE	BIRTH RATE TENDS TO BE LOW 34 PER 1000 23 OF 25 COUNTRIES(0.92) ARE BELOW	P=0.0000 CHI=29.3164
13) BIRTH RATE TENDS LESS TO BE LOW 47 PER 1000 84 OF 108 COUNTRIES(0.78) ARE BELOW	BIRTH RATE TENDS MORE TO BE LOW 47 PER 1000 25 OF 25 COUNTRIES(1.00) ARE BELOW	P= 0.0073 CHI= 6.7788

TABLE 1 (continued)

[Per Cap GDP below 700 Dollars]   [Per Cap GDP above 700 Dollars]

#	Variable	Per Cap GDP below 700 Dollars	Per Cap GDP above 700 Dollars	Statistics
14)	DEATH RATE	81 OF 105 COUNTRIES(0.77) ARE BELOW — TENDS LESS TO BE LOW 19 PER 1000	25 OF 25 COUNTRIES(1.00) ARE BELOW — TENDS MORE TO BE LOW 19 PER 1000	$P=0.0041$ CHI=7.0081
15)	INFANT MORTALITY	57 OF 96 COUNTRIES(0.59) ARE ABOVE — TENDS TO BE HIGH 69 PER 1000	25 OF 25 COUNTRIES(1.00) ARE BELOW — ALWAYS LOW 69 PER 1000	$P=0.0000$ CHI=28.0640
16)	POPULATION GROWTH RATE	98 OF 104 COUNTRIES(0.94) ARE ABOVE — TENDS MORE TO BE HIGH 9 PER 1000	13 OF 25 COUNTRIES(0.52) ARE ABOVE — TENDS LESS TO BE HIGH 9 PER 1000	$P=0.0000$ CHI=29.9382
16)	POPULATION GROWTH RATE	62 OF 104 COUNTRIES(0.60) ARE ABOVE — TENDS TO BE HIGH 21 PER 1000	21 OF 25 COUNTRIES(0.84) ARE BELOW — TENDS TO BE LOW 21 PER 1000	$P=0.0001$ CHI=15.3447
17)	CALORIE INTAKE	21 OF 26 COUNTRIES(0.81) ARE BELOW — TENDS TO BE LOW 2660 PER DAY	19 OF 20 COUNTRIES(0.95) ARE ABOVE — TENDS TO BE HIGH 2660 PER DAY	$P=0.0000$ CHI=26.0084
17)	CALORIE INTAKE	25 OF 26 COUNTRIES(0.96) ARE BELOW — TENDS MORE TO BE LOW 3085 PER DAY	12 OF 20 COUNTRIES(0.60) ARE BELOW — TENDS LESS TO BE LOW 3085 PER DAY	$P=0.0060$ CHI=9.3891
18)	CALORIE REQUIREMENTS MET	17 OF 26 COUNTRIES(0.65) ARE BELOW — TENDS TO BE LOW 104 PERCENT	19 OF 20 COUNTRIES(0.95) ARE ABOVE — TENDS TO BE HIGH 104 PERCENT	$P=0.0000$ CHI=17.3055
19)	PROTEIN INTAKE	16 OF 26 COUNTRIES(0.62) ARE ABOVE — TENDS LESS TO BE HIGH 57 GRAMS	20 OF 20 COUNTRIES(1.00) ARE ABOVE — TENDS MORE TO BE HIGH 57 GRAMS	$P=0.0024$ CHI=9.8291
19)	PROTEIN INTAKE	17 OF 26 COUNTRIES(0.65) ARE BELOW — TENDS TO BE LOW 73 GRAMS	19 OF 20 COUNTRIES(0.95) ARE ABOVE — TENDS TO BE HIGH 73 GRAMS	$P=0.0000$ CHI=17.3055

TABLE 1 (continued)

[Per Cap GDP below 700 Dollars]

20) FATS INTAKE   TENDS TO BE LOW 58 GRAMS
18 OF 26 COUNTRIES(0.69) ARE BELOW

20) FATS INTAKE   TENDS TO BE LOW 91 GRAMS
24 OF 26 COUNTRIES(0.92) ARE BELOW

20) FATS INTAKE   ALWAYS LOW 124 GRAMS
26 OF 26 COUNTRIES (1.00) ARE BELOW

23) DEATHS DUE TO DISEASES TENDS LESS TO BE LOW 90 PER 1000
27 OF 48 COUNTRIES(0.56) ARE BELOW

26) ILLITERATE POP OVER AGE 15 TENDS TO BE HIGH 25 PERCENT
54 OF 70 COUNTRIES(0.77) ARE ABOVE

27) STUDENTS AGE 5-14, PRIMARY TENDS LESS TO BE HIGH 32 PERCENT
75 OF 111 COUNTRIES(0.68) ARE ABOVE

27) STUDENTS AGE 5-14, PRIMARY TENDS TO BE LOW 61 PERCENT
78 OF 111 COUNTRIES(0.70) ARE BELOW

29) STUDENTS OVER 19, TERTIARY TENDS TO BE LOW 495 PER 100000
79 OF 88 COUNTRIES(0.90) ARE BELOW

29) STUDENTS OVER 19, TERTIARY TENDS MORE TO BE LOW 990 PER 100000
88 OF 88 COUNTRIES(1.00) ARE BELOW

[Per Cap GDP above 700 Dollars]

20) FATS INTAKE   TENDS TO BE HIGH 58 GRAMS
19 OF 20 COUNTRIES(0.95) ARE ABOVE
P= 0.0000 CHI=19.2367

20) FATS INTAKE   TENDS TO BE HIGH 91 GRAMS
17 OF 20 COUNTRIES(0.85) ARE ABOVE
R=-0.0000 CHI=27.8669

20) FATS INTAKE   TENDS TO BE HIGH 124 GRAMS
12 OF 20 COUNTRIES (0.60) ARE ABOVE
P= 0.0000 CHI=21.1059

23) DEATHS DUE TO DISEASES TENDS MORE TO BE LOW 90 PER 1000
22 OF 22 COUNTRIES(1.00) ARE BELOW
P= 0.0001 CHI=13.7500

26) ILLITERATE POP OVER AGE 15 TENDS TO BE LOW 25 PERCENT
7 OF 8 COUNTRIES(0.88) ARE BELOW
P= 0.0006 CHI=14.4289

27) STUDENTS AGE 5-14, PRIMARY TENDS MORE TO BE HIGH 32 PERCENT
25 OF 25 COUNTRIES(1.00) ARE ABOVE
P= 0.0003 CHI=11.0270

27) STUDENTS AGE 5-14, PRIMARY TENDS TO BE HIGH 61 PERCENT
20 OF 25 COUNTRIES(0.80) ARE ABOVE
P= 0.0000 CHI=21.6806

29) STUDENTS OVER 19, TERTIARY TENDS TO BE HIGH 495 PER 100000
15 OF 25 COUNTRIES(0.60) ARE ABOVE
P= 0.0000 CHI=20.8325

29) STUDENTS OVER 19, TERTIARY TENDS LESS TO BE LOW 990 PER 100000
21 OF 25 COUNTRIES(0.84) ARE BELOW
P= 0.0020 CHI=14.5962

TABLE 1 (continued)

[Per Cap GDP below 700 Dollars]

30) PUPILS PER TEACHER,PRIMARY TENDS TO BE HIGH
81 OF 107 COUNTRIES(0.76) ARE ABOVE   31 PER TCHR

31) NEWSPRINT   ALWAYS LOW
87 OF 87 COUNTRIES(1.00) ARE BELOW   91 KG PER CAP

31) NEWSPRINT   TENDS MORE TO BE LOW
87 OF 87 COUNTRIES(1.00) ARE BELOW   182 KG PER CAP

31) NEWSPRINT   TENDS MORE TO BE LOW
87 OF 87 COUNTRIES(1.00) ARE BELOW   273 KG PER CAP

32) RADIO RECEIVERS   TENDS TO BE LOW   235 PER 1000
107 OF 109 COUNTRIES(0.98) ARE BELOW

33) ENERGY CONSUMPTION   TENDS TO BE LOW
105 OF 109 COUNTRIES(0.96) ARE BELOW   2070 KG PER CAP

33) ENERGY CONSUMPTION   TENDS MORE TO BE LOW
108 OF 109 COUNTRIES (0.99) ARE BELOW   4136 KG PER CAP

39) FOOD AS PRCNT OF GNP TENDS TO BE HIGH   24 PERCENT
19 OF 20 COUNTRIES(0.95) ARE ABOVE

43) AGRICULTURE, PRCNT OF GDP TENDS TO BE HIGH
46 OF 57 COUNTRIES(0.81) ARE ABOVE   23 PERCENT

[Per Cap GDP above 700 Dollars]

30) PUPILS PER TEACHER,PRIMARY TENDS TO BE LOW   31 PER TCHR   P=0.0013 CHI=12.0623
15 OF 25 COUNTRIES(0.60) ARE BELOW

31) NEWSPRINT   TENDS TO BE HIGH   91 KG PER CAP   P=0.0000 CHI=76.0589
17 OF 23 COUNTRIES(C.74) ARE ABOVE

31) NEWSPRINT   TENDS LESS TO BE LOW   182 KG PER CAP   P=0.0000 CHI=32.6343
15 OF 23 COUNTRIES(0.65) ARE BELOW

31) NEWSPRINT   TENDS LESS TO BE LOW   273 KG PER CAP   P=0.0082 CHI=11.6660
20 OF 23 COUNTRIES(0.87) ARE BELOW

32) RADIO RECEIVERS   TENDS TO BE HIGH   235 PER 1000   P=0.0000 CHI=80.0763
17 OF 23 COUNTRIES(0.74) ARE ABOVE

33) ENERGY CONSUMPTION   TENDS TO BE HIGH   2070 KG PER CAP   P=0.0000 CHI=76.0830
18 OF 23 COUNTRIES(0.78) ARE ABOVE

33) ENERGY CONSUMPTION   TENDS LESS TO BE LOW   4136 KG PER CAP   P=0.0006 CHI=18.9775
18 OF 23 COUNTRIES (0.78) ARE BELOW

39) FOOD AS PRCNT OF GNP TENDS TO BE LOW   24 PERCENT   P=0.0000 CHI=25.9392
15 OF 17 COUNTRIES(0.88) ARE BELOW

43) AGRICULTURE, PRCNT OF GDP   TENDS TO BE LOW   23 PERCENT   P=0.0000 CHI=30.3113
19 OF 22 COUNTRIES(0.86) ARE BELOW

TABLE 1 (continued)

[Per Cap GDP below 700 Dollars]

[Per Cap GDP above 700 Dollars]

43) AGRICULTURE, PRCNT OF GDP TENDS LESS TO BE LOW 41 PERCENT
37 OF 57 COUNTRIES(0.65) ARE BELOW

43) AGRICULTURE, PRCNT OF GDP TENDS MORE TO BE LOW 41 PERCENT
21 OF 22 COUNTRIES(0.95) ARE BELOW   P= 0.0048 CHI= 7.5872

44) MANUFACTURING PERCENT GDP TENDS TO BE LOW 17 PERCENT
39 OF 57 COUNTRIES(0.68) ARE BELOW

44) MANUFACTURING PERCENT GDP TENDS TO BE HIGH 17 PERCENT
21 OF 22 COUNTRIES(0.95) ARE ABOVE   P= 0.0000 CHI=25.9102

44) MANUFACTURING PERCENT GDP TENDS TO BE LOW 31 PERCENT
50 OF 57 COUNTRIES(0.88) ARE BELOW

44) MANUFACTURING PERCENT GDP TENDS TO BE HIGH 31 PERCENT
12 OF 22 COUNTRIES(0.55) ARE ABOVE   P= 0.0002 CHI=15.5230

46) GDS AS PERCENT OF GDP TENDS LESS TO BE HIGH 14 PERCENT
18 OF 35 COUNTRIES(0.51) ARE ABOVE

46) GDS AS PERCENT OF GDP TENDS MORE TO BE HIGH 14 PERCENT
16 OF 18 COUNTRIES(0.89) ARE ABOVE   P= 0.0077 CHI= 7.2532

46) GDS AS PERCENT CF GDP TENDS TO BE LOW 20 PERCENT
30 OF 35 COUNTRIES(0.86) ARE BELOW

46) GDS AS PERCENT OF GDP TENDS TO BE HIGH 20 PERCENT
11 OF 18 COUNTRIES(0.61) ARE ABOVE   P= 0.0010 CHI=12.3668

47) AVERAGE INVESTMENT RATIO TENDS TO BE LOW 18 PRCNT GDP
23 OF 44 COUNTRIES(0.52) ARE BELOW

47) AVERAGE INVESTMENT RATIO TENDS TO BE HIGH 18 PRCNT GDP
18 OF 20 COUNTRIES(0.90) ARE ABOVE   P= 0.0019 CHI=10.3223

TABLE 2

Real Types of "Soviet Bloc" and "Non-Soviet Bloc" Countries.

Comparison Variable: [Within the Soviet Bloc]		Comparison Variable: [Not in Soviet Bloc]	

201 COUNTRIES

ADEN	AFGHANISTAN	ALGERIA	AMER SAMOA	ANGOLA	ANTIGUA	ARGENTINA	AUSTRALIA	AUSTRIA	BAHAMA
BAHRAIN	BARBADOS	BASUTOLAND	BECHUANALAND	WEST BERLIN	BELGIUM	BERMUDA	HHUTAN	BOLIVIA	NO BORNEO
BRAZIL	BR BORNEO	BR GUIANA	BR HONDURAS	BRUNEI	BURMA	BURUNDI	CAMBODIA	CAMEROON	CANADA
CANAL ZONE	CAPE VERDE	CAYMAN ILS	CEN AFR REP	CEYLON	CHAD	CHANNEL ILS	CHILE	CHRIST ILS	COCOS ILS
COLOMBIA	CUMORO ILS	CONGO BRAZ	CONGO LEOP	COOK ILS	COSTA RICA	CYPRUS	DAHOMEY	DENMARK	DOMINICAN REP
DOMINICA	ECUADOR	EL SALVADOR	ENGLAND	ETHIOPIA	FAEROE ILS	FALKLAND ILS	FIJI ILS	FINLAND	FRANCE
FR POLYNESIA	FR SOMALI	GABON	GAMBIA	W GERMANY	GHANA	GIBRALTER	GILBERT ILS	GREECE	GREENLAND
GRENADA	GUADELOUPE	GUAM	GUATEMALA	GUINEA	HAITI	HOLY SEE	HONDURAS	HONG KONG	ICELAND
IFNI	INDIA	INDONESIA	IRAN	IRAQ	IRELAND	ISLE OF MAN	ISRAEL	ITALY	IVORY COAST
JAMAICA	JAPAN	JOHNSTON IL	JORDAN	KENYA	SOUTH KOREA	KUWAIT	LAOS	LEBANON	LIBERIA
LIBYA	LICHTENSTEIN	LUXEMBOURG	MACAU	MADAGASCAR	MALDIVE ILS	MALI	MALTA GOZO	MARTINIQUE	MAURITANIA
MAURITIUS	MALAYA	MEXICO	MIDWAY ILS	MONACO	MONTSERRAT	MOROCCO	MOZAMBIQUE	MUSCAT OMAN	NAURU
NEPAL	NETHERLANDS	NETH ANTIL	NEW GUINEA	NEW ZEALAND	NICARAGUA	NIGER	NIGERIA	NIUE	NORFOLK IL
NORWAY	PACIFIC ILS	PAKISTAN	PALESTINE GS	PANAMA	PAPUA	PARAGUAY	PERU	PHILIPPINES	PITCAIRN
PORTUGAL	PORT GUINEA	PORT INDIA	PORT TIMOR	PUERTO RICO	REUNION	RHODESIA NY	RWANDA	RYUKYU ILS	ST HELENA
ST KITTS	ST LUCIA	ST PIERRE	ST VINCENT	SAO TOME	SARAWAK	SAUDI ARABIA	SENEGAL	SEYCHELLES	SIERRA LEONE
SIKKIM	SINGAPORE	SOLOMON ILS	SOMALIA	SO AFRICA	SOUTH ARABIA	S W AFRICA	SPAIN	SPAN EQUAT	SP NO AFRI
SPAN SAHARA	SUDAN	SURINAM	SWAZILAND	SWEDEN	SWITZERLAND	SYRIA	TAIWAN	TANGANYIKA	THAILAND
TOGO	TOKELAU ILS	TONGA	TRIN TOBAGO	TUNISIA	TURKEY	TURKS ILS	UGANDA	UAR	USA
UPPER VOLTA	URUGUAY	VENEZUELA	S VIETNAM	VIRGIN IS UK	VIRGIN IS US	WAKE ISLAND	WEST SAMOA	W NEW GUINEA	YEMEN
ZANZIBAR PEM									

15 COUNTRIES

ALBANIA	BULGARIA	CHINA	CUBA	CZECH	E BERLIN	E GERMANY	HUNGARY	NORTH KOREA
POLAND	RUMANIA	USSR	N VIETNAM	YUGOSLAVIA				MONGOLIA

TABLE 2 (continued)

[Within the Soviet Bloc] [Not in Soviet Bloc]

10) POPULATION UNDER AGE 15 TENDS MORE TO BE LOW 42 PERCENT
12 OF 12 COUNTRIES(1.00) ARE BELOW

POPULATION UNDER AGE 15 TENDS LESS TO BE LOW 42 PERCENT
82 OF 142 COUNTRIES(0.58) ARE BELOW
P= 0.0035 CHI= 8.3069

11) POPULATION AGED 15-64 TENDS TO BE HIGH 58 PERCENT
9 OF 10 COUNTRIES(0.90) ARE ABOVE

POPULATION AGED 15-64 TENDS TO BE LOW 58 PERCENT
72 OF 127 COUNTRIES(0.57) ARE BELOW
P= 0.0061 CHI= 8.1194

11) POPULATION AGED 15-64 TENDS TO BE HIGH 64 PERCENT
6 OF 10 COUNTRIES(0.60) ARE ABOVE

POPULATION AGED 15-64 TENDS TO BE LOW 64 PERCENT
103 OF 127 COUNTRIES(0.81) ARE BELOW
P= 0.0076 CHI= 9.1570

12) LIFE EXPECTANCY AT BIRTH ALWAYS HIGH 59 YEARS
8 OF 8 COUNTRIES(1.00) ARE ABOVE

LIFE EXPECTANCY AT BIRTH TENDS TO BE LOW 59 YEARS
45 OF 78 COUNTRIES(0.58) ARE BELOW
P= 0.0018 CHI= 9.6811

26) ILLITERATE POP.OVER AGE 15 TENDS TO BE LOW 25 PERCENT
7 OF 8 COUNTRIES(0.88) ARE BELOW

ILLITERATE POP.OVER AGE 15 TENDS TO BE HIGH 25 PERCENT
65 OF 92 COUNTRIES(0.71) ARE ABOVE
P= 0.0020 CHI=11.0914

36) GOV. DISPOSABLE INCOME ALWAYS HIGH 22 PRCNT GDP
7 OF 7 COUNTRIES(1.00) ARE ABOVE

GOV. DISPOSABLE INCOME TENDS TO BE LOW 22 PRCNT GDP
36 OF 40 COUNTRIES(0.90) ARE BELOW
P= 0.0000 CHI=26.9187

36) GOV. DISPOSABLE INCOME TENDS TO BE HIGH 36 PRCNT GDP
6 OF 7 COUNTRIES(0.86) ARE ABOVE

GOV. DISPOSABLE INCOME ALWAYS LOW 36 PRCNT GDP
40 OF 40 COUNTRIES(1.00) ARE BELOW
P= 0.0000 CHI=39.3031

36) GOV. DISPOSABLE INCOME TENDS TO BE HIGH 50 PRCNT GDP
5 OF 7 COUNTRIES(0.71) ARE ABOVE

GOV. DISPOSABLE INCOME ALWAYS LOW 50 PRCNT GDP
40 OF 40 COUNTRIES(1.00) ARE BELOW
P= 0.0000 CHI=31.9728

TABLE 2 (continued)

[Within the Soviet Bloc]

[Not in Soviet Bloc]

40) GROWTH OF TOTAL GDP TENDS TO BE HIGH
7 OF 8 COUNTRIES(0.88) ARE ABOVE 65 PER 1000

GROWTH OF TOTAL GDP TENDS TO BE LOW
51 OF 60 COUNTRIES(0.85) ARE BELOW 65 PER 1000
P= 0.0001 CHI=20.6207

42) PER CAPITA GROWTH OF GDP ALWAYS HIGH
8 OF 8 COUNTRIES(1.00) ARE ABOVE 36 PER 1000

PER CAPITA GROWTH OF GDP TENDS TO BE LOW
45 OF 59 COUNTRIES(0.76) ARE BELOW 36 PER 1000
P= 0.0000 CHI=18.5824

42) PER CAPITA GROWTH OF GDP TENDS TO BE HIGH
5 OF 8 COUNTRIES(0.63) ARE ABOVE 65 PER 1000

PER CAPITA GROWTH OF GDP TENDS TO BE LOW
55 OF 59 COUNTRIES(0.93) ARE BELOW 65 PER 1000
P= 0.0006 CHI=18.8094

44) MANUFACTURING PERCENT GDP ALWAYS HIGH
9 OF 9 COUNTRIES(1.00) ARE ABOVE 17 PERCENT

MANUFACTURING PERCENT GDP TENDS TO BE LOW
40 OF 70 COUNTRIES(0.57) ARE BELOW 17 PERCENT
P= 0.0010 CHI=10.4176

44) MANUFACTURING PERCENT GDP TENDS TO BE HIGH
8 OF 9 COUNTRIES(0.89) ARE ABOVE 31 PERCENT

MANUFACTURING PERCENT GDP TENDS TO BE LOW
59 OF 70 COUNTRIES(0.84) ARE BELOW 31 PERCENT
P= 0.0000 CHI=23.3767

44) MANUFACTURING PERCENT GDP TENDS LESS TO BE LOW
5 OF 9 COUNTRIES(0.56) ARE BELOW 45 PERCENT

MANUFACTURING PERCENT GDP TENDS MORE TO BE LOW
70 OF 70 COUNTRIES(1.00) ARE BELOW 45 PERCENT
P= 0.0001 CHI=32.7704

and 2 four real types which refer to states of the world in the 1950's and early 1960's. However, we might have been interested in those variables which are important to a society's ability to maintain itself or to expand. Each one of these considerations will lead to a different initial set of data and a different final print-out. If that final print-out is not satisfactory, it will then lead to additional data being considered or to some revised criteria for the selection and suppression of information. However, our process can be of no help to the intellectual historian who wishes to discover the essential ideas of a society, ideas which serve to prescribe conduct and make for changes in customs and laws. A real type cannot handle that kind of inquiry.

X. FURTHER PROBLEMS

The discussion to this point thus suggests at least two areas which require investigation. The first is programming of types when naming of types depends not on the values of only one comparison variable but on many. The second is the criteria used to select some types from the set of possible types which can be manufactured from a field of data. The historian will undoubtedly suggest a third area which requires investigation. What happens to the problem of constructing types when the variables are descriptive not of single periods of time, but instead cover long time-periods (as in "mercantilist societies")? The first and the third problems do not seem to be intractable, although to have taken them up in this paper would have led to greater complexity in what may seem to many already a fairly complicated discussion of something which on the face of it appears simple. We suspect that consideration of the second point entails some of the thorniest problems in historical technique.

XI. SOME GENERAL CONCLUSIONS

Our investigation does lend itself to some broad conclusions. The first is that there is no doubt that we can, to some extent, simulate on the computer familiar cognitive processes which historians use. Undoubtedly, the need to instruct a machine to perform the necessary processes leads to a great gain in the clarity of understanding of the technique being used. Furthermore, once a computer program is written and a data field is known, anyone interested in a specific problem can rapidly acquire the raw material of historical inquiry. Data which might take the historian years to consider before he finds a descriptive system to organize them can be rapidly scanned by the computer. Once a field of data has been established, other computer programs can be used to gain insights from it. Thus, it may be possible that the historian who is willing to find out under what conditions such techniques are applicable may find that certain procedures which are time-consuming to him may be performed by an electronic computer with a concomitant gain in precision and accuracy.

5. Notes on the historical study of social mobility*

STEPHAN THERNSTROM †§

In recent years sociological work in the field of stratification and social mobility has become, in at least one sense of the term, impressively cosmopolitan. National sample surveys which include data on inter-generational occupational mobility have been carried out in every major Western nation and in a good many non-Western societies as well, and those have inspired some ambitious comparative analyses of social mobility. This development, as S. M. Miller puts it, has had the virtue of making "the study of mobility one of the few fields of sociology which has overcome national parochialisms."[1] True as this is, however, it must be said that there are forms of parochialism other than national. Much contemporary research into social mobility suffers from one of these—a parochialism of time rather than of place, as it were, the parochialism of presentism. My purpose here is to suggest what is lost as a result of that parochialism, and to argue that a sense of the past, an ability to see his subject in historical depth, is not a luxury but a necessity for the student of social mobility.

I

Let me begin with a simple, obvious, uncontroversial point—so obvious, indeed, that I would blush to make it but for the fact that so few students of social

---

* "Notes on the Historical Study of Social Mobility" was reprinted from *Comparative Studies in Society and History,* January, 1968, by kind permission of the author and the publisher, Cambridge University Press.

†Stephan A. Thernstrom, currently Visiting Professor of Urban History at the University of California at Los Angeles, received his Ph.D. from Harvard University in 1962. His publications include: *Poverty and Progress: Social Mobility in a Nineteenth Century City,* Harvard University Press, 1964; and *Poverty, Planning and Politics in the New Boston,* Basic Books, 1969.

§ An earlier version of this paper was delivered at the 1964 annual meetings of the American Sociological Association. I am very much indebted to Charles Tilly for critical suggestions.

[1] S. M. Miller, "Comparative Social Mobility: A Trend Report and Bibliography," *Current Sociology,* 9 (1960), 2.

mobility seem to have taken it to heart. This is simply that some of the most interesting questions we might ask about the nature of a class structure today cannot be answered without reliable information about the nature of that class structure yesterday—and the day before yesterday, and even the century before yesterday! And that nowhere has the research necessary to supply such knowledge about class and mobility been carried out in sufficient historical depth. Despite the recent avalanche of empirical research on social mobility, appallingly little is known about the process of social mobility in the past and about long-term mobility trends in any society—certainly not in our own.

Consider the familiar controversy over the blocked-mobility hypothesis advanced by the Lynds, Warner and others some decades ago.[2] The question of whether or not American society is on the verge of succumbing to arterio-sclerosis has been repeatedly discussed ever since. Clearly this is a question of considerable interest—to the general public as well as to the scholarly world, if the success of such books as *The Status Seekers* be any index. And yet the issue remains largely unresolved, despite some recent studies demonstrating that there has been no diminution in mobility rates in the past two decades.[3] Valuable though this work is, its time perspective is so foreshortened as to be irrelevant to the issue of long-term changes in the openness of the American social order. Rogoff's Indianapolis study reaches farther back into the past, but even that begins no earlier than 1910, while the explicit or implicit point of comparison chosen by proponents of the blocked-mobility theory was *nineteenth-century* America, and there is the further limitation that Rogoff did not study intra-generational mobility at all.[4] Systematic studies of social mobility in nineteenth-century America are still woefully absent. True, the social origins of members of the national business elite of the era have been examined in some detail, and Aronson has recently explored the social composition of the higher civil service in the first four decades of the Republic, but little, regrettably, can be learned about the range of mobility opportunities at the lower and middle levels from surveys of those who rose to the very top.[5]

The debate about mobility trends in the United States has been conducted without any solid grasp of the nature of the American class structure in the past,

---

[2] W. Lloyd Warner and J. O. Low, *The Social System of the Modern Factory* (New Haven, 1947); Robert S. and Helen M. Lynd, *Middletown: A Study in American Culture* (New York, 1929) and *Middletown in Transition: A Study in Cultural Conflict* (New York, 1937); Elbridge Sibley, "Some Demographic Clues to Stratification," *American Sociological Review,* 7 (1942), 322-330; D. H. Anderson and P. E. Davidson, *Occupational Mobility in an American Community* (Stanford, 1937); J. O. Hertzler, "Some Tendencies Towards a Closed Class System in the United States," *Social Forces,* 30 (1952), 313-323.

[3] E. F. Jackson and H. J. Crockett, "Occupational Mobility in the United States: A Point Estimate and Trend Comparison," *American Sociological Review,* 29 (1964), 5-15; O. D. Duncan, "The Trend of Occupational Mobility in the United States," *American Sociological Review,* 30 (1965), 491-498.

[4] Natalie Rogoff, *Recent Trends in Occupational Mobility* (Glencoe, Ill., 1953).

[5] Sidney Aronson, *Status and Kinship in the Higher Civil Service* (Cambridge, 1964). The business-elite literature is conveniently summarized and analyzed in S. M. Lipset and R. Bendix, *Social Mobility in Industrial Society* (Berkeley, 1959), Chapter IV.

or indeed any knowledge that much the same argument about the level of opportunities has been going on in this country for approximately a century! Thus this typical contribution to the debate:

The man at the bottom of the ladder leading up to the social heavens may yet dream that there is a ladder let down to him; but the angels are not seen very often ascending and descending; one after another, it would seem, some unseen yet hostile powers are breaking out the middle rungs of the ladder.[6]

These are not the words of Lloyd Warner or the Lynds observing Newburyport or Muncie in the Great Depression, but the gloomy verdict of an obscure Boston minister in 1885. Similar complaints about declining opportunities were voiced by artisans threatened by economic change in the Jacksonian era.[7]

That the blocked-mobility hypothesis advanced by modern social scientists is not a blinding new discovery but a restatement of an age-old American complaint does not necessarily discredit the notion, but it should make us wonder a little. If the middle rungs of the social ladder were being wrenched out in the 1880's or in the age of Jackson, how many could have been left for the later destruction described by Warner and the Lynds? If, on the other hand, Reverend Smyth and Jacksonian labor leaders were mistaken in their diagnosis, victims of an innate American tendency to judge the imperfections of the present against a fictitious vanished Golden Age of perfect opportunity in the past, might not the same predispositions shape the perceptions of later American social scientists as well? The ironic coincidence that the idyllic past conjured up by Lloyd Warner in *The Social System of the Modern Factory* was just the period in which Reverend Smyth was lamenting the death of the American Dream strongly suggests that this was indeed the case. Popular mythology about the character of the social order is well worth careful study in its own right, to be sure, but some writers have reflected it instead of reflecting upon it.[8]

A large-scale, systematic quantitative study of social-mobility patterns in nineteenth-century America will be required to allow us to gauge whether any of these dire prophecies of constricting mobility opportunities had any foundation in fact, and, more important, to assess the influence of a host of different variables singled out by those who have speculated about long-term mobility trends in the United States. Was it the mechanization of industry and the consequent destruction of older craft hierarchies which produced the changes Reverend Smyth deplored, and if so, had these processes advanced as far and in the same form in Boston in the 1880's as in Muncie and Newburyport four to

---

6 Newman Smyth, *Social Problems: Sermons to Workingmen* (Boston, 1885), 12-13.

7 Norman Ware, *The Industrial Worker, 1840-1860* (Boston, 1934; paperback edition, Chicago, 1964), *passim.* For similar fears in the latter half of the nineteenth century, see the documents in Leon Litwack, *The American Labor Movement* (Englewood Cliffs, N.J., 1962), 3-14. Both Ware and Litwack were insufficiently critical of the testimony they cite, and assumed that if contemporary witnesses *thought* that opportunities were declining, they must have been in fact, an assumption questioned below.

8 For further development of this point, see Stephan Thernstrom, " 'Yankee City' Revisited: The Perils of Historical Naïveté," *American Sociological Review,* 30 (1965), 234-242.

five decades later? What of the closing of the frontier, the blocking of mass immigration to our shores, or the narrowing of class differences in fertility? The first of these, difficult though it is to date precisely, was taking place at just about the time at which Reverend Smyth wrote, while the other two had yet to occur at all. Since the *timing* of these and other historical developments which might have influenced the shape of the class structure varied greatly, historical inquiry affords us the opportunity to assign priority to certain variables and to dismiss others.

It is a truism, of course, that the comparative method serves this end. What is not a truism, however, at least not one which conspicuously influences the actual course of social research today, is that additional depth of knowledge about one society can be as fruitful for comparative purposes as additional cross-cultural breadth.[9] Perhaps more fruitful, for it does not rest upon the questionable premise that all societies pass through similar stages of development and that in the absence of sufficient historical knowledge about social patterns in the early years of industrialization in the West we may apply models derived from the study of the class structure of underdeveloped countries today. Such models may or may not be relevant; their possible relevance can only be demonstrated on the basis of thorough acquaintance with the historical record. The two research strategies are complementary, of course, but what requires emphasis is that the one is a poor substitute for the other.

II

The blocked-mobility hypothesis provides a convenient illustration of another point which underlines the importance of understanding social mobility in historical context. The question of how the Industrial Revolution and a host of subsequent economic and technological changes have affected the social position of the ordinary workingman has generated an enormous historical and sociological literature, much of it marred by the failure to grasp that in a mobile society a decline in the status of a particular occupation is often accompanied by a corresponding shift in the social stratum from which the occupation draws its labor force. Thus writers like the Hammonds, Norman Ware, the Lynds, and Warner misunderstood the implications of their discovery that the position of the semi-skilled operative in a modern textile mill or shoe factory was in many ways inferior to that of the artisan who produced similar products prior to industrialization. They saw industrial change as the engine of "status degradation" for a large sector of the working class. But this assumed a simplistic model of an occupational structure in which all skilled crafts were being wiped out and in which there were no opportunities for upward social mobility, so that the

---

9 For a good example from the field of demography, see Aaron Antonovsky, "Social Class, Life Expectancy, and Overall Mortality," *Milbank Memorial Fund Quarterly,* 45 (1967), 38-39. For further discussion of the advantages of longitudinal studies over static cross-sectional ones, see Nathan Goldfarb, *An Introduction to Longitudinal Statistical Analysis* (Glencoe, Ill., 1960), and Norman B. Ryder, "The Cohort as a Concept in the Study of Social Change," *American Sociological Review,* 30 (1965), 843-861.

artisans and their children had no alternative but to suffer status degradation and accept a semi-skilled factory job.

This model, however, is of doubtful validity. Convincing evidence that it was the skilled craftsmen of old or their children who made up the new semi-skilled factory labor force has never been produced by adherents of the cataclysmic view of industrialization. Recent research suggests that status degradation was a rare phenomenon, that the skilled have commonly been able to preserve their position and that their sons have been likely to find other skilled niches or quite often to enter a white-collar position of some kind. The new factory labor force, it appears, has characteristically been recruited by a process overlooked by earlier observers, a process with very different implications for the social structure. By and large it was not declassé artisans but unskilled newcomers—immigrants and migrants from rural areas—who moved into the factories, men for whom factory employment generally meant improved status. An essential aspect of the complex of changes we refer to as urbanization and industrialization has been a cycle of migration and social mobility which has filled the least attractive and least well-rewarded industrial positions with successive waves of newcomers, who appraise their situation with standards formed not in the proud world of the independent artisan but in a subsistence agrarian economy.

We cannot speak too dogmatically about this matter, given the paucity of evidence currently available, but this generalization does hold for the United States, I think. (More about the rest of the world in a moment.) My investigation of working class social mobility patterns in Newburyport, Mass. in the 1850-1880 period reveals this mobility cycle at work there,[10] and my current work with a sample of 8000 residents of Boston between 1880 and the present, as yet unpublished, has yielded much the same result. Few skilled workmen in the community suffered downward mobility as a result of technological and other developments at any time in this period. Furthermore, the sons of skilled craftsmen rarely dropped down into the ranks of the unskilled or semi-skilled themselves; close to half of them, indeed, attained middle class status.

The same conclusion is suggested by Rogoff's Indianapolis study. This goes back no earlier than 1910, unfortunately, but it is the most comprehensive inquiry available for the period with which it deals, and it has the further advantage of dealing with a Hoosier city quite similar to nearby Muncie, the site of the Middletown research, thus providing a rough check of the accuracy of the Lynds' assumptions about the status degradation wrought by industrialization. Rogoff's tables reveal that fully 49 percent of the sons of skilled craftsmen in the Indianapolis sample for 1910 were themselves in skilled callings, and another quarter of them had moved into the rapidly expanding non-manual occupations. Few of them had been downwardly mobile in the way foreseen by proponents of the blocked-mobility hypothesis.[11] We can infer from Rogoff's tables and what the Lynds tell us about the precipitous growth of the Muncie population

---

[10] Stephan Thernstrom, *Poverty and Progress: Social Mobility in a Nineteenth Century City* (Cambridge, 1964).

[11] Rogoff, *op. cit.*, 44.

that the semi-skilled factory labor force in both cities was actually composed predominantly of newcomers of lowly origin.

This mobility cycle, in which newly-created jobs of rather lowly status tend to go to those who previously held even lowlier jobs, is easiest to observe in cities with two distinguishing features. If a city's population increased dramatically during industrialization, and if many of the newcomers were members of highly visible ethnic groups, this relationship between immigration, industrialization and social mobility should leap to the eye. Doubtless it was not accidental that the two major community studies which advanced the blocked-mobility theory—the Yankee City inquiry and the Middletown volumes—were carried out in American cities which happened to lack one of these traits. In the case of Newburyport, whose total population was little more in 1930 than it was in 1855, it was natural—though utterly mistaken—to assume that the *composition* of the population had changed very little, and that this was a self-contained, static "old New England community." In fact, however, this was a radical misconception. Though its total population levelled off in 1855, the composition of the population underwent a number of fundamental changes. The stable net figure concealed staggeringly high rates of gross movement. A substantial fraction of the city's inhabitants left Newburyport each decade; others—the Irish, later the French-Canadians, the Italians, and so forth—poured in to take their places, a steady stream of newcomers to occupy the lower rungs of the occupational ladder.[12]

That the total Muncie population grew very rapidly during the years of the Middletown study was not conducive to the illusion that the community was sealed off from the larger society in the manner dear to the heart of the anthropologist. But the fact that the Lynds selected a community without a large foreign-born or Negro population—they sought to exclude racial change as a variable and to isolate the social effects of industrialization—blinded them to this mobility cycle in much the same way. In fact, Kentucky, Tennessee, and rural Indiana served as the functional equivalent of the Old World as a source of migrants with little status to lose; it was much easier to overlook newcomers like these, however, and to assume that the sons of the highly-skilled glassblowers of old Muncie were necessarily a prime source of the new semi-skilled factory labor force.

The bald assertion that factory employment generally meant improved status for migrants like these does raise a troubling problem sociologists are only now beginning to grapple with, the problem of how to evaluate movement from an entire social setting to one utterly different. It seems simple enough to say that a foreman enjoys higher status than a factory laborer, and that the owner of the factory ranks above both of them, but the shift of agricultural workers into urban industrial employment obviously defies easy evaluation. There can be a series of distinct clusters of positions which differ in their relationship to the market, life chances, etc. and yet which are roughly equivalent in power, wealth,

12 Thernstrom, *op. cit.,* 84-86, 167-168, 195-196.

or prestige. The concept of "situs" has been developed to describe such a situation.[13] The movement of workers from the agricultural situs to the industrial one may sometimes entail no vertical mobility in either direction, but only horizontal movement into a slot of equivalent rank. This means that it is necessary to investigate in detail the social milieu from which the migrants came in any particular instance, to specify the distribution of social types—large landlord or small, tenant or farm laborer—within the migrant stream, and to employ these categories in examining the experiences of these men after they enter the industrial world. Such a procedure will make it possible to distinguish cases in which migration brought no improvement or even status loss from what I suggest is the more common pattern of general advance.

The sketchy evidence cited above pertains to the United States in the past century. That a similar process has been at work in other societies as well we know from the work of Lipset and Bendix, Morris D. Morris, and others, but this work constitutes the barest beginning toward a full understanding of the matter.[14] One wonders if some of the societal differences which were invisible through the crudely-ground lenses of Lipset and Bendix's microscope, and which they consequently interpreted as variations in national values unsupported by actual differences in social structure, might not be rooted in differences in the way this process operated in different countries. One suspects, for example, that the pace and volume of immigration and internal migration was spectacularly high in the American case, and that the proportion of the urban labor force with prior exposure to the artisan and yeoman traditions that inspired the militant labor protest of the Industrial Revolution in Britain was distinctively low, and that this has a good deal to do with the continuing popular belief that New World society has been uniquely open.[15] Too little is known at present to press this argument very far, but the whole issue demands study by sociologically-inclined historians and historically-minded sociologists.

III

Something should be said about the problem of finding data from which historical studies of social mobility can be written, and about the historian's approach to such data. It has often been assumed that systematic historical

---

[13] Paul K. Hatt, "Occupation and Social Stratification," *American Journal of Sociology,* 55 (1950), 539. For an excellent historical illustration, see Charles Tilly's discussion of the dual class structure of the Vendée in the 1790's; *The Vendée* (Cambridge, 1964), 79-80, 98-99.

[14] Lipset and Bendix, *op. cit.,* 203-226; Gideon Sjoberg, "Rural-Urban Balance and Models of Economic Development," in Neil Smelser and S. M. Lipset, *Social Structure and Mobility in Economic Development* (Chicago, 1966), 235-261; Gunnar Boalt, "Social Mobility in Stockholm: A Pilot Investigation," *Transactions of the Second World Congress of Sociology* (London, 1954), II, 67-73; Morris D. Morris, "The Recruitment of an Industrial Labor Force in India, with British and American Comparisons," *Comparative Studies in Society and History,* II (1960), 305-328; Ronald and Deborah Freedman, "Farm-Reared Elements in the Non-Farm Population," *Rural Sociology,* 21 (1956), 50-61.

[15] Cf. E. P. Thompson, *The Making of the English Working Class* (London, 1963).

studies of social mobility are rare because of the absence of satisfactory evidence. In a great many instances, at least, this is more a rationalization than a reason. True, there are times and places irrecoverably lost to history. But for most relatively modern societies, and some traditional ones (such as ancient China), vast amounts of usable material are still untapped. Thus, for the United States there is a wonderfully rich and virtually untouched source for mobility research—manuscript schedules of the federal census, which from 1850 on provide a primitive social survey of the entire population of the United States. There are city directories, well used by Sidney Goldstein and his colleagues in the Norristown study, which for many communities extended back a century and a half or more; the problem of reliability with early city directories is severe but not insurmountable, and they offer the special advantage for sample studies that respondents are arranged by alphabetical order.[16] Reaching even farther back into the past are local tax and voting records—even when these lack adequate occupational information they made it possible to stratify a community according to property ownership and political participation. In many Western European countries, of course, historical records with relevant fragments of data have survived even longer.

There are maddening difficulties in employing this data, to be sure. Occupational designations are sometimes appallingly vague by modern standards. Until well into the nineteenth century in England and the United States, a "manufacturer" could be a manual employee or his employer; it was not until the twentieth century that the French "ouvrier" received its present definition.[17] Where the available records do not supply further information to make the distinctions which we regard as crucial, analytical possibilities are obviously sorely limited.

Instead of bewildering vagueness, we sometimes encounter puzzling concreteness. Consider the difficulties of devising an occupational classification scheme to employ in analyzing Patrick Colquhoun's enumeration of the London population at the close of the eighteenth century, enumerations which include such intriguing occupations as mudlark, scufflehunter, bludgeonman, morocco man, flash coachman, grubber, and bear baiter.[18] Obviously the findings of Inkeles, Rossi, Reiss and others who have investigated the prestige ranking of occupations is of little avail in grappling with the problem. If the example is not very serious, the point is. Whatever the difficulties they create, however, there is the consolation that the curiously antique or exotic labels which often appear in the sources convey a very useful warning. The problem of the mudlark and the scufflehunter suggests two general principles: (1) the need to employ finely calibrated instruments in reconstructing a social structure now vanished; (2) the necessity of paying close attention to the entire social context in which the particular phenomenon under consideration was embedded.

---

[16] Sidney Goldstein, *Patterns of Mobility, 1910-1950: The Norristown Study* (Philadelphia, 1958).

[17] George Rudé, *The Crowd in History, 1730-1848* (New York, 1964), 196-197.

[18] Thompson, *op. cit.*, 55.

At this level of abstraction, these principles seem singularly harmless platitudes, but they are not, I think, without a cutting edge. If we abide by them in examining some vast problem—changes in the openness of the American social structure since 1700, let us say—I think we would proceed in a manner somewhat different from that in which many contemporary sociologists would proceed. Rather than taking the currently fashionable index of social mobility, the rate of inter-generational movement between manual and non-manual occupations, computing occupational mobility rates at selected intervals, and constructing a simple time series, the historian would insist that a scrupulous examination of the class structure at several strategic points in time and an assessment of the extent of social mobility in terms of categories appropriate to each point in time would be required, and that to arrive at a simple conclusion about trends might be impossible because of the lack of comparability of the historically specific categories used. Did the Polish peasants in the mills of Gary in 1910 hold the same relative position in the class system as the indentured servants of Salem in 1710? What was the mobility equivalent in 1910 of the purchase of a farm in the Connecticut River Valley in 1710? Merely to contemplate the multitude of meanings of the occupational designation "farm owner" through the course of American history is to see some of the inescapable complexities of the problem.

This is not to say that there would be nothing of interest in a crude table which purported to summarize changes in the rate of inter-generational movement between manual and non-manual occupations in America since 1700, any more than that there is nothing of interest in a similar table summarizing crude occupational data for post-World War II Europe and the United States. But this would be but a small first step, and it may not be the wisest step to take first. The concept of social mobility, after all, is an exceptionally rich and complex one, and simple one-dimensional indices which facilitate immediate comparisons of social mobility in radically different social orders may not yield the most rewarding comparisons. The alluring comparability attained by passing disparate sets of data through a sieve so crude that it allows essential features of each set to trickle away is purchased at a very heavy price.

In my own work on working class mobility in nineteenth-century America I quickly found that some of the most important elements of the problem could not be discerned through the lenses of a two-class occupational scheme —or, indeed, any occupational scheme at all. Not only was it useful to distinguish unskilled, semi-skilled, and skilled positions within the broad rubric of manual occupations; it was essential to devote extensive attention to another dimension of social mobility entirely. By far the most important form of upward mobility in the setting I examined was movement between the floating, unstable, propertyless sector of the working class and the settled, respectable, property-owning working class group. Whether these were indeed distinct social classes or different strata of the same class seems to me a verbal rather than a substantive problem. Certainly they were distinct social groups, with different life chances and different styles of life, and movement between them must be regarded as social mobility. To move from the first of these into the second was a less dramatic upward advance than to leap directly into the world of the middle class, but it happened much more often and was in this sense a more important feature of the social scene. Without attention to social mobility of this kind, which requires investigation of patterns of home ownership, savings, and residential continuity among other things, we would know very little about social mobility in this milieu. For other times, other places—seventeenth-century England let us say—a somewhat different conception of social mobility would be required, as the famous controversy inspired by Tawney's paper on "The Rise of the Gentry" suggests, and categories appropriate to that specific historical configuration should be utilized.[19] In developing these categories, major boundaries of the stratification system of the particular society—power, wealth, style of life—can be specified, and then inquiry can be made about rates of movement and processes of movement across these boundaries, as well as about shifts in the boundaries themselves which take place in the course of historical development.

Such concern for fidelity to a particular historical context implies a certain chastening of the aspiration to construct a general theory of social mobility through comparative research, but certainly not an abandonment of sociological models and systematic comparative analysis. My aim is not to urge the inviolable uniqueness of each historical moment, but rather to argue that historical data should be employed to edit and refine social theory to make it more sensitive to social reality past and present.

---

[19] A judicious review of the controversy and selections from the leading contributions is available in Lawrence Stone, ed., *Social Change and Revolution in England, 1540-1640* (London, 1965). For splendid examples of the sort of historical analysis I have in mind, see Stone's essay on "Social Mobility in England, 1500-1700," *Past and Present,* 33 (1966), 16-55, and his book *The Crisis of the Aristocracy, 1558-1641* (Oxford, 1965).

6. United States: the 'new' political history*

ALAN G. BOGUE†

Thousands of scholars study, teach, or write American history. Score upon score of commercial and scholarly presses speed the researches of these scholars to an audience provided by their professional colleagues and the general public. To search for trends or to look for common denominators in this massive outpouring is a task for the brave, the gifted, or the foolish. On occasion, however, accident or incident reveals a purposive current in the relentless tide even to those who lack the ideal qualifications of the historiographer. So was it recently, when a political scientist searched in his midwestern University for a scalogram computer programme and learned that the only deck on campus belonged to a historian. His discovery reflected the growing interest in quantification and social-science theory and method that has been developing among American political historians for some years now.

American historians experimented with quantification in earlier years. Frederick Jackson Turner and some of his Wisconsin students, most notably Orin G. Libby, were industriously mapping election returns and analysing legislative roll calls at the turn of the century. Libby's plea for the systematic study of congressional roll calls appeared in the Annual Report of the American Historical Association in 1896.[1] Turner never lost his enthusiasm for such methods and the imprint of his influence shows in the major publications of a number of scholars. Work in this tradition appeared as late as 1941, but the early interest in quantification and political ecology among historians subsided, perhaps because of the inadequate statistical methods of the pioneers.

At present a small number of historians are trying to apply social-science

* Reprinted from the *Journal of Contemporary History,* III (January, 1968), pp. 5-27, by permission of the author and the publisher.

† Allan G. Bogue, Frederick Jackson Turner Professor of History, University of Wisconsin, received his Ph.D. from Cornell University. He is the author of *Money at Interest: The Farm Mortgage on the Middle Border; From Prairie to Corn Belt: Farming on the Illinois and Iowa Prairies in the Nineteenth Century.*

[1] Orin Grant Libby, "A Plea for the Study of Votes in Congress," *American Historical Association Report,* 1896, I (Washington, 1897).

methods and theory in American political history with varying degrees of rigour. The nine men who were early members of the American Historical Association's ad hoc committee for the collection of the basic quantitative data of American political history, and others who have since become associated with the committee's work in one way or another, are at the centre of the movement. Their seminars are producing recruits for the cause, as are the seminars of some other historians who allow their graduate students to apply methods learned in satisfying the requirements of minor or related fields. During the summer of 1965, thirty-five historians gathered at Ann Arbor for a three-week seminar on voting and legislative behaviour under the auspices of the Inter-University Consortium for Political Research.[2] This group certainly did not include all the professional historians who are interested in such matters and only representative doctoral candidates were invited. Not all those in attendance, however, were deeply dedicated to a quantitative approach. It was an assembly composed in undetermined proportions of prophets, converts, neophytes, seekers, and scoffers. In the argot of the political scientist, slightly corrupted, political historians today number an overwhelming majority of standpatters, a small group of dedicated switchers, and a growing number of their new votaries. Some believe that the members of the last two categories are sufficiently different from the majority of American political historians to justify calling them behavioural historians—understanding behavioural to connote, in this instance, a strong interest in the methods, results, and implications of measurement, combined with some desire to produce research that is respectable by social-science criteria.[3] I realize that the term raises problems, but for our purposes it is a convenient label.

The behavioural historians have not yet produced an impressive body of literature bearing upon American politics. There are in print various voting studies using ecological correlations, most of them quite simple in method;[4] two books and a number of articles in which scaling techniques or simpler methods of roll-call analysis are used;[5] a number of collective biographies of political

[2] This conference is described in a report prepared by Samuel P. Hays and Murray Murphey, "Research Conference on Political Data: Historical Analysis of Quantitative Data—July 26-August 13, 1965, Ann Arbor, Michigan" (mimeographed, 1965).

[3] Robert A. Dahl defines the term in political science in "The Behavioral Approach in Political Science: Epitaph for a Monument to a Successful Protest," *American Political Science Review*, December 1961, p. 767.

[4] George Daniels, "Immigrant Vote in the Election of 1860: The Case of Iowa," *Mid-America*, July 1962; Robert P. Swierenga, "The Ethnic Voter and the First Lincoln Election," *Civil War History*, March 1965; Stanley Parsons, "Who Were the Nebraska Populists?" *Nebraska History*, June 1963; Howard W. Allen, "Studies of Political Loyalties of Two Nationality Groups: Isolationism and German-Americans," *Journal of the Illinois State Historical Society*, Summer 1964; Thomas B. Alexander, Kit C. Carter, Jack R. Lister, Jerry C. Oldshue, and Winfred G. Sandlin, "Who Were the Alabama Whigs?" *The Alabama Review*, January 1963; Thomas B. Alexander and Peggy J. Duckworth, "Alabama Black Belt Whigs During Secession: A New Viewpoint," *Ibid.,* July 1964; Aida DiPace Donald, "The Decline of Whiggery and the Formation of the Republican Party in Rochester, 1848-56," *Rochester History*, July 1958.

[5] Joel H. Silbey, *The Shrine of Party: Congressional Voting Behaviour, 1841-1852*

elites;[6] a couple of articles dealing with the characteristics of the national electorate between 1800 and 1840 and another surveying voting trends in presidential elections;[7] a path-breaking monograph on the importance of the time dimension in evaluating election returns, as well as a major reassessment of the political ideology and voting behaviour of the Jacksonian period;[8] and several contributions concerned with the methods, problems, and promises of quantitative history.[9] This is the type of work which the behaviouralists have published so far.

What kind of findings are emerging from their endeavours? In two important articles Richard P. McCormick has shown that the Jackson elections did not represent the revolution in popular voting behaviour that historians have so confidently assumed for so many years, and that economic class affiliation apparently had little influence in affecting the party choice of voters during the

---

(Pittsburgh, 1967); David Donald, *The Politics of Reconstruction 1863-1867* (Baton Rouge, 1965); John L. Shover, "Populism in the Nineteen-Thirties: The Battle for the AAA," *Agricultural History*, January 1965; Edward L. Gambill, "Who Were the Senate Radicals," *Civil War History*, September 1965; Gerald Wolff, "The Slavocracy and the Homestead Problem of 1854," *Agricultural History*, April 1966; Howard W. Allen, "Geography and Politics: Voting on Reform Issues in the United States Senate, 1911-1916," *Journal of Southern History*, May 1961; Glenn M. Linden, " 'Radicals' and Economic Policies: The Senate, 1861-1873," *Ibid.*, May 1966.

[6] Pioneering work of this type appeared in George Mowry, *The California Progressives* (Berkeley and Los Angeles, 1951), pp. 86-104; Alfred D. Chandler, Jr., "The Origins of Progressive Leadership," in Elting Morison *et al.* (eds.), *The Letters of Theodore Roosevelt* (Cambridge, 1951-54), VIII, App. III, pp. 1462-65; David Donald, "Toward a Reconsideration of Abolitionists," *Lincoln Reconsidered* (New York, 1961). See also Grady McWhiney, "Were the Whigs a Class Party in Alabama?" *Journal of Southern History*; Ralph A. Wooster, "Notes on the Georgia Legislature of 1860," *Georgia Historical Quarterly*, March 1961; "Membership in Early Texas Legislatures, 1850-1860," *Southwestern Historical Quarterly*, October 1965; Gerald W. McFarland, "The New York Mugwumps of 1884: A Profile," *Political Science Quarterly*, March 1963; William T. Kerr, Jr., "The Progressives of Washington, 1910-12," *Pacific Northwest Quarterly*, January 1964; E. Daniel Potts, "The Progressive Profile in Iowa," *Mid-America*, October 1965; Herbert J. Doherty, Jr., *The Whigs of Florida, 1845-1854, University of Florida Monographs:* Social Sciences, 1, Winter 1959, pp. 63-72. Robert A. Skotheim discusses some of the methodological problems involved in this type of study in "A Note on Historical Method: David Donald's 'Toward a Reconsideration of Abolitionists,' " *Journal of Southern History*, August 1959.

[7] Richard P. McCormick, "Suffrage Classes and Party Alignments: A Study in Voter Behavior," *Mississippi Valley Historical Review*, December 1959; "New Perspectives on Jacksonian Politics," *American Historical Review*, January 1960; Charles Sellers, "The Equilibrium Cycle in Two-Party Politics," *Public Opinion Quarterly*, Spring 1965.

[8] Lee Benson, "Research Problems in American Political Historiography," in Mirra Komarovsky (ed.), *Common Frontiers of the Social Sciences* (Glencoe, 1957); *The Concept of Jacksonian Democracy: New York as a Test Case* (Princeton, 1961).

[9] Lee Benson, *Turner and Beard: American Historical Writing Reconsidered* (Glencoe, 1960); Samuel P. Hays, "History as Human Behavior," *Iowa Journal of History*, July 1960; "New Possibilities for American Political History: The Social Analysis of Political Life" (prepared for the American Historical Association meeting, 29 December 1964 and lithoprinted by the Inter-University Consortium for Political Research); very similar to the latter is "The Social Analysis of American Political History, 1880-1920," *Political Science Quarterly*, September 1965; "The Politics of Reform in Municipal Government in the Progressive Era," *Pacific Northwest Quarterly*, October 1964.

early national period.[10] Lee Benson carried reassessment of Jacksonian democracy still further when he found that content analysis revealed basic ideological differences between Whigs and Democrats, and particularly when he discovered that the multivariate analysis of election returns in indicator precincts in New York showed ethno-cultural conditioning to have been the most important variable associated with party choice in that state.

The writings of McCormick and Benson are perhaps the most impressive exhibits of the new historical persuasion, but a few other studies are representative. Using the Guttman scale as his major analytical tool, Joel Silbey assessed the significance of sectional and party ties in Congress during the 1840s and early 1850s, finding that party ties withstood the impact of the slavery expansion issue much better than some of the conventional literature leads one to expect. George Daniels probed the problem of ethno-cultural loyalties and the 1860 election, and his analysis of precinct voting returns in Iowa reinforced Joseph Schafer's rather neglected findings of a generation ago that a majority of German voters in Wisconsin and Illinois remained true to their Democratic party allegiance in the 1860 election.[11] Using multiple correlation techniques, Stanley Parsons destroyed a truism of Populist folklore by showing that Populist votes in Nebraska and mortgage interest rates were only slightly correlated, and that in so far as they were associated the correlation was negative rather than positive. In one of the better collective biographies published by a historian to date, William T. Kerr, Jr. has shown that the Progressive leaders of Washington differed not only in the major sources of their support from their conservative counterparts. Thomas B. Alexander and his students have published the initial results of what has since become an elaborate least-squares analysis of social and economic attributes and voting preference in ante-bellum Alabama and which contradicts the old generalization that the 'Democrats became the party of poverty and numbers, and the Whigs the party of property and talents.'

A number of theses and dissertations dealing with similar or related problems are now complete. Samuel P. Hays drew upon some of these in suggesting that the urban reform movement of the early twentieth century was essentially upper class in origin, and also in proposing an ethno-cultural interpretation of national voting behaviour in the period 1865-1929.[12] Joel Silbey found support in similar materials for his contention that sectionalism was not the only major influence shaping American politics during the 1850s.[13] Much other research

---

10 Unless otherwise stated, the contributions discussed in the next two paragraphs are those appearing under their authors' names in footnotes 4 through 9.

11 Joseph Schafer, "Who Elected Lincoln," *American Historical Review,* October 1941. Schafer was a student of Turner and much of his work exemplifies the empirical side of the Turner tradition.

12 Samuel P. Hays, "The Politics of Reform," and "Political Parties and the Local-Cosmopolitan Continuum, 1865-1929," prepared for the Conference on American Political Party Development, Washington University, 1966, and cited here by permission of Professor Hays and William Nesbit Chambers.

13 Joel H. Silbey, "The Civil War Synthesis in American Political History," *Civil War History,* June 1964.

with a strong quantitative element is under way. These studies include roll-call analyses of Congress in the early national period, during the 1850s, 1860s, and 1870s, and the progressive period, as well as of the Confederate Congress and midwestern state legislatures during the nineteenth century. Historians are preparing studies of the evolution of party structure during the nineteenth century, and others are studying popular voting behaviour in states and regions in the nineteenth and early twentieth centuries. There has also been completed, or is under way, work which has important implications for political history even though its focus is not primarily political—most notably research in historical demography and population mobility, both spatial and social.[14]

Much of the new quantitative history is unsophisticated in social-science terms. A member of the AHA committee on quantitative data estimated recently that there were no more than several dozen members of the history profession at the faculty level who are conversant with statistics through multiple correlation and regression analysis, and if one omits the new breed of economic historian that is, I am sure, true.[15] This state of affairs is changing as history graduates attend statistics courses and social science methodology seminars, but it will be some time before there is a sizable cadre of historians confidently aware of both the promises and the pitfalls inherent in quantification.

Social scientists find the theoretical assumptions of the behavioural historians rather elementary. They are not trying simply to describe 'what happened,' in the parlance of the old 'scientific' historian, but their methods hardly conform to the basic rules of the behavioural approach sketched by David Easton in *A Framework for Political Analysis*.[16] Few behavioural historians are consciously looking for findings with predictive value, or purposefully giving their research a theoretical frame which the results may in part verify, modify, or contradict. Instead, most are still problem or topic-oriented, using social-science techniques or theory to refute or build on the work of past historians or to probe new areas which catch their fancy. Lee Benson is an exception. To a far greater extent than any of the other historical behaviouralists, he tries to make his theoretical commitments explicit and believes that a historian can make a major contribution to the social sciences. He has for instance suggested certain basic propositions which, he argues, illuminate the behaviour of the founding fathers:

(1) The behavior of men is determined more by the ends they seek than by the means they use to achieve those ends; specifically, men favored the

---

[14] Stephan Thernstrom, *Poverty and Progress: Social Mobility in a Nineteenth Century City* (Cambridge, 1964); Samuel B. Warner, *Street-Car Suburbs* (Cambridge, 1962). For those interested in the rural community the work of James C. Malin is still essential; see "The Turnover of Farm Population in Kansas," *Kansas Historical Quarterly,* November 1935, and *The Grassland of North America: Prolegomena to its History* (Lawrence, 1947), pp. 278-315. Several studies bearing on Iowa are summarized with additional data of my own in Chapter I of *From Prairie to Corn Belt: Farming on the Illinois and Iowa Prairies in the Nineteenth Century* (Chicago, 1963).

[15] Samuel P. Hays speaking on "Computers and Historical Research," Purdue Conference on the Use of Computers in the Humanities, 29 October 1965.

[16] David Easton, *A Framework for Political Analysis* (Englewood Cliffs, N.J., 1965), p. 7.

Constitution largely because they favored a Commercial Society, they opposed the Constitution largely because they favored an Agrarian Society. (2) The ends men choose are positively related to the 'modes and processes' by which they gain their livelihoods, the social environments in which they live, the social roles they occupy, the groups with whom they identify, and the groups with whom they regard themselves in conflict. (3) In certain historical situations, men who choose certain ends are more likely than their opponents to possess the qualities and resources needed for victory; specifically, in the United States during the 1780s, commercial-minded men like Hamilton possessed the qualities and resources needed to defeat agrarian-minded men like Clinton.[17]

Such behavioural models are rare indeed in the work of historians. Despite his concern for theoretical explication, Professor Benson's work sometimes falls short of the standards that many behavioural scientists consider essential. One searches the first edition of *The Concept of Jacksonian Democracy* in vain for any detailed discussion of the methods by which he selected his indicator precincts, or of the numbers of voters in his sample, or of correlations or significance tests underlying the party preference percentages which he ascribed to the various ethno-cultural groups living in New York during the 1830s and 1840s.[18]

It can indeed be argued that social scientists have written almost as much, if not more, behavioural history than have the political historians. Walter Dean Burnham, William Nesbit Chambers, Robert A. Dahl, Manning J. Dauer, V. O. Key, Theodore J. Lowi, Duncan MacRae, John Schmidhaeuser, and Ruth C. Silva, have all probed significantly beyond the contemporary scene and produced work that any political historian must use if he wishes to view this nation's political history in fullest perspective.[19]

More significant perhaps than the research achievements of behavioural historians has been their contribution to the building of the historical data archives of the Inter-University Consortium for Political Research, made in cooperation with political scientists. As a number of historians became

---

[17] Lee Benson, *Turner and Beard,* p. 228.

[18] In the introduction to the paperback edition of *The Concept of Jacksonian Democracy* (New York, 1964), Benson includes a specific description of his methodology.

[19] The following list is not intended to be comprehensive: Walter D. Burnham, "The Changing Shape of the American Political Universe," *American Political Science Review,* March 1965; William N. Chambers, *Political Parties in a New Nation: The American Experience, 1776-1809* (New York, 1963); Robert A. Dahl, *Who Governs? Democracy and Power in an American City* (New Haven, 1961); Manning J. Dauer, *The Adams Federalists* (Baltimore, 1953); V. O. Key, Jr., "A Theory of Critical Elections," *Journal of Politics,* February 1955; "Secular Realignment and the Party System," *ibid.,* May 1959; with Milton C. Cummings, Jr., *The Responsible Electorate: Rationality in Presidential Voting, 1936-60* (Cambridge, 1966); Theodore J. Lowi, *At the Pleasure of the Mayor: Patronage and Power in New York City, 1898-1958* (Glencoe, 1964); Duncan MacRae, Jr. and James Meldrum, "Critical Elections in Illinois: 1888-1958," *American Political Science Review,* September 1960; John R. Schmidhaeuser, "The Justices of the Supreme Court: A Collective Portrait," *Midwest Journal of Political Science,* February 1959; "Judicial Behavior and the Sectional Crisis of 1837-1850," *Journal of Politics,* November 1961; Ruth C. Silva, *Rum, Religion, and Votes: 1928 Re-Examined* (University Park, La., 1962).

interested in quantification some years ago, they discovered in discussion that they were wasting their time in searching out and processing quantifiable information which others had already recorded. They agreed that historians needed an inventory of the basic quantitative data of American political history and ultimately, perhaps, a central data archives on which all interested scholars might draw. Following such discussions, Lee Benson, Charles Sellers, Samuel P. Hays, and William Riker (three historians and a political scientist) submitted a memorandum to the Social Science Research Council. In response the Council invited W. Dean Burnham to assess the problems of collecting election statistics in a number of states.

While these developments were taking place, the Inter-University Consortium was also beginning to consider the establishment of a data archives, having as a nucleus the data collected by the Survey Research Center of the University of Michigan. When Professor Burnham's initial investigation was encouraging, the SSRC commissioned him to spend an additional year on the task of inventorying and undertaking an exploratory recovery of data. His labours were so successful that additional organization seemed necessary. Lee Benson organized a committee of historians to assist the Consortium in developing a historical data archives, and the American Historical Association gave it status by designating it an ad hoc committee. In turn the committee organized state committees that undertook to exhume the county election returns from 1824 to the present and other materials. Under the imaginative leadership of its director, Warren Miller, the Consortium obtained funds from the National Science Foundation for the development of the archives and the SSRC continued to be helpful. Dr. Miller appointed a historian, Howard W. Allen, as director of data recovery at the Consortium, and it was hoped that almost all the county election and referenda returns would be available for use by the late fall of 1966. The historians and archivists engaged in this work may be helping to transform one area of history into a cumulative discipline, in which, for the first time, the careful historian need not duplicate every step of the research of predecessors who were interested in the same problem.

While the work of collecting and recording has gone forward at the Consortium, planning conferences have considered the problems of adding legislative materials, primarily roll call votes, to the archives, and various types of economic and ethno-cultural materials which seem necessary for any considered analysis of the basic election data. At the Ann Arbor seminar in 1965, a number of historians expressed interest in essaying the difficult task of retrieving the election returns of the early national period and this work is now under way. The extent to which these collection and service programmes can be maintained and extended will largely depend, of course, on the willingness of granting agencies to subsidize the work and this in turn must depend to a considerable degree on the interest which historians and social scientists show in using the archives.

Its concrete achievements and the ambitiousness of its programme clearly mark the combined Consortium-AHA committee project as the most impressive evidence of the development of a quantifying and behavioural bent in the historical profession. It is not the only organized effort in that direction, however. In 1964 the Mathematics Social Science Board, an offspring of the Social Science Research Council and the Institute for Advanced Study in the Behavioural Sciences, sponsored the organization of a history committee, headed by Robert Fogel of the University of Chicago.[20] The AHA ad hoc committee is concerned primarily with the development of a data archives and with training programmes geared to its use. The history committee of the MSSB is seeking ways of encouraging the spread of mathematical and statistical expertise within the history profession.

The behavioural movement among American political historians reflects in part a recent tendency among historians to draw more heavily upon the social sciences for method and theory. In his reader, *American History and the Social Sciences,* published in 1964, Edward N. Saveth presents two dozen historians, writing on concepts which are more usually considered to be of primary interest to social scientists. A large number of other scholars could be added to Saveth's list, whose writings in some way reflect the influence of social-science thought or methods. The political behaviouralists, however, are prepared to introduce considerably more quantification and rigour into their work than most such historians.

A few years ago, in a paper paying tribute to a successful revolution—the advent of behaviouralism in political science—Robert Dahl devoted some attention to the causes of this development.[21] He stressed the pioneering work of Professor Merriam at Chicago, the contributions of the European emigré scholars who came to this country during the 1930s, the practical experience of political scientists in government and military service during the Second World War, the empirical promise of survey research techniques, the leadership of the SSRC, and the helping hand of the foundations. No doubt he would agree that the recent tremendous advances in computer technology have helped to confirm the trend.

There are both similarities and differences between the early developments in political science and those now occurring in history. If political science lagged behind sister fields in moving toward behaviouralism, the lag in history has been greater. The commitment of historians to theory was of course typically less than that of political scientists even in the most unsystematic days of political science. There is among the behavioural historians no group analogous to the European emigrés of the 1930s, trained in a different tradition from their American colleagues. Nor can we point to any history department occupying the pre-eminent position of the political science department at the University of Chicago as a disseminating centre of behavioural ideas and methods. For a time in the late 1950s three historians at the University of Iowa were stressing quantification in their seminars and sending their graduates into the methods

---

[20] The members of this committee are Robert W. Fogel, Lionel W. McKenzie, Frederick Mosteller, William O. Aydelotte, Oscar Handlin, and Allan G. Bogue.

[21] Robert A. Dahl, *loc. cit.,* note 3.

seminars of their colleagues in political science and sociology. But this group is now dispersed.

There is no pioneer of quantifying techniques in the historical profession comparable in stature to Charles Merriam. But there were a number of historians, active during the 1930s, and 1940s, whose writings or seminar offerings anticipated a quantitative approach. During the 1930s James C. Malin used manuscript census rolls to prepare demographic studies that modified conventional interpretations of frontier population movements and influenced a considerable number of other scholars either directly or indirectly. This work, plus Malin's emphasis on the intensive study of the local and regional unit, make him one of the progenitors of historical behaviouralism in America, even though in his later work he specifically repudiated the aims and methods of social science.[22]

In reaction against the conventional history fare that he had suffered as a graduate student, Thomas C. Cochran immersed himself during the 1930s in social-science literature, particularly sociology. Exasperated by the traditional views of the craft which several eminent historians expressed at the meeting of the American Historical Association in 1947, he advanced his rebellious ideas in 'The "Presidential Synthesis" in American History' (*American Historical Review,* July 1948). This article was a resounding attack on the traditional method of describing American political history, presidential administration by presidential administration, and a plea for a ' "social science" synthesis of American history.' Cochran argued that our political history should be viewed as an outgrowth of fundamental cultural developments, and that it could be attacked most conveniently at the state level. By the 1940s Oscar Handlin at Harvard was emphasizing ethnic group dynamics and their relationship to politics, and a number of students followed his lead, undertaking detailed studies of politics at the local level. At Cornell University, Paul Wallace Gates, although primarily interested in institutional economic history, was asking his graduate students to spend time in other social science departments. No doubt there were others trying to direct the interests of their students into new channels.

If the writings or teachings of Malin, Handlin, Gates, Cochran and others have helped to provide a favourable climate for a more intensive approach to American political history, I must also mention an early research project that had considerable influence upon the profession. During the late 1940s, Merle Curti conceived the idea of studying a frontier county in Wisconsin intensively, and providing a rigorous test of the suggestion that the frontier was a significant factor in shaping American political institutions, the thesis stated so attractively by Frederick Jackson Turner in the 1890s. Professor Curti was a graduate student under Turner at Harvard and was familiar with his interest in systematic political analysis. One of the handful of scholars who established American intellectual history on a firm foundation, he became chairman of the committee

---

[22] James C. Malin, *op. cit.,* note 14. Professor Malin's position on historiographic problems is developed in *Essays on Historiography* (Lawrence, 1946), and in *On the Nature of History: Essays about History and Dissidence* (Lawrence, 1954).

on historiography of the SSRC, organized in 1942-43, which prepared the Council's *Bulletin 54,* entitled *Theory and Practice in Historical Study: A Report of the Committee on Historiography,* published in 1946. This report clearly brought out the concern over the problems of objectivity and relativism which had perplexed and disturbed thoughtful American historians during the previous couple of decades. Both the work of his committee and the somewhat acrimonious discussions which its report provoked, turned Professor Curti's mind to the problems of objectively validating historical fact and theory. By this time also he had concluded that study of the frontier hypothesis had reached an impasse. Margaret Curti, a psychologist with sound training in statistics, had long maintained that historians should concern themselves to a greater extent with quantitative research and with the application of statistics to historical problems. This was the background of a study of Trempealeau county in western Wisconsin, designed to exploit the quantifiable information in the county records and in the manuscript censuses; *The Making of an American Community: A Case Study of Democracy in a Frontier County,* was published in 1959.

Professor Curti's statistical methods were less rigorous than some social scientists demand today and some historians have disputed the study's conclusions, but it is a milestone in American historiography. That a man who had done so much to establish intellectual history should turn his talents to such research gave respectability to quantification, as well as testifying to the versatility and liveliness of Professor Curti's mind.

As in the field of political science, the SSRC has had considerable influence in changing the outlook of historians. It has always aided historians in projects with an inter-disciplinary character. During the last twenty years it has sponsored three monographs concerned with the problems of writing history. *Bulletin 54* looked back to the relativist controversy of the 1930s; in *Bulletin 64, The Social Sciences in Historical Study,* and in the more recent *Generalization in the Writing of History,* we find a real commitment in some of the contributors to both social-science methods and theory.[23] I am not aware that any foundation has been uniquely concerned with promoting behaviouralism among historians, but the action of the Ford Foundation in supporting the Institute for Advanced Study in the Behavioural Sciences has contributed to that end. Since its establishment, the administrators have generously allocated places to historians. Many if not most of the quantifiers among American political historians today have been assisted to some degree either by the SSRC or the Stanford Institute.

There are few more difficult tasks than that of explaining why one man adopts new techniques and another does not. We can point to general conditioning factors and to encouraging elements in the intellectual milieu, and we can discern apparent predispositions in the individuals who innovate, but it is

---

[23] Social Science Research Council, *Theory and Practice in Historical Study: A Report of the Committee on Historiography, Bulletin 54* (New York, 1946); *The Social Sciences in Historical Study: A Report of the Committee on Historiography, Bulletin 64* (New York, 1954); Louis Gottschalk, ed., *Generalization in the Writing of History: A Report of the Committee on Historical Analysis of the Social Science Research Council* (Chicago, 1963).

hard to explain in the final analysis why some take the plunge and others do not. If the SSRC has aided many of the behavioural historians it has also assisted dozens of others in the historical profession who have shown no disposition to change their approach. But aid from that agency or from the Stanford Institute must be regarded as one of a number of predisposing or confirming factors.

To some extent the behavioural historians appear to have had a broader training than usual: one was a classics major, another majored in psychology, another had a good training in mathematics and still another a double major. The prodding of graduate directors in the direction of inter-disciplinary work is remembered by members of the group. It is probably no accident that a number of them were initially interested in economic history, which has always had a body of theory and statistical method to draw upon, and in which far-reaching developments have occurred during the last fifteen years.

One learns in discussing the origins of their interests with the behaviouralists that they experienced recurrent dissatisfaction with conventional political history and searched for concepts or methods that would give them greater confidence in the results of research or provide a more satisfying framework in which to present them. A number of them were particularly impressed by the work of Lazarsfeld and Key, and probing produces the names of other social scientists who set the thinking of one or more of them on a new track—Rice, Merton, Duverger, Weber, Michels, Lubell, Hannah Arendt, and Riesman. There was some reaction, too, against the practice of borrowing concepts from the social scientists and applying them without rigorous proof. In *The Age of Reform,* for instance, Richard Hofstadter suggested that declining social status was a major motivating factor among both the Populists and the Progressives. Soon status revolution threatened to become a universal historical solvent, applied unfortunately with little resort to the careful quantification that would either corroborate or disprove the hypothesis.

The most influential of the historical behaviouralists specializing in American history is Lee Benson. Having completed a doctoral dissertation on the economic and political background of the Interstate Commerce Act, he went to Harvard to study location theory; there he was greatly impressed by the rigour and precision with which Walter Isard was attacking the problems of location theory, and by the more systematic approach of social scientists in comparison to historians. Moving to Columbia, he met Paul Lazarsfeld and found him appalled both by the flaccidity of historical analysis and by the ignorance of history among social scientists. Professor Lazarsfeld provided funds and encouraged Benson to investigate more precise approaches to American political history. From Benson's work at the Columbia Bureau of Applied Social Research came his long article 'Research Problems in American Historiography,' which provided concrete illustrations of the way in which simple time series of election results might be used to explode generalizations long cherished by historians. A few historians were already stressing quantification in their seminars, but it is with the publication of this article that the behavioural trend becomes clearly evident in American historical writing. Other research which Lee Benson began in the

1950s matured as papers on the causation of the Civil War and *The Concept of Jacksonian Democracy: New York as a Test Case.* Benson was a committed economic determinist when he began his doctoral work but, particularly in his study of Jacksonian democracy in New York, he discovered that his formula was inadequate. Ethno-cultural conditioning seemed to explain more than did economic interest.

Stimulated by a small group of social scientists at the State University of Iowa during the late 1940's, William O. Aydelotte conceived the idea of a massive study of the Corn Laws Parliament in which biographical data were to be gathered for the 800-odd members of this assembly, and these materials related if possible to party affiliation and voting behaviour. The Rockefeller Foundation launched the project with a grant and Professor Aydelotte has pushed it steadily forward, searching first for basic biographical information both here and abroad, working out satisfactory classifications of the class and business backgrounds of the members of parliament, recording the divisions, subjecting data first to correlation analysis (with rather discouraging results), then moving to scaling techniques, and along the way teaching himself social statistics and learning the technology of data processing and computer research. Given his subject matter, one is tempted to look to Namier for Professor Aydelotte's inspiration, but he maintains that his early work owed much more to Lazarsfeld and to *The People's Choice* than to Namier's studies of the British Parliament. Aydelotte has not yet summarized his research in a book-length monograph, but he has delivered a number of important papers at historical meetings, publishing some of them as articles, and he has discussed the problems and rewards of such research in numerous informal contacts with specialists in both American and European history. Once a historian recognizes that he must explain why men behaved as they did in the past, he must turn if he is a thorough scholar to the disciplines that concentrate on the explanation of human behaviour; the quantification movement in American political history is one aspect of this change of direction, but commitment to quantification is not equally strong among the members of the AHA committee; one of them wrote recently:

... I am not an enthusiast for quantification. Quantifiable data make up only a portion of the evidence available to the historian. Moreover, if quantifiable data are to be used intelligently, one must have a vast knowledge of the historical context of the situation; the data are not self-interpreting. Another grave danger with quantification is that it can lead to an extremely imbalanced emphasis on those factors that can be quantified, to the exclusion of others of equal or greater significance. Quantification, in other words, is merely one tool in the historian's kit; he must not misuse it or throw the other tools away.

In a series of papers and articles, Samuel P. Hays has tried to articulate and to some extent shape the new trend in American political historiography. He has indicted 'conventional political history' as 'so preoccupied with the outward and formal, the episodic, the unique and the individual, that it has failed to draw

attention to some of the most significant developments of our political past.' [24]
Historians, he urges, must study political structure in detail: the voters, their
socio-economic and ethno-cultural groupings, the pressure groups, the leadership
cadres and the systems of decision-making that operate at every level of the
American political system, as well as the inter-relationships of these elements. By
studying these components of American politics in action through time, by
pushing beyond the mere description of political institutions and by penetrating
the fog of rhetoric and ideology we can, he promises, reach the basic facts of
political motivation, influence, and power. In particular Hays emphasizes the
need for study of politics at the grass roots in contrast to the national scene, and
the benefits to be gained by distinguishing between political rhetoric and
political reality. Recently he has settled upon the term, 'the social analysis of
politics' as the most appropriate description of this approach. He emphasizes
that quantitative data are important tools in this analysis and has also stressed
the usefulness of drawing upon the social sciences for both method and theory.
Even 'conventional' historians can argue that much of this prescription describes
their current operations. The procedures which Professor Hays recommends
differ from normal practice in American political history mainly in the relative
emphasis that is placed upon local case studies, quantification, and social science
theory. His articles describe what behaviouralists and their students have been
doing in varying degree for some time. But if his role so far has been primarily
that of publicist and synthesizer, his emphasis on the historian's obligation to set
his findings within some sort of conceptual perspective has been salutary. On the
other hand, his unfavourable assessment of traditional history seems unnecessary
or overdrawn to some behaviouralists.

We can say, quite accurately I believe, that a large proportion of our political
historians expend their energies in writing the biographies of individual
politicians, and that others pursue their research on political bodies, groups, and
movements, almost solely in personal manuscripts, newspapers, and legislative
debates. Usually American historians have studied elections as unique expressions of the popular will rather than as parts of a time series, and limited their
consideration of roll calls to final votes, and perhaps those on major
amendments. We have as historians frequently been more impressed by what our
subjects have said than by what they have done. As a group we have been
unsystematic in our generalizations and too little interested in comparisons and
categorization. We often fail to make our assumptions adequately explicit, and
in trying to understand human motivation we often ignore the more sophisticated theorizing of the behavioural sciences. The challenge confronting the
behavioural historian is to exploit the body of hard quantitative data that exists
in election returns, legislative roll calls, court archives, census data (published
and unpublished), state, county, and municipal records, and the great accumulation of biographical facts available in other types of sources. This involves both
learning the methods necessary to master and manipulate these intimidating

[24] Hays, "New Possibilities," *loc. cit.*

sources of information, and becoming more sophisticated in the techniques of research design which are necessary to set findings in useful and defensible theoretical frameworks.

Behavioural history does not promise short cuts or easy answers. If historians have over-emphasized some types of source materials, these cannot be ignored by the historian who quantifies. The scales or other devices which reveal legislative voting patterns can be interpreted fully only if we read the preceding debates. Tables, graphs, and correlations do not explain themselves; they are the product of a particular research design and are subject to various interpretations. The politician's oratory may be designed to conceal or obfuscate his behaviour no less than to explain it, and the scholar who uses the *Congressional Globe* is rather like the prospector who examines a salted claim. Manuscript collections, some will say, are more reliable; here the politician lays bare his motives. He may indeed, but again he may not, and it is shocking to discover how little some of the manuscript collections, regularly cited as major sources in historical monographs, actually reveal about the men who accumulated them. In addition, any manuscript collection is at best an accidental historical accretion, pointing perhaps to conclusions that are completely different from those we would reach if all the related manuscript collections had been preserved. It is sobering also to remember that whenever a politician evaluates his election chances correctly (few run in anticipation of defeat), there are usually one or more opponents who judge the situation incorrectly. Remembering this, we will treat the explanations of politicians with caution. But the interplay of contemporary observation and explanation with quantitative evidence should allow us to push our understanding further than either type of source can carry us by itself.

In writing of cultural sources and economic change, Thomas C. Cochran points out that no one has yet developed a model in which all the variables can be quantified. 'One cannot,' he writes, 'speak of units or doses of personality or values.'[25] We will no doubt become increasingly ingenious in developing ways to measure attitudes or values indirectly; the quantifier may build some dams and breakwaters in what Matthew Arnold unfairly termed 'that huge Mississippi of falsehood called history,' but there are rapids he will not tame, tributaries he cannot explore, and quicksands he still cannot plumb by quantification. So American political historians are not all going to become quantifiers, and not only for this reason. Much biography and so-called conventional political history is useful and will continue to attract many in the profession. The fact that quantification calls for extra effort rather than a substitution of effort will discourage some from essaying it.

For those who find the fascination of political history in a smooth and colourful narrative, the injection of numbers, tables, and scales may be jarring and unpleasing. The new political history must make its way by appealing to the intellectual curiosity of the reader; its impact must flow from the ideas and the sense of understanding that it imparts rather than from the colourful incident or

25 Thomas C. Cochran, *The Inner Revolution: Essays on the Social Sciences in History* (New York, 1964), p. 142.

well-told anecdote. Even so, behavioural historians need not jettison the idea that history is a literary art. There is no reason why political history should not still employ the well-turned phrase or striking illustration, even though based on a foundation of measurement.

For a time in the testing period ahead the behavioural historians may find editors suspicious and cold; their graduate students will encounter difficulties in obtaining proper training in statistics and the use of computers; both faculty and students may find it difficult to obtain financial aid because the National Science Foundation has not officially recognized historians and granting agencies of humanistic temper are not likely to support behavioural history enthusiastically. These problems may in the end be less disturbing than the limitations of the quantitative data of American history and the inadequacies of the techniques now available for analysing them. Since the behavioural historian cannot interview the dead politician of yesteryear, he is forced to place considerable emphasis on the study of aggregate data, particularly in election analysis. Here he encounters the problem of ecological correlations which W. S. Robinson described some fifteen years ago. One cannot, on the basis of correlation analysis, deduce the behaviour of an individual from the behaviour of the aggregate. There is, as Austin Ranney has pointed out, a good deal to be learned from the study of aggregates as aggregates.[26] What is more, it is possible in some instances to produce refined aggregate data. In some states, for instance, poll lists of the nineteenth century and census data can be combined so that we know precisely the voters represented in precinct totals and many of their social characteristics—in contrast to situations in which we know only that voters represent a certain proportion of an electorate that has as a group certain demographic, socio-economic, or ethno-cultural characteristics. Must we stop there, or can we minimize the limits of possible error in moving from aggregate to individual, or work with probabilities rather than correlation analysis? Ferreting out virtually pure ethno-cultural or socio-economic constituencies seems offhand to be a commonsense solution, which election forecasters have used successfully on occasion; but the very purity of such units may impart bias. Assuming that we can use aggregate data in good conscience, we have fewer of them than we would like. One is hard put to it to find historical measures of some of the variables that survey research has found to be important. The emphasis which behavioural historians are placing on the importance of ethno-cultural groups may in part reflect the fact that the ethno-cultural reference group is the easiest to identify in historical data. Moreover, the statistics of social research are unfortunately much more useful in showing the relationships between variables at a particular moment than in demonstrating change over time. Ideally, the behavioural historian requires a statistics of time series, of lag, of transition matrixes, of growth models, and of indirect relationships where the association of two factors is measured by substituting a

---

[26] Austin Ranney, "The Utility and Limitations of Aggregate Data in the Study of Electoral Behavior," in Austin Ranney, ed., *Essays on the Behavioral Study of Politics* (Urbana, 1962), discusses the problems inherent in the use of aggregate data.

third for one or the other. Since most social scientists restrict their research to the findings of survey research, there are few outstanding scholars in the behavioural disciplines who are interested in developing or refining the kind of statistical methods that historians would find particularly useful.[27]

Aggregate election data provide evidence of a single act, although to some extent the preparation for this act can be deduced from examination of other variables. The modern panel survey yields information about the period of preparation and sometimes adds retrospective interpretations by the actors as well. Can content analysis of newspapers or other historical documents be refined to the point where it serves in some measure as a substitute for the questionnaire? Its advocates believe that this technique has been greatly improved during the present generation. Contingency and qualitative content analysis in particular seem to promise results that are more interesting to historians than the rather mechanical exercises that were common some years ago. The imaginative and flexible analyst can indeed deduce political values, class structure, influence and power systems, and key election issues from even the highly partisan newspapers of the nineteenth century, provided he remembers that historical evidence may come in all shapes and sizes. But it seems doubtful that content analysis will soon reach the stage where it can be used to detect the exact turning points or the precise importance of the various issues in election campaigns.[28]

If the American political historian faces problems in finding adequate quantifiable data and in discovering appropriate statistical techniques, he runs other dangers in using political theory in planning and interpreting his research. In effect he may allow such theory or its related concepts to dehumanize his work. When he writes in terms of social role or status revolution, for instance, he may produce a deterministic history in which his central characters are denied the power of choice or the freedom to make rational decisions, but seem instead the captives of forces beyond their control. The predatory railroad tycoon who bribes a legislature may appear as the guardian of his stockholders, and the representative of a peer group of railroad executives rather than as a calculating offender against the ethics or law of the community. The abolitionist or progressive leader becomes a man in unconscious revolt against the societal changes that are depriving him of the position of leadership which his father enjoyed, rather than a public-spirited reformer trying to improve society from rational and philanthropic motives. 'If powerful groups are denied access to formal power in legitimate ways,' writes Samuel P. Hays, 'they seek access through procedures which the community considers illegitimate. Corrupt government, therefore, does not reflect the genius of evil men, but rather the lack of acceptable means for those who exercise power in the private community

[27] Gösta Carlsson comments on the "timelessness" of much social theory in "Time and Continuity in Mass Attitude Change: The Case of Voting," *Public Opinion Quarterly,* Spring 1965.

[28] Ithiel De Sola Pool, *Trends in Content Analysis: Papers, Work Conference on Content Analysis* (Urbana, 1959), is a relatively recent survey of the state of the technique.

to wield the same influence in governmental affairs.'[29] Such explanations may present old material in a new light, but in careless hands they may fit facts to theory rather than using them to test theory; and certainly such analysis gives little hint of the moral indignation that some historians have found in the progressive period. Once such pitfalls are recognized, however, they can be avoided.

Some historians may consider behavioural history to be 'consensus' history. In the introduction to *The American Political Tradition*, Richard Hofstadter noted in 1949 that 'the common climate of American opinion' had 'been much obscured by the tendency to place political conflict in the foreground of history,' and showed, in the essays that followed, the very considerable agreement that had existed among American political leaders irrespective of section or party. A few years later John Higham detected a growing 'cult of "American consensus" ' in both the intellectual and political history of America, and argued that 'current scholarship' was 'carrying out a massive grading operation to smooth over America's social convulsions.'[30] It seems inevitable that the rather precise measurements and the detailed case studies of behavioural history will qualify the bold conclusions reached in some older general studies. The result need not be homogenized history, however. To prove consensus in our political history, the historian must define politics, political ideas, and the American political system narrowly. In reality it is as much a political act to exclude a racial or an economic minority from participation in formal political institutions, or to keep a depressed sector of the population in bondage by failing to provide adequate educational and economic opportunities, as it is to share in the task of choosing a presidential candidate. With this understood, American political life becomes once more the scene of fundamental political conflict. And some of the behaviouralists do bring this broad view to their study of American political history.

Critics of quantification are common in the historical profession. Some of them suspect inter-disciplinary research on general principles. Arguing by aphorism and analogy, one of my colleagues points out that the supreme achievement of hybridization in the animal world is the mule—a creature without pride of ancestry or hope of progeny. Recently Professor Aydelotte discussed quantification in history in a temperate and closely-reasoned article in the *American Historical Review* (April 1966). He divides the arguments of the most vociferous critics of quantification into four categories, questioning specifically: (1) the value of the work that has been done; (2) the feasibility of this approach in view of the admittedly limited materials available to historians; (3) the reliability of the results obtained by these techniques; and (4) the usefulness or significance of the results. There can, in the end, be only one convincing answer to such criticisms: the usefulness and intrinsic interest of the

---

29 Hays, "Politics of Reform," *loc. cit.*, p. 166.

30 John Higham, "The Cult of the 'American Consensus': Homogenizing Our History," *Commentary*, February 1959.

publications of the behavioural historians will determine whether quantification flourishes or withers as a historical technique.

Lee Benson was sanguine about the future of the new political history when he wrote recently, 'the prediction does not seem absurd that . . . by 1984, a significant proportion of American historians will have accepted Buckle's two basic propositions: (1) past human behaviour can be studied scientifically; (2) the main business of historians is to participate in the overall scholarly enterprise of discovering and developing general laws of human behaviour.'[31] The date is ominous and the future perhaps less assured than Benson believes. But the methods and theory of the social science disciplines seem to promise much. If the behaviouralists retain the broad and critical knowledge of sources found among conventional political historians, their keen awareness of the range of cultural and socio-economic differences at different times, and their willingness to search widely for alternative hypotheses, they may indeed contribute to a richer and more vital political history of the United States.[32]

---

[31] Lee Benson, "Quantification, Scientific History, and Scholarly Innovation," *AHA Newsletter,* June 1966, p. 12.

[32] I am indebted to J. Rogers Hollingsworth and Joel Silbey for critical advice during the preparation of this article. I would also like to thank the many colleagues with whom I have discussed this subject, or who have replied to my enquiries, in particular Thomas B. Alexander, William O. Aydelotte, Lee Benson, Thomas C. Cochran, Merle Curti, Richard P. McCormick, and Rowland L. Mitchell.

PART II

Bureaucrats, deputies, and decision makers: studies in elite history

Elites have always been a predominant concern of traditional history. Histories of countries, periods, or institutions have typically been studies of the most visible and powerful individuals. The notion that these persons, together with many others who are only slightly less exalted, form political, social, and economic classes called "elite" is in some respects new. Not long ago, in fact, the assumption was current that elites in progressive societies would become a thing of the past; that, being one with the aristocracy, higher clergy, and landed gentry, they would disappear with the societies that harbored these institutions.

The growth of democracies did not fulfill all the expectations of democratic theorists. In increasing numbers, students of modern society have pointed out that the great and minor institutions of democracy are also dominated by elites. Moreover, reactions against democracy and socialism, such as National Socialism, have generated political and intellectual interest in the general theory of elites, their interrelations as classes, their relations with subelites (relatively exclusive, special interest groups that operate at a lower level of prestige and power) and society at large. Although many theorists and social analysts have contributed to this renewed interest in elites, the most influential studies have probably been those of Gaetano Mosca, *The Ruling Class* (New York, 1939), and Vilfredo Pareto, *The Mind and Society. A Treatise on General Sociology* (New York, 1935).

In some respects, however, elite studies themselves have not fulfilled their promise. If the value of elite studies is based on the assumption that knowing a great deal about elites and their interrelationships is the most efficient method of uncovering the distribution of power, prestige, and authority in society, this has not been thoroughly verified by empirical studies—whether survey-based or historical. Perhaps too many of the most recent approaches to elites have been descriptive. Such description—e.g., discussing social backgrounds and attitudes of elites either qualitatively or quantitatively—however fascinating, does not necessarily explain *why* power should rest on a particular basis in a given society or *how* authority and power are actually translated into social, political, or economic outcomes in a given social situation.

During the past two decades, increasingly sophisticated attempts have been made to deal with these objections. Notable among these have been studies by Harold D. Lasswell, Daniel Lerner, and C. Easton Rothwell, *Comparative Study of Elites: An Introduction and Bibliography* (Stanford, 1952), Ithiel de Sola Pool, *Satellite Generals; A Study of Military Elites in the Soviet Sphere* (Stanford, 1955), and Carl Beck and James M. Malloy, *Political Elites: A Mode of Analysis* (Pittsburgh, n.d.).

Two of the studies presented in this section are descriptive in orientation—and, again, fascinatingly so. Moreover, they have in common with other elite studies a heavily biographical orientation. Indeed, as the Higonnet brothers point out, one of the things that has happened to this type of scholarship is that computers have facilitated immensely the task of collectivizing and synthesizing detailed biographies. Indications are that we may look forward to more studies that penetrate deeply into the collective details of classes such as political elites—groups relatively small in comparison with society at large but numerically significant and immensely important from the viewpoint of elite theory. The article by Professor Silberman, in addition to having a quantitative and collective orientation, also employs a rather elaborate social science methodology at a relatively high level of aggregation and abstraction.

1. Class, corruption and politics in the French Chamber of Deputies, 1846–1848*

PATRICK L.-R. HIGONNET AND
TREVOR B. HIGONNET†§

Whether it is to be considered in the narrow context of the reign of Louis-Philippe or the broader one of the history of French political institutions, the parliamentarianism of the July Monarchy is an important phenomenon. In a recent article, Charles Pouthas has demonstrated numerically the importance of the lower chamber in the political life of the period.[1] He finds, for example, that from 1830 to 1848 the proportion of ministers who were or had been deputies when they obtained their portfolios was more than twice what it had been during the Restoration; and in 1846 all seven of the nonmilitary members of the cabinet had received mandates to the lower house.[2] More generally, it was also during the July Monarchy that France attempted its only real experiment in parliamentarianism before the Third Republic, which partly explains why the period 1830-1848 was a seed-bed for the development of modern France, particularly its political institutions. Suffice it to say in this respect that France's final formulation of parliamentary government, the Third Republic, was originally conceived largely by men, like de Broglie or Laboulaye, who had been marked directly or indirectly by the experience of bourgeois parliamentarianism. In short, then, the Chamber of Deputies was a crucial—perhaps *the* crucial—

---

* Reprinted from *French Historical Studies*, V (Fall, 1967), pp. 204-24, by permission of the authors and the publishers.

† Patrick Louis-Rene Higonnet received his Ph.D. from Harvard University, where he is now assistant professor of history. He is currently involved in research on the European international state system in the last decades of the *ancien régime*. Trevor Higonnet is presently completing a doctorate in computing science at the Institut Henri Poincaré.

§ The authors would like to thank Harvard University, for the help given under the auspices of the Clark Fund, and the National Science Foundation, for funds made available for research by Grant No. GP 2723. They also wish to thank Janet Higonnet, Suzanne Berger, and David Landes, whose suggestions were very useful but who are, of course, in no way responsible for the views expressed in this article.

[1] Charles Pouthas, "Les Ministères de Louis-Philippe," *Revue d'histoire moderne et contemporaine*, I (1954), 102.

[2] *Almanach royal et national, 1846* (Paris, 1846), p. 83.

institutional element of Louis-Philippe's regime, and the methodical study of its membership is obviously of some consequence.

Important in itself, the methodical analysis of the deputies' backgrounds can involve more than straightforward tabulations of their characteristics: it can also serve as the basis for more involved and revealing statistical operations. Groups of deputies (e.g., all southerners, or members of the oppositions) can be compared with each other in terms of their other characteristics. Straightforward counts can tell us how many of the deputies were landowners or bankers, but from there we can go on to ask exactly how these two groups varied in terms of wealth, age, attitude toward religion, politics, parliamentary experience, and so forth. Moreover, statistical tests can then be used to determine the precise significance of these differences.

The quantity and the accuracy of the information that can be obtained for each deputy is impressive. In addition to what has already been mentioned, we know when he was born and when he died, as well as his place of birth, his rank in society, the scope of his political influence, the role that was to be played by his descendants, and even where he lived while in Paris. From all of this it is a simple task to establish for each member a detailed and convincing "profile." By the same token, the amount of information could—and did in the past—reach unmanageable proportions, since there are about fifty "characteristic" questions, each of which can be answered in as many as ten different ways for almost 500 deputies.[3] Today this problem can easily be resolved if the information is coded onto IBM cards in a way which is already familiar to many historians.[4] Computer programing makes it a simple task to obtain from these cards tabulations and statistical tests for any or all of the assemblies of the period, or for any group or combination of groups into which they can be subdivided. Numerical calculations that would have been intolerably tedious can now be achieved almost instantaneously; a vast range of historical and statistical hypotheses can be tested quickly and precisely in a way that was technically inconceivable only a few years ago. The conclusions that are presented here on the nature of Louis-Philippe's regime or on the importance in the Chamber of birth as the principal criterion of social class or of economic and regional characteristics as the determinant of political opinion would without computers have required months of incessant calculation.

For the years 1830-1848 the Assembly elected in 1846, which ended with the regime itself, is the one for which most information is readily available; it is also the most interesting, since its composition and political structure epitomize the course of Louis-Philippe's monarchy. Between August 6, 1846, the date of the general election, and the Revolution of 1848, 473 men were elected to serve as deputies. Since the number of constituencies, set at 459 in 1831, never varied during the regime, all 473 men never sat together at any one time, but in a study

---

[3] A list of these characteristics together with a description and critique of sources can be found in Appendix 1. Unless otherwise footnoted, all information used in this paper is derived from these data.

[4] See American Council of Learned Societies, *Newsletter*, XVI, No. 5 (May 1965).

of the legislature as a whole they can all be considered as forming a single group.[5]

The deputies were fairly young and vigorous men, for although their average age at the time of the general election in August, 1846, was only forty-nine, their average age at death would be sixty-six. Moreover, this was true not just of a small and hardy group but of the Assembly as a whole, which was a very homogeneous body in terms of age. Although previous assemblies had included many very young and old men, especially in 1815 and in 1831 when new political generations had entered political life, in 1846 nearly half of the deputies had been born in the years 1789-99, and only 13 per cent of them had been born either before 1780 or after 1809. It is possible, then, to speak here of a single and post-revolutionary generation whose political formation dated back not to the Revolution or even the Empire but to the later years of the Restoration. It was a generation that had matured during the July Monarchy itself: very few of the deputies had begun their parliamentary career during the Restoration, but in 1846 more than three out of four deputies had had previous parliamentary experience in the period after 1830. In fact, one out of four deputies had been sitting continuously since that date. The deputies were men who had done well in the only political system they really knew, and it is understandable that many of them had little desire to change it.

A class analysis of the Chamber of 1848 is especially surprising in so far as it reveals the continued importance of the aristocracy and a noble birth in political life. More than a third of the deputies were aristocrats; and this proportion had increased steadily since the general election of 1831, when less than a tenth of the newly elected members had been from the aristocracy. Most of the aristocrats had been born into families that had or claimed to have a lineage that antedated at least the fall of the *ancien régime*.[6] Since 1831 the increase in the Chamber of the number of aristocrats of this kind had been sizable, and it had more than offset the gradual but steady decline of the other kind of aristocrats, the Napoleonic nobles, which as a group had failed to renew itself socially or politically. In any case, it remains one of the great ironies of Louis-Philippe's regime that it should have so markedly evolved from its revolutionary and resolutely antiaristocratic origins in an elitist direction. Even if the word "bourgeois" is to be defined in a non-Marxist and traditional sense of "non-noble," so as to encompass landowners and members of the established professions, it remains obvious that the July Monarchy was not a "bourgeois

---

[5] The actual election of the deputies will be dealt with in these pages only in so far as it bears direct relation to the characteristics of the Assembly. The election itself has in any case been very well described by A. Roubaud, "Les Elections de 1842 et de 1846 sous le ministère Guizot," *Revue d'histoire moderne*, XIV (1939), 271-86, and by André-Jean Tudesq in *Les Grands Notables en France (1840-1849)* (Paris, 1964), pp. 853-95.

[6] For the sake of readability, precise figures have often been replaced by more euphonic expressions such as "most of the aristocrats." In *every* instance, however, implicit reference is in fact being made to a very exact statistic. In this case, for example, "most of the aristocrats" means that 38.1 per cent of the deputies were aristocrats; that of these, 26.5 per cent had Napoleonic titles; and that of the remaining nobles, 72.1 per cent had titles that supposedly harked back to the *ancien régime*. See also Appendix 1, Postscript 2.

monarchy." The great Orleanist notables may themselves have felt somewhat uneasy about this trend, for although *ancien régime* aristocrats were numerous on the back benches, they were not to be found in positions of importance. These were throughout taken up by bourgeois or by the remaining first-generation Napoleonic notabilities. *Ancien régime* aristocrats could be counted on to support the regime but not to run it.

A straightforward distinction between bourgeois and aristocrats is not a sophisticated one and would appear to be more characteristic of political life before 1830. Nonetheless, it is one that can be shown statistically as still valid for the years 1846-1848. This can be done if reference is made to the professional structure of the Assembly. About a fourth of all aristocrats had some professional capacity, usually law; but most of them were landowners or, more often, soldiers and eminent servants of state in the Conseil d'Etat, the Cour des comptes, or the prefectoral corps. In contrast, the professional structure of the bourgeoisie was the exact inverse of the aristocracy's. Typically aristocratic occupations account for less than a fourth of the total; half of the bourgeois deputies were lawyers, a tenth had "other professions" such as medicine or journalism, and little more than a tenth again were in business.

This last figure is surprisingly small for a regime that was not inappropriately described by Marx and Tocqueville as a joint-stock company ruling the many for the material advantage of a selected few. It is true that the number of deputies involved in business can be inflated a bit if one includes those persons who were directors of banks or railways, like the aristocratic Legitimist Jean Paul de Villeneuve-Bargemont; but under the best of circumstances it remains evident that the great majority of deputies had no direct connection with the business world. If the new industrial bourgeois magnates did run the July Monarchy, they were surely doing it vicariously. It has already been pointed out that the parliamentary personnel of the July Monarchy was not as "bourgeois" as has often been thought, and here we can add that even in so far as it was bourgeois its economic and professional structure was still traditionally oriented.

That there should have been so few businessmen-deputies is readily explicable in terms of the economic characteristics of the electoral constituencies. In the 1840's only 25 per cent of the population of France lived in the so-called urban areas, which were arbitrarily defined as towns of more than two thousand inhabitants. Only a third of the constituencies were situated in departments whose percentage of urban population was greater than the national average; and this third includes districts in departments, like the Seine-Inférieure, that comprised constituencies that were exclusively rural. Moreover, the 459 districts can be roughly averaged as including 80,000 people; but constituencies that included an industrial population of more than 10,000 men, women, and children only make up 7 per cent of the total. It follows, therefore, that although fewer than one in five of the deputies was in some way connected with business, businessmen, however few, were still overrepresented in the Chamber, since the proportion of industrial or even urbanized constituencies was also very low. Only a few representatives of the new industrial bourgeoisie participated in the workings of a regime that was supposedly their servant, but in a sense there were still more of them in the Assembly than in the country at large. Deputies of genius like Tocqueville may well have realized that the Industrial Revolution was reshaping the structure of French society, but this could hardly have been obvious to the great majority of deputies whose professional, social, and regional milieu was still completely foreign to the new economic upheaval.   In any case, most businessmen, like most lawyers and most members of the professions, were bourgeois, and comparisons of social-professional groups corroborate the idea of a basic cleavage between the aristocracy and the bourgeoisie. In terms of the social, professional, and economic criteria at our disposal, aristocrats who were bureaucrats, for example, were in most ways similar to aristocrats who were landowners, or soldiers, or to any other group of aristocrats at all.[7] Most curiously, comparisons reveal an unexpected homogeneity between *ancien régime* and Napoleonic nobles. Although the Napoleonic nobles, in contrast with other aristocrats in the Chamber, were less sympathetic to the Church and better connected politically because they were more often related to former and present deputies or to persons important in politics, the similarities far outweighed the differences. The imperial nobles, many of whom were one or even two generations removed from their founding fathers, were very much like their pedigreed brethren as regards profession, income, politics, or indeed any of the other tabulated characteristics.

Comparisons among bourgeois social-professional groups reveal a similar if somewhat less pronounced uniformity. Bourgeois lawyers, businessmen, and professional men when contrasted with bourgeois landowners, soldiers, and bureaucrats do differ in some ways. Although their politics were similar, the second group, which was more oriented to the service of the state, enjoyed greater prestige as measured by rank in the Legion of Honor, and of course more of them were, ex officio, functionaries. In terms of other personal characteristics, however, the two groups are quite alike. An even greater similarity exists between those bourgeois deputies who had some connection to business and those who had some other professional activity, usually law. Here again, as might be expected, there were very few deputies who were both businessmen and bureaucrats. Another and more peculiar difference is that businessmen were either older or younger than the professional men, perhaps because they had, when elected, either inherited their fortune or long since earned it. But in other and more important respects (wealth, geographical origin, role played in local politics, attitude toward the Church, political connections) the professional men and businessmen were similar. What matters here is not the professional division but the common social class. The personnel of the Assembly can of course be divided into other basic groups: social class is only one criterion. In fact the number of possible divisions at our disposal is truly infinite: income alone presents 1023 possible subdivisions. But none of the distinctions that readily spring to mind provide results that are consistently significant in terms of the

---

[7] For a statistical explanation of this contrast see Appendix 2.

other tabulated "social-personal" characteristics. Very meager or nonexistent differences appear from comparisons that oppose all businessmen, regardless of class, to all nonbusinessmen, regardless of class; and the same is true for divisions that oppose the rich to the poor, the young to the aged, the experienced to the inexperienced, the devout to the indifferent, or the left to the right.

In the Chamber, then, the aristocracy was a very homogeneous group regardless of vintage or profession. So was the bourgeoisie, if to a lesser degree. Consequently, it is to be expected that bourgeois deputies should be very different from their aristocratic colleagues, and that is indeed the case. Income provides in this respect the most surprising cleavage between the two groups.

The available statistics are imperfect here, because they emphasize the importance of landed wealth. But they can be used with confidence in cases such as this one, where differences are very characteristic (see Appendix 1, Postscript 3). All deputies were perforce fairly rich men, since the law defined as eligible for election only those who paid at least 500 francs in property taxes. To obtain an idea of the meaning of this sum, it is useful to recall that a tax of 500 francs represented an unearned income of 2500 to 5000 francs, when the average annual wage of a worker was at best 750 francs and of a professor in a lycée, 1500 francs. But if the deputies were all rich when compared with the nation at large, they were far from being all in the same "income group." Some were much richer than others, and there were significant differences in this respect between bourgeois and aristocrats. In the Assembly as a whole, the average tax was 1100 francs; one-fourth of the deputies paid less than 750 francs, and one-fourth paid more than 2000. This was a wide spectrum and it is one that is to be found in every social, professional, regional, or political group. There was, therefore, as wide a gap between the income of aristocrats rich and poor as there was for the bourgeois deputies, but the point here is that it was not the same gap. Aristocrats as a whole were significantly richer than bourgeois as a whole. Although it can be estimated that 40 per cent of the bourgeois deputies had an income of less than 7500 francs a year, an equal proportion of aristocrats had an annual income of more than 15,000 francs. (See Table 1.)

Income was only one of the personal characteristics that separated aristocratic and bourgeois deputies. Another was age. Aristocrats were not only richer, they were also younger. During the debate on the heredity of the peerage in the fall of 1830, Thiers had foretold that if the prerogatives of the upper chamber were curtailed, the *jeunesse dorée* would flock to the lower one instead, and this is indeed what occurred. The beginnings of the regime had also seen an influx into the Chamber of young men, like Thiers himself, but the younger men of 1846 were very different from the younger men of 1830-31. They were scions of the great rather than clever young bourgeois on the political make. This too reinforces the idea already outlined of a single political generation which was renewing itself only by becoming more inbred.

Another contrast between the two classes is provided by political connection. A breakdown of the number of deputies who were themselves the descendants of other deputies, senators, or peers or who were relatives of important persons still living also corroborates the impression of aristocratic immobilism. Here again the nobility was favored and had far better connections. Generally speaking, "pull" and a tradition of familial political involvement were important elements of electoral success, but it is interesting to see that during the reign of the bourgeois king, pull was still of greater use to the aristocrats than to the bourgeois. One can add, however, that this was a transitory situation. Under Louis-Philippe, because of the Empire and the Restoration, aristocratic deputies of all sorts still had more political connections than did their bourgeois colleagues; but if the Assembly of 1846 is taken as a whole, it is the rich regardless of class or profession who were founding political dynasties. Social class was giving way to income as the criterion of sustained political eminence.

But this would only occur in the next forty years. For the moment, wealth, age, and family politics still separated the two classes, and so did residence and place of birth. The peculiar position of Paris in national French politics has often been pointed out, but it can be added here that it affected different social classes very differently. One-third of the aristocratic deputies were by birth Parisians, and this was three times more than the corresponding figure for the bourgeoisie. Nor, for that matter, did the two social classes live in the same part of the capital once they were there. The notion of rigorous frontiers that delineated the quarters of the aristocracy in the Faubourg Saint-Germain and of the industrialists around the Chaussée d'Antin is unfortunately something of a legend, since nearly half of the deputies lived in the newly built areas that stretched from the Champs-Elysées to the Parc Monceau. But for those who did not, the legend does hold true. The criterion of exclusive domicile, in so far as criteria existed, was not income—for the richest and poorest deputies lived next door to each other—but social class. One aristocrat in three did live in the Faubourg Saint-Germain, and there were indeed many bankers and businessmen who lived in what were then the second and third *arrondissements,* the district of the banks and of the Bourse. Ninety per cent of the deputies lived to the west of the axis now set by the Boulevards Saint-Michel and Sébastopol.

Surprisingly, however, and regardless of its pronounced characteristics, the dichotomous social division of the Assembly did not for all that have significant political consequence. Comparisons between supporters of the government and opposition do not reveal that either bourgeois or aristocrats were to be found more numerous on one side of the political fence rather than on the other, or in any one "party" (see Appendix 1, Postscript 1). Contemporaries would not have been surprised by this, for it was popularly held at the time that corruption, not social class, was the mainstay of Guizot's power: corruption at the polls where minuscule constituencies were controlled by the government, and corruption in the Chamber where deputies were bribed with government jobs.

Our data provide some information about these accusations. That in some cases the government actually bought off voters with promises or threats has always been known. A general survey also shows that most elections in 1846 were not hotly contested: in more than a third of the constituencies the winner was elected unopposed or with more than two-thirds of the vote. Four-fifths of the deputies were elected on the first round, and only one in ten was unable to secure a majority of more than 10 per cent. Obviously, these figures could be used to demonstrate that political life was strangely atrophied, but others suggest a different interpretation. They clearly show that in this period national politics were usually dominated by men who enjoyed strong and even unassailable local prestige: more than half of the deputies on both the left and the right played a role in local politics either at the departmental level in the Conseils généraux or, less often, at the local level, in the municipal councils and as mayors. No less relevant is that nearly three-quarters of the deputies resided in the department that they represented in the Chamber (see Appendix 1, Postscript 4). The clear inference here is that if political life seemed unnaturally sluggish, it was not because of the interference of the government but more simply because politics, at the local level, revolved around men rather than issues.

The accusation of corruption at the polls has not, however, rested primarily on the intensity of electoral contests but on the size of the constituencies within which they were held. The argument there is that the government men were elected in the smaller constituencies where voters could be more easily bribed. Again, statistics show that this was not necessarily so. Undeniably, a difference in size did exist. About 60 per cent of the districts comprised more than four hundred voters, but those that did not returned 44 per cent of Guizot's men and only 25 per cent of the others. Yet this does not prove the accusation of corruption, for these small constituencies were not scattered evenly throughout France; they were usually to be found in the more traditional and conservative areas of Southern and Central France. Since it is well known that political opinion varies greatly from region to region, it can easily be argued that the deputies who represented smaller constituencies were more conservative not because the number of voters in their constituencies was small but because their constituencies were in the places they were. That the government was able to bribe or coerce voters in small constituencies *generally* was certainly not true. A comparison of the 103 most loyal government men returned by constituencies with less than four hundred voters with their 43 similarly elected members of the opposition reveals very significant regional differences. Fifty-eight per cent of the opposition's small constituencies were in the Eastern and North Central departments as against 17 per cent for Guizot's people. By contrast, 39 per cent of the government's small constituencies were to be found south of a line running from Poitiers to Valence as against only 5 per cent of the opposition's. It is obvious that the government did not succeed in bribing voters at will, even in small constituencies; and the regional distribution of the smaller districts that the government did control suggests that even there corruption was not the essential factor.

Electoral statistics do not therefore necessarily corroborate the accusation of corruption that has so often been leveled against Guizot's regime. The same is true but to a lesser degree as regards the deputies who were also bureaucrats. They were very numerous in the Chamber, and as a group they showed a pronounced political bias in favor of the government (see Appendix 1, Postscript 5). A fifth of the bureaucrats in the Chamber sat with the opposition, but enough of them were left to make up about half of the government's side. A large number of Guizot's men were therefore paid by the state, something that is particularly suggestive in view of the fact that the bureaucrats were, by the Assembly's standards, extremely poor men.

It is nonetheless very possible that the opposition was wrong to deride Guizot, who had claimed that the presence of so many functionaries in the Chamber was not "un abus choquant." It can be countered that the bureaucrats who voted against the government were just as poor as those who did not, so that poverty was not an inevitable source of corruptibility. More important, however, are the social-professional and regional characteristics of the deputy bureaucrats. More than a third were magistrates, and this group when compared with all lawyers as a whole did not in any way stand out as being anomalous either socially, economically, or politically. In other words, magistrates may very well have decided to vote with the government not because they had been "corrupted" but rather because they belonged to a particular social-professional group. Moreover, a closer look at the regional origins of these functionaries reinforces our impression of their relative independence. Those among them who approved were often elected in conservative areas like the Southwest, which also returned unsalaried but pro-government deputies. Similarly, those bureaucrats in the Chamber who voted against Guizot represented regions, like North Central France, that were characteristically more liberal. Thus, there are many reasons to suppose that if a magistrate from the Aveyron voted with Guizot, it was not so much because he was a magistrate but because most lawyers from the Massif Central generally voted that way. Since the distinction "bureaucrat-nonbureaucrat" was a very visible one, it was taken up by the opposition to prove that the government had bought Parliament off. But the distinction may have been more visible than true.

The personnel of the Assembly is clearly divisible into two social classes. Yet this does not explain political allegiance. If we also admit that bribery and corruption were not by any means the exclusive determinants of parliamentary opinion, why then did members come to side with the left or the right? The answer, as has already been implied, is regionalism and economics.[8] A comparison of government and opposition shows that the two groups differed as regards age and bureaucratic status, so that, consequently, one can find a slight difference in terms of profession. But in other respects left and right do not differ significantly, either in class, income, political connections, or place of birth. Attitudes toward the Church are similarly inconclusive. Of the deputies who were elected in 1846, 146 had promised to support in the Chamber the Church's efforts to open secondary schools. The signatories are slightly more numerous on the left than they are on the right. Younger men who would have more difficulties at the polls were more favorable, and older men who had been

---

8 For precise statistics on this point see Appendix 2.

active in politics during the Restoration were more hostile; but there was no discernible connection between religion and politics. Nor is it possible to claim as Marx did that politics varied according to profession, and that bankers, for example, were more sympathetic to the regime than manufacturers or merchants. There is a slight indication of this, but it is almost negligible.

On the other hand, nearly every available regional economic criterion reveals vast differences between right and left. The deputies of the opposition were elected in departments that tended to have a higher rate of urbanized population. They were also returned by departments that showed the greatest increase in the number of commercial and industrial *patentes;* and the actual electoral districts where they had won were also those with the highest number of industrial workers. Concurrently, there were sizable political variations from one region to the next. Paris, reversing the stand it had taken in the first years of the regime, now voted with the opposition. So did North Central France (Ile-de-France, Champagne, Berry, Nivernais, Orléanais), the Northwest (Normandy), the Rhône-Saône region, and finally the West (Brittany, Anjou, the Vendée), where the bourgeoisie was dominated by its hatred and fear of the aristocracy and the peasants. On the other hand, the government was strong in the East, in the Massif Central, and in all of France south of Lyon. If we except the Eastern departments, the contrast is very marked between the more progressive Northern France and the more traditional rural and poor areas of the South. How important this distinction is could be shown in many ways. One example perhaps will suffice: a comparison of lawyers on the right with lawyers on the left reveals, of course, no difference in terms of profession or even class, but neither does it show a difference of income, age, political connection, attitude toward the Church, or parliamentary experience. For the reasons that have been outlined above, there is a significant difference in terms of bureaucratic status, but it is completely overshadowed by regional cleavage: 71 per cent of Guizot's lawyers came from the area that has been described as pro-government; 72 per cent of the opposition lawyers came from Northern France. Since this case is quite typical, it follows that social and professional cleavages may have clearly divided the Assembly into two groups, but distinctions and similarities of this sort were overlapped and nullified by the force of regionalism and its concomitants, the conditions of local economic and social life.

On the whole, then, a methodical analysis of the Chamber of Deputies speaks well for French parliamentarianism and for Guizot's system. The deputies, it seems, were usually honest men whose politics often transcended their private concerns. If the system failed, it was not because it was corrupt or because it was unresponsive. Its problem, in fact, was that it was too responsive to the wishes of a country that was at once progressive in parts and, as a whole, very rural and economically backward.

This is an important point and so are many of the conclusions that are to be immediately derived from a computer analysis of the Chamber. It is also useful to know that in this period many of the deputies belonged to a single generation whose parliamentary experience had begun after the Revolution of 1830, that religion was not a determinant of political opinion, and that in this supposedly bourgeois monarchy a large and increasing number of deputies were aristocrats, better connected politically, richer, and more cosmopolitan, because they were more oriented to Paris than to the provinces. Similarly, it is of some use to see that although most deputies were indeed bourgeois, the old myth of a bourgeois-industrialist monarchy does not hold up, for although the bourgeois deputies did have incomes and professions that differed from those of the aristocrats, they were not manufacturers or bankers, or even merchants and *négociants*. Like the aristocrats, the bourgeois members of the Assembly had social and economic roots that were still sunk in the soil of *la vieille France*.

But more interesting than these conclusions are the ones that can be inferred from the assembled data. Much of the criticism, contemporary and historical, of the "system" of Louis-Philippe and of Guizot assumes as its basis, firstly, that France was a governable entity and, secondly, that the institutional system must therefore have been at fault. Hence it follows that if the franchise had been widened, if Guizot had been less obstinate, and if the deputies had been less corrupt, revolution and dictatorship could have been easily avoided. Perhaps. But a better and less conjectural case can be made for a less optimistic point of view.

Within the Assembly, the persistence of a basic gap between the bourgeoisie and the aristocracy illustrates the failure of the July Monarchy to achieve social synthesis even for the upper classes alone. Because of its monarchic principle, its "quasi-legitimacy," and the absence after 1837 of active opposition for the extreme left, and because of the many personal ties which bound individual bourgeois and nobles to the crown, the July Monarchy like the Second Empire at a later time appeared to have achieved some measure of consensus at the top. But this was in fact illusory. In the 1870's the old cleavages between the Orleanist *grande bourgeoisie* and the aristocracy appeared anew, and it is important to see that this cleavage existed latently in the 1840's as well. More important, the relationships of politics and geography, even for the limited suffrage of the 1840's, are yet more proof of the persistence of the regional and deep-seated divisions that have set the French at odds with each other since 1789. Divided vertically into distinct and antagonistic classes, France, or at any rate the *pays légal*, was also divided horizontally from place to place.

In the last years of the July Monarchy, hopeful critics like Tocqueville or small-minded ones like Duvergier de Hauranne may have accepted the idea of institutional failure because they feared or could not grasp the conclusions that were implied by the inadequacy of this superficial and mechanistic solution. Yet, it is more than likely that they were wrong and that in a way it was Guizot who was right. He was not only justified in claiming that his system was working adequately, but he may also have been right in thinking that order and liberalism were no longer compatible in France at that time. How then could we dispute his conclusion that rigid conservatism had now become the necessary condition of monarchism and the rule of the *grands notables?*

APPENDIX I

Listed below are the characteristics that were coded for each of the 473 deputies. To simplify the presentation the subcategories of each characteristic are not described. For example, although the rubric "profession" is presented as a characteristic, the nine different ways in which this question could be answered are not included. The capital letter or letters to the left of each characteristic correspond to letters in the section headed "Sources." Thus, for example, the category "profession" is preceded by the letters ABD, which indicates that in this particular instance the information that was coded was derived from A (Robert, Bourloton, and Cougny), B (The National Archives), and D (The National Almanach).

I

A   Political "party" (for this and the following four rubics see Postscript I)

AF   For or against the government

G   Opposition on vote 1

H   Opposition on vote 2

I   Signed petition for banquets

A   Importance of role in parliamentary affairs

D   Role in parliamentary committees

O   Attitude toward Church schools

A,F-I   Constancy of opinion during the legislature

II

AB   Date of birth

AC   Date of death

AB   Place of birth

A   Social class (see Postscript 3)

ABD   Profession

AB   Religion

B   Income (see Postscript 3)

BCD   Rank in the Legion of Honor

AB   Political ascendants

A   Political descendants

A   Relative of important persons

BD   Bureaucratic status (see Postscript 5)

ABD   Parliamentary experience for
     (1) every assembly of the July Monarchy

     (2) preceding regimes since 1789 and subsequent regimes to 1890

D   Residence in Paris

III

B   Department represented

N   Percentage of rural population represented for 1831

N   Percentage of change in above from 1836 to 1851

N   Absolute population for department in 1831

N   Percentage of change in above from 1831 to 1846

—   Region

M   Wealth of department (measured by number of enfranchised voters)

E   Change in number of *patentes* in department from 1835 to 1846

LN   Urban character of electoral district

E   Number of industrial workers in electoral district in 1847

IV

B   Date of election

BK   Size of electoral constituency

B   Size of electoral majority

B   Number of electoral turns needed for election

BD   Role in local politics

ABD   Place of residence (see Postscript 4)

SOURCES

A The basic source is Adolphe Robert, Edgar Bourloton, and Gaston Cougny, *Dictionnaire des parlementaries francais* (5 vols.; Paris, 1891). In spite of many errors (at least one per deputy on the average) these volumes are invaluable.

B Archives nationales, C 1165 A 2 to C 1323 A 175.

C Archives de la Légion d'honneur.

D *Almanach royal et national, 1847* (Paris, 1847)

E France, Bureau de la Statistique générale, 1e Série, Vols. X-XIII, *Industrie* (Paris, 1847-52).

F *Journal des débats* (Paris), Aug. 8, 1846

G *Le National* (Paris), Jan. 23, 1848

H *Le Constitutionnel* (Paris), Feb. 25, 1848.

I *Le National,* Feb. 21, 1848.

J *Journal officiel,* VI (May 10, 1847), 329 (gives a list of deputies who were also directors of railway companies).

K Prosper Duvergier de Hauranne, *De la Réforme parlementaire et de la réforme électorale* (Paris, 1847).

L Sherman Kent, *Electoral Procedure under Louis Philippe* (New Haven, 1937).

M Paul Meuriot, *La Population et les lois électorales en France de 1789 à nos jours* (Paris, 1916).

N Charles Pouthas, *La Population francais pendant la première moitie du XIXe siècle* (Paris, 1956).

O Henry de Riancey, *Compte rendu des élections de 1846* (Paris, 1846).

Postscript 1

The use of the word "party" here is somewhat misleading. In the Chamber of 1846 there were, of course, no parties in the sense that would exist even thirty or forty years later. Yet one could then already find cohesive parliamentary groups like the Legitimists, for example, or to some degree the Opposition Dynastique, whose members centered around Odilon Barrot and did have a common program of sorts. The 1840's, in this respect, mark off two periods. Before then, parliamentary politics had chiefly revolved around a few leaders: Molé, Guizot, Thiers, and de Broglie. By the end of the reign, however, loyalties had become less fleeting. This was particularly true during the political. institutional, and economic crisis of 1846-47.

In August, 1846, the *Journal des débats* published lists of deputies who were for or against the government (this vote is entered beside the letter "F" on our list of sources). Of the deputies who were listed there as sympathetic to the opposition, only 5 per cent can be found on the side of the government in any of our other three votes that provide the basis of our division between pro-government and pro-opposition. These three votes are (1) the division in the Chamber on Auguste Rodolphe Darblay's amendment to the Address to the Throne in January, 1848, (2) the "mise en accusation" of Guizot that was moved in Parliament on February 23, 1848, and (3) the list of deputies who supported the campaign for the banquets.

In order to clarify the meaning of these votes, one can cite the example of Tocqueville and Thiers on the moderate left, who sided against the government on Darblay's amendment only. A second group would be composed of men, like Lamartine and Subervie, who voted with Thiers on Vote 1 but also supported the campaign for banquets. A third and more extreme group would include men who sided against the government on all three issues, some of them republicans like Crémieux, Dupont de L'Eure, and Garnier-Pagès, others members of the Opposition Dynastique like Odilon Barrot and Francois Mauguin. Robert, Bourloton, and Cougny's *Dictionnaire* was used to identify the Legitimists.

Postscript 2

The characteristic "social class" was subdivided into the following categories: titled aristocrats before 1789, aristocrats before 1789, Napoleonic nobles, *grande bourgeoisie,* middle urban bourgeoisie, rural bourgeoisie, lower middle class, self-made men, and unknown. Inevitably, coding was in this respect somewhat subjective. It is, however, completely rigorous as regards the Napoleonic nobility, whose claims are easily verifiable. The most difficult cases are the thirty-odd nontitled men with compounded names like Balzac's Cruchot de Bonfons in *Eugénie Grandet,* who were passing from one class to the next. Our criterion there was the credibility of the claim. In this respect, income, residence, and status can all serve to corroborate more subjective judgments. It can also be pointed out that many tabulations of social class for this period are based on an article in the *Revue d'histoire politique et constitutionnelle,* Nouvelle Série, No. 11, July-Sept., 1948, by J. Bécaud, entitled "La Noblesse dans les Chambres, 1815-1848." The figures that are to be found in this article for the years 1846-48 are 50 per cent off, even for the Napoleonic nobility, about whose identity there can be no mistake.

Postscript 3

Our figures for income are extrapolations from the *cens électoral* that was paid by the deputies, or rather for 464 of them, since we were unable to find information about the nine others. It is important, for two reasons, to realize that these figures are only estimates. The first reason is that the proportion of income that was taxed varied from department to department. In the case of very rich men who owned property in many parts of France, the differences canceled each other out, but it would be difficult to attach great credibility to any single estimate. The second reason is that the *cens* was levied primarily on landed wealth (for a detailed discussion of this problem, see Kent, *Electoral Procedure under Louis Philippe,* chapter 2). The income of merchants and manufacturers was therefore underestimated and that of landed proprietors was overestimated. A more complete discussion of the relationship of *cens* to income can be found in Tudesq, *Les Grands Notables,* pp. 89-94.

Postscript 4

A.-J. Tudesq, in an article entitled "L'Attraction parisienne sur les députés de la monarchie censitaire," in *Politique: Revue internationale des doctrines et des institutions,* Nouvelle Série, No. 3, July-Sept., 1958, cites figures that differ markedly from our own. Tudesq believes that Paris played a very great role in French political life and cites that 41 per cent of all deputies resided in Paris. Our own figures are somewhat different. Although our tabulations indicate that eighty-five deputies were born in the Seine, as against seventy-five according to Tudesq, our contention is that 70 per cent of the deputies "resided" in the department that they represented in Parliament. This is surely because we have included in this category persons who ordinarily lived in Paris but whose families had regional ties that they themselves had kept up.

Postscript 5

The number of deputy-bureaucrats in the Assembly of 1846-48 is none too clear. Guizot himself counted 189 (Douglas Johnson, *Guizot* [London, 1963], p. 228). Tudesq finds that there were 188, to whom should be added seven deputy ministers. Duvergier de Hauranne (in his *De la Réforme parlementaire,* p. 149) counted 193 for the Assembly as it then stood. Our figure is somewhat larger, since we find that there were 202 deputy-bureaucrats: 74 were in the judiciary, 29 in the army, 60 in the higher echelons of the central administrations (35 members of the Conseil d'État, 14 *maîtres des requétes,* and 11 members of the Cour des comptes). There were 39 "other bureaucrats," five of them members of the University. To this could be added 18 mayors who were appointed by the state, but we did not include these deputies in our tally of bureaucrats. The discrepancy between our figure and those to be found elsewhere is probably because ours deals with all of the 473 deputies elected from 1846 to 184, whereas the others take into account only the 453 deputies elected at the general election.

APPENDIX 2

For any characteristic, it is a simple matter to determine the number of deputies who fall into each of the subcategories for that characteristic. For example, for the two groups "opposition" and "government men" a breakdown of this kind for regional origin will yield the following table.

Regional Origin	Government (per cent)	Left Opposition (per cent)	Regional Origin	Government (per cent)	Left Opposition (per cent)
North	6.1	4.9	Rhône-Sâone	6.8	7.7
West	7.8	11.2	Paris Region	11.7	31.5
Northwest	7.4	16.8	South (Pyrénées-		
East	12.9	7.0	Mediterranean)	12.0	3.5
Massif Central	9.1	4.2	Jura-Alps	7.4	2.1
			Aquitaine Basin	18.8	11.2

The chi-square test of independence can in this case be considered as a test to indicate if opposition and government men are similarly distributed as regards the regional location of the departments that they represent in the Assembly. If the characteristic allows for N subcategories (N $\leqslant$ 10) we have a situation with N - 1 degrees of freedom. Knowing the degree of freedom, we can determine whether the chi-square statistic for the table is significant at any given level, e.g., 1 per cent, 2 per cent, 5 per cent, etc., where significance is tabulated in any general text on statistics (see, for example, E. S. Keeping, *Introduction to Statistical Inference,* Princeton, N.J., 1962, p. 321). Significance at the x per cent level indicates that the two groups have *different* distributions for that characteristic with a probability of error of x per cent.

For example, when distribution of left-opposition and government men was tested in this way, on the following characteristics the following significant chi-squares were obtained.

Rank in the Legion of Honor	73.8 at 7 levels of freedom
Regional location of department	53.4 at 9 levels of freedom
Bureaucratic status	43.1 at 5 levels of freedom
Number of industrial workers in electoral district in 1847	21.5 at 9 levels of freedom
Change in the number of *patentes* for department from 1835 to 1846	26.6 at 9 levels of freedom
Percentage of change in proportion of urbanized population	16.3 at 7 levels of freedom
Profession	18.5 at 8 levels of freedom
Residence	14.0 at 6 levels of freedom

TABLE 1
Amount of Property Tax Paid by Deputies in 1849 (in per cent)
(used in estimating their income)

In Francs	Bourgeois	Aristocrats Including Napoleonic Nobles	Bureaucrats	Nonbureaucrats
Under 500	1.0	0.0	1.0	0.4
500-700	22.8	15.1	29.7	12.7
700-1000	20.5	13.3	24.8	12.7
1000-1300	10.7	12.0	9.9	11.9
1300-1500	6.8	6.6	6.9	6.9
1500-2000	12.4	10.2	9.4	13.5
2000-3000	12.1	15.7	5.4	19.2
3000-5000	7.2	12.0	6.9	10.4
Above 5000	4.9	12.7	4.5	10.0
Unknown	1.6	2.4	1.5	2.3

TABLE 2
Supplementary Statistics for the Chamber of 1846-1848

Deputy Characteristic	*Government (per cent)**	*Left Opposition (per cent)**
Attitude on Church Schools in 1846		
Agreed to support Church schools	26	33
No commitment	71	63
Not applicable (elected after 1846)	3	4
Social Class		
Titled aristocrats before 1789	19	14
Other aristocrats before 1789	7	6
Napoleonic nobles	10	8
Grande bourgeoisie	15	18
Middle urban bourgeoisie	25	32
Rural bourgeoisie	20	17
Lower middle class	0	1
Self-made men	2	3
Unknown	2	1
Profession		
Bureaucrats	19	8
Journalists, Intellectuals	6	11
Doctors, Engineers	1	4
Businessmen	13	12
Lawyers	35	43
Landowners	9	7
Military	15	13
Unknown	2	2
Amount of *Cens* (Property Tax) Paid in 1846, in Francs (Used to Measure Income)		
Under 500	1	1
500 to 700	21	22
700 to 1000	18	16
1000 to 1300	11	11
1300 to 1500	6	8
1500 to 2000	12	11
2000 to 3000	14	13
3000 to 5000	9	8
Above 5000	6	8
Unknown	2	2
Bureaucratic Status		
Central administration (prefects, Conseil d'État, Cour des comptes, ministries)	16	5
Judiciary	19	10
Army	8	3
Other	9	5
No function	48	77

* All figures are rounded out to the nearest 1 per cent.

TABLE 2 (continued)

Deputy Characteristic	Government (per cent)*	Left Opposition (per cent)*
Change in the Number of *Patentes* for the Department Represented (1835-1846)		
Declined by more than 20 per cent	4	1
Declined by 19 to 10 per cent	3	2
Declined by 9 to 5 per cent	9	3
Declined by 4 to 0 per cent	12	10
Rose 0 to 3 per cent	14	15
Rose 4 to 9 per cent	8	9
Rose 10 to 12 per cent	15	18
Rose 13 to 19 per cent	5	6
Rose by 20 per cent	2	11
Unknown	28	25
Date of Birth by Decades		
1760-1769	0	1
1770-1779	5	5
1780-1789	22	7
1790-1799	37	50
1800-1809	29	31
1810-1819	7	6
Rank in the Legion of Honor		
No rank	22	55
Chevalier	34	33
Above	44	12
Residence in Paris by *Arrondissement*		
1	42	34
2	15	20
3	3	3
4	1	3
5-9	1	2
10	25	18
11	2	11
12	1	0
Not accounted for in the 1847 *Almanach*	10	9
Percentage of Rural Population in Department Represented (in 1831)		
Under 50 per cent	4	8
50.1 to 67 per cent	19	14
67.1 to 75 per cent	14	8
75.1 to 85 per cent	42	37
85.1 to 90 per cent	16	22
Above 90 per cent	5	11

* All figures are rounded out to the nearest 1 per cent.

TABLE 2 (continued)

Deputy Characteristic	Government (per cent)*	Left Opposition (per cent)*
Number of Industrial Workers per Electoral District in 1847		
0-1000	30	16
1000-2000	33	28
2000-3000	14	27
3000-5000	8	10
5000-7000	4	3
7000-9000	2	2
9000-11,000	4	3
11,000-16,000	1	3
16,000-21,000	1	3
21,000 and up	4	6
Number of Registered Voters per Electoral District in 1846		
0-100	0	0
100-200	5	2
200-300	16	7
300-400	23	17
400-500	19	20
500-600	14	17
600-700	9	8
700-800	4	11
800-900	3	4
Above 900	7	14
Number of Electoral Turns Needed for Election		
1	84	74
2	10	22
3	6	4

* All figures are rounded out to the nearest 1 per cent.

2. Bureaucratic development and the structure of decision-making in the Meiji Period: the case of the Genrō*

BERNARD S. SILBERMAN †

One of the most recurrent themes in the descriptions and analyses of political development in Japan during the Meiji period (1868-1912) is the emergence of the *genrō* as the primary decision and policy-making group. Surprisingly, however, while a great deal has been written by both Japanese and Western scholars concerning the individual members of the genrō, very few attempts have been made to explain the origins of the group and especially the form which it took. A major obstacle to the analysis of this problem appears to be the failure to distinguish clearly between the *genrō* as an informal collegial decision and policy-making body and membership or participation in the organization.[1] Failure to view membership and organizational structure as two separate aspects of the development of the *genrō* has had serious consequences for those attempting to explain the place of the *genrō* in Japanese political development. The emphasis placed on the nine men who are usually designated as the *genrō* has diverted attention from the more important problem, from the viewpoint of political development, of why the *genrō* as a decision-making structure emerged at a particular time and took a particular form. Absence of serious concern over the origins of the *genrō* structure on the part of historians has led them to ignore the question completely or to assign the informal collegial character of the *genrō* to the general tendency in Japanese society to make decisions through group consensus. The latter is too general an explanation since it does not tell us why

* Reprinted from the *Journal of Asian Studies,* XXVII (November, 1967), pp. 81-94, by permission of the author and publisher.

† Bernard S. Silberman, associate professor of history, Duke University, received his Ph.D. from the University of Michigan. He is the author of *Ministers of Modernization: Elite Mobility in the Meiji Restoration, 1868-1873.*

1 See for example, Jackson Bailey, "The Origin and Nature of the Genrō," in Robert K. Sakai (ed.), *Studies on Asia, 1965* (Lincoln, Nebraska: 1965), pp. 129-41; Oka Yoshitake, *Kindai Nihon seijishi* (Tokyo: 1963), I, 254-55; Nihon Gaikō Gakkai (comp.), *Taiheyō sensō genin ron* (Tokyo: 1953), pp. 32-33; Yamada Shikazo, *Seiji kenkyū* (Tokyo: 1926), pp. 35-36.

consensus in this case should be arrived at through an informal collegial body rather than through some other structural form.

The weakness of this explanation is made even more manifest by the absence of an institutional precedent for this type of decision-making structure and by its failure to persist or to become institutionalized. If, however, the *genrō* is viewed primarily as a decision-making structure, we may then use concepts derived from the study of decision-making structures in contemporary Western societies to seek another, and perhaps more satisfactory, explanation of why this particular type of structure evolved at a specific stage of political development. Utilization of such concepts may indicate that the emergence of the *genrō* structure was the consequence of the unique decision-making situations facing the government and its leaders in the years following the Meiji Restoration of 1868. At the same time, analysis of this structure through the application of concepts derived from decision-making and organizational theory may indicate the general validity of these concepts for explaining in part the emergence of historical decision-making structures.

On a more specific level, it is the aim of this analysis to indicate through the use of data relevant to both the emergence of decision-making structures and the Japanese bureaucracy, some of those factors which led to the emergence of that unique institution known as the *genrō*. The major concern here, then, is to attempt to determine what conditions made it possible for an informal collegial structure, for which no institutional precedent existed, to evolve as the primary structure of decision and policy-making and political integration. To this extent it should be made clear that this analysis is *not* concerned with elucidating the mode of decision-making and the means by which these decisions were made binding, or any of the other functions of the *genrō* structure. Rather, we are concerned here with attempting to determine the most salient features of decision-making issues which affected and formed the structure and process of decision-making in the period 1868-1900. It is of the greatest importance to bear in mind this distinction between structure and function. Since the functions of any specific structure may undergo modification and change over time, examination of functions alone cannot indicate with any degree of accuracy when or under what conditions the structure first appeared. For this reason the emphasis of this analysis is placed on the structural characteristics of the *genrō* and the attempt to indicate the conditions under which such a structure could emerge.

The *genrō*, as it is usually described in the literature, was an informal structure consisting of, at first, seven men: Kuroda Kiyotaka (1840-1900), Matsukata Masayoshi (1835-1924), Saigō Tsugumichi (1843-1902), Oyama Iwao (1842-1916), Itō Hirobumi (1841-1909), Inoue Kaoru (1836-1915), and Yamagata Aritomo (1838-1922). Two others, Saionji Kimmochi (1849-1940) and Katsura Tarō (1848-1913), are usually described as later additions to the group. All of the original seven members between them, at one time or another prior to 1900, held all the major posts in the civil and military bureaucracy and the government. The origins of this group in the bureaucracy and their continued influence over it made the dividing line between bureaucracy and government almost indistinguishable for the greater part of this period. The general consensus is that the *genrō* did not emerge as a decision-making organization until the early eighteen nineties, apparently operating on the basis of an informal but consistent set of rules—equality of participation and voting, equal access to information, and acceptance of a majority decision as binding on all members.[2] The *genrō* acted as the primary day-to-day and long range decision-making body until approximately 1900, when the original seven members retired from active participation in governmental administration but continued to play a major role in determining long-range policy and in solving leadership crises in the government and bureaucracy. Their role in these areas weakened as their ranks were thinned by old age and death. By the mid-nineteen twenties the structure ceased to exist except in the person of Prince Saionji who acted primarily as a kind of political referee-advisor for the next two decades.

The most significant structural characteristics of the *genrō* as they appear in this brief resumé may be summed up in the following manner: 1) it was an informal structure having no legal constitutional or organizational status; 2) it was a structure originating in the bureaucracy; 3) its decisions were binding on the bureaucracy and the government as a whole; 4) as a structural type it could be described as a collegial group and; 5) as a decision and policy-making structure it did not become institutionalized. Assuming that these are the most significant aspects of the *genrō* structure then the problem concerning its emergence may be stated in the following manner: *What factors or variables relating to bureaucratic development combined to produce an informal collegial decision-making structure which was effective for only a relatively short period of time?*

A major difficulty in pursuing this problem is determining what are the significant factors or variables which affect the form of decision-making structures. In this regard a recent analysis of decision-making structural types suggests that two variables in organizational decision-making are crucial in determining the structure or strategy of decision-making.[3] Thompson and Tuden suggest that the form of any particular decision-making structure will in large part be determined by the predominance of agreement or disagreement within the organization with regard to: 1) the hierarchy of preferences or goals and 2) the knowledge available or thought to be available to achieve the expected results.[4] When these two variables are related to each other on the question of agreement-disagreement it is possible to construct a four-fold typology of

---

[2] There is very little evidence available to support or deny the existence of these rules. However, it is difficult to see how any decision-making group in which all the members were approximately equal could operate otherwise. Consistent flouting of any or all of these rules would lead to either dissolution of the group or a state of constant conflict in which decisions could not be reached.

[3] James D. Thompson and Arthur Tuden, "Strategies, Structures, and Processes of Organizational Decision," in James D. Thompson, *et. al.* (eds.), *Comparative Studies in Administration* (Pittsburgh: 1959), pp. 195-216.

[4] *Ibid.*, p. 197.

decision issues the persistence of which largely determines the structure of decision-making. Most relevant to this discussion is the situation in which a hierarchy of goal preferences is generally agreed upon in an organization but where knowledge or beliefs about causation are disputed or uncertain.[5] In the absence of clear proof of the merits of one alternative over another in achieving desired results the organization must rely on judgment. In this kind of decision situation the structure most likely to emerge is one emphasizing "wisdom" as the major criterion for choosing the decision-makers. The structure, ideally, will be made up of wise and knowing men capable of making judgments as to which kinds of knowledge or systems of cause and effect will produce the results inherent in the goal preferences. These men, if conflict is to be avoided must obey at least the following rules: 1) they must be faithful to the agreed upon scale of goal preferences; 2) all members must be able to participate in each decision; 3) pertinent information on how to achieve goals must be routed to each decision-maker; 4) each member must have roughly equal influence over the final choice and; 5) the group must abide by the decision of the majority. It is this structure, decision-making by a collegial group, such as juntas and boards of regents, which appears to approximate most closely the *genrō* as a decision-making structure. If this typology is valid, then we may assume that the

---

[5] The remaining three types may be described as follows: 1) *Decision by Computation* —when there is agreement on goals and when knowledge is available or believed to be available, decision-making is a technical or mechanical matter. The solution appears to be largely a matter of common sense. The structure emerging from such a situation will be one of specialists, one for each computational problem that can be anticipated. Their behavior will tend to be constrained by the following rules: a) specialists are constrained from making decisions on issues lying outside their competence; b) each specialist is bound to the organization's hierarchy of preferences; c) all pertinent information must be routed to each specialist; d) every issue must be routed to the appropriate specialist. Such a structure closely approximates the Weberian rational-legal bureaucrate type. It should also be noted that computational decision-making may also exist in situations dominated completely by traditional and customary behavior. Thus, in a relatively undifferentiated and diffuse social system where custom and tradition fix the goals and the means for achieving them, decisions are a mechanical matter. However, since custom and tradition rather than economy and efficiency are dominant norms, different types of structures emerge depending on the content of tradition and custom. 2) *Decision by Compromise*—when there is agreement on knowledge and its expected consequences but not on goal preferences, a bargaining or compromise structure is likely to emerge since the only alternative to conflict is arriving at a common preference. Since bargaining or compromise involves detailed and subtle exploration of the different goal preferences, the decision unit must be small enough to permit sustained exchange. At the same time the unit must be large enough to include all important factions. The type of structure which emerges is some kind of representative organization embodying the following rules: a) each faction must be represented in the structure; b) each faction must have as its top preference the desire to reach agreement; c) each faction must have veto power and; d) each faction must be given all pertinent information regarding the means to achieving varying preferences. 3) *Decision by Inspiration*—when there is neither agreement on preferences or on knowledge and its expected consequences or pertinent knowledge is simply not available, the result is likely to be organizational breakdown leading to the emergence of a charismatic leader who by his personal mystique is able to impose his own goal preferences and create or decide what knowledge and/or kinds of knowledge are most pertinent to achieve these goals. It is for this reason that charismatic organizations are notoriously unstable. Knowledge is contested or unavailable and consequently the chances of a charismatic leader making major policy blunders are very great.

emergence of the *genrō* structure is a consequence of the persistence of a decision-making situation in which goals were agreed upon but consensus about knowledge and its consequences was lacking and/or where sufficient knowledge was unavailable. On the basis of this assumption we may then propose, in a more specific manner, that the emergence of the *genrō* can be attributed primarily to the presence of agreed upon goals and the absence of consensus concerning knowledge and/or sufficient relevant knowledge in that organization in terms of which the *genrō* acted and made binding decisions—the bureaucracy, especially the civil bureaucracy. Is this in fact the case? Essentially then the basic problem which emerges is to determine whether this type of decision-making situation existed.

With regard to goal preferences, the existing literature tends to agree that by approximately 1880 a consensus on goal preferences had been arrived at within the bureaucracy and therefore within the government, the two being indistinguishable prior to 1889.[6] The departure of Saigō Takamori and his followers from the bureaucracy in 1873 over questions of policy with regard to Korea, the departure from the bureaucracy by 1873 of the great majority of court nobles and former *daimyō*, and finally the victory of government troops over a samurai army in the Satsuma Rebellion of 1877, eliminated all traditional and alternative views of goal preferences. By 1880 it is clearly evident that internal development rather than external expansion was the primary goal. More specifically, internal development was embodied in the following preferences: industrial development as opposed to agricultural development, political centralization as opposed to political particularism, military development as opposed to military adventurism, and the achievement of equality in international relations through elimination of the "unequal" treaties. It is important to note that all of these goals involved the use of Western institutional models and the utilization of Western systems and categories of causation or knowledge since no other meaningful alternative models of development then existed. Against the background of the emergence of these preferences evolved the problem of making day-to-day and long range decisions consonant with these preferences.

Turning now to the problem of whether there existed a consensus on knowledge and its expected results and whether related knowledge was available, we may examine this question through analysis of the educational backgrounds of those in the civil bureaucracy who participated most directly in the decision-making process.[7] This approach is based on the view that: 1) consensus on knowledge and its expected consequences in an organization will be directly related to the degree of uniformity of education and knowledge possessed by those most directly involved in the decision-making process and; 2) availability

---

[6] In English see for example Hugh Borton, *Japan's Modern Century* (New York: Ronald Press, 1955), pp. 93-110. In Japanese this view is summed up well by Oka Yoshitake, "Seiji," in Yanaihara Tadao (ed.), *Gendai Nihon shoshi* (Tokyo: 1952), I, pp. 70-77.

[7] The civil bureaucracy is the focus of this analysis primarily because given the goal preferences which emerged by the early eighteen eighties nearly all of the major decisions and their implementation took place within the civil bureaucracy.

of pertinent knowledge in an organization will be directly related to the possession of knowledge relevant to the goal preferences of the decision-makers.

METHODOLOGY AND DATA

For the purposes of this analysis the term "education" is defined broadly as the acquisition of knowledge considered by the society to be appropriate for the preparation of the individual for the assumption of his adult role. The focus of this analysis is on governmental-administrative roles and consequently our concern is limited to education considered appropriate to the assumption of this role type. During the period under consideration there were two types of education which were considered appropriate to the assumption of high governmental administrative roles. The first of these, Confucian-dominated moral education, combined with traditional military training, was the mode of education considered necessary for those eligible for governmental administrative roles in the Tokugawa period (1615-1868) when the vast majority of those in administrative positions between 1868 and 1900 were educated.[8] Since eligibility for administrative roles prior to 1868 was limited to those of samurai status, education for administrative roles took place primarily in the domain schools created for the purpose of providing this class with minimal preparation for assumption of these roles. The second type of education came to be considered increasingly appropriate in the last half-century of the Tokugawa period. Known as *jitsugaku* or education for practical affairs, the content of this education became, in the last years of the Tokugawa, increasingly associated with Western knowledge and education.[9] With the advent of the Meiji Restoration in 1868, Western-style education, with its emphasis on techniques and technology, came to supersede the traditional educational style. By the early eighteen eighties, a nationwide structure of Western-style education had come into existence.[10] Recognition of Western-style education as the only appropriate preparation for governmental-administrative roles came with the establishment of the civil service examination structure in 1887. The examinations, passage of which become the major means of entrance to the higher civil service, were based completely on Western categories of legal and jurisprudential knowledge and assumed a Western-style university education.

Prior to approximately 1887, then, there were two kinds of education and knowledge which were considered appropriate for the assumption of governmental-administrative positions. The vast majority of those most directly involved in decision-making in the period 1868-1900 thus had acquired and

---

8 For a description of this education see Ronald Dore, *Education in Tokugawa Japan* (Berkeley, California and London: 1965).

9 Harry D. Harootunian, "*Jinsei, Jinzei, and Jitsugaku:* Social Values and Leadership in Late Tokugawa Thought," in Bernard S. Silberman and Harry D. Harootunian (eds.), *Modern Japanese Leadership: Transition and Change* (Tucson, Arizona: 1966), pp. 83-86.

10 For a description of this development see Karasawa Tomitarō, *Nihon no kyōikushi* (Tokyo: 1955). Also Herbert Passin, *Society and Education in Japan* (New York: 1965).

completed their education in a period when not one but two types of education and knowledge were considered as appropriate for the assumption of their roles. To the extent that this description is basically correct, then two propositions may be suggested for examination: 1) there will be significant differences in the types of education and knowledge possessed by those most directly involved in the decision-making process. More specifically, we should expect to find significant numbers in both samples with Western education in addition to or instead of traditional education.[11] 2) There will be a relative scarcity, given the goals which emerged by the early eighteen eighties, of relevant knowledge among those most directly involved in the decision-making process. We should, therefore, expect to find very few in either sample with the type of education which came to be considered as appropriate for those assuming decision and policy-making roles in the civil bureaucracy after 1887—education culminating in a degree from a university with a Western-style curriculum. On the basis of these propositions the analysis is concerned with only two kinds of data: a) type of knowledge and education (traditional—Western) acquired before the assumption of a position in the civil service by those most directly involved with the decision-making process, and b) the possession of a Western-style university education by those most directly involved in the decision-making process.

In this analysis "those most directly involved in the decision-making process" are defined as those occupying the highest administrative positions in the Japanese civil service in the period 1868-1900. More specifically the group chosen for analysis is limited to those holding the positions of cabinet minister, vice-minister and prefectural governor. The selection was made on the basis of several considerations: Ministers and vice-ministers were those who, by virtue of their positions, were most directly involved in the decision and policy-making process.[12] Prefectural governors, who held approximately the same civil service rank as vice-ministers, were those most directly involved with decision and policy-making in terms of implementation of decisions made at the central level of administration. Since ministers—vice-ministers-represented one level and type of decision-making and prefectural governors another, they were treated as two distinct groups.

Analysis of these two groups is based on samples chosen at random within each group. Sample I (ministers, vice-ministers) is composed of a 50 percent random sample of 76 chosen from an incumbent population of 152.[13] Sample II

---

[11] Western education is defined in this context as the knowledge of a Western language and/or knowledge of some aspect of Western categories of science, military or civil technology, economics, political economy and law, or residence and/or travel in the West for a period of six months or longer. Traditional education is defined as knowledge acquired through attendance at domain, Bakufu or court schools to the exclusion of all Western knowledge as defined above.

[12] It should be noted that prior to 1900 all cabinets with the exception of the short-lived Okuma-Itagaki cabinet of 1898 were bureaucratic cabinets, that is, all ministers were drawn from the bureaucracy.

[13] The incumbent population was determined from the following sources: Ijiri Tsunekichi, *Rekidai kenkanroku* (Tokyo: 1925); Shishido Shinzan, *Meiji shokkan enka-kuhyō* (Tokyo: 1886-93), 19 vols.; Naikaku Insatsukyoku, *Shokuinroks* (Tokyo:

(prefectural governors) is composed of a 25 percent random sample of 80 chosen from an incumbent population of 320.[14]

Turning to an analysis of the types of education acquired by the members of the two samples, our expectation is that there will be significant numbers within these two groups who possessed traditional education only and significant numbers who possessed some type of Western education instead of, or in addition to, traditional knowledge. Examination of the two samples on the basis of this question indicates that our expectations are fulfilled. The data presented in Table 1 suggests that in both samples there were significant variations in the types of education and knowledge.

TABLE 1
Type of Education of Upper Civil Servants, 1868-1900

	Education					
	Traditional		*Western*		*N.A.*	
	N	%	N	%	N	%
Sample I	23	30.3	46	60.5	7	9.2
Sample II	58	72.5	18	22.5	4	5.0
Samples Combined	81	52.0	64	41.0	11	7.0

The presence, in significant numbers, of both types of education indicates very strongly that there was a lack of consensus with regard to knowledge and its expected consequences within the civil bureaucracy.

The lack of uniformity and its suggested corollary, a lack of consensus, is brought into sharper focus when it is noted that there was considerable variation in the way traditional and Western knowledge was presented and acquired. While the curriculum of the domain schools focused around moral education and thus achieved a certain level of uniformity, the quality and resources of the schools

1886-1900), annual. Biographical data was obtained from a large number of sources of which the major ones are: Heibonsha, *Dai jinmei jiten* (Tokyo: 1957-58), 10 vols. in 5; Igarashi Eikichi, *Taishō jinmei jiten* (Tokyo: 1914); Ishin Shiryō Hensankai, *Gendai kazoku fuyō* (Tokyo: 1929); Jinki Kōshinjo, *Jinji kōshinroku* (Tokyo: 1903, 1908, 1911); Shibusawa Eiichi, *et al.* (eds.) *Meiji Taishōshi: jinbutsu hen* (Tokyo: 1930), vols. 13-15; Teraishi Masaji, *Tosa ijin den* (Tokyo: 1923), 2 vols.; Osatake Takeshi, *Bakumatsu ishin no jinbutsu* (Tokyo: n.d.); Yamaguchi Ken Jinkai, *Yamaguchi ken jinbutsu shi* (Tokyo:1933), 3 vols.; Araki Kuwano, *Kumamoto ken jinbutsu shi* (Tokyo: 1959). In addition to these a large number of other regional biographical dictionaries, prefectural histories and biographies were utilized.

[14] The population was determined on the basis of: 1) all those who were appointed by the central government as governors of officially designated prefectures in the period May, 1868 to December 31, 1899; 2) the exclusion of the 273 *daimyō* who retained their positions until their domains were reorganized and amalgamated into new prefectures by the end of 1871. The population was determined from the following sources: Ijiri, *Rekidai kenkanroku;* Naikaku Insatsukyoku, *Shokuinroku,* 1886-1900; Naikaku Kiroku Kyōku, *Meiji shokkan enkakuhyō.* The biographical data were derived for the most part from sources identical with those used for Sample I.

varied with the wealth and resources of the domain. Furthermore, since the predominant principle of domain school organization was personal discipleship, there was quite probably considerable variation in the approach to traditional knowledge. Lack of uniformity was much more marked in the case of Western knowledge. Prior to the early eighteen seventies, schools teaching Western studies had no uniform curriculum. Although there were several private and domain schools which taught "Dutch" and Western studies in the eighteen fifties and eighteen sixties, the teachers' knowledge of Western subjects was far from proficient and was indeed haphazard.[15] This would seem to suggest that even among those who had acquired some Western knowledge, there was a lack of consensus as to what would be the consequences of the application of the knowledge they possessed.

In view of these data it must be concluded that among those most directly concerned with decision and policy-making in the period 1868-1900 there was quite probably a lack of consensus with regard to knowledge and its expected consequences. Generally speaking those with some Western knowledge perceived decision-making increasingly as questions of pertinent technical and rational-scientific knowledge while those with traditional knowledge only continued to perceive decision-making as questions of what customary behavior was applicable.[16]

We have not only suggested that there was a lack of consensus concerning knowledge and its expected consequences but also that sufficient pertinent knowledge was not available. The absence of an institutionalized system of Western-styled higher education prior to the eighteen seventies indicates that those most directly concerned with decision-making in the civil bureaucracy in the period 1868-1900 did not have, in terms of the agreed upon goals, sufficient knowledge for making decisions and policy in a relatively automatic and "bureaucratic" manner. The lack of sufficient pertinent knowledge can be viewed in two ways. First, from the view of the impartial observer, the educational structure and the institutional availability of Western knowledge were not capable of providing enough trained personnel to engage in a program of industrial, military and political development designed to insure Japan's autonomy vis-à-vis the Western powers. Nor did Japan, at this point have the facilities to produce technicians and experts of a sufficient level of sophistication to carry out extensive programs of development. That this is, in fact, the case is indicated by the great number of foreign experts in almost every field hired by

---

15 Ronald Dore, *Education in Tokugawa Japan*, pp. 160-75.

16 This conflict is perhaps best exemplified by the split among government leaders in 1873 over the so-called "Korean Question." Saigō Takamori of Satsuma *han* and a number of supporters were convinced that the road to development lay by way of immediate external expansion in the direction of Korea through the use of a traditional samurai army. His attempt to force the new government to undertake this venture in 1873 was foiled by those in the government committed to internal development by means of applying Western technology and techniques. Saigō attempted to put the question to a test in 1878 by raising an army of samurai in Satsuma and challenging the new Western-style conscript army. The government's victory was a major milestone in proving the wisdom of the commitment to Western knowledge and internal development.

the new government to provide technical training and aid in the various programs of development.[17]

Secondly, the question of what sufficient knowledge consisted of may be seen from the point of view of the Japanese themselves. The institution of the higher civil service examination system in 1887 which presumed a university education emphasizing expertise in Western jurisprudence and law is perhaps the best indication of what knowledge the Japanese leaders felt sufficed to assume high administrative roles. The question then emerges, did the leaders of the civil bureaucracy have the kind and extent of training which they came to believe was necessary for assuming the positions which they then held? The data in Table 2

TABLE 2
University Education of Upper Civil Servants, 1868-1900

	University		Non-University		N.A.	
	N	%	N	%	N	%
Sample I	4	5.0	65	86.0	7	9.0
Sample II	2	2.5	74	92.5	4	5.0
Samples Combined	6	5.0	139	88.0	11	7.0

clearly indicates that this was not the case. Among ministers and vice-ministers (Sample I) during the period 1868-1900 only four (5%) could be said, with any certainty, to have had a university education of the type required for high administrative positions after 1887. Only two (2.5%) prefectural governors (Sample II) had a university education of the type required. From these two types of evidence—the widespread hiring of foreign advisors prior to 1900 and the absence of university education in general among the decision-makers—it may be concluded that members of the highest ranks of the upper civil service did not possess enough of the right kinds of knowledge to made decisions in a relatively automatic and "bureaucratic" fashion; and therefore decision-making was primarily a question of judging as to which kind of knowledge would achieve desired results and where to go to acquire such knowledge.

From these data on educational background, several tentative conclusions may be presented. First, if the specific conclusions regarding lack of consensus on knowledge and its expected consequences and lack of sufficient relevant knowledge are basically correct, then we must conclude that decision and

---

17 In the area of government and administration, the lack of expertise and of even general knowledge was reflected in the journeys of high civil servants to Europe in the eighteen seventies and eighteen eighties, especially Germany, to seek guidance in creating a viable centralized administrative system. Subsequently, a number of German constitutional and administrative experts, most notably Hermann Roesler and Albert Mosse, were brought to Japan to teach and provide technical aid in developing the administrative system and the governmental structure. See Suzuki Yasuzō Kempō seitai to Roesler (Tokyo: 1942); Suzuki Yasuzo, *Kempō rekishiteki kenkyū* (Tokyo: 1934). Also see the recent and most definitive study of the establishment of the Meiji Constitution. Inada Masatsugō, *Meiji kempō seiritsushi* (Tokyo: 1960-62), 2 vols.

policy-making were basically questions of judgment. That is, judgments had to be made as to what kind of knowledge (traditional or Western) was to be used and within this choice, in the absence of sufficient knowledge, what course was to be followed to acquire the knowledge necessary to achieve a given goal. In view of this situation, what alternatives were available? For several reasons such judgments could not be made by a single individual. To place such enormous power in the hands of one man would have required widespread belief in and acceptance of his abilities to make such judgments. In Japan in the period after 1868, there was no one who, by his training or charismatic qualities, could qualify for this type of commitment. Perhaps more important was the restraint laid upon the appearance of such a leader by the position of the emperor. The emperor represented a kind of institutionalized charisma—an individual who was assigned, by virtue of ascription and tradition, all those qualities of the charismatic leader. No challenge to this symbol could be presented without undermining the legitimacy of the Restoration and the new government. Furthermore, the Meiji Emperor was not equipped either institutionally or by education to make necessary decisions about day-to-day administration or long range policy. By virtue of his exalted origin and position, the Emperor could not be allowed to make mistakes in decision and policy-making. The only manner in which the Emperor could be kept from making mistakes was to exclude him, with the exception of keeping him informed, from the decision and policy-making process. Others had to bear the onus of actual authority and responsibility. Nor, even if the institutional restrictions on the Emperor's ability to participate significantly in making decisions were absent, did his traditional court education make it possible for him to make decisions in terms of the goals which had emerged by the early eighteen eighties. In effect, then, judgmental decisions could not be made by the Emperor or any single individual.

Since decision and policy-making could not rest in a single individual, it, perforce, had to be a group function. For several reasons the group had to be small and collegial rather than large and representative in character. First, since there was an absence of consensus within the bureaucracy with regard to knowledge and its consequences and a lack of sufficient pertinent knowledge, even though there was general agreement on goals, the basic problem of decision-making was judging which system of knowledge was most likely to achieve the required results and in the absence of relevant knowledge how to go about acquiring such knowledge. These judgments, in the absence of a single leader, would have to be made by a group of men who were relatively equal in terms of status and prestige. The equality of the "judgers" imposed certain rules or restraints on the behavior of the participants or acceptable judgments could not be arrived at. The minimal rules are those enumerated earlier—equality of participation, voting and access to information, commitment to the agreed upon goals, and acceptance of majority decisions. Secondly, since the goals and their priority ranking had been decided and agreed upon within the ranks of the upper civil and military bureaucracy, all others had to be excluded since there was no assurance that nonbureaucrats would be or would remain committed to the goal preferences.[18] One might also suggest that, insofar as this conclusion is correct, a major reason for delimiting the powers of the Diet and establishing the independence of the Cabinet from the Diet was to insure the predominance and integrity of the goals which the bureaucracy had decided upon.[19] Third, the group making the most significant decisions had to be limited to those within the civil and military bureaucracy with the highest status and prestige or their decisions would be disputed by their peers and subordinates. Fourth, the group had to be small enough so that decisions could be made quickly. Often overlooked, speed in accomplishing national autonomy, independence and power vis-à-vis the Western powers was a factor which permeated every aspect of decision-making. Too large a group a decision-makers would inevitably have slowed the entire process of decision-making and development. For these reasons, then, the ultimate decision and policy-making group had to be collegial and of bureaucratic origin, and within this group had to be limited to those with the highest prestige and status so that their judgments would be binding on the civil and military bureaucracy.

The latter criterion immediately raises the question as to what constituted high prestige and status within the bureaucracy. This might be answered tentatively by examining the seven men who became clearly identified as the more or less permanent members of the *genrō* in the eighteen nineties and projecting on this basis. All seven were among the most active of those from the two most influential domains (Satsuma and Chōshū) involved in the Restoration Movement and all held positions in the new government from the very beginning. Being on the "right" side in the Restoration Movement and committing themselves to the new government endowed them with an aura of wisdom and foresight and coming, as they did, from two of the most powerful domains added further to their prestige. Since there were many others from the same domains who were active in the Restoration Movement, there must have been other delimiting criteria; otherwise, the decision-making group would have been considerably larger. Here we might suggest that in view of the emergence, after approximately 1873, of goals requiring some Western knowledge and education the criteria of prestige and wisdom must also have come to include

---

[18] The emergence of the Jiyūminken or People's Rights Movement in the eighteen seventies from which the political parties in large part evolved made it very evident that nonbureaucrats could not be trusted to support completely the goals which the bureaucracy had decided upon. The Jiyūminken political party leaders had somewhat different goals. In political terms they wanted less centralization of power and in economic terms they tended to support short-term rather than long-term developmental goals. The latter reflected in the demands of the Jiyūtō supporters for lighter land taxes—the major source of government development capital. See Nobutake Ike, *The Origins of Political Democracy in Japan* (Baltimore: 1950), pp. 83-85.

[19] Thus for example Itō Hirobumi, the member of the *genrō* chiefly responsible for framing the Meiji Constitution, pointedly remarked in a speech on June 2, 1899 that:

In the next place we must know the aims and policies of our country. Political parties and others may have their arguments and views about the government, but these must be kept within the bounds of the goals and policies of the government.

Itō Hirobumi, *Itō Kō zenshu* (Tokyo: 1928), II, 144.

some Western knowledge.[20] Indeed all seven of those usually designated as the original *genrō* had acquired by 1875 a comparatively extensive knowledge of the West or of various categories of Western knowledge. From this evidence it is possible to conclude that the criteria for wisdom and prestige were not only being on the right side and from the right domains but also possessing fairly extensive acquaintance with some type of Western knowledge. The combination of these elements in individuals would be rare enough to exclude all but a few. Those remaining would possess as a group a particular constellation of attributes which would, in the eyes of their contemporaries, endow them with sufficient "wisdom" to make judgments as to which knowledge and its consequences might be expected to achieve desired ends.

The suggested criteria for entrance into the group also offers a clue to at least one basic reason for its failure to persist. If a major criterion for entrance into the group was prestige derived from being among the most active participants in the Restoration, then passage of time alone would make it impossible for others to acquire this attribute. A new Restoration Movement could not be reproduced in every generation merely for the sake of providing a test of ability or wisdom. What then could then be substituted? Education and passage of a civil service examination could not be used since these attributes came to be considered as criteria for all those entering the upper civil service after 1887. Furthermore, prestige and wisdom acquired in this fashion was institutional not personal and therefore were capable of being acquired by many. Political party leadership also could not serve since such men were outsiders and could not be relied upon, in the long run, to remain committed to the bureaucracy's hierarchy of goal preferences.

For much the same reasons the *genrō* as a decision-making structure could not be formalized or given legal constitutional existence. To do so would have required an explicit if not formal set of criteria for recruitment. Again, this would have raised the question of what criteria could be used to supplant one that would disappear with time (participation in the Restoration) and another that would be so generalized (Western-style education) as to no longer be sufficiently exclusive. Other problems no less insoluble would also be raised by formalization of the structure. Who would be responsible for choosing successors? Selection by cooptation would have left the members of the *genrō* constantly open to the criticism of dynasticism, self-serving, and even *lese majesté*. Any other method of selection would have opened the possibility that nonbureaucrats might be appointed—precisely that which was to be avoided. Formalization would also have raised major problems of integration in the

---

20 This view is supported by the data on educational backgrounds of those in Sample I (Table I). Two-thirds of this group had some Western knowledge or education—an extraordinarily large number in view of the restricted opportunities to acquire such knowledge. Further support is provided by the fact that by 1873 all of those who left the upper civil service were characterized by traditional education. Bernard S. Silberman, *Ministers of Modernization: Elite Mobility in the Meiji Restoration 1868-73* (Tucson, Arizona, 1964), pp. 50-55.

political structure after the promulgation of the Constitution in 1889 which formalized the cabinet system, the Privy Council, and created a Diet.

If a *genrō* were to exist what would be the function of the Cabinet? This, of course, raises the question of why the *genrō* did not cease to exist after the development of the Cabinet system. In large part this was due to the nature of the Cabinet structure. If the Cabinet were to replace the *genrō* as the primary decision and policy-making body, it would have to be made up of "wise and knowing" men whose decisions would be binding on the bureaucracy. The number of men to whom this epithet could apply was so small that only two alternatives would be left for Cabinet development: 1) either Cabinet posts would be filled by the same men year after year or 2) any new cabinet minister would automatically become and remain a member of the decision-making group even though he no longer held a cabinet post. The problems posed by either alternative were clear. In the case of the former there would have been complete rigidification of the cabinet membership which would have allowed for little flexibility in the recruitment of high level expertise. Furthermore, open identification of the whole group with specific policies would have delimited the ability to change policy since such shifts would be admission of error which might, if sufficient changes occurred, lead to a loss of confidence in the group. [21] The second alternative would have been equally impossible since expansion of the group by a constant flow of new men would have vitiated the effectiveness, status, and prestige of the decision-making group.

In effect, then, given the lack of consensus on knowledge and lack of sufficient relevant knowledge within the higher ranks of the bureaucracy in the period 1868-1900, some type of collegial decision-making structure was necessary. The content of the criteria for entrance into the group required that the structure be informal and at the same time insured its noninstitutionalization and its inability to be integrated into formal structures of decision and policy-making.

At the same time bureaucratic development conspired to undermine the need for the usefulness of the *genrō* structure. By 1900, recruitment into the upper civil service had come to be based primarily on the acquisition of a systematic

---

[21] As it was the constant presence of the *genrō* behind the scenes and the presence of several of their members in every Cabinet but one before 1900 evoked considerable bitterness and some loss of faith in their ability among the second level bureaucrats. Witness Itō Miyoji's comments in his diary in 1901:

Although the *genrō* have controlled politics since 1881, their power today is not what it once was. Nevertheless, the glow of their great achievements lingers so that they are immediately called on whenever a problem arises. This practice was not questioned in the past but now people are tired of these kinds of activities on the part of the *genrō*. Furthermore, without the help of others the efforts of the *genrō* lead to nothing. When they are arrogant and ignore those of the second level and below then it must be said that the *genrō* role in politics will decline. Haven't you and others experienced this kind of treatment for many years? . . . While we must respect the *genrō*, we should allow them to reveal their incompetence to the nation by letting them fend for themselves. Popular support for the *genrō* will disappear and public opinion will demand that the second level statesmen step forward.

As quoted in Kurihara Hirota, *Hakushaku Itō Miyoji* (Tokyo: 1940), p. 353.

and uniform educational experience culminating in graduation from the legal faculty of a university, usually Tokyo Imperial University—an education tested by a uniform system of examinations. This resulted in the emergence of an upper civil service in which there was an extremely high consensus on knowledge and its expected consequences and one in which there was, in terms of the goals, a sufficiency of knowledge. To this extent it was no longer necessary to seek judgments from "wise and knowing" men. It is no coincidence that the *genrō* retired from active day-to-day decision-making after 1900. Nor is it surprising then to find Yamagata Aritomo, the leading member of the *genrō*, writing in 1900 that, "We have reached the point where laws are already highly developed, where there is little room left for arbitrary decisions by officials and where at last administration is becoming a specialized technique."[22] Here Yamagata was admitting that the nature of the bureaucracy had changed drastically in his generation, that decision-making had become increasingly automatic or "computational" and thus no longer required the imminent presence of the *genrō*. In more categorical terms, Yamagata's admission was a reflection of the fact that as a consequence of the development of the bureaucracy into a much more "rational" structure its functions had changed, becoming more inclusive, thus modifying the functions of the *genrō* structure.

In view of the tentative conclusions arrived at here concerning factors contributing to the emergence of the *genrō*, we must also conclude that such a decision-making structure emerged considerably earlier than the eighteen nineties, the date usually assigned. Consensus on goals appears to have emerged at least by the early eighteen eighties and probably earlier. This would seem to suggest that a collegial decision-making structure was in existence throughout the eighteen eighties even though its membership was less consistent and not as well reported as it was to be in the eighteen nineties.[23] This conclusion should not be considered as a mere afterthought but rather as the logical end of this mode of analysis. Examination of political functions such as decision-making through analysis of the characteristics of the structures performing these

---

[22] As quoted in Okurashō Insatsu Kyoku, *Gikai seido nanajūnenshi: kenseishi gaikan* (Tokyo: 1963), p.34.

[23] Thus, for example Itō Miyoji in the quote cited in footnote 21 above suggests that the *"genrō* have controlled politics since 1881 . . . ." This conclusion raises the question of why the activities of *genrō* members were given much wider publicity in the eighteen-nineties than in the eighteen-eighties. This may be explained in part by the growing and evident discrepancy between those who formally and those who actually made decisions after the institution of the cabinet system in 1885. After several Cabinets had made their appearance, it became clear that each did not include all those who seemingly held positions of power. Under these conditions it would have been extremely surprising if the newspapers of the period, which had become well developed, had not become curious about the exact status of these men who appeared to have great power and influence but who did not consistently hold office. Their status would have become an even greater object of curiosity by the appointment of several of these men as *genkun* or elder advisors by the Emperor. From this point of view the newspapers' assiduous pursuit, in the late eighteen-eighties and early eighteen-nineties, of the activities of these men is easily understood. I suggest that it was the emergence of this discrepancy which resulted in increased publicity not the emergence of the institution itself.

functions appears to make it possible to specify with greater accuracy the conditions under which various kinds of structures emerge and, consequently when they emerge. With regard to the *genrō* the problem of determining precisely when the conditions described here obtained requires another study which I hope to present in the near future.

The analysis presented here has, I believe, further implications for the study of political development in Japan. Insofar as the conclusions stated above are essentially correct, then we can proceed to examine with greater conceptual clarity such questions as: what was the full range of functions performed by the *genrō* during the full period of its existence, that is, did it also perform interest aggregation, political recruitment, system maintenance and rule application functions in addition to decision-making functions; how did it perform such functions given the collegial nature of the structure; did changes in the functions of the *genrō* structure occur as has been suggested above; under what conditions and when did these changes occur; and finally, what effect did these changes have on other political structures and their functions? These are questions which require further examination and research if we are to have a clear understanding of the nature of political development in the Meiji and succeeding periods.

Finally, on a broader level, to the degree that this analysis is valid it suggests that the structural-functional approach and the typology of decision-making issues and their relationship to the emergence of decision-making structures utilized here is also valid and may be used with especial profit as a means by which we may reexamine the development of political institutions in Japan in the whole modern period.

3. The introduction of industrialists into the British peerage: a study in adaptation of a social institution *

RALPH E. PUMPHREY †

"To create a peer is to invest a line of men with irresponsible power over the Legislature for, it may be, half a dozen centuries.... Such an act is important, we might almost call it solemn."[1] The Parliament Act of 1911 placed definite limits upon the legislative powers of the House of Lords. It was a logical sequel to three reforms of the House of Commons which had brought that body into closer conformity with the composition and spirit of the country. The House of Lords had remained an essentially hereditary institution and, as such, was too little responsive to changes in the political climate of the nation.

Did this mean that the peerage, from which most of the members of the House of Lords were drawn, had been totally unaffected by the changes in the life of the nation during the nineteenth century? Since 1911 Labour peers have been created with a minimum of either wealth or family connections, while other new peers possessing substantial wealth have been "self-made" men from industry and commerce. Much of the pamphleteering literature that preceded the 1911 reform referred in opprobrium to "Beer Barons,"[2] indicating that at

---

* Reprinted from the *American Historical Review*, LXV (October, 1959), pp. 1-16, by permission of the author and the publisher.

† Ralph E. Pumphrey, professor of social work, George Warren Brown School of Social Work, Washington University (St. Louis), received his Ph.D. from Yale University. Professor Pumphrey was one of the founders, and for several years the chairman of the Social Welfare History Group.

1 London *Times*, Aug. 2, 1856, quoted from the Manchester *Examiner*.

2 The origin of this term is not clear. As early as 1851 Sir John Cam Hobhouse, second Bart., a partner in Whitbread and Company, London brewers, received a peerage as Baron Broughton. G. E. C. [George Edward Cokayne], *The Complete Peerage of England, Scotland, Ireland . . .*, ed. Hon. Vicary Gibbs (new ed., 13 vols., London, 1910-53), II, 343-44. Hereafter cited as *CP*. It seems likely, however, that the use of the term was stimulated by the granting of several later titles, namely, Sir Arthur Guinness, second Bart., and his brother Sir Edward Guinness, first Bart., Dublin brewers, respectively created Baron Ardilaun in 1880 (*ibid.*, I, 194-95) and Baron Iveagh in 1891 (*ibid.*, VII, 78-79); also Sir Henry Allsopp, first Bart., and Sir Michael Bass, first Bart., rival brewers of Burton-on-Trent, in 1886 created Baron Hindlip (*ibid.*, VI, 525-26) and Baron Burton (*ibid.*, II, 439-40), respectively.

that time, in the popular mind at least, the nobility was no longer exclusively a landed aristocracy. How valid was such an impression, and to what extent did it arise from the introduction of new families, reflecting the newer bases of economic and social prestige?

Actually, the English nobility had never been a closed caste. The feudal nobility based on military power and prestige became a landed aristocracy transmitting estates, titles, and political power through a system of primogeniture. While death without heirs terminated some lines, others were constantly being started by the exercise of the sovereign's prerogative to summon whom he chose to sit as members of the House of Lords. To be so summoned had always represented the ultimate in upgrading of social status attainable by most Englishmen. Although some people tried to endow all noble families with feudal or aristocratic beginnings, it had long been common knowledge, as Samuel Smiles was quick to point out, that some of these lines had originated with persons who had acquired commercial or industrial wealth, invested heavily in land, and, in two or three generations through marriage and politics, become integrated into the landed gentry.[3]

By the twentieth century this process of gradual assimilation over a period of generations has been so foreshortened for some individuals that they can complete at least its formal aspects in their own lifetimes. Much of this foreshortening took place during the long reign of Queen Victoria. It is our purpose here to review some of the considerations affecting the creation of peerages during the period of nearly seventy-five years from the accession of Victoria in 1837 to the end of 1911, the year that saw the capitulation of the Lords as well as the coronation of George V. Particularly, the family backgrounds and careers of the 463 individuals who received new titles of nobility during these seventy-five years[4] are examined in order to clarify this aspect of the responsiveness of the nobility to the changing times.

---

[3] Samuel Smiles, *Self-Help; with Illustrations of Character, Conduct, and Perseverance* (rev. ed., Boston, n.d.), 232-52. In this chapter on "Industry and the Peerage." as elsewhere, Smiles equates "industry" with the personal characteristics of hard work and perseverance rather than with particular forms of the production of goods, and is concerned to show that by the application of these characteristics persons of low estate could rise to the highest ranks. Except for members of the legal and military professions, none of the persons he cites achieved the peerage themselves, but they established the fortunes on which their descendants ascended the social scale. Among the nonlegal or military peerages mentioned, only those of Lords Overstone and Belper were contemporary examples (see *infra*, fns. 16-19). Nearly all the rest were created between 1600 and 1750. This correlates closely with Habakkuk's argument that the movement of the merchant class to buy land in the late sixteenth and early seventeenth centuries contributed to the strains producing the Civil War. H. J. Habakkuk, "English Landownership, 1680-1740," *Economic History Review*, X (Feb., 1940), 2-17.

[4] Of these, twenty-eight received titles on two occasions, and three received titles on three occasions during the period studied. A total of 497 titles were thus received by the 463 individuals, apart from inherited titles or ones received prior to or following the period studied. Titles of nobility included are duke, marquess, earl, viscount, and baron. Baronet, though hereditary, is not included in this study because it does not confer any right to a seat in the House of Lords. For a more complete discussion of the subject of this article, see the author's unpublished doctoral dissertation "The Creation of Peerages in England,

Many influences affected the granting of titles. Nearly all fall into one of three groups: the requirements of the House of Lords for new members to carry out its constitutional functions; the impulse to give national recognition to great men; and the exigencies of partisan politics.

The House of Lords in the nineteenth century was still a vital participant in the legislative and judicial processes of the Empire. Individuals with special talents in government, business, and forensics were needed to carry on its essential political functions. Especially as the court of final appeal, for the dominions and colonies as well as for Great Britain, the House of Lords required a constant replenishment from among the ablest lawyers and judges of the nation. But the legal profession traditionally had been an open one that provided opportunity, however circumscribed, for social advancement. The limited number of persons of middle- or lower-class backgrounds receiving peerages primarily for their judicial ability during the period studied would hardly have created a popular sense of institutional change.[5]

The granting of a peerage also represented the traditional method by which a grateful sovereign recognized outstanding contributions to the national welfare by statesmen, military leaders, and others. Diplomacy, the army, and the navy had all been, like the law, favorite occupations of scions of the landed gentry and nobility, but had never been reserved exclusively for members of those classes. Hence it was little shock to social standards when such activities enabled some persons to move upward into the nobility without previous high-landed status.[6]

1837-1911," Yale University, 1934, which includes an appendix with annotated biographical data on each of the peerage recipients. Data about individual peers, here not otherwise annotated, was taken from obituaries in the London *Times* or from *CP*.

[5] In all, fifty-four "law lords" received sixty-one titles during the period studied. Of these, fifteen were lord chancellors and sixteen were lords of appeal in ordinary (life peers under legislation first enacted in 1876). The majority came from the gentry, but twenty, or three-eighths, came from commercial or professional backgrounds. Included in the latter group were such eminent jurists as Lord St. Leonards, whose father was a hairdresser (an example cited by Smiles); Lord Romilly, the son of Sir Samuel Romilly, member of a Huguenot merchant family; and Lord Robertson, the son of a Scottish parish minister. The Romilly family was cited as an example "of the facility with which persons of foreign extraction in one or two generations can work their way into the foremost ranks of society." London *Times*, Dec. 24, 1874.

[6] During the seventy-five years, sixty-eight persons received seventy-seven titles for services overseas (diplomatic, administrative, judicial, military, naval); six speakers of the House of Commons received viscountcies upon retirement; and fifteen devoted civil servants received peerages—a total of eighty-nine persons so honored. Of these, twenty-three were already members of the nobility (twenty-two in the foreign service), fifty (including two who afterwards succeeded their brothers in peerages) came from the gentry, and only sixteen, less than one-fifth, came from professional or commercial backgrounds. Among the distinguished noblemen included here were the Marquess of Dalhousie, Governor General of India; the Earl of Elgin, Governor General of Canada; the Marquess of Ripon, first commissioner to settle the *Alabama* claims; the Marquess of Dufferin and Ava, Viceroy of India; and Viscount Downe, who had a notable military record. Those who were not of gentle background included Lords Clyde and Lawrence, military commanders in India during the Mutiny, the first the son of a cabinetmaker and the latter the son of an army officer; Baroness Macdonald, widow of a prime minister of Canada; and Lord Haliburton,

Above all, considerations of party politics were reflected in the creations that occurred sometimes at a trickle, sometimes at a flood of more than twenty per year. Years with numerous creations occurred irregularly, but tended to increase in frequency, so that the average rate, as shown in Table 1, increased from a little over four per year before 1886 to nearly ten per year after 1897.

TABLE 1
Peerages Created, 1837-1911
by Fifteen-Year Periods

Period	Peerages Created	Annual Rate
1837-1851*	62	4.3
1852-1866	62	4.1
1867-1881	105	7.0
1882-1896	125	8.3
1897-1911	143	9.5
1897-1911	497	6.7

* This period is shortened by six months, beginning with the accession of Queen Victoria, June 20, 1837.

If the administration in power was sure of itself, it tended to put a premium on outstanding qualifications, and to give few peerages. Sir Robert Peel, who recommended the creation of only seven titles in five years, wrote to one person who was seeking a peerage:

I am resolved to be very sparing in the grant of civil honours, and, uninfluenced by any personal objects or private wishes, to consider the power of conferring them as a great public trust, to be administered on some public principle, such as, for instance, the strengthening of the Administration by rewarding those who do not hold office, or, in the case of those who do hold office, bestowing honours as the reward of public service, distinguished either by the length and fidelity of it, or by the eminence of such service....
With respect to the advantage to children, my language to my own is, to gain distinction, and establish the claim for honours (if they covet them) by their own personal exertions and public service.[7]

A ministry that had a comfortable majority in the Commons but faced a hostile majority in the Lords had to give serious consideration to "the

---

son of a Canadian jurist, who had risen from service in the commissary department of the army to become Undersecretary for War.

[7] Sir Robert Peel to George R. Dawson, P.C., Sept. 19, 1, in *Sir Robert Peel, from His Private Papers,* ed. Charles Stuart Parker (3 vols., London, 1891-99), III, 431-32. Peel inaugurated a mid-century lull in peerage creations which extended through the administrations of Russell, Derby, Aberdeen, and into that of Palmerston. During more than fourteen years a total of only twenty-eight new titles was created. As for Sir Robert's children, one, the youngest, became Speaker of the House of Commons and was created Viscount Peel on his retirement in 1895. The second viscount was raised to an earldom in 1929.

strengthening of the Administration" by judicious creation of peers. It was generally more liberal in granting titles, although it might adhere to general criteria similar to Peel's. Lord John Russell explained his policy thus:

3.... In my opinion, if [Peel's] course had been followed for fifty years, the House of Lords would have been at an end at that time; for these men of distinguished merit are not, in these days, men of much property; and a House of Lords, the Majority of which neither possess large property nor represent large masses, would be so factious, mischievous, and restless that public opinion would step in and put it down.

4. The real difficulty has arisen from the profusion of Pitt and his successors. In forty-six years they created about forty earls and viscounts and about 120 barons, altogether an addition of 160 to the House of Lords. In this body the Tory element was so predominant that Lord Grey and his cabinet advised the creation of fifty peers at once. We who advised the measure all thought it a very dangerous one, but it was the sequel of the Pitt profusion.

5. Lord Grey and Lord Melbourne remedied the evil to some extent by copious creations. Sir R. Peel again in a quarter of a year's administration made three or four peers. When he returned to power in 1841 he came in as the champion of the cause of Protection, the cause most dear to the House of Lords, and had, therefore, no occasion to make peers.

6. There does not seem to me to be at present any occasion to make a considerable number of peers. But, though it may be very well for you, who have got a comfortable seat in a front row, to call out "Shut the door and don't let any more in," it is not fair to the great body of English, Irish, and Scotch gentlemen to say that they shall ever be excluded from honours unless they command in a field of battle or distinguish themselves in the government of a colony.[8]

Still a third situation prevailed when a prime minister, having majorities in both houses, was nevertheless uncertain of the loyalty of his followers. When the Conservative party split over the repeal of the Corn Laws, most of the leaders sided with Peel and eventually found their way into the Liberal party, leaving to the Earl of Derby and Benjamin Disraeli the difficult task of building a new and well-disciplined political organization. The use that these men made of peerage creations as a means of binding their followers to them was well recognized; but since these followers were, in the first years, primarily landed gentlemen who had not achieved distinction in public life, it was hard to select recipients for titles who measured up to Peel's standards of merit.[9]

---

[8] Lord John Russell to the second Marquess of Westminister, Sept. 9, 1847. Sir Spencer Walpole, *Life of Lord John Russell* (2 vols., London, 1891), I, 458-59. Russell had just recommended the creation of four new peerages which, he pointed out, merely replaced four recent extinctions.

[9] The London *Times* was caustic in its comments on some of these creations. "Sometimes we are inclined to think the Peerage is bestowed on the same principles as give such inestimable value to the Garter,—that merit is carefully excluded from consideration." Aug. 14, 1858. "Three gentlemen of ample landed estate, but of no very remarkable ability . . . have just been raised to the peerage. . . .[It is] reported that the honour has been . . . acknowledged by an ample contribution to the election fund of the party. . . .[They] have

TABLE 2
Peerages Created, 1837-1911
by Fifteen-Year Periods
and by Parties Recommending the Creations*

	Whig-Liberal			Conservative-Unionist		
Period	Years in Office	Titles	Rate/Year	Years in Office	Titles	Rate/Year
1837-1851	9.8	55	5.8	4.8	7	1.5
1852-1866	10.3	42	4.1	2.7	20	7.4
1867-1881	6.9	54	7.8	8.1	51	6.3
1882-1896	6.8	51	7.5	8.2	74	9.0
1897-1911	6.1	71	11.6	8.9	72	8.1
1837-1911	39.9	273	6.8	32.7	224	6.8

*Excludes Aberdeen coalition ministry, 1852-1855, with no creations.

The result of these and other political factors was an increase in new creations which is shown in relation to the parties recommending them in Table 2. [10] While the prime ministers of both parties knew that almost every honors list might call forth accusations of "lavish creations," they all faced the demands of individuals for recognition and, in the case of the Liberals, urgent need to strengthen the party in the upper house.[11]

For the total period each group was in office, the Whig-Liberals and the Conservative-Unionists had identical annual rates of creations. Both parties showed substantial increases but, due to Peel's austerity, that of the Conservatives was the more striking. Consistently, an increase or decrease in the Conservative rate was reflected by an increase or decrease in the Liberal rate in the following period.

Who were the recipients of these peerage titles? To what extent did they violate traditional qualifications for such high honors? In Table 3 an attempt is made to classify them according to the degree to which they previously had been associated with the nobility. Three out of ten, already members of the

done little more for their country than bestow upon it the honour of witnessing their birth, their education, and the uniform flow of their tranquil and prosperous lives." Apr. 26, 1859. "They all belong to the seminoble order of baronets . . . are all . . . wealthy; and they are all Members of Parliament . . . whose names call up all that is most unyielding in Toryism. . . .It is pleasant to see unshrinking fidelity to party rewarded." Mar. 17, 1868.

[10] This increase should be judged partly in relation to the increase in the total population. From 1841 to 1911 the United Kingdom increased nearly 70 per cent, while Great Britain alone, excluding Ireland, increased over 125 per cent.

[11] In the vote of 1893 on the Home Rule bill, the Liberals had a majority against them in the Lords of 419 to 41. The thirteenth Earl of Pembroke, himself a Conservative, recognized the possibility that such a disparity would lead to the abolition of the House of Lords. He wrote: "It must never be forgotten that, whenever the House of Lords comes to be seriously regarded by the country as the mere instrument of the political party which happens to predominate within its walls, its doom is sealed. The party to which it is hostile will sweep it away the first time that it obtains a large majority at the polls, and there will be no one to say it nay." "Reform in the House of Lords," *Nineteenth Century*, XVII (Feb., 1885), 247.

TABLE 3
Individuals Receiving Peerages, 1837-1911
According to Family Background

Period	Total	Nobility	Gentry	Other
1837-1851	60	27: 45%	27: 45%	6: 10%
1852-1866	58	23: 40%	25: 43%	10: 17%
1867-1881	103	42: 41%	45: 45%	15: 14%
1882-1896	118	26: 22%	51: 43%	41: 35%
1897-1911	124	16: 13%	55: 44%	53: 43%
1837-1911	463	134: 29%	204: 44%	125: 27%

nobility,[12] were receiving augmented honors. More than two-fifths were members of the gentry[13] —sometimes intermarrying with the nobility, sometimes in distant succession to titles—but they never had a sure claim to any hereditary title higher than the seminoble baronetcy that did not carry with it a seat in the House of Lords. The remaining fourth came from other backgrounds which would not customarily have brought close social relations with the nobility.[14]

In each period between 43 and 45 per cent of all those receiving titles came from backgrounds classified as "gentry." A few of these maintained commercial or banking connections which they had inherited along with a landed status acquired during the previous generation or two. But most came from well-established landed and professional families, many closely related by blood or marriage to the nobility. The gentry, then, were an intermediate group between the nobility and the "other" classes, with ties in both directions.

The shift in the balance between the nobility and the "other" group is of particular interest. At first the nobility receiving augmented honors outnumbered the "other" group by more than four to one. During the third quarter of the century the ratio remained more than two to one. It would seem that as late as 1881 few "new" families were being introduced into the nobility without a substantial probationary period in the landed gentry. On the other hand, after 1882 the "other" group outnumbered the nobility receiving augmented honors,

---

[12] Those classified as "nobility" include princes and persons who themselves were, or whose children were destined to be, holders of titles that might permit them to sit in the House of Lords without reference to the creations that brought them into this study, namely, princes created royal dukes; nobles in their own rights in the peerages of England, Scotland, Ireland, Great Britain, or the United Kingdom; wives, husbands, and eldest sons of such nobles.

[13] The "gentry" classification includes members of noble families not eldest sons of peers, persons with inherited baronetcies, and persons whose fathers' landed status was indicated in entries in the *Complete Peerage,* in obituaries or other notices in the London *Times,* in J. Bernard Burke, *A Genealogical and Heraldic Dictionary of the Landed Gentry...* (London, various editions appearing under slightly different titles, 1853-1953), or in John Bateman, *Great Landowners of England and Ireland* (4th ed., London, 1883).

[14] The "other" classification includes persons whose fathers, without evidence of substantial landed status, had been engaged in the professions (law, medicine, the church, military), commerce, industry, trades, or labor.

TABLE 4
Individuals Associated with Commerce and Industry
Receiving Peerage Titles (by Ministries)

Ministry		Party *	All New Peers	Recipients from Commerce and Industry			
				Nobles	Gentry	Other†	Total†
1837-1841	Melbourne	W	38	0	0	1: 3%	1: 3%
1841-1846	Peel	C	7	0	1	0	1: 14%
1846-1852	Russell	W	16	0	2	1: 6%	3: 19%
1852	Derby	C	3	0	0	0	0
1852-1855	Aberdeen	W–P	0	0	0	0	0
1855-1858	Palmerston	W (L)	13	0	0	2: 15%	2: 15%
1858-1859	Derby	C	11	0	0	0	0
1859-1866	Palmerston and Russell	W (L)	24	1	2	0	3: 13%
1866-1868	Derby and Disraeli	C	19	0	1	0	1: 5%
1868-1874	Gladstone	L	41	1	3	2: 5%	6: 15%
1874-1880	Disraeli	C	37	1	2	0	3: 8%
1880-1885	Gladstone	L	32	2	2	1: 3%	5: 16%
1885-1886	Salisbury	C	13	1	1	1: 8%	3: 23%
1886	Gladstone	L	9	0	0	2: 22%	2: 22%
1886-1892	Salisbury	C	45	0	2	10: 22%	12: 27%
1892-1895	Gladstone and Rosebery	L	20	0	2	5: 25%	7: 35%
1895-1905	Salisbury and Balfour	U (C)	70	2	8	11: 16%	21: 30%
1905-1911	Campbell-Bannerman and Asquith	L	65	2	5	19: 29%	26: 40%
1837-1911			463	10	31	55: 12%	96: 21%

* C: Conservatives; L: Liberal; P: Peelite; U: Unionist; W: Whig.
† Percentages are of all new peers.

and after 1897 it did so by three to one. Thus, although most persons receiving the honors of nobility possessed inherited landed wealth, by the close of Victoria's reign the doors had been opened to permit persons with other forms of wealth and influence to obtain honors.

A wide range of background and personal qualifications for the peerage characterized the "other" group, which short-cut the steps in the passage between social classes. Some of the noted military leaders and judges whose fathers had been professional men before them were not far removed from the gentry. The real challenge to established patterns was found in those who were raised to the peerage without long-established landed connections but with backgrounds of personal or family activities in commerce and industry. The incidence of these people among the total group of peerage recipients is indicated in Table 4, which also shows substantial numbers of recipients from the nobility and gentry who had commercial or industrial connections of importance.

The first Salisbury ministry in 1885-1886 appears to have been the turning point so far as the introduction of persons with commercial and industrial connections into the peerage is concerned. For the first time, and always thereafter, 20 per cent or more of all recipients had such connections. Furthermore, at least 16 per cent always came thereafter from backgrounds other than the nobility and gentry, a hitherto unprecedented percentage.

Until 1885 there had been only seven new peers with "other" backgrounds who had been associated with commerce and industry. Three of these had come from commercial families,[15] but in each case their public services had been outstanding. Since in the past persons with commercial backgrounds had used the public service as a means of social advancement, and since each of these three died childless, it is doubtful that their elevation to the peerage had much impact on social institutions. Much the same might be said of the three bankers in this group of seven, as two had strong aristocratic family connections and the third exercised an important behind-the-scenes influence on government.[16]

The remaining individual, Edward Strutt, was the only true product of the new industry among the seven, since his grandfather had started the family fortune by a partnership with Sir Richard Arkwright. Edward appears to have devoted much of his time to politics and government rather than the direct management of the family enterprise, but there is little doubt that he was identified in the public mind as one of the great manufacturers of the

---

15 Charles Edward Poulett-Thomson, a younger son in a mercantile family long engaged in the Russia trade, had already had extensive experience in business both at home and abroad when, at the age of thirty-one, he became a member of the government as vice-president of the Board of Trade. Eight years later he was selected to pacify Canada after the rebellions of 1837 and 1838, and his success in unifying Upper and Lower Canada brought him a peerage in 1840 as Baron Sydenham. Unmarried, he died the following year without having returned to England. *CP*, XII, pt. 1, 589-90. Thomas Babington Macaulay, son of a Sierra Leone merchant, was created Baron Macaulay in 1857 and died unmarried in 1859. "Well known as a Whig statesman, he was far more famous as a writer." *CP*, VIII, 327. Edward Cardwell, son of a Liverpool merchant, had had an outstanding parliamentary record of more than thirty years. In 1874, rather than take the leadership of the Liberal party, which Gladstone wished to relinquish, he took a peerage as Viscount Cardwell. John Morley, *The Life of William Ewart Gladstone* (2 vols., London, 1908), II, 78.

16 Samuel Jones Loyd, head of the banking firm of Jones, Loyd and Company, was created Baron Overstone in 1850. He exercised substantial influence as the confidential adviser to Sir Charles Wood, Chancellor of the Exchequer. *The Dictionary of National Biography from the Earliest Times to 1900* (22 vols., London, 1921-22), XII, 225. The peerage became extinct at his death in 1883, but two years later his son-in-law and heir was created Baron Wantage. George Carr Glyn, head of the banking firm of Glyn, Mills, Currie and Company, whose wife was a granddaughter of the first Viscount Doneraile, was created Baron Wolverton in 1869. His father and grandfather had been Lords Mayor of London, and his son was "whip" in the House of Commons from 1868 to 1873. Glyn and his firm were important in financing railways; he was chairman of the London and Northwestern Railway. Leland Hamilton Jenks, *The Migration of British Capital to 1875* (London, 1927), 130 ff.; *The Complete Peerage of England, Scotland, Ireland ...*, ed. G. E. C. [George Edward Cokayne] (8 vols., London, 1887-98), VIII, 196. Hereafter cited as *Old CP*. Sir Dudley Coutts Marjoribanks, first Bart., first cousin of David Robertson, who had been created Baron Marjoribanks in 1873, was created Baron Tweedmouth in 1881. His father had been a partner in the Coutts Bank for seventy years. *Old CP*, VII, 441.

country,[17] the first of them to receive a peerage. Contemporary comments indicate the recognition given the event:

We have much pleasure in announcing that it is Her Majesty's gracious intention to elevate the Right Hon. Edward Strutt, late M.P. for Nottingham to the Peerage, with the title of Lord Belper—a name which will ever be identified with the manufacturing industry of the country, as well as with the family of the right hon. gentleman, by whose enterprise it was first raised to importance.[18]

A few days later the London *Times* quoted at length from the Manchester *Examiner:*

It is as a manufacturer, and to mark the interest which the Queen takes in the manufacturing pursuits of the country, that Mr. Strutt is metamorphosed into Baron Belper. As such it is a graceful and prudent act. It shows a wise appreciation of the signs of the times. It is something for those who claim to be regarded as the descendants of the mailed barons of England to admit into their order a man who not only has made but is making his fortune by spindles and looms .... Lord Belper is the first "millowner" who has been elevated to the peerage, but a considerable number of noble lords have long been quite willing to co-operate with our manufacturers and pocket their money.... They have no objection to supply our factories with fuel, and carry our goods to market.... The worst enemy of the peerage could desire nothing better than the perpetuation of the ancient schism between land and commerce, ploughs and spindles.[19]

"One robin does not make the spring," and a quarter of a century passed before, in 1880, "the surrender of feudalism to industry" which the Belper peerage had been supposed to herald was marked by any further peerages granted to persons engaged in manufacturing. Even then the two men so honored had each inherited baronetcies and had married into the higher aristocracy, so that they are here classified as "gentry."[20] It was not until 1886 that three industrialists without aristocratic connections were elevated to the

---

[17] The magnitude of the operations is indicated by a notation that early in the nineteenth century the Strutts installed at their Belper mills a breast-type water wheel forty feet wide and twelve and a half feet in diameter. Eric Hodgins and F. Alexander Magoun, *Behemoth* (Garden City, N.Y., 1932), 21.

[18] London *Times,* July 26, 1856. The patent of creation was issued August 29, 1856.

[19] *Ibid.,* Aug. 2, 1856. The acceptance of this millowner's family into the aristocracy received its ultimate confirmation in 1937, when Edward Strutt's great-granddaughter, daughter of the third Baron Belper, married the Duke of Norfolk. London *Times,* Jan. 7, 28, 1937.

[20] Sir Ivor Bertie Guest, second Bart., created Baron Wimborne in 1880, was head of the Dowlai Ironworks, which had been in the family since 1747. His mother was the daughter of the ninth Earl of Lindsey; his wife, the daughter of the seventh Duke of Marlborough and sister of Lord Randolph Churchill. London *Times,* Feb. 23, 1914. Sir Arthur Edward Guinness, second Bart., a brewer, was created Baron Ardilaun in 1880. His wife was a daughter of the third Earl of Bantry. See fn. 2.

peerage[21] to inaugurate a period when such men would be found in increasing numbers and in larger proportion to all the new peers being created.

After 1885 persons connected with commerce and industry represented, on the average, nearly a third (31.1 per cent) of all the new peers, compared with one tenth (10.4 per cent) previously. Among these, those without noble or gentle backgrounds now were more than a fifth (21.6 per cent) of all new peers, compared with less than 3 per cent before. Among these new peers a wide range of commercial and industrial activities was represented—railways,[22] armaments and machinery,[23] the publication and dissemination of news,[24] metallurgy and chemicals,[25] shipping,[26] textiles,[27] building,[28] mining,[29] brewing,[30] and others, as well as the traditional banking and mercantile interests.

Some among the new peerages seemed to indicate that opportunities for an extremely rapid rise in the social scale were increasing. Lord Herschell's father was a converted Polish Jew who became a nonconformist clergyman in London;[31] Lord Mount Stephen,[32] who promoted the Canadian Pacific Railway, and his cousin Lord Strathcona and Mount Royal,[33] who obtained control of the Hudson's Bay Company, were both obscure emigrants from Scotland who utilized their great business talents to take leading parts in the development of Canada. Lord Pirrie, on the other hand, had been born in Canada but brought back to Ireland after the death of his father. Rising from apprentice to head of the great shipbuilding firm of Harland and Wolff, he

---

21 For Sir Henry Allsopp and Sir Michael Bass, created respectively Baron Hindlip and Baron Burton, see fn. 2. Sir Thomas Brassey, son of a noted international railway contractor, created Baron Brassey in 1886, received an earldom at the coronation of George V in 1911. *CP,* II, 281-83.

22 Barons Mount Stephen (1891), Knaresborough (1905), and Joicey (1906); Viscount Colville (1895, 1902); Earl Brassey (1886, 1911). *CP, passim;* Pumphrey, "Creation of Peerages," 180-85.

23 Barons Armstrong (1887), Kelvin (1892), Rendel (1894), Armstrong (1903), and Merthyr (1911). *Ibid.*

24 Barons Glenesk (1899), Burnham (1903), Northcliffe (1905), and Faber (1905); Viscountess Hambleden (1891). *Ibid.*

25 Barons Swansea (1893), Overtoun (1893), Airedale (1907), Ashby St. Ledgers (1910), and Glenconner (1911). *Ibid.*

26 Barons Inverclyde (1897), Nunburnholme (1906), Pirrie (1906), Furness (1910), and Inchcape (1911); Viscount Ridley (1900); Earl Egerton (1897). *Ibid.*

27 Barons Cheylesmore (1887), Masham (1891), Denleath (1892), Marchamley (1908), Rotherham (1910), and Emmott (1911). *Ibid.*

28 Barons Ashcombe (1892) and Cowdray (1910). *Ibid.*

29 Barons Joicey (1906), Glantawe (1906), Allendale (1906), and Aberconway (1911); Viscount Allendale (1911). *Ibid.*

30 See fn. 2; also Barons Blyth (1907) and Marchamley (1908). *Ibid.*

31 Farrer Herschell, created Baron Herschell in 1886, was Lord Chancellor in the Liberal ministries of 1886 and 1892-1895. His maternal grandfather was a Scottish merchant, so that Herschell "was never a poor man." *Encyclopaedia Britannica,* 11th ed., XIII, 395.

32 George Stephen, created Baron Mount Stephen, 1891. *CP,* IX, 363-64.

33 Donald Smith, created Baron Strathcona and Mount Royal in 1897, having no sons, obtained a new patent of creation for the same title, but with special remainder to his daughter, in 1900. *CP,* XII, pt. 1, 377-79.

moved on to still wider shipping interests and was hailed at his death as a prototype of captains of industry.[34] Lord Glantawe's obituary was headed "A Tinplate Worker's Rise,"[35] while of the Earl of Inchape, "a great ship owner," it was said that "he rose from obscurity to great wealth and position."[36]

What had happened to bring about this sudden increase in the commercial and industrial elements among those receiving peerages? The selection of particular individuals was undoubtedly largely determined by their personalities and careers, and by the tempestuous politics of the period. But, since the obtaining of a peerage usually represented the culmination of a substantial political career, it may be postulated that the observed phenomenon of a substantial increase in the number of persons with commercial and industrial backgrounds elevated to the peerage in the middle and late 1880's was a lagging secondary reflection of a primary change that had occurred at least a political generation earlier. The suddenness of the change in the 1880's might suggest an equally sudden earlier shift, possibly related to the Reform Act of 1867.

Two contemporary comments by astute political writers, as well as the political careers of the recipients themselves, tend to support this point of view. In 1872 Walter Bagehot wrote:

The Reform Act of 1867 has, I think, unmistakably completed the effect which the Act of 1832 began, but left unfinished. The middle class element has gained greatly by the second change, and the aristocratic element has lost greatly.... The spirit of our present House of Commons is plutocratic, not aristocratic; its most prominent statesmen are not men of ancient or of great hereditary estate; they are men mostly of substantial means, but they are mostly, too, connected more or less closely with the new trading wealth.[37]

---

[34] London *Times,* June 9, 1924. William James Pirrie had been created Baron Pirrie, 1906, and Viscount Pirrie, 1921.

[35] *Ibid.,* July 28, 1915. John Jones Jenkins, created Baron Glantawe in 1906, had as a boy followed his father's occupation. He, too, became a proprietor, expanded his activities, became Mayor of Swansea and an M.P. (Liberal, Liberal-Unionist, then Liberal again).

[36] *Ibid.,* May 24, 1932. James Lyle Mackay, created Baron Inchcape in 1911 (a coronation peerage), Viscount Inchcape in 1924, and Earl of Inchcape in 1929, was the son of a small Scottish shipper. He moved ahead rapidly as a youth after assuming exceptional responsibilities while serving as a clerk in the Bombay office of the British India Steamship and Navigation Company of which he became chairman and managing director twenty years later.

[37] Walter Bagehot, *The English Constitution and Other Political Essays* (rev. ed., New York, 1877), "Introduction to Second Edition" (1872), 20. Bagehot was here carrying forward the argument he had previously stated (pp. 231-35) that the impediments to active political participation experienced by commercial and industrial leaders were, in the 1860's, becoming unbearable and contributed to the pressure for reform. See also the description of Edward Bates, the member for Plymouth, in the "London Letter" to the New York *Herald:* "Mr. Bates is a conservative of the new type—a wealthy, one ideaed merchant, who feels that he has a stake in the country, and that he must protect his interests. The House of Commons is just now swamped with such as these. . . .Mr. Disraeli . . . cannot afford to irritate the plutocrats, shippers, merchants, and others who are the backbone of the conservative party." Aug. 8, 1875. This letter, attributed to Edmund Yates, is quoted in R. J. Hinton, *English Radical Leaders* (New York, 1875), 202. However, the persons retiring from active political life and receiving peerages between 1867 and 1886 were carry-overs from the preceding period and the outstanding qualifications of some of them give the

In 1891 the author of the leading article in the London *Times* concurred in Bagehot's judgment:

It is characteristic of modern Conservatism that a man like MR. SMITH should have held his high position in the party. Conservatism in England was wont to be aristocratic, and bound up with the fortunes of the great landed class. The Tories of fifty years ago disliked PEEL; their successors hated DISRAELI, though they were obliged to follow him; and in both cases the origin of the feeling was that the leader was a man who did not belong to the old aristocratic English caste. The modern spirit and the Act of 1867 have changed all that; and our age has seen the Conservative party in the House, and the House itself, following ...with positive affection, a simple man of business, without any pretensions to "family." It is significant that his first entry into the House of Commons should have occurred in 1868, in the very year after the "leap in the dark," and that the reformed constituency of Westminster should have preferred the unknown Conservative who sold books to the famous Liberal—JOHN STUART MILL—who wrote them.[38]

The changes that had been taking place in the economic life of the nation for more than a century and that the political structure reflected through marked changes in the composition of the House of Commons after the Reform Act of 1867 thus began to show clearly in the peerage creations after 1885. But changes in an ongoing, hereditary institution such as the nobility occur slowly. The tendency is to absorb new additions and mold them into the existing pattern. The introduction of less than fifty unlanded families among more than two hundred receiving new creations over a twenty-five-year period, 1885-1911, probably did not by itself greatly modify the body of the nobility, which already consisted of over six hundred families at the beginning of the period. This would be especially true in view of the magnitude of the estates of some of the landed gentlemen who were stepping up into the nobility.[39] One would

---

impression that this was an Indian summer of the aristocracy. During Gladstone's first administration alone, for instance, the list of distinguished persons of noble or gentle family who received peerages included: Barons Lawrence, Howard of Glossop, Acton, Kildare (later fourth Duke of Leinster), Lisgar, Dalling and Bulwer, Blachford, Ettrick (tenth Lord Napier of Merchistoun), Selbourne, Moncreiff, Coleridge, and Cottesloe; Baroness Burdett-Coutts; Viscount Ossington; the Earl of Dufferin; and the Marquess of Ripon.

[38] Oct. 7, 1891. This article was written on the occasion of the death of William Henry Smith, Conservative leader of the Commons. Smith's widow, Emily Danvers Smith, was created Viscountess Hambleden, in recognition of his services. Smith, whose father had been a prosperous bookseller in the Strand, attained great wealth by developing the system of railway bookstalls throughout the country. The *Complete Peerage*, VI, 253, says that, supposedly, the following lines in *HMS Pinafore* referred to his appointment as First Lord of the Admiralty, 1877-1880:

> I always voted at my Party's call,
> And never thought of thinking for myself at all;
> I thought so little they rewarded me
> By making me the Ruler of the Queen's Navee.

[39] It was reputed that Wentworth Blackett Beaumont, created Baron Allendale in 1906, could travel thirty miles in an almost direct line over his own lands, which included important mining properties. London *Times*, Feb. 14, 1907. His son, the second Baron, received a coronation peerage as Viscount Allendale in 1911. *Cp*, XIII, 74.

hardly expect to observe marked changes in the characteristics of the nobility arising from the new creations until the increased rate of commercial-industrial peerages granted by the Liberals after 1905 could have a cumulative effect in the second and third decades of the century.[40]

However, the introduction of "new" families was not the only way in which the nobility could adapt to the times. People in all grades of the landed aristocracy could shift their own patterns and standards closer to those prevailing in other wealthy groups. That this was taking place throughout the nineteenth century is indicated fragmentarily by those persons from the gentry and nobility who received peerages after engaging in one capacity or another in commerce or industry. Two instances serve to point up different ways landed classes were making this adaptation.

The Earl of Ellesmere illustrates the great landlord, with large investments in mining and transportation,[41] whose sense of *noblesse oblige* led him to undertake benevolent activities on behalf of his tenants not unlike those recommended by Disraeli in *Sybil.*[42] Ellesmere was the younger son of the first Duke of Sutherland and heir, through a trust arrangement, to the "princely income" of a large part of the estates, including the Worsley and the Liverpool and Manchester canals with their attendant mining and industrial developments that the Duke of Bridgewater had built up in the last half of the eighteenth century.[43] Egerton built a hundred-thousand-pound residence at Worsley to identify himself with the estates. His brother-in-law Charles Greville, the diarist, after listing all the undesirable features of the surroundings, including canal and railway, chimneys and furnaces, flat clay soil, lack of hunting and society, says: "They have done this and much more from a sense of duty, from fully recognizing the authority of the maxim that 'property has its duties as well as its rights.'" He went on to say that Egerton had had to pay £45,000 to secure the

[40] For a discussion of this trend at the later period, see Harold J. Laski, "The Prime Minister's Honors Lists," *Nation and Athangum,* XXXI (July 15, 1922), 528-29.

[41] See quotation from the Manchester *Examiner* fn. 19. See also David Spring, "The English Landed Estate in the Age of Coal and Iron: 1830-1880," *Journal of Economic History,* XI (Winter 1951). 3-24.

[42] Benjamin Disraeli, first Earl of Beaconsfield, *Sybil; or The Two Nations* (3 vols., London, 1845). The entire novel is devoted to the problem of social relations of the rich and the poor; the activities of the hero, Lord Egremont, resemble those of Lord Francis Egerton.

[43] Lord Francis Egerton, created Earl of Ellesmere in 1846, received only the income, the estates themselves being held in a trust established in 1803 under the will of the Duke of Bridgewater. The trust did not expire, and the then Earl of Ellesmere received full possession of the property until 1903. *Encyclopaedia Britannica,* 11th ed., IV, 558. The extent of the industrial operations in 1837, when Lord Francis took over, is seen in a statement attributed to him: "Everything in which timber and iron are concerned, my people (whom I pay and can remove at pleasure) fashion and provide. We burn lime, supply all railroads with coke, make bricks, boats, etc., etc., all this under my immediate nose. All this, perhaps, would be more economical if done by contract, etc., but I should lose much of the amusement, and all the influence, which it now gives me over the immediate destinies of between three and four thousand people, not to mention mules and horses, which influence I find after all very agreeable to have." Bernard Falk, *The Bridgewater Millions, a Candid Family History* (London, 1942), 162.

resignation of one of the trustees of the estate who refused to cooperate in improving conditions for the laboring class tenants.[44]

Another type of adjustment—perhaps a more significant one in the long run—is typified by the Vivian family, which for more than three centuries had been among the lesser gentry of Cornwall and Devon. The family does not appear at any time to have been very affluent, and at the beginning of the French wars near the end of the eighteenth century an eldest son left the university to enter the army. By purchase, by merit, and by politics he reached the highest ranks in military circles, and eventually received a peerage.[45] In the meantime, the task of managing the family estates devolved upon his younger brother. By hard work and good business management the latter built up a large copper-smelting works which his son Henry expanded still farther until, about 1895, it employed more than five thousand men. As head of such a large establishment Henry's income must have exceeded by far the wildest dreams of his grandfather when that gentleman purchased a commission in the army for his first-born, Henry's uncle. Henry, of course, had much local influence, was drawn into politics, and in also receiving a peerage[46] illustrated the diversity of routes by which men of the same ancestry might achieve upward social mobility.

It is clear that while the passage of the Parliament Act of 1911, with its limitation on the power of the House of Lords to block legislation, sealed the fate of the political power of the nobility, the social structure of the nobility, too, was in a process of change accomplished by internal adjustment as well as by the introduction into it of persons whose power and prestige did not rest on inherited landed wealth. The impression that the aristocracy had become by the beginning of the twentieth century a "middle class institution"[47] is justified by the direction in which the aristocracy was moving rather than by a completed transformation.

------

44 Charles Greville, *The Greville Memoirs (Second Part)*, 3 vols., ed. Henry Reeves (London, 1885), II, 302-306.

45 General Sir Richard Hussey Vivian, first Bart., created Baron Vivian in 1841, had moved from a brilliant career in the Napoleonic wars into twenty years of political-military activity as a Whig M.P. London *Times*, Aug. 26, 1842.

46 Sir Henry Hussey Vivian, first Bart., created Baron Swansea in 1893. London *Times*, Nov. 30, 1894. The attraction of business as a prelude to politics for young men of good social position and high education is discussed in the London *Times*, June 15, 1865.

47 For a succinct statement of this widely held concept, see William Ralph Inge, *The Victorian Age* (Cambridge, Eng., 1922), 52.

PART III

Social history and social change

Until fairly recently, social history has had a perplexing identity problem. In many universities, it was an intellectual hybrid taught in combination with either economic history or intellectual history. If it aspired to a more independent status as a form of cultural history, the difficulties of establishing a separate identity were enlarged by the suspicion that it did not concern itself with "tested and tangible facts," but rather with moods, styles, and other evanescent substances.[1] When social history did deal with the real and extremely tangible facts of daily existence in terms of how people dressed, ate, and how they amused themselves, an equally deep suspicion was generated that it was a trivial subject, best left to popularizers and amateurs. It was perhaps the lack of a wider theoretical perspective that produced the pithy undergraduate definition of social history as "history with the politics and the ideas left out."

That phase of social history's identity crisis seems to have ended. Historians on both sides of the Atlantic are now hailing the emergence of a "new social history" whose object is the study of society in all its complex relationships.[2]

---

[1] Jacques Barzun, "Cultural History: A Synthesis," in Fritz Stern (ed.), *The Varieties of History* (Cleveland: The World Publishing Co., 1956), p. 388.

[2] Compare Ernest Labrousse's remarks in *L'Histoire sociale: sources et méthodes* (Paris: Presses universitaries de France, 1967), p. 4, with Mario S. DePillis, "Trends in American Social History and the Possibilities of Behavioral Approaches," *Journal of Social History*, I (Fall, 1967), pp. 38-60.

What is new about much of the new social history is the extent to which its practitioners are indebted to sociology for many of their theories and concepts.[3] Social groups, social structure, social conditioning factors, social mobility, career-line analysis, to mention some of the more common borrowings, are terms so widely used that a graduate history student would have to be unsophisticated indeed not to have a nodding acquaintance with most of them. In fact, the lack of a theoretical perspective that constituted a problem for earlier social historians is thought by some critics to have been transformed into a problem of too many perspectives.[4] This need not be seen as an insurmountable obstacle but as an opportunity for historians to make a substantial contribution to present-day social theory by including that much-neglected feature—the dimension of time. In any event, the attractions of a wider theoretical framework coupled with more sophisticated analytical tools are an undeniable force in the reevaluation of the tasks and boundaries of the new social history.

The diversity and complexity of the social historian's viewpoint are amply illustrated by the studies in this section. In other contexts, the subjects that here have fallen under the canon of "social history" and "social change" might be regarded as studies in developmental economics, urbanization, or sociocultural mobility, depending on one's social science viewpoint. Yet, they reflect a concern for the history of social movements and for patterns of change in society in terms of their influence on the social order, a basic theme of the new social history.

Unlike some examples of a quantitative analysis, these essays are methodologically straightforward. Their sophistication lies in the choice of materials to be analyzed and in the broad design according to which the analysis is to be accomplished. The data analyzed here are by no means unique: similar material has long been available to historians. However, as Stearns and Tilly, in particular, are at some pains to point out, the level of precision and the consistency with which concepts in social history have been related and analyzed have been traditionally inadequate. This view accounts for the somewhat reconstructive attitude taken by these two authors. While the Smith article does not use a highly complex system of data analysis, it does exemplify the value of certain kinds of information which historians occasionally use in a rather offhanded fashion. Moreover, it is an interesting example of the way in which socioeconomic mobility—in what some historians might consider a relatively narrow arena—may reflect on the broader issues of social change. Stone, on the other hand, deals with the problems of mobility as they relate to very broad issues of social and economic change over an extended period of time. In so doing, he attempts to combine the social scientist's concern for statistical accuracy with the historian's traditional interest in socially significant generalizations.

---

[3] Richard Hofstadter, "History and Sociology in the United States," in Seymour Martin Lipset and Richard Hofstadter (eds.), *Sociology and History: Methods* (New York: Basic Books, Inc., 1968), pp. 14-15.

[4] Mario S. DePillis, *op. cit.*, pp. 45-46.

1. The analysis of a counter-revolution*

CHARLES TILLY†

Just as a theory of heredity which could not account for the occasional appearance of dramatically new genetic traits would be considered incomplete, a theory of revolution, or an analysis of a specific revolution, which provides no understanding of the presence of counter-revolutionary forces in the midst of a society in revolt must leave us unsatisfied. If a theory purports to tell us when and why a society is ready for rebellion, it also ought to tell us which sectors of the society will resist the rebellion, and why. Exceptions prove the rule. Counter-revolutions test our explanations of revolutions.

If this is true, it is of no small interest to examine the ways that historians have handled the problem of counter-revolution. There is no "theory of counter-revolution" as such, but most analyses of counter-revolutions have relied implicitly on general conceptions of the nature of revolution. Almost always, furthermore, the historian's attitude toward the revolution in question has shaped his understanding of the counter-revolution which arose in its shadow.

One might think that everyone would agree with Meusel's description of counter-revolution as "an attempt to reverse the transformations effected in a revolution; its success signalizes the triumph of the upper class, which has been endangered and temporarily displaced by the revolution."[1] Yet this description rests on a particular (if popular) theory of revolution, one which leads to the conclusion that "When a great revolution finally breaks, it encounters virtually no internal opposition; it appears to unite the people rather than to separate them into hostile camps."[2] It no longer seems indubitable that this is the case,

* Copyright © 1963 by Wesleyan University. Reprinted from *History and Theory*, III, No. 1, by permission of Wesleyan University Press and the author.

† Charles Tilly, professor of sociology and history, University of Michigan, received his Ph.D. from Harvard University. He is the author of *The Vendée,* and numerous studies on French history and urban sociology.

[1] Alfred Meusel, "Revolution and Counter-Revolution," *Encyclopedia of the Social Sciences,* XVIII, 368.

[2] *Ibid.,* 371.

even for the most frequently cited model, the great French Revolution. There is accordingly room for doubt about the corollary propositions on the nature of counter-revolution.

One reasonable way to deal with this doubt would be to assemble information about a number of counter-revolutions, in order to discern any uniformities in their personnel, circumstances or organization. That would be an absorbing venture, but it is not the task of this paper. For there is another problem, more obscure but equally interesting, whose outline is flickering in the background. How have historians conceived the problem of explaining counter-revolution, and how have their conceptions of the problem influenced the results they have obtained? If we were lucky enough to stumble onto valid answers to these questions, we would greatly increase our ability to evaluate the available explanations, both general and particular, of revolution and counter-revolution. I wish to present some possible answers to these questions. They are derived very largely from reflection on one major instance of resistance to the French Revolution, and therefore cry out for comparison and correction.

I

The instance is the counter-revolution of the Vendée. Despite the eagerness with which they have disagreed over the origins of the Vendée, historians have commonly agreed on what was to be explained. They have displayed a bent that is at once psychological and judicial, seeking to accumulate evidence on the mentalities and motives of a very limited number of "actors" (consisting of either outstanding personalities or groups seen as moving in unison), and striving by means of judgments of motives to assign responsibility for the events. The motives supplied have often been in the form of articulated beliefs about the nature of the world—ideologies. Perhaps the most important point is that these conceptions of the nature of the problem have strongly influenced the kinds of explanations that have been seriously considered, the forms of historical craftsmanship that have been employed, and the conclusions at which students of the counter-revolution have arrived. There are other ways of defining the problem, and they lead to other sorts of explanations, other methods of dealing with the available documents, even to somewhat different conclusions. I shall attempt to substantiate this claim by displaying the results of defining the problem as many sociologists would be inclined to see it.

The case for discussion, the counter-revolution of the Vendée, is important in itself. The first, and probably the most potent, concentration of provincial opposition to the Revolution, the revolt in the West which began in 1793 threatened the work of the new regime, hindered the prosecution of the war, provided the occasion for enactment of some of the terrible legal instruments of the Terror, and intermittently distracted the central government from other tasks until 1799. In the course of the year 1793, there were at one time or another 50,000 to 100,000 rebels under arms in the section of western France south of the Loire. The inhabitants of the area most intensely involved in the counter-revolution—below the Loire—comprised some 2% of the entire population of France. By its sheer bulk, the Vendée rebellion commands attention.

How shall we explain the existence of this massive counter-revolution? The commonsense answer is: find out exactly who rebelled, and then look for evidence of their motives when the rebellion began. This is, in large part, what historians of the Vendée have sought to do.[3] Their agreement on the task at hand does not mean they have reached a happy consensus on the identities of those most responsible, or on their motives. Writers on the Vendée have generally been just as partisan as their zealous protestations of impartiality would lead a cynic to suspect. Yet until the very recent and very important work of Paul Bois, they had uniformly sought to place the *responsibility* for the Vendée on one group or another.[4] This was true whether they thought this responsibility a badge of honor or a mark of shame. To assign the responsibility, they undertook the almost-judicial reconstruction of the motives and conscious actions of the relevant groups: the peasants, the nobles, the clergy. It is no great surprise to learn that Célestin Port, in his introduction to his partisan, lively and valuable *Vendée angevine,* presented what he regarded as the most important conclusion of the book in these terms:

For my part, I pursued this study for a long time with the considered prejudice that the whole war had been fomented by the clergy. I have left it with a contrary conviction.[5]

The conviction was that the nobility, by means of a far-flung plot, had done the job themselves. In his change of views, Port had not left behind the assumption that explanation meant finding a responsible group, and proving that responsibility by reconstructing its motives and intentional activities.[6]

---

3 The main works to which the following discussion applies are: H. Baguénier-Désormeaux, *Les origines et les responsabilités de l'insurrection vendéenne* (Fontenay-le-Comte, 1916); Alphonse de Beauchamp, *Histoire de la Guerre de la Vendée* (Paris, 1820), 4 vols.; P. V. J. Berthre de Bourniseaux, *Histoire des guerres de la Vendée et des Chouans* (Paris, 1819), 3 vols.; Ch.-L. Chassin, *La préparation de la guerre de Vendée* (Paris, 1892), 3 vols.; Joseph Clémenceau (F. Uzureau, ed.), *Histoire de la guerre de la Vendée (1793-1815)* (Paris, 1909); J. Crétineau-Joly, *Histoire de la Vendée Militaire* (Paris, 1851), 4 vols.; Félix Déniau, *Histoire de la Guerre de la Vendée* (Angers, 1878), 6 vols.; Léon Dubreuil, *Histoire des insurrections de l'Ouest* (Paris, 1929), 2 vols.; Émile Gabory, *La Révolution et la Vendée* (Paris, 1925), 3 vols.; Pierre de la Gorce, *Histoire religieuse de la Révolution française* (Paris, 1911), vol. II; Théodore Muret, *Histoire des guerres de l'Ouest* (Paris, 1848), 3 vols.; Henri de Malleray, *Les Cinq Vendées* (Angers and Paris, 1924); Célestin Port, *La Vendée angevine* (Paris, 1888), 2 vols.; J. J. M. Savary, *Guerres des Vendéens et des Chouans contre la République française* (Paris, 1824-27), 6 vols.

4 Paul Bois, *Paysans de l'Ouest* (Le Mans, 1960); Bois, *Cahier de doléances du tiers état de la Sénéchaussée de Château-du-Loir pour les États généraux de 1789* (Gap. 1960); Bois, "Réflexions sur les survivances de la Révolution dans l'Ouest," *Annales historiques de la Révolution française,* XXXIII (Avril-Juin, 1961), 177-186.

5 Port, *op. cit.,* I, xii-xiii.

6 It is equally significant that a conscientious, if not wholly sympathetic, reviewer of *La Vendée angevine* summarized the book as follows: "Two principal conclusions appear to emerge from M. Port's analysis: 1. the uprising of March, 1793 . . . was prepared and fomented by the nobility and the émigrés; the responsibility is theirs; 2. the rôle of Cathelineau in that first uprising is purely imaginary." L. de la Sicotiére, *Étude historique et*

Even those willing to present as forthright an explanation as Célestin Port's have to contend with the fact that a large number of men who were neither nobles nor priests took up arms in the rebellion. As a result, almost all analysts of the Vendée have tried to reconstruct the mentality of the mass of the rebels, considering them to be a representative selection of the region's peasantry. And this raises a new problem. It is not easy to argue that narrow self-interest—often taken for granted in the case of nobles or priests—drove the bulk of the population into counter-revolution. Mathiez, to be sure, made a gesture in that direction, but in the end his analysis came to: a) deep peasant malaise, plus b) agitation by priests and nobles.[7] It is possible, however, to insert an ideology into the same logical structure. One can explain a group's behavior on the basis of its distinctive beliefs and attitudes, even if one finds those beliefs and attitudes tainted.

In this context, the problem of ideology is not the usual (if horrendously complex) one of analyzing the origins and functions of a set of beliefs about the social world.[8] Rather, the (no less vexing) question is the extent to which it is possible to explain major actions of large collections of men by reference to such beliefs. Certainly historians of both the Revolution and the counter-revolution have undertaken such explanations; witness Crane Brinton's insistence on the analogy between the revolutionary view of the world and eschatological religion, as well as Gabory's portrayal of the counter-revolutionary peasants as defenders of their own view of organized religion.[9] The most fully ideological explanations of the Vendée have been the work of writers, like Gabory, sympathetic to the counter-revolution. In response to such explanations, historians closer to the Republican mainstream have often been moved to distinguish, with disconcerting confidence, between "true religion," on the one hand, and superstition, mindless fanaticism or blind ritualism, on the other. In his illuminating review of counter-revolutionary doctrine and action in France, for example, Jacques Godechot remarks that "...generally speaking, the peasant of the West was quite attached to religious practice, if not to religion itself..."—an echo to Savary's contention, a century and a half earlier, that to the Vendean peasant, religion meant lighting "a candle for St. Michael, and one for his serpent."[10]

Why these inquiries into faith and reason? Pro-revolutionary historians appear to be uncomfortable with *any* assertion that the Vendeans acted in accordance with a well-articulated set of beliefs. Perhaps that is because such a conclusion

---

critique sur l'ouvrage de M. Port, *La Vendée angevine* (Angers, 1889), 6. In the heat of disagreement over its conclusions, author and critic agreed whole-heartedly on the problem of the book, and the criteria for judging its success.

[7] Albert Mathiez, *La Révolution francaise* (Paris, 1954), II, 190-195; *La Vie chère et le mouvement social sous la Terreur* (Paris, 1927), 163.

[8] See the excellent review of recent work in this field by Norman Birnbaum, "The Sociological Study of Ideology (1940-60)" *Current Sociology*, IX (No. 2, 1960).

[9] Crane Brinton, *The Anatomy of Revolution* (New York, 1957), esp. 192-207; Gabory, *op. cit.*, II, 19 ff.

[10] Jacques Godechot, *La Contre-révolution* (Paris, 1961), 220; Savary, *op cit.*, I, 31. See the nearly identical assertion in Dubreuil, *op. cit.*, I, 64.

raises some doubt about the universal acceptability of the Revolution's point of view to the French masses. At any rate, rejection of the premise that an ideology existed has barred pro-revolutionary historians from seriously considering the character of the Vendean *Weltanschauung.* Those who have not rejected the premise (who are, of course, mainly counter-revolutionary in their leanings) have considered the Vendean view of the world to be so evident that they, too, have neglected to analyze it in any detail. The bizarre outcome is that no one has presented a careful and cogent argument that the rebels acted in accordance with a distinctive ideology. If it is true, as Peter Paret contends, that "in the Vendée the young Republic for the first time encountered an opponent possessing a somewhat comparable ideological élan," this is a remarkable oversight.[11]

Ideology, in short, has appeared in accounts of the Vendée as an alternative to a) interest, b) other attitudes and feelings excited by the Revolution. It has been an explanatory device, rather than an object of study. And its use confirms the general tendency to see the crucial problem in explanation as the identification of the states of mind of the principal participants at the moments of decisive action. The historiography of the Vendée offers a fairly pure example of the common propensity to conceive of historical process and historical explanation psychologically. This propensity is certainly far from disreputable. It is, indeed, the foundation of such well-built philosophies of history as Collingwood's: "Reflective acts may be roughly described as the acts which we do on purpose, and these are the only acts which can become the subject-matter of history."[12] But it is a foundation on which one cannot build any sort of structure one pleases.

This simple observation returns us to the main point. The "psychological" conception of the problem of explanation implies a distinctive form of argument. It implies the selection of units of analysis which can reasonably be thought of as acting consciously and collectively, the identification of a limited number of principal actors, the attribution of suitable motives, and the assignment of a personal sort of responsibility for critical events. These features of the argument, in turn, encourage the investigator to select, use and present those data which can be taken most directly as evidence of the intentions of participants in the critical events. Finally, they increase the probability that the major issues over which historians will disagree will be questions of motivation and responsibility. There is an internal logic to the Vendée's historiography.

The first element of this logic is the selection of the units whose action is to be explained. From the beginning, there have been three groups almost no writer on the Vendée has neglected: the nobles, the priests and the peasants. As early as the year of the rebellion itself, Momoro was declaring:

Criminal priests, taking advantage of the credulity of the inhabitants of the country, succeeded in making them rebel against the authority of the nation in

---

[11] Peter Paret, *Internal War and Pacification, The Vendée, 1789-1796* (Princeton, 1961), 34.

[12] R. G. Collingwood, *The Idea of History* (London, 1946), 309.

the name of religion. But those priests, the horror of all humanity, remained hidden behind a screen, as did the former nobles who crowded into the region from the four corners of France; they waited for the favorable moment to appear and put themselves at the head of the rebellious peasants.[13]

The language has moderated since that time, but the principle has not changed very much: identify a small number of groups whose members can be thought of as acting collectively, with common intentions. Generally, these are groups which were already acting collectively before the Revolution rather than, for example, latent interest groups suddenly sensing their common destinies, or organizations formed and recruited from diverse origins during the Revolution itself. In the account offered by the soundest of the "Catholic" historians, Gabory, the cast of characters consists of the clergy, the nobles, the peasants and the bourgeoisie:

In the Vendée, resistance to the Revolution was in a way the struggle of the nobles and the peasants against the bourgeois....[14]
Much more so than the nobles, the clergy contributed *indirectly* to the uprising.[15]

But as Gabory's account proceeds, the bourgeois role shrinks to that of an unhappy target, rather than an active participant.

In the years since the Revolution, the number of actors that historians have felt compelled to distinguish in order to account for its general course has greatly increased. With Michelet, there is only one: The People. By the time we reach Taine, we must at least distinguish the plotting bourgeois from the furious masses. The heirs of Jean Jaurès have worked persistently at increasing the cast by dividing up the role once assigned to a single player, the Third Estate. Georges Lefebvre separates the Aristocratic Revolution, the Bourgeois Revolution, the Popular Revolution and the Peasant Revolution from each other. And now a new generation of historians is at work subdividing the role of the urban populus.[16] The parallel evolution in the historiography of the Vendée has been much more irregular and sluggish. (Maybe if more historians in sympathy with the Left could interest themselves in such a reactionary movement, the process of subdivision would advance more rapidly.) In the last significant general history of the counter-revolution, now more than thirty years old, Dubreuil offered distinctions between the upper and lower clergy, among several types of

13 A. F. Momoro, *Rapport sur l'état politique de la Vendée* (Paris, 1793), 2.

14 Émile Gabory, *Napoléon et la Vendée* (Paris, 1914), 7.

15 Émile Gabory, *La Révolution et la Vendée* (Paris, 1927), II, 19.

16 Jules Michelet, *Histoire de la Révolution francaise* (Paris, 1847-53), 7 vols.; Hippolyte Taine, *La Révolution* (Paris, 1878-84), 3 vols.; Jean Jaurés, *Histoire socialiste de la Révolution francaise* (Paris, 1901-1904), 4 vols.; Albert Mathiez, *La Révolution francaise* (Paris, 1924-27), 3 vols.; Georges Lefebvre, *The Coming of the French Revolution* (Princeton, 1947); Lefebvre, *La Révolution francaise* (Paris, 1951); Albert Soboul, *Les Sans-culottes parisians en l'an II* (La Roche-sur-Yon, 1958); George Rudé, *The Crowd in the French Revolution* (Oxford, 1959); Kare Tønnesson, *La Défaite des sans-culottes* (Oslo and Paris, 1959).

bourgeois, and even among a few different kinds of peasants. But these distinctions faded in the course of the analysis, leaving Dubreuil with the traditional nobles, peasants, priests and bourgeois.[17]

One of the postulates of this type of analysis is that the groups distinguished are homogeneous in motivation. The model group assumed by the author resembles a single-minded individual more than it does, say, a modern political party composed of people from a variety of social positions or a factory within which conflict and contention flourish. As a result, the existence of a few individuals who do not fit the pattern (such as nobles who buy church properties) often embarrasses the author a good deal.[18] For the advantage of working with a small number of actors is that it is possible to define their motives boldly and simply, and then to watch them blend or clash.

The motives assigned are critical, because so many writers treat them as the fundamental causes of the counter-revolution. Therefore, to make explanation of the Vendée convincing, one should offer some evidence that one has attributed the correct motives to the actors. The motivations of the nobles have almost always been taken to be self-evident, and this has often been the case for the clergy. The motives of the bourgeois have received little attention, and that mainly in the form of attributing personal ambition, frustration or enlightened patriotism to them on general grounds, without specific evidence. It is the motives of the peasants—or rather of everyone but the nobles, clergy and bourgeois—that have attracted the greatest interest.

A weak, if common, form of argument for a particular motive is the simple assertion that it is consistent with all the actions of the group in question. A closely related tactic is first to provide a description of the "character" of the inhabitant of the counter-revolutionary area, and then to use that character as an explanation of his actions in 1793; that is the procedure of the Abbé Déniau:

Confined in their Bocage as a result of the difficulties of communication with the adjoining territories, the Vendeans lived a familial existence; people from the same neighborhood ordinarily met only on Sunday and the days of markets or fairs... These sedentary habits had naturally preserved them from the pernicious influences of the so-called civilization of the time; so they were profoundly religious, full of lively and simple faith, always faithful to their Christian duties: celebration of all the holy days, prayers morning and evening, participation in the sacraments, fasts and abstinence, recitation, at vespers, at Rosary, everything was accomplished punctually and with the most edifying piety.[19]

After a good deal more description in this vein, the author goes on to portray the Vendean as the spontaneous defender of wronged religion.

When there is specific evidence offered for motivations, as one might expect, it is ordinarily in the form of informed observation on the mood and intentions of the rebels, or actual declarations of the counter-revolutionary leaders. The

---

17 Dubreuil, *op. cit.,* esp. I, 1-95.

18 E.g. Baguenier-Désormeaux, *op. cit.*

19 Déniau, *op. cit.,* I, 32-33.

1791 report of the emissaries of the National Assembly, Gallois and Gensonné, who reported that it was mainly the recent religious changed that were agitating the West, has been cited innumerable times as evidence that the basic motivations of the counter-revolution were religious.[20] The response of the Vendean generals to British inquiries about their intentions has had a similar popularity.[21]

It is precisely at this point that the lines between causes, motives and ideologies have become hopelessly smudged. One of the key passages in Muret's explanation of the counter-revolution runs:

When the news of the king's death resounded like a thunderbolt through the Bocage, it aroused a sentiment of horror and deep shock ... Everything that had happened in the last three years must have accustomed men's minds to crimes, and yet this one was beyond imagining. People could hardly believe that the scoundrels had dared to stain their hands with the blood of the Lord's anointed, and they wondered what plague would strike the earth after such a transgression. No more than an occasion was needed to touch off the emotions that were boiling in everyone's heart.[22]

With the greatest of ease, Muret swings among the levels of ideology (royalism), motives (righteous indignation) and causes (this state of mind plus the "occasion" offered by the imposition of conscription). These gymnastics are quite impressive, since they allow the author to judge the counter-revolution, assign the responsibility for its occurrence, judge the intentions of the principal participants, and explain it, all at the same time.

II

The implicit structure of explanation has also influenced the historical craftsmanship of writers on the Vendée: the kinds of data they have sought and found, the ways they have used the data, the manners in which they have presented their accounts. Aside from the personal testimonies which the earliest chroniclers claim to have collected, and which are hardly subject to verification now, the sources of direct information actually available may be classified roughly as follows:

1. administrative records and correspondence:
   a. deliberative and judicial bodies (e.g. minutes, court proceedings);
   b. executive bodies:
      1) governmental, especially fiscal and regulatory (e.g. tax rolls);
      2) economic, especially seigneuries, firms, and religious establishments (e.g. rent rolls);
2. extraordinary surveys and compilations (e.g. the 1790 survey of the National Assembly's Comité de Mendicité);

[20] E.g. de la Gorce, *op. cit.*, II, 365-376. The text of the report itself is in *Réimpression de l'Ancien Moniteur*, X, nos. 314 and 316.
[21] E.g. Gabory, *Révolution et la Vendée, op. cit.*, I, 203-204.
[22] Muret, *op.cit.*, I, 42-43.

3. official registration of private acts, especially notarial minutes, parish registers (e.g. records of property transfers);
4. contemporary observation and comment: newspapers, pamphlets, personal correspondence, journals, memoirs, histories.

The reason for enumerating these sources, all of which are available in considerable volume for the West, is that the historians of the Vendée have given so much of their attention to two related classes of sources: those that presented direct accounts of the presumedly critical events of the counter-revolution, and those that seemed to offer direct testimony as to the intentions of the participants in those events. Memoirs, interrogations of prisoners and refugees, personal letters, public declarations and official correspondence have been the center of attention. In the torrent of writings on the Vendée, analyses of such sources as notarial minutes or even election records have been no more than a trickle.

The selective attention given to documents of this sort is not something one can demonstrate with an apt quotation or two. Those writers who have described their methods, however, have indicated that such preferences guided them. Crétineau-Joly, the uncompromising Royalist, boasts that he is the first historian to offer "judgments that one can support with certitudes."[23] Then he describes his sources: the reports and correspondence of Republican generals, edicts of emissaries of the central government, contemporary memoirs, letters of the rebel leaders and even some interviews with aged veterans of the counter-revolution. Chassin offers another admirable test case, since his history of the Vendée is essentially a huge series of commented documents.[24] The documents are almost entirely memoirs, letters, reports, interrogations and public pronouncements. Furthermore, at the crucial points in the argument, Chassin relies heavily on contemporary commentary and memoirs, notably those of Mercier du Rocher.[25]

Célestin Port's *Vendée angevine* is another case in point. I have already mentioned the great attention Port gives the *cahiers de doléances,* and could have added that he draws heavily on the reports on local conditions prepared for the provincial Commission Intermédiaire just before the Revolution. The best indication of the sources which he regards as necessary to support his analysis, however, is the set of documents reprinted in his voluminous appendixes. It consists, by a very rough classification, of 114 depositions or minutes of interrogations, 63 letters (mostly administrative), 13 eye-witness narratives of critical events, 10 formal reports by various officials, 7 minutes of formal actions or deliberations, and 2 public declarations by municipalities. In short, it is the

23 *Op. cit.,* I, 2.

24 Chassin, *op. cit.; La Vendée patriote* (Paris, 1893-95), 4 vols.; *Les Pacifications de l'Ouest* (Paris, 1896-99), 3 vols.

25 The ironic note is that when the editor of this great mass of documents reaches his quintessential conclusion—that the rebellion was the result of a plot—he has practically no authority to offer other than the opinions of Mercier du Rocher. E.g. *Préparation, op. cit.,* 312-313.

documents which permit inferences about motivated behavior that find the greatest favor.

Such a selection of sources suggests a distinctive way of working with the available materials and constructing an explanation. Port's comments on his method offer an insight, if not exactly the one he might have intended, into that procedure. "I have worked as everyone does," he declares,

and at least no one would accuse me of *parti pris*. A long time ago, in the course of classifying a series of documents ... I was able to gain a distinctive understanding, quite different from the conventional view, of the region, its customs and its people. The unexpected conquest of the parish *cahiers* illuminated the very sentiments of these populations ... Groups of original documents encountered by chance, letters, reports, depositions of witnesses and actors, protested loudly against all the legends ... At first, the texts only speak in whispers; one must listen to them closely to understand, look at them again, confront them with each other, compare their messages, and then question some more. Little by little, for the investigator who follows them, the light changes. One hesitates, one returns, one moves on. All of a sudden, at some turn, the horizon changes, and the path opens up into a light-filled clearing.[26]

What is to be explained goes without saying. The means of explaining it goes without saying. The investigator begins by concentrating on documents which offer accounts, partial or general, of the crucial events, and puts together his own account of the sequence of actions involved, his eye alert for errors in previous reconstructions of the events. He then tries to analyze the motives of the actors, relying on the documents which report the facts themselves, on more general sources which give evidence of the character and outlook of the actors, and on his own understanding of human nature. With a continuous account of the actions of the principal participants, and a consistent set of motives for them, the job is done.

The actual presentation of accounts reflects this sort of method. Writers on the Vendée have typically begun with a description of the "character" of the region which joined the counter-revolution, and more particularly of its inhabitants. The number of categories the writer distinguishes in assigning "character" to the population normally corresponds to the number of actors he will identify in the counter-revolution. Those who claim the whole region rose as a man, for example, describe the entire population as if it were composed of one peasant type.[27] After this preliminary description, the Vendée's historians have ordinarily begun a chronological narrative. The narrative has set the actors already identified into motion, explaining their intentions and changes of intention in terms consistent with their character, and treating the significant events as combined consequences of their intentional actions. Occasionally the narrative has paused for a reassessment of motives, or the introduction of new

---

26 Port, *Vendée angevine, op. cit.*, I, viii-ix.
27 E.g. Beauchamp, *op. cit.*

actors—in the shape of outstanding leaders, each accompanied by his own character sketch. The basic design of the historical account is part and parcel of a "psychological" conception of the problem.

The evaluations that historians give such accounts rest on the same shared premises about the nature of explanation. For example, Georges Lefebvre, in reviewing three important books about the counter-revolution, remarked:

M. Dubreuil is far from denying the influence of the preaching of the Refractory clergy, but he does not think that was the only cause of the uprising. Nor do we: it seems to us that it would have been good to describe the deportation of the Refractories in September: the Vendean peasants did not rise to defend the "good priests" . . . .

We think, then, that the Vendean peasant rose, not to defend the Refractory priest or avenge the king, but to escape the demands of the central government . . . Even admitting that the noble conspiracy was a reality, I do not think that the insurrection of the peasants against conscription was incited by it: obviously, the nobles and priests must have contributed to fomenting it by exciting peasant discontent; then they exploited it and took it over.[28]

If religious motivations are the explanation, in Lefebvre's view, they should have worked in 1792 as well as in 1793; moreover there is no great evidence, nor is there any need to maintain, that the peasants were greatly attached to the nobles, the priests or the old regime. In other words, it is the state of mind of the peasantry that matters, and there is some doubt whether the authors reviewed have portrayed it correctly.

In such an attempt at simultaneous judgment, explanation and assignment of responsibility, the issues which historians hotly contest are likely to be, at bottom, questions about the intentions of the peasants, the clergy, or the nobles. There have been four such questions that have impassioned the chroniclers of the Vendée: 1) the attitudes of the peasants to the Old Regime and the early Revolution, 2) the actions of the nobles from 1789 to 1793, 3) the identities of the real leaders of the counter-revolution, 4) the existence of a plot to organize a rebellion in the West.

None of these is a trivial question. It may be that the first one, the attitude of the peasants to the Old Regime and the early Revolution, is doubly important, since it impinges on the broader problem of the acceptability of the Revolution to rural France as a whole, as well as indicating whether some specific action of the later Revolution turned the peasants away from its path. The early Royalist writers (such as Crétineau-Joly, Bourniseaux and Beauchamp) agreed with the first Republican reporters (in this case, Choudieu and Richard of the Convention) that "The Revolution hardly made itself felt here, and Liberty found only a small number of friends," even if they disagreed with the contention that "When the Revolution called the French to freedom, ignorance

---

28 Review of Léon Dubreuil, *Histoire des insurrections de l'Ouest,* Emile Gabory, *L'Angleterre et la Vendée* and Charles Le Goffic, *La Chouannerie,* in *Revue historique,* CLXIX (Jan.-Feb. 1932), 196-197.

and fanaticism dominated the region now in revolt."[29] But by the middle of the nineteenth century truly Royalist accounts of the Vendée were passé, counter-revolutionary writers were stressing the devastating effects of the religious reforms of 1790-91, and their revolutionary opponents were insisting that a fundamentally good people had been perverted by a counter-revolutionary elite. That is, all writers were contending that peasant attitudes changed between 1789 and 1793. How great the shift in sentiment was, when it occurred, and how great an opposition to the work of the Revolution as a whole it involved remained vividly at issue.

Célestin Port's analysis of the *cahiers de doléances,* for example, argues a) that the rural sections that later joined the counter-revolution were miserable under the old regime, b) that they welcomed, and indeed demanded, the major Revolutionary reforms.[30] From this base, Port proceeds to the proposition that, while there were some small reasons for the peasants of Anjou to be unhappy with the Revolution, the actions of the nobles and the émigrés accounted for the greater part of the shift in the attitudes of the peasants. Port's most systematic critic, on the other hand, concedes to his adversary that the country people began by favoring reform, but urges the view that the transformation of opinion occurred when the administrators of the West began to enforce the Civil Constitution of the Clergy.[31] The two principal rightist historians of the rebellion posterior to Port, de la Gorce and Gabory, subscribe to the same view. Early in his analysis, Gabory declares that, "A traveler who, after having voyaged through the other French provinces, had visited those of the West in 1789, would hardly have found any differences in spirit. No doubt he would have found the latter more Catholic, but that would not have seemed of any political significance."[32] Following a host of other writers, he offers the demands for reform in the *cahiers* and the orderliness of the sales of church properties as evidence for the favorable popular attitude toward the early Revolution. The corollary: the change in attitude must have come later.

Dubreuil, Gabory's contemporary, counters with the assertion that peasant opinion underwent an unsteady evolution toward open hostility to the Revolution once the first great reforms had satisfied rural needs.[33] Revolutionary taxes, the advantages that the bourgeois gained from the sale of church properties, and the agitation of the parish priests successively pushed the peasant farther from his initial attitude. Dubreuil and Gabory certainly disagree. Yet they agree that it is supremely important to evaluate the feelings of the peasants of the Vendée from 1789 to 1793. Their colleagues have been of one mind on that point.[34]

---

[29] F. Aulard, ed., *Recueil des actes du comité de salut public* (Paris, 1890), III, 431-432, report from Angers dated 24 April, 1793.

[30] Port, *op. cit.,* I, chapter 2.

[31] De la Sicotiére, *op. cit.,* 7-16.

[32] Gabory, *Révolution et la Vendée, op. cit.,* I, 18.

[33] Dubreuil, *op. cit.,* I, esp. chapters 2-5; cf. Godechot, *op. cit.,* 220-223.

[34] See the interesting debate between Georges Lefebvre and A. Lajusan: "Origines immédiates et lointaines de la Vendée," *Bulletin de la Société d'histoire moderne,* XXXVIII

This first issue foreshadows a second one: exactly how did the nobles behave after the beginning of the Revolution, and what does their behavior reveal of their intentions? The unspoken part of the question is: did they calculatingly exploit the peasants? One way of determining this is to decide whether the nobles were pious before 1793. According to Alphonse Aulard,

To amalgamate the better with the Vendean peasantry, the royalist gentlemen, up till that time for the most part Voltairian in their language, or indifferentists in matters of religion, affected an exalted piety, and, in order to obtain the support of the Roman Catholic Church in their attempt to restore the throne, made common cause with the refractory priests.[35]

But the traditional history of the Vendée presents every one of the noble leaders as a religious man.[36]

This dispute over the piety of the nobles is largely a war of epithets, waged at best with quotations from memoirs and contemporary commentaries on the counter-revolution. But it has approached some questions of fact in the debate over purchases of church properties by nobles who later joined the rebellion. Two problems are intertwined here. Were the gentlemen really so religious? When the tide was favorable to them, were they willing to profit by the Revolution they later execrated? Port took sardonic pleasure in citing Bonchamps and d'Elbée, the Vendean generals, as buyers of church lands, and Baguénier-Désormaux bent every effort to explain away the purchases in question as attempts to keep the properties out of unworthy hands.[37]

The favorite form of the debate over the intentions of the nobles, however, has been a quarrel that seems incredibly petty. Did the peasants, already in arms and ready to revolt, march to the châteaux and ask the nobles to lead them? "The uprising . . ." declared Muret, "was entirely popular. The peasants sounded the tocsin and gathered, with what arms they could find. The most determined, the most able found himself captain. For higher officers, they went to fetch the nobles, the landlords, the former officers, whose position and character won them everyone's confidence."[38] This is an old, old idea. Larevellière-Lépeaux had already stated a standard retort around 1820:

The argument that the peasants went to look for the nobles in their châteaux, and almost seized them by force to make them lead, when in fact [the nobles] had no other thought in mind but to begin a civil war . . . is of no value. Who can

---

(May-June, 1938), 3-13 and "Communication de M. Lajusan," *Bulletin de la Société d'histoire moderne,* XXXVIII (Nov., 1938), 5.

[35] Alphonse Aulard (Bernard Miall, tr.), *The French Revolution, A Political History* (London, 1910), II, 307-8.

[36] Gabory (*op. cit.,* I, 9) felt impelled to comment on this at the beginning of his account: "People have repeated *ad nauseam* that there were many atheists among the nobles of the West; the breath of Voltaire was supposed to have dried up their souls. Is that correct? Although less Catholic than today, the nobility retained a basic fund of belief that events were to revive at one blow."

[37] Port, *op. cit.,* I, 109-111; Baguénier-Désormeaux, *op. cit.*

[38] Muret, *op. cit.,* I, 46.

be made to believe that ridiculous assertion? Could the population of one or several provinces revolt on the same day without leaders and a concerted plan?[39]

In 1888, Célestin Port gave *his* version of one of the stirring scenes so often recounted by royalist historians:

The same day, in the very heart of the Mauges, d'Elbé, to whom a son was born that very morning, received, like Bonchamps, the visit of some of the insurgent peasants. Like [Bonchamps], he accepted the command—without any more pretense of strong scruples, despite what others have taken pleasure in saying—and immediately created an energetic center of action (which was in fact already prepared) at Beaupréau.[40]

Nor was the issue dead in 1961, when Godechot revealed some of its significance in writing "What tends to prove that the insurrection was not spontaneous and caused entirely by conscription is that at the beginning one sees the nobles take the lead."[41] Yet the frequent reiteration of these objections has not kept writers of another persuasion from saying, with de la Gorce,

The rising was that of an entire people pushed to its limit and seizing . . . the pretext of conscription to rebel in the name of outraged religion. The peasant had been the workman of the first hour. It was time for the hour of the nobles to sound.[42]

Once again, there is drastic disagreement on the facts, but great accord on the significance of the issue—if the peasants did come to demand the leadership of the nobles, then the revolt was "spontaneous," not the result of the self-interested manipulations of the nobility.

The third issue complements the second: who were the real leaders of the counter-revolution army? How many of them were men of the people? More specifically, was Cathelineau, that humble waggoner of Le Pin-en-Mauges, actually generalissimo of the Vendean armies? As Dubreuil says:

In spite of appearances, the affair is important. If Cathelineau was the instigator of the uprising, one can maintain that the Vendean war was essentially religious in origin. If, on the contrary, it is established that the nobles continued and intensified their gathering of support, directly after the seizure of the papers of La Rouairie, if they were involved in the affair before the one called "the Saint of Anjou," the war was royalist in origin.[43]

Célestin Port felt strongly enough about the point to devote a whole book to an attack on the "legend of Cathelineau."[44] Yet conservative writers have continued to honor Cathelineau's credentials.

[39] *Mémoires de Larevellière-Lépeaux* (Paris, 1895), I, 109.
[40] Port, *op. cit.*, II, 104.
[41] Godechot, *op. cit.*, 228-9.
[42] De la Gorce, *op. cit.*, II, 433.
[43] Dubreuil, *op. cit.*, I, 132.
[44] E.g. De la Gorce, *op. cit.*, II, 429; de la Sicotière, *op. cit.*, 28-39.

The final issue—the existence of a counter-revolutionary plot—is also far more than a question of fact. Just as the *thése du complot* applied to the Revolution as a whole tends to discount the significance of popular discontent with the old regime, the theory of conspiracy applied to the counter-revolution expresses doubt that there was grave and general opposition to the Revolution in the West. The antithesis has always been that the counter-revolution was "spontaneous"— an ambiguous term, to say the least.

"Enough of these fairy tales!," expostulates Célestin Port. "The Angevin insurrection . . . did not develop at random, in a small village, under the inspiration of a well-intentioned fanatic. It was the fatal explosion of a conspiracy of nobles and émigrés."[45] But his critic, de la Sicotière, is there at once to contradict him: "We persist in believing that the uprising of the Vendée was not at all the work of the émigrés or of the local nobility."[46] The same kind of division separated the last two important general historians of the counter-revolution, Gabory and Dubreuil.

The curious fact is that no recent writer has denied that there was a conspiracy to organize a counter-revolution, centering on a colorful Breton royalist, a minor hero of the American Revolution, the Marquis de la Rouairie.[47] Nor is there much contestation over the gathering of a group of conspirators around the Marquis de la Lézardière in Vendée.[48] What the advocates of the plot thesis insist on is the direct connection between these machinations and the outbreak of the counter-revolution. They frequently bridge considerable gaps in the evidence to make that connection. Paul Bois remarks of Dubreuil that "He insists on the royalist conspiracy of La Rouairie but cannot, any more than anyone else can, discover its ramifications in the Vendée; he is simply convinced of their existence."[49] The critics of the plot thesis have worked just as tenaciously to deny any significance to the conspiracy. Gabory's conclusions show very well what the disputation is about:

It was the peasants who kindled the general conflagration the agents of La Rouairie had been unable to light. In the thought of the Breton agitator, the nobles should begin, and the peasants follow; in fact, the peasants began, the nobles only obeyed.[50]

What is at issue is not merely the existence of a little plotting or some fond hopes for counter-revolution on the part of the nobles. The basic dispute is over the attribution of various combinations of motives, strength and responsibility

---

45 Célestin Port, *La Légende de Cathelineau* (Paris, 1893), 13-14; see Paul Bois' critique of the plot thesis, which he aptly calls "la thése de la responsabilitié nobiliaire," *Paysans de l'Ouest, op. cit.,* 584-588.

46 De la Sicotière *op. cit.,* 28.

47 A. Goodwin, "Counter-Revolution in Brittany, The Royalist Conspiracy of the Marquis de la Rouérie 1791-93," *Bulletin of the John Rylands Library,* XXXIX (March, 1957), 326-355.

48 See Dubreuil, *op. cit.,* I, 122-4.

49 Bois, *Paysans de l'Ouest, op. cit.,* 587.

50 Gabory, *Révolution et la Vendée, op. cit.,* I, 198.

to the elite and the mass among the rebels. At the one extreme, the plot thesis assigns intention, power and responsibility to a self-interested elite, and no more than gullibility to the rest of the population.[51] At the other extreme, the spontaneity thesis denies the disjunction between elite and mass.[52] It has them share intentions, power and responsibility. The problem is not the existence of a plot, but the treatment of the rebellion as the *result* of a plot. The trick is to divine the intentions of the participants, and this divination is peculiarly susceptible to the influence of political predilections.

III

It is no news that historians have disagreed about the Vendée, or that their positions have been related to their general attitudes toward the Revolution. The point I want to urge is that the deeply divisive issues are judgments of the motives of the principal participants—rather than such still-open questions as the distribution of power before 1789 or the extent of the actual participation of various elements of the population in the counter-revolution—and that the accentuation of these issues is the result of a structure of explanation in terms of intention and responsibility.

This way of seeing the problem of explanation has some serious drawbacks. For one thing, it seems to discourage the analyst from making careful distinctions among the groups whose behavior he is explaining. The egregious example is the "peasantry." When looked at close up, the non-noble, non-clerical mass of the rebels turns out to be quite heterogeneous, and far from strictly peasant in composition. The prominence of such chiefs as Stofflet (a game warden), Cathelineau (a carter), Cady (a physician), and Souchu (a minor official), gives fair warning of that fact. A large proportion of the rebels were rural artisans (around 40 percent, according to the best estimates I have been able to prepare for Southern Anjou). And the peasants themselves ranged from landless laborers to substantial leaseholders. It is not evident *a priori* that one can attribute a uniform set of motives to such a group, even if they did all join the rebellion. Yet the method of analysis itself resists the conception of the rebels as a collection of men with diverse, even inconsistent, intentions, varying over time, linked by power, personal influence or common enemies—as reasonable as such a description might seem for contemporary rebellions, armies or political factions. Even Dubreuil, who begins with a description full of nuances, ends by abandoning all but the most elementary distinctions.

Another difficulty is that a whole range of problems tends to evaporate in the course of the analysis, even when the writer intuits their importance. They are the problems that cannot be readily subsumed under the states of mind of the principal actors during the times of critical actions: the effects of kinship ties, the residues of previous conflicts, the existence of party alignments, the presence of group pressures, and so on. The tension between urban and rural is such a

---

[51] E.g. Jaurès, *op. cit.*, vol. VII; Chassin, *op. cit.*, esp. II, 501-527.

[52] E.g. Bourniseaux, *op. cit.*, Baguénier-Désormeaux, *op. cit.*

problem in the Vendée. Both Dubreuil and Gabory sensed its importance, Gabory labeling the counter-revolution a "struggle of the countryside against the cities."[53] But except as the analysis of bourgeois and "peasant" behavior absorbed it, nothing more came of the insight. The consequence is that the historians of the counter-revolution (even those who, like Célestin Port, had plenty of evidence before them) have neglected the significance of local rural-urban conflicts in the process that led to rebellion.[54]

The problem of ideology also disappears, all too quickly. Of course, many writers have felt the importance of a distinctive view of the world in the Vendée; military historians seem to have been particularly sensitive to it, perhaps because they had to explain how "insurgents beginning without cannon, without cavalry, without material, without munitions, armed in part with scythes, with sickles and with ploughshares, operating in a small theater that one can cross in four marches, [accumulated] triumph after triumph, not in simple skirmishes . . . but in pitched battles."[55] General Turreau, who was in a position to know the ferocity of the Vendeans, hinted that their particular way of looking at the world was important:

A way of fighting that no one had known before . . . an inviolable attachment to their party; unlimited confidence in their chiefs; such fidelity to their promises that it could take the place of discipline; indomitable courage . . . this is what made the Vendeans fearsome enemies and has placed them in history among the first rank of warrior peoples.[56]

Despite all this, no historian of the Vendée has distinguished sharply enough among motives, causes and ideology to investigate how and when the distinctive outlook of the rebels was formed, how widely it was accepted, and in what way (if any) it constrained the course of the counter-revolution.

Explanation via intention and responsibility contains an even more serious defect, its discouragement of comparative analysis. So long as one holds an individualistic, psychological view of the actors, he will find it hard to see the relevance of systematic comparison with other actors: what seems to matter is the sympathetic understanding of those who did something, not of those who did not. Many writers have noted that the people of the larger cities, the Loire Valley and the plains surrounding the Vendée generally supported the Revolution. Then they have passed on to what they regarded as the business at hand, the description of the men who resisted the Revolution. They have not given serious attention to the most searching question of all: why the Vendée, and not somewhere else? In the rush away from this question, historians of the counter-revolution have also left behind the tasks of delineating accurately the

---

[53] *Napoléon et la Vendée, op. cit.,* 7.

[54] See Charles Tilly, "Local Conflicts in the Vendée Before the Rebellion of 1793," *French Historical Studies,* II (Fall, 1961), 209-231; "Some Problems in the History of the Vendée," *American Historical Review,* LXVII (October, 1961), 19-33.

[55] De Halleray, *op. cit.,* 20.

[56] Louis Marie Turreau, *Mémoires pour servir à l'histoire de la guerre de la Vendée* (Paris, 1924, originally published in 1795), 19.

territory whose inhabitants took active part in the fighting, as well as determining exactly what sorts of people participated most vigorously. Without these tasks accomplished, it is hard to see how a valid explanation could even begin. And until statements of the order of "The peasants were religious" are translated at least into others like "The peasants were *more* religious than those elsewhere, and religious peasants are more likely to resist revolution", it is even harder to see how any explanation could be verified.

The viewpoint that has prevailed in the analysis of the Vendée involves an extremely rationalistic model of human behavior—at least that part of human behavior which is worthy of historical analysis—and sets the historian the immensely difficult task of reconstructing states of mind. It drastically limits the part that systematic theory can play in historical explanation, since the relevant theories must be of a very special sort: theories of motives and states of mind. Instead, it encourages the analyst to introduce, implicitly, general propositions of an exceedingly simple order (e.g. "Men act in accordance with their material interests"). Furthermore, it draws the historian's attention away from alternative ways of defining his problem which may be equally profitable, and less likely to draw him into bootless debate. Perhaps it is significant that just as it was de Tocqueville, who never wrote a history of the Revolution itself, but brilliantly anticipated later forms of analysis of the Revolution, it was André Siegfried, who never wrote a history of the Vendée, who provided the most exciting ideas for further research on the counter-revolution.[57] For it is Siegfried's intuitive, journalistic, often inaccurate observations on the relationship between social organization and political action in the West that offer the beginnings of a comparative sociological analysis of the counter-revolution.

A critical examination of what Siegfried had to say, in the course of which a great many of the important details turned out to be entirely wrong, started Paul Bois on his monumental comparative study of political life in the Sarthe.[58] The re-examination of Siegfried eventually led him to reject some of the most cherished assumptions writers have made about rural life in the West: the predominance of noble landlords, the frequency of noble residence in the countryside, peasant resistance to the sale of church properties, and so on. Not all of Bois' conclusions are definitely established, but they are certainly powerful enough to expose the feeble foundation on which a great deal of previous writing has been based.

Bois' study of the Sarthe shows unremitting labor. However, it is not its thoroughness which is its most distinctive feature. The author did not just offer a "new interpretation." He asked new questions. The questions he asked did not focus on intention and responsibility, but on the characteristics that distinguished the areas of counter-revolutionary activity (in this case, the guerrilla of Chouannerie rather than the full-scale war of the Vendée) from those that

---

[57] André Siegfried, *Tableau politique de la France de l'Ouest sous la Troisième République* (Paris, 1913).
[58] *Op. cit.*

remained calm after 1793.[59] In doing so, he painstakingly tested each of the major variables Siegfried and other commentators had alleged to be related to the presence or absence of rightist politics and counter-revolutionary spirit. One by one, the idols fell: there was no correlation between large property and rightist voting;[60] no fatal relationship between dispersed settlement (that producer of "independent character" and preserver of "religious spirit") and counter-revolution;[61] nothing to the supposed influence of sharecropping in maintaining patriarchal relations between nobles and their tenants.[62] There is room for doubt whether the data justify all the conclusions—for instance, the allegedly greater rivalry between bourgeois and peasants for the acquisition of land in the areas that were vigorously counter-revolutionary.[63] It is far from certain that the conclusions can be transferred wholesale to the Vendée. And the final element of the analysis, an ill-defined *prise de conscience* on the part of the substantial peasantry of one section of the department, is a reversion to unverified explanations in terms of states of mind.[64] Still, a new logic is there, and it works magnificently in clearing away the debris of earlier discussions of counter-revolution in the West.

The new logic is not, of course, entirely of Bois' invention. With all his inaccuracies, Siegfried saw clearly enough the principle that regional variations in political orientation in the West should be related to variations in social organization.[65] Jacques Godechot has recently stressed the necessity of analyzing the "economic and social structure of the insurgent areas," an observation anticipated by Marc Bloch, thirty years before.[66] Over the last few years, a number of careful scholars have been working to accumulate the essential information on local social organization and regional variation in the West.[67] The great tradition represented by the *Annales* is finally making its weight felt.

The basic logic is one that is almost second nature to sociologists.[68] When

---

[59] *Ibid.*, 580-581.

[60] *Ibid.*, 94-96.

[61] *Ibid.*, 98, 581-584.

[62] *Ibid.*, 97.

[63] *Ibid.*, 340-358. By Bois' own logic, one should conclude that the most intense competition was between peasants and ecclesiastics.

[64] *Ibid.*, 658-678.

[65] Siegfried, *op. cit.*, esp. 362 ff.; Siegfried, "Le régime et la division de la propriété dans le Maine et l'Anjou," *Musée social* (no. 18, 1911), 195-215; Siegfried, "En Vendée," *Le Figaro,* 17 July, 1950, pp. 1, 7.

[66] Godechot, *op. cit.,* 217-18; Marc Bloch, book review in *Annales d'histoire économique et sociale,* IX (July, 1937), 393-396.

[67] E.g. Louis Merle, *La Métairie et l'évolution agraire de la Gâtine poitevine de la fin du moyen âge à la Révolution* (Paris, 1958); Marcel Faucheux, "Les élections de 1869 en Vendée," *Bibliothèque de la Révolution de 1848* (Paris, 1960), 127-162; Abel Châtelain, "Évolution des densités de population en Anjou (1806-1936)," *Revue de géographie de Lyon,* XXXI (No. 1, 1956), 43-60, as well as the older R. H. Andrews, *Les Paysans des Mauges au XVIIIe siècle* (Tours, 1935).

[68] I shall not pretend to reveal the nature of sociological knowledge; I merely wish to

explaining the existence of a phenomenon, a sociologist is likely to begin by asking of exactly what kind of social unit (traditional bureaucracies? marginal individuals? high-ranking cliques?) it is characteristic. He is likely to proceed immediately to an analysis of the distinguishing characteristics of such social units (elaborate hierarchy? dual allegiances? powerful controls over membership?) and thus to a systematic comparison of units which display the phenomenon with otherwise comparable units which do not. He tends to search for reliable evidence (often, but by no means necessarily, in the form of quantitative measures) that the differences actually exist. Then he seeks to explain the phenomenon in question in terms of the distinguishing characteristics of the unit in which it appears. This leads him to an analysis of the way the elements of that unit fit together, or the subsumption of the case at hand under some broader generalization, or (more likely) both.

There is nothing occult, or even uncommon, about such a logical procedure. The important elements to retain are: the careful identification of the units of analysis, the concern for the identification of reliable differences, the use of generalizations already established, the stress on systematic comparison. These have obvious implications for the study of a counter-revolution. The most powerful new questions they lead to are these: 1)What were the real differences between the areas in which the counter-revolution sprang up in 1793 and those which remained calm, a) under the Old Regime, b) during the early Revolution? 2) What was distinctive about both the organization and the composition of the *groups* which actively supported the Revolution, and those which actively resisted it, over the period 1789-93? 3) What significant changes in the social situation occurred during the same period? 4) Is there any general knowledge available that helps to assemble coherently the answers to these three questions and the fact of counter-revolution?

These questions are by no means already definitely answered, but the very fact that they are now being asked is leading to rapid increases in our understanding of the Vendée. Like Bois' immense study of Chouannerie in the Sarthe, my own more modest work on the counter-revolution in Southern Anjou illustrates the utility of asking new questions. Within the section of Anjou south of the Loire, some 700 square kilometers in area, appeared the most concerted counter-revolutionary outburst of 1793, as well as sharp divisions between the areas and the groups supporting and opposing the counter-revolution. A valid explanation should account for these divisions. It should also relate them to the process which culminated in counter-revolution.

Even asking the prior question—"Precisely what *are* the divisions to be explained?"—is quite useful. Although characterizations of the rebels are legion,

---

point out that sociologists (in common with some kinds of historians) have an habitual way of looking at a problem which offers a useful alternative to the logic heretofore dominant in analyses of the Vendée. For stimulating discussion of related theoretical problems, see Robert K. Merton, "Notes on Problem-Finding in Sociology," in Robert K. Merton, Leonard Broom and Leonard S. Cottrell, eds., *Sociology Today* (New York, 1959), ix-xxxiv, and Kingsley Davis, "The Myth of Functional Analysis as a Special Method in Sociology and Anthropology," *American Sociological Review,* XXIV (Dec. 1959), 957 ff.

the only studies remotely approaching the careful description of the supporters of revolution and counter-revolution in the West are Donald Greer's valuable compilations, by department and social category, of individuals officially designated as émigrés, and of people executed during the Terror.[69] Those studies yield the following statistical description of these two categories of presumed opponents of the Revolution for all of western France:[70]

Category	Percent of All Émigrés	Percent of Those Executed
Clergy	35	2
Nobility	23	2
Upper Middle Class	5	3
Lower Middle Class	2	3
Working Class	10	41
Peasants	20	48
No Status Given	5	1
Total	100	100

Even when taken for individual departments these figures provide only the most unreliable of guides to the divisions to be explained, since they necessarily mix counter-revolutionary and revolutionary sections of departments; since they comprehend only opponents, not supporters, of the regime; since the categories themselves do not correspond closely to the major social divisions in the West; since they do not indicate which categories had more than their shares of execution and emigration; and since neither emigration nor execution is tantamount to participation in the rebellion. We need other social categories, finer geographic divisions, further measures of opposition and support.

There are, as it happens, quite a few materials in the archives which will with careful handling turn themselves into measures of this sort. Eighteenth-century records of births, deaths and marriages, voting lists for 1790 and 1791, and population enumerations from the early Revolution all make possible some estimates of the distribution of occupations and its variation from one section to another, in Southern Anjou. Rosters of the National Guard, records of enlistments in the army, local election returns, and some curious *listes des bons patriotes* provide some information as to the identities of the supporters of the Revolution. The lengthy interrogations of refugees and prisoners during the counter-revolution, the registers made up from them, and the captured rosters of counter-revolutionary army units offer information on the character of the rebels. Some of the more easily handled items of this sort are in the following table, summarizing tentative findings for all of Southern Anjou:

[69] *The Incidence of the Emigration During the French Revolution* (Cambridge, 1951); *The Incidence of the Terror during the French Revolution* (Cambridge, 1935).

[70] *Incidence of the Emigration*, 128; *Incidence of the Terror*, 164. As Greer points out, the lists of émigrés are far from an accurate enumeration of those who actually left the country. The reservations that follow are not meant as criticisms of Greer, who never intended to prepare materials for the analysis of the Vendée.

Percent Distribution by Major Social Category[71]

Category	Estimated Occupational Distribution of Adult Males Rural Communes	Army Volunteers 2792	Bearing Arms with Rebels (Revolutionary Sources)	Bearing Arms with Rebels (Counter-Rev. Sources)	Aiding Rebels (All Sources)
Noble	0.29	0.0	0.61	0.0	1.95
Priest	1.28	0.0	0.0	0.0	8.87
Bourgeois	8.03	28.96	14.72	1.62	21.00
Hired Hand	14.28		6.75	9.43	3.68
		4.52			
Other Peasant	44.77		20.86	53.91	37.88
Weaver	10.62		31.29	14.56	8.44
		66.51			
Other Artisan	20.73		25.77	20.48	18.18
Number Identified	——	221	1121	841	801

The statistics do not speak for themselves, but they do seem to make muffled noises. They suggest, for example, the nearly total absence of peasants, nobles and priests from the patriotic camp. They raise serious reservations about the depiction of the Vendée as a "peasant" rebellion. They tend to confirm Greer's general conclusions about the victims of the Terror in the West. And the discrepancies between the revolutionary and counter-revolutionary sources of information about the rebels (undoubtedly affected by the fact that the counter-revolutionary sources are communal rosters, while the revolutionary ones are mainly the minutes of interrogations and deposition) bring into play some absorbing new problems. Not the least of the fruits of this sort of investigation are the inquiries it stimulates concerning the actual social relations among the diverse groups actively opposing the Revolution. It leads naturally to an analysis of the structures and relations of the revolutionary and counter-revolutionary parties of Southern Anjou.

In order to understand the party divisions, however, one must understand the regional divisions. A number of writers have, with apparent nonchalance, joined maps displaying the boundaries of the insurrection to their accounts of its course.[72] The basis of such historical cartography is almost always a mystery. But there are some ways to reduce the mystery. For most of the period of the Revolution that concerns us here, the province of Anjou (alias the department of

[71] Sources: 1) occupational distribution: A.D. (Archives Départementales) de Maine-et-Loire, B (parish registers), 6 L 19, 7 L 98 (population enumerations), Andrews, *op. cit.,* 163 ff.; 2) volunteers: A. D. Maine-et-Loire, 1 L 590 bis (enlistment registers, Second Battalion of Volunteers); 3) characteristics of rebels: compilations from A. D. Maine-et-Loire 1 L 750, 1 L 835 bis, 1 L 840 bis, 1 L 1018, 1 L 1028, 1 L 1039, 1 L 1094, 1 L 1125 bis, 9 L 84, 9 L 86, 15 Q 272-273, plus small numbers from a variety of other sources. "Other artisan" here actually includes several occupations, such as Carter and Miller, which are hard to place anywhere in this condensed set of categories.

[72] E.g. de la Gorce, *op. cit.*

Maine-et-Loire) was divided into districts averaging some 60,000 persons, which were subdivided into cantons, themselves generally composed of three or four communes and four or five thousand people. The districts, cantons, and communes provide a convenient standard set of units for a wide variety of comparisons.

Given these units for comparison, the first task is the uneasy one of designating them as "revolutionary" and "counter-revolutionary." Paul Bois identified the significant divisions in the Sarthe by classifying official reports on the political tempers of the various cantons of the department.[73] In the Vendée, one may also map the reported incidence of armed opposition to the Revolution in the first weeks of 1793's great outbreak. The same can be done with the counter-revolutionary incidents of 1790 and 1791. Likewise, it is possible to map the residences of the rebels identified in the documents already discussed, and to use the numerous claims for reward presented during the Restoration by Vendean veterans for the same purpose. These various tests agree with each other fairly well, and therefore identify the groups of communes, cantons and districts whose characteristics must be compared.

For purposes of illustration, one of the more easily quantifiable of these criteria appears in the following table with some measures of other forms of significant response to the Revolution. The units, in this case, are the most uniformly counter-revolutionary district of Southern Anjou (Cholet) and the most undividedly revolutionary district (Saumur):[74]

	Counter-Revolutionary	Revolutionary
Number of reported rebels per 1,000 population	9.83	0.04
Émigrés reported per 1,000 population	4.1	7.1
Percent of priests taking Civil Constitution oath	5.3	64.7
Army enlistments per 1,000 population, 1791-92	2.3	7.0

The table has the virtue of being disconcerting. Considering that emigration is so widely taken as a sign of opposition to the Revolution, that the counter-revolutionary sections of Anjou have so often been portrayed as teeming with

---

[73] Bois, *op. cit.*, 161-164.

[74] Principal sources of these compilations: 1. reported rebels: analysis of 2106 individuals positively identified as bearing arms in Archieves Départementales de Maine-et-Loire 1 L 750, 1 L 835 bis, 1 L 840 bis, 1 L 1018, 1 L 1028, 1 L 1094, 1 L 1125 bis, 9 L 84, 9 L 86, 15 Q 272-3, 1 L 1039, plus small numbers from a variety of other sources; 2. émigrés: analysis of A. D. Maine-et-Loire 1 L 398 bis, *Relevé général des émigrés portés sur les listes arrêtées par le Département de Maine-et-Loire jusqu'au premier octobre 1793, vieux style;* Civil Constitution oath: see Charles Tilly, "Civil Constitution and Counter-revolution in Southern Anjou," *French Historical Studies,* I (No. 2, 1959), 172-199; 4. enlistments: based on allowances made in the setting up of draft quotas for March, 1793, A. D. Maine-et-Loire, 1 L 551.

resident nobles in *bonne entente* with their peasants, and that the persecution of the clergy is supposed to have driven so many of them out of the country, one might have expected a much higher rate of emigration for those sections. Not so. This bit of serendipity leads to a re-examination of the question of noble residence, and to the (tentative) conclusion that the gentlemen were actually more numerous in the revolutionary sections of Southern Anjou, as well as to the hunch, plausible but untested, that emigration was most frequent where a determined counter-revolutionary minority met a determined revolutionary majority.[75] One of the advantages of using systematic comparison and well-defined measures is that the results so often prove one's easy assumptions wrong.

Despite a few such contretemps, however, the general result of a variety of comparisons is to reinforce the conclusions a) that there was a relatively well-defined boundary between revolutionary and counter-revolutionary sections of Southern Anjou; b) that the two areas differed significantly in political behavior for several years before the counter-revolution; c) that it therefore makes sense to investigate further the contrasts in social organization between the two areas defined in this way.

At this point, a sociological view of the problem is especially useful. Many commentators, especially those mainly concerned with writing descriptions, rather than histories, of the region, have detailed their intuitions of a drastic difference:

Between the Mauges and the neighboring Saumurois on the east, the difference is great. Distant, wide horizons succeed the plateau cut with valleys and ravines; wastes and orchards disappear, replaced by rich fields of hemp and vineyards. After a dark, rather hard Anjou comes a bright, light, sunny, blooming, flowering Anjou, a country of small property, a country of substantial people, individualistic, conscious of their liberty, egalitarian, a place where the Vendean insurrection was never able to take serious root.[76]

The intuition of a contrast appears in a slightly different form in the frequent assertion of the intense isolation of the Vendée. But no one could seriously hold that the West as a whole, the setting of such cities as Nantes, Angers, La Rochelle, Niort, Laval, Saint-Malo or Le Mans, was completely rural or completely isolated. Nor was the counter-revolution simply the response of the most "backward" sections to the Revolution.[77] One element of the contrast, to

---

[75] Analysis of the rolls of the *capitation nobiliaire,* of communal reports of "privileged residents," of parish registers and of population reports for 1790 (A. D. Maine-et-Loire B [parish registers], C 191-193, IV C 3, 1 L 402) yields this estimate, unworthy of overwhelming confidence; 67 households per thousand noble in the revolutionary district, and 39 households per thousand in the counter-revolutionary district.

[76] A. Le Moy, *L'Anjou* (Paris, 1924), 15-16.

[77] Given the immense volume of writing on the Vendée, the richness of the documents shedding light on the social organization of western France that have never been exploited is nothing short of amazing. There are extensive manorial records, abundant notarial archives full of information about property transfers and social alignments, plentiful parish registers, numerous minutes of court proceedings, and adequate records of the sales of church and

be sure, was the difference between localized, subsistence agriculture (in the Vendée) and market-oriented, rationalized agriculture (in the surrounding area). But another, often neglected, element is the eighteenth-century development of nuclei of trade and manufacturing in the midst of the traditional farming areas. One more statistical fragment, again comparing the extreme districts of Southern Anjou shows the results:[78]

Estimated Occupational Distribution of Adult
Males; Rural Communes (per cent)

Category	Revolutionary	Counter-Revolutionary
Noble	0.47	0.16
Priest	1.42	1.10
Bourgeois	1.69	8.43
Hired Hand	29.19	11.26
Other Peasant	51.11	41.13
Weaver	2.35	21.27
Other Artisan	13.77	16.64

The important fact to notice is the higher proportion of artisans and bourgeois (largely merchants and petty manufacturers) in the counter-revolutionary section, surrounded by peasants little involved in the money economy (as the low proportion of hired hands suggests). To put the matter all too baldly, such a social situation is much more favorable to violent local conflict between "old" and "new," "backward" and "progressive" than is a uniformly advanced, or a uniformly backward, social setting. In fact, it is not far off the mark to say that throughout the West, the peaks of counter-revolutionary activity were not in the backward sections so much as at the junctions of rural and urban ways of life.

Even if this simple formula explained the variation from revolutionary to counter-revolutionary sections of the West, it would still be necessary to analyze the changes in the social situation from 1789 to 1793. This returns us to one of the traditional issues, but from a new direction. Rather than asking whether the *cahiers* of the Vendée asked for any reform (when, after all, each commune was asked explicitly to state its grievances), we may ask whether there was any significant difference in the *cahiers* of the two sections of Southern Anjou that were later to disagree so acridly over the Revolution. The answer: yes. On almost every significant issue on which there was a difference, the counter-revolutionary section made fewer demands for reform.[79] In this case, a statistical criterion

émigré properties. The last, at least, are now, finally, being studied. See Joseph Denecheau, "La vente des biens nationaux dans le district de Vihiers," *Mémoire pour le Diplôme d'Études Supéieures d'Histoire*, Université de Poitiers, 1955, and the forthcoming study by Mme. Vendre of the sales in the district of Cholet.

[78] Sources: A. D. Maine-et-Loire, B (parish registers), 6 L 19, 7 L 98, Andrews, *op. cit.*, 163 ff.

[79] See A. Le Moy, *Cahiers de doléances des corporations de la ville d'Angers et des paroisses de la sénéchaussée particulière d'Angers pour les États Généraux de 1789* (Angers, 1915), vol. II. Conclusions drawn from this comparison are weakened by the fact that

does barbaric injustice to the pithy content of the cahiers, but is still convenient. 63% of the revolutionary communes opposed the *droit de chasse,* while 13% of the counter-revolutionary communes opposed it. On the question of reform or suppression of the manorial courts it was 31% against 22%. When it came to opposing the fiscal rights of the seigneurs, it was 52% versus 15%. 14% of the *cahiers* of communes from the revolutionary area proposed the sale of church lands, and 26% complained about the tithe collected by outsiders, while the figures for the counter-revolutionary territory were 2% and 11%. In short, in regard to issues that mattered a great deal in the years to follow, there were already notable differences in the positions taken in 1789 by the spokesmen of communities of the two sections of Southern Anjou.

Nevertheless, clearly defined revolutionary and counter-revolutionary *parties* did not form in the area until later. To summarize very briefly, a nucleus of revolutionary leaders, drawn especially from the mercantile bourgeoisie, emerged fairly early in the section that joined the counter-revolution, and steadily increased its share of the available public offices, and its control of the political apparatus. The organized opposition to the revolutionaries crystallized much more slowly, locally and erratically. That opposition was a good deal more heterogeneous than the revolutionary nucleus. A series of public issues drove more and more of the population into commitment to one party or the other, and increasingly drastic conflict both reinforced that commitment and drove the parties further apart.[80] This happened somewhat independently within most localities of the Vendée. In fact, a process like that which Gregory Bateson calls schismogenesis—the increasing polarization of the norms of two groups as a result of their interaction—occurred. The level of conflict mounted erratically to the apex, counter-revolution.

IV

My purpose in laying out these segments of an analysis of the Vendée here is not to present a convincing and comprehensive explanation of the counter-revolution, but to demonstrate that a sociological conception of what is to be explained, and how it is to be explained, leads to different ways of dividing up the problem, different types of data, different methods of handling the data, different crucial issues, and new conclusions. It clarifies a number of the traditional debates that historians who begin by concentrating on the personal motives of the rebels get into, and deflates the importance of some of those

---

almost none of the communal *cahiers* from the vicinity of Saumur have been found and deposited in public archives. In this case, the "counter-revolutionary section" consists of all communes of Southern Anjou west of the Layon River and not touching the Loire.

[80] See Charles Tilly, *"Rivalités* entre bourgs et l'alignement des partis dans les Mauges," *Revue du Bas-Poitou* (forthcoming); "Local Party Conflicts," *op. cit.*; "Some Problems," *op. cit.*; "Civil Constitution and Counter-Revolution," *op. cit.* One of the dividends of the close study of the character of the opposition to the patriots has been to discover how widespread were unemployment and agitation among the textile workers in the vicinity of Cholet during the years just before the counter-revolution.

debates. For example, the dilemma of "plot" vs. "spontaneity" in the explanation of the rebellion appears unreal when one considers the numerous, bitter combats between the parties in the years before 1793. As a result, even those who ask the traditional questions have something to gain from the sociological approach.

Some caveats are in order. A sociological approach does not banish motives. Sociologists (and the numerous historians who share the general method I have called "sociological," many of whom would reject both the appellation, and the implication of a prior claim by sociology) discuss motives, norms, values, and interests with considerable confidence. But they see motives as differentiated, complex and variable, as strongly limited and influenced by social structure, and they do not give the detection of motives nearly the prominence in their methods of explanation that traditional political historians do.

Furthermore, a sociological approach by no means sweeps away the problem of ideology. Instead, it reduces the indiscriminate use of articulated beliefs as explanations of collective social actions, and calls attention to the necessity of analyzing the development of an ideology, its function for the group which adheres to it, and, more generally, the conditions under which a group of men will fight in the name of a set of beliefs. In the case at hand, it seems that the beliefs about the virtues of the old regime and the intentions of the rebellion which have so often been retroactively imputed to the rebels actually emerged from the stress of battle, that once defined they did influence the movement, that they were later elaborated by elite apologists of the old regime and powerfully affected the region's political life in the nineteenth century.[81] It does not seem that one can explain the counter-revolution by alleging the personal attachment of the peasants to Throne and Altar.

Of course, to the extent that one wishes to assign moral responsibility for historical events, or to encourage modern readers to empathize with historical figures, a sociological conception of explanation is unsatisfying. Either of these is a legitimate end for an historian to pursue. They are, however, ends which are declining in importance—or at least, whose pursuit is becoming more and more subtly blended with other aims—in the historiography of the French Revolution. The important new work of historians like Cobb, Rudé and Soboul stresses a range of questions whose significance stands out boldly in the light of the previous discussion: Exactly who were the participants in crucial actions of the Revolution? How did they differ from other people? How were they organized? What were their relations to other significant groupings? And only then comes the old question: what were their motives?[82] The result is that great masses of new sorts of documents (long available but rarely explored before), new methods of handling the documents, and even new ways of presenting analyses of the Revolution are coming into use. The increasing prominence of expert

---

[81] See Paul Bois, "Reflexions," *op. cit.*

[82] See the convenient review of recent writing in Marcel Reinhard, "Sur l'histoire de la Révolution francaise," *Annales; Économies, Sociétés, Civilisations,* XIV (July-Sept. 1959), 553-570, and the books of Soboul, Rudé and Tφnnesson already cited.

demographers like Marcel Reinhard among the historians of the Revolution is itself a sign of the change.

What seems likely to result from this trend in the historiography of the Revolution and the parallel, if weaker, trend in the historiography of the counter-revolution is a much greater integration of our knowledge of the two of them. Both can be subsumed under an unsubtle question with subtle ramifications: in France as a whole, what social conditions led to acceptance or rejection of the Revolution and the party in power? This question, in turn, opens the way to a comparative sociology of political upheaval and change. [83] No doubt it would be an act of sociological chauvinism to declare that this should be the aspiration of all studies of the Revolution. Yet I cannot escape the conviction that it is a worthy aim, and a feasible one.

Not so long ago, Alfred Cobban remarked that, with increasing awareness of the multilithic character of the Revolution they once treated as a monolith, historians are enormously complicating their explanations, and that the "result may be something which it is difficult to list as a series of causes in a text-book, and in this sense the search for causes of the French Revolution may well be at an end."[84] This is surely true. What seems to be happening, however, is not so much the withering of all causal inquiry as the following of a new understanding of the way to explain the events of the great revolution and, indeed, of all revolutions and counter-revolutions.

---

[83] Harry Eckstein, "An Introduction to the Study of Internal Wars" (unpublished paper, Princeton University), contains a good review of current thinking on internal political disturbances. See also the bibliography in Reinhard Bendix and Seymour M. Lipset, "Political Sociology," *Current Sociology*, VI (No. 2, 1957), and the marvelously stimulating work of E. J. Hobsbaum, *Primitive Rebels* (Manchester, 1959).

[84] *Historians and the Causes of the French Revolution* (London, 1958), 39.

2. Aspects of mobility in pre-industrial Japanese cities*

ROBERT J. SMITH †

A very great deal of our knowledge of urban life in Tokugawa Japan relates to the "happy society" of Genroku in the early 18th century, to the life of the theater and the gay quarters, and to the activities of the great merchant houses and the more extravagant and colorful of their heads. Extensive coverage is given theories of the state, administrative arrangements, and the discrepancies between the actual and theoretical positions of the classes of Tokugawa society. Ordinarily, mobility is treated in passing, partly because vertical social mobility is rightly presumed to have been a minor feature of that society until at least its closing period, and partly because the materials required are so difficult to unearth and so resistant to rigorous analysis. Bellah's observation that ". . . mobility was largely within classes rather than between them,"[1] is apt, although Taeuber reminds us that ". . . movements of surplus youth from the rural areas to the cities were adjustments of population to resources and employment opportunities that ante-dated modern industrialization by some centuries."[2] Lampard completes the thought with respect to its implications for the transition to industrialism in his remark that ". . . old commercial-administrative centers [provide] ready markets, some tradition of urban life, and constant pressure to secure a livelihood from non-farming activity."[3]

* Reprinted by permission of the editors from *Comparative Studies in Society and History*, V (July, 1963), pp. 416-23. The research of which this paper is a partial report was supported by the Wenner-Gren Foundation for Anthropological Research in New York, the Social Science Research Council, and the Cornell University Committee on Faculty Research Grants.

† Robert J. Smith, professor of anthropology and chairman, Department of Anthropology, Cornell University, received his Ph.D. from Cornell University in 1953. He is coauthor of *Two Japanese Villages*, with John B. Cornell, and co-editor of *Japanese Culture: Its Development and Characteristics*, with Richard K. Beardsley.

[1] Robert N. Bellah, *Tokugawa Religion: The Values of Pre-Industrial Japan* (Glencoe, 1957), p. 25.

[2] Irene B. Taeuber, *The Population of Japan* (Princeton, 1958), p. 27.

[3] Eric E. Lampard, "The History of Cities in the Economically Advanced Areas," *Economic Development and Cultural Change*, 3 (1955), 130.

The three great cities of Tokugawa Japan did indeed provide a tradition of urban life, no small part of which is closely related to the pressure on old residents and new migrants to secure a livelihood from non-agricultural activities. It is a curious feature of much of the less defensible literature on the pre-industrial city that it argues so forcibly for the view that such cities are simply not urban. This position can, in my opinion, be held only by defining into the term urban some features of the industrial system, thereby auto-matically excluding the cities of pre-industrial societies. It is, as I have observed elsewhere, apparent that if the cities of Tokugawa Japan were not like the cities of contemporary industrial states, neither were they like the villages of Tokugawa Japan.[4] Edo, Osaka and Kyoto, with their highly variegated life, very large populations, and the drama and excitement of the bustling amusement and business centers (*sakariba*), which provided a large measure of anonymity in the pursuit of this wide range of activities, were at a considerable remove from the villages of the countryside.[5] To be sure, the organization of the wards and quarters (*chōnai*) might be tight, and their control frequently lodged in the hands of conservative wealth, but neither the individual nor the household was bound to the urban quarter in anything like the firm way in which a farmer was tied to the area in which his fields were located.

There was, in short, what appears to have been a considerable mobility of the city population in Tokugawa Japan, both geographically and horizontally within the class into which one was born or adopted early in life. For the urban dweller (*chōnin*), then, while the scope for movement was great, it was primarily if not entirely limited to movement within the broadly defined activities of the *chōnin* group. The system of primogeniture, commonly but not rigidly observed among the *chōnin*, made it necessary for children other than the successor to find a place in society. Of these children, the second and third sons have been made out to be a rather special population, their personalities and psychologies the object of much attention for signs of an achievement motivation thought to be lacking in their more settled elder-brother successors. But, of course, the careers of these non-successor children are by no means simply reflections of a drive toward success brought on by independence training. To be sure, there is some belief in Japan that successors *are* differently trained and differently treated and this belief is sometimes given half ironic recognition in the naming of offspring. I am reminded of a second son of a business house, now a university professor, whose name—Tokio—may be translated "Go, with good fortune", and his younger brother, Tomoo, "Go and prosper".

Nakano provides us with a succinct listing of the possible careers open to a son other than the successor among the townsmen:[6] (1) If the house had the

[4] Robert J. Smith, "Pre-industrial Urbanism in Japan: A Consideration of Multiple Traditions in a Feudal Society," *Economic Development and Cultural Change*, 9 (1960), 241-257.

[5] John Friedmann, "Cities in Social Transformation," *Comparative Studies in Society and History*, 4 (1961), 86-103.

[6] Nakano Takashi, "Shōnin no shakai" ["Merchants' Society"] in Fukutake Tadashi, ed., *Nihon no shakai* [Japanese Society] (Tokyo, 1952), p. 88.

financial means, he might be made head of a branch family (*bunke*); (2) He might be adopted out at an early age, or go later as the adopted husband (*muko-yōshi*) of the daughter of another house; (3) He might be sent to serve (*hōkō*) in another business house, for training; (4) He might be sent as an acolyte (*kozō*) to a Buddhist temple to prepare for a career in the priesthood. A daughter could hope for one of a similar variety of futures: (1) The most common, of course, was simply to go as a bride to another house; (2) She might be adopted out early to another family; (3) If the family could afford it, her family might take one of their clerks (*tedai*) as her adopted husband and set up the couple as a branch house (*bunke*); (4) She might be sent as a maid to serve another house, with hopes for a good marriage through their good offices; (5) In a variety of circumstances affecting normal succession of the eldest son, her family might take an adopted husband for her and make him the successor to headship of the main house (*honke*).

It seems well at this juncture to point out a common feature of all these solutions to the problem of what to do with the surplus sons and daughters who were not to succeed to the headship of the house. It has, perhaps, been overlooked in the many analyses of the effects on non-heirs of the system of single-heir inheritance. In every case, it is the family which assumes initial responsibility for the placing of the children in some context within which it is hoped they will be able to prove themselves. While he begins with an early disadvantage, the non-inheriting son may, through a combination of the care with which he is placed by his family and by the exercise of his own initiative, once given a position from which to pursue his career, rise to heights nearly equal to or even beyond those attained by the successor in his native house. The temple acolyte is potentially an abbot; the trusted clerk may, through marriage to the daughter of his master, himself become the head of a main house; the cautiously selected adopted husband may be a candidate for high status. Similar concerns for the future of the daughters of a house are reflected in the disposition which the family makes of them. A girl who goes as a maid in a wealthy house may herself become the wife of a son or clerk who later becomes a house-head; a girl may be married into a good family for business and other considerations, but her status there is of some concern to her family; she may even, through a combination of circumstances, be the individual through whom the continuity of her family line is assured, if it proves necessary to take for her an adopted husband in the absence of a regular successor. In short, the non-inheriting children are not, as is so often implied, simply thrown out upon the world to make their mark. Quite the contrary, much care may be taken to assure their futures by cutting them off early from the family in order, actually, to guarantee them a degree of success which might be denied them if kept too long in their family. In any event, it is usually the family which makes the decision, not the child.

Both sons and daughters might marry in the city of their birth, and sons might go into the same trade or business as their fathers and elder brothers, but there was a significant amount of movement between cities and trades for purposes of both marriage and apprenticeship. Furthermore, as we shall see, there appears to have been a great deal of moving about within the cities, changes of business location, and shifting of business activities from one trade to another. All this suggests that the constant pressure to secure a livelihood necessitated some flexibility of commitment not only on the part of the individual but the household as well, particularly among small business houses, a flexibility perhaps under-reported for pre-industrial Japan.

The under-reporting, if that is what it is, may be attributed in large part to the tendency to concentrate on the great merchant houses and the rather rare families of very long genealogy at the expense of the small merchants and artisans. It is my intention to direct attention to some scattered data for the city of Kyoto in the late 18th and the first three quarters of the 19th century, which although fragmentary, do seem to me to suggest the outlines of a situation of great importance for our understanding of the nature and extent of mobility in this, presumably the least stable of the three great urban centers of Tokugawa Japan. I shall lean heavily on the inestimably valuable work of Nakano and Yokoyama,[7] reinterpreting some of their extremely interesting data. The conclusions are my own.

We are fortunate in having fairly good data for the 82-year period 1786-1867 for an area called *Koromo-no-tana-chō* in Kyoto. Table 1 gives the total population figures for the *chō*:

TABLE 1
Koromo-no-tana-chō: Changes in Population from 1786-1867

Factors	1786	1866	Loss
Population	206	135	-35%
Number of houses (*ie*)	35	24	-32%
Number of houses with servants, apprentices, clerks, etc.	18	13	-28%
Number of male employees	105	59	-44%

The decline in all figures is the striking aspect of these data, which are taken from annual registrations.

The figures of Table 1 reveal change, but say nothing directly about mobility. In Table 2 is shown the length of duration of the total number of houses registered throughout the 82-year period, 343 in all. The registers from which these figures are taken, called the *shūmon nimbetsu-chō*, were compiled annually. It was the responsibility of property owners to present to an official the required information, comprising the name of the house-head, his place and date of birth, and his temple affiliation. All family members and quasi-family (*jun-kazoku-nin*) members were also listed by name, age, and temple of

---

[7] Nakano, "Shōnin no shakai," pp. 79-136; Yokoyama Sadao, "Kinsei toshi shūraku no dōtaisei to shūdansei" ["Movement and Grouping in the Urban Community of the Late Modern Period"] in *Gendai shakaigaku no shomondai* [*Problems of Modern Sociology*] (Tokyo, 1949), pp. 523-546.

TABLE 2
Duration of Houses (ie) in *Koromo-no-tana-chō:* 1786-1867

Number of Years Appearing in Records	Number of Houses	Percent
1	96	28.0
2	69	20.5
3	43	12.5
4-5	33	9.4
6-10	58	16.9
Total 1-10	299	87.3
11-20	19	5.4
21-30	7	2.2
31-70	13	3.6
71-	5	1.5
Total 11-and over	44	12.7
Total	343	100.0

affiliation (which might differ from that of house-head). A daughter who had married out was listed, as well as the place and family into which she had married, and the date of the marriage. For quasi-family members, the name of their guarantor (*mimoto, yadomoto, oyamoto*) was given, with the date on which they entered service and the reason for which they were taken in. The figures reveal a startling rate of turn-over, with only 12.7% of the houses registered for longer than 10 years and almost half (48.5%) registered for only 1 or 2 years.

This rapid turn-over is highlighted by the figures for the same 82-year period in terms of the number of generations of duration of all the houses reported in the same registers (Table 3):

TABLE 3
Generation of House-Heads: *Koromo-no-tana-chō,* 1786-1867

Generation	Number of House-Heads	Percent
1st	312	91.0
2nd	17	5.0
3rd	6	1.7
4th	6	1.7
5th	2	.6
Total	343	100.0

Thus, less than 10% of the house-heads reported in the registers represented any generation of succession to the headship above the first. These small merchant houses do not participate in the claims to genealogical longevity of the larger, wealthier houses. Virtually the entire population of the quarter in the last 80 years of the Tokugawa period were members of small families, with neither claim nor pretensions to the legitimacy of antiquity. They have left no house-codes and few of them have left house-names (*yagō*). That there was a considerable difference between these small merchants, liable to fail in business or to move on to try their luck elsewhere or to find themselves without a successor, and the larger, wealthier merchants is pointed up by the comparative figures contrasting all other merchants of Koromo-no-tana-chō with the one large *yagō* of the quarter, Chigiriya (Table 4), established in 1650.

TABLE 4
Duration of Houses for Period 1786-1867 in *Koromo-no-tana-chō:*
Total Compared with Largest and Most Powerful

Number of Years	Total		Chigiriya	
	Number	*Percent*	*Number*	*Percent*
Up to 5	241	70.4	32	59.9
6-10	58	16.9	8	15.4
11-30	26	7.6	6	11.5
31-and over	18	5.1	7	13.2
Total	343	100.0	53	100.0

It is clear that the life expectancy of even those houses bearing the name Chigiriya was not great, for only about 25% lasted longer than 10 years. It is worthy of note, however, that in comparison to all other houses in Koromo-no-tana-chō, the Chigiriya *yagō* was easily the most likely to endure. Whereas only about 5% of the other houses lasted longer than 30 years, 13% of the houses of Chigiriya had a life span longer than 30 years. The advantages of solid financial backing and the presence of a large number of bearers of the same *yagō* to help out in emergencies are doubtless reflected in the tendency of Chigiriya to persist.

Koromo-no-tana-chō was a quarter in which there was no concentration of a single trade or business. We have figures for 1864, just before the great fire called *teppō-kaji* of that year, which show that for the area called Minami-chō there were 21 shops, representing 10 different trades and specialties. The largest single business was that of clothier (*gofuku-ya*), represented by 6 houses. Of the 21 households, 17 were tenants. All the evidence suggests that the economic life of the smaller independent businesses was extremely precarious and it is, of course, these very houses which fail to make a comeback in the records subsequent to the fire which wiped them out.

It might be objected that the *chō* is not the unit with which we should be dealing, but rather that the *kabu-nakama* (guilds) of various kinds represented the stable units of the time. That this is hardly the case is illustrated by the examples of the Nijō drug-wholesalers' *kabu-nakama* in Kyoto (Table 5). The situation here is rather like that of the mixed trades of Koromo-no-tana-chō, for almost half of the names listed are represented by only one house. Only two are really very large, one with 13 member houses and one with 14. Clearly the 20 years which elapse before the next figures are available were ones of great change in the world of the Japanese merchants, but several features of the shift

TABLE 5
Membership in the *Nijō-gumi* Drug-Wholesalers' *Kabu-nakama*
Kyoto: 1866 and 1887

Number of Member Houses of a Given Yagō (Bunke – Bekke)	1866	1887
1	20	15
2	4	7
3	5	3
4	3	2
5	3	4
6	1	1
7	2	1
8	1	2
9	–	–
10	–	1
11	–	–
12	–	–
13	1	–
14	1	–
Totals	41	36

stand out—and structurally they are highly reminiscent of the changes noted during Tokugawa. There are now five fewer names, and the proportion of one-house listings is now 42%, not 50%. Eleven of the groupings have remained stable, with the same number of members, at least; 13 have declined in numbers; only 5 have increased; 7 have appeared on the scene; 12 have disappeared completely. What stands out is this: no groupings which in 1866 had more than one member-house had disappeared by 1887. The two groupings which in 1866 were largest were also among the three largest in 1887. Like Chigiriya of the other district which we have discussed, they weathered change while their smaller, less tightly organized and more independent guild fellows fell by the wayside, victims of the changing commercial system as their counterparts had been to other pressures in the Tokugawa period.

We have not dealt with questions of vertical mobility in the foregoing pages because trustworthy evidence is extremely scarce. What we have done is to illustrate by some selected examples a situation which suggests that the movement of people, the shuffling of households and individuals, and the swift pace of change, all part of a pattern so often cited as characterizing the brave new world of Meiji Japan, was no stranger to the townsman of the late Tokugawa. For at least a hundred years before the official beginning of Japan's industrial effort and the growth of her industrial cities, important learning had gone on—the cities waxed and waned in size as did their constituent parts; businesses succeeded or failed; workers came and went; new households budded off from old ones within the trade or into some other business; a man of parts could hope to make his mark; the less talented or less fortunate slipped into less rewarding activities, and were shunted from place to place, finally to drop from the registers of their own or their adoptive houses.

The very little that we have of autobiographical material for men of the small-merchant class shows varied patterns of success and failure, rise and fall of fortune, and above all a sense of movement within the confines of their class in terms of their personal fortunes which, save for details of practice, has all a very modern ring and could, indeed, be duplicated with little difficulty for commercial enterprise of the period since the beginning of Japan's "modern century."

3. Patterns of industrial strike activity in France during the July Monarchy*

PETER N. STEARNS†

During the Restoration and July Monarchy, factory workers and artisans formed fairly distinct groups. Their methods and places of work differed, obviously. Instead of the small shops and manually operated tools of the artisan, relatively large plants with relatively complex machinery surrounded the factory worker. More important, artisans, particularly in the cities, had far firmer traditions, including many traditions of mutual organization and protection, than did the factory workers. There were, to be sure, many artisans of peasant origin filling expanding cities such as Paris, but even the newcomers encountered a large nucleus of established artisans, accustomed to the city and to the work, who helped educate them in the ways of their new life. In contrast, factory workers for the most part had no traditions and no traditional elements to direct them when they entered a new plant, often fresh from the countryside. Their standards of living might differ little from those of urban artisans, but their behavior necessarily differed considerably. Among the many areas of activity where such differences prevailed was that of agitation and strikes. The simple fact was that most of the strike activity of the period, both in quantity and quality, was conducted by urban artisans. For very good reasons, most factory workers protested their lot collectively far less often and, usually, in different ways than did their brethren in the crafts. It is, then, misleading to discuss "the workers" in a study of labor movements in the early years of French industrialization. Such a discussion obscures the bases of the agitation that did

* Reprinted from the *American Historical Review*, LXX (January, 1965), pp. 371-94, by permission of the author.

† [Formerly] an assistant professor at the University of Chicago, Mr. Stearns is interested mainly in modern European social history. He has written "The Nature of the *Avenir* Movement (1830-31)" (*American Historical Review*, LXV [July 1960]). Editors Note: Presently a professor of history, Rutgers University, Stearns received his Ph.D. from Harvard University. He is the author of *European Society in Upheaval, Social History Since 1800*, and *Priest and Revolutionary: Lamennais and the Dilemma of French Catholicism*. The article that appears here won the 1966 Koren prize from the Society for French Historical Studies.

take place, and, equally important, it prevents an understanding of the conditions that would later allow the development of strike activity among factory workers. This essay concentrates on sectors of manufacturing labor directly affected by mechanization. By implication it shows many of the factors separating these workers from the urban artisans. It does not, however, discuss the labor movement as a whole because such a single movement really did not exist. The experience of artisans was, at this time, largely irrelevant to factory workers. Only by separating the two classes can the activities of either be properly understood.

Any student of the factory worker in the first decades of French industrialization is struck by an obvious if superficial anomaly. In the midst of conditions of such misery that extreme and frequent protest might be expected, the French industrial worker was almost totally quiescent. Certainly the factors favorable to strikes and other forms of industrial agitation were numerous. In the first place, challenges to the social order had a clear precedent in the traditions of the Great Revolution and even in the events of 1830. Furthermore, the increase in numbers of industrial workers provided a greater quantitative opportunity for strikes to occur; in some fields, such as mining, the labor force actually doubled in the period, though usually the increase was not so great. Growing concentration of industry around certain urban centers also facilitated contacts among workers and was a potential spur to organization. Most important, the workers had ample cause for complaint. In a period when the wealth of the middle classes was increasing noticeably, the lot of most factory labor remained stagnant and depressing. In the plant, the worker was kept under the discipline of both machine and foreman for thirteen hours or more a day. The rewards of this labor were meager. Some workers, in fact, did not earn enough to subsist without charity. The majority could pay for bread, a few clothes, and a tiny apartment, but little or nothing remained after these were provided. Illness, and industrial crisis, or even old age might lower this minimal standard of living still further. Yet, in this period, when industrial conditions were at their worst, protests by factory labor were almost nonexistent.[1]

This is not to say, of course, that there was no strike activity by industrial workers. Jean-Pierre Aguet, in his description of strikes during the July Monarchy, has counted 98 strikes by workers who might be called industrial.[2] Actually, consideration of local reports of agitation reveals a number of strikes

---

[1] For descriptions of labor conditions in general, see L. R. Villermé, *Tableau de l'état physique et moral des ouvriers employés dans les manufactures de coton, de laine, et de soie* (2 vols., Paris, 1840), and André Lasserre, *La Situation des ouvriers de l'industrie textile dans la région lilloise sous la Monarchie de Juillet* (Lausanne, 1952).

[2] Jean-Pierre Aguet, *Contributions à l'histoire du mouvement ouvrier francais: Les grèves sous la Monarchie de Juillet (1830-1847)* (Geneva, 1954). This is a useful narrative account of all strike activity as reported to the government in Paris. As a supplement to Aguet, and to the BB[18] series of the Archives Nationales [hereafter cited as AN] that he employed, the most fruitful sources are the Series M in departmental archives, plus scattered references in economic journals such as the *Moniteur industriel* and in records such as the Archives de la Compagnie des Fondéries et Forges d'Alais [hereafter cited as ACF] and the Archives des Établissements Haussman à Logelbach [hereafter cited as AEH].

not recorded in Aguet's count; at least 40 additional cases can be added to the list as a result of this information, and quite possibly that many more could yet be found by diligent searching. Nevertheless, even a total count of 130 or 150 industrial strikes results in an average of only 7 or 8 a year. And analysis of what is usually included in the category "industrial" detracts even further from the impact of the figures. Aguet, for example, quite sensibly includes in his category mining, metallurgy, machine building, and textiles—all industries affected by the new mechanical methods and organized in part at least in a factory system of production. Of the industries in the group, however, textiles provided the largest number of strikes (82 in Aguet's count). But the textile industry was incompletely transformed by modern industrial methods and systems. To be sure, cotton and wool spinning were vastly altered, but weaving was still largely done by hand, and whole areas of production, such as silk and ribbons, were untouched either by power machinery or by factories. Such industries, particularly the silk manufacturing of Lyons, were among the most productive of strikes; furthermore, their strikes were unusually forceful and well organized. Even aside from such well-known cases, a high percentage of textile strikes were conducted by workers, particularly weavers, who produced either at home or in very small shops. In fact, of the 128 industrial strikes that I have been able to count, 51 of them were conducted by domestic or small shop labor. Actual factory labor was engaging in merely 4 or 5 strikes a year on the average. This paucity is particularly startling because labor as a whole, including artisans, was definitely increasing its activity during the July Monarchy. Aguet has counted 284 strikes by artisans and construction workers, virtually three times the number produced by the industrial categories. To be sure, artisans outnumbered industrial workers, even broadly construed, possibly by as much as two to one; nevertheless, it is clear that industrial labor was not keeping pace with its brethren in the crafts. Both on the basis of absolute numbers of strikes and of relative activity, the sluggishness of industrial labor is clear.[3]

The nature of most industrial strikes, moreover, demonstrates still further the ineffectiveness of factory workers at the time. In the first place, few strikes boasted any real organization or planning; they were usually spontaneous responses to an immediate subject of discontent. Often they were conceived in a tavern the evening before, or even on the same morning as they took place. There was no real leadership, no funds to support the effort. As a result, it was rare for a strike to last more than a single day. In Lille, for example, during the crisis year 1837, workers on short time had the habit of attending band concerts in the late afternoon; one afternoon they replaced the concert with a riot—and that was the extent of Lille's labor agitation that year. In 1838 the thread piecers in Cateau-Cambrésis were incited by some spinners not to work on Ash Wednesday; they spent all day in a bar and then rioted around closing time. Strikes of this sort served mainly to vent a complaint for the satisfaction of the

---

[3] Aguet, *Mouvement ouvrier,* 365; Henri Sée, *La Vie économique de la France, 1789-1914* (Paris, 1927), 87; Edgard Allix, *La Concentration industrielle et son influence sur le sort des classes ouvrières* (Paris, 1909), 54-55.

strikers themselves. They could not be the vehicles of a prolonged or intensive effort. In addition, they could not hope to attract large numbers. Without planning or organization, many strikes did not go beyond a single plant. Usually strikers in one plant would attempt to arouse their colleagues in neighboring factories, and sometimes they would succeed. But even in a major industrial city such as Lille, worker demonstrations never boasted more than three or four hundred participants; most strikes affected only a few dozen workers. The average strike was brief, small, disorganized, and lacked formal leadership.[4]

It is obvious that workers were in no position to sustain any elaborate links with their fellows in other places. To be sure, workers in Thann sometimes imitated riots by workers in Mulhouse; workers in Bédarieux had even more active contacts with their neighbors in Lodève. And there were reports of some general awareness of the major riots in Lyons and Paris. But seldom did any action result, and almost never was any coherent contact maintained. What initiative there was came from the individual town or city, often even from the individual factory.[5]

Methods employed by strikers naturally reflected the lack of planning and real strength. Labor protests usually took one of two courses. The first was an appeal to the authorities, usually the local government but sometimes the employer himself. A group of workers would abandon the plant, march to city hall, and present a verbal petition. A soothing speech from the mayor, urging patience and resignation, would calm all passions, and the workers would disperse in an orderly manner. This was the pattern of most labor agitation in Tourcoing during the depression year 1847. Workers there, and often elsewhere, were simply too resigned to do more than briefly demonstrate in the hope that some higher power would solve their problems. When the higher power refused, they had no other recourse. Often, however, workers went beyond the humble petition or did not attempt it at all. In such cases, a strike usually involved considerable violence against property. Frequently the windows of the employer's home or of the factory would bear the brunt of the anger. In Elbeuf in 1846, employees of a man who had introduced a new wool-cleaning machine massed around his home, shouting threats and breaking windows; troops were required to break up the riot. But the attack could focus on machines or on bakers' shops as well. No matter what the target, the pattern was usually the same: an hour or two of intense violence, and then the strike would be over. Again, there was no possibility of constructive or prolonged strike action. At

---

4 AN BB[18]1220, report from Louviers, Nov. 1833; *ibid.*, 1245, Lille report, May 1837; *ibid.*, 1389, report on Hardinghen miners, Jan. 1841; Archives départementales [hereafter cited as AD] du Nord, M620–6, Cateau-Cambrésis report, 1836; Charles Engrand, "Les Ouvriers lillois de 1829 à 1832," unpublished thesis, Faculté des Lettres, Université de Lille, 1957, 147.

5 Édouard Dolléans and Gérard Déhove, *Histoire du travail en France: Mouvement ouvrier et législation sociale* (2 vols., Paris, 1953-55), I, 210; Marie-Madeleine Kahan-Rabecq, "L'Importance de la classe ouvrière alsacienne en 1848," in *Deux siècles d'Alsace française, 1648-1848* (Strasburg, 1948), 409, 414; Aguet, *Mouvement ouvrier,* 341; AD, Haut-Rhin, 1M126-1, 1831 report.

best, it could be hoped that a show of wrath would induce concessions out of fear. But usually the thinking of strikers did not seem to go this far. The strike, with its violence, was an expression of pent-up emotion and hostility; it was not a tool to achieve lasting improvements in conditions. Once passions found expression in an hour or two of howling riot, and were perhaps calmed by a certain amount of fatigue, there was nothing left of the strike.[6]

Seldom did striking factory workers have any long-range goals in mind. Here again, the basic weakness and inadequacy of industrial agitation in the period were reflected. Workers generally struck for a single purpose only; they could not formulate a series of demands. More important, they were seldom capable of envisaging long-range improvement in their conditions. As a result, most industrial strikes were protests against some immediate change in the workers' situation. In most cases, strikes were called solely to protest a lowering of pay, and all that was usually demanded was a return to the previous level. A reduction of wages provided a definite issue and a definite purpose. Further, the announcement of reduction was the sort of clear-cut, single event against which grievance could be most easily directed, particularly since the announcement usually found workers assembled or assembling for work. Most strikes, then, took place immediately upon workers' hearing the news of a pay cut, or within the next twenty-four hours, after a night of rising excitement and hasty planning. Characteristically, spinners in Dornach in 1830 walked out as a result of an announcement of salary reduction, which was made in particularly unsympathetic terms; in 1847, wool spinners of the Ménage plant in Elbeuf struck the day after a similar announcement.[7]

In a smaller number of cases, other changes provided the goals for some strikes. Often, agitation focused on a rise in food prices, the introduction of machines, or rising unemployment. Sometimes even changes in systems of work that had no particularly adverse effect on workers would give rise to strike. Again, change was the only phenomenon clear enough to rouse factory labor, however rarely, from its lethargy. Industrial strikes were overwhelmingly designed simply to defend the *status quo* against deterioration. Hence most industrial strikes took place during business slumps. Then alone was change sufficiently drastic to goad apathetic workers into brief protest. In many cases the workers who struck were simply expressing the abysmal misery of unemployment and hunger. Tragically, however, a strike or riot during a crisis period was almost doomed to failure because employers had neither desire nor need to improve conditions of labor when their own profits were often being reduced or even eliminated. Only a strike in prosperous times had a real chance of effecting permanent improvements in conditions. But in prosperity industrial workers were incapable of formulating demands because there was no adverse change to provide the goal for action. In contrast, strikes of artisans increased in number during prosperous years, for many artisans could plan and organize for

---

6 Lasserre, *Situation des ouvriers,* 222; Aguet, *Mouvement ouvrier,* 11; AN BB[18]1442, report from Elbeuf, May 23, 1846.

7 *Ibid.,* 1192, report on Dornach, 1830; *ibid.,* 1456, report on Elbeuf, Oct. 1847.

the future and could understand something of the economic forces under which they operated. During the boom months from September 1833 to April 1834, for example, Aguet counted fifty strikes by artisans, only nine by industrial labor—far above the ratio for the period as a whole. For factory workers, protest during relatively good times was years in the future. During the July Monarchy, they remained quiet unless given an obvious stimulus in the form of some alteration of their lot. And even then, the vast majority of pay reductions and dismissals passed by without a hint of protest from their victims.[8]

Factory labor, lacking the ability to act except under the stimulus of immediate deterioration of conditions, was not in a position to be stirred by doctrinal influences. In contrast, leaders of artisan movements, especially in Paris and Lyons, often had a definite, if hazy, ideological bent; as a result their approach was more diversified and even stronger, in the sense that it did not depend so heavily on specific economic changes. There were, of course, a number of active socialist propagandists who tried occasionally to make contact with factory workers, but they were almost always completely unsuccessful. The workers were neither ready nor able to be roused by any talk of rights or justice. What industrial protest there was lacked any support from general ideas or programs.

The confused quality of the sporadic industrial agitation was reflected, finally, in the lack of any consistent object of attack. Most commonly, to be sure, grievances were directed against employers. But there were several other directions that protest could take. In cases where rising prices competed with falling wages for workers' attention, bakery shops and their owners were as likely to be attacked as were the plant and its director. The only real agitation in the whole period on the part of Troyes cotton workers focused on bakers alone. There were several instances, also, of attacks on machines as the cause of misery; it was felt that destruction of machines would result in an improvement of conditions for workers generally. Hence in 1830 Lille thread twisters expressed their discontent at the unemployment and low pay that were part of the industrial crisis of that year by demonstrating against machines. Finally, there were a number of riots against other workers, particularly foreigners—another possible scapegoat for unsatisfactory conditions. In sum, the protests of factory labor in this period expressed much bitterness and generalized unhappiness. But there was no clear focus for this intense feeling, and no clear conception of what improvements could be brought about and by what methods.[9]

Thus, despite a number of factors that seemed to favor protest by industrial workers, strikes during the July Monarchy were rare and weak in almost every respect. As a result, they had almost no success in improving the workers' lot. To be sure, employers were aware that workers might riot and in some cases were

---

[8] *Ibid.*, 1264, report on Saint-Quentin strike; AD, Nord, M626-3, report on Anzin strike, Oct. 1847; Aguet, *Mouvement ouvrier*, 123, 370, 375; Georges Créveuil, "La Condition ouvrière et la crise de 1847, à Nantes," *1848 et les évolutions du*, xixe *siècle*, XXXIX (Feb. 1948), 50.

[9] André Colomés, *Ouvriers du textile dans la Champagne troyenne, 1730-1852* (Paris, 1943), 135; AD, Nord, M620-4, 1830 report.

mildly influenced by this awareness in the setting of labor policy. In few instances, though, did the possibility of a strike inhibit employers; for strikes were unlikely and could easily be defeated if they occurred. There were, however, a small number of strikes that ran counter to the general trend of weakness and disorganization. An unusual number of such outbreaks took place in a very few areas and industries. Any effort to understand the factors involved in protest in this period must, then, devote some attention to the exceptional efforts of a few groups of workers and to the factors that allowed such efforts.[10]

The criteria by which relatively strong strike action may be judged are numerous, relating to goals, organization, and frequency. A few cases approached real vigor by any standards save those of the period itself. But compared to the average, they stand out as exceptional indeed. In the first place, there were certain instances in which the purposes of labor agitation indicated some solidity and breadth of vision. In such instances, workers did not totally rely on a direct, immediate change to determine their goals. In some cases a strike was initiated over a single issue, as a result of a recent innovation, but later it developed a broader range of demands going beyond the original problem. In 1844, for example, coal miners at Rive-de-Gier struck against the threat of a pay cut for workers in two of their company's many pits, but soon the strike turned into a demand for a twenty-five-centime raise for the majority of the workers. Similar developments occurred in strikes at Anzin in 1833 and at Lodève in 1834. Other strikes sought indemnities for the time lost in protest. In 1833 Lodève wool workers sought such an indemnity for the two and a half months of their strike; workers in Castres made the same demand in 1841. Again, the strikes had been motivated by a direct change—a reduction in pay—but had gone beyond this to develop other goals.[11]

There were other ways in which the purposes of agitation occasionally expressed greater complexity than usual. In some instances the past was used as a standard, but not in an immediate sense. Strikes occurred for restoration of past conditions, but not as the direct result of an unfavorable change. In 1840, for example, wool workers in both Lodève and Castres struck for higher pay in a period of prosperity. They sought primarily to compensate for wage declines of the previous year; they did not anticipate absolutely new wage levels. But their strikes did represent the ability to retain past standards as a goal over a relatively long period of time, rather than an instinctive reaction to change when it first occurred. Again in 1845 workers in Lodève were able to use a sense of tradition in an unusually sweeping manner. In their strike they sought a cessation of mechanization, a return of industry to domestic production, and an increase both of the number of small manufacturers and of their opportunities in the industry. Here was a list of purposes far more complex and varied than most industrial labor could have produced, it envisaged the local economic structure

---

10 J. Veneday, *Reise und Rasttage in der Normandie* (2 vols., Leipzig, 1838), II, 480.

11 AN BB[18]1437, report on the Compagnie générale des mines de la Loire, May 1844; *ibid.*, 1406, report on Rouen metallurgical strike, Sept. 1842.

as a whole. The demands were totally archaic, relying completely on the past. But they clearly represented a use of past standards in more than the usual immediate and single-minded way.[12]

In a few cases, finally, workers were able to formulate demands for better conditions that went beyond past standards altogether. In 1831, for example, miners at Alais struck for higher pay not because of a previous deterioration in their own position, but because they simply hoped for better wages than they had ever before received. In 1837 Anzin miners similarly sought a raise not to compensate for an earlier change in conditions, but because the price of coal had risen, and they deserved to share in the greater prosperity that this rise had brought the company.[13] In these and a few other instances (less than ten in all) workers were clearly able to seek improvements in their lot beyond what the past had offered.[14]

Most strikes seeking more than an immediate return of previous conditions involved not only a relatively firm sense of purpose but also a relatively advanced understanding of the bargaining position of labor. For workers who were able to strike for more than a restoration of past standards, or who could agitate on the basis of tradition without the spur of a change of conditions immediately preceding the protest, were capable of timing their action to coincide with situations favorable to success. Their strikes were more than emotional reactions; they were planned with an eye to the economic position of the industry. The Alais strike of 1831 was brought about because the miners realized that their employer was in desperate need of coal production. The wool workers of Lodève and Castres who reacted to the pay cuts of 1839 not by immediate protest but by a strike when prosperous times had returned to their industry showed a similar understanding of the economic pressures on manufacturers.[15]

Strikes in which goals were relatively complex and farsighted inevitably demanded better organization than did a defensive strike called in sudden anger over a specific issue. Such strikes had to be arranged in advance. Furthermore, there were instances in which even defensive strikes elicited a relatively solid organizational effort, sometimes developed after the strike began. Hence cases of interesting strike organization are somewhat more common than cases of comparative complexity of purpose. The key feature of good organization, indeed of any significant organization at all, was the attempt to set up a strike fund. Only by this means could workers hope to give their strike duration and numerical strength. In 1839 in Lille, for example, cotton workers boasted a strike fund offering twelve francs a week to every striker, though it is doubtful

---

[12] AD, Hérault, 4M247, report on Lodéve, Jan. 1834; Frank E. Manuel, "L'Introduction des machines en France et les ouvriers; la grève des tisserands de Lodève," *Revue d'histoire moderne*, X (Sept.-Oct. 1935), 371.

[13] ACF report, Nov. 18, 1831; AD, Nord, M626-1, July 1837, report.

[14] Government officials and employers often claimed that a strike was for a pay raise, when actually it was a case of defensive reaction to a recent pay reduction. The number of truly offensive industrial strikes was very low.

[15] ACF report, Nov. 18, 1831; Aguet, *Mouvement ouvrier*, 179.

that this sum could have been long maintained; even so, the fund and the organizational effort behind the action as a whole allowed the strike to last five days, an unusually long time for cotton workers. In 1835 wool workers in Bédarieux used a mutual-aid group as a cover for a strike fund sufficient to permit a three-week effort; the same device was used by Castres wool workers in 1840 and 1841. Several other textile strikes, including most of the many actions by Lodève labor, were covered by strike funds, and coal miners at Anzin and Rive-de-Gier made at least some attempt to support their agitation by a common purse.[16]

Organization was evident not only in financial planning, but also in coordination and tactics. Only a strike with some leadership and direction could intelligently appeal to a large number of workers. In 1847, for example, miners at Anzin planned a strike and began in advance to contact workers in other companies to increase their strength. Miners at Rive-de-Gier in 1840 and 1844 made great efforts to involve their colleagues at Saint-Étienne, with some success. Hence mining strikes both in the Nord and in the Saint-Étienne region often involved one or two thousand workers. Cases of such numbers in textile strikes were rare, though in 1833 the wool workers of Louviers managed to involve eleven hundred people in their strike. However, Lodève workers attempted far more coordination than even the coal miners. Lodève weavers maintained contacts with workers at Bédarieux, and even at Carcassonne; they occasionally managed to encourage strikes paralleling their own and also sought to dissuade labor in other areas from attempting strikebreaking employment in Lodève.

The relatively elaborate organization of miners, particularly at Rive-de-Gier, and of Lodève and Castres wool workers also permitted efforts of exceptional duration and tactical subtlety. In 1833 and again in 1845 Lodève workers managed to strike for over two months; miners in Rive-de-Gier did the same in 1844. The mining strikes at Rive-de-Gier and to an extent at Anzin displayed definite organization and control in their prevention of any particular striker violence despite great provocation and even bloodshed caused by government troops. In Castres and Lodève worker tactics also showed considerable planning. Lodève workers often struck a few key plants alone, in an effort to break employer unity and win general gains. Castres weavers, in 1840, carefully coordinated demands in all shops at once. They also managed, at least briefly, to put the most offensive plants under interdict, preventing them from acquiring labor for any purpose even after the strike had ended in most shops. Such tactics were not always successful, but they indicated both planning and intelligence on the part of their sponsors. In sum, certain areas on some occasions did see a real effort at coordination in industrial strikes. Exactly what form labor organization

---

16 Jean-Paul Courtheoux, "Naissance d'une conscience de classe dans le prolétariat textile du Nord (1830-1870)?" *Revue économique,* XXXI (Jan. 1957), 136; AD, Hérault, 4M247, Sept. 1847, report; AD, Tarn, IVM231-34, report on Castres, Nov. 1840. Strike funds were also reported among Vienne wool workers in 1843 (AN BB[18]1409) and among Roanne cotton spinners (*ibid.,* 1455, Aug. 1847, report).

took in such cases is not known. The source and type of leadership are also unknown, though there are occasional and doubtful government reports of outside and often republican agitators at the helm. Even the duration of these organizational efforts cannot be certain. In the case of Lille in 1839, the organization obviously did not survive the strike; there were no coordinated efforts by Lille labor during the rest of the July Monarchy. The same is true of most of the textile regions, such as Vienne and Roanne, which offer one clear case of some organization. The mining regions undoubtedly had some continuing or at least repeating leadership since signs of planning appear several times. And some of the southern wool centers, such as Lodève, undoubtedly had even more continuous worker groups, often behind the facade of a mutual-aid society.[17]

In essence, then, there were a few cases of a single important strike effort, in terms of organization, tactics, and occasionally purpose, in a small number of regions. In even fewer areas, there was an obvious ability to mount even more important efforts repeatedly. The industrial areas in which more than one major strike was conducted in the period fall into two clear categories: the regions of large coal mines and the southern wool cities of Lodève, Bédarieux, and Castres. Lodève workers struck at least eight times in the period, often for considerable lengths of time and with a powerful organization. Miners in the Rive-de-Gier and Saint-Étienne region struck four times, and again usually with large numbers and for a relatively long time; Anzin miners struck three times and agitated again in 1847. Miners of the Grand'-Combe struck twice, and several other mines were struck importantly at least once. In contrast, there were only two or three strikes in metallurgy and machine building in this period, none of them notable. Similarly, in textiles, the great cotton city of Mulhouse saw only one small strike and a bread riot; the Nord witnessed only two textile strikes plus several bread riots. Many important manufacturing centers, such as Troyes, experienced no real strikes at all, though there was often a bread riot in 1847. To be sure, a few textile regions outside the south did see more than one or two strikes by the same type of workers. This was true, for example, in Cholet, where rural weavers struck on several occasions. But the Cholet strikes were short, disorganized, and caused simply by the decline of domestic weaving, and so of wages, in the area. Their relative frequency was largely a sign of a desperation greater than that of more modern textile centers. True strength of industrial labor, by the standards of the period at least, was exhibited only in the wool industry of one region and in the coal industry more generally.[18]

---

[17] Aguet, *Mouvement ouvrier,* 106, 332, and "Les Grèves de mineurs en France sous la Monarchie de Juillet (1830-1848)," *Schweizerische Zeitschrift für Geschichte,* XXI (May 1954), 384; AN BB[18]1388, report on Castres, 1841; *ibid.,* 1444, report on Anzin, Feb. 1847; AD, Hérault, 4M247, Jan. 1831, and Jan. 1834 reports; E. Tarlé, "La Grande coalition des mineurs de Rive-de-Gier en 1844," *Revue historique,* CLXXVII (Mar.-Apr. 1936), 257.

[18] Aguet, *Mouvement ouvrier,* 337; Colomès, *Ouvriers du textile,* 135; Courtheoux, "Naissance d'une conscience," 136. Obviously, the silk industry of Lyons and the ribbon industry of Saint-Étienne were also areas of real labor strength according to the criteria used in this essay. The peculiar and largely artisanal organization of these industries makes it

Any explanation of strike movements by factory labor must, then, cover the two aspects of protest activity. On the one hand, it must account for the infrequency and weakness of agitation by most industrial workers. At the same time, it must show why much greater labor power existed in a very few cases. Fortunately, such an explanation is possible. It can be shown that, while there were certain general factors inhibiting strike activity in all cases, there were other factors affecting much of the textile industry, and metallurgy and machine building, far more than they affected coal mining and the southern wool industry. The general factors account for the fact that labor even in the exceptional cases was badly organized and relatively lethargic. The special factors explain why a few groups of workers were able to stand out so notably compared to most industrial labor in the July Monarchy itself.

The two most obvious general factors operating against all labor activity were the attitudes and policies of government and industrialists. The national government had long held strikes to be illegal and stiffened the provisions against worker and other associations during the July Monarchy. The cabinet ministers concerned with such matters were unanimous in fearing strikes as hostile both to proper economy and to the stability of the government itself. Some officials were even more inflexible in their stance than most industrialists, and, when the latter occasionally yielded to a strike, the government could be loud in its denunciations of their weakness. To be sure, some prefects occasionally saw the justice of the strikers' demands and attempted to promote at least a compromise settlement. This occurred, for example, in a weavers' strike in Rennes in 1839; the prefect held that wages were unjustly low and induced the employers to yield.[19] More commonly, however, the government reacted to a strike by sending soldiers and arresting and prosecuting the leading workers involved. A large number of strikes, including mining strikes and other vigorous efforts, were only broken up by troops who were perfectly willing to use arms against the strikers. A substantial number of strikers were brought to trial, and while they seldom suffered sentences of more than a year, their example was undoubtedly sufficient to intimidate many prospective strikers. In 1832, for instance, 522 workers were brought to trial, with 304 actually sentenced. Furthermore, several more general governmental policies inhibited strike action. The enforcement of the *livret* as virtually a license to obtain a job, with the possibility open to employers to withhold it in cases of bad conduct, was a powerful means of controlling worker behavior generally, though it was not universally utilized. The common effort by local governments to send away unemployed workers during slumps was another powerful deterrent to coordinated protest during the worst times. In general, government viewed workers with great distrust and acted

needless and confusing to include them in a study of factory workers. But it should be noted that many of the elements of labor's strength in both cities resemble those of the wool industry in the south.

19 AN BB[18]1263, report on Rennes, Nov. 1839; David H. Pinkney, *"Laissez-Faire* or Intervention? Labor Policy of the First Months of the July Monarchy," *French Historical Studies,* III (Spring 1963), 123-28.

accordingly to control and to intimidate. Though not all workers were always or equally deterred, most were powerfully influenced by the government's policies.[20]

Even more immediate to most workers was the power exercised over them by their employers. Quite obviously, almost all employers hated and feared strikes. In their eyes, strikes were symptoms of ingratitude that could only end in worsening the workers' lot by disturbing industry. More important, manufacturers feared the effects that strikes would have on the cost and discipline of labor. They also opposed the interruption of production and the potential violence that strikes represented. Employers were, furthermore, able to implement their hostility to labor agitation. They were often instrumental in calling in troops and seeking prosecution of strikers in the courts. Even more commonly, they simply fired strike leaders, at least temporarily. Occasionally, industrialists in a city facing a generalized strike banded together to fight it, though mutual jealousy often prevented any real coordination. Industrialists in Lodève, for example. in 1845 locked out workers from plants that had not been struck. Later in the strike they even sought to bring in machines to replace the striking workers permanently. On other occasions, these and other industrialists sought to break strikes by importing scab labor. Truly, the power of industrialists, backed by government, to resist strikes and to prevent protest through their ability to intimidate, was impressive. Nothing indicates this more clearly than the fact that most strikes, and particularly industrial strikes, failed completely. Workers faced formidable odds in their protest efforts; small wonder that such efforts were so rare.[21]

Employers possessed another type of authority over many workers that undoubtedly had an effect in limiting strikes. Most industrial enterprises were still small. There were some huge firms, particularly in metallurgy and mining, but even in iron production the average company in the 1840's employed only 51 people. Spinning plants, in both wool and cotton, employed an average of 60-70 workers in the same period, while shops for weaving and other branches of textile production seldom assembled more than 30 or 40 workers. There were only 6,000 firms in France with more than 20 employees, and only 3,200 with more than 50.[22] Many industrialists thus could know most of their workers and through daily relations with them could create an impression of a community of interests in the same work. A number of industrialists, particularly in the larger plants, were interested in a wide range of paternalistic efforts to assist their workers. Company housing, health plans, and the like were fairly common. Many workers were profoundly grateful for these and other efforts and felt a

---

[20] Pierre Laroque, *Les Rapports entre patrons et ouvriers* (Paris, 1938), 67-79; Dolléans and Déhove, *Travail en France*, I, 245.

[21] AEH, Jan. 30, 1843, report; Manuel, "Machines en France," 359; Aguet, *Mouvement ouvrier*, 65 et passim.

[22] Ministère de l'agriculture et du commerce, *Statistique de la France: Industrie* (4 vols., Paris, 1847-52), *passim;* M. A. Moreau de Jonnès, *Statistique de l'industrie de la France* (Paris, 1856), *passim;* Eugène Flachat et al., *Traité de la fabrication du fer et de la fonte* (Paris, 1842), 73-86.

genuine devotion to their employer; sincere expressions of grief by workers at the death of many industrialists was a sign of this sort of feeling. To be sure, many workers, even those who never actively protested, did not feel kindly toward their employer. And some of the most paternalistic companies, such as the big mines, had the worst strike records. However, as one factor among many, employer paternalism, often partially adopted to prevent disorder, undoubtedly helped to turn many workers away from agitation. The exceptionally low strike record of the big metallurgical firms, and the textile firms of the Haut-Rhin, may well have been partially caused by the exceptional interest that the industrialists took in their labor force.[23]

Though both government and employers were important in keeping the level of strikes low, they cannot be regarded as the only factors involved. After all, their power bore on artisans as well as factory workers, but the former managed to agitate far more frequently and with greater organization. Their hostility was just as great during most of the Second Empire as during the July Monarchy, but the pace of labor activity was increased notably. Obviously, some more specific factors must be sought.

The condition of industry during the July Monarchy was an important deterrent to strike activity, particularly of a constructive or offensive variety. A successful strike, winning permanent improvements in conditions, could take place only in a period of prosperity. Only then would industrialists be anxious to continue production in order to take advantage of steady or rising business levels. Only then would they be likely to have a sufficient profit margin to afford, albeit grudgingly, some concessions to their workers. During the July Monarchy a large number of industrial areas were not prosperous. Many of the older regions, such as Cholet, were being bitterly pressed by competition from modern factories. Even such centers as Rheims and Louviers, while able to bear up under competition, were too backward in methods to enjoy extensive prosperity. Workers in these regions might strike, and occasionally did out of desperation, but their protests would be in vain, and usually they would not bother to try.[24]

In the more modern centers, such as Mulhouse and Lille, levels of prosperity were of course far higher. But this advantage was modified by the fact that prosperity was not steady. Excessive competition, leading to overproduction on occasion, caused five years of major slumps and a number of other lesser declines during the eighteen years of the July Monarchy. The instability of the economy affected industrialists and workers alike. Industrialists even in a boom year were unlikely to relax their hostility to strikes because concessions might weaken their position when the apparently inevitable slump occurred. Workers, for their part, were discouraged from developing any expectations of real improvement in the future, from developing any long-range plans at all, by the knowledge that a crisis would come to wipe away any advance. Thus the textile industry

[23] Engrand, "Ouvriers lillois," 47; Courtheoux, "Naissance d'une conscience," 122.
[24] AN BB[18]1388, report on Castres, 1841; Arthur L. Dunham, *The Industrial Revolution in France, 1815-1848* (New York, 1955), *passim*.

particularly, in which most industrial workers were engaged, was dominated by a mixture of decline and instability—an important factor in discouraging more than occasional and halfhearted protest efforts.[25]

The conditions of industry were, however, less important in inhibiting strike activity than were three related aspects of the conditions of workers themselves. In the first place, a number of potential worker leaders were being drained off into the ranks of industrialists or foremen. This early industrial period was still sufficiently open, particularly in the production of textiles, to enable an exceptionally active worker to set up on his own without too much difficulty. The number who actually did so was relatively small, but if they had not had this outlet they might well have turned their energies to their own class. And the number of workers recruited as foremen and top-grade workers, while obviously a minority of the whole, was quite large, particularly since the general lack of training and discipline required an unusually large number of supervisors. The larger textile factories, for example, used at least one foreman for each room in the plant; furthermore, workers such as top-grade spinners and miners were given supervisory functions. Foremen and top workers alike were encouraged to represent the interests of management and were distinguished from ordinary workers by salaries at least triple the average in the firm. Finally, a number of workers beyond even those who had risen believed in the possibility of their own rise to at least lower-middle-class ranks and were correspondingly disinterested in specifically worker efforts.[26] Hence many worker groups were deprived of their natural leaders and could not organize or act. And many of the strikes that did occur were essentially leaderless and unplanned. To be sure, the upper echelons of the labor force did not necessarily share the interests of management. In many cases, relatively wellpaid and experienced workers such as spinners took the lead in agitation. But there is no record of any involvement of foremen in labor protest, except on occasions when they resisted it out of loyalty to their employers. And in general the opportunity of rising in the industrial hierarchy undoubtedly impeded any sense of labor solidarity on the part of many able workers. In fact, some of the scant agitation that occurred was incited and led by teenagers, who were of course abundantly employed in industry at the time. Several coal strikes were instigated by young coal haulers, rather than the miners themselves. Agitation among textile workers, as in Lille in 1837, was often led by apprentice spinners. In other words, the energy of youth was sometimes substituted for the experience and possible wisdom which, in the person of active, intelligent, and mature workers, were frequently drained away into other pursuits.[27]

Even more important than a partial absence of potential leadership was the fact that almost all workers were too poor and too busy to strike often, or for

---

[25] *Ibid.;* Villermé, *Tableau de l'état physique et moral*, I, *passim.*

[26] Charles Noiret, *Mémoires d'un ouvrier rouennais* (Rouen, 1836), *passim;* Oger, *Traité élémentaire de la filature du coton* (Mulhouse, 1839), *passim.*

[27] AD, Nord, M616-2, 1837 report; AD, Loire, 92M4, report on coal miners' strike, 1844.

more than a day or two, or even to strike at all. Most laborers in the textile industry worked thirteen hours a day and were in the plant fourteen or fifteen hours. Metallurgical workers seldom worked more than twelve hours, and miners sometimes worked still less, but the labor was physically harder. With such hours, it was unlikely that many workers had the energy to plan a strike; further, so much time spent under the supervision of foremen and employers was another deterrent to the possibility of real organization. This is undoubtedly one of the principal reasons that the majority of industrial strikes were defensive, unplanned reactions to a specific event.

But the material circumstances of most workers made even this type of strike a risky matter. Even aside from the possibility of losing a job as a result of a strike, most workers could ill afford to lose even a day's pay. Their wages were simply not sufficiently above subsistence needs. Though many urban factory workers earned a bit more than was absolutely necessary to live, they were unable to amass enough savings to carry them for more than two or three days without either work or charity. Few workers had any savings. The average laboring family in 1848, in the unlikely event that illness or unemployment did not limit the employment of either man or wife to less than an entire year, earned 765 francs. Three hundred francs of this went for bread, another 100 or 200 for other food; 150 for rent, heat, and a few furnishings; another hundred for clothes. This was life above the subsistence level, but with no frills and no margin of safety. Certainly there was little chance in this situation to strike for positive improvements in conditions because the risk of failure was great, and the result would simply be precious days of income lost. Only to prevent a worsening of income might a short and passionate protest be launched. During crises, desperation at the prospect of a wage reduction or of unemployment could induce some workers to forget their normal caution. Anger had to be vented, despite the risk of loss of pay. But strikes of this sort were almost invariably brief, again because no prolonged protest could be afforded. And most workers did not strike at all even during crises; rather, they clung tenaciously to what jobs and pay they had. In fact, much of the agitation during crises came not in the form of strikes, but of riots. And in the riots unemployed workers commonly took a prominent role for they had little to lose. A riot by men either without jobs or on short time was, for example, the only agitation by labor in Lille during the crisis of 1837. Workers who had jobs generally kept at them in good times and bad for survival depended on earning without fail.[28]

Obviously, not all industrial employees were in the same material situation as was the average worker. Some earned more and had correspondingly more margin. There is evidence that, other things being equal, such workers were more

28 E. Vuilemin, *Les Mines de houille d'aniche* (Paris, 1878), 250; Charles Beaugé, "Évaluation rétrospective des dépenses et des salaires de la classe ouvrière en France en 1840," *Journal des économistes*, LXXVII (Mar. 1924), 361; Jean Fourastié, *Machinisme et bien-être* (Paris, 1951), 42-47; Comité de l'Association formée à Mulhouse pour la défense du travail national, *Réponses aux questions de l'enquête industrielle ordonée par l'Assemblée nationale* (Mulhouse, 1848), 9; Emile Levasseur, *Histoire des classes ouvrières et de l'industrie en France de 1789 à 1870* (2 vols., Paris, 1903-1904), II, 274.

likely to strike. In certain areas, such as both Mulhouse and Lille it was pointed out that the best-paid workers generally led what strikes and agitation as did occur. For similar reasons, spinners in cities were more likely to strike than weavers because they earned more. The strikes by miners in the Saint-Étienne region were far better organized and of longer duration than those of Anzin, largely because Saint-Étienne miners earned over half again as much as their counterparts in Anzin. Lille cotton workers conducted a relatively well-organized strike in 1839, a year of high bread prices but also of high employment; there was reason for complaint, but also some margin to allow the risk of complaint. In the far more severe crisis of 1831-1832, when there was no margin at all, Lille workers were quiescent; in 1846-1847, they risked only a brief bread riot. It is indisputable, then, that the low levels of average conditions prevented strikes and that most strikes aside from brief expressions of misery involved workers enjoying conditions above the average.[29]

Material conditions, however, are not the magic key to an explanation of strike activity in the period. It is impossible to correlate agitation with income levels in any consistent way, even leaving aside the misery riot of a crisis year or a particularly poor area. For the fact is that the best-paid group of industrial workers, those in metallurgy and machine building, almost never struck. Their incomes averaged almost twice the level of industrial pay for adult males; they undoubtedly had the means to strike, but they did not choose to do so. Relatively high income was necessary for a vigorous strike, but its possession was no guarantee that the vigor was present. One final general factor must be sought.

Most industrial workers were new to their jobs, to their urban environment, and to each other. In the most modern industrial centers, the very areas in which standards of living for labor were likely to be above average, the vast majority of workers were of first or at most second generation even in 1848. Even in older centers such as Lille much of the factory labor was new not only to the plant but also to the city. Most of the new work force was ignorant; their literacy rates were far lower than those of native urban populations. In Mulhouse in the 1840's almost three-quarters of the illiterates had been born outside the city. In Lille in 1848 only a tenth of the workers were literate, though many more had had a brief educational experience. Many of the new workers were also unusually impoverished and unhealthy when they entered the factory labor force. Thus they were cut off from much possibility of intelligent protest not only by their lack of education but also often by physical weakness. But most of all they were confused. Their traditions were those of the countryside, which no longer had much meaning for them. In some cases they may have retained peasant habits of resignation. This was fortified, for those who attended church, by constant recommendations of patience and orderliness. It was further fortified by the fact that conditions of factory labor, in terms of income, hours,

---

[29] Aguet, "Grèves de mineurs," 380; Lasserre, *Situation des ouvriers,* 96; AD, Marne, 186M5, Apr. 1837, report.

and the like, represented little deterioration and often positive improvement when compared to conditions in the countryside.[30]

What was most upsetting to the new workers was the change in their psychological environment. The older norms of marriage and family, of religion, and of recreation had less meaning in the factory city. The new and rapid pace of work, the discipline of the factory, the strangeness of the people, and the fact that the members of a family now usually worked apart were far more disturbing than bad food or inadequate clothes. But it was terribly hard to express complaints about such matters. There was no tradition to fall back on, and the people from the country had relied on tradition. There was little motivation to join forces with strangers, who happened to be fellow workers, since the presence of such strangers was one of the newest aspects of factory life. The habit of a substantial minority of workers to return to the country occasionally, especially at harvesttime or during crises, further impeded adjustment to urban conditions and joint action to protest the difficulties of the new life. And there was little chance even fully to realize what the trouble was, since the novelty of the situation was so great. Hence the considerable discontent that undoubtedly existed in the period was expressed primarily in individual ways; the heavy consumption of alcohol, the decline of religious practice, and the increase in crimes against property, including thefts in the plant, were the most important forms of protest. Of necessity, they were individual forms, thus precluding much effort at cooperative action. Many strikes were born or ended in a bar; far more were drowned there. The individual disorientation of a substantial number of the early industrial workers was the final factor inhibiting vigorous strike activity. [31] These workers often felt themselves debased. They lacked the moral energy to rise in protest. Fundamentally apathetic, they relieved any resentment they clearly felt by an occasional bout at the tavern. Beyond this, workers could not think: "When we grow old the hospital will receive us, or we'll die, and then everything will be over."[32]

A large number of workers had simply lost their accustomed standards and had not found anything to replace them. At most, they attempted to apply some of the canons of rural life to their new situation. This is why so much worker agitation in the newest industrial centers is indistinguishable from peasant riots. In Mulhouse in 1847, in Lille in 1830 and 1847, and in many other regions, the appalling conditions of the industrial slump were protested not by a strike, but

---

[30] Raymond Oberlé, "Étude sur l'analphabétisme à Mulhouse au siècle de l'industrialisation," *Bulletin du Musée historique de Mulhouse,* LXVII (1959), 105; Courtheoux, "Naissance d'une conscience," 124; Marie-Madeleine Kahan-Rabecq, *La Classe ouvrière en Alsace pendant le Monarchie de Juillet* (Paris, 1939), 402.

[31] Villermé, *Tableau de l'état physique et moral,* I, 86, 292; Armand Audiganne, *Les Populations ouvrières et les industries dans le mouvement social du xixe siècle* (2 vols., Paris, 1854), I, 93; H. A. Frégier, *Des Classes dangereuses de la population dans les grandes villes, et des moyens de les rendre meilleures* (2 vols., Paris, 1840), I, 34, 284.

[32] J. P. A. Villeneuve-Bargemont, *Le Livre des affligés ou douleurs et consolations* (3 vols., Paris, 1841), II, 28 (statement by a Lille worker).

by an attack on the bakers. As in peasant agitation, the most immediate apparent villain was attacked, often violently, as the only response to unexpected misery. In fact, the same type of bread riots occurred in a number of rural areas during 1847. The many industrial areas that had little or no worker agitation beyond an attack on food merchants during a famine year were simply areas in which the workers continued at best to apply peasantlike responses to cases of outright hunger. When so clear a grievance was not presented, the worker had no standards to follow. Further, his environment was so different from the rural that even many periods of real misery passed without response. [33]

In addition, then, to the pressure of government and employers, subsistence conditions and the newness of the situation inhibited active labor protest. In the case of most textile centers, these factors were supplemented by the fact that a large minority of the working force was composed of women and children. Both were, naturally, more docile than male workers—one of the reasons for their wide use. Only a few regions escaped the multiple burdens of poverty and disorientation. Metallurgical workers, of course, were not poor; nor were they hampered by many women and children in their ranks. Their industry was far more consistently prosperous than the textile industry, though it had its crises, particularly prior to the building of railroads. Most important, however, was the fact that metallurgical workers were new to their situation for the most part. The most experienced workers were often foreigners, usually British, and were highly paid. They had little contact with most of the new labor. Even so, one of the few metallurgical strikes on record was led by experienced British workers. Aside from the British, skilled workers were either brought in from a number of different parts of France or were newly trained locals. Neither group had sufficient roots in the new situation to feel particularly clear about its needs and strengths. And the unskilled labor that composed over half the work force in new centers like Le Creusot was brought in from the local peasantry. These workers, far more highly paid than ever before in their experience, lacked any real sense of being workers and any grievances that could be expressed in collective protest. In metallurgy there was neither the need for hunger riots or defensive strikes, given the relatively good conditions, nor the experience and orientation necessary for constructive strikes. [34]

There remained coal mining and some of the major southern textile centers, notably Lodève and Castres. Not all the southern centers were involved in intensive strike activity. Carcassonne workers were too poor to strike. Workers in Mazemet, though very near Castres, were located in a new industrial center; they lacked the experience and sense of tradition of Castres and Lodève. Both the latter cities were relatively old wool centers. They brought in some new labor from the outside, but the majority of their labor force was local. This majority represented a nucleus of firm tradition of a semiartisanal nature. Hence the

---

[33] AD, Nord, M616-3, 1846 report.

[34] Courtheoux, "Naissance d'une conscience," 122; Engrand, "Ouvriers lillois," 99; Georges Lefranc, *Histoire du travail et des travailleurs* (Paris, 1957), 273; AN BB[18]1406, report on Rouen, 1842.

workers of Lodève expressed their desire to return to a purely artisanal organization; they had a memory of past standards and a tradition of craft closeness that would serve them even in a partially mechanized period. In this they differed from their colleagues in northern textile centers. At the same time, their own pay was relatively high, allowing some margin for protest activity. And their employers were engaged in an industry for which there was remarkably steady demand, though crises were not unknown. For both Lodève and Castres produced extensively for the French Army, and government orders could not be ignored, at pain of violation of contract and the loss of vital business. As the workers well knew, therefore, employers would often have to yield to strikes in order to meet definite business commitments. Finally, Lodève and Castres employed fewer women and children than was the average in textile manufacture; their hours of work were also lower by two or more, allowing more time for thought or planning. A group of relatively prosperous male workers, most of them accustomed to their work, their city, and each other, engaged in an industry that was fairly steadily prosperous; such was the formula that induced the exceptional strike activity of Lodève, Castres, and to an extent Bédarieux. [35]

The mining industry presented many similar features. It was far more consistently prosperous than textiles or even metallurgy; hence coal prices fell very little during the July Monarchy. Mineowners were often pressed with orders that they could scarcely fill; in fact, France had to import coal because its domestic production was insufficient. Several miners' strikes took place in periods when manufacturers were swamped with orders. Miners were, moreover, seldom called upon to work more than ten hours and sometimes worked only eight. Their work was, of course, far more tiring than labor in textiles or even metallurgy. But at least their waking hours were not totally devoted to work and travel to work; many miners, for example, were regularly able to spend some time gardening. Correspondingly, they had at least some time away from the job, which could be used for reflection on conditions and for actual organization. Few women and children worked in the mines. Miners earned a wage well above that of textile workers, and usually above subsistence as well. Often they could purchase some garden land; this could be a source of support in time of strike. Miners were not totally new to their work or their area. In the Saint-Étienne region particularly, while some new miners were hired during the July Monarchy, probably only a fifth of the workers in the 1840's were of first generation. At Anzin the labor force was increased by one-third during the July Monarchy, but the company dated from the eighteenth century, and at least half of the labor force consisted of families that had been associated with the company for two generations or more. So with coal mining, too, there was often a large nucleus of workers with a real sense of tradition, in a profession that had long relied heavily on such tradition. Through this tradition the extensive disorientation and confusion that weakened industrial labor generally could be avoided. Interestingly, newer mining regions such as Alais saw no strike activity

---

[35] AD, Tarn, IVM²31-34, 1845 report; Manuel, "Machines en France," 371.

comparable to that of the more traditional centers. In such regions the skilled workers were imported, and so were new to the area, whereas most of the labor force, recruited locally, was new to the trade; little real sense of tradition could exist. Finally, the mining companies most often struck were huge concerns, remote from the worker. They were less paternalistic and more often exploitative than metallurgical firms of great size. And they were often under public attack because of their size; miners both at Anzin and at Saint-Étienne operated in an atmosphere of widespread public sympathy. These specific factors were simply a further addition to situations already comparatively favorable to strike activity.[36]

Relative prosperity, both of industry and workers, and a sense of tradition were sufficient to allow the few real industrial challenges to government and employers that occurred in the July Monarchy. The same factors were, of course, present in the comparatively active ranks of artisans in Paris and Lyons. They were, further, factors that were likely to become increasingly introduced in the ranks of textile and metallurgical workers as time went on. Both industries, in the more modern centers, tended to become increasingly prosperous and, in many instances, to offer rising standards of living to the workers. Both tended to decrease hours of work in the 1840's, and the textile industry curtailed its use of children in the same decade. Most important, workers in these industries increasingly developed a set of values appropriate to their new situation; they were no longer lost newcomers. Their orientation was often aided by contact with the more traditional and active worker groups. Most of the fruits of these developments were seen only after the July Monarchy had ended; they required more time than the period itself offered. Some halting advance may be seen, however, in a few areas by the 1840's. In Lille, for example, the slump around 1830 had seen only scattered agitation, led, interestingly, by the thread twisters; here a traditional, artisanal group, albeit very ill-paid, was more active than factory labor. By 1839 factory workers were capable of mounting a really organized strike, and they were far more active in the crisis of 1847 than they had been in 1830, though their vigor was certainly limited. Similarly, Mulhouse workers reacted more massively to the crisis of 1847 than to that of 1828-1830; admittedly, this may have been partly because the crisis was more severe. The most interesting case of clearly increased activity among textile workers occurred, however, in Elbeuf. This was a relatively prosperous wool center, with a new factory labor force. There was no history of agitation among the workers prior to 1846. In that year and the next, however, guided partly by agitators from Paris, the workers were in considerable ferment. They were led by the spinners, a relatively well-paid group with a long record of docility. Their action consisted of a number of strikes and riots, for the purpose of higher pay and protection against undue mechanization. Under the immediate impulse of the economic collapse, but fortified also by a generation or more of experience in

---

36 AN BB[18] 1437, reports on the Compagnie générale des mines de la Loire, Apr. 4 and Nov. 1845; *ibid.*, C956, 1848 inquiry on the Loire; ACF, *passim.*

industry, the workers of Elbeuf for the first time frightened both government and employers. Clearly, there is no pervasive trend of heightened worker activity in the July Monarchy itself. But there are indications that some of the causes of labor weakness were being modified, in a few areas at least.[37]

For the July Monarchy as a whole, the impotence of industrial labor remains the outstanding fact. The few factors favoring protest action generally were greatly outweighed by the vast number of inhibiting forces. Some of these forces came from outside labor itself, some from conditions within. In a few cases the confusion and poverty of workers were absent to a sufficient extent to permit unusually active and elaborate labor movements. But even the miners of Rive-de-Gier, even the workers of Lodève, were too poor to afford more than occasional and loosely organized efforts. Even they lacked a clear picture of what they wanted for the future; the workers of Lodève, who could present demands relating to the very structure of their industry, looked really to the past. And against miners and southern wool workers, the force of employers and especially of government troops could always be applied. This outside force could defeat most efforts whenever internal weakness was not sufficient. The miners of Anzin, however, managed to win a number of wage raises through strike action; those of Rive-de-Gier were partially successful. Workers of Lodève and Castres also achieved some gains through strikes. Clearly, the example would spread. For many of the most important weaknesses of industrial labor were not permanent. Time and experience would decrease the debilitating sense of newness. Industry itself would create greater prosperity and so a greater possibility of taking vigorous action. As these factors changed, the external barriers to worker protest would have to yield.

---

[37] AN BB[18]1456, report on Elbeuf, Oct. 1847; Engrand, "Ouvriers lillois," 139.

4. Social mobility in England, 1500-1700*

LAWRENCE STONE†

The purpose of this paper is fourfold: firstly to sketch the configuration of a western traditional society at a fairly advanced stage of its development, a model that might be applicable to any European society from the sixteenth to the eighteenth centuries; secondly, to produce the evidence for believing that between 1540 and 1640 English society experienced a seismic upheaval of unprecedented magnitude; thirdly to postulate some reasons both for the development of this upheaval and for its termination; and fourthly to speculate about the political and religious consequences. The paper attempts—perhaps rashly—to take a broad overview of the society as a whole, and therefore ignores the important local variations which undoubtedly existed.

I. MODELS

The first problem is what sort of a visual image we have of this early modern English society. Sociologists tend to describe pre-industrial societies in terms of a stepped pyramid, the lower classes forming the bottom step, and the aristocracy or plutocracy the apex (because of the erosion of the poor and the growth of the middle-class in contemporary western society, it has turned into a stepped lozenge). But one may reasonably doubt whether this model fits a traditional pre-industrial society. Two alternatives present themselves. The first—let us call

* This article is reprinted with the kind permission of the author and of the Society from *Past and Present*, No. 30 (April, 1966).

† Some of the many errors of sense and logic in early drafts of this paper were pointed out to me by David Bien, Christopher Hill, Michael Walzer, Jerrold Seigel, John Shy and Joan Thirsk. Daniel Baugh went to great trouble in helping me to guess at the number of office-holders. I am very grateful to them for their assistance. An earlier version of this article was circulated for the 1965 Past and Present Annual Conference. Editors Note: Lawrence Stone is Dodge Professor of History and Chairman, Department of History, Princeton University. He is also Director of the Shelby Cullom Davis Center for Historical Studies. Among his major publications are: *The Crisis of the Aristocracy, 1558-1641; An Elizabethan: Sir Horatio Palavicino;* and *Sculpture in Britain: The Middle Ages.*

it the United Nations model—is a tall skyscraper erected on top of a vast low podium. Within the podium, which extends over many acres, live 95% or more of the population, who are free to move along wide corridors and to rise and descend very shallow staircases within this limited level. The skyscraper itself, within which dwell the remaining 5% or less, is composed of a series of floors for status groups based on the ownership of land. Within it is a single infrequent elevator which always goes down with a full load of failures and superfluous younger sons, but often rises half empty. Around the skyscraper itself, however, there wind several ascending ramps, labelled Church, Law, Commerce, and Office. Some people camp out on the ramps, but it is draughty and wet out there, and most of them struggle upwards and then take shelter inside at the highest floor they can comfortably reach.

The second—the San Gimignano model—is a series of vertical towers upon a hill. In this model the hill represents the amorphous mass of the poor and the humble, and the towers a series of more or less independent economic and status hierarchies with their own internal elevators: land, church, law, commerce, and government office are the most conspicuous of these towers.

Neither of these models exactly fits the observed facts, but both are an improvement on the conventional stepped pyramid image. It will be argued in this paper that between 1500 and 1700 English society was moving from the United Nations towards the San Gimignano model as the status of business and professions rose in the eyes of the landed classes.

II. CATEGORIES

The hierarchy of status

In the sixteenth century there was a status hierarchy, not the loose competitive status agglomerations to which we are accustomed today.[1] Though there existed a few completely non-integrated groups—artists and stage-players, for example—and four semi-independent occupational hierarchies, the vast mass of the population was fitted into a single hierarchy of status defined by titular rank, and to a certain extent by legal and fiscal privilege. The most fundamental dichotomy within the society was between the gentleman and the non-gentleman, a division that was based essentially upon the distinction between those who did, and those who did not, have to work with their hands. This is a critical division in all societies where human labour is the principal power-unit, apart from the horse and the ox, wind and water. The more extreme conservatives, heralds and others, argued that it took three generations for a family to purge its blood from the taint of inferiority and to become an accepted member of this upper class. In practice such notions seem to have had

---

[1] L. Stone, *The Crisis of the Aristocracy, 1558-1641* (Oxford, 1965), pp. 49-53, is an earlier attempt to tackle this problem. The present analysis provides what is hoped to be a more sophisticated model.

little effect, but the fact that they could be seriously propounded is evidence that an element of caste theory was to be found in Tudor England.

Within the dual system of gentlemen and non-gentlemen contemporaries recognized a rough sixfold status division:—

Group 1. The dependents on charity, whether widows, aged, or unemployed; also the apprentices and living-in servants, domestic, agricultural, or industrial, who composed as much as 15% to 25% of the adult male population.[2]

Group 2. The living-out labourers, both rural and urban, agricultural and industrial.

Group 3. The husbandmen, the lesser yeomen (both tenants and freeholders), and the more substantial yeomen; also the artisans, shopkeepers and small internal traders.

Group 4. The lesser, or parish, gentry.

Group 5. The county élite: squires, knights and baronets.

Group 6. The peers: barons, viscounts, earls, marquises, and dukes.

This sixfold status hierarchy is based on the values of a primitive rural society. At the lower levels of groups 1-3 there already existed two parallel hierarchies for urban and rural society, but they can be roughly matched without too much difficulty. But both contemporaries and ourselves are faced with the more vexing problem of fitting into this scheme four semi-independent occupational hierarchies, whose precise relationship to the basic reference groupings was never fully clarified. These were:—

Group A. The Merchants. The middling and large-scale exporters of London, Exeter, Bristol, Hull and Newcastle, the wholesalers, the large retailers of the main cities, the customs farmers and government contractors, and the financiers of London. In the sixteenth and early seventeenth centuries they were still regarded in many quarters as distinctly inferior in status to a gentleman. As late as 1669 Edward Chamberlayne stated flatly that "Tradesmen in all ages and nations have been reputed ignoble," and a generation earlier there had been a brisk pamphlet discussion whether or not a gentleman's son lost his gentle status by becoming an apprentice. Because of this attitude the merchants were a mobile group of transients, very many of whom moved into and out of the group in a single lifetime, and nearly all in two generations; as a contemporary put it at the time, merchants "do attain to great wealth and riches, which for the most part they employ in purchasing land and little by little they do creep and seek to be gentlemen." In other words, the most successful tended to merge into groups 4 and 5.[3]

---

[2] A. J. and R. H. Tawney, "An Occupational Census of the Seventeenth Century," *Econ. Hist. Rev.,* v (1934-5), p. 47. P. Laslett, "Clayworth and Cogenhoe," in *Historical Essays, 1600-1750,* ed. H. E. Bell and R. L. Ollard (London, 1963), p. 169; and data extracted from "Lay Subsidy Rolls, 1524-25," *Sussex Record Society,* lvi (1957).

[3] L. Stone, *op. cit.,* p. 40. W. G. Hoskins, "The Elizabethan Merchants of Exeter," in *Elizabethan Government and Society,* ed. S. T. Bindoff *et al.* (London, 1961), pp. 166-70, 176, 185-6. W. T. MacCaffrey, *Exeter, 1578-1640* (Cambridge, Mass., 1958), pp. 260-4. P. McGrath, "Records relating to the Society of Merchant Adventurers of the City of Bristol in

Group B. The Lawyers. These ranged all the way from the local attorney and solicitor to grandees like the Master of the Rolls and the Lord Chancellor. Over three-quarters of those trained at the Inns of Court, that is the barristers and above", were of gentry or clergy stock, but we know little about the social origins, economic prospects, or accepted status of the local attorneys.[4]

Group C. The Clergy. These ranged in income and position from the curate to the archbishop, and varied in social origin from the copyholder to the squire. Even in a prosperous and socially and intellectually advanced area like Oxfordshire or Worcestershire, between three-quarters and two-thirds of the early seventeenth-century parish clergy were still of non-gentry origin. Though most rectors were comfortably off, and though the overall average real income probably remained much the same, substantial numbers of vicars and curates were existing on an income hardly different from that of unskilled labourers.[5] The higher clergy were ruthlessly plundered under the Tudors, and their social origins were generally inferior to those of the lawyers. For example, of twenty-eight bishops in the 1630s, the fathers of only nine were gentry; eight were clergymen, seven were merchants, one was a yeoman and three were artisans or below.[6] It seems that the highest ranks of the clergy were generally regarded as inferior in status to the highest ranks of the legal profession, despite the presence of the former in the House of Lords. The precise reason for this lowly status is hard to determine. Was it the vigorous and widespread anti-clericalism of the age which both lowered respect for the profession and frightened off prospective entrants of gentry stock? Or the lack of assured tenure during a period of theological upheaval? Or the substantially reduced financial rewards to be expected even from a successful career? We do not know, but it is probable that all three factors interacted one upon the other.

Group D. The Administrators. These are the office-holders in the royal household, the major departments of state, and the army and navy, men to whom administration was a professional life commitment. This definition includes all those dealt with by Professor Aylmer in *The King's Servants* except the courtiers at the apex of the system. By the early seventeenth century, these royal servants were predominantly of squirearchy or gentry origin, but with a

the Seventeenth Century," *Bristol Rec. Soc.,* xvii (1953), pp. xxviii-xxx. *V.C.H., Yorks., The City of York* (London, 1961), *pp. 180-1.* T. S. Willan, The Muscovy Merchants of 1555 (Manchester, 1953), pp. 69-74. Willan casts some doubts on the truth of this picture, but he offers no hard statistical evidence to back up his suspicions.

[4] L. Stone, "The Educational Revolution in England, 1560-1640," *Past and Present,* no. 28 (July, 1964), pp. 58-9. R. Robson, *The Attorney in Eighteenth Century England* (Cambridge, 1959).

[5] D. M. Barratt, "The Condition of the Parish Clergy between the Reformation and 1660" (Oxford D.Phil. thesis, 1949), pp. 18, 180-206. F. W. Brooks, "The Social Position of the Parson in the Sixteenth Century," *Brit. Arch. Ass. Jl.,* 3rd ser., x (1948). W. G. Hoskins, "The Leicestershire Country Parson in the Sixteenth Century," in his *Essays in Leicestershire History* (Liverpool, 1950), pp. 1-23.

[6] Stone, *Crisis,* pp. 40, 405-11. This social pattern (the information about which I owe to Mr. F. S. Odo, a member of my research seminar at Princeton) hardly differs from that of the pre-Reformation church of the 1520s and '30s.

substantial leavening from yeoman, merchant, and miscellaneous non-gentry stock.[7]

What we have, therefore, is a rural-based status hierarchy running from 1 to 6, the clarity and utility of which is marred by the existence of four occupational hierarchies, A, B, C and D, whose exact positions within this standard system of reference were, and are, uncertain.

Moreover, it is unhappily true that 1, 2 and 3 include well over 90% of the population—perhaps as much as 95%—which means that a great deal of horizontal, and even some vertical, mobility within the vast mass of the population goes unrecognized. In such a society one cannot expect there to be very much upward mobility at the lower levels. Most of the population was living on the land, enjoying a very low income and tied to the soil by the needs of manual labour for food production and distribution. A reasonable guess is that about 95% of the population was still rural in 1500, and about 85% in 1700.[8] Now in a society in which 90% of the population are manual workers or petty rural artisans, even if every other job and office is filled by one of their sons, still only 11% can expect to change occupations.[9] Under such circumstances it is evident that the chances of upward economic mobility for the great majority of the population must be very small indeed.

The task of the historian of social mobility is complicated by a variety of difficulties. The degree to which a society appears open or closed both to contemporaries and to posterity depends partly on the prevailing myth, and partly on hard facts. For lack of anything better on which to base their judgements, historians tend to see a society much as the contemporaries saw it. Thus if seventeenth-century Englishmen and nineteenth-century Americans thought of their society as exceptionally mobile, then exceptionally mobile they appear in the history books. But there is also the social reality underlying the myth, a reality which cannot be too remote from the image without creating severe psychic tensions. The general contentment of the greater number is probably most strongly determined by the possibility of minor movement up and down at the lowest levels of groups 1, 2 and 3. But the quality of the society as it is seen by the historian is determined by two quite different factors. The first is the proportion of the lower and middling classes who are able to filter through into the élite; that is the number of ambitious youths who can move up from group 3 to group 4, the speed of acceptance of upwardly mobile elements of A, B, C and D by 4 and 5, and the degree to which income, political power, and status are open to talent among 4, 5 and 6. The second factor is the method by which this filtration occurs. Is it "sponsored mobility" of youths selected for

7 G. E. Aylmer, *The King's Servants* (London, 1961), p. 263.

8 Gregory King's figures suggest that in 1690 only about 15% of the population was living in towns of more than 1,000 (two-thirds of whom were crowded into London). D. V. Glass, "Two papers on Gregory King," in D. V. Glass and D. E. C. Eversley, *Population in History* (London, 1965), pp. 174, 178.

9 S. M. Lipset and R. Bendix, *Social Mobility in Industrial Society* (Berkeley, 1959), p. 27.

advancement at an early age, an upward movement planned and controlled by the existing élite for its own purpose of functional efficiency and the preservation of status lines? Or is it "contest mobility," the chance product of prolonged and open competitive struggle?[10]

The hierarchy of income

Tax data and other contemporary records suggest that the hierarchy of status corresponded roughly with the pyramid of incomes, and that the same was true within the four anomalous occupational categories of merchant, lawyer, official and clergyman.[11] It should be noted that the spread of income distribution after taxation was enormous by modern standards, perhaps as many as 1,000 families enjoying a net income after tax of £1,000 a year or more, which was a hundred times greater than that of the unskilled labourer.

The hierarchy of power

Political power was rather less intimately linked to status than was income, but it was still close. Groups 3-6 and A, B, C and D, nearly all enjoyed the franchise, but in practice contests for seats in Parliament were fairly rare, and political affairs at the local level were run in towns exclusively by A and in the county by 5 and 6, with some support and occasional competition from elements of 4.[12] At the national level, power was exercised by courtiers and officials: that is, a select minority of groups 5 and 6, and the whole of group D.

At Court, a knight from the lower gentry like Sir Walter Raleigh ranked higher in status, wielded more power, and might even enjoy a larger income than a backwoods earl like Bath. But this top Court élite of politicians was too ephemeral in its composition and too amateur in its interests to be regarded as a permanent part of the official class.

III. PATTERNS

The evidence is twofold, contemporary comment and statistics. The former is unreliable, firstly because what seems like great social mobility to contemporaries may appear very small to us; secondly because, when dealing with a small élite class, a numerically very small opening into it may seem gigantic to the élite but insignificant to the outsiders; and lastly because the individual example, which may be quite exceptional, cannot be used to prove a generalization.

---

10 For this distinction see Ralph H. Turner, "Sponsored and Contest Mobility and the School System," *Amer. Soc. Rev.*, xxv (1960), pp. 855-67.

11 T. Wilson, "The State of England Anno Dom. 1600," *Camden Misc.*, xvi (1936). C. B. MacPherson, *The Political Theory of Possessive Individualism* (Oxford, 1962), pp. 280-1.

12 MacCaffrey, *op. cit.*, pp. 16-17, 22-5, 251-6. Hoskins, "Elizabethan Merchants of Exeter," *loc. cit.*, pp. 163-6. J. E. Neale, *The Elizabethan House of Commons* (London, 1949), *passim.*

Finally, myth may not correspond to reality. The rags-to-riches legend of Dick Whittington may bear little relation to the actual life-prospects of an apprentice, although the fact that the legend first appears in 1605 may indicate growing aspirations for upward mobility.

There are three kinds of mobility, of which the first is the rise and fall of certain groups in relation to others. When studying this kind of change, it must be remembered that there are four elements in social stratification: the relative numbers, income, status and political power of each group. It is very unlikely that the four will change together in perfect harmony and it may be necessary to construct four different profiles of mobility over time for each group.

The second consists of changes in the profile of stratification, that is to say in the distances between the groups: thus there can be yawning gulfs or barely perceptible cracks separating one social group from another in terms of income, status or power; and the third consists of changes in the scale and range of individual mobility. This last, which is the one which usually attracts most attention but is historically in some ways the least important, has three variables: the direction, upwards or downwards; the height, that is to say the number of steps in the hierarchy to which the individual can climb or descend; and the frequency, the proportion of individuals in the group who are socially mobile.

Changes in group profiles

(1) Numbers. The great growth of population up to 1620, coupled with the continued engrossing of holdings by rich farmers, and heavy regressive taxation after 1642, must have caused a substantial increase in the size of groups 1 and 2 at the bottom of the heap, and an all too obvious growth of structural unemployment and underemployment which provoked the introduction of exceptional measures of poor relief and social control. Even in 1522-4 about one half of the population of Coventry, one third of that of Leicester and Exeter, and a substantially smaller proportion of the lesser country towns was reckoned to be below the poverty-line, and therefore not taxable. In 1688 Gregory King estimated that over half the total population, rural and urban, earned less than was needed for subsistence. The late seventeenth-century Hearth Tax returns for one Midland village show 30% of all households below the tax level altogether, and a further 46% with only one hearth. In a town like Exeter conditions were even worse, with some 40% of households below the tax level.[13]

Secondly, there was a remarkable increase in the number of the upper classes,

---

[13] D. C. Coleman, "Labour in the English Economy in the Seventeenth Century," *Econ. Hist. Rev.*, 2nd ser., viii (1955-6), pp. 280-95. W. G. Hoskins, *Provincial England* (London, 1963), p. 83. J. Cornwall, "The People of Rutland in 1522," *Leics. Arch. Soc. Trans.*, xxxvii (1961-2), p. 15; "English Country Towns in the 1520s," *Econ. Hist. Rev., 2nd ser., xv (1962-3), p. 66. MacPherson, op. cit.,* pp. 280-1. W. G. Hoskins, *The Midland Peasant* (London, 1957), p. 195. C. H. Wilson, *England's Apprenticeship 1600-1763* (London, 1965), pp. 231-6, 343-7. W. G. Hoskins, *Industry, Trade and People in Exeter, 1688-1800* (Manchester, 1935), pp. 115-6.

which trebled at a period when the total population barely doubled. The number of peers rose from 60 to 160; of baronets and knights from 500 to 1,400; of squires from perhaps 800 to 3,000; of armigerous gentry from perhaps 5,000 to around 15,000. This was due partly to the increase of land in private ownership, partly to the abnormally high reproduction rate of the upper classes, partly to the generation of new wealth in trade, the law, office and agriculture, and partly to the casual government attitude towards the inflation of honours.[14]

Thirdly, there were striking fluctuations in the numbers of the clergy. The profession contracted sharply—perhaps by 50%—with the elimination of the regular clergy at the Reformation and the subsequent plunder of the Church. In 1560, with no monks or chantry priests left, and perhaps as many as 2,000 of the 9,000 livings unfilled, the clergy were fewer in numbers than they had been for centuries. Thereafter numbers expanded again as vacant livings were filled, curacies increased, and a surplus of talented preachers were taken on as lecturers. The peak of the revival must have been in the 1640s, but the post-Restoration slump in both university education and religious enthusiasm, and the suppression of lecturers, must have cut the numbers back again.

The other professions showed sustained and striking increases in size. In particular the lawyers grew by leaps and bounds. The numbers called to the bar at the Inns of Court increased by over 40% between the 1590s and the 1630s. At the same time there were complaints about the proliferation of attorneys and solicitors. An official survey of 1633 stated that the number of attorneys enrolled in the court of Common Pleas had risen from 342 to 1,383 since 1578, and in 1689 John Aubrey said it was thought that there were nearly 3,000 in England. In 1688 Gregory King reckoned the entire legal profession at 10,000.[15] In addition, the medical profession grew very rapidly, and there may have been as many as 1,000 doctors, surgeons and apothecaries practising medicine between 1603 and 1643.[16]

Though statistics are wholly lacking, it is likely that there was an equally important proliferation of secretarial and administrative jobs. The rise of literacy stimulated the rise of record-keeping, the rise of record-keeping the increase of record-keepers. An increasingly specialized society demanded ever more specialized services. The Court and central royal bureaucracy seems to have been stabilized at about 600 persons up to the Civil War, and showed only limited signs of increase in minor and unauthorized clerical posts, while in the provinces

---

14 A. G. Dickens, *The English Reformation* (London, 1964), pp. 163-6. Stone, *Crisis,* ch. iii. J. Cornwall, "The Early Tudor Gentry," *Econ. Hist. Rev.,* 2nd ser., xvii (1964-5), pp. 457-61. MacPherson, *op. cit.,* pp. 280-1.

15 W. R. Prest, "Some Aspects of the Inns of Court 1590-1640" (Oxford D.Phil. thesis, 1965), p. 385. E. Foss, *Lives of the Judges* (London, 1857), v, pp. 107-8, 421-4; vi, pp. 35-7, 234-6. *H. M. C. Rutland MSS.,* iv. p. 216. *Cal. State Papers Dom., 1633-4,* p. 251. J. Aubrey, *The Natural History of Wiltshire,* ed. J. Britton (London, 1847), part ii, ch. xvi. MacPherson, *op. cit.,* p. 180.

16 J. H. Roach, *A Directory of English Country Physicians, 1603-43* (London, 1962). R. S. Roberts, "The Personnel and Practice of Medicine in Tudor and Stuart England," *Medical History,* vi (1962); viii (1964).

there were about another 600 petty and part-time officials. But the English Revolution—like all revolutions—demanded a great expansion of state employees, partly as soldiers to hold down the defeated party and ward off external threats, partly as officials to exact taxes to pay for the war, and to handle the bold projects of social engineering that revolutionary governments always embark upon. Much of this expansion survived the emergency, and Restoration England found itself saddled with a large navy, a small standing army, and a new force of excisemen, Hearth Tax collectors, Customs officers, Treasury officials, and dockyard workers whose political rôle as obsequious government supporters soon aroused the alarm of the Country Party.

How far these new offices were an avenue of upward mobility is uncertain but they certainly expanded enormously the numbers of the professional and administrative classes during and after the Civil War. By the late eighteenth century the number in these new central offices enjoying fees and salaries of over £100 a year was perhaps around 1,000, while those earning between £50 and £100 ran into several thousands. As for local officers, nothing whatever is known, but here again there must have been several thousand of them. Although the major increase in the number of officers occurred in the hundred years after the accession of William III, there is still some reason to believe that there must have been up to three or four thousand local and central office-holders in 1690 with incomes over £100 and at least as many again with incomes between £50 and £100.[17]

Perhaps equally important was the increase throughout the whole of the sixteenth and seventeenth centuries in the numbers of secretaries and agents of private landlords and businessmen.[18] Lastly, it can hardly be doubted that urbanization and greater commercial activity both at home and abroad must have caused a very substantial increase in the numbers of merchants and shopkeepers.

(2) Income. Throughout the sixteenth century the pressure of excess supply of labour relative to demand not only increased unemployment but also forced down real wages to an alarming degree, the Phelps Brown index suggesting a decline by as much as 50%.[19] Even if this is an unduly pessimistic calculation,

---

[17] W. T. MacCaffrey, "Place and Patronage in Elizabethan Politics," in *Elizabethan Government and Society*, ed. S. T. Bindoff *et al.* (London, 1961), pp. 106-8. Aylmer, *op. cit.*, p. 254; and "Place Bills and the Separation of Powers," *Trans. Roy. Hist. Soc.*, 5th ser., xv (1965), pp. 65-6. These very rough guesses for 1690 I owe to the kindness of Professor Daniel Baugh. The firm figures for central office-holders in the late eighteenth century are derived from *The Report of the Commissioners on Fees, 1786-7* (P.P., 1806, vol. vii). *Reports of Committees*, vol. xi, pp. 114 ff., 200 ff. *Commons Journals*, vol. xli, pp. 9 ff.; vol. xlii, pp. 48 ff.

[18] Stone, *op. cit.*, pp. 274-94. Wilson, *op. cit.*, p. 17. Examples of the new kind of secretarial/professional careers in private and royal service are those of Edward Palavicino at a lower level and John Pym and Sir Benjamin Rudyard at a higher: L. Stone, *An Elizabethan: Sir Horatio Palavicino* (Oxford, 1956), pp. 316-20; M. F. Keeler, *The Long Parliament, 1640-41* (Philadelphia, 1954), pp. 318-9, 329.

[19] B. H. Phelps Brown and S. V. Hopkins, "Seven Centuries of Prices of Consumables compared with Builders' Wage-rates," *Economica*, xxiii (1956), repr. in *Essays in Economic History*, vol. ii, ed. E. M. Carus-Wilson (London, 1962).

the fall was undoubtedly of a magnitude for which there is no parallel in English history since the thirteenth century. The living standards of the labouring classes went down sharply in the sixteenth century, and stayed down throughout the seventeenth. On the other hand, throughout the whole of the sixteenth century and much of the seventeenth there was a striking rise in the material comforts of all classes from the yeomen upwards, groups who benefited from rising agricultural prices, increased commercial activity, and increased demand for professional services. This is shown by the increase in the amount of domestic equipment mentioned by William Harrison and others and proven by the study of probate inventories; and by the increased number of rooms in housing erected during what has been described as "The Great Rebuilding."[20] At the gentry level, there is some rough statistical evidence to suggest that the years 1575-1625 saw more country-house building than any other 50-year period in our history,[21] which is itself significant proof of a "rise of the gentry."

It is probable, but not yet proven, that the average income and capital value of the London monopoly merchants and financiers, rose considerably throughout the period.[22] The income of nobles and courtiers certainly fell sharply in the late sixteenth century but recovered in the early seventeenth.[23] And lastly the income of the higher clergy was sharply curtailed at and after the Reformation, the process only stopping at the accession of James I. Although the income of some of the lower clergy kept pace with prices, that of the others, particularly vicars and curates, probably fell.[24] We do not yet know enough about lawyers or administrators to reach a firm conclusion, although the impression is that their economic position was improving, as was certainly that of medical practitioners. It is an ill wind which blows nobody any good, and the increase of smallpox and venereal disease brought wealth to many doctors' pockets.[25]

For one hundred years after the Restoration, however, there is reason to believe that the fortunes of the various levels of the landed classes were dramatically reversed from the trends of the previous century. The holdings of

---

20 W. Harrison, *Description of England,* in R. H. Tawney and E. Power, *Tudor Economic Documents* (London, 1924), iii, pp. 68-72. R. Reyce, *The Breviary of Suffolk,* ed. Francis Lord Hervey (London, 1902), pp. 49-52. F. Bacon, "Observations on a Libel," in J. Spedding, *Life and Letters of Sir Francis Bacon* (London, 1890), i, pp. 158-9. W. G. Hoskins, ed., *Essays in Leicestershire History* (Liverpool, 1950), pp. 132-6, 179-83; "Elizabethan Merchants of Exeter," *loc. cit.,* pp. 178-83. M. W. Barley, *The English Farmhouse and Cottage* (London, 1961), pp. 38-179. W. G. Hoskins, "The Rebuilding of Rural England, 1570-1640," *Past and Present,* no. 4 (Nov., 1953); *The Midland Peasant* (London, 1957), pp. 185-6, 296-8.

21 This observation is based on a survey of the evidence in the counties covered so far by N. Pevsner in the Penguin *Buildings of England* series.

22 For the wealth of the Jacobean aldermen, see R. G. Lang, "The Greater Merchants of London in the early Seventeenth Century" (Oxford D.Phil. thesis, 1963). Some figures for officially recorded personal incomes are given in W. K. Jordan, *The Charities of London, 1480-1660* (London, 1960), pp. 53-4.

23 Stone, *Crisis,* pp. 156-64, 470-6.

24 C. Hill, *Economic Problems of the Church* (Oxford, 1956), ch. ix.

25 *The Journal of James Yonge,* ed. F. N. L. Poynter (London, 1963).

the aristocracy and greater landlords steadily increased, those of the small yeomen and freeholders were converted into leaseholds, and the smaller gentry were economically depressed by the stagnation of food prices and the rise of taxation on the land.[26]

(3) Status. After a severe slump in the sixteenth century, there was a marked rise in the middle of the seventeenth century in the status of the lesser clergy, as they became better educated, better paid, and of more genteel social origins;[27] secondly, there was an improvement in the status of lesser legal officials like country attorneys, culminating in the formation in 1739 of a professional organization, "The Society of Gentlemen Practisers";[28] thirdly, there was a rise in status of the medical profession as a whole as its professional and educational standards improved; and fourthly, there was a slow but steady rise in the standing of the merchant class in the eyes of the gentry. By the middle of the seventeenth century, the old view that the younger son of a gentleman lost his gentility by becoming an apprentice was still held only by a few legal pedants, heralds, and other social conservatives.

These changes were all the product of the upgrading of trade and the professions relative to the landed classes. What cannot at present be determined is whether this was a result of an influx of superfluous younger sons of gentry, who had to be provided for somehow or other; or whether the influx was the result not so much of economic necessity as of a change in attitude towards occupations whose utility to society as a whole was increasingly being recognized. The probability is that the ideological and the economic changes marched hand in hand, thus relieving the historian of the responsibility of distinguishing horse from cart.

Thirdly, at the upper levels there was a striking though temporary fall in the prestige of the peers in the early seventeenth century, demonstrated by a decline in tenant loyalty, gentry deference, and electoral obedience. This decline prepared the way for the abolition of the House of Lords in 1649.[29] And lastly there was a similar decline in the status of courtiers, as a "Country" interest and a "Country" morality, expressed in "Country Party," emerged as a self-conscious interest group with a well-defined idological content.[30]

(4) Power. In the sixteenth century, thanks to the growing strength of the Crown, there was a decline in the political authority of peers; in the seventeenth century, thanks to the growing power of Parliament, there was a decline in the political influence of courtiers; the beneficiaries of both movements were the greater gentry, although the peers were recovering some of their power again

---

[26] H. J. Habakkuk, "English Landownership, 1680-1740," *Econ. Hist. Rev.*, x (1940); "La Disparition du Paysan Anglais," *Annales E.S.C.*, xx (1965).

[27] See above, note 5.

[28] R. Robson, *op. cit.*, ch. iii.

[29] Stone, *op. cit.*, pp. 119-22, 163-4, 266-70, 476-81, 662-8, 743-53.

[30] P. Zagorin, "The Court and the Country," *Eng. Hist. Rev.*, lxxvii (1962), pp. 306-11. Aylmer, "Place-bills," *loc. cit.*

towards the end of the century.[31] Secondly, the political influence of the clergy was virtually eliminated at the Reformation, a loss which was only partially and temporarily made up in the 1630s. And thirdly there was a marked increase in the influence of the merchant community over English policy—especially foreign policy—thanks to the leverage it could exercise over any government by the offer or withholding of its facilities for credit.

By dividing this analysis of changes in group profiles into four distinct sections, the two important shifts in English society have tended to be lost to view. The first was a polarization of society into rich and poor: the upper classes became relatively more numerous, and their real incomes rose; the poor became relatively more numerous and their real incomes fell. The second was a greater equality among the upper classes: firstly the wealth and power of the greater gentry increased relative to those of the aristocracy; and secondly members of the trades and professions rose in wealth, numbers and social status relative to the landed classes. How far this last development had proceeded can be glimpsed by looking at Gregory King's not implausible guesses about the structure of society in 1688. He estimated that there were 10,000 merchants by land and sea, 10,000 clergy, 5,000 greater and 5,000 lesser officials, 10,000 lawyers, 16,000 persons in the sciences and liberal arts, and 9,000 army and navy officers, making 65,000 in all. When one considers that he reckoned there were only 16,000 gentlemen and above, plus 40,000 wealthier freeholders, and that (if his figures are to be trusted) the total income of the professional and commercial groups was now nearly as great as that of the landed proprietors, it becomes clear that English society no longer conformed to the traditional pattern.[32] The landed classes might continue to wield political power and be the arbiters of social status for another two hundred years, but they had now to temper the exercise of this authority with a careful regard for these newer elements in the society.

Changes in individual mobility

(1) *Horizontal.* Individual mobility may be horizontal from one geographical area or occupation to another, or vertical, up or down the social and economic scale. The two are interrelated in that although most people move horizontally to avoid slipping downwards, there are still some who do so in the hope of also moving vertically upwards. To the extent that horizontal mobility reflects the second motive rather than the first, therefore, it is an indicator of rising aspirations, though by no means necessarily of rising achievements.

(a) Internal. There is good reason to suppose that physical mobility, even in the village, was far greater than is generally supposed. Both the muster rolls and the detailed census returns of two individual villages suggest a turnover as high as

---

31 Stone, *op. cit.*, ch. v. M. E. James, *Change and Continuity in the Tudor North* (Borthwick Papers, xxvii, York, 1965).

32 MacPherson, *op. cit.*, p. 280. Professor Baugh tells me that he thinks King substantially overestimated the number of officials in the upper category.

50% to 60% in ten years. If removal by death accounted for some 20%, there are still some 30-40% who moved on in a given 10-year span, which indicates that the seventeenth-century village was very far from being a static or isolated unit.[33] This mobility can partly be explained by the high proportion of the community who worked as living-in servants. These would move away from home to take service and move on again to change employers or to get married. Partly it was caused by a steady process of buying and selling of small properties and engrossing of holdings. A good deal of it, however, was caused by two major trends. There was a movement from the more densely-settled areas into undeveloped land in the forests, the fens and the Highland zone; and there was perhaps an even more massive drift from the countryside to the towns, and especially London. The first movement is difficult to document statistically, but is evident from many local and estate records.[34] Moreover there was a very great increase in the volume of food production over these two centuries, so great that England became a net exporter of corn on a very large scale by the end of the seventeenth century, despite the doubling of its population. This has to be explained mainly by the opening up of virgin lands by a restlessly mobile population seeking a living wherever opportunity offered.

The flow into the towns is more easily demonstrated. As one would expect if the population doubled, most towns show some growth after 1550. In the early sixteenth century London had a population of about 60,000, there was one other town of more than 10,000, and not more than fourteen of more than 5,000. Between 1550 and 1650 a few places like Norwich, Newcastle, York and Bristol may have doubled or trebled to between 12,000 and 20,000, but London and its suburbs increased sixfold to about 350,000. By now London was clearly in a class by itself, and it went on growing to about 550,000 by the end of the century. In other words, London comprised perhaps 2% of the population of England and Wales in 1500, 5% in 1600 and 10% in 1700. In view of the very high urban death rates, this massive increase is evidence that a large proportion of the surplus population in the countryside was annually pouring into the capital city. Even when the city was devastated by plague and lost some 15% of its inhabitants, as occurred in 1603 and 1625, so great was the influx that the losses were made up within two years, to judge from the statistics of baptisms, marriages and burials.[35] A London parson in the reign of Elizabeth remarked

---

[33] E. E. Rich, "The Population of Elizabethan England," *Econ. Hist. Rev.,* 2nd ser., ii (1949-50), p. 259. P. Styles, "A Census of a Warwickshire Village in 1698," *Univ. of Birmingham Hist. Jl.,* iii (1951), pp. 45-8. Laslett, "Clayworth and Cogenhoe," *loc. cit.,* p. 183. L. M. Marshall, "The Rural Population of Bedfordshire, 1671 to 1921," *Beds. Hist. Rec. Soc.,* xvi (1934), pp. 53-64.

[34] G. H. Tupling, *The Economic History of Rossendale* (Manchester, 1927), pp. 42-97. J. Thirsk, *Fenland Farming in the Sixteenth Century* (Leicester, 1953), pp. 21-2. M. Campbell, *The English Yeoman* (New Haven, 1942), pp. 72, 93-7. P. A. J. Pettit, "Charles I and the Revival of Forest Law in Northamptonshire," *Northamptonshire Past and Present,* iii (1961), p. 54. E. Kerridge, "The Revolts in Wiltshire against Charles I," *Wilts. Arch. Magazine,* lvii (1958), pp. 66-70.

[35] C. Creighton, "The Population of Old London," *Blackwood's Magazine,* cxlix (Edinburgh, Apr., 1891). N. G. Brett-James, *The Growth of Stuart London* (London, 1935), ch.

that every twelve years or so "the most part of the parish changeth, as I by experience know, some goinge and some comminge"—a situation which resembles nothing so much as Los Angeles in the mid-twentieth century.[36] What effect this enormous shift of population had upon status or living standards is entirely unknown, but it may well have been downward on both counts. Many of these wanderers failed to find a permanent home either on the wastes and forests or in the towns, and there is plenty of evidence—if of a non-quantitative character—for a serious increase of vagabondage.

One rung up the social ladder, however, horizontal mobility was probably more rewarding. It was certainly so for craftsmen trained in a skill through the expensive and tedious process of apprenticeship, for the Hearth Tax returns indicate that the income of the urban craftsman was a good deal higher than that of his rural counterpart.[37] In this connection some interesting conclusions emerge from an analysis of the apprenticeship records of London companies. These show that between the early sixteenth and the early eighteenth centuries there was a striking change in the geographical distribution of recruitment. Professor Thrupp had noted that in the late fifteenth century nearly half the apprentices of two London companies had come from the North, and there is evidence that this pattern persisted for another 100 years. The only early sixteenth-century records are what survives of the list of men who had completed their apprenticeship and were admitted to the Freedom of the City, mostly between 1535 and 1553. They show that over half came from north and west of a line Trent-Severn Bournemouth. The pattern is conformed by the later records of apprenticeship in the Carpenters' and Fishmongers' Companies. Both recruited about 40% from the Highland zone up to the Civil War, but only 20% or less by the end of the seventeenth century. There was a corresponding rise of apprentices from London and the four home counties from less than 20% before the Civil War to well over 50% by 1700, rising to 70% or more by 1750. This contraction of the area of recruitment receives striking confirmation from the records of the Cutlers' Company at Sheffield which show that recruits from over 31 miles away fell from 22% to 5% between the second and the fourth quarter of the seventeenth century, and did not rise above 12% for another hundred years. The second important trend over these years was from sons of agricultural workers and smallholders—yeomen, husbandmen and labourers—to the sons of artisans and small tradesmen. This movement was most intense in the late seventeenth century, the proportion of sons of artisans among apprentices rising

xx. Wilson, *op. cit.*, p. 47. W. G. Hoskins, *Provincial England* (London, 1963), ch. iv. MacCaffrey, *Exeter*, pp. 12-13.

Date	London	England and Wales	%
1500	60,000	3,000,000	2%
1600	225,000	4,500,000	5%
1700	550,000	5,500,000	10%

36 *The Writings of John Greenwood, 1587-90*, ed. L. H. Carlson (London, 1962), p. 198.

37 P. Styles, "The Social Structure of Kineton Hundred in the Reign of Charles II," *Birmingham Arch. Soc. Trans.*, lxxviii (1962), p. 100.

from 50% to 74% in the Carpenters' Company between 1654 and 1693, and from 39% to 63% in the Fishmongers' Company between 1641 and 1704.[38]

Just what these two movements mean is not entirely clear. These apprentices were a fortunate élite who were only a tiny minority of the mass of migrants to London and only about a third of whom were destined to stay and become Freemen of the City after their apprenticeship had expired. But the startling decline of immigrants from the north and west, and the almost equally impressive rise in the proportion of sons of artisans, surely indicate a closing of both horizontal and occupational mobility channels. Why this should be so we do not know. Was it due to changing opportunities for employment in the north and west, or to declining attraction of apprenticeship in London; or was it the automatic product of the expansion of numbers of both artisans in general and Londoners in particular, which made internal recruitment more possible? Whatever the cause, it is clear that a phase of very active horizontal mobility both in geographical range and in occupational shift was replaced by conditions of relative quiescence.

(b) External. Between 1620 and 1640 some 80,000 Englishmen emigrated to America and the West Indies. Those who survived the first harsh years in America received very much greater land than they could ever hope for at home, and there is evidence to suggest that for the humble the move involved some general but modest upward status (and perhaps also economic) mobility.[39] Mid seventeenth-century Massachusetts was a rural society of small yeomen farmers, without either landed gentry above or landless poor below.[40]

Far more significant mobility was achieved by colonial exploitation of Ireland. Those who entered the Irish scene in the 1590s, obtained rich pickings in land grants and government offices, and lived to profit by the economic growth of the early seventeenth century, found themselves endowed with great wealth which was easily converted into status by the purchase of an Irish title. The richest man in England in 1640 was almost certainly Robert Boyle, earl of Cork, who had landed in Dublin fifty-two years before as a penniless adventurer.[41] By emigration in the seventeenth century, whether to Ireland, or

---

[38] S. L. Thrupp, *The Merchant Class of Medieval London* (Chicago, 1948), p. 211. C. Welch, *Register of Freemen of the City of London in the Reigns of Henry VIII and Edward VI* (London, 1908). Kahl, *op. cit.,* pp. 17-20. C. Blagden, "The Stationers' Company in the Eighteenth Century," *Guildhall Miscellany,* x (1959), pp. 36-52. Bower Marsh, *Records of the Worshipful Company of Carpenters* (Oxford, 1913-39), vols. i and vi. Guildhall Library, MSS. 5576/1-3 (Fishmongers); 5184/1 (Bakers). For a discussion of the changing social and economic role of apprenticeship and freedom of a Company, see J. R. Kellett, "The Breakdown of Guild and Corporation Control over the Handicraft and Retail Trade of London," *Econ. Hist. Rev.,* 2nd ser., x (1957-8). E. J. Buckatsch, "Places of Origin of a Group of Immigrants into Sheffield, 1624-1799," *Econ. Hist. Rev.,* 2nd. ser., ii (1949-50), p. 305.

[39] *Cambridge History of the British Empire* (Cambridge, 1929), i, p. 179. S. C. Powell, *Puritan Village* (Middlebury, Conn., 1963), pp. 18-29, 92-116. M. Campbell, *op. cit.,* pp. 279-80.

[40] I owe this point to Dr. Kenneth Lockridge.

[41] T. O. Ranger, "Richard Boyle and the making of an Irish fortune, 1588-1614," *Irish*

to America, or to the West Indies, horizontal mobility often became a means of moving upwards.

(2) *Vertical.* (a) Upward (economic and status). The basic evidence to support the hypothesis that this period saw a phase of unprecedented individual mobility, upwards and downwards, followed by a fresh period of stability, lies in the statistics for the purchase and sale of land. They rise to a peak in the 1610s, 250% higher than in the 1560s. This great movement had spent itself before the Civil War, and land transfers had begun to slow up after 1620. By 1700 the land market was once again almost as tight as it had been in the early sixteenth century.[42]

For those who were not gentlemen there were various ways of moving upwards. University education on a scholarship, followed by entry into the church, certainly led to improvement in status, but only in the late seventeenth century did it normally lead to a reasonably well-paid or secure position.[43] Shrewd manipulation of the land and the agricultural produce market was far more important: the social and economic rise of many yeomen into the lesser gentry was a well-established feature of the society, at any rate before rents began rising steeply in the early seventeenth century.[44] Success in the servicing and retail trades offered some limited opportunity for self-improvement, though this was rarely the road to substantial wealth and power. Service as agent or steward of a large landed estate sometimes brought both status and financial rewards.[45] Apprenticeship to a leading merchant was a common way to rise quite high in the social scale. Commerce was the origin of the family wealth of two out of the fourteen richest Yorkshire squires in 1642, one out of twenty-five leading Somerset squires in the 1630s, 7% of the Early Stuart baronetage, and 4% of the new Early Stuart peerage. These figures suggest that both contemporaries and posterity have exaggerated the scale of the movement, but how it compared with earlier or later periods we do not know.[46]

As for the post-Restoration period, the remarkable commercial expansion of the late seventeenth century clearly created a great deal of new wealth. What is

---

Historical Studies, x (1957). A. B. Grosart, *The Lismore Papers, 1886-88*, 2nd ser., iv, p. 259. Brit. Mus., Harleian MSS., 991, p. 8.

[42] Stone, *op. cit.*, p. 37, fig. 1. That this rise and fall is a solid reality is supported by a study of the mobility of manorial property in Surrey between 1480 and 1700, carried out by Mr. F. M. Brodhead, a member of my research seminar at Princeton. He has shown that the market for this sort of property was all but dead before the Dissolution of the monasteries, and that it was this political act which set the process in motion; he has also confirmed that the movement reached its peak in the early seventeenth century and then died away again.

[43] M. Curtis, "The Alienated Intellectuals of Early Stuart England," *Past and Present*, no. 23 (Nov., 1962). Hill, *op. cit.*, ch. ix.

[44] Campbell, *op. cit.*, ch. v.

[45] MacCaffrey, *Exeter*, pp. 269-70. W. G. Hoskins, *Essays in Leicestershire History* (Liverpool, 1955), ch. iv, and "An Elizabethan Provincial Town: Leicester," in his *Provincial England*, p. 107. Stone, *Crisis*, pp. 285-94.

[46] *Op. cit.*, p. 190. J. T. Cliffe, "The Yorkshire Gentry on the Eve of the Civil War" (London Ph.D. thesis, 1960), p. 96.

not so certain, however, is how it was distributed. Was it concentrated in the hands of a few men like Sir Josiah Child and Sir John Banks, or was it spread over the mercantile community as a whole? The closing down of the land market suggests that, however it was distributed, less of this wealth than before was being converted into social status by the purchase of an estate, and more of it was being reinvested in long-term mortgages, commerce and banking.[47] Thus neither the expansion of the bureaucracy nor the expansion of trade are incompatible with the hypothesis of an increasingly immobile society.

For a young man of gentle birth, the fastest ways of moving up the social scale were the lotteries of marriage with an heiress, Court favour, and success at the law. The first of the three is usually neglected or ignored by social historians, but it was probably the commonest method of upward movement for gentlemen. The second, which was only open to a tiny handful of the horde of aspirants, could lead to dizzy heights of wealth and grandeur—witness the careers of the earl of Leicester under Elizabeth, and the duke of Buckingham under James. An analysis of the available evidence suggests that royal bounty reached a peak in the reign of James and then declined. The top positions in the law were also very rewarding in terms of wealth and status, but we have no way of telling what changes occurred over time in the numbers who benefited or the amount of profit they realized. Lastly the commonest, but certainly the slowest, of all the status elevators was thrift and diligence in estate management, a force which carried many gentry upwards into the squirearchy, and one or two squires upwards into the peerage.[48] It is worth noting that if we substitute India for Ireland, these avenues of upward mobility are precisely those operating a hundred years later, in the middle of the eighteenth century: four fast elevators: marriage, the law, high government service, and the colonies; three medium fast: trade, government contracting and finance; and two slow: estate management, and professions other than the law.[49]

(b) Downward (economic and status). Downward mobility was the lot of those who were improvident or incompetent, extravagant or unlucky. History, however, rarely records, and even more rarely pays attention to, such tragedies. The victims sink without trace or comment. The fact that they were extremely common between 1560 and 1640 is proven by the dizzy rise of land sales up to 1620, before the other factors came into play to reduce again the likelihood of ruin and to shut off the supply of land for the market.

The final question, to which no firm answer can be given, is the degree of stability achieved by the socially and economically mobile at this period. Plenty of examples can be instanced of wasteful and dissolute sons of self-made men, who ran through the fortune accumulated by their father and so reduced the

[47] H. J. Habakkuk, "The English Land Market in the Eighteenth Century," in J. S. Bromley and E. H. Kossmann, ed., *Britain and the Netherlands,* ii (London, 1959), pp. 168-73.

[48] Stone, *op. cit.,* pp. 191-4.

[49] L. B. Namier and J. Brooke, *The House of Commons, 1754-1790* (London, 1964), p. 104.

family to the status from which it began. And it may well be that the status-seeker of the Tudor age experienced considerable difficulty in founding a family that would last. But when the land market closed down in the late seventeenth century, when the pressures of demographic growth and price revolution eased off, when the strict settlement made alienation of property extremely difficult, when institutional road blocks had been erected to confine power to the existing élite, then it may well be that families were established which were capable of withstanding for generations all but the ineluctable processes of biological failure in the male line. Professor Tawney discovered that in ten counties one third of all manors changed hands by purchase and sale at least once every forty years between 1561 and 1640. He also found that of sixty-two large landowning families in the area in 1640, over half were still large landowners in 1874.[50] These two pieces of evidence put together suggest that those who rose in the social scale in the early seventeenth century, towards the end of the great phase of mobility, had a good chance of establishing their family on the new level of income and status once the avenues of mobility were closed. Indeed, it may have been just these social climbers who were most anxious to slam the door behind them, a suggestion which is supported by the socially very exclusive marriage patterns of the children of the newly risen Henrician and Jacobean peers in the mid-sixteenth and mid-seventeenth centuries.[51]

The argument that the period 1560-1640 was an exceptionally mobile one depends upon the statistical evidence, but it is also supported by the weight of contemporary comment running from Thomas Fuller, William Habington and Robert Reyce to the playwrights like Marston and Massinger. In 1665, Edward Waterhouse published his *Gentleman's Monitor, or a sober Inspection into the Virtue, Vices and ordinary means of the rise and decay of men and families.* Though not a very profound analysis, and though sloppily organized, so far as I know this is the first full-scale study of social mobility ever to have been attempted in Europe, and possibly in the world. It is surely no mere coincidence that Waterhouse should have written at the end of this period of maximum upheaval.

IV. CAUSES

Universal factors

We have very little precise data about social mobility in traditional societies. All we do know is firstly that before the nineteenth century towns failed to reproduce themselves because of the high wastage rate from disease, and that as a result there is bound to be a good deal of horizontal mobility from rural to

---

50 R. H. Tawney, "The Rise of the Gentry, 1558-1640," *Econ. Hist. Rev.,* xi (1941), repr. in *Essays in Economic History,* vol. i, ed. E. M. Carus-Wilson (London, 1954): pp. 173-4, 192.

51 Stone, *op. cit.,* pp. 629-32.

urban areas if town life is to survive at all.[52] Secondly we know that the random distribution of sterility and intelligence (or lack of it) creates some vertical mobility in all societies, however highly stratified and caste-ridden they may be. There is a high probability that any one family over a period of one or two hundred years will fail in the direct male line; there is also the certainty that the distribution of inherited intelligence and stupidity will not conform to the existing status hierarchy and that inequality of opportunity cannot always prevent consequential mobility upwards or downwards. Thirdly we know that in all societies the most promising avenues of upward mobility, apart from the lottery of marriage, are through occupational Groups A, B, C and D. Both the amount and the range of this mobility will depend partly on the psychological attitudes of the entrants into these occupations (whether they are active risk-taking entrepreneurs, or cautious conservatives with limited ambitions); partly on major long term changes in the demands by society for their services; and partly on changes in the legal and psychological obstacles to assimilation into the élite of the upwardly mobile. If this is the normal situation, there were certain peculiar features operating in sixteenth- and seventeenth-century England that gave English mobility its special character, and dictated the remarkable changes that took place over these two hundred years.

Factors particular to early modern England

(1) Primogeniture. In all the upper ranks of society primogeniture was the rule.[53] Eldest sons usually inherited the great bulk of the estates of peers, gentry and yeoman farmers. Moreover, eldest sons received a better and longer education, and were better placed to obtain rich wives and good jobs at court and in government, thanks to the more energetic patronage of their fathers. Their life chances were therefore very good. In the sixteenth century younger sons were often left small landed estates, either in outright gift or for life or lives, but by the seventeenth century they could normally expect no more than a modest life annuity which expired at their death. They were therefore downwardly mobile from the very beginning of their careers, and were obliged to feed into the professional and business groups if they were to make their way in the world. If they failed, their children were liable to sink still further down the scale and disappear into the great mass of labourers and small tradesmen. Examples can be found of this downward process, but the paucity of evidence makes it virtually impossible to demonstrate the trend in statistical terms.

(2) Family patterns. Much more research is needed on this subject but, so far as we can tell, marriages were arranged by parents with an eye to material advantage. At the upper levels among the heirs male there was relatively little interstratal marriage, although great wealth could often buy a socially good

---

[52] J. Le Goff and R. Romano, "Paysages et Peuplement rural en Europe après le XIe Siécle," Comité International des Sciences Historiques, XIIe Congrès International, 1965, *Rapports*, iii, pp. 21-2.

[53] Stone, *op. cit.*, pp. 178-83.

marriage for a daughter: thus between 1600 and 1659 some 4% of all marriages
of peers were to the daughters or widows of aldermen. Some two thirds of the
younger sons and daughters of peers were obliged to marry below them,
presumably mostly into the squirearchy. At the lower levels of society, we know
virtually nothing about marriage, and until some such study as Charles Tilly has
just published on the Vendée has been completed, our ignorance will remain.[54]

The two main requirements for upward mobility—capital and patronage—
both hinged on the family. At a time when the interest rate was 10% and
long-term credit hard to come by, the easiest road to riches was through
inheritance or marriage: for example some 8% of London Jacobean aldermen
had, when apprentices, married their master's daughter, while several of the
richest merchants of Elizabethan Exeter had got a start by capturing the fancy
of a rich widow.[55] Similarly family connections usually provided the initial
leverage to get a man started on a career in this deferential society where success
hinged on patronage, as is well exemplified in the case of Pepys.

(3) The value system. Societies are profoundly affected by the way people
think of themselves, regardless of objective criteria such as wealth. The most
important aspects of sixteenth- and seventeenth-century thinking which affected
social mobility were:

(a) The great chain of being. The official theory, which was very widely
accepted, was that everyone had his place in the social system and that it was his
duty to stay in it. Both upward and downward mobility was deplored. This
theory was clearly at variance with the facts and in the early seventeenth century
there began to be heard more egalitarian ideas which culminated in the social
and political thinking of the Levellers. These views were egalitarian in that they
expressed hostility to the concept of hierarchy, and a desire to reduce the
distinctions that cut one group off from another: only the early Renaissance
humanists had wished to preserve the hierarchy but to throw it open to talent.
Both of these were minority opinions and the more common view was that the
functional needs of a modern state could and should be matched to the
traditional hierarchy of birth by educating each social group to meet its
inherited responsibilities. This re-vamping of medieval social ideals to fit the new
political conditions led to an intensification of hostility towards social mobility,
which was at the same time undoubtedly on the increase. There was a flood of
laments about the decay of ancient families, there was widespread and
embittered comment on the ostentatious upward mobility of the merchant class,
and there was also a good deal of complaint that consumption standards and
patterns of life no longer conformed to the ideal status hierarchy.[56] This

54 *Op. cit.,* App. xxx. T. H. Hollingsworth, *The Demography of the British Peerage,*
Supplement to *Population Studies,* xviii (1965), p. 9. H. Tilly, *The Vendée* (Cambridge,
Mass.), 1964, p. 97.

55 R. G. Lang, "The Greater Merchants of London in the early Seventeenth Century"
(Oxford D.Phil. thesis. 1963). Hoskins, "The Elizabethan Merchants of Exeter," *loc. cit.,* p.
167.

56 Stone, *op. cit.,* pp. 21-36.

criticism made it very difficult for the arriviste to achieve social acceptability in his own person, although it was usually easy enough for his son.

On the other hand, we shall see that these traditional views were undergoing considerable modification, and attitudes towards the professions were softening markedly by the middle of the seventeenth century. The decline of war and the church as the two major occupations for the upper classes, the rise in educational standards, the shift to an ideal of administrative and political service to the state or local community, the growing realization of the potentialities for upward mobility of trade and the professions, all led increasing numbers of the gentry class, both elder and younger sons, to seek an outlet for their energies in a career in the law and government office, and some in trade and medicine. For both functional and social reasons, the status of the professions was rising relatively to that of the landed classes, so that by the late seventeenth century the church and the armed services were again becoming popular.

(b) *Consumption as a test of status.* All commentators stressed the obligation to maintain a suitable display as a mark of gentility or nobility. The cost of such displays rose under pressure from below, and there developed a double standard of consumption, that of the old feudal lord with open house and numerous servants in the country, and that of the cultivated Maecenas at Court. Either could be ruinous, and those who tried to maintain both usually spent in excess of income. Excessive consumption was thus one of the principal causes of downward mobility,[57] and the obligation to spend to maintain status was a powerful brake on rapid upward economic mobility. At each stage the new rich had to pause and spend freely in order to establish themselves in their position in society.

Destabilizing factors, 1540-1640

There was a whole series of strongly disruptive forces at work on society between 1540 and 1640, but which were not present to anything like the same degree before or after.

(1) Demographic growth. Firm statistics are impossible to come by, but the best guess is that between 1500 and 1620 the population of England and Wales nearly doubled, from between 2½ and 3 million to 5 million. This added enormously to the labour force and caused horizontal mobility and urbanization. After 1620, however, there is every sign that, except perhaps in the north-west, plague, land hunger, commercial difficulties, family limitation, and emigration combined to reduce the increase to far more modest proportions.[58]

---

[57] *Op. cit.,* pp. 184-8, 547-86.

[58] *V.C.H., Leics.* (London, 1955), iii, pp. 137-47. W. G. Hoskins, "The Population of an English Village, 1086-1801: a study of Wigston Magna," in his *Provincial England,* pp. 185-200. Lionel Munby, *Hertfordshire Population Statistics, 1563-1801* (Hertfordshire Local History Council, 1964), p. 21. L. Owen, "The Population of Wales in the Sixteenth and Seventeenth Centuries," *Trans. of the Cymmrodorion Society* (1959), pp. 113. W. G. Howson, "Plague, Poverty and Population in parts of North-West England, 1580-1720," *Lancs. and Chesh. Hist. Soc. Trans.,* cxii (1960), pp. 29-55.

(2) Differential fertility. Between 1500 and 1630 there was almost certainly a differential fertility pattern by which the upper classes produced more children than the poor—the exact opposite of today. Thus an Elizabethan census of some 450 poor families with children in Norwich shows an average of 2·2 children per household, against between 4·25 and 4·7 children per household of well-to-do merchants of Norwich and Exeter. In the countryside the same discrepancy emerges from such data as are available.[59] The causes of this striking difference are not hard to find.

(a) There was a difference in the average age, duration, and frequency of marriage. For the eldest sons of peers (and probably also of squires) in the late sixteenth century, the average age of marriage (of those who did marry) was 21, and for all children and grandchildren of peers, including both heirs male and younger sons, it was 25 to 26. For yeomen and below, however, the average age of marriage in the early seventeenth century was 27 to 28. Far more important for fertility is the age of marriage of women, and it is here that the contrast is most marked. Between 1550 and 1625 the daughters of the upper classes married at 20 to 21, whereas daughters of the lower classes had to wait till they were 24 to 25. The reproduction period of the latter was therefore significantly shorter than that of the former, and in the absence of contraception would have resulted in between one and two children fewer per family. The reasons for this pattern of delayed marriage among the lower classes are fairly clear. In the artisan class the seven-year apprenticeship system put a stop to marriage before the age of 25 or thereabouts; in the countryside most young people began as living-in servants for either domestic or agricultural work, while the eldest sons of freeholders or tenant farmers had to wait for the death of their father before they could afford to marry. This pattern determined the female age of marriage, since it seems to have been a convention from top to bottom of seventeenth-century society to marry women only about three years younger than oneself.[60]

Equally important in producing greater upper class fertility was the very high rate of re-marriage at this level of society, so that the interruption of the procreative process by death of husband or wife (which was an extremely frequent occurrence) was reduced to a minimum. There is reason to believe that both marriage and re-marriage was less easy for those in less favourable economic circumstances, and indeed at Lichfield at the end of the seventeenth century as many as 31% of all women in the fertile age-group between 25 and 44 were either widows or spinsters.[61]

(b) There was a difference in natural fertility: there is clear evidence that lactation impedes fertility, although the precise share of this effect between the

59 J. F. Pound, "An Elizabethan Census of the Poor," *Univ. of Birmingham Hist. Jl.*, viii (1962), p. 142. P. Laslett, *The World We Have Lost* (London, 1965), p. 69.

60 Hollingsworth, *op. cit.*, p. 25. Laslett, *op. cit.*, p. 83. Stone, *op. cit.*, App. xxxiii and further information from peerage genealogies extracted by Mrs. J. C. Stone. Glass and Eversley, *op. cit.*, pp. 153, 454, 468. P. Styles, "A Census of a Warwickshire Village in 1698," *Univ. of Birmingham Hist. Jl.*, iii (1951), p. 38.

61 Stone, *op. cit.*, pp. 619-23. Glass and Eversley, *op. cit.*, p. 181. Hollingsworth, *op. cit.*, p. 20. Styles, *op. cit.*, p. 40.

physiological prevention of ovulation and a social taboo on sexual intercourse with a suckling woman is at present unknown.[62] Now in the upper classes infants were put out to lower-class wet-nurses at birth, whereas prolonged lactation by the mother for up to two years was normal among the poor.

(c) There was a difference in infant mortality: more upper-class children survived to a marriageable age, since the death rate among upper-class infants was almost certainly lower than among the poor. In one parish of the city of York in the healthy years 1572-85, children under the age of two made up 34% of all burials. The genealogical records of the peerage suggest a considerably lower rate, the expectation of life at birth at that period being about 35 for boys and 38 for girls.[63] This was presumably because these children lived in the countryside rather than in towns, and were better housed, better clothed and better fed (though they were admittedly exposed to the attentions of feckless wet-nurses and of doctors, who often did more harm than good). Moreover, in the seventeenth century, there grew up institutions whose practical achievement, if not ostensible purpose, was to eliminate the unwanted children of the poor: both foundling hospitals and workhouses were highly effective infanticide agencies. In early eighteenth-century London, the latter were killing off some 88% of their children, and indeed in some parishes it was reported that "no infant had lived to be apprenticed from their workhouses."[64]

As a result of all these factors, fertility among the upper classes was very high indeed, and the peers had an effective generation replacement rate of unparalleled magnitude—as high as 1·5 for those born between 1550 and 1600. In other words between about 1580 and 1630 the children of peers were producing 50% more children per generation.[65] The intense competition for jobs and offices in the decades before the Civil War can best be understood in the light of this remarkable demographic phenomenon.

(3) Price revolution. Largely, but not entirely, as a result of this demographic growth, prices rose by between 400% and 650% from 1500 to 1640. Food prices (and therefore agricultural profits) soared, wages and other less adaptable revenues lagged behind. Whole social and occupational groups rose or fell as a result.

(4) Free land market. Between 1534 and 1650 the Crown seized all the revenues of the monasteries and the chantries, and substantial portions of those of the bishops. To pay for war, it immediately sold much of it, the rest being disposed of at intervals under financial stress. Including all sales of Crown and Church lands, as much as 25% or 30% of the total landed area of the country, which had previouslybeen locked up in institutional hands, may have been

---

62 P. Vincent, "Recherches sur la Fécondité Biologique," *Population*, xvi (1961), p. 112. L. Henry, "La Fécondité Naturelle," *Population*, xvi (1961), p. 633.

63 *V.C.H., Yorks., loc. cit.*, p. 121. Hollingsworth, *op. cit.*, pp. 56-7.

64 Wilson, *England's Apprenticeship, 1600-1763*, p. 352.

65 Hollingsworth, *op. cit.*, pp. 32-4.

released on to the private market between 1534 and 1660. By the Restoration the process was virtually complete.[66]

This throwing of Crown and Church lands onto the market was accompanied by an equally important development which released a huge mass of private property, which had previously been tied up by legal restrictions against alienation. In the late middle ages the entail was a fairly effective barrier against the free disposition of property by the current owner; in the late seventeenth century the strict settlement served the same purpose. Between 1530 and 1660, however, there were relatively few and weak legal obstacles to the alienation of property. The result of this legal situation and of various economic pressures was the massive transfer of land by purchase and sale, which reached a peak in the 1610s. It should be noted that both factors involved, the seizure and dispersal of Church lands and the freeing of private property from restrictions on alienation, were the result of politico-legal action supported and encouraged by the landed classes themselves.

(5) Increased commercial activity. Foreign trade expanded in sudden bursts, particularly fro, 1603 to 1620, and 1660 to 1688. More important, but less easy to document, may have been the growth of credit and transport facilities, and the consequent expansion of market activity inside the country. Their development increased both the numbers and the amount and range of mobility of the merchants.

(6) Increased litigation. The end of violence, the growth of commercial activity, and the opening of the land market enormously increased the volume of litigation, the main result of which was to transfer wealth from the landed classes to the lawyers.[67]

(7) The puritan ethic. The Puritans took a strongly moralistic—indeed medieval—approach to economic affairs, and the puritan merchant was consequently subject to almost intolerable psychological pressures as he strove both to maximize profits and to conform to ethical doctrines of the just price.[68] On the other hand, insistent puritan indoctrination on self-discipline and the virtue of striving in the calling could hardly avoid producing personalities with strong anal-erotic characteristics and a high achievement motive. Once the children were grown up, their obsession with thrift and hard, rationally planned, work carried them inexorably along towards the corruptions of wealth and upward social mobility.

There is some reason to believe, however, that this ideological factor did not become fully operative until the 1630s, for its best theoretical expression comes from Richard Baxter. Moreover, evidence of close association of religious Dissent with commercial success does not become plentiful until after the Restoration. Even then the association may have been as much an incidental by-product of

---

[66] Stone, *op. cit.*, p. 166.

[67] *Op. cit.*, pp. 191, 240-2.

[68] The autobiography of the pious London and Boston merchant Robert Keayne is the *locus classicus* of this dilemma: B. Bailyn, ed., *The Apologia of Robert Keayne* (New York, 1965).

exclusion from social and political life under the Clarendon Code as a direct consequence of religious ideology.

More important than this possible economic link, are the indirect and accidental consequences of Puritanism. One is the stress the Puritans laid on Bible-reading, and hence the spread of elementary education. Another is the self-confidence and sense of righteousness arising from contract theology and the doctrine of the Elect, which gave men the assurance to aspire high and to challenge their social, economic and political superiors. Furthermore the democratic, or at the very least oligarchic, tendencies of Puritan church organization worked against the hierarchical and authoritarian concept of society and was thus a destabilizing force. "Purity is Parity" was the slogan of their Anglican enemies, and there was something in the taunt.

Finally one can point to certain chronological correspondences which are, at the very least, suggestive of interconnections. The great age of social mobility precisely coincides with the great age of Puritanism. It is also, perhaps, rather too much of a coincidence that a content analysis of popular literature reveals a high peak of achievement motifs at precisely the same period.[69] This period of widespread challenges to the official system of values contrasts sharply with the post-Restoration development of Divine Right and Passive Obedience notions, and still more with the smug complacency with which Englishmen regarded the existing social and political order after the Glorious Revolution of 1688.

(8) Educational expansion. The period 1560 to 1640 saw an unprecedented educational boom, which affected all but the lowest levels of society. This did not only produce quantitatively a remarkably literate society; it also turned out an educated gentry and aristocracy in excess of the capacity of government service to absorb them, and lower-class clergymen in excess of the cures of souls available. If for many the fruits of this educational expansion were bitter, the spread of literacy and the increased opportunities for higher education for the children of yeomen and artisans, must have increased the possibility of upward mobility for intellectual talent.[70] The secularization of the state may have destroyed the opportunity for the occasional child of the moderately humble to shoot up via the church to high political office, but the growth of education and of the professions opened up other and wider avenues to hardly less exalted positions.

After 1640 first the disturbance of the Civil War and then the social reaction of the Restoration put an end to the expansion of secondary and higher education, which went into a decline. After 1660 opportunities for social advancement via the professions must have been proportionately reduced, and confined to those who could still gain access to this narrowed educational ladder.

(9) Revolutionary political action. One would have supposed that the

[69] M. Walzer, *The Revolution of the Saints* (Cambridge, Mass., 1965), *passim.* D. McClelland, *The Achieving Society* (New York, 1961), p. 139.

[70] Stone, "Educational Revolution," *loc. cit.*

political upheavals of the English Revolution between 1640 and 1660 must have produced far-reaching social changes. Now it is certainly true that revolutionary activity was itself a vehicle for social mobility, in that previously submerged individuals, low-born parsons like Stephen Marshall, backwoods gentry like Oliver Cromwell, frustrated petty bourgeois like John Lilburne, found an opportunity to take the centre of the stage and even to seize power from their social superiors.

But the temporary collapse of the traditional order and the temporary inversion of rôles had no lasting effect upon English society. It has been shown conclusively that the old landlords, even the royalists, survived the Interregnum far better than might have been expected. No new class of successful generals, entrepreneurs and parliamentary committee men arose out of the 1650s, if only because Church, Crown, and Royalist lands were nearly all restored to their former owners at the Restoration.[71] Lower down the social scale the schemes of the Levellers for converting copyhold tenure into freehold were defeated, and the tenantry and small freeholders were probably depressed by the burden of war taxation, plunder and billeting, rather than elevated by any new official concern for their welfare. The rising government debt and the expansion of government services enhanced the prestige and increased the fortunes of financiers, contractors and leading officials, but the significance of these factors does not seem to have been very great. Society in 1660 looked much as it had in 1640, and the number of new families who had risen, or old families who had fallen, over the previous twenty years does not seem to have been at all exceptional. In terms of permanent social change (as opposed to a permanent legacy of ideas) the English Revolution was the least successful of all the "Great Revolutions" in history.

Stabilizing factors, 1650–1700

During the course of the late seventeenth century, a series of stabilizing factors became operative which severely dampened the process of social mobility, and at the same time eased social tensions.

(1) Of the main destabilizing factors, demographic growth, price revolution, free land market, educational expansion, Puritan ideological enthusiasm, and revolutionary activity had all been substantially reduced by 1660, some of them beginning to decline as early as 1620.

(2) There was a sharp drop in fertility and a sharp rise in mortality among the upper classes, so that cohorts born between 1625 and 1674 were barely reproducing themselves, and those between 1675 and 1749 were actually falling behind.[72] This dramatic change from the pre-Civil War condition of an excess of

---

71 J. Thirsk, "The Sale of Royalist land during the Interregnum," *Econ. Hist. Rev.,* 2nd ser., v (1952-3), pp. 188-207; and "The Restoration Land Settlement," *Jl. Mod. Hist.,* xxvi (1954), pp. 315-28. H. J. Habakkuk, "Landowners and the Civil War," *Econ. Hist. Rev.,* 2nd ser., xviii [1] (1965), pp. 130-51.

72 Hollingsworth, *op. cit.,* pp. 32-3.

children to be accommodated in a relatively static job market must enormously have reduced social competition twenty-five years later, that is after 1660.

(3) The natural result of a long period of social mobility, followed by civil war and violent political and social upheaval, was a determination in the minds of all classes to put a damper on change, and to reassert traditional control by traditional authorities.[73] Although in some respects it only accelerated trends already visible in Early Stuart society, this post-Restoration conservative reaction was perhaps the most striking practical consequence of the Revolution. The results can be seen most clearly in the field of education, which was now carefully adjusted to the needs of the élite. Between 1570 and 1650 secondary and university education had been running wild, resulting in a free-for-all competitive struggle uncontrolled by the existing élite, which produced a surplus of qualified men for the available élite jobs, and which failed to indoctrinate them with élite values and élite behaviour patterns. Hence the lamentations of conservatives like Bacon and Hobbes in the early seventeenth century that education was undermining the basis of established society. After the Restoration, however, educational opportunities at this higher level were sharply reduced, and English educational patterns settled down to that tradition of "sponsored mobility" which it has retained ever since. By this system a minority of youths are selected by the élite and their agents at an early age for training in classical studies and aesthetic appreciation, in preparation for admission into this exclusive world. The eighteenth-century grammar schools and universities with their limited scholarship facilities, and the public schools of the nineteenth century, both performed this task of indoctrinating the aspiring few with the ideals and values of the existing élite. A recurrence of the dangerously competitive situation of the early seventeenth century has consequently been avoided ever since.

This adjustment of the educational system was only achieved, however, at considerable intellectual cost. It was not only in terms of quantity that English education declined: qualitatively, the Ancients triumphed over the Moderns, and enforced their view of the rôle of classical studies in the curriculum; socially the Royal Society, after a promising beginning as an intellectual group open to talent regardless of rank, degenerated into a club for gentlemanly dilettantes.[74] By 1720 England had lost its scientific pre-eminence, and the Universities had sunk into a torpor which only the pen of Gibbon could adequately describe.

Parallel to this development, rule by a narrow élite was strengthened at all levels of government. Control of the parish fell into the hands of select vestries of "the better sort." County administration, for example in Northamptonshire, was confined to a smaller, more stable and more closed-off élite group of families.[75] In the towns the same process had long been at work as control of

---

[73] Stone, *Crisis,* pp. 30-1.

[74] Stone, "Educational Revolution," *loc. cit.* M. 'Espinasse, "The Decline and Fall of Restoration Science," *Past and Present,* no. 14 (Nov., 1958), pp. 71-89.

[75] W. E. Tate, *The Parish Chest* (Cambridge, 1946), pp. 18-19. A. Everitt, "Social Mobility in Early Modern England," *Past and Present,* no. 33 (Apr., 1966).

both guilds and civic government passed into the hands of an ever smaller and less fluid oligarchy. At the Freeman level the same thing was happening, and at York the closing of the ranks seems to have occurred before the end of the sixteenth century. In 1509–18, only 16% of Freemen were sons of Freemen, but the proportion had jumped to 38% by 1594–1603, and to 43% by 1675–99. The same trend is visible at Leicester, and its continuance is indicated by the rise of patrimony and purchase as means of entry into several of the Livery Companies of London in the eighteenth century.[76]

In both the Church and government service, hereditary succession became more marked. In the former this was an inevitable by-product of clerical marriage and growing respect for the dignity of the cloth. In the dioceses of Oxford and Worcester, the proportion of parish clergy who were the sons of clergymen rose from 5% in 1600 to 23% in 1640. In the 1630s, over a quarter of the bishops were sons of clergymen.[77] By 1660 the Anglican Church was well on the way to becoming a markedly hereditary profession.

Well before the Civil War there is evidence of considerable nepotism in government service. In the early seventeenth century, patrimony and patronage were the two principal keys to entry into government service, with purchase a bad third. The rôle of patrimony is shown by the fact that the fathers of more than half the officials who were sons of peers or knights had themselves been in government service. Of the whole body, 18% were second generation in the royal service. Almost half came from the squirearchy and above, and about two thirds from the gentry or above. The critical question is whether or not the situation was getting worse, and this we just do not know. Charles I was certainly reacting against this tendency in the 1630s, but this may be evidence of a new political attitude towards the bureaucracy by the absolute monarch rather than of any actual change in recruitment patterns.[78] All one can say is that an increasing trend towards nepotism and social exclusiveness is what *a priori* one would expect to result from the very high reproduction rate of the landed classes over the previous sixty years.

V. CONSEQUENCES

The century of mobility, 1540–1640

Modern societies are learning slowly that widening opportunities and rapid mobility are not necessarily conducive to human contentment. Given the traditional and conservative value system of the age, the great increase in

---

76 A. H. Johnson, *The History of the Worshipful Company of Drapers* (Oxford, 1914-22), ii, pp. 54-5, 197 n. 1; iv, pp. 253-4, 634, 643. *V.C.H. Yorks, loc. cit.,* pp. 128, 166. W. G. Hoskins, *Provincial England,* p. 109. W. K. Kahl, "Apprenticeship and the Freedom of London Livery Companies, 1690-1750," *Guildhall Miscellany,* vii (1956), pp. 17-20.

77 Barratt, thesis cited note 5, p. 241. Information supplied by Mr. F. S. Odo.

78 Aylmer, *op. cit.,* ch. iii and pp. 263-5.

mobility of all kinds in the hundred years from 1540 to 1640 probably created discontent rather than satisfaction, due primarily to the wide discrepancies which developed between the three sectors of wealth, status and power.

(1) Social discontent.   This was felt by both the upwardly and the downwardly mobile. One economically rising group, the merchants, felt themselves denied social prestige, and resented the affront. Other economically advancing groups, the successful lawyers and the greater squires, felt themselves excluded from power by the Court, and also resented the affront. Of the declining groups, the wage-earners were in a state of abject misery which found intermittent relief in rioting and mob-violence. The clergy lamented their loss of income and status relative to those of the laity, and under Laud they allied themselves with the Crown in a vain attempt to recover both. An economically static group, the humble parish gentry, resented their stagnation and were consumed with envy at the conspicuous success of merchants, courtiers and squires. Those nearest London felt the resentment most keenly, since they were most aware of the discrepancy in opportunities. Though the gentry of the home counties were better off economically than those of the north and west they were more bitter since they knew what they were missing. Hence the loyalty to Church and King of the poor backwoodsmen of the west and north in the Civil War, and the rallying to the Independent cause of a section of the small gentry of the home counties.

(2) Religious discontent. How Puritanism affected mobility has already been discussed, but we must now examine how mobility affected Puritanism. After all, the two rose and fell together in extraordinary unison, and a reciprocal feed-back system of causation is by no means theoretically impossible. Professor Walzer has suggested that rigid self-discipline at the service of an ideology is one possible response to a condition of anxiety induced by the overthrow of stable social relationships and agreed political, ethical and religious ideals; cheerful opportunism, quietistic withdrawal, and fierce nostalgia for a lost world are others.[79] It is not difficult to understand the predicament of late sixteenth- and early seventeenth-century Englishmen as the ancient props of their universe fell away. Competing religious ideologies shattered the unquestioning and habit-forming faith of the past; the failure of the Anglican Church to put its house in order left it open to every enterprising undergraduate to draw up an alternative scheme for ecclesiastical organization; constitutional conflicts between Commons and Crown disturbed conventional notions of the rôle of the state and posed the insoluble question of sovereignty; the collapse of the quasi-feudal ties of hereditary dependence left men free to seek clientage where they could find it; the decline of the craft guilds freed labour from both rules and companionship; the bonds of kinship were loosened under pressure from new religious and political associations, and from new ideals of love and freedom within the nuclear family. The upsetting of the hierarchy of status as a result of rapid social

---

[79] Walzer, *The Revolution of the Saints, passim.*

mobility was thus just one of many factors which generated unease, anxiety, anomie.

At present, it is hardly possible to identify Puritanism as the ideology of groups clearly moving in any particular direction. Many were undoubtedly members of upwardly mobile groups seeking security, companionship and assured status in the emerging society of the seventeenth century. There were newly risen Henrician peers and officials like the Dudleys, Cecils, Norths; rich squires at last freed from dependence on aristocratic power, like Knightley, Barrington and Hampden; new academics and preaching ministers like Laurence Chaderton and Anthony Gilby; new merchants, shopkeepers, and artisans in the flourishing towns. Others were members of the static small gentry class bewildered by the transformation around them and seeking some support, like Oliver Cromwell. Both revolutionary Puritanism and the reactionary "Church and King" conservatism of Laud, Stafford and the backwoods royalists are alternate responses to identical pressures of social change. On the other hand many of the key figures in the movement, like their Huguenot counterparts in France, seem to belong to rich, ancient, self-confident families, who should have been immune from such fears. The thesis is an attractive one, but there are still many loose ends to be tidied up.

The decades of revolution, 1640-1660

I have argued at length elsewhere that it was the temporary decline in status and income of the nobles relative to the gentry which allowed the House of Commons to take the centre of the political stage; and that it was this decline in prestige, together with a similar decline of the higher clergy and the ineptitude of the remedies adopted by the Stuarts, which allowed the gentry in the Commons successfully to challenge the establishment in Church and State in 1640. Furthermore it was their vision of an increasingly corrupt, wealthy, wasteful and wicked Establishment which galvanized the squirearchy into action. Finally, it was the rise in education and in numbers of the urban petty bourgeois, especially of London, which made possible the development of the Leveller Party and of Leveller ideas in the late 1640s. If these hypotheses are correct, the shifts in wealth and prestige among the various status and occupational groups, and the "contest mobility" created by the expansion of education during the previous hundred years, played no small part in generating the tensions that led to political breakdown in 1640, to Civil War in 1642, and to the emergence of radicalism in 1647.

Post-Restoration stability, 1660-1700

One of the obvious conclusions of this paper is that much more, and more sociologically and statistically sophisticated, research is needed before we will be in a position to confirm or refute some of the most basic assumptions that are commonly made about the character of early modern English society.

Contemporaries asserted, and posterity has followed them in believing, that by European standards England was an exceptionally mobile society in the sixteenth, seventeenth and eighteenth centuries, and that this was perhaps the main reason why England was the first European nation to industrialize and why it was successful in avoiding bloody revolution in the process. Now there is no doubt that primogeniture and the confining of a title to the eldest son ensured a steady flow of downwardly mobile younger sons, and so made English society at all times different from that of Europe. But recent work on France has revealed a hitherto unsuspected degree of upward mobility in the apparently caste-structured society of the *ancien régime*. It was Turgot who remarked that "il n'est aucun homme riche qui sur le champ ne devienne noble; en sorte que le corps de nobles comprend tout le corps des riches."[80] It may well be that it was only in the century 1540-1640, when land was changing hands at a speed which was quite unprecedented between 1200 and 1900, that there was any unusual mobility in the upper ranks of English society as a whole. Could it be that English society closed ranks a century earlier than France, in the late seventeenth instead of the late eighteenth century, and that the reputation enjoyed by pre-industrial England as an unusually mobile society is largely an illusion based on false assumptions and a dearth of statistical evidence?

If high mobility was only a temporary phenomenon, however, it effected certain structural changes which had profound and lasting results, and which undoubtedly made England rather different from France in the age of Voltaire. The first was the increase in numbers of the squirearchy and gentry, which had far-reaching political and social consequences. Politically, it meant a massive numerical extension of the political nation and so provided the basis for the eighteenth-century constitutional system, which was operated in rough conformity to the interests and aspirations of this broad-based class.

Socially, it meant that for the first time in history the majority of the population were living directly under the eye of a member of the ruling élite. If we may generalize from Buckinghamshire and Rutlandshire, in 1522 only about one village in ten had a resident squire; by 1680 the proportion in the whole country had risen to over two thirds.[81] The potentialities for social and political control were thus greatly increased over what they had been two hundred years before.

The second structural change was the rise of the commercial and professional classes in numbers and wealth, and their consequent acquisition both of a share in political decision-making and of social recognition. The massive increase in numbers had the important social function of absorbing the younger sons pushed out of the landed classes by the primogeniture system. The merchants

---

[80] F. L. Ford, *Robe and Sword* (Cambridge, Mass., 1953). P. Goubert, *Beauvais et le Beauvaisis de 1600 à 1730* (Paris, 1960). G. Bluche, *Les Magistrats du Parlement de Paris au XVIIIe siècle* (Paris, 1960). Turgot is quoted by Betty Behrens in *Hist. Jl.*, viii (1965), p. 123.

[81] J. Cornwall, "The Early Tudor Gentry," *Econ. Hist. Rev.*, 2nd ser., xvii (1964-5), p. 460. Laslett, *The World We Have Lost*, pp. 62-3.

had little formal power but their economic interests closely interlocked with those of the landed classes, thanks to the dependence of the price of land on the price of wool, in turn dependent on the cloth export trade. The maintenance of this trade was also of vital concern to the government, since a slump not only created a threat to social stability in the clothing areas due to unemployment, but also reduced government revenue from the customs. Furthermore, the growing role of the leading London merchants as government creditors and contractors, culminating in the foundation of the Bank of England, gave them considerable behind-the-scenes influence. As a result, foreign, military, and economic policies were increasingly conducted with an eye to the interests, and with the advice, of this merchant élite.[82]

Along with their admission to the political nation went a rise in their social status. There was a slow but steady shift of attitudes on the part of the landed classes, a growing recognition that the previously anomalous occupational categories formed a series of semi-independent and parallel status hierarchies—the "San Gimignano model." By the late seventeenth century merchants, lawyers, clergymen and officials were held in much less contempt than they had been a century earlier. The hypothesis (which has yet to be proved) that many of these middle-class occupational groups were of gentry origin would make it that much easier for the landed classes to treat them with respect. It was perhaps this which gave foreigners the illusion that England was a more mobile society than their own.

Three consequences followed from this rise in status. Firstly, there was much more intermarriage between the landed classes and the appropriate economic strata of these occupational groups. Thus of the 105 armigerous gentry of Warwickshire recognized by the heralds in 1682, two-thirds had mercantile connections (mostly with London) built into their pedigrees somewhere, though only a handful may have owed their economic prosperity primarily to this source. Secondly, the gentry lost their earlier reluctance to put their sons into trade. By the middle third of the seventeenth century nearly half the Freemen of the Drapers' Company of Shrewsbury and nearly a fifth of the London Stationers' Company apprentices were coming from gentry stock.[83] Thirdly, the business or professional man could acquire the title of "Gent.," and on occasion even "Esquire," without having to buy an estate and cut himself off from his economic roots. As early as 1635, there were nearly 1,200 persons resident in London who described themselves as gentlemen, the great majority of whom were engaged in trade or in some professional occupation. In one hundred of Warwickshire, in the late seventeenth century, a third of the "gentlemen" of the

---

[82] B. E. Supple, *Commercial Crisis and Change in England, 1600-42* (Cambridge, 1959), ch. x. R. Ashton, *The Crown and the Money Market, 1603-40* (Oxford, 1960), pp. 67-78.

[83] Laslett, *op. cit.,* pp. 186, 191. P. Styles, "The Heralds' Visitation of Warwickshire in 1682-3," *Birmingham Arch. Soc. Trans.,* lxxi (1953), pp. 131-2. T. C. Mendenhall, *The Shrewsbury Drapers and the Welsh Wool Trade in the Sixteenth and Seventeenth Centuries* (Oxford, 1953), pp. 89-91, and App. C. Calculations from the figures supplied in D. F. Mackenzie, "Apprentices in the Stationers' Company, 1555-1640," *The Library,* 5th ser., xiii (1958), pp. 296-7.

area were now resident in the town of Warwick, and most of them were probably earning their living there.[84] The substantial shrinkage of land offered for sale on the market thus coincided with a distinct, if less pronounced, shrinkage of demand. A country house on its own grounds was still essential for entry into the restricted élite who wielded political and administrative power at both county and national levels, but no longer had the whole of the family capital to be sunk in the purchase of a substantial country estate. At a lower level even possession of a country house was no longer necessary in order to be recognized as the social equal of a minor landed gentleman. If 1540-1640 saw the rise of the gentry, 1600-1700 saw the rise of the "pseudo-gentry."

A striking example of this development is Henry Bell. He was born in 1647, his father being an Alderman of King's Lynn, a mercer by trade, and twice mayor of the town. Henry was educated at the local grammar-school and at Cambridge, then spent his life as a merchant and civic dignitary of Lynn, following in his father's footsteps as alderman and twice mayor of the town. But despite this impeccably bourgeois family and career, Bell had gone on the Grand Tour, and was a virtuoso whose great passion in life seems to have been the arts. He wrote a treatise on the invention of painting before the Flood, he was one of the half-dozen Englishmen with a good professional knowledge of Italian architecture, and he practised as an architect on the side. On the other hand his clientele was as urban as himself, being the corporation of Northampton, who enlisted his services in the rebuilding of the town after a disastrous fire, and the authorities and dignitaries of his home town of Lynn.[85] Here in the flesh is the true *bourgeois gentilhomme,* the self-assured townsman and tradesman with the education, the values and the interests of the cultivated aristocrat. He is a peculiarly English phenomenon, impossible before the late seventeenth century, whose like was unknown to Molière.

Further evidence of this trend rather further down the social scale may be seen in the blurring of that previously crucial division between gentlemen and others by the emergence of a new titular group, sandwiched in between, and comprising parts of, the lesser gentry on the one hand and the upper yeomanry and shopkeepers on the other. These were the people, the numbers of whom were steadily increasing as the seventeenth century wore on, whose names in official lists, etc. were prefixed by the word "Mr."[86] By 1700 the topmost elements of Group 3 and the lowest elements of Group 4 were beginning to form another status group of their own.

These two structural changes caused by the mobility of the previous hundred years were accompanied in the late seventeenth century by that deliberate restriction of mobility channels which has already been described. At the upper

---

84 J. Grant, "The Gentry of London in the Reign of Charles I," *Univ. of Birmingham Hist. Jl.,* viii (1962), pp. 197-201. P. Styles., "The Social Structure of Kineton Hundred...," *Birmingham Arch. Soc. Trans.,* lxxi (1953), p. 106.

85 H. M. Colvin and L. M. Wodehouse, "Henry Bell of King's Lynn," *Architectural History,* iv (1961), pp. 41-62.

86 Styles, "Kineton Hundred," *loc. cit.,* pp. 107-8.

levels there was the narrowing of the avenues of mobility, partly by legal changes devised to preserve existing fortunes and property, and to restrict to established families access to positions of wealth and power; partly by biological changes which caused the striking reduction of the reproduction rate of the upper classes between 1630 and 1740; and partly by economic changes which shut off the disturbing forces of demographic growth and price inflation. At the lower level there was the attempted restriction of horizontal mobility by the pass-law system introduced by the Act of Settlement of 1662; the reduction of educational opportunities to a pattern of carefully sponsored mobility for a selected few; the reduction of the last remaining democratic elements in parish, guild and urban government; and the perversion of the national electoral process by the extravagant use of corruption. These developments prepared the way for the political and social stability of the century following the Glorious Revolution of 1688, during which England was governed by a broad-based but relatively closed oligarchy, part landed, part monied, under the leadership of a still narrower élite of extremely wealthy and influential noble landowners.

PART IV

Historical
demography

From the time of Herodotus, historians have asked questions about the origins and movement of population, and by asking have implied that demographic information is a useful form of historical knowledge. Still, there has been a wide gap between research in historical demography and its reception and exposition in works of general history. Why is it, asks one observer of this problem, that historians avoid seeking "the ultimate explanation which birth and death alone can provide?"[1] One explanation that has been offered is that demographers have failed to demonstrate the relevance of their work to historians whose principal involvement is with the consequences of demographic change rather than with the changes themselves.[2] Whether this explanation is valid or not, there is currently among historians a growth of interest in demographic data that suggests that in the future the problem of a gap may be resolved to the mutual benefit of demography and history.[3] Such collaboration involves qualitative as

---

[1] Louis Chevalier, "Towards a History of Population," in D. V. Glass and D. E. D. Eversley (eds.), *Population in History: Essays in Historical Demography* (Chicago, 1965), p. 71.

[2] David Landes, "The Treatment of Population in History Textbooks," *Daedalus*, 97 (Spring, 1968), p. 379.

[3] As Landes points out, pp. 371, 380-81. His optimism with respect to future collaboration between history and demography, however, is tempered by a feeling that

273

well as quantitative approaches, which should go far beyond the range of what are now conceived to be standard techniques of demographic investigation.[4]

A mixture of demographic styles is illustrated by the selections reprinted here. Russell's essay is by far the most quantitatively oriented, combining economic theory with demographic analysis in what is a rather innovative methodological approach. The other two essays, while somewhat less numerically oriented, more clearly illustrate the use of demographic variables as tools for analyzing social development from a historical perspective.

---

esoteric character of demographic techniques and language will continue to be a barrier for nonquantitative historians.

[4] David V. Glass, *Population in History, op. cit.,* p. 19; also Roger Reville in the introduction to the volume of *Daedalus* cited above, p. 362.

1. A quantitative approach to Medieval population change*

J. C. RUSSELL†

Geographers and city planners, endeavoring to explain or foretell changes in urban population, sometimes use an approach called basic-nonbasic.[1] A basic factor is one which brings in money from outside of the city and which usually sells its products beyond the city limits. The nonbasic factor furnishes services and supplies to the city. Thus a factory would normally be a basic factor, while grocery stores, barber shops, and similar institutions, together with most professional groups, would be nonbasic. A factory employing a thousand workmen would add to the city not merely the workmen's families but about an equal group of nonbasic families, perhaps a total of six or seven thousand persons. This concept is a very useful one in modern society and is worth testing for its possibilities for medieval settlements.

In the Middle Ages life was simple. Instead of a thousand-employee mill as a possible basic factor, there were fairs, markets, fisheries, and guilds which attracted buyers from the countryside; and castles, courts, and monasteries where people were supported by outside money. The question is whether nonbasic groups appeared inevitably alongside or near these basic factors and, if they did, what size did they attain with respect to the basic groups. Should we be surprised at the appearance of a village under a castle, explaining it as existing under the protection of the lord, or should we learn to expect it as a normal nonbasic complement to the basic castle? This study will consider the hypothesis

* Reprinted from the *Journal of Economic History*, XXIV (March, 1964), pp. 1-21, by permission of the publisher and the author.

† Josiah C. Russell, professor of history, Texas A. & I. University, received his Ph.D. from Harvard University. He is the author of *Late Ancient and Medieval Population; British Medieval Population;* and *Dictionary of Writers of Thirteenth Century England.*

[1] For modern use, see, for instance, J. W. Webb, "Basic Concepts in the Analysis of Small Urban Centers of Minnesota," in *Annals of the Association of American Geographers,* XLIX (Mar. 1959), 55-72, especially 61-63; J. W. Alexander, "The Basic-Nonbasic Concept of Urban Economic Functions," *Economic Geography,* XXX (July, 1954), pp. 246-61.

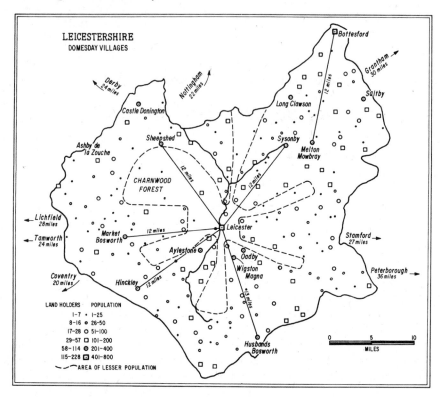

LEICESTERSHIRE
DOMESDAY VILLAGES

of a basic-nonbasic pattern, largely from the evidence of Domesday Book of England of 1086.[2]

Domesday Book provides a very large amount of data about villages and market towns in the rather primitive eleventh century. The principles of local organization thus stand out with some clarity. The second volume, concerned with Norfolk, Suffolk, and Essex, often presents information for three times: that of King Edward just before 1066 (TRE), that just after the Conquest, and that of the Survey in the reign of King William (TRW). The first, second, and third times are referred to frequently in Domesday as then (*tunc*), after (*post*), and now (*modo*). From these data in some instances short-period changes can be seen. Unfortunately, Domesday Book does not present detailed information about the boroughs; and even when a city such as Colchester was included, little

---

[2] References "D. B.," following, are to *Domesday-book seu Liber Censualis Willelmi Primi regis Angliae...* (London, 1783, 1816). A series of geographical studies of Domesday is referred to as follows (each being published at Cambridge by the Cambridge Univ. Press in the year indicated): Darby, *Eastern England,* for H. C. Darby, *The Domesday Geography of Eastern England* (2d ed., 1957); Darby and Terrett, *Midland England,* for Darby and I. B. Terrett, *The Domesday Geography of Midland England* (1954); Darby and Maxwell, *Northern England,* for Darby and I. S. Maxwell, *The Domesday Geography of Northern England* (1962); Darby and Campbell, *Southeast England* for Darby and Eila M. J. Campbell, *The Domesday Geography of Southeast England* (1962).

besides the agricultural holdings of the inhabitants is given. Its information about monasteries and monastic villages will be supplemented by data of later periods.

The boroughs and market towns were set amid agricultural villages whose size varied with local circumstances but in general was small.[3] The surplus grown in the villages was the ultimate support of the larger settlements which were scattered over the countryside. The map of Domesday Leicestershire illustrates the pattern. At a distance of eight to twelve miles from the county borough, Leicester, there appears a series of market towns of a few hundred people. Other boroughs, comparable to Leicester in size, occur approximately twenty-five to thirty-five miles away. However, there were exceptions to this pattern, such as the large villages of Aystone, Oadby, and Wigston Magna, within a few miles of Leicester. That such patterns of population distribution should exist should not be surprising, especially to those who know something of the literature illustrating the distribution of modern population.[4]

The agricultural population, being largely a subsistence group, is regarded as neither basic or nonbasic but a neutral factor. It has to be isolated and subtracted from village total population in order to identify the basic and nonbasic elements. This can probably be done satisfactorily for Domesday evidence by using the number of plows as an index of the agricultural element, since nearly all tillage then characteristic of England was based on plows. The number of landholders to the plow varied from 2.1 in Herefordshire and Gloucestershire to more than 5 in East Anglia.[5] The latter was a populous and fertile area where the large number to the plow would suggest a high percentage of persons supported by nonagricultural activities. We assume that there were about 2.1 persons to the plow. In some cases Domesday indicates that there were more plows in use than were actually necessary: in those cases the lesser number would be the more correct number. The normal working team was apparently four animals handled by two men.[6]

A test of the number to the plow may be illustrated in the cases of Gorleston and Eye in Suffolk in the times of King Edward (1066) and William (1086).[7] For Gorleston and its member, Lowestoft:

---

[3] The size of English villages of Domesday can be seen in my *British Medieval Population* (Albuquerque: Univ. of New Mexico Press, 1948), pp. 306-14, and may be compared with the larger villages of Spain in my "The Medieval Monedatge of Aragon and Valencia," *Proceedings of the American Philosophical Society*, CVI (Dec. 1962), pp. 500-1.

[4] This map [opposite page] is adapted from one drawn by Jerome G. Widdeson for my article, "The Metropolitan City Region of the Middle Ages," *Journal of Regional Research*, II (1960), pp. 55-70.

[5] A. H. Inman, *Domesday and Feudal Statistics* (London, 1900), p. 14.

[6] *Ibid.*, p. 22. H. G. Richardson, "The Medieval Plowteam," *History*, XXVI (Mar. 1942), 287-94. F. W. Maitland, *Domesday Book and Beyond* (Cambridge, 1893), p. 403.

[7] *D. B.*, II, 283, 283b. There were also four freemen of the king there; p. 284b. The *villani* were serfs, *bordars* were small holders much like cotters, and the *servi* were supposed to be slaves; but see my "Short, Dark Folk of England," *Social Forces*, XXIV (Mar. 1946), pp. 340-47.

	TRE	*TRW*
Villani	25	15
Bordars	15	15
Servi	10	7
	50	37
Plows	14	9

The decline was 5 plows and 13 persons, an average of 2.6 to the plow. The loss was caused apparently because 24 persons attached to the manor were fishing at Yarmouth.

The situation at Eye was more complicated.[8]

	TRE	*TRW*
Villani	39	20
Bordars	9	16
Servi	12	0
Burgesses	0	25
	60	61
Plows	23	11

Here there was a decline of 24 persons and 12 plows in the course of a few years, 2 to the plow. The appearance of the 25 burgesses raises the question of whether they were a basic group or nonbasic. If basic, is the nonagricultural group (presumably 13—that is, 36 less 23 for the 11 plows) enough as a nonbasic group? If nonbasic, where is the basic element, assuming the hypothesis of basic-nonbasic factors? Actually, William Mallett built a castle at Eye in the period, but he was a minor lord who can hardly have built a very large one.[9] In addition, a priory of perhaps four monks was established there before 1086 but after the Conquest.[10] These are obviously basic factors: between them the need for a nonbasic group would arise.

Fortunately there is considerable evidence in Domesday and later documents to determine the number of persons about the monasteries of the time and near the castles.

Domesday Book provides detailed information about Bury St. Edmunds, one of the wealthier houses of the time. It had "75 bakers, ale-brewers, tailors, launderers, shoemakers, robemakers, cooks, porters and *dispensatores,* who daily ministered to the needs of the abbey."[11] This would be about the same as the

---

[8] *D. B.,* II, 319b-320. There are other references to Eye which bring the number of landholders to about 145 to 147. See Darby, *Eastern England,* pp. 169, 195.

[9] *D. B.,* II, 379. He also set up a market, but no value is given.

[10] *Victoria County History,* "Suffolk," II, 72-73; D. Knowles and R. N. Hadcock, *Medieval Religious Houses, England and Wales* (London: Longmans, Green, 1953), p. 65. It was established about 1080 and had four monks in 1279.

[11] *D. B., II, 372 ff.;* M. D. Lobel, *The Borough of Bury St. Edmunds* (Oxford: Clarendon Press, 1935), pp. 12-13; Darby, *Eastern England,* pp. 197-99.

number of monks.[12] The abbey also supported "thirty priests, deacons and clerks as well as 28 nuns and some poor people,"[13] who are hard to define in terms of basic and nonbasic. In the thirteenth century, Bury St. Edmunds had 80 monks and 21 chaplains served by 111 servants and others.[14] The matter is complicated because the borough was a sizable place, and it cannot be certain that others than those mentioned served the abbey.

Unlike St. Edmunds, Ely was a peculiarly isolated monastery although farmland was nearby. In 1086, 40 villeins each had 15 acres of his own; together they had 14 plows, and there were 5 plows in demesne. This complement of plows (19) was just about right for the 40 villeins. In addition there were 28 cottars and 20 *servi* in the village.[15] One suspects that they were "ministering to the needs of the abbey": but there is a problem of the number of monks in 1086. In 1093 and again in 1108, Ely had 72 monks. However, Ely was made the episcopal chapter for the new bishop of Ely in 1092:[16] probably the monastic chapter was enlarged then, so that the previous number of monks (in 1086) may have been considerably less. If, as we shall see, the ratio of one servant to one monk held then as later (and the cottars and *servi* were servants) there should have been about 48 monks in 1086. The establishment of Ely as a bishop's see seems to have stimulated the borough's growth: Cambridge demanded of Henry I (1103-35) that its monopoly of commerce in the county be not disturbed, and by 1377 Ely was about as large as Cambridge.[17]

The monastery of Abingdon, Berkshire, had 78 monks in 1117, which was probably about the number for the entire twelfth century.[18] Two lists of abbey servants remain, both for the third quarter of the century.[19] The lists include personnel of the bakery, cellar, and infirmary, and also maintenance men for the plants, and employees in the garden, the mill, and the pasture. There were 76 altogether, thus about equaling the number of monks. This was probably a minimum, since Oxford was only six miles away and doubtless provided for some the abbey's needs. Most of the servants were probably married, but enough might have been single to keep the average nonbasic family small: probably about 3.5 would be a maximum multiple to estimate the total population represented by the servants. This would mean, including the monks, that there would be a multiple for either monks or servants of about 4.5 for the whole

---

[12] Knowles and Hadcock, *Religious Houses,* p. 61.

[13] Lobel, *Bury St. Edmunds,* p. 12.

[14] Knowles and Hadcock, *Religious Houses,* p. 61; *Victoria County History,* "Suffolk," II, 69.

[15] *D. B.,* I, 192.

[16] Knowles and Hadcock, *Religious Houses,* p. 65.

[17] F. W. Maitland, *Township and Borough* (Cambridge, 1898), p. 213; Russell, *British Medieval Population,* p. 142.

[18] Knowles and Hadcock, *Religious Houses,* p. 58.

[19] *Chronicon monasterii de Abingdon,* J. Stevenson, ed. (Rolls Series; London, 1858), II, 237-43. Less helpful data are given in II, 299 ff. This and subsequent references to the Roll Series pertain to *Rerum Britannicarum medii aevi scriptores,* printed in London for the Public Record Office of Great Britain in years as designated.

village. If this holds true, the number of monks at Abingdon can be estimated as about 46 in 1086.[20]

The community about the abbey of Ramsey, Huntingdonshire, can be estimated for the late thirteenth century from information compiled apparently while William of Gomecestre was abbot (1267-85).[21] About 121 persons were then in the employ of the house. These included some agricultural workers who probably should be excluded as a neutral factor. Eliminating about twenty of these would leave about a hundred, which would still include some poor people and seven *prebendarii* (pensioners) in the hospital. The number of monks has been estimated as about eighty.[22] At about the same time, Evesham in Worcestershire included sixty-seven monks, three clerks, five nuns, and three poor, together with sixty-five servants and dependents. This would again give about one servant for each monk.[23] Evesham's monastic population of 1086 probably was about twenty.[24] About 1328, Winchcombe Abbey in Worcestershire drew up a list of the abbey's and abbot's servants, unluckily specifying merely a plural in some cases.[25] Assigning two for the plural, one gets thirty-five servants for the abbey and eighteen for the abbot, a total of fifty-three. The number of monks for the thirteenth and fourteenth centuries has been estimated at fifty to sixty, which is what the wealth of the monastery would suggest.[26] Toward the end of the century, Meaux in Yorkshire drew up a similar list. The number of servants, setting aside the purely farming element, was about forty.[27] In addition there were some dozen legal advisors and fifteen holders of corrodies (right to live at the monstery): the former probably did not live at the house. In 1393, Meaux had twenty-eight monks:[28] these together with the corrody holders would about equal the number of servants.

The evidence then suggests that there would be near the abbey gates in the

---

[20] By subtracting as follows from the 136 (*D. B.*, I, 58b, *Bertune*): 78 agriculturists (37 plows at 2.1); one basic group of 12 for 58½ shillings for mills and fisheries and another 12 as nonbasic; then some 36 persons, together with 10 merchants, or a total of 36 to 46, is left as support for the monks of Abingdon Abbey, who should number about the same. Presumably Abingdon was too close to Oxford to have more than a rudimentary market.

[21] *Cartularium monasterii de Rameseia*, W. H. Hart and P. A. Lyons, eds. (Rolls Series; London, 1893), III, 236-41. The date is the commonly held one shared by the editors. The settlement at Ramsey is apparently not included in *Domesday*. Darby, *Eastern England*, p. 321.

[22] Knowles and Hadcock, *Religious Houses*, p. 74.

[23] *Ibid.*, p. 65.

[24] *D. B.*, I, 175b, offers some interesting data for conjecture. The 27 bordars should include 15 agriculturists (for 7 plows) and 12 others (6 basic for mills worth 30s and their 6 nonbasic). This leaves those paying 20s for *census*. If the *census* was a shilling apiece (often the tax of burgages, or city lots), there should have been twenty persons, which should have been nonbasic for an equal number of monks.

[25] *Landboc sive Registrum ... de Winchelcumba* (Exeter, 1892), I, 363-66.

[26] Knowles and Hadcock, *Religious Houses*, p. 81.

[27] *Chronica monasterii de Melsa*, E. A. Bond, ed. (Rolls Series; London, 1868), III, lxvi-lxxii.

[28] Knowles and Hadcock, *Religious Houses*, p. 111. In 1336, it had 42 monks and 7 lay brothers.

local village or city about as many families as there were monks, the result of the presence of the house. This was naturally not true of the Cistercian monasteries with their lay brothers to handle the needs of the abbey. These houses were able to remove even farming populations from their manors because they could substitute these brothers for the manual labor. However, even that system seems to have broken down by the end of the thirteenth century. Perhaps before the Conquest monks did much of the work in the house, but it is unlikely that they did the specialized work, such as the care of the roofs. Furthermore, heavy farm labor has always been incompatible with long sustained religious or intellectual activity.

The cathedral constitutes a somewhat different problem, largely because of the migratory character of the episcopal retinue and the possibility of nonresidence even of the canons of the cathedral chapter.

A study of the bishop's household, dealing primarily with the more literate members, does note in passing that "Pope Alexander III in the Third Lateran Council (1179) thought it necessary to restrict archbishops, journeying on their canonical visitations, to a retinue of forty to fifty horse and bishops to twenty or thirty."[29] And there were others who kept up the episcopal palace while the bishop was away. The Bishop of Hereford, Richard of Swinefield, of the late thirteenth century, had forty paid servants: squires (*armigeri*), serving valets (*valletti* or *vadletti de ministerio*), servants (*garciones*), and pages (*pagii*) in addition to clerks.[30] If we can assume that the first two groups, totaling about twenty, were married and had sixty dependents and the others (about twenty) were single, we have a basic group of about one hundred. The cathedral chapter of St. Paul's, London, in 1381 had 108 persons paying poll tax—102 priests and 6 clerks—but it was a very wealthy chapter. However, the influence upon the cities is difficult to estimate in nonbasic terms.

Domesday presents one case where such influence may be estimated. In 1075, the Bishop of Selsey moved to Chichester and presumably his chapter with him. Unfortunately, the information about the land held *communiter* by the canons at Selsey does not give details about its inhabitants.[31] However, the number of houses (haws) in Chichester increased by another sixty from the time of King Edward to 1086.[32] If we assume that half of the increase consisted of canons and their clerks supported by the cathedral endowment, their number should have been about thirty. A small cathedral, such as that of Chichester, should then have had about fifteen to twenty canons. The bishop probably had a very modest retinue.

[29] C. R. Cheney, *English Bishops' Chanceries, 1100-1250* (Manchester: Manchester Univ. Press, 1950), pp. 1-21, especially 5.

[30] *A Roll of the Household Expenses of Richard de Swinfield, Bishop of Hereford,* John Webb, ed. (London: Camden Society, 1855), especially pp. 166-72, 194-97.

[31] Russell, *British Medieval Population,* p. 136.

[32] *D. B.,* I, 17, 23. Fishburne manor was very close to the west of Chichester, so that the city's agricultural population was small. See also Darby and Campbell, *Southeast England,* pp. 463-66.

Among the basic factors in population change was the activity of the ruling class, which drew its income from wide areas but disbursed it in small ones. They spent time in some of their favorite castles or cities or hunting lodges, even though much of their life, especially that of royalty, was migratory. Since their dignity normally found one expression in the size of their retinues, this was a factor in population. The appearance of even a baron would crowd a village, and the coming of a king and his retinue would overwhelm any but a sizable borough. Large-scale castle building brought extensive changes in cities, where great sections were torn down to make room for them, especially following the Conquest. The addition of even a small castle, as at Eye, might affect the economy.

The changes in the village of Clare, in Suffolk, illustrate what could be the result of constructing a castle which was the head of a great honour. Its owner in 1086, Richard of Bienfaite, had shared the justiciarship in 1075 and had built up a great complex of estates in the eastern counties.[33] The changes recorded in Domesday are:[34]

	TRE	1067	TRW		TRE	1067	TRW
Villeins	40	35	30	Plows	48	36	31
Bordars	10	10	30	Sheep	60		492
Servi	20	20	20	Swine	12		60
Socmen	5	5	5				
Burgesses			43				
In Castle	–	–	?				
	75	70	128				

The change from arable land to pasture for the many more sheep and swine would account for decline in the number of villeins. In the castle there were 7 secular canons[35] and, of course, the staff of the castle. Subtracting 65 as the farming group (31 x 2.1) would leave 63 to be accounted for. If there were 25 in the castle besides the canons, there would be a basic group of 32, which would still not account for 31 of the 63 persons. However, Clare was actually far enough away from its sizable neighbors, Bury St. Edmunds, Cambridge, Colchester, and Ipswich to be a tertiary center, a market town which would create another group of basic persons, merchants selling to the surrounding areas. The establishment thus of the *caput* (head) of a great honour probably triggered a potential development so that it became a market town of perhaps five to six hundred.

---

[33] Under "Clare, Richard de" in the *Dictionary of National Biography* (London: Smith, Elder & Co., 1908). He was also known as son of Count Gilbert or FitzGilbert and even as Richard of Tonbridge.

[34] *D. B.,* II, 389b.

[35] Knowles and Hadcock, *Religious Houses,* p. 84.

The castle of Clifford in Herefordshire, which was built on wasteland by order of King William, would seem to have been organized as follows:[36]

In castle		Farming		Borough	
Men	4 (or 5)	Bordars	13	Burgesses	16
Servi	6	*Bovarii*	4		
Ancille	4	Welsh	5		
	14 (or 15)		22	Value	60s
		Plows	12		

The four men holding large tracts of land were evidently the custodians of the castle: the *servi* and *ancille* (men and women slaves?) were probably associated with them in the castle.[37] This would leave about the right number of plows, twelve, for the other twenty-two persons. In two ways the number of burgesses seems correct: they are equal to the people presumed to have been in the castle and their value should be about five shillings a person. The actual value is a little low but that might be expected on the Welsh border. On the basis of the hypothesis, a village of about 150 should have been near the castle.

Using the hypothesis and on the basis of rather scant evidence in Domesday Book, a very conjectural estimate of the number of people in and about the castle of Wigmore can be made.[38] This castle was built on waste land at Merston and thus no earlier settlement was there. At Wigmore there were only four *servi* and two hides of land: no plows are mentioned so presumably the *servi* were herders. The *burgum* was worth only seven pounds: if it was rated like the Clifford community not far away there should have been about twenty-eight "merchants" there. This was the *caput*, head castle, of the Mortimer family which at the time was a relatively modest noble family: their acquisition of great holdings came later. One might well expect a retinue of twenty to thirty for such a family, which would thus match the hypothetical group of merchants. The castle and village may be estimated conjecturally as about 55 to 65 families and about 200 to 250 in total population.

In view of these examples of the size of settlements in and about castles of baronial lords of importance, the population near small *castella* must have been quite small. Domesday Book has no regular way of presenting evidence about this type of settlement, and so the data are not easy to interpret. Many of the castles in the boroughs were essentially shire-houses (county court houses)

---

[36] *D. B.*, I, 183.

[37] The *bovarii* were oxherds or cowherds. On Clifford, see also Darby and Terrett, *Midland England*, pp. 73, 103. A very small mill was there.

[38] *D. B.*, I, 179b, 180, 183b. For Ralph de Mortimer's career, see account in *Dictionary of National Biography*. Darby and Terrett, *Midland England*, p. 104.

whose complement of shire officials was about eight to twelve[39] With an equivalent nonbasic group, the county officialdom would augment the population of a borough by about fifty to one hundred in addition to what was produced by the custodians and any other residents of the castle.

The royal castle of Windsor provides a problem, since it is not certain whether the Windsor of 1086 was the old city or the new, or both. In a sense it makes little difference, since even old Windsor was only two miles from the castle: the 95 haws recorded as being there would be expected near a great royal castle.[40]

Fortunately the number of persons in the household of Henry I can be estimated very roughly at about 172, from the *Constitutio Domis Regis.*[41] This does not include the king's judicial courts, which often accompanied him on his journeys, nor such lords as might be with him as members of his council. Many of them might have been married, with families settled in London, Westminster, or Windsor; but a good part of them went with him. Walter Map asserted that on one occasion twenty ships were required to carry the court across the Channel:[42] unfortunately he did not designate the occasion, so that a clearer picture of the fleet is unavailable. When the king and his court (with their families) were in London it must have been a basic factor of at least five hundred.

Earlier, the large size of certain villages near Leicester was mentioned. All three were seats of great lords. Two were relatively simple in structure:[43]

Oadby (held by Countess Judith)		*Wigston Magne* (by Hugh de Grantesmil)			
Socmen	49	Priest	1	Socmen	31
Bordars	11	Knights	2	Freemen	4
	60	Clerk	1	Villeins	32
Plows (9			4	Bordars	12
at 2.1	19			*Servi-e*	3
	41				82
		Plows (17 at 2.1)			36
					46

[39] Mabel H. Mills, "The Medieval Shire-House," in *Studies presented to Sir Hilary Jenkinson*, J. Conway Davies, ed. (London, New York: Oxford Univ. Press, 1957), pp. 254-71; G. H. Fowler, "Rolls from the Office of the Sheriff of Bedfordshire and Berkshire, 1332-4," in *Quarto Memoirs of the Bedfordshire Historical Society*, III (1929), especially 2-8.

[40] *D. B.*, I, 56b, 62b; Darby and Campbell, *Southeast England*, pp. 279-80.

[41] *Red Book of the Exchequer*, Hubert Hall, ed. (Rolls Series; London, 1896), III, cclxxxix-ccxciii, 809-13. It is translated in *English Historical Documents*, D. C. Douglas and G. W. Greenaway, eds. (New York: Oxford Univ. Press, 1953), II, 422-27 and bibliography. See also G. H. White, "The Household of the Norman Kings," *Transactions of the Royal Historical Society*, 4th series, XXX (1948), 127-55.

[42] *English Historical Documents*, II, 390.

[43] *D. B.*, I, 232b and 236 for Oadby; I, 232 and 236b for Wigston Magna.

The socmen and bordars at Oadby were unlikely to have been members of Countess Judith's retinue and were presumably a non-basic group (except for the farmers) of the village. Forty would be about right for the retinue of a wealthy and powerful countess. On the other hand the priest, knights, and clerk were probably part of Hugh's retinue and thus of the basic group. A retinue of about forty-six would be appropriate for the seat of a great landholder whose holdings lay in many counties.

Not far away from these villages was Aylstone, a more complicated settlement.[44] There a lesser countess, Alveva, had a seat, and the Earl of Mellent a prosperous milling center together with lands of two of his vassals, Turold and

	The Countess	*The Earl*	*Turold*	*Ulnod*
Socmen	1		5	
Villeins	18	24	1	2
Bordars	8	5	2	3
Servi	1	1		
Total	28	30	8	5
Plows (8 at 2.1) 17		Plows (7 at 2.1) 15	Plows (2 at 2.1) 4	Plows (2 at 2.1) 4
	11	15	4	1

Ulnod. It would appear that the Countess had a retinue, according to the hypothesis, of about eleven; rather small, but in spite of her title she was a minor landholder. The Earl had four mills worth forty-eight shillings. If we assume one man for each five shillings, there would be about ten basic persons, leaving five to be accounted for. It seems likely that the Countess had a larger retinue, supported by the extra-sized nonbasic extra of the earl and his men. At least it is clear that there were good reasons why villages of a larger size should have been so near Leicester.

The evidence about the castles and monasteries seems to fit the basic-nonbasic hypothesis well. Only occasionally have other basic factors, such as mills and markets, been mentioned. We have mentioned without explaining that we have assumed one basic person for each five shillings value of these. This is assumed partly because it represents a 5 per cent return upon what a skilled workman would then make in a year (that is one hundred shillings, or three hundred days at four pence a day), and partly because it seems to work out satisfactorily in practice.[45] We consider the hypothesis now with respect to economic factors.

Perhaps the best example in Domesday of something approaching an industry is the salt works at Droitwich near Worcester.[46] The salt came from brine in

[44] *D. B.,* I, 231b, 237.

[45] See Table 1 and explanation upon it. Five per cent would be a shilling in a pound.

[46] On Droitwich, see E. K. Berry, "The Borough of Droitwich and its Salt Industry, 1215-1700," *University of Birmingham Historical Journal,* VI (1957-58), 39-61. Darby and Terrett, *Midland England,* pp. 251-56.

three great springs and some minor ones. The brine was evaporated in wooden sheds called *saline*. Domesday shows about 150 of them held of the king:[47] of these, a variety of lords had about 100 and the rest were presumably used by local operators.[48] The burgesses (112) and houses (38), together with 18 bordars in the adjacent manor of Wycelbold and 3 *salinarii*, given in Domesday Book, would suggest a population of about 170 families, about the same as the 151 families of the four parishes in 1563.[49] In the interval both the process of producing the salt and the volume of production remained much the same,[50] so it is reasonable that the population would remain as it was. With Worcester only four miles away and Wycelbold even closer (with certain merchants as citizens), Droitwich might well develop almost entirely through its salt works, since its weekly market and annual fair may also have been primarily for the sale of salt.[51] The question is whether the salt workers as a basic group included a proper proportion of the population.

One of the king's manors had attached to it in Droitwich thirteen *saline* and three *salinarii*.[52] Presumably the *salinarius* was a master workman, since salt making was a highly specialized operation at Droitwich, producing a very high grade of salt of which the city was proud.[53] If the ratio of *saline* to *salinarii* was typical, the 150 *saline* of the city should have been worked by about forty *salinarii*. However, some holdings had ratios of one burgess or house to two *saline*,[54] or about one half of the other ratio. This suggests that each master had an assistant to help him, as we should expect, bringing the salt workers as a group to about eighty, or half of the population. The number of persons paying the lay subsidy was 87 in 1276 and 90 in 1327.[55] These were the more substantial persons of the town, presumably the *salinarii*, which we have estimated as about forty, and a roughly equal number of nonbasic persons of some means. The full population thus can be accounted for on the hypothesis

---

[47] The earl is said to have had 51½ (*D. B.*, I, 172b), which should have been a third, as in a *wich* in Cheshire (*D. B.*, I, 268).

[48] Evidently carried away to their own landed property; it was stated as belonging to certain manors of the lords.

[49] *Victoria County History*, "Worcestershire," III, 78. Two parishes in Wich; the others at Witton and Gosford.

[50] Berry, *Borough of Droitwich*, pp. 42-43, 51. The vats increased from between 310 and 320 in 1086 to 400 in the sixteenth century.

[51] *Lay Subsidy Roll for the County of Worcester, circ. 1280*, J. W. Willis Bund, ed. (Worcester: Worcestershire Historical Society, 1893), pp. 7-8, 23-24; *Lay Subsidy . . . for 1327*, F. J. Eld, ed. (1895), pp. 15-16, 37-38.

[52] *D. B.*, I, 172. The volume of the product of these was a little above average: 23 mitts of salt to the *salina* when the average was 19.

[53] *D. B.*, I, 265b. A Cheshire place, Actun, had a "quiet house" for making salt crystallize properly. For conditions, see Berry, *Borough of Droitwich*, pp. 48-51. The customs of salt making in Cheshire are given in *D. B.*, I, 268; they are probably much like those of Droitwich.

[54] Osbert Fitz Herbert had 13 burgesses with 26 *saline*. Gilbert Turoldi had 1 burgess to 2 *saline*. *D. B.*, I, 176b, for both. Berry, *Borough of Droitwich*, pp. 48-49.

[55] *Victoria County History*, "Worcestershire," III, 78. Also n. 51.

that the salt making industry supplied the basic factor for an equally sized nonbasic group.

A second industry was fishing, of which one large center in 1086 was Wisbech in Cambridgeshire. Its quota of 33,260 eels was probably the largest in England: the village quite appropriately was held by Ely Abbey.[56] The composition of the village by classes was:

Villani	15	Total	65
Socmen	13	Plows (10 at 2.1)	21
Cottars	17		44
Fishers	20		

The plows would have been used by the villani and socmen (a special type of freeman). Wisbech was a small village in which there would be few basic operators besides the fishers.[57] The twenty fishermen plus three others (perhaps merchants) are by our estimate just about half of the forty-four in the nonagricultural group.

Another place, Seasalter, Kent, called in Domesday Book a little borough *(parvum burgum)*, was apparently based upon oyster fisheries.[58] Domesday says that the place belonged to the kitchen of Canterbury (Christchurch) Abbey and had eight fisheries. Its recorded population consisted of a priest (presumed because a church is mentioned), the feudal holder, Blize, and forty-eight bordars; a total of fifty families. The two plows mentioned would probably require the work of only four or five men. If the basic industry, here fisheries, would require as we believe the work of half of the nonagricultural people, the eight fisheries would employ about twenty-two persons, or about three to a boat. The value of the fisheries had arisen from twenty-five shillings to five pounds and was thus worth, in 1086, about five shillings a fisherman or about the average for a skilled workman. The nearness of Canterbury (five miles) must have limited the functions of Seasalter very largely to fishing: its claim to being a borough presumably rested upon its nonagricultural character.

The herring fisheries off the east coast seem to have been growing in the eleventh century, as in France.[59] Beccles, Suffolk, had the following population:[60]

---

56 *D. B.*, I.

The list of persons or religious houses to which eels were owed included: 6 fishers owing 3,500 to William Warenne (196b); 1 fisher for 5,000 to Bury St. Edmunds (192); 8 fishers for 5,260 to Ramsey Abbey (192b); 3 for 4,000 to Croyland Abbey (193); 2 for 14,000 to Ely (192); and a miscellaneous obligation for 1,500 (probably to Ely; 192).

57 King John arranged for some shipping by sea there just before his death. J. C. Holt, "King John's Disaster in the Wash," in *Nottingham Medieval Studies*, V (1961), 75-86.

58 *D. B.*, I, 52. Tait knew that it was an oyster center but called it largely agricultural. James Tait, *The Medieval English Borough* (Manchester: Univ. of Manchester Press, 1936), p. 67.

59 For the herring fisheries off the coast of France from 1030 to 1170, see M. A. Valenciennes, "Histoire naturelle du hareng," extract from *Histoire naturelle des poissons* (Paris, 1847).

60 *D. B.*, II, 283b, 369b.

Burgesses (at market)	26
Freemen	12
Villeins	7
Bordars	26
Socmen	20
and their bordars	30
	121
Plows (16 at 2.1)	34
	87

Half of these 87 should be basically employed, or about 44. If we assume that these were fishermen, there would be a quota for more than a thousand herring apiece, since they owed sixty thousand. As this was probably in the nature of a tax, the total catch must have been several times larger.

The situation at Kessingland and thirteen nearby villages in 1066 suggests that villagers fished at one place and lived at others.[61]

	Men	Plows	Farmers	Nonagri-cultural	Herring Quota
Kessingland	7	3 at 2.1	6.3	.7	22,600
Other villages	51	14.5 at 2.1	30.5	21.5	8,660

There were more plows in the villages in 1066 (18) than twenty years later. Kessingland apparently was the best fishing site: some of the villages were not on the sea. It would seem that many of the men from the villages spent at least part of their time fishing at Kessingland, and in increasing numbers.

After all, these were small fishing ports. It is unfortunate that there is so little information about the greater centers: Dunwich and Yarmouth, among others. One recalls the twenty-four men from Gorleston who were fishers at Yarmouth: were they organized as a boat company? The twenty ships of Dover which were manned by twenty-one persons apiece (the captain and a crew of twenty?) were required for royal service only fifteen days a year.[62] Were some of them fishing boats the rest of the year? No wonder the king had a sergeanty for a man to hold his head while he crossed the Channel. Few landsmen enjoy the smell of fishing boats! The herring were running heavily in the Channel at the time and must have been one of the chief sources of income for the Cinque Ports and other Channel ports.

Mills and markets were the most common form of business activity, although even about these the detailed information is limited. With mills are often

---

61 Kessingland, *D. B.,* II, 283, 407; for others, 407, 407b. Southwold also seems to have had too few men for its quota of 25,000. *D. B.,* II, 371b.

62 *D. B.,* I, 1.

associated fisheries, presumably because of the millpond. The information is presented in Table 1. Columns (a), (b), and (c) isolate the farming population which is estimated in (c). On our hypothesis, about half of the nonagricultural people should be nonbasic and are given in (d). The basic group is estimated from the values given for market, mills, and other "industries," by dividing the values by five shillings, as explained above. The data gives the strength as well as the weaknesses of Domesday data, as the notes indicate. The basic figures confirm, in the cases of Faversham, Milverton, and Oundle, the correction of the actual number of plows to a smaller figure indicating the number really needed on the manor. To fulfill our hypothesis, the numbers of nonbasic in column (d) should be somewhat near the basic in (e), as is the case for most of the examples. Some other interesting cases besides these may be considered.

The Lincolnshire village or market town of Louth presents an unusual picture of a milling center in Domesday with its eighty burgesses, forty socmen, two knights, and two villeins.[63] Eighteen plows of the village were presumably worked by the socmen and villeins. Thirteen mills were worth sixty shillings, or about five shillings apiece, about as one might expect. Assuming this represents thirteen men basically employed, there should be about twenty- seven other basically employed persons, that is, half of the eighty burgesses. However, the market was said to be worth only twenty-nine shillings, which is both a very small and a very unusual number. One suspects then that twenty-nine merchants were each charged a fee of a shilling apiece. The distance of Louth from other centers encourages one to assume that it was becoming a market town as well as a mill center.

Two other illustrations may be given. Walton in Norfolk, not far from Wisbech, belonged to a variety of lords.[64] Its 233 inhabitants, assuming that all the items are from one village, used only 29 plows which should have indicated about 61 persons, leaving 172 for other pursuits. For the basic industries, half (86) should be employed in its 39 salt works and one fishery, which would be about two persons apiece. This would follow the Droitwich pattern, although the type of salt was different. The mill at twenty shillings should add another four persons. This total would not be much different from the eighty-six estimated for either basic or nonbasic. Another case is that of Otterton, Devon, a holding of St. Michael's Mount in Cornwall, which had thirty-three *salinarii*. The other classes recorded are fifty villeins, and twenty bordars, alleged to have forty plows in addition to the six plows in demesne.[65] The "forty" plows arouses suspicion, since the land is said to be able to use only twenty-five plows! The chances are that the "xl" was a misreading of "xi" and that there were seventeen plows in use. Subtracting 36 persons, assumed to be using the plows, 34 are left, which is very near the 33 *salinarii*. However, there were three mills at Otterton

63 *D. B.*, I, 345.

64 *D. B.*, II; Ely Abbey, 213; Earl Alan, 149b; William de Warenne, 160; Roger Bigot, 173; *R. de Bello Fago*, 226; Robert Toni, 236; Hermer de Ferrers, 274b. The proportions of the Ely holding to the others are about the same.

65 *D. B.*, I, 104; III, 177.

TABLE 1

Estimate of Basic and Nonbasic Factors in Certain English Villages, 1086

Village (pages D.B I)	Farming			Nonbasic (d) (a − c) (2)	Basic (e) (f + g) (5)	Value in Shillings and Pence of:	
	Persons (a)	Plows (b)	Farmers (c) (b × 2.1)			Market (f)	Mills (g)
Alcester, Beds. (210b, 212, 214b, 218)	42	14	29	6.5	9	10	36
Basingstoke, Hants. (39, 43)	52	20	42	5[a]	16	30	50
Bolingbroke, Lincs. (351)	33	5	11	22	2[b]	??	10
Buckland, Berks. (58b)	23	4	9	7	6.5	20/6[c]	12/6
Cheshunt, Herts. (137)	78	21	44	17	15[d]	10	10
Cosham, Berks. (56b)	70	23	48	11	11	20	
Faversham, Kent (2b)	75	17[f]	36	19.5	20	80	35/10[e]
Middleton, Leics. (235b)	40	10.5	22	9	9	20	20
Milverton, Somst. (86b, 87, 94)	150	50[g]	105	22.5	27	60	25
Newenden, Kent (4)	29	5	11	9	8	39/7	77/6
Okehampton, Devon (105b)	55	24	50	2.5	2.5	5	6/8
Oundle, Nhants. (221)	36	9[h]	25	8.5	9	25	20
Spalding, Lincs. (351b)	74	17	36	19	18	40	50[i]
Tischfel, Hants. (39)	33	9	19	7	12	40	20
Ilchester, Somst. (86b)	108	28	59	54	48	220	20

[a] Apparently merchants and millers were not listed.
[b] The value of the new market is not given.
[c] Includes value of the dairy.
[d] Includes value of the fishery.
[e] Includes value of the fishery.
[f] Using farm plow potential rather than listed 26 plows.
[g] Using farm plow potential rather than the listed 69 plows.
[h] Using farm plow potential rather than the listed 12 plows.
[i] Including fisheries and salt works.

valued at forty shillings total, which should have meant another basic group of eight. This casts suspicion at those large round numbers of fifty and twenty which may well have been approximations, underestimating the labor force.

The effect of an addition of a market can be seen in the case of *Caramhalla* (Kelsale, Suffolk)[66] from the following data:

	TRE	TRW
Freemen	25	25
Villeins	15	22
Bordars	11	26
	51	73
Plows	32	32

The ratio of men to plows in 1066 was very low, about 1.5 to the plow instead of the expected 2.1. The increase of men from 51 to 73 might be in part the result of more men to the plows. This would depend upon the size of the market. Unfortunately, its value is not known. However, there were two manors there: the smaller had sixteen men in 1086 and was valued at eight pounds, while the second had fifty-seven men and was worth sixteen pounds. If the purely agricultural manor saw a ratio of one half pound value to a man, the larger might have the same and thus have 48 agriculturists, which would leave 9 for the basic-nonbasic group with half of them, or about 5, merchants. Subtracting 9 from 73 would give 64 for the 32 plows, a much more normal ratio.

The effect of change of basic elements is evident in the case of two settlements in Wiltshire—Brokenborough and Malmesbury, slightly more than a mile apart. Brokenborough was probably a century older than its neighbor: in the reign of Eadwi (955-959) it apparently had a hundred houses, which might be expected of a small borough then.[67] At the site of Malmesbury was set up a large monastery and then a royal castle,[68] both on what had previously been unsettled land. By 1086, Brokenborough had declined, although it was still a milling center.[69] Its neighbor then had at least 91 houses,[70] of which at least 25 were held of the king, an appropriate nonbasic housing near a small castle, and the remaining 65 houses would be the proper support for a large monastery of

66 D. B., II, 330b. Kelsale is suggested by Darby, *Eastern England,* p. 202.

67 *Registrum Malmesburiense,* J. S. Brewer and C. T. Martin, eds. (Rolls Series; London, 1880), II, xxxi. Its alternative name was Kairdunburgh.

68 *Ibid.,* II, xxxi. The editors note that Bishop Leuterius granted the site as "terra illa que vocabulum est Maeldunesburg" rather than as manor. *Eulogium Historiarum,* F. S. Haydon, ed. (Rolls Series; London, 1858), I, 225.

69 *D. B.,* I, 67a. It had 64 villeins, 7 cotters, 15 *cosces* (cotters), 16 *servi* for a total of 102. The 64 plows would more than employ this group. The eight mills were valued at £ 8 12s 6d. which should have indicated the employment of at least 34 millers who probably lived in Malmesbury.

70 *D. B.,* I, 64b. Long afterward, the inhabitants of Malmesbury were to keep up the borough wall. *Registrum Malmesburiense,* I, 136.

perhaps 40 monks and for the millers who apparently worked but did not live at Brokenborough.

The hypothesis of a basic-nonbasic explanation thus seems to be satisfactory for explaining population and population change from the Domesday evidence and related data. For monastic houses there seem to be about as many monks as persons holding land in the adjacent villages. This is to be expected, since monasteries were substantial buildings of considerable value. Other basic factors, such as mills and fisheries, show also about one nonbasic landholder for each workman in the basic industry. The merchants vary in classification as in function: if they are primarily buying and selling to out of town persons they would be basic: if dealing primarily with and for the townspeople, probably nonbasic.

The basic-nonbasic approach should be valuable in at least two ways. For the earlier Middle Ages it enables one to conjecture with some certainty upon the population near castles, monasteries, and other basic factors. For the later period it may be applied to study of the larger boroughs where data exist, to estimate numbers in guilds and in occupational groups. The approach makes clearer the relationship of population to the basic groups and gives a certain reasonableness to its distribution.

2. Families in colonial Bristol, Rhode Island: an exercise in historical demography*

JOHN DEMOS†

No aspect of early American history has been more badly served by unsystematic, impressionistic methods of handling source materials than the whole vast area of family life. Our understanding of the subject has begun from a set of assumptions sustained chiefly by the force of a venerable popular folklore. Many of them can be tested in quite simple numerical terms, yet only very recently has the effort to do so even been started. Perhaps the best way to illustrate the seriousness of the situation is to list some of the most prominent of these assumptions, together with the verdict that present and future research seems likely to render upon them: (1) The colonial family was, initially at least, "extended" rather than "nuclear." (This is almost certainly false.) (2) The normal age of marriage was extremely early by our own standards. (Wrong again.) (3) The average number of children per family was very high. (True, but with some qualifications.) (4) Life expectancy was generally quite low, though a few people who managed to escape the manifold hazards of the day survived to a prodigiously old age. (Largely false.) (5) The mortality rate for infants, and for mothers in childbirth, was particularly high. (Much exaggerated.) (6) Many men and women were married two or more times, owing to the death of their first spouses. (Somewhat exaggerated.)[1]

---

* Reprinted from the *William and Mary Quarterly*, XXV (January, 1968) pp. 40-57 by permission of the author and publisher.

† This article is part of a broader investigation of family life in Plymouth Colony, sponsored by Plimoth Plantation, Inc. Editors note: An assistant professor of history, Brandeis University, Demos received his master's degree from the University of California at Berkeley and is the author of several articles on American colonial history. His current research includes a study of witchcraft in 17th century America.

[1] This summation is based partly on my own work with various towns in Plymouth Colony. See John Demos, "Notes on Life in Plymouth Colony," *William and Mary Quarterly*, 3d Ser., XXII (1965), 264-286. But see also Philip J. Greven, Jr., "Family Structure in Seventeenth-Century Andover, Massachusetts," *ibid.*, XXIII (1966), 234-256, for another set of findings closely approximating most of the results for Plymouth. Note that my use of the term "extended family" is a rather formal one, comprising simply common residence "under the same roof." Greven's model of the "modified extended

But if the need for precise information on these matters is urgent, the *opportunity* to make a fresh approach has never been more promising. For some years past, in England and France, a small group of scholars has been engaged in applying new methods of demographic analysis to certain key problems of European social history. This important development has recently been accorded its first real American exposure in a long review article by Philip J. Greven, Jr., and my own task is thereby simplified considerably.[2] The reader who wishes a general initiation into the mysteries of historical demography can do no better than consult the essay by Greven. My purpose here is to offer a concrete instance of this kind of analysis within the context of a single colonial town. For a variety of reasons, chiefly reflecting deficiencies in the source materials, certain of the more significant results obtained for England and France cannot be duplicated here. Still, it may be useful to rehearse at least some of the procedures that are central to this discipline, as much to show the difficulties involved as to communicate new findings.

Before concluding these introductory comments let me try to outline in advance the basic direction in which the argument will proceed, since in a study with an underlying methodological focus there is some danger that the end product may seem somewhat spotty and disjointed. An initial set of questions will concern the membership of households in colonial Bristol. Then, in order to establish the degree to which these results are "representative," Bristol will be examined in terms of the over-all age-structure of its populace. This, in turn, will suggest certain broader conclusions about the comparative demographic profiles of "old" versus "new" towns. Finally, after treating Bristol in this fashion at two different points in time, the analysis will move briefly into a somewhat different area of family life. An investigation of "birth intervals" will be attempted—with results which, while disappointing alongside comparable European studies, will at least suggest some intriguing possibilities with regard to the sexual mores of the time.

The story of the town of Bristol reaches back to the last quarter of the seventeenth century.[3] The site had been the home of the Indian chief Ousamequin (Massasoit) and later of his son Philip, the Indian leader in King Philip's War. Settlers in adjacent parts of New England knew it as the Mount Hope Lands. With the defeat of King Philip, it fell by right of conquest into the

family," which he regards as applicable to Andover, does not then conflict with my first conclusion above. For he is referring to families in which the various conjugal units lived apart, while retaining significant economic and emotional ties to one another.

[2] Philip J. Greven, Jr., "Historical Demography and Colonial America,"*ibid.,* XXIV (1967), 438-454.

[3] There is no recent scholarly study of Bristol, but the main outlines of the story can be found in George L. Howe, *Mount Hope; a New England Chronicle* (New York, 1959). Certain 19th-century compilations are useful: for instance, Wilfred H. Munro, *The History of Bristol, R. I. . . .* (Providence, 1880); Wilfred H. Munro, *Tales of an Old Seaport* (Princeton, 1917); and James P. Lane, *Historical Sketches of the First Congregational Church, Bristol, R. I., 1689-1872* (Providence, 1872). See also Richard LeBaron Bowen, *Early Rehoboth* (Rehoboth, Mass., 1945-48), I, which contains a chapter of notes on the early years of Bristol.

hands of the English, who subsequently added it to the territory of Plymouth Colony. The General Court at Plymouth then conveyed the land to a group of four Boston merchants who undertook to perform the functions of town proprietors. The proprietors readily procured settlers, the majority coming from the adjoining towns of Rehoboth and Swansea; and by the fall of 1681 Bristol seems to have been a going concern. In 1692 Plymouth Colony was absorbed by Massachusetts Bay, the settlement at Bristol included. In 1747, however, it was one of five towns transferred to the jurisdiction of Rhode Island; there, of course, it has remained ever since.

Bristol was initially laid out as a farming community, and presumably agriculture remained a central pursuit for many of its inhabitants throughout the colonial period. However, the site offered strong possibilities as a seaport that were clearly apparent from the very beginning.[4] By the middle of the eighteenth century Bristol had become an important center of commerce, and most of its leading citizens were engaged in some form of mercantile activity. Trade with the West Indies followed lines long known to historians of early New England. The outward cargo comprised various sorts of produce, horses, and fish; these goods were exchanged for coffee, molasses, sugar, and tropical fruits. Distilleries were soon established in the town for converting molasses into rum, which became, in turn, the key item in an expanding slave trade with the coast of West Africa. Whaling was another important industry for the town's seagoing populace; and at least a few captains made a fortune at privateering. These aspects of the history of Bristol are important for the demographic profile that I shall attempt to establish. The commercial orientation of the town may well impose limitations on the opportunity to generalize from the Bristol findings. Indeed, the possibility that the demographic structure of colonial settlements varied markedly among different regions, or between town and country, should constitute a major focus in future research of this type.

The demographic data for Bristol are of two kinds. There are, first of all, the same sort of vital records that can be found for nearly every New England town—long listings of births, "intentions" to be married, marriages, and deaths.[5] Their accuracy and completeness seem to have varied considerably over time. For some periods they are rather sketchy, while for others they seem quite full and careful. It is my impression, however, that there was no time in the history of colonial Bristol when all of the pertinent events were officially recorded. One must, therefore, be reconciled from the start to working with partial data.

The second type of material, census listings, is much less common. Indeed, the complete census of Bristol residents made in 1689 may possibly be unique: I at least have never seen another such document for the seventeenth century.[6] It provides a rare opportunity to view the population structure of an early New

---

[4] Indeed, according to local traditions, it was this prospect which induced the settlers to name their town after the great English seaport of Bristol. See Munro, *History of Bristol,* 78.

[5] See James N. Arnold, *Vital Records of Rhode Island,* VI (Providence, 1894).

[6] Lists compiled for military or tax purposes are, of course, common enough, but these normally include only male citizens above the age of 16.

England community in a kind of cross section and at one given point in time. The vital records, by contrast, permit us to construct a *running picture* of the same developments, but a picture, as already mentioned, that is never complete or wholly reliable. The possibility of using these different sources to supplement each other is what makes Bristol a particularly hopeful demographic prospect.

Unfortunately the original census has long since been lost, and we have no idea for what purpose it was compiled. The material survives thanks to a copy made by George T. Paine from the records in the "Church of Christ" in Bristol, which was published in 1880 in the *Register* of the New England Historic and Genealogical Society.[7] The document begins: "1688-9. Feb. 11. All the families in New Bristol and children and servants." There follows, in a vertical column at the left, a list of names which clearly comprises all the heads-of-household in the town. Three adjacent columns, headed "Wife," "Children," and "Servants," provide the relevant figures for each family. The census shows a total population of 421 persons, distributed through 70 families. There are 68 husbands, 68 wives, 1 man without a wife or child but listed with the heads-of-family, 226 children, 56 servants (of whom 1 is identified as "black" and listed separately), and 2 unclassified men (added at the end as "Jacob Mason 1 more Zachary Cary 1 more"[8]).

The census permits a precise analysis of several important aspects of family structure. There is, first of all, the simple matter of the over-all size of Bristol households, for which the relevant data are gathered in the following table:

TABLE 1
Size of Households

Number of Persons in Household	1	2	3	4	5	6	7	8	9	10	11	12	13	14	15
Number of Families	1	6	5	11	9	13	5	7	6	3	2	1	0	0	1

The evidence on this point seems fairly clear-cut. Households of four, five, and six persons were most common, comprising almost half of the total sample, though there were many units both smaller and larger. The mean figure for these seventy households is 5.99, and the median is 5.72. It is important to anticipate

[7] See "Census of Bristol in Plymouth Colony, now in Rhode Island, 1689," *New-England Historical and Genealogical Register* XXXIV (1880), 404-405. The census has been republished in Bowen, *Early Rehoboth*, I, 75-76.

[8] The instance of the man without wife or child—one Eliaship Adams—suggests that in rare cases a single person might live alone and maintain his own domestic establishment. The vital records show that Adams was married later during the year 1689 and began to have children soon thereafter. The fact that he is listed among the original inhabitants of Bristol, in 1681, suggests that he must have been at least 30 when the census was taken. The case of the two men that I have referred to as "unclassified" is more mysterious. Clearly without wife or children, they do *not* seem to have been regarded as heads-of-family. Yet they are not likely to have been servants in the usual sense of the term—else they would have been listed in the appropriate space, as part of some other family.

one possible objection to these conclusions. The term "household" has been treated as equivalent to the "families" listed in the census, but can we be sure that some domestic units did not in fact include several families? Such households would be "extended" in the formal sense of the term. There is no *prima facie* way of eliminating this possibility, but the sum total of the evidence against it seems virtually overwhelming. First, careful study of the wills and land deeds of Plymouth Colony strongly suggests that married adults normally lived with their children and *apart* from all other relatives.[9] The sole exception was the occasional residence of aged parents in the family of some one of their children. Moreover, the census itself seems to imply the same pattern. There are, among the heads-of-family, a few sets of individuals bearing the same surname for whom we can establish a definite relationship, either as brothers or as father and sons. The respective positions on the list of the men within a given set are seemingly quite random. But if they had in fact shared the same household, there is some probability that their names would have followed one after the other. This, of course, begs the whole question of the reasons for the order in which all the families were recorded. There is no ready answer, but some possibilities can at least be ruled out. For example, the order is not alphabetical, nor does it reflect any rankings in terms of wealth or social prestige. The most likely guess, I think, would make spatial proximity the determining factor, and would assume that the census-taker moved from one house to the next until he had covered all the families intown. If this was the case, the "extended family" alternative is clearly set aside.

The category of children, which included some 54 per cent of the total population of the town, can be broken down in a similar manner:

TABLE 2
Children per Family

Number of Children in Family	0	1	2	3	4	5	6	7	8	9	10
Number of Families	7	10	11	12	9	8	6	4	1	0	1

The mean in this case is 3.27 and the median, 3.04. Nearly half of the families listed had one, two, or three children, though the "tail" of the distribution toward the higher brackets is fairly substantial. If these results seem rather on the low side, certain additional factors must be considered. The average parents produced children at roughly two-year intervals, beginning from the time of their marriage in their early or mid-twenties.[10] Birth intervals tended gradually to increase as the wife grew older and the last child would usually arrive

9 See Demos, "Notes on Life in Plymouth Colony," 279-280.

10 *Ibid.,* 271, 275. I am assuming here that Bristol conformed to the general pattern for age-at-marriage which obtained in other parts of Plymouth Colony. The comment on birth intervals is left somewhat imprecise, but its general validity can be sustained by even a cursory perusal of the vital records.

sometime between her fortieth and forty-fifth birthday. (These regularities obviously do *not* represent those families in which one spouse died before the childbearing years were over.) Families, in short, grew slowly. This means that at any given time only those parents in a certain limited age-range, about thirty-five to fifty, would be likely to show really large numbers of children. Younger couples would not yet have produced their full complement of children, whereas in the case of elderly parents some or all of the children would have reached maturity and started their own independent lives. The census listings for Bristol, therefore, do not invalidate the common notion that colonial parents usually raised many children, at least in comparison to the norm for our own day.

It remains to consider the fifty-six servants in the town. Their distribution can best be described with another simple table:

TABLE 3
Servants per Family

Number of Servants	0	1	2	3	4	8	11
Number of Families	48	8	8	3	1	1	1

Thus twenty-two Bristol families (31.5 per cent) had one or more servants. Only two men, however, possessed a really large group of servants: Captain Nathaniel Byfield, who was the first Bristol resident to cut a substantial figure in the larger affairs of Massachusetts Bay, and John Saffin, Esq. To the Byfield household was also attributed the single Negro in the town.

The analysis will now shift somewhat in order to meet certain possible difficulties bearing on the question of whether or not these findings for Bristol can be regarded as "representative" of a wider picture. It could, for example, be argued that since the town was still quite new in 1689, its demographic profile may in some respects have been atypical. In particular, there is the possibility that most of its inhabitants were quite young and that its families might therefore have been smaller than the norm for most other towns, or for Bristol itself some years later. In short, the next task is to form some impression, if possible, of the structure of Bristol's population in 1689 by age-groups.

Here the method which the European demographers call "family reconstitution" suggests itself.[11] It must be said at once, however, that the data for early Bristol are far too scanty to permit extensive work along these lines. The origins of many of its citizens cannot definitely be traced, and the sum total of precise

---

[11] The basic elements of family reconstitution are simple enough. The prime requisite is some reliable and reasonably complete data about the dates of birth, marriage, and death of all the residents in a given village or town; and fortunately in both France and England there are parish registers which meet these specifications quite nicely. This information is then arranged so as to dovetail *by families,* and the outcome is a large body of vital statistics, hopefully extending over a considerable span of time. The method has even been standardized by the use of Family Reconstitution Forms ("FRFs" to the initiated), which contain a set of spaces for recording each of the pertinent bits of data. A complete account of the method can be found in E. A. Wrigley, ed., *An Introduction to English Historical Demography from the Sixteenth to the Nineteenth Century* (New York, 1966), chap. IV. See also Greven, "Historical Demography and Colonial America," 440-442.

and reliable information about dates of birth, marriage, and death is disappoint-
ingly small. Partial reconstruction of many families is possible, but for very few
is the picture anywhere near complete.

The situation is not, however, wholly without possibilities. One can obtain at
least a general picture of the structure of the population by age-groups through a
careful study of the women of the town. The importance of women in this
connection stems from the more or less definite limits that nature has set upon
their childbearing years. Thus if one can determine the ages of at least some of a
given couple's children, it is possible to make a rough guess as to the wife's own
birth date. The word "rough" should be stressed here; in my own efforts with
the Bristol materials I have tried only to classify women in one or another
ten-year age-group. Moreover, because of the approximate nature of these
estimates, the categories have been made to overlap: they are 20-30, 25-35,
30-40, 35-45, 40-50, 45-55, and over 55. An individual woman has been placed
in whichever one of these seemed the most likely in her particular case. Some
concrete examples may be helpful. The census reports that the family of Jabez
Gorham contained in 1689 six persons—himself, his wife Hannah, and four
children. The vital records attribute nine births to this family, spanning a period
from April 1682 to October 1701. Since virtually no woman in seventeenth-
century New England had her first child before the age of 19, one can assume
that Hannah Gorham was not born later than 1663. Similarly, since nearly every
woman had ceased to bear children by the age of 45, the earliest likely birth year
in this instance is 1656. This means that Hannah Gorham was somewhere
between 26 and 33 years of age when the census was taken, and in the sample
analyzed below (Table 4) she has been included in the 25-35 category. Mary
Throop, wife of William, was a somewhat older woman. The census describes her
family as containing five children; but the only one of these whose arrival was
noted in the vital records was a daughter born in July 1686. However, two bits
of data help to establish a terminus at the *other* end of her childbearing span: a
listing in the records of Barnstable, where the Throops lived before migrating to
Bristol, of their marriage in 1666; and a notation in the Bristol records of the
birth of the couple's first grandchild in November 1688. Thus a birth year
between 1641 and 1647 can be inferred for Goodwife Throop, which places her
in the 40-50 age-category.

Similar procedures have been employed for forty-seven other Bristol women.
A few of the estimates may possibly be in error, owing to special circumstances
of which no hint remains today, but I feel reasonably certain that the great
majority are right. The final results are as follows:

TABLE 4
Age of Wives

Age-group	20-30	25-35	30-40	35-45	40-50	45-55	Over 55
Number of Women	12	10	12	11	3	1	0

(*Note:* This sample comprises 49 of the 68 wives in the town. There are no data for adult
female servants, if indeed there were any.)

The mean age here is 33.6 years. What is immediately striking about this outcome is the relative youth of the town's adult women. The table suggests that there was a fairly even distribution between the ages of 20 and 45, but very few women older than this. There remains, however, the question of nineteen Bristol women whom the sample does *not* include. In their case the data are so scanty as not to permit classification even in the ten-year groupings; but in most instances it is possible at least to infer that they fall on the younger side of 50. There are only two women among all the Bristol families for whom some shred of evidence exists that suggests a more advanced age.

These data for the women will not sustain deductions about the ages of their husbands in specific cases, for there may have been some men who were considerably older than their spouses. Still, it does seem possible to make the general inference that the great majority of the men were comparably young. There are some other pieces of information with which to fill out this picture. In the first place, it is striking that there should be in a town of over four hundred people only one widow and one widower. Of course, in the case of some Bristol couples one or both spouses may have been previously married and widowed; but I have been able to discover this for a fact in only a single instance. [12] Second, there is the matter of those couples who are listed with less than the average complement of children. As mentioned earlier, this could indicate either youth and a very recent marriage, or old age with most or all of the children grown up and on their own. But the evidence for Bristol in 1689 is heavily weighted toward the former alternative. Five of the seven couples without children and nine of the ten with only a single child seem likely to have been people in their twenties and recently married. For the remaining three cases there is simply no evidence one way or the other.

The various materials bearing on the age structure of the Bristol population may, then, be summarized as follows: (1) A majority of those listed in the census fall under the heading "children." (2) An additional category of "servants" (13 per cent of the whole) comprises persons who are likely also to have been quite youthful. (3) Nearly all of the fully adult residents, heads-of-family and their wives, were contained within a range whose upper limit seems to have been "middle age." What are the implications of all this for the question of the "representativeness" of the earlier findings about families? It seems clear that the Bristol citizenry was quite youthful; but can we assume, then, that its households will therefore prove to be smaller than in the average town? I would argue strongly *against* making any such inference. For if perhaps the considerable number of young couples (say, those under 30) created some bias in favor of small families, this effect was more than offset by the nearly complete absence of elderly couples. Moreover, the Bristol population in 1689 does seem to have included quite a number of couples at or near middle age, and, hence, most likely to show large households. Thus any distortion in the

---

12 That is, in the course of "reconstituting" the various families on the basis of the vital records.

sample may conceivably be in the direction of families slightly *larger* than the average for other towns.

The question of the age-structure of Bristol in 1689 is also pertinent in one other context; for it serves to call attention to a kind of demographic model for the process of settlement which, while not inherently new or startling, seems worth an explicit statement. The settlers of new towns were generally young people, presumably because the opportunities for gaining wealth and prestige were greater there than in the more established communities of their birth and also because the problems of town building required a youthful strength, imagination, and resourcefulness.[13] We may suspect, in addition, that when a young man left his place of origin to make an independent start in a newer settlement, he did not always take a bride with him. This can be demonstrated for about a dozen of the firstcomers to Bristol, but the most striking evidence is to be found in certain materials from the eighteenth century. The census taken for the whole colony of Massachusetts in 1765 provides a good case in point. It shows virtually all the towns of the eastern section—the older ones—with an appreciable surplus of women, while in the "frontier" parts to the west the ratio is largely reversed.[14]

Thus, in sum, the older towns were gradually left with a disproportionate number of elderly people and women. These kinds of imbalance may well have important implications for many aspects of the social history of the colonies. For example, the growth of schools in the older towns of New England may have been related to the rise of a substantial class of spinsters, who would serve as teachers. The problem of caring for elderly persons whose children had gone elsewhere may have stimulated fresh approaches in the area of welfare services. Almost certainly rates of marriage and remarriage were affected. But for the present these matters can be raised only in a speculative way.

In 1774 an official census was ordered for the whole colony of Rhode Island; and this permits us to restudy Bristol nearly a century after the compilation of the initial set of data.[15] While it is appropriate to ask the same basic questions a second time, a somewhat different set of arrangements for the later materials complicates the situation. Adjoining a list of all the heads-of-family are seven columns. Four appear under the major heading "Whites": "Males Above 16," "Males Under 16," "Females Above 16," "Females Under 16." There are separate categories for both "Indians" and "Blacks" without distinctions of age or sex, and finally there is a column marked "Total" that provides the sum of all the members in each household.

The picture for the town as a whole can be quickly summarized. In an over-all population of 1209, there were 1079 whites, 114 Negroes, and 16 Indians. Among the whites 504 were men, 575 were women. By age, 591 people were

---

13 This conclusion is in no way modified by the presence in Bristol in 1689 of a significant number of middle-aged couples. Most of these people had come when the town was founded—that is, when they were eight years younger than at the time of the census.

14 See J. H. Benton, Jr., *Early Census Making in Massachusetts, 1643-1765* (Boston, 1905).

15 The listings for Bristol are printed in full, Munro, *History of Bristol*, 188-191.

"Above 16," and 488 "Under 16." Two changes since 1689 are immediately apparent. First, the growth of Bristol as a seaport and its development of substantial trading connections with the West Indies and Africa have brought a significant nonwhite population into the town. Nearly all of these people appear as part of white households and are presumably slaves. The exceptions are 1 independent family of 3 Negroes and 1 family of 7 Indians. Second, there is among the whites a substantial preponderance of female residents. This, I believe, reflects the impact on the sex ratio of the process of settlement—a matter already discussed above. Bristol had by this time become itself an "older town"; and it is not unreasonable to infer the regular loss of some portion of its young men.

The figures for the size of the individual households in 1774 are as follows:

TABLE 5
Size of households, 1774

Total Number of Persons in Family	Total Number of Families		Total Number of Persons in Family	Total Number of Families	
	All-inclusive	Whites Only		All-inclusive	Whites Only
1	4	4	9	10	11
2	18	25	10	12	13
3	21	28	11	6	4
4	28	28	12	5	1
5	22	19	13	1	3
6	28	23	14	3	0
7	19	22	15	2	0
8	16	16	16	2	0

Table 5 provides separate listings for entire households, including Negroes and Indians, and for whites only in order to facilitate comparisons with the data for 1689. Unfortunately, such comparisons are problematical at best, but in order to examine all possibilities the relevant material for both periods has been reorganized in two further tables, with all the figures expressed as percentages of the whole sample:

TABLE 6
Comparative Size of Households in 1689 and 1774

Number of Persons Per Household	Percentage of Total Number of Households			
	1689 All-inclusive	1774 All-inclusive	1689 Without Servants	1774 Whites Only
1-3	17.1%	21.8%	25.7%	28.9%
4-6	47.1%	39.6%	45.7%	35.5%
7-9	25.7%	22.8%	25.7%	24.9%
10-12	8.6%	11.7%	2.9%	9.2%
13 and over	1.5%	4.1%	0%	1.5%

TABLE 7
Mean and Median Number of Persons per
Household in 1689 and 1774

	1689 All-inclusive	*1774 All-inclusive*	*1689 Without Servants*	*1774 Whites Only*
Mean	5.99	6.14	5.21	5.53
Median	5.72	5.70	4.95	5.21

It seems at first sight most natural to set the first against the second column and the third against the fourth, but certain distortions are inherent in this tactic. First, the all-inclusive listings for the two dates effectively conceal the addition of the non-white segment of the population during the eighteenth century. One must recognize that a Negro slave was probably a member of a 1774 household in quite a different sense from what had obtained for a white servant in 1689. Moreover, there still were some white servants in Bristol in 1774, a fact which tends to blur the possibilities of comparing the other two columns in the tables.[16] In short, the figures for "1689 Without Servants" comprise only blood-members of families, whereas those for "1774 Whites Only" include some servants as well. When this factor is taken into account, the slightly larger average for the later period shrinks to virtually nothing. Thus the following general conclusions emerge: (1) The mean and median size of Bristol families in terms of blood-members changed very little between 1689 and 1774. (2) The same observation applies for the category of all-inclusive households comprising servants and slaves too. (3) There is, however, one noticeable and interesting difference between the figures for the two periods, namely, the greater concentration of 1689 households in the middle ranges, especially the 4-6 person units, and of the 1774 households at both the lower and higher extremes. In short, the distribution of sizes of households widened considerably as time passed.

In order to be able to understand these patterns more clearly, a second effort at family reconstitution seems advisable. Fortunately the data for 1774 are somewhat more amenable to this procedure than were the earlier materials. The vital records, for example, show the year of birth of many of the white persons reported in the 1774 census. This permits construction of the following table depicting the age structure of the population at the time:

---

[16] Further discussion of the question of white servants in Bristol in 1774 appears below, p. 305.

TABLE 8
Age-Structure of Bristol, 1774
vs. United States, 1960

| | Percentage of Total Population | | | |
| | Bristol, 1774 | | United States, 1960[17] | |
Age-group	Men	Women	Men	Women
Under 10	27.6%	26.9%	21.7%	20.3%
10-19	21.8%	19.8%	17.0%	15.9%
20-29	15.2%	18.7%	12.0%	11.9%
30-39	10.9%	13.4%	13.6%	13.5%
40-49	10.6%	9.9%	12.7%	12.7%
50-59	7.5%	6.5%	10.2%	10.1%
60-69	3.2%	3.1%	7.4%	8.7%
70 and over	3.2%	1.7%	5.4%	6.9%

(Size of sample for Bristol, 1774: 348 men and 353 women.)

The sample on which these percentages are based comprises almost two-thirds of all the white residents of Bristol. This is a sufficiently large majority to give some credibility to the results, but the chance remains that certain age-groups are a little underrepresented, owing to possible defects in the vital records, etc. A partial check can be attempted by dividing the above sample at age 16 and comparing the outcome with the similar breakdown in the census itself. Thus, whereas the census shows 46.1 per cent of the men to be under 16, the sample yields a figure of 44.8 per cent; for women the comparable percentages are 44.5 and 42.5. This suggests that the sample may be slightly biased against the younger categories, but *only* slightly.

In general terms, then, the predominance of youth is still striking in the Bristol of 1774. The comparable breakdown for our own day serves only to highlight this pattern. Nonetheless there is by 1774 a significant group of older people in the town, in contrast to the situation that had obtained nearly a century earlier. This matter relates, I think, to the change mentioned previously with regard to the pattern of household sizes, that is, the shrinking of the distribution in the middle ranges, with a corresponding gain at both the lower and higher extremes. In brief, the presence of elderly couples would add to the proportion of *small* households in the town as a whole. It is also worth noting that the list of heads-of-family included no less than twenty-five widows and two widowers.

The gain in large households is more difficult to interpret. However, one possible factor immediately suggests itself, namely, the presence in many families of single people over the age of 16. Indeed, this category comprises 224 people, some 23 per cent of the town's total white population. Who were they? In many specific instances, the vital records reveal them to be older, but as yet

17 The figures for the American population in 1960 are based on tables in U.S. Bureau of the Census, *Statistical Abstract of the United States, 1965* (Washington, 1965), 23.

TABLE 9
Ages of First Marriage

Time of Marriage	Age of Men		Number in Sample	Age of Women		Number in Sample
	Mean	Median		Mean	Median	
Before 1750	23.9	23.4	(37)	20.5	20.3	(32)
After 1750	24.3	23.8	(71)	21.1	20.8	(54)

unmarried, sons and daughters of the head of the household. But it is also worth demonstrating that some of them were probably servants—witness the following very crude "proof." The various families in Bristol can be divided with regard to the possession of nonwhite servants or slaves. There are 147 families recorded as being without such slaves; of these, 54 per cent have at least one white member over 16 who cannot be identified as a parent. But the comparable figure is 75 per cent for those families which had some nonwhite membership. In short, as between families which did and did not own Negro or Indian slaves, the former were more likely also to have *white* servants. These comparisons show only that some portion of the whites over 16 living as subordinate members of larger families, were servants. Unfortunately there is no way to determine exactly *what* portion, but very probably it was less than one-half. If so, the slaves in Bristol had by this time become a larger group than the white servants.

But there yet remains a considerable number of people who were apparently older children living at home. This suggests a new question: did the average age of first marriage rise during the latter part of the eighteenth century? Table 9 offers an answer by comparing samples of marriages made before and after 1750.

The change, while in the expected direction, is very small indeed, and its utility as an explanation for the size of the "Over 16" group seems correspondingly limited. There is, however, an additional factor that may be relevant here, the imbalance in the sex ratio. As previously noted, Bristol had joined those "older" towns which showed an appreciable surplus of females, and perhaps in some families there were daughters for whom husbands were simply not available. It seems significant that in the "Over 16" group 98 were men and 126 were women. There is the further likelihood that the "white servant" category included more men than women; if so, the preponderance of unmarried daughters as against sons would be even greater. Such a pattern would have the obvious effect of adding to the total membership of at least some Bristol households.

One final set of questions will now be raised relating to the matter of "birth intervals." As the European historical demographers have shown, careful analysis of the time periods that elapsed between the births of children permits definite inferences about the practice, in certain communities, of some form of birth control.[18] It might be interesting to apply the same models to the study of

[18] See, for example, Louis Henry, *Anciennes familles genevoises* (Paris, 1956); and E. A. Wrigley, "Family Limitation in Pre-Industrial England," *Economic History Review*, 2d Ser., XIX (1966), 82-109.

Bristol. Unfortunately, however, the absence of full and precise data presents major obstacles here. One needs very exact information on the births of *all* the children in each family to be included in the sample, and the Bristol records fall badly short of this standard. The general conclusion that births occurred at roughly two-year intervals is the extent of our findings on this point.[19]

But I do want to point out one other use for information about dates of birth, which throws some light on a very different area of a people's life. I have tried with as many Bristol couples as possible to check the date of marriage against the date recorded for the birth of the first child. The purpose is to discover how many babies may have been conceived *before* a formal ceremony of marriage, and thus to develop some impression of possible changes in the sexual mores of the community. Consider, then, the following table for Bristol, which summarizes data for over one hundred cases broken down into five twenty-year time periods:

TABLE 10
Intervals between Marriage and Birth of First Child

Time of Marriage	Total Number of Couples	Number with First Child within 8 Months	Percentage with First Child within 8 Months
1680-1700	19	0	0%
1700-1720	8	0	0%
1720-1740	42	4	10%
1740-1760	35	17	49%
1760-1780	23	10	44%

The variance of these figures over time is really quite dramatic. It would seem to indicate some significant loosening of sexual prohibitions as the eighteenth century wore on, but its specific meaning in the lives of the people directly involved is hidden from us.[20] For example, in the cases where conception seems to have occurred before the marriage, what was the precise relation between these two events? Did the discovery of a pregnancy *force* a hasty wedding on the model of the "shotgun weddings" of our own day? Or were the couples in question "engaged" (or "going steady") when conception occurred? Did the

---

[20] One point with regard to changing legal practice seems relevant here. Throughout the 17th century in all the New England colonies fornication was a punishable offense, and court records for the period contain a large number of such cases. The standard "proof" of guilt was the arrival of a baby within eight months of marriage. The usual penalty was a fine and, in some instances, a whipping. In the 18th century, however, such prosecutions seem to have become steadily more rare and finally to have ceased altogether. This too, therefore, suggests a falling away from restrictive standards of sexual morality. It is my own guess that when the subject of American sexual behavior is more fully explored, the middle and late 18th century may prove to have been the most "free" period in our history. But much more research is necessary before such hypotheses can be offered with confidence. The only useful study in this whole area is one by Edmund Morgan, "The Puritans and Sex," *New England Quarterly,* XV (1942), 591-607.

[19] See above, p. 297. The pattern did not visibly change between 1689 and 1774.

community come to condone sexual relations in such cases? Is it even possible to infer here a kind of "trial marriage," an effort to establish that both partners were fertile before the actual wedding ceremony?

In short, there are many ways to interpret these results, but it is worth hoping that further research may begin to suggest some answers. The history of sexual behavior and mores is still largely unwritten, yet in our own post-Freudian era its immense significance can scarcely be questioned. The problem of data is something else again: it is clear that new source materials, and new methods of analyzing the *old* materials, will be required. All of this will call for extraordinary patience and ingenuity. Yet the effort must be made, and in the end demographic study may prove to be one of the more fruitful lines of approach.

3. Population movements and political changes in nineteenth century France*

G. DE BERTIER DE SAUVIGNY†

The political history of France, as usually recorded, appears to be a conflict of parties, ideologies and ideologists: liberals against conservatives, royalists against republicans, and radicals against politicians of moderate tendencies. The Marxian conception of history has fortunately contributed to directing scientific research toward economic factors which might explain the attitude taken by this or that social group in certain circumstances, or might account for the progress of some parties in a specific region. Yet, research in that direction does not appear to have achieved any sensational discovery: to reduce all political history to a struggle between the "haves" and the "have-nots" is oversimplification and does not account for the disconcerting complexity of political strife in nineteenth century France.

The rise of the industrial proletariat is, indeed, a social factor of prime importance, a result of economic transformation. Its progression on the political plane is due to the birth of the Socialist Party, the first Party to style itself, with some justification, a "class party." But even the evolution of this Party proves that the economic factor, powerful as it may be, is not sufficient to account all by itself for political realities.

Very quickly, in fact, this Party, which claimed to represent the "working class," included in its ranks persons who had never worked with their hands: its most famous leaders, Jules Guesde, Brousse, Jean Jaurès and Léon Blum came from the bourgeois class, its best propagandists were teachers, and, since the creation of the Third International, it has been only a white collar workers' party.

* Reprinted from the *Review of Politics,* XIX (January, 1957), pp. 37-47, by permission of the publisher and the author.

† Guillaume de Bertier de Sauvigny, professor of history, University of Notre Dame (Indiana) and Institut catholique in Paris, received his Docteur ès-Lettres in 1949 at Paris (Sorbonne). He is the author of several books on European diplomatic history and French history, including *La Restauration* and *Metternich et son temps.*

Between the ideological order and the political on the one hand, and between the economic order and the political on the other, the "human" intervenes; not the human as an individual but the social human, for man isolated is powerless on the political plane, where force means number. But men do not form groups merely because of common interests. Their economic interests are often disguised, wrapped up, so to speak, in other motives which delude the actors themselves: memories, prejudices, loyalty, friendship, passions of every kind.

Deeper even than economic forces and social ties is the influence exerted by powerful demographic factors, the more irresistible as their effects are slower and more difficult to be detected. The study of the demographic conditions of nineteenth century France in their relation to politics is a field almost unexplored by historians. And no wonder, for basic studies and even indispensable data are lacking.

Nonetheless, if I have considered it interesting to broach this subject, so impossible to deal with properly, it is because of my earnest desire to call the attention of specialists in political science to this practically unexplored domain. Thus, ventured hypotheses, controversial generalizations and unanswered questions will make up the subject matter of my essay. For this reason, it may prove all the more challenging.

That demographic conditions influence the foreign policy of a state is indisputable: when military power was tantamount to the number of soldiers drawn up in line, the foreign policy of a state depended fundamentally on the total of men of army age; when the point in question concerned imperial or colonial expansion, it was demography that commanded and conditioned the efforts of founders and leaders of empires. Doubtless Mussolini in discussing foreign policy had that fact in mind when he remarked: "Demography is the key to history." France under M. Fallières with only 9% of Europe's population in 1908, could not lay claim to the hegemony of France under Louis XIV, which then constituted 38% of Europe's population.

But what I would like to emphasize is the influence of demographic conditions over the internal policy of France in the nineteenth century. Here two essential facts are worth mentioning: the rhythm of the population's growth and the changes in its distribution.

The rate of increase dropped substantially throughout the nineteenth century, but that change manifested itself decisively between 1850 and 1860. At the beginning of the century the rate of annual increase was 66 per 10,000 people—never dropping below 41 per 10,000 until 1850, from 1860 on it declined rapidly, reaching the low of 6 or 9 per 10,000 people in the last years of the century. In other words, the French population increased by 8 million units in the first half of the nineteenth century, that is, by 31%. But in the second half it increased only by 4 millions, that is, by 9%. At this point I am not going to discuss the causes of this phenomenon; it suffices to state that it is a result of a single factor, which can be explained in many ways: the fall of the birthrate. The ratio of births which had been 308 to 10,000 during the decade 1821-1830, and was 274 to 10,000 from 1841 to 1850, reached the low point of

217 to 10,000 between 1891 and 1900. During the same period the deathrate diminished greatly, owing to medical progress: 282 per 10,000 people on the average, during the first years of the century, 178 per 10,000 in the last years.

Did this fact have any repercussions on internal policy? No one, to my knowledge, has up till now so ascertained. But if we translate those cold columns of figures into a more human language, a hypothesis will present itself. This double phenomenon, namely, the considerable decrease of mortality and the sharp decline of births, resulted in the aging of the population some generations later. This is how French society was constituted, in respect to age, at the beginning and at the end of the nineteenth century:

	less than 20	20-39	40-59	Over 60
About 1810	44%	29%	20%	7%
About 1900	33.8%	30.6%	23%	12.6%

Thus people over forty made up 27% of the population, at the beginning of the nineteenth century and 35.6% at the end of it. This difference is certainly not of huge proportions. But if we consider that in a general way, and especially in the political field, the leading and responsible positions were held by older people, we can come to this conclusion: the French democracy which came to power after 1870 had the tendency to develop into a gerontocracy. Is there no correlation between this and the fact that, from 1870 on, France enjoyed real political stability, in comparison with the revolutions, riotings, and conspiracies so frequent during the first half of the century? The revolutionary climate between 1815 and 1850 was that of a political society, where thousands of ambitious young people had no access to administrative positions, to honors and the advantages of power. These privileges were reserved for the aristocracy and wealthy classes. Beginning in 1870, however, the lack of balance between desirable positions and the number of young and ambitious individuals tended to diminish. Leaders of opposition parties were no longer exalted, venturous men, capable of staking their lives on a game of dice. Rather they were men matured by experience, hardly desirous of risking an acquired position in violent actions. Politics could no longer be a matter of conspiracies and barricades but a question of skillful tactics in which money rather than ideals would play a dominant part.

A qualitative analysis of the phenomenon of the birthrate decrease and an aging society suggests another idea, even as it reinforces our hypothesis. A study by M. Aries[1] (*History of French Populations and of Their Attitudes towards Life*) has established that voluntary birth restriction and the decline of births originated first in the upper layers of society as a characteristic feature of the bourgeois class, perpetually bent on success through ascent in the hierarchy of families and the social milieu. With the barriers confining the lower classes to their inferior conditions abolished one after another, through the actions of

---

[1] *Histoire des populations francaises et de leurs attitudes devant la vie* (Paris, 1948).

democratic institutions and a mass education, that climbing mentality which found its expression in birth restriction was bound to penetrate more and more deeply into the lower strata of society.

If, then, the devastating fall of the birth-rate and aging phenomenon affected the social elite earlier and more markedly it may be expected that the phenomenon of gerontocracy will be still more pronounced for this very reason. On the other hand, as M. Marcel Reinhard has pointed out in his *History of the World's Population, from 1900-1948,*[2] this vital weakening of the bourgeois classes, their inability to reproduce themselves as readily as the lower classes may have contributed to the triumph of democracy. Just as an ascending movement of air occurs whenever atmospheric layers of different density are superimposed, in the same manner the numerical and vital rarefaction of the upper layers of society produces and maintains that ascending current of individuals and families which is of the essence of democracy. Even in a society completely organized on democratic principles, from the legal point of view, the possibilities and consequently the desire and hope to climb the social ladder ought to be more contained, provided the leading classes themselves produce enough children to fill all the desirable situations. If, on the other hand, in a society based on birth privileges, vacancies occur in the higher ranks, competition is liable to break loose among the most ambitious elements of the lower classes and so the democratic process is set in motion. Thus, we might conclude that the decline of births is a factor working in favor of democracy, while a high birth rate, at least in the upper classes, is an element favoring the maintenance of an aristocracy *de jure* or *de facto*.

England offers a case of counterproof. Here is a country where political life presents an unquestionable stability of power vested in the nobility. It is not known whether the leading classes in that country have been less prolific than the lower classes. Still one fact is certain: on the whole, in the nineteenth century the British population did not witness a breakdown of birthrate comparable to that of the French population. This fact can be explained by a fundamental difference in the succession laws, at least as far as the leading classes are concerned. In France birth control as practiced by the upper classes was evidently a response to the desire to forestall the decline of family position, for the civil code imposed a sharing of the family estate among the children. Where primogeniture prevailed and the younger children thus became commoners, aristocratic families did not have the same motive for birth control. All the younger children of noble families formed an insulating layer between the common people and those desirable positions, to which they could more successfully aspire as long as their seniors, the members of the peerage, kept intact their political influence, based on the tenure of immense estates.

These remarks have carried us quite far away from demography. The truth is that reality cannot be analyzed in its elements except through intellectual conventions and that everything clings together from statistics on to the innermost mental attitude. Let us, however, return to the subject of our starting

---

[2] *Histoire de la population mondiale* (Paris, 1929).

point and try to find out whether the shifting of populations might have influenced the internal politics of France in the nineteenth century.

Like all other countries of Western Europe in the nineteenth century, France was the scene of a migration of populations from rural districts to cities. The following diagram shows the extreme limits of this movement:

	Urban Population	Rural Population	Towns of over 5,000 inh.
1801	15% (about)	85%	253
1901	46%	54%	648

These figures give a very rough idea of the real process of the urbanization phenomenon. Considering the curve of its evolution, we notice that the mid-century marks a decisive turning point, as in the decline of births and even to a greater extent because the question is not only a change of aspect, that is, an acceleration of a movement already under way, but of a change in its substance. During the entire first half of the century, towns grew very slowly, absorbing only the *surplus of* the rural population, which was on the increase everywhere. Thus urbanization did not progress at the expense of rural population. On the contrary, French rural districts then witnessed an increase of their stable population and seem to have never been more densely populated than between 1840 and 1850. In 1846, the rural population—this denomination referring only to communities of fewer than 2,000 inhabitants—still represented 75% of the whole nation's population.

It was the economic crisis of 1847 that set off the real movement of the rural exodus, as Professor Charles Pouthas has recently demonstrated in *The French Population during the First-Half of the XIXth Century.*[3] Thereafter, the depopulation of some rural departments was under way and after 1880 this drain assumed the character of a mass exodus depleting some regions of a fifth or even a third of their population.

Such are the facts. But what is their import on the political plane? At first we can see that the movement of rural depopulation began at the very moment when the common people were gaining access to political life through universal suffrage. Hence it is impossible to discover the relation between internal migrations and political fluctuations, because the basis of comparison cannot be established. It can only be assumed that the rapid urbanization of a half of the French nation might have contributed, as popular education did, to the penetration of republican and democratic ideas into rural masses who, under the combined influence of the aristocratic landowners and the clergy, had up till then remained in the conservative camp. Indeed, the first test of universal suffrage showed, in rural departments an overwhelming predominance in favor of conservative candidates. After 1870, on the contrary, when the urbanization

[3] *La population francaise pendant la première moitié du XIX-ème siècle—Travaux et documents de l'Institut national d'Etudes demographiques* No. 25 (Paris, 1956).

movement effected a general blending of populations, when there was no peasant who had not lived for some time in a town or whose son, brother or cousin had not become townsmen, when the products of the towns and especially the newspaper would reach the most remote rural regions, then, the republican parties, till then composed essentially of elements from lower-middle classes and from among handicraftsmen, spread their influence over the rural masses as well.

Stress has often been laid on the remarkable stability of political trends in diverse regions of France, since the foundation of the Third Republic. Among all other possible explanations of this phenomenon—each of them containing, doubtless, some truth—may we not introduce this one: namely, that the most active and ambitious elements of each generation left their native region to incorporate themselves with the anonymous urban masses, leaving behind only aged people and those youths who were contented with their lot or were inclined to follow in the beaten track of their ancestors? Thus, this rural exodus appears as a factor making for political stability in the rural areas.

Yet this conclusion is apparently invalidated by the striking example—and almost unique in France—of a region which completely changed political colors in the course of the nineteenth century: the Aquitanian and Languedocian South. In the first decades of the century that region was regarded as one of the bastions of the most fanatic royalists; yet the great-grandchildren of those royalists were to vote for the radical-socialist candidates at the end of the century. Many factors could explain that reversal. But it is noticeable that the departments of the Aquitanian South were among the most affected by rural depopulation. From this fact, we might draw a hypothetical conclusion: this depopulation when exceeding a certain level, bears witness to the deep uneasiness of a whole population, inducing it to vote for the Left parties who appear to be opponents of the established regime and who demand that "things should be changed." The other rural departments most seriously affected by emigration are those of the Paris region (*Bassin parisien*): there, too, in the second half of the nineteenth century, the peasants' votes went overwhelmingly to the Left.

In fact, upon reflection, we can see that these two hypotheses—first, that emigration from rural parts to cities might have been a factor of political stability in the rural vote, and secondly, that a mass exodus, exceeding the average rate, would be accompanied by Leftist political tendencies in the home region—do not contradict each other irremediably. Nevertheless, the absence of more precise basic studies compels us to admit that all this belongs to the realm of pure conjecture.

The case of Paris is particularly interesting and we are better equipped to discuss it, thanks to the remarkable works by M. Louis Chevalier.[4] The enormous growth of its population (547,000 in 1801, 1,053,000 in 1851, 2,660,000 in 1901) was essentially the result of an influx of elements originating from all over France and also from abroad. M. Chevalier succeeded in making a

[4] *La Formation de la population parisienne du XIX-ème siècle* (Paris, 1950).

chart, for 1831 and for 1891, of the sources of this immigration. On the first chart, for 1831, we see that the population of Paris was exclusively supplied with new elements from 27 departments, located in the northern part of France. Brittany, the Valley of the Loire, Franche Comté, the Center (except Creuse and Cantal), and the South, sent but a few individuals. After 1891, however, all French departments contributed to the increase of the population of Paris.

Confronting this fact of demographic nature, there is a fact of political nature. Between them we would like to establish a connection. At the beginning of the nineteenth century the great mass of the Paris population clearly showed a tendency towards the Left: it was in Paris that political revolutions broke out, barricades were erected and monarchic governments overthrown. On the contrary, at the end of the nineteenth century the ballots of Paris showed a distinctly conservative if not reactionary trend. The fact that the people of Paris turned out to be republicans—in the first half of the century—is perfectly comprehensible, from the demographic standpoint, if we recall that then the population of the departments in the East and in the Paris region (*Bassin parisien*) was much more "patriotic" (in the meaning of the word as used in 1789) than the rest of rural France. It is to be assumed that a massive admixture of royalist elements from the South or the East might have modified the reaction of the Paris population, in 1830, in 1848 and in 1870.

It is more difficult to explain in the same manner the fact that, at the end of the nineteenth century, Paris had become rather conservative. If the population of Paris was then the mirror of all other departmental populations, we might expect to find the inhabitants of Paris divided into two approximately equal blocs, between the Right and the Left, with a slight predominance in favor of the Left. Yet we have just stated that such was not the case. The explanation remains demographic in nature, but within the reduced boundaries of the Parisian region, or more exactly of the Seine department. At the beginning of the nineteenth century, the revolutionary masses of Paris, the artisans, shopkeepers, workers and plain beggars, used to live in the very center of Paris, elbowing the well-to-do bourgeois and aristocrats of the Faubourg Saint Germain. In the same tenements, different social layers were superimposed, tier upon tier: shopkeepers on the ground-floor, aristocrats by birth or wealth on the first floor—the "noble floor" suited for brilliant receptions—then, the bourgeois on upper levels in proportion as their fortunes were smaller, and finally poor workmen in their uncomfortable garrets. The great real estate operations in the time of Louis Philippe and even more so in the time of Haussmann put an end to that mingling of classes. Subsequently, the "bourgeois" quarters, the "workers' " quarters and the suburban communities made their appearance. The influx of industries accelerated the workers' migratory movement out of Paris; henceforth only liberal professionals and merchants, plus a certain number of artisans, lived within the very enclosure of the capital. As for the industrial workers, who nowadays form the "militia" of the progressive parties, they resided outside of Paris, in the numerous suburban communities which make up what is called "the Red suburbs."

It might be interesting to approach from the other end this problem of a connection between the demographic phenomena and politics and to try to find out the influence exercised by the internal policies of France upon the movements of her population. But that would require another study and it does not raise any timely questions. Nevertheless, let us point out two connections which are the easiest to establish.

The phenomenon of a decrease in births has long occupied the minds of a large number of sociologists. In order to explain it, all kinds of factors have been taken into consideration. Among those, it is undeniable that there are some factors originating—at least indirectly—in the political evolution of France in the nineteenth century. Voluntary restriction of births, as we have seen, is linked with families' desire to climb up the social ladder or to prevent social decline. It is therefore evident that the triumph of the Republic and of the democratic regime—by allowing the humblest families to reach out for high positions—could contribute to the permeation of the common people by the Malthusian mentality, previously confined to the upper classes. Another principle apparently linked with the democratic regime is that of absolute equality concerning succession to property. These inheritance regulations, a concrete application of the republican principle of equality, were bound to end in parcelling out landed property: in 1908 49,969,000 hectares (113,478,400 acres) of cultivated lands were subdivided into 5,505,000 farms, with an average of 9 to 10 hectares (22 to 25 acres) per farm. But average figures do not mean very much; for the quoted number of farms, the computation was 4,611,564 of less than 10 hectares (25 acres) and 2,235,000 of less than 1 hectare (about 2½ acres).

No wonder that in these circumstances, farm-owners tried to ensure the preservation of their farms by avoiding the risk of new partitions. In 1826, the reactionary government of Villele attempted to consolidate the landed aristocracy, introducing amendments to the law of succession. That attempt failed in the face of public opinion, revolting against this odious "birth right." The Vichy government, attempting to redress the demographic situation in France, devised the "family estate," inalienable and indivisible, but this innovation, considered to be inconsistent with democratic principles, was repudiated.

Another undeniable factor in the decline of births is irreligion. In a country like France where religion is practically synonymous with Catholicism, birth control is practiced less among the religious population than among those whose irreligion produces its destructive effect. It is enough to compare the chart of births with that of religious practice. In this view, is it possible to deny the fact that the triumph of the anticlerical Republic played an important part in the sphere of births?

With regard to interior migrations, the political influence does not manifest itself clearly, except in one respect: the almost monstrous growth of the Parisian agglomeration. This expansion would have taken place in any case, but there is no doubt that the policy of rigorous centralization, a legacy of the Jacobin and Napoleonic regimes, facilitated it. The royalist and conservative ideology had always—at least in theory—a decentralizing tendency; it is worth noticing that during the entire history of nineteenth century Paris no epoch witnessed a slower growth than the fifteen years of the Restoration, from 1815 till 1830. We can assume that a Socialist regime, or a regime of controlled economy, would not have permitted economic forces to play the sole determining role in the location of industries; but throughout the nineteenth century economic liberalism and political liberalism were closely associated, so that the triumph of one meant the triumph of the other.

For too long a time demographers and historians have worked side by side, ignoring one another; now, they are beginning to realize what rich historical material is wrapped up in the forbidding columns of figures provided by the classified census. In life almost everything coheres and it would be quite astonishing if we could sever the connection between other aspects of human life and those two acts, supremely important for each individual: the transmission of life and the choice of a place geographically suited for living. The historian could and should seize upon these facts in order to integrate them into the complete synthesis of the human past, which is the goal of his efforts.

PART V

"Cliometrics," the new economic history

If there is a quantitative revolution in history, it is safe to say that economic history has led the vanguard of this revolution. For more than a decade, economic history has been transforming itself into econometric history, or cliometrics.[1] In the view of some of the theorists of this movement—Douglass C. North, for example—this process has resulted in a marked decrease in the community of method—if not of interest—which formerly united economic historians and general historians.[2] Not that the new economic historian's concern for the past is any less; quite the contrary, the past has an added significance as a testing ground for economic theory—a place where economics and economic history can meet as equal contributors to a joint effort.

Several factors have characterized the development of the new economic history, but the most important have been the increased interest of economists in developmental or historical studies, and the impact of econometrics—the application of statistics to the study of economic systems. Another factor has been the explicit use of economic theory, particularly neoclassical theory, in

[1] Lance E. Davis, Jonathan R. T. Hughes, and Stanley Reiter, "Aspects of Quantitative Research in Economic History," *Journal of Economic History,* XX (December, 1960), p. 540.

[2] Douglass C. North, "Economic History," in *International Encyclopedia of the Social Sciences,* VI (New York: Macmillan Co. and Free Press, 1968), pp. 468-74.

historical explanation. The degree to which the application of economic theory to the study of economic history has been an essential feature of the new economic history needs to be emphasized. Econometric historians feel that while traditional economic historians have also utilized economic theory in their work, they have usually done so implicitly, and without engaging in the empirical verification of these theories. Econometricians regard this verification as the most significant part of the research process. Finally, the appearance of increasingly sophisticated computers combined with the availability of quantifiable historical data has made an impressive contribution to the development of a statistically oriented economic history.

There is a certain parallel between the past development of econometric history and the current development of quantitative history, granting, of course, the basic distinction that economic history has always been somewhat quantitative, though usually not explicitly theoretical or statistical. Just as economists provided a body of theory and a methodology for the use of economic historians, so other social sciences, particularly sociology and political science, have provided similar tools for quantitative historians in other areas of history. At the same time, the historians' awareness of and willingness to use quantifiable data have increased as a result of the availability of such data and the presence of techniques for its manipulation.

In this context, certain issues have arisen in the development of econometric history which may have some relevance to the progress of quantitative history in general. Like the econometric historian, the quantitative historian's justification for compressing the wholeness of his inspirations and observations into a quantitative format is the advantage of the relative exactness and explicitness of the theoretical foundations and methods of verification such a format supplies. However, if this work is socially significant—that is, if it is to make some contribution to the understanding of human behavior—then the careful scholar can quickly become involved in solving vastly complex problems that are actually analyses of dynamic systems many times the size of what he or his readers originally bargained for.

It is this situation that Meghnad Desai describes as leading to the problem of "underidentification" of economic models, and that results in ambiguities at best and erroneous conclusions at worst.[3] Although Mr. Desai's cautionary observations on the inadequacy of the economic growth theory are directed to the economic historians, by extension they also point to a problem common to all social sciences—the lack of a coherent body of tested theories of social, economic, and political growth. Since this problem increases in magnitude as the investigator deals with larger systems and more complex models of interacting social processes, a tempting research strategy would be to confine one's efforts to small-scale analysis and thus avoid the more manifest uncertainties of the

---

[3] Meghnad Desai, "Some Issues in Econometric History," *The Economic History Review,* 2nd Series, XXI (April, 1968), p. 6.

larger enterprise.[4] It is equally clear, however, that if history seeks to achieve a synthesis that will take into account the real diversity of human action, complex models that attempt to identify larger patterns of human behavior are extremely desirable. Since the decision on which research strategy to use is so obviously an individual matter, no useful purpose would be served by ruling out either approach at this stage in the development of our understanding of history. Only by the extensive and critical interplay of theory, method, and data can we avoid the danger of falling into a rigid pattern of historical analysis and interpretation.

It was with these issues in mind that we chose to include the Russet essay, an example of what might be called political econometrics, in addition to the more patent examples of economic history. Addressing itself to propositions commonly dealt with by historians, the essay illustrates how rapidly the complexities of a statistically oriented study can increase when it attempts to account for the interaction of economics and politics.

---

[4] For a brief but interesting discussion of the problem of micro- versus macroscopic approaches, see Mirra Komarovsky (ed.), *Common Frontiers of the Social Sciences* (Glencoe, Ill.: Free Press, 1957), pp. 12-18.

1. The new economic history, its findings and methods*

R. W. FOGEL†

The 'new economic history,' sometimes called econometric history or clio-metrics, is not often practised in Europe. However, it is fair to say that efforts to apply statistical and mathematical models currently occupy the centre of the stage in American economic history. The influence of this type of research in the United States is illustrated by the proceedings of the twenty-fifth annual meeting of the Economic History Association, published in the last number of the *Journal of Economic History*. [1] Of the ten major papers included in the issue, three practise the new economic history and a fourth is devoted to a discussion of it. Moreover, if the dissertations presented to the annual meeting are an index of the intellectual direction of the youngest generation of economic historians, then it is worth noting that six of these seven studies are cast in the new mode, and the seventh is a computer analysis (of a large sample of commercial papers) aimed at revealing the motivation for the colonization of the Americas. [2]

Econometric history gained its present eminence with extraordinary rapidity. Perhaps the first definitely formulated expression of the new approach is contained in a pair of essays written by Alfred H. Conrad and John R. Meyer in 1957, less than a decade ago. [3] It was not until three years later that work in

---

* Reprinted from the *Economic History Review,* XIX (December, 1966), pp. 642-56, by permission of the author.

† This paper was originally commissioned by the Economic History Society and was presented to their annual meeting on 1 April 1966. It was also presented to the Institut de Science Economique Appliquée on 26 March 1966. Editors note: Robert William Fogel, who currently holds a joint appointment as professor of economics at the University of Chicago and University of Rochester, received his Ph.D. from The Johns Hopkins University. He is the author of *The Union Pacific Railroad: A Case in Premature Enterprise* and *Railroads and American Economic Growth: Essays in Econometric History.*

[1] XXV (December 1965).

[2] *Ibid.,* pp. 680-712.

[3] John R. Meyer and Alfred H. Conrad, "Economic Theory, Statistical Inference and Economic History," *Journal of Economic History,* XVII (December 1957); and Alfred H. Conrad and John R. Meyer, "The Economics of Slavery in the *Ante-Bellum* South," *Journal of Political Economy,* LXVI (April 1958). Both essays are reprinted in Alfred H. Conrad and John R. Meyer, *The Economics of Slavery* (Chicago: Aldine Publishing Co. 1964).

cliometrics had gone far enough to warrant a conference devoted to it. In December of 1960 Purdue University sponsored a Seminar on Quantitative Methods in Economic History. Although the organizers of the meeting had difficulty in finding a score of scholars interested enough to attend, the Purdue Seminar did much to stimulate further research in the application of the mathematical and statistical models of economics to the study of history. So successful was the first meeting that the Purdue Seminar has become an annual event. The sixth meeting was held last January. This time the problem was not where to find attendees, but how to choose thirty participants from a list several times that number of scholars who wanted to attend.

Even more impressive is the fact that many of the principal American centres of post-graduate work in economic history are now devoted to, or encourage, training and research in econometric history. Among the most well known of these centres are Alexander Gerschenkron's Economic History Workshop at Harvard University, Douglass North's Economic History Seminar at the University of Washington, the graduate programme in economic history of Purdue University, the Graduate Programme in Economic History at the University of Wisconsin, the interdisciplinary programme for economic history at the University of Pennsylvania, the joint Berkeley-Stanford Economic History Colloquium, William Parker's seminar in economic history at Yale, and the Workshop in Economic History at the University of Chicago.

I do not want to give the impression that the new economic history is universally acclaimed in the United States. The growing debate on the methodological implications of the new work reflects the existence of a significant division of opinion. Fritz Redlich is one of the critics. He argues that much of econometric history is based on hypothetical models which can never be verified, and that certain of its methods are 'anti-empiricistic,' and 'anti-positivistic.' Hence, Professor Redlich concludes that the new work often produces not history but 'quasi-history.'[4] Interestingly enough, those features of which Professor Redlich is most critical are, according to George G. S. Murphy, the main virtue of the new approach. Professor Murphy contends that by rigorously developing hypothetico-deductive models the cliometricians are providing economic history with 'a really defensible set of techniques' and 'coming close to what a modern empiricist might demand of it.'[5]

---

4 Fritz Redlich, " 'New' and Traditional Approaches to Economic History and their Interdependence," *Journal of Economic History* XXV (December 1965), 480-95.

5 George G. S. Murphy, "The 'New' History," *Explorations in Entrepreneurial History* (2nd series), II (Winter 1965), 132-46. Other contributions to the discussion on the methods of the new economic history include, Conrad and Meyer, *The Economics,* chapters 1 and 2; Lance E. Davis, Jonathan R. T. Hughes and Stanley Reiter, "Aspects of Quantitative Research in Economic History," *Journal of Economic History,* XX (December 1960), 539-47; Franklin M. Fisher, "On the Analysis of History and the Interdependence of the Social Sciences," *Philosophy of Science,* XXVII (April 1960); Douglass C. North, "Quantitative Research in American Economic History," *American Economic Review,* LIII (March 1963), 128-30; Robert W. Fogel, "A Provisional View of the 'New Economic History,' " *American Economic Review,* LIV (May 1964), 377-89; Robert W. Fogel, *Railroads and American Economic Growth: Essays in Econometric History* (Baltimore:

To say that opinions are divided does not imply that the American wing of our discipline is torn by internecine warfare. While the debate is vigorous, it is also amicable. Moreover, even its severest critics believe that the new economic history has made a positive and lasting contribution to historical research. Despite his strong reservations, Fritz Redlich writes that the new approaches 'are here to stay,' and predicts an increasing interdependence between the new and the old work.[6]

THE FINDINGS

The considerable impact of the new economic history on research in the United States is due primarily to the novelty of its substantive findings. If cliometrics merely reproduced the conclusions of previous scholarship, its methods would be of trivial consequence. However, the studies of the new economic historians have substantially altered some of the most well-established propositions of traditional historiography. They have also yielded knowledge that was hitherto considered unobtainable concerning institutions and processes central to the explanation of American economic development. I cannot within the compass of this paper do justice to the many studies produced by the new economic historians during the past decade. But I will attempt to summarize briefly some typical examples of their work.[7]

The economics of southern slavery

One of the first, and one of the most influential, reinterpretations of the new economic history concerns the effect of slavery on the course of economic development in the South prior to the Civil War. Until recently most history books portrayed the *ante-bellum* South as an economically backward agricultural region that stagnated under the burden of the plantation system. By the eve of the war, it was held, slavery had become unprofitable and hence the system was moribund. Slavery was kept temporarily in existence by the transitory resolve of a class long accustomed to its peculiar social institutions.[8]

Johns Hopkins Press, 1964), pp. 237-49; Douglass C. North, "The State of Economic History," *American Economic Review,* LV (May 1965), 86-91; Robert W. Fogel, "The Reunification of Economic History with Economic Theory," *American Economic Review,* LV (May 1965), 92-98; Ralph Andreano, *New Views on American Economic Development* (Cambridge, Mass.: Schenkman Publishing Co. 1965), pp. 3-8, 13-26; Jonathan R. T. Hughes, "Fact and Theory in Economic History," *Explorations in Entrepreneurial History* (2nd series), III (Spring/Summer 1966); Douglass C. North, "Economic History" (prepared for inclusion in the *International Encyclopedia of the Social Sciences).*

[6] Redlich, " 'New' and Traditional," pp. 491-95.

[7] For representative selections of essays in the new economic history, see Robert W. Fogel and Stanley L. Engerman (eds.), *The Reinterpretation of American Economic History* (New York: Harper and Row, Spring 1967); and Andreano, *New Views.* For a more popular more interpretative survey see Douglass C. North's *Growth and Welfare in the American Past: A New Economic History* (Englewood Cliffs: Prentice-Hall, 1966).

[8] Cf. Harold D. Woodman, "The Profitability of Slavery: A Historical Perennial," *Journal of Southern History,* XXIX (August 1963), 302-25; and Stanley L. Engerman, "The

This view was sharply challenged in a paper by Alfred H. Conrad and John R. Meyer.[9] They rejected as inadequate the evidence usually presented to support the proposition that the profits of slaveowners were declining. The contention that slavery was unprofitable rested largely on the fact that the prices of slaves had risen more rapidly than the prices of the commodities that slaves produced. Conrad and Meyer pointed out that this divergency did not necessarily imply declining profits, for the productivity of slaves might have risen by an amount sufficient to maintain the original level of profits. They further argued that from an economic point of view slaves were a capital good and hence that one could compute the rate of return on an investment in them by solving the standard equation for the capitalization of an income stream; that is, by finding the rate of return which equated the price of slaves to the discounted value of the stream of annual earnings derived from their employment.

Conrad and Meyer divided the slave economy into two sectors. The first was described by a production function that related the male slaves to the output of such staples as cotton, sugar and corn. The second was a capital-goods sector in which female slaves were used to produce new slaves. Conrad and Meyer then went on to estimate separate rates of return on slaves of each sex. The computation of the return on male slaves was the simpler case. They first derived the average capital cost per slave including not only the price of a slave, but also the average value of the land, animals and equipment used by a slave. Estimates of gross annual earnings were then built up from data on the price of cotton and the physical productivity of slaves. The net figure was obtained by subtracting the maintenance and supervisory costs for slaves from gross earnings. The average length of the stream of net earnings was determined from mortality tables. With these estimates Conrad and Meyer computed rates of return on male slaves and found that for the majority of *ante-bellum* plantations the return varied between 5 and 8 per cent, depending on the physical yield per hand and the prevailing farm price of cotton. On the farms in poor upland pine country or in the exhausted lands of the eastern seaboard the range of rates was merely 2 to 5 per cent. However, in the 'best lands of the new Southwest, the Mississippi alluvium and the better South Carolina and Alabama plantations' rates ran as high as 10 to 13 per cent.[10]

The computation of the rate of return on female slaves was somewhat more

---

Effects of Slavery on American Economic Growth," *The Reinterpretation*, Fogel and Engerman.

[9] Conrad and Meyer, *The Economics*, chapter 3.

[10] An alternate approach to the estimation of the return on male slaves is contained in Robert Evans, in "The Economics of American Negro Slavery," *Aspects of Labor Economics*, H. Gregg Lewis (ed.), Conference of Universities–National Bureau Committee for Economic Research (Princeton University Press 1962), pp. 185-243. As with other capital goods, there was a market for the rental of slaves. Evans argued that the average annual hire price represented a good estimate of the annual net earnings on the investment in a male slave. He reduced the annual hire price for slaves of a given age by the proportion of the cohort that died during the course of the year. In so doing, Evans avoided the assumption that all slaves lived the average length of life. The result of his computation was a return of over 10 per cent during most of the years from 1830 through 1860.

complicated. Conrad and Meyer had to take account not only of the productivity of a female in the field, but of such additional matters as the productivity of her offspring between their birth and the time of their sale; maternity, nursery and rearing costs; and the average number of offspring. Noting that very few females produced less than five or more than ten children that survived to be sold, Conrad and Meyer computed lower and upper limits on the rate of return. These turned out to be 7.1 and 8.1 per cent respectively. Thus, planters in the exhausted lands of the upper South who earned only 4 to 5 per cent on male slaves, still were able to achieve a return on their total operation equal to alternative opportunities. They did so by selling the offspring of females to planters in the West, thus earning rates of 7 to 8 per cent on the other half of their slave force. Proof of such a trade was found not only in the descriptions of contemporaries, but also in the age structure of the slave population. The selling states had a significantly larger proportion of persons under 15 and over 50 while the buying states predominated in slaves of the prime working ages.

Of the many studies in the economics of slavery stimulated by the pioneering work of Conrad and Meyer, the most important was the one by Yasukichi Yasuba.[11] Yasuba pointed out that in order to evaluate the viability of the slave system as a whole, rather than merely the viability of slavery in a given region or occupation, one had to equate the stream of net income from slaves not with their market price, but with their cost of production—that is, with the net cost of rearing slaves. A discrepancy between the price and the cost of producing capital goods in a given industry ordinarily will not last very long.[12] The existence of an unusually high profit—of economic rent—will induce new capital-producing firms to enter or old firms to expand production until the rent is eliminated, until the market price of the capital good falls to its cost of production.

In the case of slaves, however, the demand curve for them shifted outward more quickly than supply curve. The lag in supply was due partly to the ban against the importation of slaves after 1808 and partly to the fact that the domestic expansion of supply was limited by biological and cultural factors. As a consequence of these restrictions, the rent on slaves increased over time. Yasuba estimates that during the quinquennia of 1821-25, the average capitalized rent amounted to $428 out of an average slave price of $736, the balance representing the net cost of rearing the slave to maturity. In other words, during 1821-25 capitalized rent represented 58 per cent of the market price of slaves. By 1841-45 the capitalized rent was 72 per cent of the price of slaves and by 1851-55 it was nearly 85 per cent.

By showing the existence of a large and rising capitalized rent in the price of

---

[11] Yasukichi Yasuba, "The Profitability and Viability of Plantation Slavery in the United States," *Economic Studies Quarterly*, XII (September 1961), 60-67; reprinted in Fogel and Engerman, *The Reinterpretation*. Richard Sutch independently arrived at a position similar to Yasuba's in "The Profitability of Slavery–Revisited," *Southern Economic Journal*, XXXI (April 1963). See also the discussion by North in *Growth and Welfare*, chapter 7, and Engerman's "The Effects of Slavery."

[12] The cost of production includes the normal rate of profit.

slaves over the forty years leading up to the Civil War, Yasuba effectively demonstrated the economic viability of the slave system. Moreover, the fact that Conrad and Meyer computed a return based on the market price rather than on the cost of producing slaves means that they underestimated the return to slavery as a system. Indeed, their computation showed only that slave prices adjusted so that investors who wanted to buy into the slave system could, on average, expect to earn merely the market rate of return.

Although slavery was a viable economic system, it could nevertheless have thwarted economic growth in the south by reducing the saving rate or by stifling entrepreneurship. Historians have long held that because of slavery, planters acquired extravagant tastes which led them to squander their income on high living. Slavery is also supposed to have bred an irrational attachment to agriculture. As a consequence, it is said, planters shunned opportunities for profit in manufacturing.

The alleged stagnation of the *ante-bellum* South has been thrown into doubt by recent findings. The work of Conrad, Meyer, Yasuba and others strongly suggests that the southern decision to slight manufacturing was not an absurd eccentricity. It now appears to have been a rational response to profits in plantation agriculture, that were considerably above alternative opportunities. Moreover, estimates of regional income constructed by Richard Easterlin indicate that *per capita* income grew as rapidly in the *ante-bellum* South as in the rest of the nation, averaging about 1.5 per cent per annum.[13]

The retarded development of the South during the last third of the nineteenth century and the first half of the twentieth was due not to stagnation during the slave era, but to the devastation caused by the Civil War. As Stanley Engerman points out, if *ante-bellum* growth-rates had continued through the war decade, southern *per capita* income would have been twice the level that actually prevailed in 1870. So disruptive was the war that it took the South some thirty years to regain the *per capita* income of 1860 and another sixty years to reach the same relative position in national *per capita* income that it enjoyed at the close of the *ante-bellum* era.[14] The case for the abolition of slavery thus appears to turn on issues of morality and equity rather than on the inability of a slave system to yield a high rate of economic growth.

Technology and productivity

While the issue of slavery looms large in the interpretation of American economic history, it is of limited relevance outside of that context. Of wider interest to European scholars is the new work on technology and productivity. From the time of Arnold Toynbee through that of Paul Mantoux and down to

---

[13] Richard A. Easterlin, "Regional Income Trends, 1840-1950," *American Economic History,* Seymour E. Harris (ed.) (New York: McGraw-Hill, 1961), pp. 525-47. Stanley L. Engerman, "The Economic Effects of the Civil War," *Explorations in Entrepreneurial History* (forthcoming).

[14] Engerman, "The Economic Effects."

the present day, economic historians have made technological change embodied in specific machines and processes the *sine qua non* of economic advance. As a result of their work every schoolboy has been taught that it was such inventions as the spinning jenny, the power loom, the reverberatory furnace, the rolling mill, the steam-engine and the railroad that brought about the industrial revolutions of England, France, Germany and the United States. Yet despite a considerable literature which illuminates the history of machines and their employment, we still have much to learn about the precise effects of particular innovations on productivity and about the process by which a given innovation spreads throughout an industry.

It is to the solution of these and related questions that much of the research of the new economic historians has been directed. This work falls into four main categories. The first is the attempt to 'explain' observed increases in productivity—that is, to distribute the responsibility for the increase in productivity among various factors. Typical of this approach is William Parker's analysis of wheat production.[15] He finds that between 1840 and 1911 labour productivity in wheat grew by more than three-fold. Of this increase he attributes the lion's share, 60 per cent, to mechanization; 17 per cent to the change in the regional locus of production; 16 per cent to the interaction of mechanization and regional relocation; and the remaining 7 per cent to other factors. Improvements in machines had their greatest impact on harvesting and post-harvesting operations. Professor Parker estimates that the reaper and thresher alone accounted for 70 per cent of the gain from mechanization or over 40 per cent of the increase in overall productivity.

It would be wrong to infer from Parker's study that the new work gives warrant to the preoccupation with technological change embodied in equipment that characterizes so much of the past literature of economic history. Parker's study aims not at extolling machines, but at identifying all the important factors that explain productivity advance in agriculture. It so happens that for the given period and crop, the development of two machines dominates the explanation. Other studies produced quite different results. Thus, new equipment plays virtually no role in Douglass North's explanation of the 50 per cent fall in the cost of ocean transportation that he finds for the 250-year period between 1600 and the middle of the nineteenth century. Almost all of the decline is explained by two other factors: the elimination of piracy and the increase in the size of the market. The elimination of piracy substantially reduced manning requirements since military personnel were no longer needed The increase in the size of the market lowered shipping costs by encouraging the concentration of surpluses in central markets. This development considerably reduced the amount of time ships spent in port acquiring a cargo.[16]

The second category consists of studies aimed at explaining the growth of

15 William N. Parker and Judith L. V. Klein, "Productivity Growth in Crop Production," Volume 30 of *Studies in Income and Wealth*, National Bureau of Economic Research (New York: Columbia University Press, 1966), pp. 523-80.

16 Douglass C. North, "Determinants of Productivity in Ocean Shipping," *The Reinterpretation*, Fogel and Engerman.

particular industries. One of the best examples of this type of work is Robert Brooke Zevin's analysis of the growth of the American cotton textile industry prior to 1860.[17] As Zevin points out, the seventeen years from 1816 to 1833 are the most interesting period in the early history of the industry. During this span the output of cotton cloth expanded from 840,000 to 231,000,000 yards, an increase of over 280 times. Abstracting from cyclical considerations, Zevin puts the average annual rate of growth in production at 17.1 per cent. He finds that one-third of this expansion was due to an increase in demand stimulated mainly by the growth of the urban and western populations. The remaining two-thirds was due to a downward shift in the supply curve. Zevin explains the change in supply by improvements in textile machinery, the fall in the price of raw cotton and the growth of skilled technicians. However, the improvement of machinery was the least important of the factors. It accounted for only 17 per cent of the expansion of cloth production. The fall in the price of raw cotton accounted for 28 per cent and the growing pool of skilled technicians for the remaining 22 per cent.

Zevin's study, taken in conjunction with others, points to the inadequacy of new machinery and other forms of equipment as the sole, or even the primary explanation of growth in the main manufacturing industries of Europe and America during the last two centuries. The preoccupation with machines has led to an underestimation of the role of demand in the promotion of industrial growth. It has also resulted in the slighting of such determinants of supply as the equality of labour, the stock of skills, the efficiency of industrial organization, and economies of scale.[18]

Analyses of the diffusion of technological innovations fall into the third category. The diffusion problem promises to be one of the most popular topics of the new economic history. Peter Temin's explanation of the spread of anthracite and coke blast furnaces has already become well known.[19] A more recent contribution is a paper on reapers by Paul David.[20] Although the reaper was invented in the 1830's, its diffusion proceeded at a very slow pace for two decades. The 'first major wave of popular acceptance' of the innovation 'was concentrated in the mid-1850's. The literature is ambiguous regarding the cause of this upsurge. Various writers have stressed the rise in wheat prices and the scarcity of farm lobour as factors. However, these accounts do not indicate the process by which the rise in wheat prices led to an increased demand for reapers.

David points out that if, on the industry level, the supply curve of labour is less elastic than the supply of reapers, a rise in the price of wheat will raise the

---

17 Robert Brooke Zevin, "The Growth of Cotton Textile Production after 1815," *The Reinterpretation*, Fogel and Engerman.

18 Cf. North, *Growth and Welfare*, pp. 6-10.

19 Peter Temin, "A New Look at Hunter's Hypothesis about the Antebellum Iron Industry," *American Economic Review*, LIV (May 1964), 344-51; Peter Temin, *Iron and Steel in Nineteenth-Century America* (Cambridge, Mass.: M.I.T. Press, 1964), chapter 3.

20 Paul David, "The Mechanization of Reaping in the Ante-Bellum Midwest," *Industrialization in Two Systems: Essays in Honor of Alexander Gerschenkron*, Henry Rosovsky (ed.) (New York: John Wiley and Sons, 1966), pp. 3-39.

price of farm labour relative to the price of reapers. He also notes the reapers had to be purchased rather than rented. Thus, even though the annual cost of a reaper to a farmer was independent of farm size, his average reaper cost, per acre harvested, fell as the number of acres in small grains increased, until the cutting capacity of a single machine was reached. By contrast, the cost per acre of reaping by the old method was constant because, to the farmer, the supply of labour was perfectly elastic and there were no economics of scale in the old method.

The foregoing considerations suggest the existence of a threshold function that relates the farm size at which it just paid to introduce the reaper, to the ratio between the price of a reaper and the wage of farm labour. David estimates the parameters of this function and finds that at the beginning of the fifties, the relationship of reaper and labour prices was such that it become profitable to introduce the reaper only on farms with 46 or more acres in small grains. At the time, however, the average number of acres in such grains per farm was about 25. By the mid-fifties the cost of reapers had fallen relative to the price of labour. The decline reduced the threshold size to just 35 acres. At the same time the average acreage in small grains rose to 30. Thus, within a period of about five years, the gap between the threshold farm size and the average actual farm size was reduced by over 75 per cent. It is the precipitous closing of this gap that explains the accelerated diffusion of reapers during the mid-fifties.

The final category of studies on technology and productivity consists of works which attempt to evaluate the net social benefit of particular innovations. My book, *Railroads and American Economic Growth,* belongs to this category.[21] Estimation of the net benefit of railroads involves a comparison between the actual level of national income and the level that would have obtained in the absence of railroads. The amount of national income in the absence of railroads cannot be computed directly. It is necessary to construct a hypothetico-deductive model on the basis of which one can infer, from those conditions that were actually observed, a set of conditions that never occurred.

In my book I attempted to construct such a model for the year 1890. The conceptual foundation of the model is the 'social saving' of railroads. The social saving in any given year is defined as the difference between the actual cost of shipping goods in that year and the alternative cost of shipping exactly the same goods between exactly the same points without railroads. This cost differential is in fact larger than the 'true' social saving. Forcing the pattern of shipments in a non-rail situation to conform to the pattern that actually existed is equivalent to the imposition of a restraint on society's freedom to adjust to an alternative technological situation. If society had had to ship by water and wagon without the railroad it could have altered the geographical locus of production in a manner that would have economized on transport services. Further, the sets of primary and secondary markets through which commodities were distributed were surely influenced by conditions peculiar to rail transportation; in the

---

21 Baltimore: Johns Hopkins Press, 1964.

absence of railroads some different cities would have entered these sets, and the relative importance of those remaining would have changed. Adjustments of this sort would have reduced the loss of national income occasioned by the absence of the railroad.

The computation of the social saving required both estimates of the direct payments that would have been made for boat and wagon transportation services and estimates of such indirect costs as cargo losses in transit, the expense resulting from the time lost when using a slow medium of transportation and the expense of being unable to use waterways during the winter months. Regression analysis was used to derive the cost functions of boats. The water rates that would have obtained in the absence of railroads were computed from these functions. The economic losses caused by slow service and by the vagaries of the weather were quantified by estimating the cost of expanding inventories to a size that would have permitted businesses to maintain their normal temporal pattern of distribution. The expected cargo loss was derived from insurance rates.

Because of the large amounts of data that had to be processed, my study was restricted to the social saving attributable to the transportation of agricultural commodities. The amount of this saving was estimated under three different assumptions regarding the possibility of technological adaptation to the absence of railroads. The first was that society would have relied on only the canals and roads that actually existed in 1890. The second was that at least 5,000 miles of feasible and, in the absence of railroads, highly profitable canals would have been built. The third was that common roads would have been improved. Under the first of these assumptions the agricultural social saving of railroads was $373,000,000 or 3.1 per cent of gross national product in 1890. The extension of canals and improvements of roads would have reduced the social saving to 1.8 per cent of G.N.P. It is interesting to note that the two main benefits achieved by the railroad were the reduction in inventories and the reduction in wagon transportation. Together these accounted for about 80 per cent of the social saving.

Albert Fishlow's penetrating, many-sided study of railroads during the *ante-bellum* era contains an estimate of the social saving for 1859.[22] His computation covers not merely agricultural commodities, but all other freight and all passenger traffic. Fishlow finds that the social saving of railroads was about $175,000,000 or 4 per cent of G.N.P. Of this total, agricultural commodities account for roughly one-quarter, other freight for another third, and passenger service for the balance. In comparing Fishlow's result with mine, it is important to keep in mind that Fishlow's calculation is for the case in which there would have been no technological adaptation to the absence of railroads. Given that assumption, the correspondence between our findings is extremely close. A computation of the 1859 social saving for the case of limited technological adaptation to the absence of railroads is still to be performed.

---

[22] Albert Fishlow, *American Railroads and the Transformation of the Ante-Bellum Economy* (Cambridge, Mass.: Harvard University Press, 1965), chapter 2.

I should like to conclude this section of my paper in the way that I began it—by stressing the inadequacy of my survey of the work of the new economic historians. Among the important contributions that I have slighted are studies by Robert Gallman on Southern agriculture, Jeffrey Williamson on the determinants of urbanization before the Civil War, Stanley Lebergott on the role of labour in nineteenth-century economic growth, John Bowman on the agricultural depression of the Gilded Age, and Lance Davis on the evolution of capital markets.

THE METHODS

The methodological hallmarks of the new economic history are its emphasis on measurement and its recognition of the intimate relationship between measurement and theory. Economic history has always had a quantitative orientation. But much of the past numerical work was limited to the location and simple classification of data contained in business and government records. With the exception of the excellent work on the construction of price indexes, relatively little was done to transform this information in ways that would shed light on 'rigorously defined concepts of economic analysis'[23] until the development of national income accounting techniques. The pioneers of the massive statistical reconstructions embodied in national income accounts were not economic historians, but empirical economists such as Simon Kuznets in the United States, J. R. N. Stone and Phyllis Deane in Great Britain, and Francois Perroux and Jean Marczewski in France. While economic historians made considerable use of national income measures, they did not immediately attempt to extend the process of statistical reconstruction to the vast array of issues in their domain. Most discussions of economic historians remained primarily qualitative with numerical information used largely as illustration.

The new economic historians are trying to end this long-existing void in measurement. They have set out to reconstruct American economic history on a sound quantitative basis. This objective is extremely ambitious and the obstacles to its fulfilment are numerous. The most frustrating problem is the paucity of data. Information bearing on many vital institutions and processes in the past was either never collected or has been lost. In still other cases the data are extant, but are so numerous or held in such a form that their retrieval without the aid of modern statistical methods would be prohibitively expensive.

As a consequence, statistics and mathematics are widely employed by the new economic historians. Regression analysis is perhaps the most frequently used tool. It is the principal device on which Albert Fishlow relied in his reconstruction of the investment of railroads during the *ante-bellum* era.[24] Jeffrey Williamson makes heavy use of it in his study of urbanization.[25] And

---

23 Simon Kuznets, "Summary of Discussion and Postscript," *Journal of Economic History*, XVII (December 1957), 553.

24 Fishlow, *American Railroads*, chapter 3 and Appendix B.

25 Jeffrey G. Williamson, *"Ante-bellum* Urbanization in the American Northeast,"

Paul MacAvoy employs a lagged form of the regression model in order to determine the relationship between grain prices and transportation rates.[26] Examples of the usefulness of other mathematical methods include William Whitney's employment of input-output analysis to measure the effect of tariffs on the rise of manufacturing[27] and James K. Kindahl's application of the hypergeometric distribution to estimate, from two incomplete lists, the total number of state banks that were in operation immediately after close of the Civil War.[28]

Some historians have held that there is no point in applying powerful statistical methods to economic history because the available data are too poor. In actual practice, the correlation often runs the other way. When the data are very good, simple statistical procedures will usually suffice. The poorer the data, the more powerful are the methods which have to be employed. Nevertheless, it is often true that the volume of data available is frequently below the minimum required for standard statistical procedures. In such instances the crucial determinant of success is the ability of the investigator to devise methods that are exceedingly efficient in the utilization of data—that is, to find a method that will permit one to achieve a solution with the limited data that are available.

The way in which economic theory can be employed to circumvent the data problem is illustrated by Paul David's study of mechanical reapers. Utilization of regression analysis to compute a threshold function for reapers would have required county data on the employment of reapers by farm size, on the delivered price of reapers, and on the average wage of labour. Unfortunately, such information was not available for counties. To surmount the problem, David turned to the theory of production. He first noted that a farmer would be indifferent to the choice between mechanized and hand reaping when the cost of cutting grain on a specified acreage was the same by both methods. He also noted the absence of economies and diseconomies of scale in the employment of hand labour. These specifications, together with two linear approximations, yielded a threshold function with only three parameters. The parameters were the rate of depreciation, the rate of interest and the rate of substitution between reapers and man-days of labour. The data required to estimate these parameters were available.[29]

Journal of Economic History, XXV (December 1965), 592-608; Jeffrey G. Williamson and Joseph A. Swanson, 'The Growth of Cities in the American Northeast, 1820-1870" (mimeographed).

[26] Paul W. MacAvoy, *The Economic Effects of Regulation: The Trunk-Line Railroad Cartels and the Interstate Commerce Commission before 1900* (Cambridge, Mass.: M.I.T. Press, 1965).

[27] William S. Whitney, *The Structure of the American Economy in the Late Nineteenth Century* (dissertation in progress for Harvard University).

[28] James K. Kindahl, "The Economics of Resumption: The United States, 1865-1879' (unpublished doctoral dissertation, University of Chicago, 1958); published without statistical appendices as 'Economic Factors in Specie Resumption: The United States, 1865-79', *Journal of Political Economy,* LXIX (February 1961).

[29] David, 'The Mechanization', pp. 28-39.

The union between measurement and theory is most clearly evident when one attempts to establish the net effect of innovations, institutions or processes on the course of economic development. The net effect of such things on development involves a comparison between what actually happened and what would have happened in the absence of the specified circumstance. However, since the counterfactual condition never occurred, it could not have been observed, and hence is not recorded in historical documents. In order to determine what would have happened in the absence of a given circumstance the economic historian needs a set of general statements (that is, a set of theories or a model) that will enable him to deduce a counterfactual situation from institutions and relationships that actually existed.

This is precisely the problem when one attempts to evaluate the frequent claim that railroads extended the area of commercial agriculture in the United States. It is, of course, true that the area of commercial agriculture and the construction of railroads expanded more or less simultaneously. However, it does not follow that railroads were a necessary condition for the commercial exploitation of the new lands. To settle the issue one must find a method of determining how much of the land actually settled after the advent of railroads would have been settled in their absence.

Without railroads the high cost of wagon transportation would have limited commercial agricultural production to areas of land lying within some unknown distatance of navigable waterways. It is possible to use the theory of rent to establish these boundaries of feasible commercial agriculture in a non-rail society. Rent is a measure of the amount by which the return to labour and capital on a given portion of land exceeds the return the same factors could earn if they were employed at the intensive or extensive margins. Therefore, any plot of land capable of commanding a rent will be kept in productive activity. It follows that, even in the face of increased transportation costs, a given area of farm land will remain in use as long as the increased costs incurred during a given time period do not exceed the original rental value of that land.

Given information on the quantity of goods shipped between farms and their markets, the distances from farms to rail and water shipping points, the distance from such shipping points to markets, and the wagon, rail and water rates, it is possible to compute the additional transportation costs that would have been incurred if farmers attempted to duplicate their actual shipping pattern without railroads. In such a situation shipping costs would have risen not because boat rates exceeded rail rates, but because it usually required more wagon transportation to reach a boat than a rail shipping point. In other words, farms immediately adjacent to navigable waterways would have been least affected by the absence of rail service. The further a farm was from a navigable waterway the greater the amount of wagon transportation it would have required. At some distance from waterways the additional wagon haul would have increased the cost of shipping from a farm by an amount exactly equal to the original rental value of the land. Such a farm would represent a point on the boundary of feasible commercial agriculture. Consequently, the full boundary can be established by finding all those points from which the increased cost of shipping by alternative means the quantities that were actually carried by railroads is equal to the original rental value of the land.

This approach, it should be noted, leads to an overstatement of the land falling beyond the 'true' feasible boundary. A computation based on the actual mix of products shipped does not allow for adjustments to a non-rail technology. In the absence of railroads the mix of agricultural products would have changed in response to the altered structure of transportation rates. Such a response would have lowered shipping costs and hence extended the boundary. The computation also ignores the consequence of a cessation in agricultural production in areas beyond the feasible region on the level of prices. Given the relative inelasticity of the demand for agricultural products, the prices of such commodities would have risen in the absence of railroads. The rise in prices would have led to a more intensive exploitation of agriculture within the feasible region, thus raising land values. The rise in land values would have increased the burden of additional transportation costs that could have been borne and shifted the boundary of feasible commercial agriculture further away from water shipping points.[30]

The method outlined above is the one I used to establish the boundary of feasible commercial agriculture for 1890. It turns out that given only the active waterways of that year, at least 76 per cent of the land actually employed in agriculture would have remained employed in the absence of railroads. Moreover, a 5,000-mile extension of the canal system would have increased the land in commercial agriculture to 93 per cent of that actually cultivated. The theory of rent also enables one to infer which canals would have been socially profitable. It can be shown that a new canal would have been profitable if the land it brought into the feasible region had an 1890 value which exceeded the canals' construction cost by the present value of any additional wagon transportation that would have been incurred by the absence of railroads.[31]

According to Fritz Redlich, these attempts to answer counterfactual questions by the use of hypothetico-deductive models are the most novel and the most dubious methodological aspect of the new economic history. Professor Redlich argues that counterfactual propositions are fundamentally alien to economic history. He also believes that they are untestable and hence calls essays involving such propositions 'quasi-history.'[32]

However, if we are to exclude from history those studies which are based on counterfactual propositions, we will have to expurgate not only the new work, but much of the old work as well. The difference between the old and the new economic history is not the frequency with which one encounters counterfactual propositions, but the extent to which such propositions are made explicit. The old economic history abounds in disguised counterfactual assertions. They are

[30] For a more detailed discussion of the theoretical issues see Fogel, *Railroads*, chapter 3.

[31] *Ibid.* pp. 79-84, 92-107.

[32] Fritz Redlich, ' "New" and Traditional', pp. 486-87.

present in discussions which either affirm or deny that tariffs accelerated the growth of manufacturing; in essays which argue that slavery retarded the development of the South; in debates over whether the Homestead Act made the distribution of land more equitable; in the contention that railroads expanded interregional trade; and in virtually every other discussion which makes a legal, social, technological, administrative or political innovation the cause of a change in economic activity. All of these arguments involve implicit comparisons between the actual state of the nation and the state that would have prevailed in the absence of the specified circumstance.

Indeed, the new economic historians have not been primarily engaged in launching new counterfactual propositions, but in making explicit and testing the ones they find in traditional history. One should not underestimate the task involved in demonstrating that comparisons which appear to be between events that actually occurred are in reality counterfactual propositions. Consider, for example, the arithmetic index of productivity popularized by John Kendrick. This measure of total factor productivity, now more than a decade old, is usually described as the ratio of an output index to a weighted index of inputs, where the weights are the shares of the factors in value added. However, a deft proof by Albert Fishlow shows that what appears to be purely a comparison of recorded circumstances is really a disguised comparison between the actual price of the output and the price that would have obtained in the absence of technological change.[33]

Since counterfactual propositions are merely inferences from hypothetico-deductive models, it follows that such propositions can be verified in at least two ways. The first involves the determination of whether the prosition asserted follows logically from its premises. The second requires a determination of whether the assumptions of the model are empirically valid.[34] Most of the revisions of the new economic history follow from a demonstration that one or both of these conditions for valid inferences have been violated. As noted earlier, Conrad and Meyer overthrew Phillips's proposition that slavery was moribund by showing that his conclusion rested on the false assumption that a divergence between the rates of growth of slave and cotton prices implied a decrease in profits. On the other hand, as I attempted to demonstrate in another paper, one cannot rest the case for the indispensability of railroads to the total economy on evidence which shows that railroads had the power to crush particular firms on regions. This argument involves the fallacy of composition and hence gives rise to a *non-sequitur*.[35]

The foregoing suggests that the fundamental methodological feature of the new economic history is its attempt to cast all explanations of past economic

---

[33] Albert Fishlow, 'Productivity and Technological Change in the Railroad Sector, 1840-1910', forthcoming in Volume 30 of *Studies in Income and Wealth*, National Bureau of Economic Research (New York: Columbia University Press, 1966), pp. 583-646.

[34] A third level of verification, the test of the predictive power of a model, may often be possible in historical analysis. Cf. Fogel, *Railroads*, pp. 176-89.

[35] 'Railroads and the Axiom of Indispensability', *New Views*, Andreano, pp. 232-4.

development in the form of valid hypothetico-deductive models. This is another way of saying that the new generation seeks to continue an effort that was under way long before it appeared on the scene: namely the construction of economic history on the basis of scientific methods. If the new economic historians are able to advance that objective it will be partly because of what they have inherited from their predecessors and partly because they are the beneficiaries of a series of important developments in economic theory, in statistics and in applied mathematics.

2. A quantitative approach to the study of the effects of British imperial policy upon colonial welfare: some preliminary findings*

ROBERT PAUL THOMAS†§

Historians have long debated whether the American colonies on balance benefited or were hindered by British imperial regulation. George Bancroft thought the regulations worked a definite hardship on the colonies. George L. Beer believed these regulations nicely balanced and that the colonies shared in the general advantages. Lawrence Harper, in a now classic article, actually attempted to calculate the cost and found that British policies "placed a heavy burden upon the colonies."[1] Oliver Dickerson wrote that "no case can be made ... that such laws were economically oppressive,"[2] while Curtis P. Nettels, writing at the same time to the same point, stated: "British policy as it affected the colonies after 1763 was restrictive, injurious, negative."[3] It is quite evident

* Reprinted from the *Journal of Economic History,* XXV (December, 1965), pp. 615-38, by permission of the author and the publisher.

† Robert Paul Thomas, assistant professor of economics, University of Washington, received his Ph.D. from Northwestern University. He is the coauthor, with Douglass C. North, of *The Economic Growth of the United States to 1860: A Documentary History,* and is the author of several articles on British and American economic history.

§ The paper is a progress report on one aspect of a larger study of the effects of British imperial policy upon colonial welfare. All computations in this study are preliminary and subject to revision. I have benefited from conversations with many persons, especially Douglass C. North and James Shepherd. The former was especially helpful in pointing out several errors in a previous draft. Since I did not take all his advice, he is not responsible for any errors that may remain. J. N. Sharma and James Livingston served ably as my research assistants. The National Science Foundation provided support for the project on which this paper is based. Due to space limitations an appendix explaining how the calculations were made has been deleted, but it is available to the interested reader from the author.

1 "Mercantilism and the American Revolution," *Canadian Historical Review,* XXIII (Mar. 1942), 3.

2 *The Navigation Act and the American Revolution* (Philadelphia: University of Pennsylvania Press, 1951), p. 55.

3 "British Mercantilism and the Economic Development of the Thirteen Colonies," *Journal of Economic History* XII, No. 2 (Spring 1952), 114.

that a difference of opinion exists among reputable colonial historians over this important historical issue.

In this paper an effort is made to meet this issue head on. I shall attempt to measure, relative to a hypothetical alternative, the extent of the burdens and benefits stemming from imperial regulation of the foreign commerce of the thirteen colonies. The main instruments of this regulation were the Navigation Acts, and we shall confine our attention to evaluating the effect of these Acts upon colonial welfare. Various other imperial regulations such as the Revenue Acts, enacted after 1764, the modification of naturalization and land regulations, the interference with colonial issues of paper money, and the various regulations discouraging manufacturers will not be dealt with in this paper. The assumption is that the direct effects of these regulations upon the economic welfare of the American colonists were insignificant compared to the effects of the Navigation Acts.[4]

The hypothesis of this paper is that membership in the British Empire, after 1763, did not impose a significant hardship upon the American colonies. To test this hypothesis I shall endeavor to bias the estimates against the hypothesis, thus not attempting to state what actually would have happened but only that it would not have amounted to as much as my estimate. The end result will, therefore, err on the side of overstating the real costs of the Navigation Acts to the thirteen colonies.

The traditional tools of economic theory will guide the preparation of these estimates. Two series of estimates will be prepared where possible: one, an annual average for the period 1763-1772, based upon official values; the other, for the single year 1770. The official trade statistics for the year 1770 have been adjusted to make them more accurate.[5]

I

Is it legitimate for the historian to consider alternative possibilities to events which have happened? ... To say that a thing happened the way it did is not at all illuminating. We can understand the significance of what did happen only if we contrast it with what might have happened. –Morris Raphael Cohen[6]

All attempts at measurement require a standard to which the object being measured is made relative or compared. In the case of this paper, the colonies either on balance benefited or were burdened by British imperialism, relative to how they would have fared under some alternative political situation. The problem is to pick the most probable alternative situation.

---

[4] The effects of British regulations not considered in this paper will be taken into account in the larger study now in process.

[5] The statistics on colonial exports have been adjusted in a manner suggested by James Shepherd and used by him in preparing his balance of payments for the colonial period. Imports, due to a lack of prices, were adjusted by the Schumpeter-Gilboy price index.

[6] Quoted in Robert W. Fogel, *Railroads and American Economic Growth* (Baltimore: Johns Hopkins Press, 1964), p. 17.

The only reasonable alternative in this case is to calculate the burdens or benefits of British regulation relative to how the colonies would have fared outside the British Empire but still within a mercantilist world. Considered within this political environment there is little doubt that prior to February 1763, when the Treaty of Paris was signed, the American colonies on balance benefited from membership in the British Empire. Before that date, the colonies were threatened on two sides by two superior colonial powers. C. M. Andrews has pointed out that, before 1763, in addition to remaining within the protection of Great Britain, the American colonies had only one other alternative: domination by another European power, probably France or Spain. Clearly, from a colonial point of view, belonging to the British Empire was superior to membership in any other.[7]

The French and Indian War ended the menace of foreign domination through the cession to Great Britain of Canada by the French and of Florida by Spain.[8] Immediately, thereupon, several Englishmen voiced their fears that these spoils of victory, by removing the foreign threat, made inevitable the independence of the American colonies.[9] Even the French Foreign Minister, Choisoul, lent his voice to this speculation when, soon after the Treaty of Paris, he predicted the eventual coming of the American Revolution. In 1764, Choisoul went so far as to send his agents to America to watch developments.[10] Knollenberg has pointed out that English suspicions of a desire for independence on the part of the colonies do not prove that the suspicions were well founded.[11] They do, however, suggest that an independent America was, by 1763, a distinct possibility; and thereafter the American colonists possessed another alternative to membership in a European empire. This alternative was an independent existence outside the British Empire but still within a mercantilist world.

The alternative situation that I shall employ to calculate the economic effects of the Navigation Acts after 1763 is that of a free and independent thirteen colonies outside the British Empire. This new nation would, therefore, be subject to most of the same restrictions hindering foreign nations attempting to carry on commerce with the eighteenth-century British Empire.[12]

II

Had the wealth and economic potential of the thirteen Atlantic colonies depended solely on farming, their growth history might have paralleled that of many another slowly developing agricultural settlement. However . . . an

---

[7] *Journal of Economic History*, XII (1952), 114.

[8] In 1790, nearly 80 per cent of the residents of the United States traced their origin, or that of their ancestors, to the British Isles.

[9] Bernhard Knollenberg, *Origin of the American Revolution: 1759-1766* (New York: Collier Books, 1961), p. 18.

[10] Max Savelle, "The American Balance of Power and European Diplomacy, 1713-78," in Richard B. Morris, ed., *The Era of the American Revolution* (New York: Columbia University Press, 1939), p. 162.

[11] Knollenberg p. 19.

[12] This was certainly the case after the American Revolution.

*indigenous commercial economy developed, unique in colonial history and
conducive to sustained growth.* —George Rogers Taylor[13]

This "unique" commercial economy developed within the British Empire
subject to the rules and regulations of the Navigation Acts. The American
colonies in a sense grew up with the empire, which after the successful
conclusion of the Seven Years' War in February 1763, was the wealthiest, most
populous colonial empire in the world. It included the kingdom of Great Britain
and Ireland with the outlying islands of Europe; trading forts on the Gold Coast
of Africa; enclaves in India, and some minor islands in Asia; Newfoundland,
Hudson Bay, Nova Scotia, Quebec, the thirteen American colonies, East Florida,
and West Florida on the continent of North America; the Bahamas, Bermuda,
Jamaica, Antigua, Barbados, and the Leeward and Windward groups of minor
islands in the West Indies, as well as the settlement of Belize in Central America.

The American colonies by 1763 formed the foundation of Great Britain's
Atlantic empire and had become, as a group, England's most important
commercial ally.[14] The basis of this commerce was a vigorous colonial export
trade. The total exports in 1770 amounted to £3,165,225. Trade with Great
Britain and Ireland accounted for 50 per cent of colonial exports. The West
Indies trade constituted another 30 per cent, and commerce with southern
Europe and the Wine Islands, another 17 per cent. Trade with Africa and South
America accounted for most of the residual.

The colonists, of course, used their exports to purchase imports. They were
Great Britain's most important customer and Great Britain their most important
supplier. The British Isles shipped to the American colonies in 1768 (a year for
which a detailed breakdown is available) £2,157,000 worth of goods, or nearly
75 per cent of all colonial imports, which totaled £2,890,000. Of this, £421,000
were British reexports from northern Europe.[15] The West Indies, the other
important source of imports, accounted for 20.5 per cent of the colonial
imports; southern Europe and the Wine Islands, 2.9 per cent; and Africa, a little
less than 2.0 per cent.

The thirteen American colonies carried on this foreign commerce subject to
the constraints of a series of laws designed to alter the trade of the British
Empire in the interests of the mother country.[16] This commercial system can be
viewed as being made up of four types of laws: (1) laws regulating the
nationality, crews, and ownership of the vessels in which goods could be

---

13 "American Economic Growth Before 1850: An Exploratory Essay," *Journal of
Economic History,* XXIV, No. 4 (Dec. 1964), 435.

14 B. R. Mitchell, *Abstract of British Historical Statistics* (Cambridge [Engl.]: University
Press, 1962), p. 312.

15 The values of imports are the official values f.o.b. Great Britain. For that reason, they
are probably approximately 10 to 20 per cent too low. Import figures for 1768 were used
because detailed breakdowns for 1770 were unavailable when this paper was written.

16 Sir William Ashley thought the regulations of English mercantilism were pious
formulas nullified in the actual world of commerce by fraud and evasion when they existed
contrary to national commercial habits. Studies by Lawrence Harper have indicated that the
burden of the Navigation Acts was in fact felt in transatlantic commerce.

shipped; (2) statutes regulating the destination to which certain goods could be shipped; (3) laws designed to encourage specific primary industries via an elaborate system of rebates, drawbacks, import and export bounties, and export taxes; (4) direct prohibition of colonial industries and practices that tended to compete with English industries or to harm a prominent sector of the British economy or even, occasionally, the economy of a British colony.[17] These laws, it should be stressed, did not regulate the American colonies alone, but with occasional local modifications applied equally to the entire British Empire.

The laws regulating the nationality of vessels were designed to insure a monopoly of the carrying trade of the empire to ships of the empire. In the seventeenth and eighteenth centuries the freight factor on goods traded internationally probably averaged at least 20 per cent, and these laws were designed to insure that this revenue stayed within the empire.[18] The Navigation Acts also insured, to the extent that they were effective, that England would be the entrepôt of the empire and that the distributing trade would be centered in the British Isles.

The commodity clauses of these various regulatory Acts controlled the destination to which certain goods could be shipped. These enumerated commodities generally could be shipped only to England. The original list contained tobacco, sugar, indigo, cotton-wool, ginger, fustic and other dye-woods. Later, naval stores, hemp, rice, molasses, beaver skins, furs, and copper ore were added. The Sugar Act of 1764 added coffee, pimiento, coconuts, whale fins, raw silk, hides and skins, potash and pearl ash to the list. In 1776, the law was amended to prohibit the direct export of any colonial product north of Cape Finisterre.

There were exceptions and compensations to these commodity clauses which benefited the American colonies. Rice, after 1730, could be directly exported south of Cape Finisterre and, after 1764, to South America. Tobacco was given a monopoly in Great Britain, as its local cultivation was prohibited. While the list appears extensive, of the enumerated commodities only tobacco, indigo, copper ore, naval stores, hemp, furs and skins, whale fins, raw silk, and potash and pearl ash were products of the thirteen colonies, and only tobacco, rice, and perhaps indigo and naval stores could be considered major exports of the colonies that later became the United States.

An elaborate series of laws was enacted by the English Parliament to

---

[17] The Molasses Act of 1733 was a law enacted in the interest of the British West Indies. This law taxed foreign molasses sufficiently to make the molasses of the British West Indies competitive. The law was, however, widely evaded.

[18] Export commodities shipped to the West Indies were reputed by one source to be worth £ 275,000 when they left the American colonies and £ 500,000 when they arrived in the West Indies. The freight factor is thus over 30 per cent. The return trip saw excess cargo capacity and therefore lower rates. The freight factor on the return trip was but 5 per cent. Herbert C. Bell, "West Indian Trade before the Revolution," *American Historical Review*, XXII, No. 2 (Jan. 1917), 273-74.

encourage specific industries in the interest of a self-sufficient empire. These included preferential tariffs for certain goods of colonial origin. A distinctive feature of these laws was an elaborate system of rebates and drawbacks to encourage the exports of certain commodities from England and extensive bounties to encourage the production of specific goods for export to Great Britain.

Most enumerated goods benefited from a preferential duty. These goods were thus given a substantial advantage in the markets of the mother country. Goods receiving preferential treatment included cotton-wool, ginger, sugar, molasses, coffee, tobacco, rice, naval stores, pitch, rosin, hemp, masts, whale fins, raw silk, potash and pearl ash, bar and pig iron, and various types of lumber. Certain of these goods also received drawbacks of various amounts upon their reexport from Great Britain. Foreign goods competing in the English market with enumerated colonial commodities were thus subject to a disadvantage from these preferential duties.

A system of bounties was also implemented to encourage the production of specific commodities in the colonies or to allow the British manufacturers to compete with foreign exports in the colonial markets. The production of naval stores, silk, lumber, indigo, and hemp was encouraged in the colonies with bounties. In the mother country the manufacture of linen, gunpowder, silks, and many nonwoolen textiles was encouraged by a bounty to allow these products to compete with similar foreign manufactures in the colonial markets.

Certain of the colonial commodities favored by legislation were given what amounted to a monopoly of the home market of the mother country. The colonial production of tobacco, naval stores, sugar and sugar products was so favored. In the case of tobacco, the major share of total imports was reexported, so the local monopoly proved not a great boon.

In economic terms, the Navigation Acts were designed to insure that the vast bulk of the empire's carrying trade was in ships owned by Englishmen. The design of the commodity clauses was to alter the terms of trade to the disadvantage of the colonists, by making all foreign imports into the colonies, and many colonial exports whose final destination was the Continent, pass through England. The effect was to make colonial imports more expensive and colonial exports less remunerative by increasing the transportation costs of both. Finally, through tariff preferences, bounties, and outright prohibitions, resources were allocated from more efficient uses to less.

I shall approach the problem of assessing the overall effect of the various British regulations of trade by considering their effect on the following aspects of the colonial economy: (1) exports of colonial products; (2) imports into the colonies; (3) colonial foreign commerce; and (4) colonial shipping earnings. An assessment will then be undertaken of compensating benefits arising from membership in the British Empire. Finally, an attempt will be made to strike a balance on the total impact of British imperial policy upon the colonial economy.

III

> *The enumeration of key colonial exports in various Acts ... hit at colonial trade both coming and going. The Acts ... placed a heavy burden upon the colonies.—Lawrence Harper[19]*

> *In spite of the extravagant language that has been used to condemn the system, the grower of enumerated commodities was not enslaved by the legal provisions of enumeration .... Enumeration clearly did not hamper the expansion of the tobacco raising business in America .... It has been assumed by many writers that enumeration imposed a serious burden upon rice planters. The ascertainable facts do not support this assumption.—Oliver Dickerson[20]*

The export trade between the colonies and the mother country was subjected to regulations which significantly altered its value and composition over what it would have been if the colonies had been independent. The total adjusted value of exports from the American colonies to Great Britain in 1770 was £1,458,000 of which £1,107,000, or 76 per cent, were enumerated goods. Such goods were required to be shipped directly to Great Britain. The largest part, 85.4 per cent, of the enumerated goods was subsequently reexported to northern Europe and thus when competing in these markets bore the burden of an artificial, indirect routing through England to the Continent. The costs of this indirect route took the form of an added transhipment, with the consequent port charges and fees, middlemen's commissions, and what import duties were retained upon reexport. The enumerated goods consumed in England benefited from preferential duties relative to goods of foreign production. A few of these enumerated commodities also were favored with import bounties.

The additional transport costs borne by enumerated goods upon their reexport had the effect of lowering the prices received by the colonial producer and depressing the quantity exported. In economic terms, the world market price as shown in Graph 1 would, in the absence of regulation, be P^2 and exports would be Q^2. The effect of the additional cost of shipment through England is to raise the price to the consumer to P^3. Colonial exports, consequently, are reduced to Q^1. Therefore, both consumers and producers suffer from the enumeration of colonial exports whose final destination is not England.

The incidence of this burden depends upon the elasticities of supply and demand for the product. The direct cost to the producer as shown in Graph 1 is the unit burden times the quantity produced $(P^2P^1.Q^1)$.[21] The burden on the reduced output is equal to the return that would be earned on the additional output over what the resources would earn in their next-best alternative. This cost is illustrated by the shaded triangle in Graph 1 and represents the sum of the direct and indirect burdens.

---

[19] *Canadian Historical Review,* XXIII (1942), 3.

[20] Dickerson, p. 33.

[21] Since most tobacco was exported, exports for all practical purposes equal output or production.

GRAPH 1

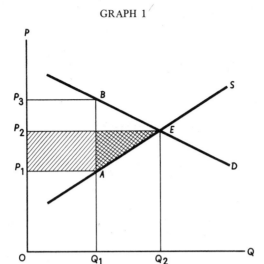

In order to calculate the direct burden borne by the colonial producers of enumerated goods that were reexported from England, we need to know three separate time series. In the case of tobacco, we need to know the world market price in a European port, the price actually received in the colonies, and the actual reexports of tobacco from England all three of which are readily available.[22]

The price that would have existed in the colonies in the absence of of enumeration can be estimated, given the above information. It was estimated by dividing the observed Amsterdam price of Virginia tobacco before the Revolution by the ratio of Amsterdam to Philadelphia tobacco prices after the Revolution.[23] The postwar ratio of prices reflects the advantages received by the colonists by shipping directly to northern Europe rather than indirectly through England. This procedure provides us with an estimate of the price of tobacco in the colonies (P^2 on Graph 1) had tobacco not been subject to enumeration. The difference between the estimated price (P^2) and the actual price (P^1) is the unit burden suffered by reexported colonial tobacco.

Calculated in this manner, the price of tobacco in 1770 colonial America, had the colonies been independent, would have been over 49 per cent higher than it actually was. The average price for the decade 1763-1772 would have been 34 per cent higher than was actually recorded. These higher prices indicate that

[22] For Philadelphia prices, Anne Bezanson, *et al., Prices and Inflation during the American Revolution: Pennsylvania, 1770-1790* (Philadelphia: University of Pennsylvania Press, 1965). For a European port, Amsterdam prices have been used as found in N. W. Posthumus, *Inquiry into the History of Prices in Holland* (Leiden: E. J. Brill, 1946). For tobacco quantities, see *Historical Statistics of the United States, Colonial Times to 1957* (Washington: U. S. Government Printing Office, 1960), series 230-37, p. 766.

[23] Albert Fishlow, discussion of a paper by Gordon Bjork, "The Weaning of the American Economy: Independence, Market Changes, and Economic Development," *Journal of Economic History*, XXIV, No. 4 (Dec. 1964), 565.

tobacco planters suffered a burden on the tobacco they actually grew in 1770 of £262,000 and, for the decade, an average annual burden of £177,000.

The direct burden is only a portion of the total colonial loss due to enumeration. The hypothetical higher tobacco prices would certainly have stimulated an increase in the supply of tobacco. Assuming that a 1 per cent increase in price would generate a 1 per cent increase in supply, the resulting increase in supply would have been about 39,000,000 pounds in 1770, or an annual average of 29,000,000 pounds for the decade.[24] The loss to the colonies of this foregone output is the calculated value of the shaded triangle in Graph 1, which is £64,000 for 1770, or an average of £30,000 for the decade.[25] Thus, the total burden on tobacco amounts to £326,000 for the year 1770, or an average of £207,000 for the period 1763-1772.

The calculation of the encumbrance suffered by rice proceeded in the same manner as the calculation of the burden on tobacco, except that Charleston prices were used instead of Philadelphia prices since South Carolina was the center of colonial rice production. The burden on the price of rice reexports was calculated to be an appreciable 105 per cent. This amounted to £95,000 in 1770, or £110,000 average for the decade 1763-1772.[26]

The indirect loss attributable to the expected increase in rice exports with the increase in price amounted to £25,000 for 1770, or an average of £29,000 for the longer period. In the case of rice, an elasticity of supply of .5 was assumed, due to the limited area of southern marshlands suitable to the cultivation of rice. The whole burden on rice products totaled £120,000 for 1770, or an average of £139,000 for the period 1763-1772.

Tobacco and rice together accounted for the vast bulk of the enumerated products that were reexported and therefore bore most of the burden. If we apply the weighted average of the tobacco and rice burden to the remainder of enumerated reexports, and adjust for the expected increase in supply, we obtain an estimated additional burden of £53,000 for 1770, or an annual average of £35,000 for the ten-year period.

However, to arrive at the total burden on enumerated exports we must allow for the benefits that colonial exports received from preferential duties or bounties. Most enumerated commodities benefited from one or the other: beaver skins, furs, and copper ore appear to be the only exceptions. Enumerated goods consumed in Great Britain amounted to £161,570 in 1770, or an average

---

[24] This amounts to assuming an elasticity of supply of one. This is probably optimistic, since the average exports of tobacco between 1790 and 1793 were 28 per cent greater than the average for the period 1763-72 and 41 per cent greater than for 1770. This suggests on a crude base an elasticity of supply between .8 and .9. Bjork also found that tobacco prices after the Revolution rose sharply.

[25] The indirect burden suffered because of the loss of exports is calculated as the unit burden times the increased output that would have been exported, divided by two.

[26] For rice, the prices are to be found in Arthur H. Cole, *Wholesale Commodity Prices in the United States, 1700-1861, Statistical Supplement* (Cambridge: Harvard University Press, 1938). The rice estimate was made on the basis of but one observation in the colonial period (1760). The author considers the rice estimate optimistic.

of £126,716 for the decade. The average preference amounted to 38 per cent of the price of enumerated products consumed in the mother country.[27] Again, assuming an elasticity of supply of one, we find that in the absence of these preferential duties the first-order effects would result in a decline in the amount of these enumerated commodities consumed in England of about £61,000 for 1770 or an average of £48,000 for the decade. The benefit of preferential duties to the colonists is the gain enjoyed by those exports that would have been sent to England in the absence of preferential duties had the colonies been independent (or £38,000 in 1770 and £30,000 average for the decade) plus the gain on the commodities actually sent that would not have been sent to England had the colonies been free. This amounted to £17,000 in 1770, or £9,000 as the annual average between 1763 and 1772. The benefit accruing to the colonies from preferential duties thus totals £55,000 for 1770, or £39,000 for the decade average.

TABLE 1
Net Burden on Colonial Foreign Commerce

	1770	1763-1772
Exports		
Tobacco	£ 326,000	£ 207,000
Rice	120,000	139,000
Other	53,000	35,000
Burden	499,000	381,000
Preference	55,000	39,000
Bounty	33,000	35,000
Benefit	88,000	74,000
Imports		
Burden	121,000	144,000
Net burden on foreign commerce	£ 532,000	£ 451,000
	or	or
	$ 2,660,000	$ 2,255,000

In addition to preferential duties, the Crown annually spent large sums in the form of bounties to promote certain industries. The recorded bounties for the year 1770, for instance, totaled £47,344.[28] These payments were designed to divert resources from more efficient uses into industries where they were employed less efficiently but where, for political purposes, they were thought

---

[27] The average preference was figured from statistics presented in tables 2 and 3, found in Lawrence Harper, "The Burden of the Navigation Acts on the Thirteen Colonies" in Morris, ed., *Era of the American Revolution.*

[28] Recorded bounty payments for the decade 1763-72 averaged:

Indigo	£ 8,065
Naval stores	32,772
Lumber	6,557
Total	£ 47,394

better occupied. Thus it was better to obtain naval stores in the American colonies at a higher cost than to rely upon foreign imports. Part of the bounty, therefore, was a payment for the inefficient allocation of colonial resources and was no gain to the colonies.

The calculation of the approximate proportion of these payments that exceeded the amount required to pay the cost of the inefficiency is not difficult. Since in every case Great Britain continued to import substantial amounts of these commodities from foreign as well as colonial sources, the demand for bountied goods from the colonies can reasonably be assumed to have been perfectly elastic. That is, the colonies could have sold as much of these goods in England as they desired without lowering the market price. This is shown in Graph 2 as a horizontal demand schedule (*D*) and *OB* is the market price of the commodity.

GRAPH 2

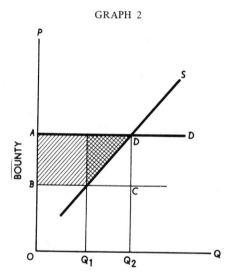

The effect of a per-unit bounty is to increase the supply of the commodity; this is shown as an increase in the quantity supplied from Q^1 to Q^2. The net benefit to the colonies of the total bounty (shown on Graph 2 as the area *ABCD*) is the shaded portion of that rectangle. The total bounty payment less the cost of an inefficient use of resources (the unshaded area of the rectangle *ABCD*) gives the net benefit, which must be less than the bounty payment. In order to measure the actual benefit derived by the colonies from the bounty payments we need know only the percentage of the market price represented by the bounty and the elasticity of supply of the commodity.

The export of colonial naval stores was stimulated by bounty payments in significant amounts. The average for the decade 1763-1772 totaled £33,000, and for the year 1770 the payment amounted to £29,803. The average bounty amounted to about 28 per cent of the price; therefore, assuming an elasticity of supply of one, the bounty was responsible for roughly 28 per cent of the exports of naval stores to Great Britain. Figured on this basis, the net gain to the colonists from the bounty on naval stores was 86 per cent of the payment.[29] This amounted to an average of £28,000 for the decade, or £26,000 for the single year 1770.

The second largest bounty payments were for the production of indigo; in 1770 this amounted to £8,732 and for the decade an average of £8,065.[30] Evidently, the indigo bounty not only stimulated increased output but was responsible for the entire output, since the production of indigo in the colonies disappeared after independence. Therefore, the net benefits of the indigo bounty are derived by calculating the value of the triangle as shown in Graph 3. In the

GRAPH 3

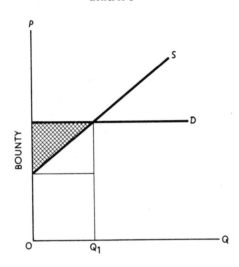

absence of the bounty, no indigo would have been exported. The effect of the bounty was to stimulate an export equal to Q^1. The net gain to the colonists from the indigo bounty at best is equal to, and is probably something less than, one half the amount of the bounty. We estimated that 50 per cent of the bounty

---

[29] The gain to the colonists from the bounty payments was figured in the following manner. The gain is in two parts. First, the unit bounty times the quantity that would have been produced without the bounty gives us the clear gain. In order to find that portion of naval stores that would have been produced without the bounty, we assumed a supply elasticity of one, reckoned the percentage of the price of naval stores that the bounty represented, and thus easily estimated that portion of the supply of naval stores for which the bounty was responsible. The other part would have been produced anyway; on this portion the full amount of the bounty was clear again. On the part stimulated by the bounty, only one half was gain to the colonists.

[30] This figure is taken from reports by the London Custom House, retained in Treasury 38, Vol. 363, Public Record Office, London, as originally stated in Dickerson, p. 28, and is accurate. Lawrence Harper "Navigation Acts" (cited in n.27) uses a figure of £ 23,086. While the Dickerson figure may possibly exclude some payments, the Harper figure is calculated on the basis that all indigo received the bounty, which was not the case. Lewis Grey quotes a British official to the effect that about seven eighths of the indigo exported from South Carolina received the bounty, but much less deserved so, being poor in quality. On this basis the payments could have reached as high as £ 20,000 a year. Lewis C. Grey, *A History of Southern Agriculture* (Washington: Carnegie Institution, 1933), p. 292.

payment for indigo was gain for indigo producers—gain they would not have enjoyed if the colonies had been independent. This totaled £4,400 in 1770, or £4,000 as the annual average for the decade.[31]

The importation of colonial lumber into Great Britain also received a bounty which, according to Beer, totaled £6,557 in 1769.[32] Sufficient data are not available to allow a calculation of the gain to the colonists from this payment, but it appears that the bounty was just sufficient to pay the added cost of shipping lumber to England. This payment was necessary to divert lumber from the West Indies, which was the colonies' natural market, and to attract it to England. It appears justifiable to assign the entire payment as the cost of a less efficient use of resources. Nevertheless we shall include 50 per cent as a net gain to the colonists, which amounts to £3,300.

The total net gain to the colonies from the bounties paid for colonial products was, therefore, £33,000 in 1770 and an average of £35,000 for the decade. Our analysis of the effect of the Navigation Acts on colonial exports has included the burden on exports, the benefit of the preferential duties, and the net gain from bounty payments. The sum total of these burdens and benefits is a net burden upon exports of £411,000 for 1770. The average annual burden for the decade 1763-1772 was calculated to be £307,000.

IV

The extra expense of importing competitive European products from England acted as a protective wall which permitted increases in English prices. . . . Those [statistics] which exist tend to confirm . . . the theory that transshipment was costly. —Lawrence Harper[33]

The clauses of the Navigation Acts that sought to make England the chief source of supply for manufactured goods were not burdensome . . . . There was a distinct effort to make the British market attractive to colonial purchasers. — Oliver Dickerson[34]

British law required that the colonies purchase their East Indian and European goods in England. The colonies actually purchased three quarters of their imports from the mother country, of which about 20 per cent were goods originally manufactured in Europe or Asia. These imported goods also bore the burden of an indirect route to the colonies, analogous to that borne by tobacco destined to be consumed in Europe. This burden was reflected in higher prices for goods of foreign manufacture in the colonies than otherwise would have been the case.

---

[31] Figured on the basis of an annual bounty of about £ 20,000. Then around £ 10,000 would have been the value of the bounty to the producers of indigo.

[32] George Louis Beer, *British Colonial Policy, 1754-1765* (New York: Macmillan, 1907), p. 224.

[33] "Navigation Acts," p. 36.

[34] P. 70.

Our method for calculating the burden borne by colonial imports of foreign manufactures is similar to the method used to calculate the cost of enumeration on colonial goods reexported to Europe. Two commodities, tea and pepper, for which both colonial and Amsterdam prices are available, were selected as our sample.[35] Tea and pepper accounted for about 16 per cent of the value of foreign goods imported into the colonies through England. The price that would have obtained in the colonies had they been independent was calculated for these goods exactly as in the case of tobacco. The alternative prices of these commodities, according to our estimates, would have averaged 16 per cent lower than they in fact were.[36] Thus, the colonists paid more for their imports of foreign origin than they would have paid had they been independent.

The colonies actually imported foreign goods to the average value of £412,000 for the decade 1763-1772 and of £346,000 for the single year 1770. The burden on the goods, according to our measurement, averaged £66,000 for the decade, or £55,000 for 1770. However, the burden on imports should not be calculated on the basis of foreign goods alone. The burden should also be calculated on goods of English manufacture which were made competitive in the colonial markets by virtue of the artificially increased cost of foreign goods forced to travel an indirect route to the colonies.

The bounty laws benefiting English manufactures which were designed to make English goods competitive with those of foreign manufacture give us a clue to the identity of these English manufactures. If goods of English manufacture required a bounty to compete with similar foreign goods suffering the handicap of an indirect shipment, then the colonists, if independent, would have purchased foreign instead of English goods. Thus, some English goods actually purchased by the colonists would not have been purchased if the colonies had been independent.

Linen was the most important of these goods; the list also included cottons and silks. The colonies thus paid more for most nonwoolen textiles than they would have if they had existed outside the British Empire. The additional monetary loss resulting from the purchase of English rather than foreign goods was calculated to average £73,000 for the decade or £61,000 for 1770 alone.[37] The colonists thus paid a total of £116,000 more in 1770 or £139,000 average for the decade for their imports than they would have if independent. If we assume, for convenience, a price elasticity of demand for imports of one, the colonists would have spent the same amount on imports but they would have received more goods for their money.[38]

---

35 Colonial prices are to be found in Bezanson and Amsterdam prices in Posthumus.

36 Bjork, *Journal of Economic History*, XXIV, (1964), 554, found that goods of foreign manufacture (his Index A) fell dramatically in price after the Revolution, while goods in which Britain had a comparative advantage fell little if at all in price (his Index B).

37 This loss was calculated by taking the percentage unit burden on the price of such imports times their total value.

38 The consumer surplus lost to the colonists because of higher import prices could be easily calculated in the Hotelling-Harberger manner.

The results of this preliminary investigation into the effects of the Navigation Acts upon the foreign commerce of the American colonies are found in Table 1. The result is an overall burden for the year 1770 of £532,000, and an average of £451,000 for the decade.

V

The fact is that colonial shipowners suffered, directly, and colonial shipowners, indirectly, under the Navigation Acts.—Lawrence Harper[39]

Instead of being oppressive the shipping clauses of the Navigation Acts had become an important source of colonial prosperity which was shared by every colony. As a device for launching ships these clauses were more efficient than the fabled beauty of Helen of Troy's face.—Oliver Dickerson[40]

The purpose of the various clauses in the Navigation Acts dealing with shipping was to insure that ships built and manned by Englishmen monopolized this aspect of the foreign commerce of the empire. Colonial vessels, for all intents and purposes, were considered English and shared in the benefits of the monopoly.

Calculation of the resultant colonial benefits was hampered by a lack of available data; therefore, the conclusions should be considered tentative. The estimate was constructed in the following manner: an estimated percentage of the total tonnage entering and clearing colonial ports in 1770 that was colonial owned was calculated from the American Inspector General's ledger. Using an estimated average earnings per ton, it was possible to approximate the shipping earnings deriving from the foreign commerce of the American colonies.[41] The total earnings from shipping the foreign commerce of the thirteen colonies were calculated to be £1,228,000, of which 59.4 per cent, or £730,000, was earned by American vessels.

The next question considered was what these earnings would have been had the colonies been independent. Using as a guide what actually did happen between 1789-1792, after the Revolution but before the outbreak of the war in Europe, I found that the colonies' share of the trade carrying their own commerce declined from 59.4 per cent to 53.2 per cent. On this basis, their shipping earnings in 1770 would have been £653,000 instead of £730,000—a difference of £77,000.

However, as we have seen, had the American colonies been independent their volume of foreign commerce would have been greater. Their ships would have carried a portion of the increased amounts of tobacco, rice, and other exports that would have been shipped, as well as a portion of the larger volume of imports.

---

[39] *Canadian Historical Review*, XXIII (1942), 4.

[40] P. 32.

[41] See James Shepherd, "Colonial Balance of Payments," p. 691, for a discussion of how this estimate was obtained.

My calculations suggest that the volume of shipping required to carry this additional output would have amounted to over 53,000 tons. If American vessels had carried the same percentage of this increased volume as they carried of the total volume in 1789, their earnings in 1770 would have increased to over £742,000—or a little more than they in fact were during the late colonial period. The composition of the trade, however, would have been different.[42]

Thus, it seems fruitless to do more with the effect of the Navigation Acts upon shipping earnings until we know more about shipping rates before and after the Revolution. The best guess, at this time, is that on balance the colonial shipping industry neither gained nor lost from the Navigation Acts.

VI

Indeed, the question ought not be separated from the larger one of the savings offered Americans by the military and naval protection of the British.—Stuart Bruchey[43]

The main obligation of the mother country to its colonies in a mercantilist world was to provide protection. In this area lies the significant benefit to the colonies from membership in an empire. The empire of course also performed certain administrative functions for the colonies from which they benefited.

Great Britain in the defense of the empire could provide for the protection of the American colonies at very little additional expense to itself. That is to say that the colonies, if independent, would have had to expend more resources in their own defense than did England, just to maintain the same level of protection. Our estimate of the value of military and naval protection provided by the British to the colonists, since it is based in part upon actual British expenditures, is therefore too low.

The value of British military protection was estimated as follows. Great Britain, before 1762, maintained a standing army in America of 3,000 officers and men. After 1762, the size of this troop complement was increased to 7,500 men.[44] These troops were garrisoned throughout the colonies, including the frontiers where they served as a defensive force against the incursions of hostile Indians. Each man stationed in America cost the mother country an average of £29 a year, or annually a total expense of at least £217,500.[45]

The colonists constantly complained about the quality of the "redcoats" as Indian fighters. Furthermore, they believed the larger standing army in the colonies after 1762 was there not primarily to protect them but for other

---

[42] Colonial vessels probably would have carried relatively less of the trade with the West Indies, assuming that (as happened after the Revolution) they were excluded from the British West Indies. However, they would also presumably have carried relatively more of the transatlantic trade.

[43] *Roots of American Economic Growth* (New York: Harper and Row, 1916), p. 74.

[44] Knollenberg, p. 34.

[45] Great Britain, *House of Commons Journals*, King George III, Vol. XXXII (1768-1770), sessions no. 1768, 1803.

reasons. However, they found after independence that a standing army of at least 5,000 men was required to replace the British.[46] Thus the benefit to the colonies from the British army stationed in America was conservatively worth at least the cost of 5,000 troops, or £145,000.

Another large colonial benefit stemmed from the protection offered colonial shipping by the British navy, which included the Crown's annual tribute to the Barbary powers. The ability of the British navy to protect its merchant ships from the ravages of pirates far surpassed anything a small independent country could provide. This the colonies learned to their sorrow following the Revolution.

The value of such protection would be reflected in the rise in marine insurance rates for cargoes carried by American vessels after independence. Unfortunately, until research in process is completed, I do not have sufficient data to directly calculate the value of the protection of the British navy in this manner.

However, this benefit can be tentatively measured in an indirect manner. Insurance rates during the 1760's on the West Indies trade one way averaged about 3.5 per cent of the value of the cargo.[47] Rates to England were higher, averaging 7 per cent. These rates on colonial cargoes existed while colonial vessels were protected by the British navy. During the French and Indian War, the risk of seizure increased the rates to the West Indies, which rose steadily until they reached 23 per cent, while rates to England climbed as high as 28 per cent,[48] indicating the influence of risk upon marine insurance rates.

The colonists upon obtaining their independence lost the protection of the British fleet. Insurance rates, as a result, must have increased over the prerevolutionary levels. To estimate the approximate rise in insurance rates, we calculated the percentage decline in insurance rates for American merchant vessels following the launching in 1797 of three frigates which formed the foundation of the small, eighteenth-century American navy.[49]

The percentage difference between the rates on an unprotected merchant marine and those charged on the merchant fleet safeguarded by our small navy was applied to the insurance rates prevailing before the Revolution. The weighted difference in rates between a barely protected merchant marine and a totally unprotected one was slightly over 50 per cent.

Applying this percentage to existing prerevolutionary rates, it appears that the average cargo insurance rate, if the colonies had been independent, would have been at least 8.7 per cent of the value of the cargo instead of 5.4 per cent, a difference in rates of 2.7 per cent. Figuring this increase in insurance charges on the value of colonial cargoes in 1770 gives a low estimate of the value derived from British naval protection of £103,000. Three ships were not the British navy

---

[46] *Historical Statistics*, p. 737.

[47] Harold E. Gillingham, *Marine Insurance Rates in Philadelphia, 1721-1800* (Philadelphia: Patterson & White, 1933), pp. 18, 64.

[48] *Ibid.*

[49] Charles Goldsbourgh, *The United States Naval Chronicle* (Washington, 1824), pp. 109-10.

and could not be expected to provide equal protection. Marine insurance rates thus probably increased more than 2.7 per cent. An estimate that rates doubled does not seem unreasonable and would raise the annual value of naval protection to £206,000.

The estimate of the value of British protection for the American colonies is thus made up of the adjusted cost of the army in the colonies, £145,000, plus the estimated value of naval protection for the merchant marine of £206,000. The estimated total value of the protection afforded the colonies by their membership in the British Empire was thus calculated to be at least £351,000.

By way of a check upon this estimate, the Government of the United States, during its first nine years under the Constitution, found it necessary to spend annually an average of $2,133,000, or £426,600, for national defense.[50] This included the purchase of arms and stores, the fortification of forts and harbors, and the building and manning of a small navy. In addition, an independent America had to bear the expense of conducting an independent foreign policy. The support of ministers to foreign nations, the cost of negotiating and implementing treaties, the payment of tribute to the Barbary nations, all previously provided for by Great Britain, now had to be borne by the independent colonies. These expenses alone cost the United States, during the last decade of the eighteenth century, annually over £60,000.

After achieving independence, the United States found it necessary to spend annually about £487,000 to provide certain functions of government formerly provided by Great Britain. This suggests that our estimate of £351,000 for the value of British protection to the American colonists is too low. It is doubtful, in the light of history, whether the new nation was able to provide this type of governmental services of equal quality to those furnished by the British. If not, even the £487,000 a year understates the value of governmental services supplied by Great Britain to her American colonies.

VII

For reasons which have been explained more fully elsewhere we shall reject Beer's claim that there was no exploitation. —Lawrence Harper[51]

Exploitation . . . by the home country is an economic myth. —Oliver Dickerson[52]

My findings with reference to the effect of the Navigation Acts upon the economy of the thirteen colonies indicate a net burden of £532,000, or $2,660,000, in 1770. The average burden for the decade 1763-1772, based upon official values, was somewhat lower—£451,000, or $2,255,000. These estimates are near the lowest estimates made by Harper and seem to strengthen his case that exploitation did exist.[53]

---

50 U.S. Congress, *American State Papers, Finance,* III, 14th Cong., 1st sess., 63, 69.

51 *Canadian Historical Review,* XXIII (1942) 2.

52 P. xiv.

53 Harper estimated that the burden on tobacco, rice, European goods imported, and

Considering for a moment only the value of the losses on colonial exports and imports, the per capita annual cost to the colonist of being an Englishman instead of an American was $1.24 in 1770. The average per capita cost for the decade based upon official values was a somewhat lower $1.20. The benefits per capita in 1770 were figured to be 82 cents, and for the decade 94 cents. Subtracting the benefits from the burdens for 1770 shows a per capita loss of 42 cents. The estimate for the decade shows a smaller loss of 26 cents a person. It is unlikely, because of the nature of the estimating procedures employed, that these losses are too low. Conversely it is not at all improbable, and for the same reasons, that the estimated losses are too high.

TABLE 2
Summary of the Results

	1763-1772		1770	
Burdens				
Burden on colonial				
foreign commerce	£	451,000	£	532,000
		or		or
	$	2,255,000	$	2,660,000
Burden per capita[a]	$	1.20	$	1.24
Benefits				
Benefit of British				
protection	£	351,000	£	351,000
		or		or
	$	1,775,000	$	1,775,000
Benefit per capita	$	.94	$	.82
Balance[b]				
Estimate I	$	-.26	$	-.42

[a]Population for the decade average was figured to be 1,881,000 and for 1770 to be 2,148,000.

[b]The balance was obtained by subtracting the per capita benefits from the per capita burden.

Suppose that these findings reflect the true magnitude of the cost of the Navigation Acts to the thirteen colonies. The relevant question becomes: How important were these losses? Albert Fishlow stated at last year's meetings that he believed that the average per capita income in the 1780's "could not have been much less than $100."[54] George Rogers Taylor, in his presidential address, hazarded a guess that per capita income did not grow very rapidly, if at all, between 1775 and 1840.[55] Therefore, assuming that average per capita income

---

the benefits of bounties together added up to a burden of between $2,560,000 and $7,038,000. Harper's estimate of the loss on tobacco and rice really measured the area $(P^1.A.B.P^3)$ in Graph 1 rather than $(P^1.A.E.P^2)$, which is the correct area. However his lower estimate is rather close to ours.

[54] *Journal of Economic History*, XXIV (1964), 566.

[55] *Ibid.*, p. 429.

hovered about $100 between 1763 and 1772, what would it have been had the colonies been independent?

The answer is obvious from Table 2: it would not have been much different. The largest estimated loss on this basis is .54 of 1 per cent of per capita income, or 54 cents on a hundred dollars. Suppose for a moment that my estimates are off by 100 per cent; then, in that case the largest burden would be slightly more than 1 per cent of national income. It is difficult to make a convincing case for exploitation out of these results.

3. Inequality and instability: the relation of land tenure to politics*

BRUCE M. RUSSETT†

I

At least since the ancient Greeks many thinkers have regarded great diversity of wealth as incompatible with stable government. According to Euripides:

> In a nation there be orders three: —
> The useless rich, that ever crave for more;
> The have-nots, straitened even for sustenance,
> A dangerous folk, of envy overfull,
> Which shoot out baleful stings at such as have,
> Beguiled by tongues of evil men, their "champions":
> But of the three the midmost saveth states;
> They keep the order which the state ordains.[1]

Alexis de Tocqueville, writing many centuries later, declared: "Remove the secondary causes that have produced the great convulsions of the world and you will almost always find the principle of inequality at the bottom. Either the poor have attempted to plunder the rich, or the rich to enslave the poor. If, then, a state of society can ever be founded in which every man shall have something to keep and little to take from others, much will have been done for the peace of the world."[2]

---

* This article is part of the research of the Yale Political Data Program, supported by a grant from the National Science Foundation. I am grateful to John Shingler and Seth Singleton for research assistance. An earlier version was presented at the Annual Meeting of the American Political Science Association, September 1963. Reprinted from *World Politics,* XVI (April, 1964), pp. 442-54, by permission of the publisher and the author.

† Bruce M. Russett, professor of political science, Yale University, received his Ph.D. from Yale University. He is the author of *World Handbook of Political and Social Indicators, Trends in World Politics* and *Community and Contention: Britain and America in the Twentieth Century.*

1 "The Suppliants," *The Tragedies of Euripides,* trans. by Arthur S. Way (London 1894), 373.

2 Alexis de Tocqueville, *Democracy in America* (Vintage edn., New York 1954), II, 266.

Many modern writers echo the same thought. Merle Kling, for example, blames political instability in Latin America on the extreme concentration of economic bases of power in what he terms "colonial economies." Land ownership, he says, is so heavily concentrated that no individual not already possessing great tracts of agricultural land can reasonably hope to achieve wealth through farming. Foreign exploitation of mineral resources effectively blocks the ambitious native from that source of wealth. Industry remains rudimentary. Of the possible sources of enrichment, only government is open to competition. Political office provides such a unique source of gain that "large segments of the population are prepared to take the ultimate risk of life, in a revolt, in a *coup d'état,* to perpetuate a characteristic feature of Latin American politics—chronic political instability."[3]

Both Plato and Karl Marx so despaired of the pernicious effects of wealth that they saw no way to abolish the evil except to abolish private property itself. Tocqueville, on the other hand, thought that he found in America a society which had been able to reach another solution: "Between these two extremes [very few rich men and few poor ones] of democratic communities stands an innumerable multitude of men almost alike, who, without being exactly either rich or poor, possess sufficient property to desire the maintenance of order, yet not enough to excite envy. Such men are the natural enemies of violent commotions; their lack of agitation keeps all beneath them and above them still and secures the balance of the fabric of society."[4]

Yet if we check the matter empirically with present-day polities the answer is not so clear-cut. Wealth is everywhere distributed unequally; even in the most egalitarian societies the income of the rich is many times that of the poor. And one can readily point to a number of instances—such as Spain—where, despite an impressionistic judgment that goods are distributed highly unequally, the polity is seemingly stable under the rule of a dictator.

Part of the difficulty stems from a conceptual problem, a lack of clarity about just what is the dependent variable. Is economic inequality incompatible with *stable* government, or merely with *democratic* or *"good"* government? If we mean stable government, do we mean regimes in which the rulers maintain themselves in power for long periods despite the chronic outbreak of violence (Colombia and South Vietnam), or simply the avoidance of significant violence even though governments may topple annually (France throughout most of the Third and Fourth Republics)? Or must "stable" government be both peaceful and reasonably long-term? Finally, what do we mean by the government? A particular individual (Spain), a particular party (Uruguay), the essential maintenance of a particular coalition (France under the system of "replastering"), or the continued dominance of a particular social stratum (Jordan)?

Another part of the difficulty stems from the absence of comparative study.

---

3 Merle Kling, "Toward a Theory of Power and Political Instability in Latin America," *Western Political Quarterly,* IX (March 1956), 21-35. Note that land distribution is only one element of the "colonial economy" defined by Kling.

4 Tocqueville, 266.

Numerous authors have examined the distribution of agricultural land in particular countries or areas, and its contribution to a particular political situation. Several books have drawn together studies giving attention to many different nations.[5] But none of these have been based on the same concepts or have presented data for the same variables in a manner necessary for true comparative analysis. Case studies are essential for providing depth and insight, but generalization requires eventual attention to many cases.

Comparative analysis is dependent on the provision of comparable data. For instance, one may know that in contemporary England the upper 5 per cent of income earners receive over 15 per cent of all current income, even after taxes.[6] Is this high or low compared with other nations? All too often the necessary data simply are not available or, if they are, they are not in comparable form. For another country one may, for instance, know the proportion of income going to the top 10 per cent and top 1 per cent of earners, but not to the top 5 per cent, as in England.

In this article we shall attempt to clarify the problem conceptually, present for the first time a large body of distribution data, and test some hypotheses about the relation between economic inequality and politics. First, the data. We shall be concerned with information on the degree to which agricultural land is concentrated in the hands of a few large landholders. Information on land tenure is more readily available, and is of more dependable comparability, than are data on the distribution of other economic assets like current income or total wealth.[7] Material on land distribution is available for many countries about which we know nothing precise or reliable in regard to income distribution. In addition, land distribution is intrinsically of major interest. Kling's theory of Latin American political instability was built in large part on land inequality; the United States government has long warned its allies in poorer nations about the need for land reform. In Japan, and to a lesser extent in South Korea, the American military government took upon itself a major redistribution of land with the intention of providing the necessary bases for political democracy.

II

I have discussed elsewhere the uses of various summary statistical measures designed to indicate the degree of inequality in a distribution.[8] Here we shall

---

[5] See, for example, Kenneth Parsons, *et al.,* eds., *Land Tenure* (Madison 1958), and Walter Froelich, *Land Tenure, Industrialization, and Social Stability* (Milwaukee 1961).

[6] Robert M. Solow, "Income Inequality Since the War," in *Postwar Economic Trends in the United States,* ed. by Ralph Freeman (New York 1960).

[7] One must always introduce comparative data, particularly on land tenure, with certain caveats. The quality of data collection is not uniform from one country to the next, and in any case it cannot indicate the quality of the land in question. Nevertheless, while these caveats may be important with regard to a few distributions, they do not fundamentally alter the character of the data shown.

Although a few of the data presented were compiled some time ago, patterns of land tenure normally change but little over the years. Only for Bolivia, Taiwan and, to a lesser degree, Italy is there evidence of a significant change between the year given and 1960.

employ three separate indices, each of which measures somewhat different aspects of land distribution. The first two are directed to the relative size of farms, the last to tenancy.

(1) The *percentage of landholders who collectively occupy one-half of all the agricultural land* (starting with the farmers with the *smallest* plots of land and working toward the *largest*).

(2) *The Gini index of concentration.* We begin with a Lorenz curve (Figure 1) drawn by connecting the points given in a cumulative distribution (e.g., the proportion of land held by each decile of farmers). All farms are ranked in order from the smallest to the largest, so that one can say what proportion of the total *number* of farms accounts for a given proportion of the total *area* of agricultural land. In Figure 1 the cumulated percentage of farms is given along the horizontal axis, and the cumulated percentage of the area along the vertical axis. The 45° line represents the condition of perfect quality, wherein each percentile of farmers would make an equal contribution to the cumulated total of agricultural land. Thus, under complete equality each 10 per cent of the population would

FIGURE 1
Lorenz Curves of Land Distribution: Austria and Bolivia

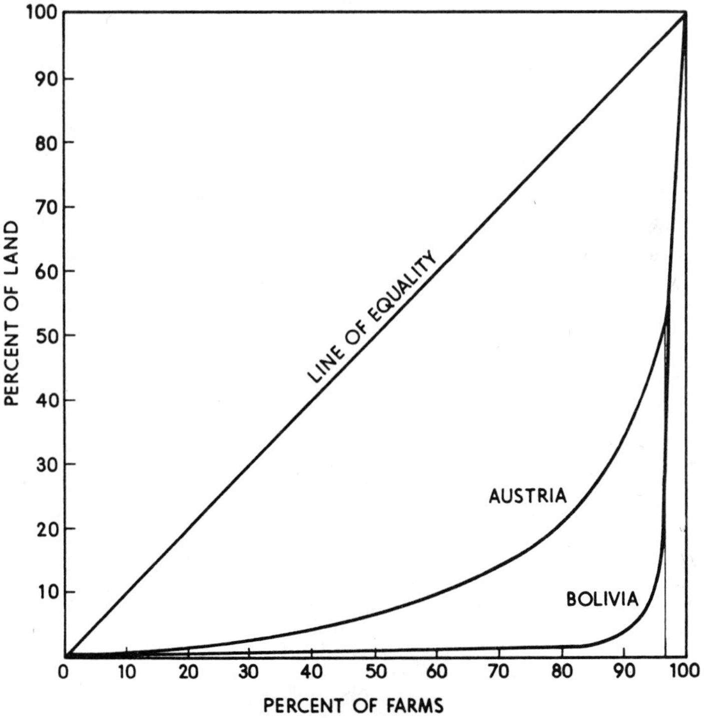

[8] Hayward R. Alker, Jr., and Bruce M. Russett, "Indices for Comparing Inequality," in *Comparing Nations: The Use of Quantitative Data in Cross-National Research*, ed. by R. L. Merritt and Stein Rokkan (New Haven 1964).

have exactly 10 per cent of the land; any two-thirds of the population would have exactly two-thirds of the land. How far in fact the curve for a particular distribution departs from the "line of equality" gives us a visual measure of the inequality involved.

The Lorenz curve provides an extremely useful way of showing the complete pattern of a distribution, but it is impractical to try to compare whole Lorenz curves for any substantial number of countries. But if we measure the *area* between the cumulated distribution and the line of equality we have the Gini index, a simple summary measure of the total inequality of a distribution.[9] The Gini index calculates over the whole population the difference between an "ideal" cumulative distribution of land (where all farms are the same size) and the actual distribution. The higher the Gini index, the greater the inequality.

Though the percentage of farmers with one-half the land is simple and useful, the more comprehensive Gini index, by examining the whole distribution, is in many ways superior. The curves for the two countries in Figure 1, for example, both show virtually the same percentage of farmers with half the land. But below the 50 per cent mark, the distribution for Bolivia is much more unequal than is that for Austria. In Bolivia the top 10 per cent of all farmers owned nearly 95 per cent of the land; in Austria the top 10 per cent of farmers owned only about 65 per cent of the land. The implications for a theory of political stability are obvious. (The Bolivian figures actually apply to 1950. Since that date Bolivia has experienced a social revolution.)

(3) Probably less important than the relative size of farms, but still relevant, is the question of *ownership*. If a farmer tills a substantial piece of land but nevertheless must pay much of the produce to a landlord, the effect may be much the same as if he actually owned a much smaller plot. Therefore we also present data, where available, on *farm households that rent all their land as a percentage of the total number of farms*.

It is even more difficult to find a satisfactory operational definition of stability than measure inequality. In our effort to account for different aspects of "stability," we shall use several quite different indices.

(A) *Instability of Personnel.* One measure of stability is simply the term of office of the chief executive. As the numerator of our index, we have used the number of years during the period 1945-1961 in which a country was independent; and, as the denominator, the number of individuals who held the

---

[9] The Gini number for a Lorenz curve is actually twice the area mentioned divided by the area (10,000 for 100 by 100 axes) of the whole square. Formula:

$$G = \frac{2\int_0^{100} (x\text{-}f(x)) \ dx}{10,000}$$

where x is the cumulated population percentage and f (x) is the height of the Lorenz curve. Cf. Mary Jean Bowman, "A Graphical Analysis of Personal Income Distribution in the United States," *American Economic Review,* xxxv (September 1945), 607-28. In Table 1 below, the Gini index is multiplied by 100.

3. Inequality and instability: the relation of land tenure to politics 361

post of chief executive during the same period. By subtracting this figure from 17 (the number of years in the period) we obtain what we shall term the index of "personnel instability." It may vary from 0 to 17; in fact, the highest figure in our sample is 16.32 for France.[10]

(B) *Internal Group Violence.* Rudolph Rummel, in his Dimensionality of Nations Project, collected data on the number of people killed as a result of internal group violence—i.e., civil wars, revolutions, and riots—during the years 1955-1957. We have extended the time period to 1950-1962, and have modified the data to allow for the size of the total population in question, making the index deaths per 1,000,000 people.[11]

(C) *Internal War.* As an alternative to the violent-death material, we shall use Harry Eckstein's data on internal war for the period 1946-1961.[12] These data include the total number of violent incidents, from plots to protracted guerrilla warfare.

(D) Quite a different problem is the *Stability of Democracy.* With few adaptations we shall use the distinctions employed by Seymour Martin Lipset. "Stable democracies" will be defined as states that have been characterized by the uninterrupted continuation of political democracy since World War I, *and* the absence over the past thirty years of a totalitarian movement, either Fascist or Communist, which at any point received as much as 20 per cent of the vote. "Unstable democracies," again following Lipset, are countries which, although unable to meet the first criteria, nevertheless have a "history of more or less free elections for most of the post-World War I period."[13] "Dictatorships" are those countries in which, perhaps despite some democratic interludes, free elections

---

10 With this definition, most of the indices fall between 11 and 17. Our use of logarithmic transformations in the correlations below compensates for this bunching.

In some ways it might have been more desirable to measure the average tenure of a party or coalition, but that solution raises other problems. When a government in the French Fourth Republic fell and was replaced by a new cabinet composed basically of the same parties, was this a new coalition or just the old one under a new Premier? The first answer immediately involves one in difficulties of comparability with other countries' experiences; the second answer would cause France to appear much more stable than any observer would agree was correct.

Measuring the tenure of the chief executive tells nothing about the *form* of government, nor about what Kling (p. 25) describes as concealed instability. A government may appear stable only as long as its repressive techniques succeed; when they fail, it may be violently and suddenly overthrown. Thus Trujillo's Dominican Republic was "stable" for several decades. Nevertheless it is difficult to see how "hidden instability" can be allowed for other than through some definition of a democratic-dictatorial continuum, which we attempt in index D below.

11 Cf. Rudolph J. Rummel, "Dimensions of Conflict Behavior Within and Between Nations," in *General Systems,* Yearbook of the Society for the Advancement of General Systems Theory (Ann Arbor 1963). The nature and limitations of the data used in this article will be discussed in Bruce M. Russett *et al., World Handbook of Political and Social Indicators* (New Haven 1964).

12 Harry Eckstein, *Internal War: The Problem of Anticipation,* a report submitted to the Research Group in Psychology and the Social Sciences, Smithsonian Institution (Washington 1962), Appendix I.

13 Seymour Martin Lipset, "Some Social Requisites of Democracy," *American Political Science Review,* LIII (March 1959), 73-74.

TABLE 1
Land Distribution and Political Stability, 47 Countries

Country	Land Data			Political Data			Economic Data	
	Gini Index	% of Farms with ½ Land	% of Farms Rented	Personnel Insta-bility	Eckstein Internal War	Deaths from Civil Group Violence per 1,000,000	GNP Per Capita ($ 1055)	% Labor Force in Agriculture
Yugoslavia	43.7	79.8	0*	0	9	0	297	67
Poland	45.0	77.7	0*	8.5	19	5.0	468	57
Denmark	45.8	79.3	3.5	14.6	0	0	913	23
Japan	47.0	81.5	2.9	15.7	22	0.1	240	40
Canada	49.7	82.9	7.2	11.3	22*	0	1667	12
Switzerland	49.8	81.5	18.9	8.5	0	0	1229	10
India	52.2	86.9	53.0	3.0	83	14.0	72	71
Philippines	56.4	88.2	37.3	14.0	15	292.0	201	59
Sweden	57.7	87.2	18.9	8.5	0	0	1165	13
France	58.3	86.1	26.0	16.3	46	0.3	1046	26
Belgium	58.7	85.8	62.3	15.5	8	0.9	1015	10
Ireland	59.8	85.9	2.5†	14.2	9	0	509	40
Finland	59.9	86.3	2.4	15.6	4	0	941	46
Netherlands	60.5	86.2	53.3	13.6	2	0	708	11
Luxembourg	63.8	87.7	18.8	12.8	0	0	1194	23
Taiwan	65.2	94.1	40.0	0	3	0	102	50
Norway	66.9	87.5	7.5	12.8	1	0	969	26
South Vietnam	67.1	94.6	20.0*	10.0	50*	1000*	133	65
West Germany	67.4	93.0	5.7	3.0	4	0	762	14
Libya	70.0	93.0	8.5	14.8	8	0*	90	75
United States	70.5	95.4	20.4	12.8	22*	0	2343	10
United Kingdom	71.0	93.4	44.5	13.6	12	0	998	5

Country						
Panama	73.7	95.0	12.3	15.6	29	25.0	54
Austria	74.0	97.4	10.7	12.8	4	0	32
Egypt	74.0	98.1	11.6	15.8	45	1.6	64
Greece	74.7	99.4	17.7	15.8	9	2.0	48
Honduras	75.7	97.4	16.7	13.6	45	111.0	66
Nicaragua	75.7	96.4	n.a.	12.8	16	16.0	68
New Zealand	77.3	95.5	22.3	12.8	0	0	16
Spain	78.0	99.5	43.7	0	22	0.2	50
Cuba	79.2	97.8	53.8	13.6	100	2900.0*	42
Dominican Rep.	79.5	98.5	20.8	11.3	6	31.0	56
Italy	80.3	98.0	23.8	15.5	51	0.2	29
Uruguay	81.7	96.6	34.7	14.6	1	0.3	37
El Salvador	82.8	98.8	15.1	15.1	9	2.0	63
Brazil	83.7	98.5	9.1	15.5	49	1.0	61
Colombia	84.9	98.1	12.1	14.6	47	316.0	55
Guatemala	86.0	99.7	17.0	14.9	45	57.0	68
Argentina	86.3	98.2	32.9	13.6	57	217.0	25
Ecuador	86.4	99.3	14.6	15.1	41	18.0	53
Peru	87.5	96.9	n.a.	14.6	23	26.0	60
Iraq	88.1	99.3	75.0*	16.2	24	344.0	81
Costa Rica	80.1	99.1	5.4	14.6	19	24.0	55
Venezuela	90.9	99.3	20.6	14.9	36	111.0	42
Australia	92.9	99.6	n.a.	11.3	0	0.0	14
Chile	93.8	99.7	13.4	14.2	21	2.0	30
Bolivia	93.8	97.7	20.0	15.3	53	663.0	72

Sources:

GNP: Norton Ginsburg, *Atlas of Economic Development* (Chicago 1962), 22.
Land, Personal Instability, Violent Deaths, and Percentage of Labor Force in Agriculture: Russett, *World Handbook* (forthcoming).
Internal War: Eckstein, Appendix I.
*Yale Data Program estimate—very approximate.
†% Area (not farms) rented.

have been generally absent. These judgments are impressionistic and do not permit precise rankings from most to least democratic; nevertheless they generally agree with those of other scholars and with widely accepted standards.[14]

Note again that our political dependent variables measure distinctly different aspects—stability of executive personnel, the incidence of violence, and "democracy." No one is by itself an adequate measure of all the conditions to which land distribution has been thought relevant.

Table 1 indicates the rankings of 47 countries (all those for which distribution data are available) on the first six of these indices. It also gives 1955 *GNP per capita,* in U.S. dollars, and the *percentage of the labor force employed in agriculture* in the most recent year for which we have data. The possible relevance of these additional variables will be discussed below.

III

Land is everywhere distributed unequally. In even the most egalitarian states, about four-fifths of the farmers are concentrated on only half the land. Still, the degree of inequality varies widely from state to state. Table 2 presents the correlation coefficients (r) indicating the degree of association between each of the three measures of land distribution and each of the first three indices of instability.[15]

For the three indices of inequality there is in each case a positive relationship

TABLE 2
Correlation Coefficients (r) for Measures of Land Equality
with Measures of Political Instability for 47 Countries

	Personnel Instability	Violent Politi- cal Deaths (per 1,000,000)	Eckstein Internal War Data
% of Farms with ½ Land	.24	.45	.35
Gini Index	.33	.46	.29
% of Farms Rented (44 countries only)	.01	.27	.11

---

[14] For a similar classification of regimes in the underdeveloped countries, see Gabriel A. Almond and James S. Coleman, eds., *The Politics of the Developing Areas* (Princeton 1960), 579-81.

Lipset's categorization is of course crude and subject to a number of criticisms. For example, cf. Phillips Cutright, "National Political Development: Measurement and Analysis," *American Sociological Review,* XXVIII (April 1963), 253-64. The alternative index that Cutright suggests, however, really deals with the complexity of political institutions— quite a different matter.

[15] For the three political variables, I used logarithmic transformations instead of the raw data.

to instability, though in two instances the correlation is extremely slight. The highest correlation is between violent deaths and the Gini index. Judged by the standards of most social science this is a fairly high correlation, with a significance level of .001 (i.e., unless there really were a positive relationship between land distribution and instability, this high a correlation would not occur, purely by chance, as often as one time in a thousand). Nevertheless, these correlations indicate that much remains unexplained. Even the highest (.46) gives an r^2 of only .21. (The squared product moment coefficient—r^2—can be interpreted as the percentage of the total variation in one index that can be explained by another.) Inequality of land distribution does bear a relation to political instability, but that relationship is not a strong one, and many other factors must be considered in any attempted explanation.[16] The degree to which farm land is rented is not a factor of great explanatory power, given the low level of the correlations of rental with all the stability indices.

A more complex hypothesis, closely related to Kling's, might read as follows: extreme inequality of land distribution leads to political instability only in those poor, predominantly agricultural societies where limitation to a small plot of land almost unavoidably condemns one to poverty. In a rich country, the modest income a farmer can produce from even a small holding may satisfy him. Or, if that is not the case, at least in wealthy countries there are, besides agriculture, many alternative sources of wealth.[17] Finally, one might assert that the *combination* of inequality *and* a high rate of tenancy would cause instability. While neither by itself would necessarily lead to violence or frequent change of government, the combination almost inevitably would.

To test these hypotheses we examined simultaneously the effect of GNP per capita, percentage of labor force in agriculture, tenancy, and land distribution on our various indices of political stability.[18] These refinements improved our

---

[16] Nor is great concentration of farmland always a prelude to violent revolution in predominantly agricultural societies. Even according to figures cited by the Communists, inequality in Czarist Russia and interwar China was less than in most of the countries listed in Table I. Cf. V. I. Lenin, *The Agrarian Programs of Social Democracy,* in *Selected Works,* III (New York, n.d.), 164-65; and Yuan-li Wu, *An Economic Survey of Communist China* (New York 1956), 119. Wu lists several estimates, the most extreme of which was the report of the Hankow Land Commission, which he alleges was Communist-dominated. The Gini indices for Russia and China were, respectively, approximately 73.0 and 64.6.

According to George Pavlovsky, in *Agricultural Russia on the Eve of the Revolution* (London 1930), chap. 4, the difficulty in Russia stemmed less from the *relative* size of farm plots than from the fact that the *absolute* size of most holdings was too small to produce more than bare subsistence. Given the technological backwardness of the Russian peasant, this may well be true.

[17] "Rich" countries and "societies where there are many alternative sources of wealth" are to some degree synonymous. Denmark and Australia, two rich nations often thought of as "agricultural," actually have only 23 and 14 per cent, respectively, of their labor forces in agriculture.

[18] The technique used was multiple regression. For a description and application of this method, see Donald Stokes, Angus Campbell, and Warren Miller, "Components of Electoral Decision," *American Political Science Review,* LII (June 1958), 367-87. This procedure also allows us to test for the independent "explanatory" power of each variable with the other variables *controlled.*

explanation rather strikingly in some cases. The strongest relationship was between the Gini index and violent deaths; r^2 was raised to .50. By far the most important variables in the equations for "predicting" instability were first the Gini index and then the percentage of the population in agriculture, as suggested by our first hypothesis. The percentage of farms rented again added little explanatory power. Qualifications of this sort help to explain the stability of a country like Australia, despite a highly unequal distribution of agricultural land. Venezuela's land distribution is also very unequal (but no more so than Australia's), yet Venezuela is somewhat poorer and has three times as many people (proportionately) employed in agriculture.[19] All the indices of instability are quite high for Venezuela. Nevertheless, even the strongest relationship found among these variables leaves over half the variance "unexplained"—as the sophisticated student of politics might expect. The old saws about equality can be accepted only with caution.

There remains one other possibility yet to be explored—that equality may be

TABLE 3
Stable Democracies, Unstable Democracies, and Dictatorships
by Degree of Inequality in Land Distribution

Gini Index	Stable Democracies	Unstable Democracies	Dictatorships
Greater than Median Equality	Denmark Canada Switzerland India Philippines Sweden Belgium Ireland Netherlands Luxembourg Norway United States United Kingdom	Japan France Finland West Germany	Yugoslavia Poland Taiwan South Vietnam Libya Panama
Median Equality or Less	New Zealand Uruguay Australia	Austria Greece Italy Brazil Colombia Argentina Costa Rica Chile	Egypt Honduras Nicaragua Spain Cuba Dominican Rep. El Salvador Guatemala Ecuador Peru Iraq Venezuela Bolivia

[19] This points up rather sharply the flaw in any attempt to use land distribution as an indicator of the degree of inequality in all wealth for *advanced* economies. Australia is widely acknowledged to be a highly egalitarian society.

related to the stability of a *democratic regime*. That is, there may or may not be sporadic outbreaks of violence; there may or may not be frequent changes of personnel at the highest level; but it is highly unlikely that a nation with a grossly unequal pattern of distribution of a major source of wealth, like agricultural land, will have a consistently democratic government. Table 3 presents a sixfold table showing each of the countries in our sample classified, after Lipset, as a "stable democracy," an "unstable democracy," or a "dictatorship,"[20] and also listed as above or below the median for the Gini index of land inequality.

The results are again quite striking. Of the 23 states with the more equal pattern of land distribution, 13 are stable democracies, whereas only three of 24 more unequal countries can be classified as stable democracies. And of these three, each is a fairly rich state where agriculture is no longer the principal source of wealth. Tocqueville's basic observation would therefore appear correct: no state can long maintain a democratic form of government if the major sources of economic gain are divided very unequally among its citizens. American policy in urging the governments of underdeveloped nations to undertake massive land reform programs seems essentially well-founded. A "sturdy yeomanry" may be a virtual *sine qua non* for democratic government in an underdeveloped land. Nevertheless there are many instances where relative equality of land tenure is not associated with stable democracy; it is no *guarantee* of democratic development. Land reform may provide the soil to nourish free institutions, but the seed must first be planted.

---

[20] Note that these definitions of stability say nothing about the rate of turnover among government personnel, but only about the stability of democratic forms of government. We have included India and the Philippines in the category "stable democracy" because, though independent only since the end of World War II, they met the above test. Nevertheless this decision is open to some question, as political conditions in these countries clearly are *not* the same as in Western Europe. If they instead were classified as "unstable democracies" it would, however, only very moderately change the pattern of the following table.

PART VI

Voters and publics: studies in legislative and electoral history

Legislative and electoral behavior comprise one of the richest areas for historical research of a quantitative nature. Public records of legislative voting exist for the last two centuries in the United States and many European countries, and in some cases are carried back even farther. Similarly, records of general and local elections, although usually more difficult to find collected in a single record or location, exist in great abundance for the 19th and 20th centuries—it being understood, of course, that the quality and quantity of the records vary considerably by country and time period.

As such, legislative and electoral materials constitute a body of information of considerable magnitude and richness about the political habits of the past. As W. O. Aydelotte puts it, these data can be considered "a kind of questionnaire which we may submit to the dead and on which they will give us their replies." This is particularly true of research in legislative behavior, which can tap an usually broad spectrum of information concerning the opinions, attitudes, and career patterns of past and present elites. Most important, as Aydelotte also points out in this context, we are not dealing with scattered individuals whose opinions may or may not be representative or even "responsible,"[1] but with

[1] Arthur Schlesinger, Jr., "The Humanist Looks at Empirical Social Research," *American Sociological Review,* 27 (December, 1962), p. 769, in his critical discussion of public opinion polling, defines "responsible opinion" as an "opinion which issues directly in decision and action."

relatively complete universes of constitutionally selected men whose votes represent the culmination of a complex decision-making process.

Drawing significant inferences from electoral behavior is a much more delicate and difficult problem because of certain limitations that are built into the data. Electoral records are aggregate records—that is they are an aggregate of hundreds and thousands of individual decisions, usually recorded in such a way that there is no direct path back to the individual or even to a group of individuals. For this reason, generalizations that commit the ecological fallacy of arguing individual characteristics on the basis of group or aggregate character-istics are properly regarded with considerable suspicion by social scientists. Yet, in many cases where survey research data, which can and do bridge this kind of gap, are lacking, the historian is obliged to go ahead and take the calculated risk rather than to do nothing because he does not have perfect or ideal data. Is he in any worse case than the historian who goes ahead and takes newspaper editorials as representing public opinion? Or is he in a better case in that he has the possibility of checking his inferences by using correlational techniques and controlling for the presence or absence of certain characteristics?

One might point out at this juncture that the historian of the future who will deal with our times will be in a much better position to say something significant about public opinion and political attitudes as a result of the increasing amount of opinion surveys that are being made. Instead of basing generalizations about what "the people" believed or what "the group" thought on highly biased and unrepresentative newspaper editorials, or scattered and even more unrepresent-ative and biased literary sources, the historian of the future may have precise, representative surveys of the attitudes of an entire public on questions vital to historical understanding. As Paul Lazarsfeld suggests in his excellent essay, "The Obligations of the 1950 Pollster to the 1984 Historian," the possibility of an interplay between polling and history might be a source of methodological and substantive innovation for both fields.

Electoral and legislative behavior are probably the areas in which the historian will be able to use a broad variety of statistical techniques, running from the simple, but useful and widely used technique of Rice indexing, through various kinds of scaling techniques, to perhaps one of the heaviest statistical weapons in the quantitative arsenal—factor analysis. This type of material, in fact, is particularly well suited to the application of quantitative methods, and does not lend itself to simple visual inspection or impressionistic description, as anyone who has ever attempted to analyze the votes of over 500 men or issues will readily testify.

Moreover, it is in these areas of research that historians have a distinctive contribution to make—to create models of political behavior which will embrace a dimension oftentimes neglected by other social scientists—namely, change over time. Until we have studies of legislative and electoral behavior for periods of time longer than we now have, our present knowledge and interpretation will lack an important element of meaning. As Professors Clubb and Allen point out in their essay, we do not really know whether high or low agreement for

American parties is normal or abnormal without this kind of important information. Professor Shover underlines once again V. O. Key's pointed reminder that analysis of foreshortened time series is dangerously misleading, and thus supports more generally the cause of a greater attention to a more systematic and comparative analysis of political behavior extending over time.

1. New perspectives on Jacksonian politics*

RICHARD P. McCORMICK†

The historical phenomenon that we have come to call Jacksonian democracy has long engaged the attention of American political historians, and never more insistently than in the past decade. From the time of Parton and Bancroft to the present day scholars have recognized that a profoundly significant change took place in the climate of politics simultaneously with the appearance of Andrew Jackson on the presidential scene. They have sensed that a full understanding of the nature of that change might enable them to dissolve some of the mysteries that envelop the operation of the American democratic process. With such a challenging goal before them, they have pursued their investigations with uncommon intensity and with a keen awareness of the contemporary relevance of their findings.

A cursory view of the vast body of historical writing on this subject suggests that scholars in the field have been largely preoccupied with attempts to define the content of Jacksonian democracy and identify the influences that shaped it.[1] What did Jacksonian democracy represent, and what groups, classes, or sections gave it its distinctive character? The answers that have been given to

---

* Reprinted from the *American Historical Review*, LXV (January, 1960), pp. 288-301, by permission of the author.

† Mr. McCormick, professor of history at Rutgers University and author of *The History of Voting in New Jersey: A Study of the Development of Election Machinery, 1664-1911*, is interested primarily in American political history. The present study was made possible by a grant from the Social Science Research Council. Editors note: McCormick, received his Ph.D. from the University of Pennsylvania. He is also the author of *The Second American Party System: Party Formation in the Jacksonian Era;* and *Experiment in Independence: New Jersey in the Critical Period*.

[1] For a concise survey of the literature on the topic, see Charles G. Sellers, Jr., *Jacksonian Democracy* (Washington, D. C., 1958) or his "Andrew Jackson versus the Historians," *Mississippi Valley Historical Review*, XLIV (Mar. 1958), 615-34. For the most recent treatment of the period, see Glyndon G. Van Deusen, *The Jacksonian Era, 1828-1848*, The New American Nation Series, ed. Henry Steele Commager and Richard B. Morris (New York, 1959).

these central questions have been—to put it succinctly—bewildering in their variety. The discriminating student, seeking the essential core of Jacksonianism, may make a choice among urban workingmen, southern planters, venturous conservatives, farm-bred *nouveaux riches,* western frontiersmen, frustrated entrepreneurs, or yeoman farmers. Various as are these interpretations of the motivating elements that constituted the true Jacksonians, the characterizations of the programmatic features of Jacksonian democracy are correspondingly diverse. Probably the reasonable observer will content himself with the conclusion that many influences were at work and that latitudinarianism prevailed among the Jacksonian faithful.

In contrast with the controversy that persists over these aspects of Jacksonian democracy, there has been little dissent from the judgment that "the 1830's saw the triumph in American politics of that democracy which has remained pre-eminently the distinguishing feature of our society."[2] The consensus would seem to be that with the emergence of Jackson, the political pulse of the nation quickened. The electorate, long dormant or excluded from the polls by suffrage barriers, now became fired with unprecedented political excitement. The result was a bursting forth of democratic energies, evidenced by a marked upward surge in voting.[3] Beard in his colorful fashion gave expression to the common viewpoint when he asserted that "the roaring flood of the new democracy was ... [by 1824] foaming perilously near the crest...."[4] Schlesinger, with his allusion to the "immense popular vote"[5] received by Jackson in 1824, creates a similar image. The Old Hero's victory in 1828 has been hailed as the consequence of a "mighty democratic uprising."[6]

That a "new democracy, ignorant, impulsive, irrational"[7] entered the arena of politics in the Jackson era has become one of the few unchallenged "facts" in an otherwise controversial field. Differences of opinion occur only when attempts are made to account for the remarkable increase in the size of the active electorate. The commonest explanations have emphasized the assertion by the common man of his newly won political privileges, the democratic influences

---

2 Sellers, *Jacksonian Democracy,* I.

3 For representative examples of this viewpoint, see Charles A. and Mary R. Beard, *The Rise of American Civilization* (new ed., 2 vols. in 1, New York, 1933), 540, 546, 550; Wilfred E. Binkley, *American Political Parties: Their Natural History* (New York, 1943), 101, 108, 111, 115, 121; John D. Hicks, *The Federal Union* (2d ed., Cambridge, Mass., 1952), 351, 363-64; William MacDonald, *Jacksonian Democracy, 1829-1837* (New York, 1906), 3, 42, 311; Richard Hofstadter, *The American Political Tradition* (Vintage ed., New York, 1954), 50-52; John Bach McMasters, *A History of the People of the United States* (8 vols., New York, 1883-1913), V, 518; Marvin Meyers, *The Jacksonian Persuasion: Politics and Belief* (Stanford, Calif., 1957), 4, 11; E. E. Robinson, *The Evolution of American Political Parties* (New York, 1924), 101; E. H. Roseboom, *A History of Presidential Elections* (New York, 1957), 91; Arthur M. Schlesinger, Jr., *The Age of Jackson* (Boston, 1947), 12-15, 36.

4 Beard, *American Civilization, 550.*

5 Schlesinger, *Age of Jackson,* 36.

6 Frederick A. Ogg, *The Reign of Andrew Jackson* (New Haven, Conn., 1919), 114.

7 Roseboom, *Presidential Elections,* 91.

that arose out of the western frontier, or the magnetic attractiveness of Jackson as a candidate capable of appealing with singular effectiveness to the backwoods hunter, the plain farmer, the urban workingman, and the southern planter.

Probably because the image of a "mighty democratic uprising" has been so universally agreed upon, there has been virtually no effort made to describe precisely the dimensions of the "uprising." Inquiry into this aspect of Jacksonian democracy has been discouraged by a common misconception regarding voter behavior before 1824. As the authors of one of our most recent and best textbooks put it: "In the years from the beginning of the government to 1824, a period for which we have no reliable election statistics, only small numbers of citizens seemed to have bothered to go to the polls."[8] Actually, abundant data on pre-1824 elections is available, and it indicates a far higher rate of voting than has been realized. Only by taking this data into consideration can voting behavior after 1824 be placed in proper perspective.

The question of whether there was indeed a "mighty democratic uprising" during the Jackson era is certainly crucial in any analysis of the political character of Jacksonian democracy. More broadly, however, we need to know the degree to which potential voters participated in elections before, during, and after the period of Jackson's presidency as well as the conditions that apparently influenced the rate of voting. Only when such factors have been analyzed can we arrive at firm conclusions with respect to the dimensions of the political changes that we associate with Jacksonian democracy. Obviously in studying voter participation we are dealing with but one aspect of a large problem, and the limitations imposed by such a restrictive focus should be apparent.

In measuring the magnitude of the vote in the Jackson elections it is hardly significant to use the total popular vote cast throughout the nation. A comparison of the total vote cast in 1812, for example, when in eight of the seventeen states electors were chosen by the legislature, with the vote in 1832, when every state except South Carolina chose its electors by popular vote, has limited meaning. Neither is it revealing to compare the total vote in 1824 with that in 1832 without taking into consideration the population increase during the interval. The shift from the legislative choice of electors to their election by popular vote, together with the steady population growth, obviously swelled the presidential vote. But the problem to be investigated is whether the Jackson elections brought voters to the polls in such enlarged or unprecedented proportions as to indicate that a "new democracy" had burst upon the political scene.

The most practicable method for measuring the degree to which voters participated in elections over a period of time is to relate the number of votes cast to the number of potential voters. Although there is no way of calculating precisely how many eligible voters there were in any state at a given time, the evidence at hand demonstrates that with the exception of Rhode Island,

---

[8] Richard Hofstadter, William Miller, and Daniel Aaron, *The American Republic* (2 vols., New York, 1959), I, 391.

Virginia, and Louisiana the potential electorate after 1824 was roughly equivalent to the adult white male population.[9] A meaningful way of expressing the rate of voter participation, then, is to state it in terms of the percentage of the adult white males actually voting. This index can be employed to measure the variations that occurred in voter participation over a period of time and in both national and state elections. Consequently a basis is provided for comparing the rate of voting in the Jackson elections with other presidential elections before and after his regime as well as with state elections.[10]

Using this approach it is possible, first of all, to ascertain whether or not voter participation rose markedly in the three presidential elections in which Jackson was a candidate. Did voter participation in these elections so far exceed the peak participation in the pre-1824 elections as to suggest that a mighty democratic uprising was taking place? The accompanying data (Table 1) provides an answer to this basic question.[11]

In the 1824 election not a single one of the eighteen states in which the

---

[9] The only states in which property qualifications were a factor in restricting voting in presidential elections after 1824 were Virginia and Rhode Island. New York did not completely abolish property qualifications until 1826, but the reform of 1821 had resulted in virtually free suffrage. In Louisiana, where voters were required to be taxpayers, the nature of the system of taxation operated to confine the suffrage to perhaps half of the adult white males. See Joseph G. Tregle, "Louisiana in the Age of Jackson: A Study in Ego Politics," doctoral dissertation, University of Pennsylvania, 1954, 105-108. To be perfectly accurate, estimates of the size of the potential electorate would have to take into account such factors as citizenship and residence requirements and, in certain states, the eligibility of Negro voters.

[10] After 1840 when the proportion of aliens in the population increased markedly and citizenship became an important requirement for voting, the adult-white-male index becomes less reliable. In order to calculate accurately the number of qualified voters in 1850, the alien adult white males would have to be deducted in those states where citizenship was a qualification for voting. Unfortunately, federal census data on aliens is not obtainable prior to 1890, except for the censuses of 1820 and 1830. In the latter year there were only 107,832 aliens out of a total population of nearly thirteen millions, a fraction so small as to be insignificant. But by 1850, according to one calculation, adult male aliens may have amounted to one-twelfth of the total voting population. J. D. B. De Bow, *Statistical View of the United States* (Washington, D. C., 1854), 50. In certain eastern states the proportion of aliens was higher than the national average. In New York, for example, 18.5 per cent of the total population in 1855 were aliens; the proportion in 1835 had been only 3.79 per cent. Franklin B. Hough, *Census of the State of New York for 1855* (Albany, 1857), xiv, xliii.

[11] The figures on voter participation have been computed from a compilation I have made of returns of state-wide elections covering twenty-five states over the period from 1800 to 1860. For the post-1836 years the returns may be consulted in the *Whig Almanacs* and *Tribune Almanacs* issued by Horace Greeley and, for presidential elections, in W. Dean Burnham's *Presidential Ballots, 1836-1892* (Baltimore, Md., 1955). For the period prior to 1836 the best general sources are the official manuals of certain states, the legislative journals, and the contemporary newspapers, For several states, among them Massachusetts, Connecticut, New Jersey, Maryland, Virginia, North Carolina, and Georgia, it is necessary to use the manuscript sources. The estimate of the adult white male population was computed for each decennial year from the federal census, and the figure for the particular election year was obtained by interpolation. I have computed for each gubernatorial and Presidential election in the twenty-five states admitted to the Union by 1836 (exclusive of South Carolina) the percentage of adult white males voting.

TABLE 1
Percentages of Adult White Males Voting in Elections

	Highest Known % AWM Voting before 1824		*Presidential Elections*					
State	*Year*	*% AWM*	*1824*	*1828*	*1832*	*1836*	*1840*	*1844*
Maine	1812g	62.0	18.9	42.7	66.2*	37.4	82.2	67.5
New Hampshire	1814g	80.8	16.8	76.5	74.2	38.2	86.4*	65.6
Vermont	1812g	79.9	–	55.8	50.0	52.5	74.0	65.7
Massachusetts	1812g	67.4	29.1	25.7	39.3	45.1	66.4	59.3
Rhode Island	1812g	49.4	12.4	18.0	22.4	24.1	33.2	39.8
Connecticut	1819l	54.4	14.9	27.1	45.9	52.3	75.7*	76.1
New York	1810g	41.5	–	70.4*	72.1	60.2	77.7	73.6
New Jersey	1808p	71.8	31.1	70.9	69.0	69.3	80.4*	81.6
Pennsylvania	1808g	71.5	19.6	56.6	52.7	53.1	77.4*	75.5
Delaware	1804g	81.9	–	–	67.0	69.4	82.8*	85.0
Maryland	1820l	69.0	53.7	76.2*	55.6	67.5	84.6	80.3
Virginia	1800p	25.9	11.5	27.6*	30.8	35.1	54.6	54.5
North Carolina	1823c	70.0#	42.2	56.8	31.7	52.9	83.1*	79.1
Georgia	1812c	62.3	–	35.9	33.0	64.9*	88.9	94.0
Kentucky	1820g	74.4	25.3	70.7	73.9	61.1	74.3	80.3*
Tennessee	1817g	80.0	26.8	49.8	28.8	55.2	89.6*	89.6
Louisiana	1812g	34.2	–	36.3*	24.4	19.2	39.4	44.7
Alabama	1819g	96.7	52.1	53.6	33.3	65.0	89.8	82.7
Mississippi	1823g	79.8	41.6	56.6	32.8	62.8	88.2*	89.7
Ohio	1822g	46.5	34.8	75.8*	73.8	75.5	84.5	83.6
Indiana	1822g	52.4	37.5	68.3*	61.8	70.1	86.0	84.9
Illinois	1822g	55.8	24.2	51.9	45.6	43.7	85.9*	76.3
Missouri	1820g	71.9	20.1	54.3	40.8	35.6	74.0*	74.7
Arkansas		–	–	–	–	35.0	86.4	68.8
Michigan		–	–	–	–	35.7	84.9	79.3
National Average			26.5	56.3	54.9	55.2	78.0	74.9

* Exceeded pre-1824 high
g Gubernatorial election
p Presidential election
\# Estimate based on incomplete returns
c Congressional election
l Election of legislature

electors were chosen by popular vote attained the percentage of voter participation that had been reached before 1824. Prior to that critical election, fifteen of those eighteen states had recorded votes in excess of 50 per cent of their adult white male population, but in 1824 only two states—Maryland and Alabama—exceeded this modest mark. The average rate of voter participation in the election was 26.5 per cent. This hardly fits the image of the "roaring flood of the new democracy . . . foaming perilously near the crest. . . ."

There would seem to be persuasive evidence that in 1828 the common man flocked to the polls in unprecedented numbers, for the proportion of adult white males voting soared to 56.3 per cent, more than double the 1824 figure. But this outpouring shrinks in magnitude when we observe that in only six of the twenty-two states involved were new highs in voter participation established. In three of these—Maryland, Virginia, and Louisiana—the recorded gain was inconsiderable, and in a fourth—New York—the bulk of the increase might be attributed to changes that had been made in suffrage qualifications as recently as 1821 and 1826. Six states went over the 70 per cent mark, whereas ten had bettered that performance before 1824. Instead of a "mighty democratic uprising" there was in 1828 a voter turnout that approached—but in only a few instances matched or exceeded—the maximum levels that had been attained before the Jackson era.

The advance that was registered in 1828 did not carry forward to 1832. Despite the fact that Jackson was probably at the peak of his personal popularity, that he was engaged in a campaign that was presumably to decide issues of great magnitude, and that in the opinion of some authorities a "well-developed two party system on a national scale" had been established, [12] there was a slight decline in voter participation. The average for the twenty-three states participating in the presidential contest was 54.9 per cent. In fifteen states a smaller percentage of the adult white males went to the polls in 1832 than in 1828. Only five states bettered their pre-1824 highs. Again the conclusion would be that it was essentially the pre-1824 electorate—diminished in most states and augmented in a few that voted in 1832. Thus, after three Jackson elections, sixteen states had not achieved the proportions of voter participation that they had reached before 1824. The "new democracy" had not yet made its appearance. [13]

A comparison of the Jackson elections with earlier presidential contests is of some interest. Such comparisons have little validity before 1808 because few states chose electors by popular vote, and for certain of those states the complete returns are not available. In 1816 and 1820 there was so little opposition to Monroe that the voter interest was negligible. The most relevant elections, therefore, are those of 1808 and 1812. The accompanying table (Table 2) gives the percentages of adult white males voting in 1808 and 1812 in those states for which full returns could be found, together with the comparable percentages for the elections of 1824 and 1828. In 1824 only one state—Ohio—surpassed the highs established in either 1808 or 1812. Four more joined this list in 1828—Virginia, Maryland, Pennsylvania, and New Hampshire—although the margin in the last case was so small as to be inconsequential. The most significant conclusion to be drawn from this admittedly limited and unrepresent-

---

12 Charles G. Sellers, Jr., *James K. Polk: Jacksonian, 1795-1843* (Princeton, N. J., 1957), 166. See also Meyers, *Jacksonian Persuasion*, 11.

13 It may be suggested that it is invalid to compare voter participation in each state in the presidential contests of 1824, 1828, and 1832 with the highs, rather than the average participation in each state prior to 1824. The object of the comparison is to ascertain whether the Jackson elections brought voters to the polls in unprecedented numbers, as has so often been asserted. Moreover, it is hardly feasible to compare average participation in elections before and after 1824 in many states because of the changes that were made in the methods of electing governors and presidential electors or—in certain instances—because the state had only recently entered the Union. However, among those states in which average voter participation was obviously higher before 1824 than it was in the three Jackson elections were Alabama, Connecticut, Georgia, Massachusetts, Mississippi, New Hampshire (1809-1817), Pennsylvania, Rhode Island, Tennessee, and Vermont (1807-1815).

TABLE 2
Percentages of Adult White Males Voting in Presidential Elections

State	1808	1812	1824	1828
Maine	Legis.	50.0	18.9	42.7
New Hampshire	62.1	75.4	16.8	76.5
Massachussetts	Legis.	51.4	29.1	25.7
Rhode Island	37.4	37.7	12.4	18.0
New Jersey	71.8	Legis.	31.1	70.9
Pennsylvania	34.7	45.5	19.6	56.6
Maryland	48.4	56.5	53.7	76.2
Virginia	17.7	17.8	11.5	27.6
Ohio	12.8	20.0	34.8	75.8

Note: No complete returns of the popular vote cast for electors in Kentucky or Tennessee in 1808 and 1812 and in North Carolina in 1808 could be located.

ative data is that in those states where there was a vigorous two-party contest in 1808 and 1812 the vote was relatively high. Conversely, where there was little or no contest in 1824 or 1828, the vote was low.

When an examination is made of voting in other than presidential elections prior to 1824, the inaccuracy of the impression that "only small numbers of citizens" went to the polls becomes apparent. Because of the almost automatic succession of the members of the "Virginia dynasty" and the early deterioration of the national two-party system that had seemed to be developing around 1800, presidential elections did not arouse voter interest as much as did those for governor, state legislators, or even members of Congress. In such elections at the state level the "common man" was stimulated by local factors to cast his vote, and he frequently responded in higher proportions than he did to the later stimulus provided by Jackson.

The average voter participation for all the states in 1828 was 56.3 per cent. Before 1824 fifteen of the twenty-two states had surpassed that percentage. Among other things, this means that the 1828 election failed to bring to the polls the proportion of the electorate that had voted on occasion in previous elections. There was, in other words, a high potential vote that was frequently realized in state elections but which did not materialize in presidential elections. The unsupported assumption that the common man was either apathetic or debarred from voting by suffrage barriers before 1824 is untenable in the light of this evidence.

In state after state (see Table 1) gubernatorial elections attracted 70 per cent or more of the adult white males to the polls. Among the notable highs recorded were Delaware with 81.9 per cent in 1804, New Hampshire with 80.8 per cent in 1814, Tennessee with 80.0 per cent in 1817, Vermont with 79.9 per cent in 1812, Mississippi with 79.8 per cent in 1823, and Alabama with a highly improbable 96.7 per cent in its first gubernatorial contest in 1819. There is reason to believe that in some states, at least, the voter participation in the election of state legislators was even higher than in gubernatorial elections.

Because of the virtual impossibility of securing county-by-county or district-by-district returns for such elections, this hypothesis is difficult to verify.

Down to this point the voter turnout in the Jackson elections has been compared with that in elections held prior to 1824. Now it becomes appropriate to inquire whether during the period 1824 through 1832 voters turned out in greater proportions for the three presidential contests than they did for the contemporary state elections. If, indeed, this "new democracy" bore some special relationship to Andrew Jackson or to his policies, it might be anticipated that interest in the elections in which he was the central figure would stimulate greater voter participation than gubernatorial contests, in which he was at most a remote factor.

Actually, the election returns show fairly conclusively that throughout the eight-year period the electorate continued to participate more extensively in state elections than in those involving the presidency. Between 1824 and 1832 there were fifty regular gubernatorial elections in the states that chose their electors by popular vote. In only sixteen of these fifty instances did the vote for President surpass the corresponding vote for governor. In Rhode Island, Delaware, Tennessee, Kentucky, Illinois, Mississippi, Missouri, and Georgia the vote for governor consistently exceeded that for President. Only in Connecticut was the reverse true.[14] Viewed from this perspective, too, the remarkable feature of the vote in the Jackson elections is not its immensity but rather its smallness.

Finally, the Jackson elections may be compared with subsequent presidential elections. Once Jackson had retired to the Hermitage, and figures of less dramatic proportions took up the contest for the presidency, did voter participation rise or fall? This question can be answered by observing the percentage of adult white males who voted in each state in the presidential elections of 1836 through 1844 (Table 1). Voter participation in the 1836 election remained near the level that had been established in 1828 and 1832, with 55.2 per cent of the adult white males voting. Only five states registered percentages in excess of their pre-1824 highs. But in 1840 the "new democracy" made its appearance with explosive suddenness.

In a surge to the polls that has rarely, if ever, been exceeded in any presidential election, four out of five (78.0 per cent) of the adult white males cast their votes for Harrison or Van Buren.[15] This new electorate was greater than that of the Jackson period by more than 40 per cent. In all but five states—Vermont, Massachusetts, Rhode Island, Kentucky, and Alabama —the peaks of voter participation reached before 1824 were passed. Fourteen of the

---

14 These summary statements are based upon an analysis of the compilation referred to in footnote eleven.

15 It can be calculated that the total of adult white males in the twenty-five states was 3,090,708. The total popular vote was 2,409,682. In the presidential election of 1896 the total vote approximated 80 per cent of the potential electorate. In 1940 and 1952 the comparable figures would be 63 per cent and 65 per cent respectively. These percentages have been calculated on the assumption that the potential electorate in 1896 included all adult male citizens and in 1940 and 1952 all adult citizens.

twenty-five states involved set record highs for voting that were not to be broken throughout the remainder of the ante bellum period. Now, at last, the common man—or at least the man who previously had not been sufficiently aroused to vote in presidential elections—cast his weight into the political balance. This "Tippecanoe democracy," if such a label is permissible, was of a different order of magnitude from the Jacksonian democracy. The elections in which Jackson figured brought to the polls only those men who were accustomed to voting in state or national elections, except in a very few states. The Tippecanoe canvass witnessed an extraordinary expansion of the size of the presidential electorate far beyond previous dimensions. It was in 1840, then, that the "roaring flood of the new democracy" reached its crest. And it engulfed the Jacksonians.

The flood receded only slightly in 1844, when 74.9 per cent of the estimated potential electorate went to the polls. Indeed, nine states attained their record highs for the period. In 1848 and 1852 there was a general downward trend in voter participation, followed by a modest upswing in 1856 and 1860. But the level of voter activity remained well above that of the Jackson elections. The conclusion to be drawn is that the "mighty democratic uprising" came after the period of Jackson's presidency.

Now that the quantitative dimensions of Jacksonian democracy as a political phenomenon have been delineated and brought into some appropriate perspective, certain questions still remain to be answered. Granted that the Jacksonian electorate—as revealed by the comparisons that have been set forth—was not really very large, how account for the fact that voter participation doubled between the elections of 1824 and 1828? It is true that the total vote soared from around 359,000 to 1,155,400 and that the percentage of voter participation more than doubled. Traditionally, students of the Jackson period have been impressed by this steep increase in voting and by way of explanation have identified the causal factors as the reduction of suffrage qualifications, the democratic influence of the West, or the personal magnetism of Jackson. The validity of each of these hypotheses needs to be reexamined.

In no one of the states in which electors were chosen by popular vote was any significant change made in suffrage qualifications between 1824 and 1828. Subsequently, severe restrictions were maintained in Rhode Island until 1842, when some liberalization was effected, and in Virginia down to 1850. In Louisiana, where the payment of a tax was a requirement, the character of the state tax system apparently operated to restrict the suffrage at least as late as 1845. Thus with the three exceptions noted, the elimination of suffrage barriers was hardly a factor in producing an enlarged electorate during the Jackson and post-Jackson periods. Furthermore, all but a few states had extended the privilege of voting either to all male taxpayers or to all adult male citizens by 1810. After Connecticut eliminated its property qualification in 1818, Massachusetts in 1821, and New York in 1821 and 1826, only Rhode Island, Virginia, and Louisiana were left on the list of "restrictionist" states.[16] Neither

---

16 There is no reliable study of suffrage qualifications, but the standard account is Kirk H. Porter, *A History of Suffrage in the United States* (Chicago, 1918). Porter erred in stating that New Jersey retained a property requirement until 1844; it was replaced in 1807 by

Jackson's victory nor the increased vote in 1828 can be attributed to the presence at the polls of a newly enfranchised mass of voters.

Similarly, it does not appear that the western states led the way in voter participation.[17] Prior to 1824, for example, Ohio, Indiana, and Illinois had never brought to the polls as much as 60 per cent of their adult white males. Most of the eastern states had surpassed that level by considerable margins. In the election of 1828 six states registered votes in excess of 70 per cent of their adult white male populations. They were in order of rank: New Hampshire, Maryland, Ohio, New Jersey, Kentucky, and New York. The six leaders in 1832 were: New Hampshire, Kentucky, Ohio, New York, New Jersey, and Delaware. It will be obvious that the West, however that region may be defined, was not leading the "mighty democratic uprising." Western influences, then, do not explain the increased vote in 1828.

There remains to be considered the factor of Jackson's personal popularity. Did Jackson, the popular hero, attract voters to the polls in unprecedented proportions? The comparisons that have already been made between the Jackson elections and other elections—state and national—before, during, and after his presidency would suggest a negative answer to the question. Granted that a majority of the voters in 1828 favored Jackson, it is not evident that his partisans stormed the polls any more enthusiastically than did the Adams men. Of the six highest states in voter participation in 1828, three favored Adams and three were for Jackson, which could be interpreted to mean that the convinced Adams supporters turned out no less zealously for their man than did the ardent Jacksonians. When Van Buren replaced Jackson in 1836, the voting average increased slightly over 1832. And, as has been demonstrated, the real manifestation of the "new democracy" came not in 1828 but in 1840.

The most satisfactory explanation for the increase in voter participation between 1824 and 1828 is a simple and obvious one. During the long reign of the Virginia dynasty, interest in presidential elections dwindled. In 1816 and 1820 there had been no contest. The somewhat fortuitous termination of the Virginia succession in 1824 and the failure of the congressional caucus to solve the problem of leadership succession threw the choice of a President upon the electorate. But popular interest was dampened by the confusion of choice presented by the multiplicity of candidates, by the disintegration of the old national parties, by the fact that in most states one or another of the candidates was so overwhelmingly popular as to forestall any semblance of a contest, and possibly by the realization that the election would ultimately be decided by the House of Representatives. By 1828 the situation had altered. There were but two candidates in the field, each of whom had substantial sectional backing. A

---

taxpayer suffrage. See my *The History of Voting in New Jersey: A Study of the Development of Election Machinery, 1664-1911* (New Brunswick, N. J., 1953), 100. Porter's statement that a freehold property requirement existed in Tennessee under the 1796 constitution is based on a misreading of that document. Porter, *Suffrage*, 24, 80; Francis N. Thrope, *Federal and State Constitutions, Colonial Charters, and Other Organic Laws* (7 vols., Washington, D. C., 1909), VI, 3418.

[17] See Table 1.

clear-cut contest impended, and the voters became sufficiently aroused to go to the polls in moderate numbers.

One final question remains. Why was the vote in the Jackson elections relatively low when compared with previous and contemporary state elections and with presidential votes after 1840? The answer, in brief, is that in most states either Jackson or his opponent had such a one-sided advantage that the result was a foregone conclusion. Consequently there was little incentive for the voters to go to the polls.

This factor can be evaluated in fairly specific quantitative terms. If the percentage of the total vote secured by each candidate in each state in the election of 1828 is calculated, the difference between the percentages can be used as an index of the closeness, or one-sidedness, of the contest. In Illinois, for example, Jackson received 67 per cent of the total vote and Adams, 33; the difference—thirty-four points—represents the margin between the candidates. The average difference between the candidates, taking all the states together, was thirty-six points. Expressed another way this would mean that in the average state the winning candidate received more than twice the vote of the loser. Actually, this was the case in thirteen of the twenty-two states (see Table 3). [18] Such a wide margin virtually placed these states in the "no contest" category.

A remarkably close correlation existed between the size of the voter turnout and the relative closeness of the contest. The six states previously listed as having the greatest voter participation in 1828 were among the seven states with the smallest margin of difference between the candidates. The exception was Louisiana, where restrictions on the suffrage curtailed the vote. Even in this instance, however, it is significant that voter participation in Louisiana reached a record high. In those states, then, where there was a close balance of political forces the vote was large, and conversely, where the contest was very one sided, the vote was low.

Most of the states in 1828 were so strongly partial to one or another of the candidates that they can best be characterized as one-party states. Adams encountered little opposition in New England, except in New Hampshire, and Jackson met with hardly any resistance in the South. It was chiefly in the middle states and the older West that the real battle was waged. With the removal of Adams from the scene after 1828, New England became less of a one-party section, but the South remained extremely one sided. Consequently it is not surprising that voter participation in 1832 failed even to match that of 1828.

Here, certainly, is a factor of crucial importance in explaining the dimensions of the voter turnout in the Jackson elections. National parties were still in a rudimentary condition and were highly unbalanced from state to state. Indeed, a two-party system scarcely could be said to exist in more than half of the states until after 1832. Where opposing parties had been formed to contest the

---

[18] The index figures in the table represent the difference between the percentages of the total popular vote secured by the two major candidates in each state. For the election of 1832, the figures represent only the difference between the votes obtained by Clay and Jackson.

TABLE 3
Differential between Percentages of Total Vote Obtained by
Major Presidential Candidates, 1828-1844

State	1828	1832	1836	1840	1844
Maine	20	10	20	1	13
New Hampshire	7	13	50	11	19
Vermont	50	10	20	29	18
Massachusetts	66	30	9	16	12
Rhode Island	50	14	6	23	20
Connecticut	50	20	1	11	5
New York	2	4	9	4	1
New Jersey	4	1	1	4	1
Pennsylvania	33	16	4	1	2
Delaware	–	2	6	10	3
Maryland	2	1	7	8	5
Virginia	38	50	13	1	6
North Carolina	47	70	6	15	5
Georgia	94	100	4	12	4
Kentucky	1	9	6	29	8
Tennessee	90	90	16	11	1
Louisiana	6	38	3	19	3
Alabama	80	100	11	9	18
Mississippi	60	77	2	7	13
Ohio	3	3	4	9	2
Indiana	13	34	12	12	2
Illinois	34	37	10	2	12
Missouri	41	32	21	14	17
Arkansas	–	–	28	13	26
Michigan	–	–	9	4	6
Average Differential	36	36	11	11	9

election, the vote was large, but where no parties, or only one, took the field, the vote was low. By 1840, fairly well-balanced parties had been organized in virtually every state. In only three states did the margin between Harrison and Van Buren exceed twenty points, and the average for all the states was only eleven points. The result was generally high voter participation.[19]

When Jacksonian democracy is viewed from the perspectives employed in this analysis, its political dimensions in so far as they relate to the behavior of the electorate can be described with some precision. None of the Jackson elections involved a "mighty democratic uprising" in the sense that voters were drawn to the polls in unprecedented proportions. When compared with the peak participation recorded for each state before 1824, or with contemporaneous

[19] Careful analysis of the data in Table 3 will suggest that there were three fairly distinct stages in the emergence of a nationally balanced two-party system. Balanced parties appeared first in the middle states between 1824 and 1828. New England remained essentially a one-party section until after Adams had passed from the scene; then competing parties appeared. In the South and the newer West, a one-party dominance continued until divisions arose over who should succeed Jackson. Sectional loyalties to favorite sons obviously exerted a determining influence on presidential politics, and consequently on party formation, in the Jackson years.

gubernatorial elections, or most particularly with the vast outpouring of the electorate in 1840, voter participation in the Jacksonian elections was unimpressive. The key to the relatively low presidential vote would seem to be the extreme political imbalance that existed in most states as between the Jacksonians and their opponents. Associated with this imbalance was the immature development of national political parties. Indeed, it can be highly misleading to think in terms of national parties in connection with the Jackson elections. As balanced, organized parties subsequently made their appearance from state to state, and voters were stimulated by the prospect of a genuine contest, a marked rise in voter participation occurred. Such conditions did not prevail generally across the nation until 1840, and then at last the "mighty democratic uprising" took place.

2. Was 1928 a critical election in California?*

JOHN L. SHOVER†

A critical election, according to the political scientist V. O. Key, Jr., occurs when the depth and intensity of electoral involvement are high, when more or less profound readjustments occur in the relations of power within the community, and when new and durable electoral groupings are formed. Using Massachusetts as a case study, Key demonstrated that two critical elections have occurred in that state since 1888. The first was in 1894, when significant realignments of voters heralded the defeat of Bryan two years later and ushered in a period of Republican party ascendancy uninterrupted until the second critical election, that of 1928. In this election, the upsurge of support for Al Smith established a pattern of Democratic party dominance that nearly forty years later still represents the prevailing alignment in Massachusetts. While Key cautiously singled out the two elections of 1894 and 1928 as particularly significant, he nonetheless suggested that rather than a single critical election, there may be a critical period extending over several elections during which important realignments occur.[1]

Few political scientists and even fewer historians have attempted to follow up

* Reprinted from the *Pacific Northwest Quarterly*, LVIII (October, 1967), pp. 196-204, by permission of the author and the publisher.

† This paper in its original version was presented as part of a panel, "Twentieth Century California Politics: A Behavioral Approach," at the 1966 meeting of the Pacific Coast Branch of the American Historical Association at Reed College. The author wishes to thank the other participant in the panel, Michael J. Rogin, for assistance with the statistics presented here, and Samuel T. McSeveney and Robert E. Burke for their suggestive critiques. Editors note: Shover, now associate professor of history, University of Pennsylvania, received his Ph.D. from Ohio State University. He is the author of *Cornbelt Rebellion: The Farmers' Holiday Association*.

[1] V. O. Key, Jr., "A Theory of Critical Elections," *Journal of Politics*, Vol. 17 (1955), 3-18. The concept of a "critical period" is developed by Duncan MacRae, Jr., and James A. Meldrum, "Critical Elections in Illinois, 1888-1958," *American Political Science Review*, Vol. 54 (1960), 669-83. Key makes passing reference to this concept when he notes: "the great reshuffling of voters that occurred in 1928 was perhaps the final and decisive stage in a process that had been under way for some time" (p. 5).

the Key model by employing it as a means for interpreting voting statistics from other states. In the case of the historians, this apparent lack of interest is particularly surprising, for Key's concepts and method seem well adapted to one of the central concerns of historical study: the rate and distribution of change over space and time.[2]

This paper is an attempt to apply Key's model to California voting data. The question raised here, "Was 1928 a critical election in California?" asks whether the same trends that Key detected in Massachusetts during the 1920's—and especially in 1928—are equally evident in California.

As a case study for voting analysis, California poses vexing problems. The first is the rapid growth and mobility of the population. The census of 1910 reported 2,377,549 Californians, and that of 1950, 10,586,223—an increase of 445 per cent. Changes due to internal migration compound the difficulties. According to the 1960 census, only 37.3 per cent of Californians were living in the same house as five years earlier, and 25 per cent were living in a different county.[3]

Analysis is further complicated by the peculiar nature of California political parties. The Progressive movement left the state a heritage of weakened party structure and a lingering distrust of partisan activities. The two major political figures in California in the 20th century, Hiram Johnson and Earl Warren, were at best apathetic partisans. Moreover, the Progressive upsurge produced within both the Republican and the Democratic parties severe internal schisms that prevailed for at least a decade.

Finally, California election data must be treated with considerable qualification. Official voting returns are assembled only on a county basis. When one considers that in 1960 the population of the fifty-eight counties in California ranged from 397 to 6,038,771 and that the largest, Los Angeles County, supplied 40 per cent of the registered voters in the state, the difficulties of analyzing election data become apparent.[4]

Accordingly, this paper will present no all-encompassing theory that will provide an ordered explanation for capricious political trends in California. The intent is to advance a hypothesis that will attempt to identify over a time sequence of fifty-six years important and significant realignments of voters in presidential elections in California. Obviously, it is not possible in an exploratory study of this kind to search behind the voting returns to investigate the

---

[2] The major studies that have made use of the Key model are: V. O. Key, Jr., and Frank Munger, "Social Determinism and Electoral Decision: The Case of Indiana," in Eugene Burdick and Arthur J. Brodbeck, eds., *American Voting Behavior* (Glencoe, Ill., 1959), 281-99; V. O. Key, Jr., "Secular Realignment and the Party System," *Journal of Politics*, Vol. 21 (1959), 198-210; and MacRae and Meldrum, "Critical Elections in Illinois," 669-83. For a historian's use of the model, see Charles Sellers, "The Equilibrium Cycle in Two-Party Politics," *Public Opinion Quarterly*, Vol. 29 (1965), 16-38. See also Lee Benson, "Research Problems in American Political Historiography," in Mirra Komarovsky, ed., *Common Frontiers of the Social Sciences* (Glencoe, Ill., 1957), 114.

[3] Warren S. Thompson, *Growth and Changes in California's Populations*, (Los Angeles, 1955), 4; Eugene C. Lee, *California Votes, 1928-1960* (Berkeley, 1963), 5.

[4] Lee, *California Votes*, A45; State of California, *California Statistical Abstract* (Sacramento, 1965), 51.

importance of economic, social, educational, or religious variables on the voting changes observed.

Regardless of what qualifications have to be made about California voting behavior, one point is certain: a voting revolution took place between 1928 and 1936. In 1928 Republican registration constituted 72 per cent of the state's 2,313,816 registered voters; in 1930, 78 per cent of California's 2,245,228 voters were registered as Republicans. Then, during the first six years of the 1930's, the Democratic party added nearly 1,500,000 registrants, an increase of 313 per cent. During the same interval, the Republicans lost 394,000 registrants, a decrease of 24 per cent.[5] In 1934 Democratic registration for the first time exceeded Republican. The Democratic party of California, weak and schism-torn through the twenties, reaped the harvest of depression discontent.

Dramatic increments in registration, however, are not necessarily indications of shifts in distribution of power. Political interest, as manifested by the percentage of the eligible adult population who actually voted, had been increasing for two elections before 1932. In 1916, 58 per cent of eligible adults voted; in 1920, 47 per cent; in 1924, 51 per cent; in 1928, 59 per cent; and in 1932, 63 per cent.[6] More important, while the Democratic gains in the thirties marked a phenomenal increase in the party's voting strength, there was no significant realignment of Democratic party support. As Eugene C. Lee has noted:

Even in the upheaval which occurred between 1928 and 1936, the relative position of the counties tended to be maintained . . . the 25 most Democratic counties in 1936 were all among the most Democratic counties in 1928, although not all of the 1928 Democratic counties are included in the later figure . . . of the 15 most Democratic counties in 1960, all were among the most Democratic counties in 1936.[7]

In short, this would indicate that the increments of the early thirties were a part of a voting cycle that had been established earlier.

If there were not significant voter realignments in the early thirties, when did the significant shift in voting loyalties take place? Such distinguished authorities as Samuel Lubell and V. O. Key, Jr., agree that the election of 1928 marked a critical realignment of American voting patterns, particularly manifested by the fact that the Democratic party for the first time marshaled a plurality of the

---

[5] Lee, *California Votes,* 28.

[6] The estimated percentage of eligible adults voting is as follows: 1912, 46 per cent; 1916, 57.6 per cent; 1920, 47.2 per cent; 1924, 50.5 per cent; 1928, 58.5 per cent; 1932, 63.4 per cent; 1936, 65.3 per cent; 1940, 74.1 per cent; 1944, 64.3 per cent; 1948, 62.5 per cent. To estimate the eligible adult population in any given election year, the number of adults over 21, excluding aliens, in a census year was determined. Intercensal population was estimated as follows: Population for 1924 equals the population of 1920 plus .4 times the population of 1930 minus that of 1920. This formula was borrowed from Burton R. Brazil, "Voting in California, 1920-1946," master's thesis (University of California, Los Angeles, 1948).

[7] Lee, *California Votes,* 71.

total vote cast in the twelve largest metropolitan centers in the United States.[8]

Most students of American political behavior concur with Lubell: "Smith's defeat in 1928, rather than Roosevelt's 1932 victory, marked off the arena in which today's politics are being fought." Key was more circumspect and offered an interpretation of voting behavior in only one section: "In New England, at least, the Roosevelt revolution of 1932 was in large measure an Al Smith revolution of 1928, a characterization less applicable to the remainder of the country."[9] The concern of this paper is to ask the question, Was there an Al Smith revolution in California? The answer is definitely No.

A first suspicion about the appropriateness of Lubell's theory in California can be raised by comparing in the election of 1928 alone the percentage vote for Smith in the metropolitan and nonmetropolitan areas of the state. The eleven largest counties in California contributed 79.8 per cent of the total vote cast in California in 1928, but only 78.1 per cent of Smith's vote. The remaining counties—less urban and rural—contributed 20.1 per cent of the total vote, but 21.1 per cent of the Democratic candidate's total.[10] This scarcely suggests an urban voting revolution.

Such first suspicions are further confirmed if the Democratic vote in the eleven metropolitan counties in 1928 is compared with the Democratic vote there in the three preceding elections.[11]

---

[8] Samuel Lubell, *The Future of American Politics,* 2nd ed., rev. (New York, 1956), 32-35; Key, "A Theory of Critical Elections," 3-18. See also Samuel Eldersveld, "The Influence of Metropolitan Party Pluralities in Presidential Elections Since 1920: A Study of Twelve Key Cities," *American Political Science Review,* Vol. 63 (1949), 1194, 1201.

[9] Lubell, *Future of American Politics,* 36; Key, "A Theory of Critical Elections," 4.

[10] A metropolitan county is defined as one that includes a city of 50,000 or more (in the 1930 census) or is adjacent to such a county and has 10,000 or more persons in nonagricultural employment. This definition is from Thomas A. Flinn, "The Outline of Ohio Politics," *Western Political Quarterly,* Vol. 13 (1960), 703 n.
All statistics used in this paper for elections before 1928 are from State of California, Secretary of State, *Statement of Vote,* for each respective election; after 1928, from Lee, *California Votes.* Rather than an urban-rural differentiation in 1928, the main significance was a north-south division. Northern California contributed 47.6 per cent of the total vote cast, but 56.7 per cent of Smith's total vote, while the eight counties of Southern California contributed 52.3 per cent of the total vote and only 43.2 per cent of Smith's vote.

[11] Lubell, *Future of American Politics,* uses a different computation—a listing of the respective pluralities in a series of elections. His figures are as follows for the twelve largest U.S. cities:

Year	Net Party Plurality
1920	1,638,000 Republican
1924	1,252,000 Republican
1928	38,000 Democratic
1932	1,910,000 Democratic

Plurality figures for the eleven metropolitan counties in California are:

Year	Plurality
1916	12,766 Republican
1920	302,823 Republican
1924	175,120 Republican
1928	458,738 Republican
1932	361,917 Democratic

TABLE 1
Democratic Vote in Eleven Metropolitan
Counties, 1916-1928

County	1916	1920	1924	1928
Alameda	45.9	20.7	37.8	33.6
Contra Costa	48.4	25.0	45.6	43.4
Fresno	54.8	37.5	55.4	44.3
Los Angeles	45.7	22.4	33.4	28.7
Orange	37.9	20.7	31.3	19.8
Sacramento	52.1	30.1	58.5	48.2
San Bernardino	44.1	29.5	41.4	24.1
San Diego	49.7	18.1	50.5	32.0
San Francisco	55.3	22.4	51.6	49.4
San Joaquin	59.3	33.8	50.5	37.9
Santa Clara	46.0	23.4	41.2	35.4

In all of the eleven counties, Smith's percentage was less than that for Wilson in 1916 or for the combined La Follette-Davis vote in 1924. The election of 1920 may be aptly classified as a "deviant election"; in all eleven counties Democratic percentages fell off sharply from 1916, but the losses were regained in 1924. It is ironic that most analyses of the 1928 election have been based on comparisons with the deviant election of 1920. A comparison with 1916 and 1924, therefore, indicates a falling off rather than a Democratic upsurge in California in 1928.

An examination of local voting statistics in the city of San Francisco, which Lubell cites as manifesting the alleged upsurge of 1928, lends no confirmation to the theory. In six of the thirteen assembly districts in San Francisco, the percentage Republican vote in 1928 was greater than that in 1924; in two, it

TABLE 2
Republican Percentage of Total Vote Cast
by Assembly Districts in San Francisco, 1920-1928

Assembly District	1920	1924	1928	Gain or Loss 1924-1928
21. South of Market	52	29	31	+2
22. South of Market	55	28	31	+3
23. South of Market	57	26	35	+9
24. Mission	61	37	45	+8
25. Mission	62	33	37	+4
26. Western Addition	64	44	44	0
27. Sunset Addition	70	57	55	-2
28. Richmond and Sea Cliff	73	64	57	-7
29. Downtown	59	34	37	+3
30. Downtown	63	45	45	0
31. Pacific Heights and Marina	74	72	60	-12
32. Nob-Russian Hill	71	64	58	-6
33. North Beach	72	55	44	-11

remained constant; and it decreased in five. Most important, however, five of the districts where the Republican vote increased were those in the Mission and South of Market areas, the working class and immigrant districts where the Al Smith revolution was supposed to have happened. In contrast, the greatest falloff in Republican vote (12 percentage points) between 1924 and 1928 occurred in the 31st, which was the strongest Republican Assembly District in San Francisco and encompassed the upper-class Pacific Heights and Marina areas. Only one district, the 33rd in the heavily Italian and Catholic North Beach area, where the Republican vote declined 11 per cent, performed in the fashion that would be expected from the Lubell analysis.

All this is sufficient to raise considerable doubt about the significance of the 1928 election. If 1928 does not meet the test of a critical election, is there some earlier or later point when a genuine realignment appears to have taken place? To answer this question, it is necessary to revert to the basic components of Key's model.

First, the counties with the greatest gains and the greatest losses for one party, in this case, the Democratic, are determined for a particular time span, for example, 1908 to 1916. Then, the average Democratic vote for each set in a series of presidential elections, in this instance from 1892 to 1944, is computed. These average figures for the two sets of counties are then represented in line graph form, and, as the time sequence is surveyed, it may be possible to determine an election in which the two "average" lines diverge widely from each other, like the opening of a scissors. If this separation persists over time, it may be concluded that the particular point where the scissors opened represented a critical election where a realignment that persisted over time first appeared.

If such a cleavage appears, it should be evident in the most extreme cases. Accordingly, a first step is to chart the most consistently Republican county and the most consistently Democratic county in California—Riverside and Plumas counties, respectively. As Figure A indicates, from 1896 to 1912 these two counties were separated by a margin of about 10 per cent, and in one election—that of 1896—Riverside was more Democratic than Plumas. The first wide difference appears in 1916, when the Democratic percentage in Plumas County rose 18 per cent and that in Riverside only 5.6 per cent. Omitting momentarily the deviant election of 1920, the two counties were separated by a wide margin of about 30 per cent from 1924 through 1944. This represents an ideal type model for the critical election phenomena. Judging from the most extreme cases, one can observe that a readjustment widening the division of political preference in these two counties had occurred in the election of 1916, and that this alignment remained over a twenty-year period. The election of 1928 was but a part of a process already underway.

As Key discovered in New England, the data for the extreme case should represent in exaggerated form the patterns occurring in other combinations of data. However, to confirm the existence of the pattern, a number of related tests have been conducted, using different base periods and different combinations of counties.

Figure B represents a comparison of the five counties with the fewest and the five counties with the most Democratic party gains, using the base years 1920 to 1928. If the election of 1928 were a critical one, it should be manifest in this example. Rather, the pattern is remarkably parallel to the ideal type. The average Democratic vote in the five counties with the most gain rose sharply in 1916, fell off precipitately in 1920, then surged back close to the 1916 total in 1924; the Smith percentage actually was less than that in either 1916 or 1924 for Democratic and Socialist candidates.[12] Again the scissors appear to diverge in the election of 1916 and with the exception of 1920 the cleavage persists until 1944.

Since the election of 1916 appears to take on a special significance, an appropriate test is to chart in the same manner the counties with the most and the least Democratic gains between the base years 1908 to 1916. Here the number of examples has been expanded, and averages have been computed for the twenty-one counties with the most Democratic increase during this period and the eleven with the least. Nonetheless, the pattern first observed in the ideal type is not significantly modified in Figure C. It is, however, worthy of note that the counties with the least gain were actually more Democratic than the counties with the most gain prior to the 1916 election. Again, with less sharp differentiation due to the increased number of causes, the alignment of 1916 basically prevailed through 1944.

Inasmuch as many of the counties used in the foregoing analyses were sparsely populated rural counties, it is desirable to examine patterns of change in the eleven metropolitan counties of California. These counties contributed 59 percent of the total two-party vote in 1896; 70 per cent in 1916, 78 per cent in 1932, and 82 per cent in 1944. The counties are divided into the six with the largest Democratic gains, 1920 to 1928, and the five with the least.[13] Again, as Figure D indicates, the pattern is replicated. After a seesawing of political allegiances from 1892 forward, a cleavage emerged in 1916 that was relatively constant through 1944.

Our analysis thus far has avoided one extremely important variable: the election of 1920. Although some of the foregoing discussion would seem to point to the Wilson-Hughes election of 1916 as a critical one, Democratic strength was not stable enough to survive the complex of new issues, such as the League of Nations, the Treaty of Versailles, and prohibition, which were interjected into the 1920 campaign. Neither is it accurate to designate the 1924 La Follette-Davis-Coolidge election as critical, since this would overlook the very close relationship of the 1924 vote to that of 1916. While the disastrous desertion from the Democratic party in 1920 does not qualify our hypothesis that there was no "Al Smith revolution" in California, it does make it difficult to identify just when a definite and permanent realignment occurred. However,

---

12 Since the Progressive electors were barred from the California ballot in 1924, to vote for La Follette one had to cast a vote for the Socialist party electors.

13 No major differences appear if the 1908-1916 rather than the 1902-1928 base is used in this example.

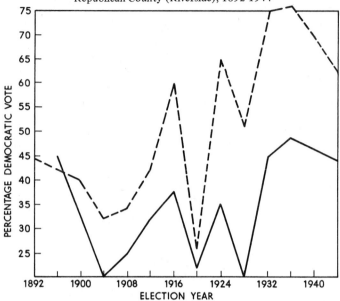

FIGURE A

Percentage Democratic Vote for President in Most Consistently
Democratic County in California (Plumas) and Most Consistently
Republican County (Riverside), 1892-1944

Broken line — Democratic gain counties
Solid line — Democratic loss counties

FIGURE B

Percentage Democratic Vote for President in the 5 Counties with
the Most Democratic Gain, 1920-1928 and in the 5 Counties with
Greatest Democratic Loss (and Least Gain). 1920-1928

Broken line — Democratic county
Solid line — Republican county

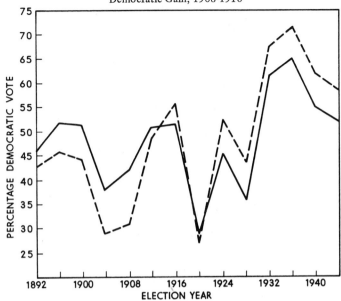

FIGURE C

Percentage Democratic Vote for President in 21 Counties with
Most Democratic Gain, 1908-1916 and in 11 Counties with Least
Democratic Gain, 1908-1916

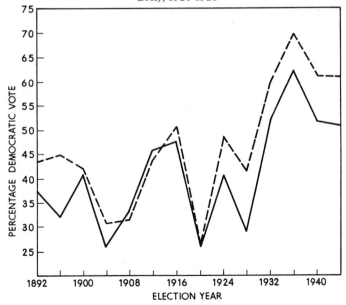

FIGURE D

Percentage Democratic Vote for President in the 6 Metropolitan
Counties with Most Democratic Gain, 1920-1928 and in the 5
Metropolitan Counties with Least Democratic Gain (or Democratic
Loss), 1920-1928

more than any other election in the time sequences presented, that of 1920 would appear to be a deviant one, in which voters were responding to short-term stimuli not present four years earlier and not present four years later.

One further methodological device, supplementary to Key's critical election model, can be employed to test the hypothesis of this paper. This is a measure of multiple correlations developed a number of years ago by the political scientist Harold F. Gosnell and adapted by Duncan MacRae, Jr., and James A. Meldrum to apply to the Key model.[14] It may best be explained by an example. Taking as an illustration the vote for the Republican candidate, Charles Evans Hughes, in 1916, we correlate the percentage vote for Hughes in each of the fifty-eight counties with the percentage vote in each identical county for Warren G. Harding in 1920. In the rare circumstances that the percentages were exactly the same, a correlation coefficient of 100 would be produced. Obviously, any correlation coefficient at the 80 level or above represents extremely close parallelism in the distribution of the votes in the two elections. Then, in the same fashion, the percentages for 1916 and 1920 are correlated with percentages for ensuing elections. By using an IBM 1620 computer, we can obtain correlations among more than one hundred separate election contests. This paper employs correlations between the presidential elections from 1884 to 1940, fifteen elections for the Republican party matrix, sixteen for the Democratic party, since the 1924 La Follette vote is included in the Democratic matrix. The correlation coefficients between county percentages in votes for president by both parties, 1884-1940, are set forth in Table 3.[15]

Before we present the results of these calculations, we offer a word of caution. Given the disparate population of California counties, the correlations reflect a geographical rather than a numerical distribution of the vote; hence, any generalizations from the correlation coefficients should be considered as suggestive, not conclusive.

When all the correlations covering the presidential elections from 1884 to 1940 are arranged in the two matrices, fifteen by fifteen and sixteen by sixteen, it is possible to observe those that cluster into high correlations blocs. A voting realignment would be indicated when a sharp drop-off in correlations appears over a short time interval. MacRae and Meldrum point out that "All the elections before the reorientation should show high correlations with one another; all elections afterward should also be highly correlated; but any election before the critical transition should show a lesser correlation with any election afterward."[16] Visual analysis of the matrix can be supplemented with a more refined statistical technique, that of elementary factor-analysis, which identifies

---

14 Harold F. Gosnell, *Grass Roots Politics: National Voting Behavior of Typical States* (Washington, D.C., 1942).

15 Each entry in the matrix represents a correlation coefficient between two elections. For example, the figure 85 in row 2, column 1 of the Republican matrix is the correlation between the distribution of votes for the presidential candidate in 1884 and the distribution of votes for the presidential candidate in 1888.

16 MacRae and Meldrum, "Critical Elections in Illinois," 670.

TABLE 3

Correlation Coefficients between County Percentages in Votes for President,
1884-1940 (decimals deleted)

Republican Party Matrix

	1884	1888	1892	1896	1900	1904	1908	1912	1916	1920	1924	1928	1932	1936	1940
1884		85	72	69	74	73	70	31	42	52	26	10	34	39	42
1888	85		76	52	69	72	68	26	47	44	31	26	42	17	18
1892	72	76		58	76	76	62	22	42	58	30	23	25	47	12
1896	69	52	58		79	74	75	54	48	54	34	15	44	14	21
1900	74	69	76	79		92	90	56	63	70	49	36	53	20	27
1904	73	72	76	74	92		90	61	69	75	59	42	55	27	36
1908	70	68	62	75	90	90		62	78	70	65	49	66	39	46
1912	31	26	22	54	56	61	62		63	54	64	52	56	39	35
1916	42	47	42	48	63	69	78	63		71	86	75	83	66	71
1920	52	44	58	54	70	75	70	54	71		66	51	57	43	50
1924	26	31	30	34	49	59	65	64	86	66		85	82	68	75
1928	10	26	23	15	36	42	49	52	75	51	85		81	76	76
1932	34	42	25	44	53	55	66	56	83	57	82	81		75	74
1936	39	17	47	14	20	27	39	39	66	43	68	76	75		89
1940	42	18	12	21	27	36	46	35	71	50	75	76	74	89	

Democratic Party Matrix

	1884	1888	1892	1896	1900	1904	1908	1912	1916	1920	1924 (D)	1924 (S)	1928	1932	1936	1940
1884		85	69	69	74	82	70	47	42	66	62	03	10	34	04	04
1888	85		80	52	69	83	68	43	47	56	51	13	26	42	17	18
1892	69	80		31	56	76	63	47	58	57	43	14	54	51	37	32
1896	69	52	31		79	67	75	52	48	65	68	05	15	44	14	21
1900	74	69	56	79		84	90	55	63	77	62	27	36	53	20	27
1904	82	83	76	67	84		89	65	70	70	64	33	46	62	33	35
1908	70	68	63	75	90	89		64	78	78	62	10	49	66	39	46
1912	47	43	47	52	55	65	64		57	49	60	29	45	52	38	24
1916	42	47	58	48	63	70	78	57		71	48	73	75	83	66	71
1920	66	56	57	65	77	70	78	49	71		64	52	46	60	40	45
1924 (D)	62	51	43	68	62	64	62	60	48	64		00	29	53	19	24
1924 (S)	03	13	14	05	27	33	10	29	73	52	00		80	67	66	71
1928	10	26	54	15	36	46	49	45	75	46	29	80		81	76	76
1932	34	42	51	44	53	62	66	52	83	60	53	67	81		75	74
1936	04	17	37	14	20	33	39	38	66	40	19	66	76	75		89
1940	04	18	32	21	27	35	46	24	71	45	24	71	76	74	89	

those elections that cluster together around some common relationship and
permits us to estimate the extent to which each election is "loaded" with some
particular factor, such as the "Bryan vote" or the "New Deal vote."[17]

---

[17] The method used here is a highly simplified form of factor analysis that selects
"reference factors" rather than the more complex computation. It is outlined in Louis L.
McQuitty, "Elementary Factor Analysis," *Psychological Reports*, Vol. 9 (1951), 71-78. The
"clusters" are determined by marking the highest entry in each row of the matrix, then
selecting the highest single duo of entries in the entire matrix (e.g., in the Democratic party

Examining Republican party correlations first, one notes that the factor analysis reveals four clusters of highly interrelated elections: first, 1884 and 1888; second, all elections between 1892 and 1908 and the election of 1920; third, the elections of 1912, 1916, 1924, 1928, and 1932; and finally, the elections of 1936 and 1940. This analysis would point to the election of 1912 (when Theodore Roosevelt, although a Progressive nationally, was the Republican nominee in California) as an important turning point, when an older Republican constituency present since 1892 gave way to a different alignment which, except for the election of 1920, prevailed until the depression. It therefore seems appropriate to conclude on the basis of this data that the geographical distribution of the Republican party voting constituency was relatively well established, that the sharpest break had come in 1912, and that the election of 1928 marked no major change.

Analysis of the Democratic party matrix presents a similar, although less clear picture. The three elections from 1884 to 1892 form one bloc. Then, there is high correlation between the five elections from 1896 to 1912. For the purposes of this analysis, the next bloc is the most important. The election of 1916 does not fit into the earlier set; rather, four elections—1916, the 1924 Socialist vote for La Follette, 1928, and 1932—form a set of their own. The 1920 vote and the vote for John W. Davis in 1924 appear as a part of the older pre-1912 orientation. This would suggest again the same conclusions reached through the Key model. A new Democratic alignment, harbinger of the New Deal coalition, appeared in the vote for Wilson in California in 1916, was temporarily shattered in 1920, only to emerge hesitantly in the Socialist vote of 1924 and the Smith vote in 1928. With the 1940 vote as 100 representing a "New Deal" factor, the 1916 vote shows a loading of 71; the 1920 vote only 45, the Davis vote only 24. The La Follette vote, loading at 71, shows the same relationship as that of 1916 to the New Deal vote, and the Smith vote loads at 76.

---

matrix, the highest is the 90 correlation between the 1900 and 1908 votes). These are the first two members of the first cluster. Then by reading across the rows for each of these first entries, we can bring in all other elections which have their highest single correlation with one of these elections. These entries are then checked to bring in all elections that have their single highest correlation with one of them. This is done until all possible elections are incorporated.

The specific clusters are as follows:

Republican

   I. *1884*-1888
  II. 1892-1896-1900-1904-*1908*-1920
 III. 1912-*1916*-1924-1928-1932
 IV. 1936-*1940*

Democratic

   I. 1884-1888-*1892*
  II. 1896-1900-*1904*-1908-1912-1920-1924D
 III. *1916*-1924S-1928-1932
 IV. 1936-*1940*

The reference factor for each of these clusters is the column in each cluster with the highest total when all correlations are added. These are italicized above.

TABLE 4
Reference Factor Loadings
California Democratic Party

Year	Pre-Bryan	Bryan Period	1916 Shift	New Deal
1884	69	82	42	04
1888	80	83	47	18
1892	100	76	58	32
1896	31	67	48	21
1900	56	84	63	27
1904	76	100	70	35
1908	63	89	78	46
1912	47	65	57	24
1916	58	70	100	71
1920	57	70	70	45
1924 D	43	64	48	24
1924 S	14	33	73	71
1928	54	46	75	76
1932	51	62	83	74
1936	37	33	66	89
1940	32	35	71	100

Conclusions should be drawn from this data only with extreme caution. Its principal value is for comparative purposes. For example, the "New Deal" factor, the highest column total in the cluster bloc that includes the elections of 1936 and 1940, is more closely related to the Democratic constituency most evident in the "1916 shift" than to the constituency of either the Pre-Bryan or the Bryan period. Also, comparing the column entries, the 1924 Socialist vote is more parallel to the "New Deal" factor than to the 1924 Democratic vote for John W. Davis.

It is probably neither necessary nor possible to identify any single California presidential election as the "critical" one. The alignment in 1916 does not qualify, for it was not permanent; to choose the 1924 Socialist vote would overlook the close correlation of the Wilson percentage to later Democratic votes. But if any single election could be classed as critical, it is clear that either 1916 or 1924, not 1928, constituted a crucial realignment point in California politics. This conclusion is consistent with the suggestion of MacRae and Meldrum that electoral realignments may take place over an extended "critical period," rather than being sharply manifested in any single critical election.

As I have indicated earlier, it is not the purpose of this paper to inquire into motives and to ask what caused voter alignment or lack of it in California. The design of this paper is predicated upon an assumption of Lee Benson: "Once historians know what happened and where and when it happened, it seems reasonable to believe they are in a better position to detect what caused it to happen."[18] Nevertheless, one possible clue is provided by comparing the correlations of Democratic party votes subsequent to 1900 with such ecological factors as the rural and urban population, males in manufacturing, and such

[18] Lee Benson, *Concept of Jacksonian Democracy,* 1st Atheneum ed. (New York, 1964), 270.

sample reference factors as the No vote on the Hot Cargo referendum in 1942 representing pro-labor sentiments. Although these correlations are not high, they indicate in general an increasing relationship of the Democratic vote to the urban population, to the percentage of industrial workers in a county and sympathy for organized labor. It is no startling hypothesis, but it can be suggested that the California Democratic party was gradually shifting from a rural base and was becoming an urban party with substantial labor support. This evolution began around 1916 and was still in process in 1940.

One final question is appropriate. Is an interpretation that identifies significant political realignments which took place in California before 1928 consistent with what has been learned about the politics of the state from nonstatistical methods? The years between 1912 and 1924 marked the zenith and the nadir of the Progressive party in California. After a brief third party flurry, the Progressives had returned as unwelcome guests to the Republican party, and from 1916 until the early thirties the bitter factional battles within the Republican party constituted the most significant political contests in California. The Progressives, more than the weakened and ineffective California Democratic party, represented the major political alternative. Except in 1920, the Progressive leaders were lukewarm supporters of the national Republican party presidential candidates. Given this shattering of traditional party organizations in California, it is not implausible to conceive that large numbers of voters, either from confusion or choice, made new political commitments between 1916 and 1928.

In summary, to prove that the election of 1928 was critical in California, it would be necessary to demonstrate that new alignments took place in that year unlike those in immediately preceding elections. It would be necessary to show that the percentage distribution of votes by counties correlated higher with all elections after 1928 than with any elections before 1928. It is the hypothesis of this paper that such proof cannot be found. In California, the election of 1928 brought Democratic losses from their totals in two preceding elections, and these losses were particularly evident in the metropolitan areas where the ostensible Smith revolution was supposedly most manifest.

The election of 1928 in California was a backward step in the process that led in 1932 to the emergence of a Democratic constituency whose existence was presaged in the elections of 1916 and of 1924.

A single case study of this type is insufficient to challenge the widely held assumption that a nationwide political realignment occurred in 1928. However, two facts should be noted: first, the conclusions about the Smith election are based upon analysis of only the largest urban centers; and second, most of these studies compare 1928 only with the deviant election of 1920. If the conclusions of this paper can be sustained, it would be wise to suspend final judgment about the importance of the election of 1928 until detailed studies of other metropolitan states identify more clearly the patterns of voting behavior.

3. The simulmatics project*

ITHIEL DE SOLA POOL† AND ROBERT ABELSON§

This is the first report on a program of research conducted for the Democratic Party during the 1960 campaign. The research used a new technique for processing poll data and included computer simulation of likely voter behavior. The immediate goal of the project was to estimate rapidly, during the campaign, the probable impact upon the public, and upon small strategically important groups within the public, of different issues which might arise or which might be used by the candidates.

THE DATA

This study is a "secondary analysis" of old poll results. Students of public opinion are becoming aware that the growing backlog of earlier polls provides a powerful tool to aid in the interpretation of new poll results. Polling has now been routine for three decades, but poll archives are just beginning to be assembled. The main one is the Roper Public Opinion Research Center in Williamstown, the existence of which made feasible the project here described.[1]

The first step in the project was to identify in that archive all polls anticipating the elections of 1952, 1954, 1956, and 1958. (Pre-election polls on

* Reprinted from *The Public Opinion Quarterly*, XXV (Summer, 1961), pp. 167-83, by permission of the authors and the publisher.

† Ithiel de Sola Pool, chairman, political science department, Massachusetts Institute of Technology, received his Ph.D. from the University of Chicago. He is the coauthor, with Robert P. Abelson, of *Candidates, Issues, and Strategies: A Computer Simulation of the 1960 and 1964 Presidential Elections;* and, with Raymond A. Bauer and Lewis A. Dexter, of *American Business and Public Policy.*

§ Robert P. Abelson, professor of psychology, Yale University, received his Ph.D. from Princeton University in 1953. He is the coauthor, with Ithiel de Sola Pool, of *Candidates, Issues, and Strategies: Computer Simulations of the 1960 and 1964 Presidential Elections;* and editor of *Theories of Cognitive Consistency: A Sourcebook.*

[1] We wish to express our gratitude to that Center, as well as to the MIT Computation Center, and to the men who originally assembled the data, especially George Gallup and Elmo Roper.

the 1960 contest were added later when they became available.) We selected those polls which contained standard identification data on region, city size, sex, race, socio-economic status, party, and religion, the last being the item most often missing. Further, we restricted our attention to those polls which asked about vote intention and also about a substantial number of pre-selected issues such as civil rights, foreign affairs, and social legislation. From 1952 to 1958 we found fifty usable surveys covering 85,000 respondents. Sixteen polls anticipating the 1960 elections were added to this number. The sixty-six surveys represented a total of well over 100,000 interviews.

PROCESSING THE DATA

To handle such massive data required substantial innovations in analytic procedures. In essence, the data were reduced to a 480-by-52 matrix. The number 480 represented voter types, each voter type being defined by socio-economic characteristics. A single voter type might be "Eastern, metropolitan, lower-income, white, Catholic, female Democrats." Another might be, "Border state, rural, upper-income, white, Protestant, male Independents." Certain types with small numbers of respondents were reconsolidated, yielding the total of 480 types actually used.

The number 52 represented what we called in our private jargon "issue clusters." Most of these were political issues, such as foreign aid, attitudes toward the United Nations, and McCarthyism. Other so-called "issue clusters" included such familiar indicators of public opinion as "Which party is better for people like you?" vote intention, and nonvoting. In sum, the issue clusters were political characteristics on which the voter type would have a distribution.

One can picture the 480-by-52 matrix as containing four numbers in each cell. The first number stated the total number of persons of that voter type asked about that particular item of information. The other three numbers trichotomized those respondents into the percentages pro, anti, and undecided or confused on the issue.

We assembled such a matrix for each biennial election separately and also a consolidated matrix for all elections together. Thus, it was possible by comparison of the separate matrices to examine trends.

The reduction of the raw data to this matrix form was an arduous task. The first step was to identify in each survey those questions which seemed to bear on any of the fifty-two issue clusters we had listed as relevant to the campaign. One such cluster was attitude toward domestic communism or, as we called it for shorthand, McCarthyism. Over the past decade many questions have been asked on this and related matters in many different polls. One survey might ask, "Are you in favor of permitting a Communist to teach in the school system?" Another would ask, "What do you think of Senator McCarthy?" Another would ask, "Do you think McCarthy has done more good or harm?" The problem was to determine which questions tapped essentially the same attitude, domestic anticommunism. The decision was made by a two-step process. First, questions were grouped together *a priori* on the basis of intuitive judgment, and then this grouping was empirically tested.

The empirical test was conducted as follows: Replies to each questions were separately trichotomized. Typically, the replies had previously been coded in up to thirteen categories. Where more than three replies had been coded, the codes had to be regrouped. On the McCarthyism issue, replies were classified as McCarthyite, anti-McCarthyite, and indeterminate. A reply opposing retention of a Communist in the school system would be classified as McCarthyite. In the case of such a question as "How well do you like McCarthy?" for which a scale had originally been used, cutting points had to be set depending on the distribution.

For each pair of questions in the presumed cluster we then correlated the percentage "pro," and separately the percentage "anti," across voter types yielding two correlation matrices. (The voter types for this operation were 15, a reconsolidation of the 480. Since this operation dealt with percentages on questions from single surveys, consolidation was essential to obtain base numbers in each voter type large enough so that the percentages being correlated would be reasonably stable.) Only those questions which showed high correlations with each other were retained in a cluster. Thus, our assumption that a question about Communist teachers in the schools could be treated as equivalent to a question about McCarthy was subject to empirical validation.

In many instances questions which *a priori* seemed alike had to be discarded from the clusters. Some clusters had to be broken up into two or more. Indeed, in the particular example we have been using here, it turned out that replies to the identically worded question "How well do you like McCarthy" ceased tapping the same attitudes the minute the Senate censured him. Clusters thus represented questions which could be regarded as in some sense equivalent, both on the grounds of political common sense and on the grounds of empirical correlation.[2]

It should be emphasized that empirical correlation was not enough. Such a question as "Which party is better for people like you?" and a question about the image of Adlai Stevenson would correlate strongly because they were both

---

[2] We should qualify. What has been described is what we started out to do and what we did for most issue clusters. In the end, however, we were forced to compromise on certain foreign-policy clusters. This in itself is an interesting finding. On almost all domestic questions, primarily because they were party-linked or left-right linked, it was possible to validate empirically the equivalence of questions which *a priori* seemed alike. On certain foreign-policy issues this was quite impossible. The political scientist looking at a half-dozen questions about foreign aid or about the UN might conclude that they all should reflect a common underlying attitude toward that matter. However, empirically, in many instances the distribution of replies was highly sensitive to conjunctural influences or shades in wording of the question. Rather than completely abandon the hope of doing any analysis of foreign-policy issues in the campaign, we retained some clusters which failed to meet the correlational test, labeling them *a priori* clusters, not sure of what we would do with them (in fact we did very little), but feeling it better to retain them on the computer tape than to discard the data from the start.

party-linked. However, they were not included in a single issue cluster unless they also seemed politically equivalent.

The final step in the preliminary data processing—the step which gave us our matrices—was to take all cards in any one of the 480 voter types for a particular biennial period and tabulate for each issue cluster the number of replies pro, con, and indeterminate, and the number of cards on which such replies appeared. That last number varied for each cluster since some questions (e.g. turnout) were asked on virtually every survey we used, while other questions were asked only occasionally.

PURPOSES OF THE METHOD

The reader may wonder what purposes were served by reorganizing the data into the standard format just described. That handling of the data lent itself to three main uses: (1) A "data bank" was available from which one might draw the answer to any one of a vast number of questions at a moment's notice. (2) The consolidation of separate surveys made available adequate data on small, yet politically significant, subsegments in the population. For example, we wrote a report on Northern Negro voters based upon 4,050 interviews, including 418 with middle-class Negroes. The typical national sample survey contains no more than 100 interviews with Northern Negroes, a number clearly inadequate for refined analysis. (3) The data format and its transfer to high-speed tape facilitated its use in computer simulation of the effects of hypothetical campaign strategies. This aspect of the project is the most novel and is the one to which we shall return later in this article.

THE HISTORY OF THE PROJECT

Before we illustrate those uses of the data, let us detour to examine the history of the project: the fact that it was sponsored and actually used by a partisan group makes the story of its management of some interest to students of public opinion research.

The project was initiated in the early months of 1959 by William McPhee and the authors. Our plan for computer simulation (on a different version of which McPhee had already been working)[3] was presented to Mr. Edward Greenfield, a New York businessman actively engaged in Democratic politics. Through his intervention, a group of New York reform Democrats who had taken major responsibility for raising money for the Democratic Advisory Council became interested.[4] Before this group of private individuals was willing to secure funds, however, they wanted to be sure that the results were likely to be valid and useful. In May of 1959 the project was discussed in Washington at a meeting

---

[3] William McPhee, *A Model for Analyzing Macro-dynamics in Voting Systems,* Columbia University, Bureau of Applied Social Research, undated.

[4] We wish to express our particular thanks to Thomas Finletter, Robert Benjamin, Joseph Baird, and Curtis Roosevelt for encouragement and cooperation.

attended by Mr. Charles Tyroler, Executive Secretary of the Democratic Advisory Council; the members of the Council executive committee; Paul Butler, Chairman of the Democratic National Committee; several other officials of that Committee; Mr. Neil Staebler, Michigan State Chairman; and a number of social science consultants, including Samuel Eldersveld, Morris Janowitz, and Robert Lane. This group was interested but reserved. It was suggested that the project should be supported for four months initially and at the end of this period a further review should be made.

The Williamstown Public Opinion Research Center agreed to permit the use of polls in their archives on two conditions: First, all basic data tabulated by Simulmatics from their cards were to be made available to the Center so the Republican Party would have an equal opportunity to use such data if they wanted them. We provided a print-out of the data on the computer tape, but not, of course, the programs for simulation nor supplementary data obtained from other sources (e.g. the census) and used in our system. Second, and demanded by both the Roper Public Opinion Research Center and the social scientists engaged in the study, all results could be published for scientific purposes after the election. This article is part of our program to meet that condition.

Given the green light to carry out the project, the principals organized themselves as The Simulmatics Corporation, for although the objective of the project constituted scientific research, it was clear that universities would not and should not accept financing from politically motivated sources or permit a university project to play an active role in supplying campaign advice to one party.

The summer of 1959 was devoted to the data reduction job described above. In October 1959, when the preliminary data processing had been substantially completed, a review meeting in New York was attended by many of the same persons who had been at the Advisory Council meeting in May plus a number of social science consultants, including Harold Lasswell, Paul Lazarsfeld, Morris Janowitz, and John Tukey. Although the degree of confidence in the basic approach ranged from enthusiasm to doubt, a decision to proceed was quickly reached.

The next step was the development of computer programs, some of which will be discussed below. One objective was to make possible rapid incorporation of new data which might, we hoped, become available during the campaign. Our hope, as we shall see, was only slightly fulfilled.

By June of 1960 we were able to prepare a first report as a sample of the kind of thing which might be done by the Simulmatics process. That was the report on the Negro vote in the North.

Our contractual arrangements with our sponsors ended with the preparation of the process and of this report illustrating it, shortly before the 1960 convention. It was understood that actual use of the service in the form of further reports on specific topics would be purchased by appropriate elements of the party in the pre-campaign and campaign period at their discretion. In the immediate pre-convention period, the National Committee felt that it should not make decisions which would shortly be the business of the nominee. After the convention, the Kennedy organization, contrary to the image created by the press, did not enter the campaign as a well-oiled machine with a well-planned strategy. Except for the registration drive, which had been carefully prepared by Lawrence O'Brien, no strategic or organizational plan existed the day after the nomination. It took until August for the organization to shake down. No campaign research of any significant sort was therefore done in the two months from mid-June to mid-August, either by Simulmatics or by others. In August, a decision was made to ask Louis Harris to make thirty state surveys for the Kennedy campaign. However, because of the late start, data from these surveys would not be available until after Labor Day. On August 11, the National Committee asked The Simulmatics Corporation to prepare three reports: one each on the image of Kennedy, the image of Nixon, and foreign policy as a campaign issue. These three reports were to be delivered in two weeks for use in campaign planning. Along with them we were to conduct a national sample survey which, in the minds of the political decision makers, would serve to bring the Simulmatics data, based as they were on old polls, up to date. (It should be mentioned that one of the most difficult tasks of the Simulmatics project was persuading campaign strategists that data other than current intelligence could be useful to them.) The national survey by telephone was conducted for the project by the Furst Survey Research Center and was indeed extremely useful in guiding the use of the older data. It confirmed the published Gallup finding that Nixon was at that point well in the lead, though we disagreed on the proportion of undecideds (we found 23 per cent). It made us aware that Nixon's lead was due to women. It also persuaded us that voters were largely focusing upon foreign policy at that point in the campaign.

The relationship between the use of such current intelligence and the use of a simulation model developed out of historical data is analogous to the relationship between a climatological model and current weather information. One can predict tomorrow's weather best if one has both historical information about patterns and current information about where one stands in a pattern. While it would be presumptuous to assert that in two weeks of intense activity we approached an effective integration of the two sets of data, that was the ideal we had in mind and which in some limited respects we approximated.

It should be added that the introduction of the national survey data was possible only because of prior preparation for rapid data analysis. The survey was ordered on a Thursday, the field interviewing took place between Saturday and the following Thursday, by Friday morning all cards had been punched, and by Friday night the pre-programmed analysis had been run and preliminary results were given to the National Committee.

The three reports that had been ordered on August 11 were delivered on August 25. The speed of the entire operation is, of course, a testimony to the advantages of a high-speed computer system. Nonetheless, such intense pressure is not an optimum condition for research work, even though rapid analysis was one of our objectives from the start. The reader who suspects that under those circumstances clerical errors inevitably occurred is quite right. It was our good fortune that none of those which we have found since in rechecking have turned out to alter any conclusion, but we do not recommend such limited schedules as a normal mode of work. Nevertheless, with well-prepared computerized analysis, it can be done when necessary.

The reader may ask whether the large preparatory investment was justified in terms of the quantitatively limited use of the project. When we planned the project, we—perhaps unrealistically—anticipated active campaign work from the beginning of the summer until about September 15. (Anything done later than that would hardly be useful.) How far the investment was justified by the two weeks of work actually done is a question which we find impossible to answer. An answer depends on an estimate of how much impact the contents of the reports had on the campaign. The reports received an extremely limited elite circulation. They were seen during the campaign by perhaps a dozen to fifteen key decision makers, but they were read intelligently by these talented and literate men.

Despite the contraction of our effort, our own feeling is one of relative satisfaction that the Simulmatics project was able to provide research on demand concerning the key issues at perhaps the critical moment of the campaign. While campaign strategy, except on a few points, conformed rather closely to the advice in the more than one hundred pages of the three reports, we know full well that this was by no means because of the reports. Others besides ourselves had similar ideas. Yet, if the report strengthened right decisions on a few critical items, we would consider the investment justified.

EXAMPLES OF USE OF THE SYSTEM

Earlier in this article we listed three uses of the method herein described: providing a "data bank," rapidly available; providing data on small, politically significant groups; permitting computer simulation. The first of these advantages has perhaps already been adequately illustrated. Let us turn to the other two.

Our report on Northern Negro voters did not use a computer simulation but rather illustrated the capability of the process to provide information about small subgroups of the population. Compare here a number of quotations from the report with what we could have said working from a single survey containing responses from perhaps 100 Northern Negroes. The report demonstrated, for example, that between 1954 and 1956

[A] small but significant shift to the Republicans occurred among Northern Negroes, which cost the Democrats about 1 per cent of the total votes in 8 key states [a shift which continued in 1958]. In those years, the Democratic Party loss to the Republican Party was about 7 per cent of the Northern Negro vote—enough to cause a one half per cent loss in the *total* popular vote in the eight key states. In addition, among Northern Negro Independents, only about one quarter actually voted Republican in 1952, but about half voted Republican in 1956, enough of a shift to cause an additional loss of a little less than one half per cent of the total popular vote in the eight key states.

. . .

The shift against the Democrats is more marked among the opinion leading middle class Negroes than among lower-income Negroes.

. . .

Anti catholicism is less prevalent among Negroes than among Northern, urban, Protestant whites.

. . .

The most significant point of all is the fact that the shift is not an Ike-shift: it is a Republican Party shift. It affects Congressional votes as much as Presidential votes.

In addition, the report demonstrated that Northern urban Negroes vote as often as whites of comparable socio-economic status, and that "there is no sharp difference between Negroes and comparable whites in their feelings about Nixon."

This report was made available to all the leading Democratic candidates, to the Democratic National Committee, and to the drafters of the Democratic platform. Probably no one can say what influence, if any, it had upon them. Those men themselves would not know which of the many things they read or heard shaped their decisions. As outside observers, we can assert only that the report was placed in the hands of the platform framers in the ten days preceding the drafting of the platform, and was read.

The most dramatic result, however, was, as indicated above, the finding that Eisenhower had not generated among Negroes the kind of personal following that he had among most white voter types. This suggested that the Negro vote presented far more of a problem to the Democratic campaign than appeared at first glance; it could not be assumed that the losses in recent years would be recovered with Eisenhower out of the picture.

SIMULATIONS

We turn now to what was perhaps the most novel aspect of the study—the use of computer simulations. We describe, first, how we simulated state-by-state results and, second, how we simulated the impact of the religious issue.

One of the benefits gained from the large number of interviews we used was the possibility of approximating state-by-state results. A national sample survey—even a relatively large one—has too few cases from most states to permit any significant analysis of state politics. The same would have been true, however, even for our voluminous data if we had attempted to do a state-by-state analysis in a simple way. We had an average of about 2,000 interviews per state, but that is a misleading figure. In a small state there might have been no more than 300 or 400 interviews, and on a particular issue cluster that had occurred, for example, in only one-tenth of the surveys, there would be too few cases for effective analysis. We therefore developed a system for creating synthetic, or simulated, states.

By an elaborate analysis of census, poll, and voting data—made more difficult because 1960 census results were not yet available—we developed a set of estimates on the number of persons of each voter type in each state. (Note that since *region* was one of the defining characteristics for the 480 voter types, there were at most only 108 voter types in any given state.) It was assumed that a voter of a given voter type would be identical regardless of the state from which he came. A simulated state therefore consisted of a weighted average of the behaviors of the voter types in that state, the weighting being proportional to the numbers of such persons in that state. For example, we thus assumed that the difference between Maine and New York is not truly a difference between New Yorkers and inhabitants of Maine as such, but a difference in the proportions of different voter types which make up each state. We assumed that an "upper-income Protestant Republican rural white male" was the same in either state, and that a "small-city Catholic Democratic lower-income female" was also the same in either. This assumption enabled us to use all cases of a voter type from a particular region in arriving at a conclusion for a state.

We do not assert that the assumptions on which this simulation is based are true. On the contrary, we can be sure that they are partly false. The interesting question intellectually is how good were the results obtained with these partially true assumptions. The test is, of course, how far state-by-state predictions made on these assumptions turn out to correspond to reality. To the extent that they do, they suggest that the essential differences between states in a region are in distributions of types rather than in geographic differences, even within a voter type.[5]

Upon this simulation of states was built a second and more interesting simulation, one which attempted to assess the impact of the religious issue. Since the one simulation rests upon the other, the effectiveness of the state simulation is simultaneously tested by examination of the religious simulation. The latter, the main simulation actually carried out during the campaign, represented a hypothetical campaign in which the only issues were party and Catholicism. Our report of this simulation was limited to the North because of the peculiar role of party in the South. The outcome was a ranking of thirty-two states ranging from the one in which we estimated Kennedy would do best to the one in which we estimated he would do worst. The ranking was:

1.	Rhode Island	8.	California
2.	Massachusetts	9.	Arizona
3.	New Mexico	10.	Michigan
4.	Connecticut	11.	Wisconsin
5.	New York	12.	Colorado
6.	Illinois	13.	Ohio
7.	New Jersey	14.	Montana

---

[5] The states where the simulation was most notably off included Arizona, Nevada, New Mexico, Idaho, and Colorado, states mostly of small population, and states which, in the absence of a "Mountain Region" in our classification, we attempted to treat as Western or Midwestern. Clearly, the assumption of regional uniformity was misleading as applied to them.

15. Minnesota	24. Nebraska
16. Missouri	25. Indiana
17. Pennsylvania	26. South Dakota
18. Nevada	27. Vermont
19. Washington	28. Iowa
20. New Hampshire	29. Kansas
21. Wyoming	30. Utah
22. Oregon	31. Idaho
23. North Dakota	32. Maine

The product-moment correlation over states between the Kennedy index on the simulation (not strictly speaking a per cent) and the actual Kennedy vote in the election was .82. It should be emphasized that this satisfying result was based upon political data not a single item of which was later than October 1958. Surveys on the 1960 election were not available soon enough to be incorporated into this analysis.

The basic method in this simulation was a fairly straightforward application of the cross-pressure findings of earlier election studies.[6] These findings enabled us to improve our estimate of how a particular voter will behave if we know the cross-pressures he is under. With such knowledge, an analyst should feel more comfortable making guesses about how voters under particular kinds of cross-pressure will shift in an election than he would about making an over-all intuitive guess at the outcome. The method of this simulation was to make a series of such detailed estimates and then let the computer put them together to give an over-all outcome.

To make these detailed estimates we classified our set of 480 voter types into 9 possible cross-pressure subsets arising from a 3-by-3 breakdown on religion and party: Protestants, Catholics, and others; Republicans, Democrats, and Independents. For each of the nine resulting situations we made a prediction. For example, take the Protestant Republicans. They were not under cross-pressure. Since our data had revealed no substantial dislike of Nixon as an individual among such voters, we saw no reason why their vote in 1960 should differ substantially from their vote in 1956, even though Eisenhower was not running. Thus for them we wrote two equations:

$$V_k = P_{56} (1 - P_{35})$$
$$V_n = Q_{56} (1 - P_{35})$$

meaning that the predicted Kennedy percentage (V^k) in any voter type of this Protestant-Republican sort would be the percentage of persons in that voter type who had indicated a preference for Stevenson in the 1956 polls (P^{56}), reduced by the nonvoting record of that voter type $(1 - P^{35})$.[7] The equation for the

---

[6] Bernard R. Berelson, Paul F. Lazarsfeld, William N. McPhee, *Voting: A Study of Opinion Formation in a Presidential Campaign,* Chicago. University of Chicago Press, 1954.

[7] Since we trichotomized results, $P^{56} + Q^{56}$ do not add up to 100 per cent. The reader may wonder why a turnout correction is added: are not the residuals the nonvoters? The answer is that a turnout correction is needed because many more persons express a candidate preference on a poll than actually turn out to vote.

expected Nixon percentage (V^n) was the same except that it used the 1956 Eisenhower supporters (Q^{56}).

The above was the simplest set of equations used. Let us now turn to a more complicated set, that for a group under cross-pressure—Protestant Democrats. First, we decided that, barring the religious issue, 1958 vote intentions would be a better index of the Protestant Democrats' 1960 vote than would their 1956 vote intentions. Too many of them were Eisenhower defectors in 1956 for us to believe that 1956 was a good indicator of normal behavior. On the other hand, 1958 polls would overestimate their Democratic vote, since many of them would defect again against a Catholic. However, it would not suffice merely to subtract the percentage who gave anti-Catholic replies on poll questions, for perhaps those very Democrats who were anti-Catholic were the ones who in practice voted Republican anyway. In short, the question was: Were the bigot defectors right wingers whose vote the Democrats would lose even without a Catholic candidate? Our system could not give us that information for each respondent incorporated into our data. While one respondent in a voter type might have been polled in a survey in 1958 about his vote intentions, another man of the same voter type, on a different survey, might have been polled on whether he would vote for a Catholic for President. To estimate the correlation between these two variables we had to find one or more surveys on which both questions appeared. We then ran anti-Catholicism by 1958 vote for each of the more numerous Protestant Democrat voter types. We found that among them the ratio *ad/bc* in the following fourfold table averaged about .6. With that information we could estimate how many of the anti-Catholics were hopeless cases anyhow (i.e. had gone Republican even in 1958) and how many would be net losses only in a campaign dominated by the religious issue.

1958 Vote Intentions	*Anti-Catholic*	*Not Anti-Catholic*
Democratic	*a*	*b*
Republican	*c*	*d*

It should be added here that we decided to take poll replies on the religious issue at face value. We were not so naïve as to believe that this was realistic, but since we were not trying to predict absolute percentages, but only relative ones, all that mattered was that the true extent of anti-Catholicism, voter type by voter type, should be linearly related to the percentage overtly expressed. Even this could only be assumed as a promising guess.

Finally, in predicting the vote of the Protestant Democrat voter types, we took account of the established finding that voters under cross-pressure stay home on election day more often than voters whose pressures are consistent. Therefore, for our 1960 estimate we doubled the historically established nonvoting index for these types.

Thus we arrived at equations applied to each Protestant Democratic voter type:

$$V_k = (P_{58} - a)(1 - 2P_{35})$$
$$V_n = (Q_{58} + a)(1 - 2P_{35})$$

The estimate of anti-Catholic 1958 Democratic voters (i.e. persons in cell a in the fourfold table above) was arrived at by the computer, given that

$$a + b = P_{58} \qquad a + c = P_{14}(P_{58} + Q_{58})$$

$$P_{14} = \text{per cent anti-Catholic} \qquad \text{and} \ \frac{ad}{bc} = .6$$

Space precludes a similar examination of each of the other of the nine conditions.[8] Suffice it to say that one other set of serious guesses had to be made, namely what proportion of those Democratic Catholics who had voted Republican in 1958 would switch back to their party to vote for Kennedy and what proportion of Republican Catholics who had voted Republican in 1958 would also switch to Kennedy. After an examination of the trial-heat data from

---

[8] With the above information, the remaining equations should be decipherable and are reported here for the record:

Protestant Independents, same equations as Protestant Democrats.
Catholic Democrats and Catholic Independents:

$$V_k = (P_{58} + \frac{Q_{58}}{3})(1 - P_{35})$$

$$V_n = \frac{2Q_{58}}{3}(1 - P_{35})$$

Catholic Republicans

$$V_k = (P_{58} + \frac{Q_{58}}{3})(1 - 2P_{35})$$

$$V_n = \frac{2Q_{58}}{3}(1 - 3P_{35})$$

All others:

$$\frac{ad}{bc} = .6$$

$$a + b = \frac{P_{58} + P_{56}}{2}$$

$$c + d = \frac{Q_{58} + Q_{56}}{2}$$

$$a + c = P_{14}\frac{(P_{58} + Q_{58} + P_{56} + Q_{56})}{2}$$

$$b + d = (1 - P_{14})\frac{(P_{58} + Q_{58} + P_{56} + Q_{56})}{2}$$

$$V_k = \left(\frac{P_{58} + P_{56}}{2} - a\right)\left((1 - 2P_{35})\right)$$

$$V_n = \left(\frac{Q_{58} + Q_{56}}{2} + a\right)\left((1 - 2P_{35})\right)$$

polls which asked about Kennedy vs. Nixon, we decided to use one-third as the proportion in each case, and to use that figure also as an estimate of the proportion of Catholic independents who would be won back by the religious issue.

The simulation required that the computer make 480 separate calculations, each one using the appropriate set of equations from above. During each of the 480 calculations, the computer put into the equations values for turnout record, 1958 vote intention, 1956 vote intention, and anti-Catholicism, derived from the data which had been assembled about that particular voter type. This gave a 1960 vote estimate for each voter type for the particular hypothetical campaign being investigated. Weighted averages of these gave the state-by-state estimates.

These estimates, as we have already noted, turned out to be close to the actual November outcome. They were not intended to be predictions. Or, rather, they were *contingent* predictions only. They were predictions of what would happen if the religious issue dominated the campaign. We did not predict that this would happen. We were describing one out of a set of possible types of campaign situation. But by August, when we took our national survey, comparison of our simulation and the survey results showed that this situation was actually beginning to occur. And the closeness of our contingent prediction to the final November result suggests that, indeed, the religious issue was of prime importance.

How close was the religious-issue simulation to the actual outcome compared to alternative bases of prediction? A full exploration of this remains to be made. We must, for example, further vary the parameters used in the simulation to determine which ones affect the results most critically and which values of those give the best prediction. For the present we look only at the one set of values and equations on which we relied during the campaign and which has already been described. (A few variations were tried and dismissed during the campaign, but none that made much difference.) How did this one simulation compare with other predictive data?

An obvious comparison is with the Kennedy-Nixon trial heats on polls taken at the same time as the latest polls used in the simulation. The correlation between the state-by-state result of these polls and the actual outcome is but .53 as compared to .82 for the simulation. The simulation, in short, portrayed trends which actually took place between the time the data were collected and election day. The uncorrected polls two years before the election explained but one-fourth of the variance in the real results, while intelligent use of them taking into account the cross-pressure theory of voting behavior allowed us to explain nearly two-thirds of the variance.

A more stringent comparison would be with Kennedy-Nixon trial heats run in August 1960, when the simulation was run on the computer. Such a comparison would answer the question of whether the Democratic Party would have gotten as good information at that date by the conventional means of up-to-the-minute field interviewing as it got by reanalysis of old data. Very likely it could have, if it had chosen to invest in a large enough national sample survey to give it state-by-state results, for as far as we can now tell the Catholic issue exerted most of its impact by shortly after the conventions. However, until poll data for that period becomes available we can only speculate. We wish to emphasize, however, that at some point in the history of the campaign, poll data certainly came into close correlation with the November election results and thus with our simulation. The date the raw poll results became as or more predictive than the simulation would be the point in the campaign at which mechanisms of voter behavior anticipated in the simulation became reality.

Besides simulation and polls, what other indices might have forecast long in advance the state-by-state order of voting in 1960? Results of previous elections would be one such index. Perhaps the rank order of the states in a previous election is a good forecast of rank order in future ones, even if the electoral outcome changes. (The whole country could move one way or the other, leaving the order of the states much the same.) But, if one is to use this device, which election should one use? The year 1956 was a presidential election year, as was 1960, but in 1956 the Eisenhower phenomenon was operating. 1958, although more recent and less affected by Eisenhower's idiosyncratic appeal, was a Congressional election year. In our simulation, too, we faced this problem. We resolved it for some voter types one way, for some another. But what happens if one relies on a single simple over-all assumption of continuity between elections? The result is not very good, though slightly better using 1956 than 1958. The product-moment correlation of Northern results between 1956 and 1960 was .39, between 1958 and 1960, .37. The multiple correlation using both earlier years was .44 with the 1960 election. So far our simulation clearly was superior as a forecast.

Perhaps one might have made a good prediction of the impact of the religious issue by a simple slide-rule method of calculation instead of by an elaborate computer procedure. One could correct the 1956 or 1958 vote by some crude percentage of the Catholic population of each state. That would have worked and worked well if, by some act of intuitive insight, one could have hit on the right percentage correction. One would have had to decide first of all to use 1956, not 1958, as the base, for no simple correction of the 1958 results gives a good correlation with the actual outcome. If one had that correct flash of intuition, one could have surpassed our complex simulation with a correction of exactly 34 per cent of the Catholic percentage of the population added to the Democratic vote. The correlation with the actual outcome achieved by this process is .83. The simulation was better, however, than any correction except 34 per cent. It is better than 33 or 35 per cent. At corrections of 32 and 40 per cent the coefficients of correlation for the simple correction procedure drop below .80.

There was, in other words, a "lucky guess" way of estimating the effect of the religious issue in the campaign which would have given an excellent prediction. But even if we had tried to make such an overall estimate and had somehow arrived at the right "lucky guess," we could not have defended it against skeptics. What the simulation did was to allow competent political analysts, operating without inspired guesses, to make sober, scientifically explicable estimates that they were willing to commit to paper before the facts. As the accompanying table shows, the simulation gave results about as good as the very best which hindsight now tells us could have been reached by simpler methods if infused by the right lucky guesses.

Correlations with Actual Election Results

Trial heats contemporaneous with simulation data	.53
Continuity with 1956	.39
Continuity with 1958	.37
Continuity with 1956 and 1958	.44
1956 results with optimum, or "lucky guess," correction for Catholic vote	.83
Simulation as done during campaign	.82

The essence of the simulation was to treat each voter type separately. Under what conditions should one expect that procedure to obtain a better result than an optimal across-the-board correction applied to the total? Clearly, if the process at work in each voter type was uniform it would make no difference whether we applied correction factors voter type by voter type or to the total. One could add 34 per cent of each Catholic voter type to the Democratic vote for that type or add 34 per cent of total Catholics to the total Democratic vote and come out with the same result. Where there are complex interactions of several variables on a voter type, however, then calculations done the two ways are no longer equal. If, for example, turnout varies between voter types and party voting also varies, then an equation applied to each voter type could not equally well be applied to total voters.

It is clear that we did not use the most predictive values for all parameters in our simulation. Determining what these were with the aid of hindsight is part of our present research program. But before election day we had no way of knowing what they were. (The one-third of 1958 Catholics casting Republican votes likely to go Democratic in 1960 according to our equations should not be confused with the 34 per cent of all 1956 Catholic voters, which turned out to be a good across-the-board correction.) The fact that our result came out on a par with the optimum simple correction which hindsight has enabled us to make is a crude measure of the gain from working voter type by voter type, with account taken of interactions within each type, that is, the gain from the computer operations.

The test of any new method of research is successful use. The outcome of the present study gives reason to hope that computer simulation may indeed open up the possibility of using survey data in ways far more complex than has been customary in the past. The political "pros" who commissioned this abstruse study were daring men to gamble on the use of a new and untried technique in the heat of a campaign. The researchers who undertook this job faced a rigorous test, for they undertook to do both basic and applied research at once. The study relied upon social science theories and data to represent the complexity of actual human behavior to a degree that would permit the explicit presentation of the consequences of policy alternatives.

This kind of research could not have been conducted ten years ago. Three new elements have entered the picture to make it possible: first, a body of sociological and psychological theories about voting and other decisions; second, a vast mine of empirical survey data now for the first time available in an archive; third, the existence of high-speed computers with large memories. The social science theories allow us to specify with some confidence what processes will come to work in a decision situation. The backlog of survey data permits us to estimate the parameters of these processes with fair precision and great detail for each small element of our national population. The computer makes possible the handling of this mine of data. More important still, it makes possible the precise carrying out of long and complex chains of reasoning about the interactions among the different processes. In summary, we believe that conditions now exist for use of survey data in research far more ambitious than social scientists are used to. If it is possible to reproduce, through computer simulation, much of the complexity of a whole society going through processes of change, and to do so rapidly, then the opportunities to put social science to work are vastly increased. It is our belief that this is now possible which was put to a test by the campaign research reported here.

4. Voting patterns in the British House of Commons in the 1840s*

WILLIAM O. AYDELOTTE†

In the 1840s, the time of Sir Robert Peel's great ministry, the British House of Commons debated and voted upon a number of substantial political issues. The Parliament of 1841-47 not only repealed the Corn Laws; it also placed on the statute books important legislation regulating factories, banks, railways and mines. It approved the income tax, reintroduced by Peel in 1842, and the Poor Law, which was renewed in 1842 and again in 1847. It discussed and voted upon, though it was far from approving, proposals for the extension of the franchise, the adoption of the secret ballot and the restriction of the special legal privileges of landowners. There were divisions as well on various aspects of the Irish question, religious questions and the position of the Church of England, army reform, fiscal reform and other matters.

The magnitude of these questions, the richness of content of the politics of the 1840s, make this decade of exceptional interest for the study of the development of modern political attitudes. Many of the most significant issues that arose as a consequence of Britain's transformation from an agricultural to an industrial state were raised, even if only in a preliminary form, in the debates in this Parliament. The relations between these questions constitute a problem of historical interpretation of great interest. This problem, the general character of the ideological patterns of the period has, however, been relatively little studied in detail.

Yet there exists a source, a body of materials, on this subject which is not only readily available but is also fuller and more reliable than most sources which historians have at their disposal. This is the division lists in Hansard. The peculiar value of these lists is that they contain expressions of opinion upon important subjects from men who are no longer available for questioning. It does

* Reprinted by permission of the editor from *Comparative Studies in Society and History*, V (January, 1963), pp. 134-63.

† William O. Aydelotte, professor of history at the University of Iowa, received his Ph.D. from the University of Cambridge, England, in 1934. He is the author of numerous articles on the theory of history and on British political history in the mid-19th century.

not strain terms too much to say that, imaginatively used, they can constitute a kind of questionnaire which we may submit to the dead and on which they will give us their replies. Further, the information about the votes of members of Parliament is perhaps more complete and more certain than anything else that is known about them. Their social background, their economic interests and their relations with their constituents can be studied with profit, but on such matters the information is and always will be fragmentary and there are nuances which it is difficult now to recapture. By contrast, the stands which these men publicly adopted on the major issues of the day are documented by the division lists with a wealth of detail, repeated corroboration and, I have reason to believe, a relatively high degree of accuracy.

It is important, also, that the division lists give information for all the men in Parliament, so far as they voted in the issues in question. Doubtless the opinions of a limited number of prominent individuals could be gleaned from their biographies or private papers; this would not, however, be possible for more than a small fraction of the group since, for the majority, detailed biographical materials are not available. Yet one may not generalize about a large group of men on the basis of a few individual cases, and an undue concentration on the principal characters may be misleading about the rank and file. Dr. G. Kitson Clark rightly criticizes the facile generalizations and over-simplified stereotypes about the opinions of the governing class in some of the older works on this period, and asserts that: "The old bland confident general statements about whole groups of men, or classes, or nations ought to disappear from history."[1] To say this, however, is not to say that the ideas and opinions of the governing class cannot be investigated. The point is that we must make sure of our ground, and base generalizations about a group upon information that applies to all members of it, so far as such information exists. It is in this context that the division lists appear to be a source of peculiar interest and value. Their merit is that they yield information, and comparable information for the entire group.

The division lists have never been fully exploited. Whatever may be the reasons for this, certainly the bulk and the complexity of the materials make them difficult to use. It is hard to see the wood for the trees or to obtain a general view that will at the same time do justice to the richness of the information. Most members of Parliament did not vote consistently "liberal" or consistently "conservative" on all issues: only a small minority, those on the extreme left and the extreme right did this; the great majority approved of reform on some questions and disapproved of it on others. Nor were all men "liberal" or "conservative" in the same sense: some (though by no means all) of those liberal in the sense of supporting free trade were conservative in the sense of opposing factory legislation; some (though by no means all) of those conservative in the sense of opposing free trade were liberal in the sense of supporting factory legislation. It seems hard to make sense out of all this, and these complexities have been more fully appreciated as the period has come to

---

[1] G. Kitson Clark, *The Making of Victorian England*, London, 1962. pp. 13, 4.

be studied more carefully. Writers of some of the older texts sought to interpret the political history of the time in terms of some "angle," some general principle that would tie together a number of diverse happenings. Early Victorian politics have been variously explained as a battle between the poor and the rich, between agriculture and industry or between the principles of laissez-faire and state intervention. As our knowledge has increased these general schemes have come somewhat under a cloud—though one still hears of them—and they have been replaced by a new realization of the complexity of events and by a scepticism about the possibility of describing what happened in any readily intelligible pattern or formula. This feeling of scepticism is one that I myself shared until recently. As I wrote in an earlier article, "the prevailing social and political objectives of this age form a rich and complex pattern which is as stimulating to study as it is difficult to characterize."[2] My views on this subject have changed, however, and I now think that I can begin to characterize it.

By borrowing a technique worked out in a different field for a different purpose I have been able to find patterns that embrace a large amount of this material and, I believe, aid substantially in its interpretation. I had glimmerings of such a pattern some years ago when I observed a relationship between votes on several issues in the House of Commons: I found that some men supported all three; others opposed the first but supported the second and third; others opposed the first and second but supported the third; while a fourth group opposed all three proposals. Although I did not know it I had stumbled upon a central feature of the Guttman scale.[3] At that time, I lacked both the technical skills and the theoretical knowledge to proceed further, and I did not appreciate the significance of what I had found; I dropped the subject and turned to other matters. Some years later, as a result of a suggestion made by a colleague in another department,[4] I decided to try a Guttman scalogram analysis on my data, not with great hope of profit, but as an experiment to see what would happen. To my surprise a pattern emerged which even at the first attempt could be clearly distinguished, and which much further work has now brought into sharply defined focus.

The basic property of a Guttman scale is that it ranks in cumulative order two things: the issues voted upon and the men voting upon them, and, furthermore, ranks each of these terms in terms of the other. The issues that fit a scale may be ordered according to the proportion of favorable votes each received, the one having the least support—i.e. the hardest to vote for, the mst radical proposal—coming first, and the one having the most support coming last. The men are then ranked according to the number of issues each supported, those voting positive or "liberal" on all being placed at the top, and those against

[2] W. O. Aydelotte, "Nineteenth Century British Pamphlets at the Newberry Library," *The Newberry Library Bulletin*, 2nd ser., no. 6, May 1951, pp. 179-80.

[3] See the articles by Louis Guttman in *Studies in Social Psychology in World War II*, vol. IV, *Measurement and Prediction*, Princeton, 1950.

[4] Frederick Waisanen. I am also indebted, for stimulating conversations on these problems, to David Gold, Martin U. Martel and Duncan MacRae, Jr.

TABLE 1
First Scale

	Chartism, 1842		Corn Laws, 1843		Income Tax, 1842		Corn Laws, 1846		Duty on Livestock, 1842	
	+	–	+	–	+	–	+	–	+	–
Chartist petition 3 May 1842 +	51	0	37	2	43	2	40	0	32	1
–	0	289	26	224	48	195	117	111	197	62
Repeal of Corn Laws, 15 May 1843 +			127	0	93	4	111	0	94	2
–			0	383	31	247	119	194	209	98
Opposition to Income Tax Bill, First Reading, 18 April 1842 +					190	0	146	8	126	19
–					0	287	87	138	183	63
Corn Law Repeal Bill, 3rd Reading 15 May 1846 +							349	0	223	15
–							0	251	91	78
Rejection of proposal that duty on imported livestock be taken by weight, 23 May 1842 +									115	0
–									0	382

everything at the bottom. It is by no means a foregone conclusion that these procedures will create a scale: the technique is, properly speaking, not a means of establishing a scale but a means of testing for the existence of one, discovering whether such a pattern is intrinsic in the material. If a scale does exist, however, this double ranking should produce a reasonably consistent pattern in which all persons voting positively on a given issue will prove to have voted positively on all issues lower in the scale and will also have higher ranks than all those who voted on this same issue negatively. By the same token, all those voting negatively on a given issue will prove to have voted negatively on all issues higher in the scale and will have lower ranks than all those who voted on this issue positively. In a perfect Guttman scale every fourfold table showing the relation between two items in the scale has an empty cell, since no one who responds negatively to the more popular or lower item will respond positively to the less popular or higher item.[5]

The scheme can be readily understood from Table 1. This table compares the votes in five divisions with each other and shows how those voting positively or

[5] Bert F. Green, "Attitude Measurement", in Gardner Lindzey, ed., *Handbook of Social Psychology*, Cambridge, Mass., 1954, vol. I, pp. 353-4. There is also a useful general description in Samuel A. Stouffer, *"An Over-view of the Contributions to Scaling and Scale Theory"*, Measurement and Prediction, pp. 3-45.

negatively in each one voted in each of the other four. The selection and ordering of the issues were determined only after considerable investigation. A comparison of these five issues with each other produces ten fourfold tables. If the issues are arranged in the order indicated, it turns out that those who voted positively on the first item also voted positively on the remaining four, so far as they voted on them at all. Those voting positively on the second item also voted positively on the last three, though they were divided on the first item, 37 of them being for it and 26 against it. The remaining items fall into a similar pattern. Each of the ten fourfold tables contains one cell that is empty or almost empty, this being the upper right-hand cell in every case. In the ten fourfold tables shown in Table 1 the upper right-hand cell is completely empty in two cases, it is less than one-half of one percent in four others, and it is 2% or less in two others. The upper right-hand figures in the last two tables, 19 and 15, look somewhat larger but on a percentage basis they are also insignificant, 4% and 3% respectively, a relatively trifling proportion of exceptions to the general pattern.

Not all issues will fit together in a cumulative scale of this kind. Thus, for example, a man's vote on the Corn Law motion of 1846 tells nothing about his vote on the Ten Hours division of 1844; votes in the two divisions are quite irregular with each other. (The figures are given in Table 4.) If, however, such cumulative patterns can be found, as I have found them in great quantity here, a scalogram analysis can be useful in that it reveals a relation between a number of different questions, some of which received very different degrees of support. It thus incorporates into a single intelligible scheme a far larger amount of information than could be brought together by a simpler method, and points the way to generalizations based not on votes in one division or on one issue only but on much wider information on a number of issues considered together in terms of their relationship with each other. This is, I think, the particular interest of scalogram analysis that it permits the continuation of the search for uniformities, for wider patterns, on a reasonably secure foundation of accuracy and reliability. The result of detailed research can be disheartening: it often destroys existing theories without offering anything to replace them. What is useful about scalogram analysis is that it helps to reverse this trend. It makes possible a concrete, precise and detailed description of the larger patterns of voting behavior and political choice in this Parliament and it may also, by revealing these patterns, suggest some insights into the ideas, preconceptions or working political assumptions that underlay them.

The operations performed in preparation for this report may be briefly summarized as follows:

(1) The votes cast by the 815 men who sat in the House of Commons between the general elections of 1841 and 1847 in a total of 114 divisions were recorded on IBM cards.[6] Recording and checking this information, which

---

[6] In none of the divisions analysed did this entire "population" of 815 men take part. Only 658 of them could be in Parliament at any one moment; only 656 after the disfranchisement of Sudbury in 1844. There was also a considerable turnover: of the 658 whom I have counted as elected at the general election of 1841 only 513 were sitting at the

comprised nearly 93,000 items of data (92,910, to be exact) proved a formidable task involving several years work and the help of a number of assistants. Every division was checked at least three times; some had to be checked as many as ten times to run down all discrepancies. I am satisfied that the information now on my cards is substantially correct. No formal sampling procedure was used in the selection of issues. I simply tried to get in at least one division on each of what seemed the most important questions, and tried also to cover more thoroughly certain highly controversial subjects of particular interest by including a considerable number of divisions on each. These last included such topics as: political reform, free trade, the Poor Law, the income tax, Irish questions, religious questions and the regulation of working hours in factories. Most of the divisions tabulated took place during the lifetime of the Parliament of 1841-47, but I included a number from earlier and later Parliaments as well.

(2) A conjunction count[7] was made on a 650 IBM machine showing the relation of the votes cast by men in the Parliament of 1841-47 in each of these 114 divisions to their votes in each of the others. In other words, a set of fourfold tables was prepared showing the extent to which those who voted positively or negatively in each division voted positively or negatively in each of the others. This resulted in a total of 6,441 fourfold tables, each of which was punched on a separate card which gave the frequencies, marginals, totals and percentages. This seems like a wholly unmanageable amount of information; however, I had the tables classified mechanically and then printed up in a form in which it was not too difficult to do a good deal of work with them manually. These procedures necessitated the invention of a certain number of techniques on which I will not elaborate here. It should be made clear, however, that the method I have used for deriving scales is that of paired comparisons, rather than any other of the variety of means that have been suggested for scaling. My method differs from those employed by others also in the point that I have not used a single group or sample of the individuals in the population throughout the operation. I have, on the contrary, included in each paired comparison all the men who voted on both the issues in question. This meant using not one sample but as many samples as I had pairs, or a total of 6,441, though probably a number of them included nearly the same men. Though this procedure may appear unconventional it has the advantage that it permits the use, for each paired comparison, of all the evidence available.

(3) From an inspection of these tables I attempted to build such scales as the evidence permitted. The method was to begin with two divisions that stood in a

---

time this Parliament was dissolved in 1847; still others entered Parliament at by-elections after the general election and left it before the dissolution. I have also included divisions from earlier and later Parliaments in which a number of the men of the Parliament of 1841-47, the only group whose votes are considered here, did not sit. Nor, of course, did all those in Parliament at a given moment necessarily vote in every division. For these various reasons, none of the divisions used included more than three-fourths of the population of 815, many included less than half, and some so few as one-eighth.

[7] I am indebted to John P. Dolch of the Computer Center of the State University of Iowa who arranged for this count to be made and also wrote the program for it.

scale relationship to each other in the sense that the fourfold table comparing the votes in the two divisions had an "empty" cell in the upper right-hand or lower left-hand corner. An "empty" cell was defined, after a certain amount of experimentation, as one containing less than 6% of the total of the figures in the four cells put together. It was also a criterion of a scale relationship that each of the figures in the other three cells should be 6% or more and that each should be more than twice as large as the figure in the "empty" cell. Two items that proved to be related in this way could then be shown to be related to a third, and so on, and a scale could be built up. These steps may sound more elaborate in description than they proved in execution: I was able to devise a number of short cuts by which the work could be expedited.

Certain decisions in this process had to be made, of course, on an arbitrary basis. This is true, for example, of the criterion of scalability just described, which is rather more strict than others that have been used and in fact excludes as irregular some relationships that are rather interesting; I purposely adopted a rather stringent criterion in order to be reasonably sure of my ground. The length of a scale is also an arbitrary matter. In each of the two principal scales described here five divisions were used as cutting-points which separate the men who voted in these divisions into six groups or "scale-types." Each scale could have been made somewhat longer or somewhat shorter. In each scale some items (not shown in the tables) fall between two steps and these could have been used, if that had seemed desirable, to designate additional steps: this would have produced scales with more steps, but the steps would have been less sharply differentiated from one another. On the other hand, it would have been possible to collapse either scale simply by eliminating certain items from it: this would have produced scales with steps more sharply differentiated, but the number of items falling between them would have been increased. A five-issue scale seemed to be, everything considered, a reasonable compromise. In matters of this kind there is no rule for deciding between the various alternatives. Any arrangement of the evidence will presumably yield some information of value. The problem is to decide what arrangement is most useful to help answer what prove to be the most important questions.

The procedure described here is more empirical than that ordinarily followed. It is more usual to start with a hypothesis and then verify it; to define, on the basis of an inspection of the subject-matter of the items, a "universe of content" and then to test whether the items that seem to belong to it fall into a scale. I have, however, gone at the problem in the opposite way. I obtained my scales first, from the paired comparisons, without regard to my own notions of which items belonged together and which did not, and then considered whether these relationships could be explained by postulating a "universe of content" to which all the items in a given scale might plausibly be supposed to belong. Doubtless some hypothesizing was implicit in the original selection of divisions for analysis, but this was only of a very general kind.

The proper defense of an empiricism so strict as this is that it helps to emancipate the student from his own preconceptions. This seems particularly advantageous when one is attempting to describe the attitudes of a body of men removed at some distance in time and whose political assumptions, as the following discussion will show in detail, were rather different from those prevailing today. It is only too easy to misinterpret the views of men living a century ago, to believe that what seems important or what seems reasonable to us must have appeared in the same light to them and to read our own assumptions or prejudices into the past.[8] A quantitative analysis of attitudes serves to bring out the discrepancies between present and past opinions, and gives a means of evaluating issues which, a hundred years ago, could have had a very different meaning from what they do now. It brings out connections that one might not have expected and also reveals that some connections that one might have expected did not in fact exist. The difficulty of comprehending the opinions of men in the past century, whose ideas were in many ways so like ours but in many ways so different, suggests that it is advisable to lean as far as possible in the direction of objectivity and empiricism. In dealing with problems and with a body of materials which are so complex and about which so much is still unknown, there would seem to be a strong case for making the original investigation an exploratory one.

From this analysis there emerged a great number of different scales. What also emerged, however, and what makes it possible to present in an article a general view of the results of a rather complicated investigation, was the fact that many of these scales coincided with one another. Voting patterns in the British House of Commons in the mid-nineteenth century were, in striking contrast to those revealed by studies of the United States and France in the mid-twentieth century,[9] relatively simple, regular and comprehensive. What I have found is that the great majority of the divisions analysed, over four-fifths, belonged to one or the other of two principal scale patterns. These two scales are illustrated in Tables 1 and 2. It will be noted that, in each, the proportion of votes that do not fit the scale—the figures in the upper-right corners of the fourfold tables—is extremely small. Table 1 contains 2,989 pieces of information; of these, 2,939 or 98.3% fit the pattern. In Table 2, of the 1,554 pieces of information presented, 1,517 or 97.6% fit the pattern. It will be observed also that it is possible for two divisions on the same subject, at two different dates, to fit at different points in the same scale. Those supporting Corn Law repeal in 1843 continued to support it in 1846 but by then they had been joined by others and the 1846 Corn Law vote, in which a considerably larger proportion favored repeal, comes at a lower point in the scale. A similar change took place on the Ten Hours question between 1844 and 1847.

---

[8] The problem of objectivity has been more fully discussed, in relation to this period, by G. Kitson Clark in the first chapter of *The Making of Victorian England* and, in more general terms, by myself in a volume of essays on generalizations in history edited by Louis Gottschalk, published by the Chicago University Press in 1963.

[9] See the account by Duncan MacRae, Jr., in chapter II of his book, *Dimensions of Congressional Voting: A Statistical Study of the House of Representatives in the Eighty-first Congress,* Berkeley and Los Angeles, 1958; also his article, "Intraparty Division and Cabinet Coalitions in the Fourth French Republic", in this issue of *CSSH,* pp. 164-211.

TABLE 2
Second Scale

		Poor Law, 1847		Lace Factories Bill, 1846		Ten Hours, 1844		Ten Hours, 1847		Roebuck's resolution, May 1844	
		+	−	+	−	+	−	+	−	+	−
Vote against 2nd Reading of Poor Law Bill, 21 May 1847	+	44	0	23	1	22	7	26	1	24	3
	−	0	220	17	69	64	62	71	46	88	40
Duncombe's Lace Factories Bill, 20 May 1846	+			68	0	37	6	48	0	40	2
	−			0	153	24	73	20	52	65	33
Ten Hours, 1844: clause 8 of bill specifying "12 hours" per day, 22 March 1844	+					194	0	104	6	109	5
	−					0	191	13	48	94	41
Ten Hours, 1847: rejection of Hume's proposal for post-ponement, 17 Feb. 1847	+							197	0	105	6
	−							0	89	24	35
Rejection of Roe-buck's resolution against interfer-ence with contrac-tual power of adult labourers, 3 May 1844	+									284	0
	−									0	78

It turned out, however, that many other divisions belonged to one or the other of these two patterns. Each item in each of the two illustrations was selected out of a number of possible alternatives, any of which could have been substituted for it without impairing the symmetry of the scale. Instead of using the division on the Chartist petition as the first item on the first scale, it would have been possible to use the division on Roebuck's motion to exclude earned incomes from the income tax on 17 February 1845, or the division on the motion to abolish parliamentary oaths on 30 March 1843, or Roebuck's motion against the privileged status of Irish landowners of 8 March 1847. A positive vote in any of these three divisions predicts a positive vote on all four of the other divisions used in the illustration. Similar substitutions could have been made at other points on both scales. The exact figures are as follows. An analysis was made of a total of 114 divisions. Four of these could not be used for scaling, since the votes on only one side were recorded. Of the 110 usable divisions, 72 or 65.5% fit the first scale and 28 or 25.5% fit the second. For the most part the scales are quite unrelated, as appears from Table IV; it turned out, however, that 11 items or 10% could be fitted into either scale, a curious fact to which I shall revert. Between them the two scales included a net total of 89 items or 81% of the usable divisions; 21 items or 19% did not fit either scale.

These patterns of association appear to have been relatively stable. They were not of course inevitable or permanent: they differ decidedly, for example, from those that prevail today, in England or elsewhere. Even in the limited period covered by my data there were some changes. The income tax is a notable example: it was opposed by the Liberals when the Conservatives brought it up in 1842 and 1845; but in 1853 the Liberals supported it and it was opposed only by a small group on the extreme right. The political reasons that may account for this change of heart are not difficult to conjecture. Yet the case of the income tax appears to have been exceptional. On most issues I have been able to find divisions either before Peel's accession to office in 1841 or after his fall in 1846 that fit the appropriate scales. On the whole these patterns, so far as my evidence shows, altered very little from the late 1830s to the early 1850s. It appears that a change of government did not greatly affect the composition of the groups mobilized to support or oppose various policies, and certainly did not involve any immediate general ideological re-alignment.

Space precludes discussion of all the findings of this inquiry or all the questions raised by it. It would be impracticable to attempt here a detailed discussion of all the divisions, the 72 that fit the first scale and the 28 that fit the second, and the reasons for their appearing where they do in the scales. Nor can I at the moment discuss the possibility of the existence of additional dimensions, though I should like to say that I have reason to believe that the two described here do not constitute an exhaustive account of the findings, and that I have observed some features of the evidence that seem to suggest additional variables. An account of the characteristics of the individuals in the different scale-types must also be postponed, since this is a large subject that requires separate treatment.

The following remarks will deal principally with what seems the most interesting feature of the findings, the fact that divisions on different subjects occur together in the same scale. That a number of issues which seem to us unconnected should prove to be related may at first appear surprising. If all the items in a scale concerned one question only, the pattern would be easier to understand. If, for example, the central question in the scale had been the amount of duty on a given article of import, some would perhaps want a certain amount, others this much and more and so on, and there might be a regular progression through a number of steps. In the first scale, however, it turns out that divisions on very different subjects are brought together in this same intimate fashion. To take only the items used in the illustration, almost all those who voted for the Chartist petition favored Corn Law repeal so early as 1843, almost all those who voted for Corn Law repeal in 1843 opposed the income tax and so on. Votes on these different questions were associated together as they might have been if they had all been votes on the same question, and it is not easy to see why this should have been the case.

Yet these associations between diverse issues were actually far more extensive than is indicated by the illustrations given. The first scale, which is the more comprehensive of the two, includes divisions on, among other things: free trade, not merely in corn but also in articles like sugar and cattle; religious questions, such as the abolition of parliamentary oaths; the opening of public exhibitions on Sunday; the temporalities of the Church of Ireland, the Ecclesiastical Courts Bill of 1844, Roman Catholic Relief, and the removal of Jewish disabilities; Irish questions; the income tax; proposals affecting the status and privileges of landowners, such as Elphinstone's motion in 1842 that legacy and probate duties on the succession to real property be equated with those on the succession to personal property, or Roebuck's motion in March 1847 attacking the privileged status of Irish landlords; the abolition of flogging in the army; the reduction of the national debt; the Health of Towns Bill; Russell's education proposals in 1847; and the Masters and Servants Bill of 1844. These different topics seem to have been closely associated in the minds of men living at the time. Members of Parliament, though they disagreed as to the merits of these questions, yet apparently possessed a set of common views or shared assumptions regarding the relation to each other in which they stood. The existence of these associations and their great extent constitutes a principal finding of this investigation and present a difficult but challenging problem of historical interpretation.

Connections or relationships between some of these questions have been observed or at least surmised by other scholars. Some of these connections were also identified in debates in Parliament at the time: I have often noticed that a speech on one of the issues in the scale may bring in several of the others. Thus, for example, Sharman Crawford, speaking on reform of the representation, found occasion to mention also the national debt, the privileged legal position of the landowning class, the Corn Laws and the Irish question, and the context in which he introduced these subjects suggests that to him they were almost inseparable from one another.[10] The scale, however, provides a more weighty demonstration than could be obtained from other sources of the connection of these questions in the minds of members of this Parliament and also a more exact account of which issues were related to each other and—what has proved very important—which ones were not related. Nor, I believe, has it been shown before what a number and variety of different questions were tied together in this general scheme.

The problem is to find a theory that will account for these relationships. The most plausible interpretation, and one that is commonly advanced for such findings, is that the items in the scale represented to the men who voted on them different aspects of or different ways of stating some larger general question.

---

[10] Speech by W. Sharman Crawford on "Reform in the Representation", 21 April 1842, *Hansard's Parliamentary Debates,* 3rd Series, vol. 62, pp. 907-921.

The usual interpretation of a scale is that it represents either a single variable or else several closely correlated ones. Although a scale is not regarded as necessarily demonstrating the existence of a single variable, it is consistent with this hypothesis, and to postulate such a variable may turn out to be the most reasonable and convincing way of accounting for the evidence. It seems difficult to explain the results except by assuming the existence of some more general question or issue which was reflected in or in some way related to all these divisions and which was also important enough so that it might plausibly be regarded as the determining consideration in the voting in each.

To suggest that the many subjects in the first scale all reflect a single variable or several closely correlated ones may appear to be an over-simplification. It might be objected that a vote or any other political choice is often a complex matter, perhaps a compromise between pressures pulling in different directions and, therefore, reflecting a number of different objectives. Doubtless this is often the case. Yet it is also possible that a single issue or a single variable may be reflected in men's votes on many questions, and the great number of issues that fit the first scale affords a strong presumption that this was the case here. A certain caution in regard to generalizations is right and proper, but it should not induce us to ignore uniformities in the evidence when they are handed to us on a silver platter. It may be instructive, then, to consider whether these issues have in any sense a common content or a common denominator that may account for the observed relationship between them.

This, however, is a more difficult matter. It is easier to demonstrate the presence of a scale than to identify the variable or variables it contains. The existence of the first scale (or the second) can scarcely be disputed. It is no chimera of the imagination nor a theoretical model that may or may not fit the evidence. On the contrary, it is a general description of the behavior of these men that can be verified with about as much certainty as we ever get in historical investigations. Yet it may be capable of more than one interpretation and, like other massive factual findings, it presents questions rather than answering them. The scale shows only that certain arithmetical relationships obtain; to translate these arithmetical relationships into substantive generalizations or into answers to substantive questions is not easy. Thus, though the existence of a scale may be incontestable, the interpretation of its meaning may be extremely controversial. In contrast to the immense concreteness of the scale itself, its interpretation is at best hypothetical and tentative, a matter of the best judgment that one can make and the most convincing arguments that can be found to support it.

It is tempting to describe the first scale, by analogy to a scale that has appeared quite prominently in modern dimensional studies, as a rural-urban conflict. Or, perhaps, in the terms more commonly used in the 1840s, it might be described as a conflict between agricultural interests and business and professional interests, between the aristocracy and the "middle classes." This, of course, is not the kind of class controversy we think of in connection with modern politics, between rich and poor, but rather one between rich and rich, between the great landowners and the great merchants and industrialists, between the old and the new forms of wealth. Though I am not entirely happy about such an interpretation, for reasons which I will explain, there are certainly some features of the evidence that make it plausible.

It seems supported, in the first place, by an analysis of the content of a number of issues that belong in the first scale. Radical attacks by Roebuck or Elphinstone on the special privileges of the landowners fit the scheme easily enough. The free trade cause and particularly the movement for the repeal of the Corn Laws were regarded in many quarters at the time, whether rightly or wrongly, as directed against the interests of the landowners and as favoring the commercial and manufacturing interests. The moderate proposals for political reform in this decade could be regarded as designed to establish a reliably middle-class electorate and thus to increase the influence of the newer interests in the House of Commons.

Perhaps the many divisions relating to religious subjects and the Church of England and a number of the large divisions on certain aspects of the Irish question could also be comprehended in a scheme of this character. It is often said that the conflict between the Establishment and Dissent was as much a social question as a theological one. Admittedly the connection between religious and social questions was occasionally contrived as, for example, in the case of Cobden's success in enlisting the support of a large number of dissenting ministers for the anti-Corn Law cause. Yet the fact that such a maneuver was even feasible, that it was possible to line up religious sentiment behind a political objective of this kind, tells something about the associations of ideas that seem to have been acceptable at the time. As for the Irish question, it could be and apparently was regarded, by some at least, as a kind of paradigm of ideological and social questions in England, an area in which they could be fought out in a preliminary way. Irish problems were, in particular, closely related to two sensitive points of general controversy that the first scale seems to represent. They raised the question of the position of the landlords and constituted a field in which Radicals could pursue their attacks on the landed class, as Roebuck in fact did in his amendment to the Landed Property (Ireland) Bill on which a division took place on 8 March 1847. Religious issues also played a prominent part in Irish affairs and attacks on the Establishment could be carried on in debates over the position of the Church of Ireland, as for example in the debate over H. G. Ward's motion for a committee on the temporalities of the Church of Ireland, on which there was a division on 12 June 1844.

Furthermore, the notion that politics represented a general class controversy of this kind was widely held at the time, though just how widely I will not undertake to say. The class interpretation of early Victorian politics is not a theory imposed by historians at a later date but is derived from the opinions of contemporaries. The existence of such a controversy was an important part of the message of the classical economists. Class arguments were a commonplace of the political pamphlet literature of the 1830s and 1840s, as I have observed from my reading of this material in the collection at the Newberry Library.

Propagandists for repeal of the Corn Laws played extensively on the theme. Class arguments frequently occurred in the debates in Parliament, and were used on both sides of the House. That they should have been found serviceable by the right as well as by the left is rather interesting, since it is generally said that class arguments are a more useful weapon for the left because the poorer or more underprivileged classes, to which the left appeals, are in a majority. Yet in Parliament in the 1840s it was apparently a powerful argument that a given proposal represented a threat to the landowning interest; the reason was, presumably, that at least four-fifths of the members of the House of Commons belonged to or were immediately related to the gentry, the baronetage or the peerage.

There is one obvious difficulty here which seems on consideration, however, to be without great weight. It may be objected that the conflict between the aristocracy and the "middle classes," whoever they were, is a *cliché* of the textbooks, a foggy generalization based on assumptions which, so far as they have any meaning at all, are untenable in the light of modern knowledge. The class concepts in terms of which the political history of this age has commonly been described are crude and unsatisfactory and have been energetically attacked by a number of recent students, myself included.[11] It is better understood now than it used to be that class is a relative matter, that the boundaries between different social groups are not easy to ascertain, and that different indicants of status may cut across one another and divide a population in different ways. This is not to say that notions about class divisions are nonsense, but rather that these matters must be carefully investigated and statements about them cautiously formulated. Even if they were nonsense, however, this would be immaterial to the present argument, for the fact that an issue is unreal does not necessarily prevent its being a subject of political controversy, and would not exclude the possibility of its being the central variable in a scale. A scale is a psychological thing which reveals not the facts of social history but what men thought about them. That men believed one thing while the reality was apparently something rather different would be an interesting finding but not an incredible one, for there is no reason to suppose that men are never mistaken. Politics may and sometimes do revolve around an illusion.[12] In the general confusion men may embrace a theory that seems to offer some insight into what is otherwise unintelligible, and they may particularly welcome a theory that provides a scapegoat, an enemy on whom their troubles may be blamed and against whom their energies may be concentrated. The idea of a controversy between aristocratic and middle-class interests, even if the question was rather more complicated than is suggested by the polemical arguments at the time,

---

11 W. O. Aydelotte, "The Business Interests of the Gentry in the Parliament of 1841-47" printed as an appendix in G. Kitson Clark, *The Making of Victorian England,* pp. 290-305.

12 John Howes Gleason, *The Genesis of Russophobia in Great Britain,* Cambridge, Mass., 1950, pp. 272-90. J. Roland Pennock, "The Political Power of British Agriculture", *Political Studies,* vol. VII, no. 3, October 1959, pp. 291-6.

apparently served for a number of contemporaries as a point of orientation of this character. Why this was so, why class theories should have seemed more plausible in the middle decades of the nineteenth century than they did earlier, is an interesting question and one on which several historians have already presented some suggestive evidence and comment.[13]

The real difficulty about a class interpretation of the first scale is that it fails to cover a certain amount of the evidence about the scale itself. Though it seems persuasive to regard a class conflict of this kind as part of the content of the first scale, it is difficult to regard it as the whole content. A number of issues in the scale do not fit so neatly into such a scheme as do those already mentioned. The income tax, for example, would, one might suppose, have borne with equal severity upon all those who had taxable incomes, and it is not easy to see at once why it should have been more unwelcome to those whose incomes came from trade or industry than to those whose incomes came from rents. One wonders whether the county members who voted for it did not do so more out of a desire to support a Conservative government than out of consideration of the advantages of the tax for them or for their constituents; there is some evidence in the debates to show that they accepted the measure with reluctance. It may be forcing the evidence to fit even some of the questions just discussed into a scheme of this kind. The common modern view that religious issues merely embodied social issues may be a gloss of our own which we, with our secular assumptions, have imposed upon the nineteenth century; if we go by what men said at the time, religious questions were important in their own right.[14] There was perhaps more to the Irish question than the role of the landlords and the church, however important these matters might be. Other issues in the first scale might also be difficult to fit a class pattern of this kind such as, for example, education, army reform, public health or the Masters and Servants Bill.

The evidence of the debates also suggests that the issue was a broader one. It would not be practicable to offer here a detailed analysis of the debates and the arguments used in them. It is enough for present purposes to say that, though class arguments often appeared, other kinds of arguments were frequently used as well. To this it should be added that references to classes in this period are often vague, so that it is difficult to be sure what men meant, or whether they all meant the same thing.

Beyond this, however, so simple an answer appears meagre and unsatisfactory in comparison to the richness of content revealed by the analysis. Though it is reasonable to suppose that class interests were involved in some of the items in

---

[13] G. Kitson Clark, "The Repeal of the Corn Laws and the Politics of the Forties", *Economic History Review,* 2nd Series, vol. IV, no. 1, 1951, pp. 3-4. Asa Briggs, "The Language of 'Class' in Early Nineteenth-century England", in Asa Briggs and John Saville, eds., *Essays on Labour History, in Memory of G. D. H. Cole,* London, 1960, pp. 43-73. I understand that a student of John Harrison's at the University of Wisconsin is making a further study of this problem.

[14] This point has been more fully discussed by G. Kitson Clark, *The Making of Victorian England, s,* p. 20.

the scale, much more seems to have been involved as well.[15] To dismiss the results in a sterile and empty formula may be to miss taking advantage of what is perhaps the most interesting aspect of the findings, the elaborate interconnections that they reveal. What is striking about the first scale is not that it makes everything simple but rather that it shows the richness of the ideological pattern of mid-century politics and the way in which this pattern was, so to speak, embroidered upon. It may be more illuminating to regard the scale not as reducing many questions to a common denominator but rather as showing the connection of these questions with each other. There are, as has been mentioned, two common interpretations of a scale: that it reflects one variable, or that it reflects several closely correlated ones. The variety of subject matter in the scale described here seems to make the second of these interpretations the more reasonable one. To assign to this group of issues a single descriptive name would be difficult and, indeed, misleading.

This view may appear overly conservative. That these questions were all tied together in this way is a striking finding: one might expect it, then, to lead to a new interpretation, a key to the period that would suddenly unlock its secrets. Scalogram analysis, however, is no gimmick to answer all questions. It is merely a means of placing in some kind of intelligible order a mass of evidence too profuse and too complex to be clearly observed without the aid of such a device. Further, as I have tried to insist, the interpretation of a scale is a controversial matter. A scale gives no ready answer to problems of historical interpretation; its function, rather, is to provide a concrete basis, a firm foundation, on which argument about these problems can be effectively carried forward.

However, the results of such an investigation do not necessitate a position of agnosticism. The analysis makes several things clear that were less clear before. It is something to show that certain earlier interpretations of the politics of the period will not work: a simple class interpretation is not enough; nor may we explain in terms of the principle of laissez-faire a scale that includes the Health of Towns Bill, one of the most considerable interventionist proposals of the nineteenth century. Beyond this, however, the analysis yields concrete information as to what issues were connected together and what were not connected. As a result, though we cannot summarize the subject of political controversy in a magic formula, we can at least say what were its constituent elements, what were the particular questions that, combined together, made up the central ground of political contention.

The issues in the first scale occupied a considerably larger share of the time and attention of Parliament than did the issues in the second, as will be discussed more fully below when the two scales are compared. The importance of the subject-matter of the first scale is also, however, underlined by another finding, which is that the issues contained in it were those around which party conflict tended to crystallize.

---

[15] The fact that the correlations I have found between vote and personal background or constituency are, though substantial, far from complete also suggests the presence of additional variables.

The fact that it was possible even to make a comparison between the voting of different parties on issues in a single scale represents in itself a striking contrast to findings for the most recent period in both the United States and France. MacRae, in his analysis of the 81st Congress and again in his analysis of the Fourth French Republic, discovered that he could not build a single scale for the entire population but that, on the contrary, he had to build separate scales for each party, since the parties did not agree on the order in which they placed the issues. In the House of Commons in the 1840s, on the contrary, almost all men in the House, including members of both the main party groups, put the items in both scales in the same order so far as they voted on them. The common frame of reference, the set of shared assumptions about the ordering of issues, which in modern America or modern France appears to extend only to individual parties, extended in mid-nineteenth century Britain to the entire legislative body. I have at the moment no pat explanation for this interesting difference, although I have speculated that this common frame of reference extending across party lines might be related to such matters as the physical proportions of the chamber (inadequate seating accommodation for all the members), the direct confrontation from opposite benches and, what follows from these, the intimate and businesslike tone of the debates. However this may be, the nature of the findings makes it possible to attempt for this population, what MacRae says he could not attempt for the 81st Congress,[16] to test how the two party groups stood on the set of issues in each scale and to give a precise answer to the often debated question whether the members of the parties differed on the issues.

It proves that party affiliation was closely related to votes in the divisions that fit the first scale. This does not mean, of course, that either party voted unanimously in all these divisions. If this had been the case, there would have been no point in a scalogram analysis, for there would have been only two possible ideological positions. There were, on the contrary, important cleavages of opinion within each of the two general party groups. Yet in a more general sense an unmistakable pattern does emerge. This consists in the fact that each party occupied a different section of the ideological spectrum defined by the scale. The five issues used in the scale divide the members of Parliament who voted on these questions into six scale-types. It turns out that almost all those in the first three scale-types, i.e. those voting positive on the first, second or third items, belonged to the Liberal group; while almost all those in the last three scale-types, i.e. voting negative on the third, fourth or fifth items, were Conservatives. The break between Liberals and Conservatives comes at a clearly

---

[16] MacRae, *Dimensions of Congressional Voting*, p. 222. It should be added that, while scales cannot apparently be built for the entire U.S. House of Representatives without the sacrifice of a good deal of information, it has proved possible to construct scales for smaller legislative bodies in the United States that do include the whole group. Most of the studies of the U.S. Senate have scaled the parties together, and MacRae was also able to scale the parties together in his study of the Massachusetts House of Representatives. See his article, "Roll Call Votes and Leadership", *Public Opinion Quarterly*, vol. XX, no. 3, Fall 1956, pp. 543-558.

defined point on the scale, and the ideological gamuts of opinion in each party radiate away from this central point: the Liberals in one direction and the Conservatives in the other. Some questions, such as the income tax bill of 1842 in the illustration given, were voted upon almost exactly according to party lines. Other questions, such as the first two in the illustration, split the Liberals and on these some Liberals voted with the Conservatives. Still others, such as the last two in the illustration, split the Conservatives and on these some Conservatives voted with the Liberals. However, questions in the scale that divided one party never divided the other. On the first two items, as will be seen from Table 3, the Liberals disagreed but the Conservatives were unanimously negative; on the last two the Conservatives disagreed but the Liberals were almost unanimously positive.

TABLE 3
Party Votes on Issues in Both Scales

	Liberals		Conservatives	
	+	−	+	−
First Scale:				
1. Chartism, 1842	51	68	0	221
2. Corn Laws, 1843	127	52	0	331
3. Income Tax, 1842	186	6	4	279
4. Corn Laws, 1846	235	10	114	241
5. Live Cattle, 1842	169	29	213	86
Second Scale:				
1. Poor Law, 1847	11	120	33	100
2. Lace Factories Bill, 1846	16	64	52	89
3. Ten Hours, 1844	94	56	100	135
4. Ten Hours, 1847	77	55	120	34
5. Roebuck's resolution, 1844	56	73	228	5

Thus, in terms of the divisions in the first scale, the conflict between the two main party groups clearly had an ideological content. Despite their internal differences of opinion parties did, in the sense described here, differ substantially on major questions of the day, and can be clearly distinguished from each other in terms of program, in terms of the causes they supported or opposed. The main line of political cleavage and the main line of ideological cleavage in this Parliament appear to have been closely related to each other, and it was in terms of the issue or nexus of issues in the first scale that the principal lines of political battle were drawn.

This finding may seem to suggest a simpler interpretation of the scale. This is that the relationship between these issues can most easily be accounted for not in terms of their substantive content but in terms of party maneuver and political opportunism: that the content of the scale, the central variable, consisted not in the subject-matter of the issues or connections that we now believe we can see between them, but in political objectives quite unrelated to them. This view, which is certainly accepted to a considerable extent by students of party history, implies an instrumental interpretation of issues: they are to be regarded not as ends in themselves, but as means by which political leaders and politically active groups seek to promote their own interests: to build majorities, to retain power or to secure it and to mobilize support behind them for these purposes. Issues, then, need have no logical connection except for their convenience in serving the purposes of party politics. Attitudes on them might be determined by the political exigencies of the moment, party coalitions and alliances, efforts of the government to secure its position or efforts of the opposition to obtain a majority against the government. By this view, any general ideological scheme such as might be inferred and frequently was inferred from the group of causes supported by a particular party might be not an animating principle but an improvised rationale devised after the event, an attempt to bring into a coherent plan, as plausibly as the circumstances permitted, a variety of matters that had no logical connection apart from the fact that they had all proved politically serviceable.

Such a view is in many ways attractive. It would be idle to deny the presence of opportunism in the politics of Early Victorian England. Cases can be cited readily enough where the struggle for political advantage appears to have dictated both the selection of issues to debate and the positions taken on them. I doubt, however, that anyone who has read widely in the debates in Hansard would regard opportunism as the whole story. It would be difficult to credit that the animated and acrimonious discussion of the various measures proposed, and the way in which they might be expected to affect the interests of different groups in the community, was nothing more than an external facade. It is also relevant here that, as mentioned earlier, the scales proved to be relatively stable and did not greatly change with changes of government, as might have been expected if nothing more than opportunism was involved. Doubtless, also, motives may be mixed, and men may pursue at the same time both their own advantage and what they conceive to be the public good, and these objectives may be combined in different proportions in different individuals in a way that it would be difficult now to disentangle. I cannot in any case discuss the question of motives here, since I am not presenting evidence on correlations between political choice and personal or political background.

The point to make here is, rather, that the argument about political opportunism does not necessarily refute the suggestion already made about the content of the scale and about the relationships between the issues that make it up. One may admit, and must admit in part, that political leaders made use for political purposes of issues or causes to which they were personally indifferent or even hostile. To concede this, however, is not to concede that these causes were a matter of indifference to everybody. Exactly the opposite is the case. A completely instrumental theory of issues, that they served no other purpose than that of rallying men to the support of a party or coalition, runs up against the difficulty that issues can be offered as a kind of political bait only to those who take them seriously. It would be useless for party leaders to take up causes out of strategy unless others were ready to support them out of conviction. Even if it is admitted that political stands were often taken for reasons of opportunism or demagoguery it would have to be admitted at the same time that there were groups in the political community, whether in the electorate or in Parliament, who supported these causes for their own sakes. Otherwise the "opportunism" would be pointless or useless. The very fact that issues could be used for opportunistic purposes by some implies that they served substantive purposes for others. Whether these substantive goals were real or fictitious, whether men's reasons for wanting a particular measure were good or bad, intelligent or silly, based on a reasoned calculation or on a neurotic compulsion unrelated to reality, is irrelevant. The point is that it would be useless for a politician to make an instrumental use of an issue unless it represented something that a considerable group of the electorate or of Parliament wanted. In view of this, it is clearly unsatisfactory to propose an explanation in terms of what might be called a "vulgar" opportunism: i.e., a theory that the connection of issues in the scale and the votes of members of Parliament on these issues can be explained exclusively in terms of competition for office and majority-building, or that the connection between these issues was wholly unrelated to their content or to the expressed interests or desires of anybody in the political community.

The point can be put even more strongly. If politicians adopt a certain policy it may make little difference in practice whether they do so from conviction or because they realize that there is no political future for those who continue to oppose it. Even if politicians are wholly opportunistic, pressing certain causes exclusively for political advantage, to gain support in the electorate or in Parliament, they may still be very much concerned with the merits of these questions, and may argue strenuously about their details and their anticipated impact on the interests to which the politicians wish to make their appeals. Even if attitudes were manipulative, arguments could still be about content. To say that politicians were opportunist—which may or may not be true, but was very likely true in part—has no bearing on the question whether the issues in the scale were related in their substantive content.

The second scale is more limited both in the number and the variety of the topics it includes. It consists principally of divisions on the regulation of working hours in factories and on the Poor Law. Its general character can be gathered from Table 2. Here, again, each item was selected from a number of possible alternatives. Other divisions that could be fitted into the second scale included several additional ones on the Poor Law in 1842 and 1845, a number of other divisions on factory questions in 1844 and 1847, the Mines division of 1843 (but not that of 1842, when Ashley's bill was passed). Besides this, several items that fit the first scale also fit the second. Except for this small group of divisions that fit both scales, the two scales were unrelated to each other. This appears from Table 4 which compares the votes on the determinants used for the first scale with the votes on those used for the second: the pattern, as can be observed, is largely irregular.

It is tempting to regard the second scale as equivalent or at least comparable to another dimension that figures prominently in studies of modern periods, the

TABLE 4
Comparison of Votes on Issues in First and Second Scales

		Second Scale:									
		Poor Law, 1847		Lace Factories Bill, 1846		Ten Hours, 1844		Ten Hours, 1847		Roebuck's resolution, May 1844	
		+	−	+	−	+	−	+	−	+	−
First Scale:											
Chartism, 1842	+	7	14	8	12	18	10	15	7	12	11
	−	13	90	25	79	100	95	75	36	164	20
Corn Laws, 1843	+	9	54	12	29	48	32	36	30	29	41
	−	21	98	37	80	114	131	97	33	216	13
Income Tax, 1842	+	7	78	11	42	60	40	50	35	38	52
	−	17	71	31	67	78	105	70	23	175	5
Corn Laws, 1846	+	13	141	15	123	106	103	84	77	111	64
	−	29	59	51	24	66	57	100	6	133	3
Live Cattle, 1842	+	18	130	23	100	107	131	89	61	161	61
	−	9	28	20	14	42	29	34	4	59	5

"welfare-state" or "labor-management" scale. The theme of the second scale, so far as it can be conjectured, appears to be the welfare of the underprivileged classes and the use of the powers of the state to assist them. The second scale is also, like the modern "welfare-state" scale, irregular with the rural-urban dimension.

Yet a closer inspection reveals more differences than similarities between the second scale described here and the modern "welfare-state" scale. It is difficult to push the comparison too far, and the differences cast some light on the special political circumstances of Britain in the 1840s.

For one thing, the "social legislation" of this period was trifling and inconsiderable in comparison to what has come since. To say this is not to deny its existence or its importance. The notion, which can still be found in the older books like those of Dicey or Cheyney, that the middle third of the nineteenth century was an age of "laissez-faire" when the general direction of legislation was to remove restrictions rather than to impose them, has been thoroughly refuted by recent research. The interventionist legislation of the mid-century proves substantial when all the information about it is gathered together, as has been done by David Roberts in his recent study. Yet, as Mr. Roberts also brings out in his account, these measures were, in comparison to the social legislation of the twentieth century, limited, tentative and hesitant. They generally involved regulation rather than the supply of social services. The powers of the new agencies were insufficient to deal with the problems they were assigned to cover, the staffs allotted to them were inadequate, and the administrative design of this early "welfare state" was ramshackle and inefficient, since the legislation authorizing it was based on hasty improvisation rather than on the development of a coherent general plan. It was found necessary to revise this legislation extensively by a series of consolidating acts in the 1870s.[17]

Doubtless the minor and limited social measures of the mid-nineteenth century were important as precedents. In the sixties, writes G. M. Young, "one social observer laid his finger not on the Repeal of the Corn Laws in '46, but on the Factory Act of '47, as the turning point of the age and, with our longer perspective, we can hardly doubt that he was right."[18] What makes these precedents important, however, is the fact that in the century between then and now these small beginnings have swollen into a torrent. In view of the direction taken by British politics and British legislation during this past century, they have a significance for us that they could scarcely have had for contemporaries. Actually the question of "social legislation," though central to the politics of most western democracies at the present time, appears to have been peripheral to the main business of Parliament in the 1840s. The interest of Parliament in the subject, measured by the crude tests of amount of legislation enacted and hours of debate devoted to it, seems to have been only minor. The first of the two scales considered here contains a far larger number of the divisions analysed and a far larger number of different topics than appear in the second.

This finding may of course be due to a bias in the sampling procedure, but I do not believe this to be the case. In view of the importance that recent students have attached to the rudimentary social legislation of the mid-nineteenth century, I was particularly on the lookout for this kind of thing. I have reason to suppose that the bias, if any, was in the other direction and that issues fitting the second scale, far from being under-represented in the sample, are probably over-represented and, despite their small number, give an exaggerated impression of the amount of attention that Parliament devoted to these matters.

Furthermore, the divisions that fit the second scale were for the most part relatively small, in contrast to the many huge divisions in the first scale. Some questions were apparently not controversial enough to necessitate a recorded division. On other questions only the votes of the small minority opposed to the measure were recorded, as was the case with the rather important Factory Act of 1844. For the most part it was only the Poor Law and the Ten Hours question that brought out votes of any size.

The secondary role of "condition-of-the-people question" in the politics of the 1840s is also shown by the fact that party affiliation was almost entirely unrelated to the voting on the issues in the second scale. Although members of both parties did apparently agree on the ordering of issues in this scale, there was no consistent party vote. This may be observed from Table 3, which shows the party vote on the issues used here to illustrate each of the two scales. While the first scale, as has been noted, is quite regular with party, the issues in the second

[17] David Roberts, *Victorian Origins of the British Welfare State*, New Haven, 1960.
[18] G. M. Young, *Victorian England: Portrait of an Age*, Oxford and London, 1936, p. 47.

scale divided both parties in an irregular fashion and there is no clear pattern.

These points supply a useful corrective to an assumption which it is easy for modern students to make about the mid-nineteenth century and which has been held by a number of progressive historians of the last generation, the Webbs, for example, or the Hammonds. This assumption is that the central political issue of a modern state is and must necessarily be the conflict between the rich and the poor. A modern student of the 1840s is apt to find himself more involved emotionally in the basic questions of social adjustment represented by Early Victorian social legislation than in the quarrels between protectionists and free traders. It seems clear, however, that for members of Parliament in the 1840s the emphasis was just the other way round and that the central issue of politics was not the welfare of the poor but the divergent interests of the rich, so far as the first scale may be regarded as centered on this latter problem. To attribute to the "social question" in the 1840s the weight and importance that it has for the politics of the twentieth century is to read the present into the past.

The most interesting problems regarding the interpretation of the second scale turn on the relationship of the two scales to each other. This is because a number of efforts have been made to explain or to provide a rationale of the issues appearing in the second scale in terms of the issues that appear in the first. To do this, of course, is to assume a unidimensional pattern. My argument here is that the politics of the 1840s can be better understood by thinking of them in terms of a multi-dimensional pattern, and I will try to show why this seems to be a more useful approach.

There are three interpretations of the "social legislation" of the mid-nineteenth century which, though they have been considerably qualified by responsible students of the period, have had and continue to have a fairly wide currency. They may be summarized as follows: (1) Social legislation was supported by protectionists and opposed by free traders for reasons of ideological consistency. Free traders who opposed government regulation of commerce would, by the logic of their position, also oppose government regulation of industry as, for example, in the factory acts. Protectionists, on the other hand, being committed to intervention in trade, could have no objection to it in industry. The principles of laissez-faire and state intervention were general ones that could readily be transferred from one sphere of economic activity to another, and that were consistently applied to all. (2) Social legislation was supported by the aristocracy or the landowners, or by spokesmen for the landed interest, whether from sentiments of *noblesse oblige* and a sense of responsibility for the whole body politic, or whether for the more practical object of attacking the manufacturers in an area where the interests of land were not involved; whereas the businessmen and the manufacturers, and those who spoke for them in Parliament, were sturdily reactionary on questions of social legislation and the regulation of working hours in factories because of their desire to exploit the working classes for their own economic benefit. (3) Leadership in social reform came from the Conservatives rather than from the Liberals, since the Conservatives were presumably identified with the cause of protection and the interest of the landowners, while the Liberals, presumably identified with the cause of free trade and the interest of the merchants and industrialists, opposed such legislation.

The common feature of these three propositions is that they assume, though this assumption is not always made explicit, a direct relationship between the issues in the first scale and the issues in the second. A "conservative" in terms of the first scale is, as has been shown, a man who tends to support protection, the landed interest and the Conservative party: a "liberal" in terms of the first scale is the opposite of these. To demonstrate the three propositions it would have to be shown that those most "liberal" in terms of one scale were also the most "conservative" in terms of the other or, in other words, that the two scales could be fused into one with the items in one of them simply inverted. It is implied in the three propositions that the two scales represent not two dimensions but only one, that they are not incommensurable but related in reverse, and that the second scale is simply an inversion of the first.

A somewhat different view that occasionally appears is that leadership in social legislation was taken not by the Conservatives alone but by a "Tory-Radical alliance," the extreme right and the extreme left combining together to push through legislation dealing with the regulation of factories and other matters. This pattern, in which extremes unite against the center, is sometimes described as a "curvilinear" one.

These views are not altogether nonsense. Some evidence can be found to support them, and doubtless they would not have obtained so wide a circulation if this had not been the case. It is easy to cite examples of Radical industrialists like Bright or Cobden who opposed factory legislation or of protectionists like Disraeli or Lord George Bentinck who to some extent favored it. Some of my own evidence lends support to the notion of an inverse relationship between the two general sets of issues represented by the two scales. It can be seen from Table 4, by those who care to puzzle the matter out, that the first and the last items in the second scale, the Poor Law division of 1847 and the division on Roebuck's resolution in 1844, would both, if they were turned upside down, come close to fitting the first scale, though neither would fit it exactly, and that each would, so far as it fits the first scale, occupy there almost the opposite position from what it does in the second: Roebuck's resolution, reversed, would come near the top; the Poor Law vote, reversed, would come near the bottom. I have also, as was mentioned, found a few other items that fit both scales: all but one of these (and the exception is a very small division) fit the two scales in reverse: in other words a negative vote on one of these issues in terms of one scale is a positive vote in terms of the other, and *vice versa*. These divisions which have opposite meanings in the two dimensions include several on free trade, all in 1849 or later, and several on the regulation of factories. They do not by any means include all the divisions on either of these two subjects. I have also found some evidence to support the theory of a "curvilinear" pattern: a few cases where factory legislation was supported both by the extreme left and the extreme right. What needs to be said here, perhaps, is that to qualify a theory is not necessarily to reject it entirely. Insights of this kind, even if they have been pressed too far, may still have some value, and the problem is to define the limiting conditions, to ascertain the degree to which they are valid.

In view of the total evidence, however, it is clear that such theories can have at most only a very limited and partial application. The number of items that fit both scales in reverse is small, and most of these questions were voted upon after the end of the Parliament of 1841-47. They do not include the majority of items fitting either scale. Nor can the theory of a "curvilinear" pattern be carried very far: the reality is more complicated. A few proposals for social legislation, it is true, received support from both the extreme left and the extreme right. This is the case for the divisions regarding Ashley's Mines Bill in 1842 and 1843 (these were both, however, very small divisions), the division on Fielden's Ten Hours Bill in 1846, and the first of the four main divisions on the Ten Hours Bill of 1847. However, only the left and not the right voted positive on the Poor Law divisions of 1842 and 1843 and on the five main Ten Hours divisions in 1844. On the other hand only the right and not the left voted positive on the 3rd Reading of the Poor Law Bill of 1847, the three remaining Ten Hours divisions in 1847, and the Ten Hours divisions in 1850. Thus, while social legislation did receive support from both the extreme left and the extreme right, there seems also to be a time element involved: the left supported it more before 1846 and the right more after 1846, while the year 1846 itself represents a kind of turning point when both groups supported social legislation and the curvilinear pattern was for a brief period in existence.

Apart from these exceptions, which form only an insignificant part of the whole picture, the two scales were unrelated. Both supporters and opponents of the Ten Hours Bill can be found among those who were liberal in terms of the first scale, those who were conservative, and those who occupied intermediate positions. Free traders disagreed on questions of social legislation and so did Protectionists. Although Bright opposed the Ten Hours Bill, it was vigorously supported by other free-trade manufacturers like Fielden and Brotherton. Nor is there any clear relation between the support of Ten Hours and Protection. Ashley, the main sponsor of the Ten Hours Bill, was converted on the Corn Law question and had to give up his seat in consequence, which is why he was not in Parliament for the final Ten Hours battle. Bentinck, the Protectionist leader, was still voting against Ten Hours in 1844, though he came to support it in 1846 and 1847. Support of Ten Hours was not inconsistent with any position on the first scale, nor was it directly related to any position on the first scale either.

In the light of this evidence, the three theories sketched above, which purport to give a rationale for the limited "social legislation" of the 1840s, appear on the whole to be entirely unacceptable. Although something can be found to support them, or at least to give them a slight color of plausibility, they can be stretched to cover at the most only a small proportion of the total evidence. Though they may have represented the thinking of some individuals in this group, they clearly did not represent the thinking of all.

These considerations suggest another way of describing a scale: that it reflects only relationships between a set of issues regarding which all the members of the population who voted on these issues were agreed. This is not to deny that there may have been other relationships existing in the minds of certain individuals, and that some of these may have been important. For some Radicals a vote for political reform necessarily implied a vote for the regulation of factories: for other Radicals it implied exactly the opposite. Some protectionists regarded the cause of protection as linked to that of factory regulation; others did not. Some members of Parliament, and conceivably all, appear to have believed that there was a logical connection between the two sets of issues in the two scales; but members of Parliament as a whole did not agree as to what this connection was. A scale, then, does not reveal all the associations of this kind that were present in the minds of individuals, but only a limited number about which there appears to have been general agreement, and which represented assumptions that everyone in the group was willing to accept. It is surprising, perhaps, that Parliament as a whole agreed on so much.

This view necessitates some qualification of what was said earlier. It may not be quite correct to say that those two dimensions were unrelated to each other: a more exact statement might be that many individuals (and, for all I know, the whole group) believed that there was such a relationship, but that they disagreed with each other as to what it was. For many individuals (and perhaps for all) there may have existed only a single dimension, and all the votes of a given individual may have seemed to him justifiable by a single rationale, which he regarded as consistent and all-embracing. Yet these rationales do not appear here since they were different for different men and the scales show only patterns on which almost all men were in agreement. To put it differently, general agreements about relationships between issues or sets of issues are reflected in the scales; disagreements on these matters are reflected in the incommensurability of the scales, in the existence of apparently unrelated ideological dimensions.

I wish, finally, to suggest how a multi-dimensional analysis can throw light on a problem that has bothered some students of the period: the fact that men who were radical in some respects were not radical in others. As the complexity of the period has been more clearly perceived it has led, as I mentioned at the outset, to a scepticism about the possibility of reducing these varieties of political choice to any intelligible pattern. One sophisticated modern critic has put the problem as follows:

Political spectrum-making on the basis of programmes is invariably plagued by difficulties. Shaftesbury, Oastler, and Peel, Newman and Blomfield, Disraeli and Cecil make unmanageable gaps in Conservatism; Owen and Mc Culloch, Fielden and Bright, Mill and Martineau make a meaningless hodge-podge of Radicalism. What can one do about Cobbett or Feargus O'Connor? One must either suppose a capricious incidence of radicalism or resort to what Professor Hexter in another connection has called "apologetic epicycles"—Tory Radicals, Radical Conservatives, breeds of Chartists—to save the appearances. The polarities of conservative and radical are better used to describe tempers or approaches. To classify (for what it is worth) by approach rather than programme, if it does not solve the problem entirely, at least simplifies it.[19]

I believe, however, that for the 1840s at least these difficulties are not so formidable as this quotation would suggest. Actually it is perfectly easy to meet this problem if we think of the men who sat in this Parliament as being divided not by one issue but by two or several, and if we think of not one radical-conservative dimension but two or more. By this means it is quite possible to define radicals and conservatives not in terms of approaches but in terms of concrete political objectives. The use of two scales as alternative and unrelated dimensions provides a conceptual framework in which it is possible to take account of men who were "radical" or "conservative" in different ways and on different issues, and replaces the apparently chaotic picture of political attitudes with a reasonably simple and comprehensive scheme. What emerges is not an unmanageable multiplicity of different attitudes but a simpler pattern: only two kinds of behavior, or a small number, which are unrelated, but which taken together offer an entirely adequate description of the evidence. The argument that radicals and conservatives cannot be described in terms of program presupposes that only a single dimension exists. If this assumption is abandoned the problem is readily resolved.

The existence of unrelated political dimensions both operating at the same time has been frequently observed in studies of twentieth-century politics. In the United States at the present day, for example, it has been found that economic "liberalism" does not always coincide with "liberalism" in the sense of support for civil liberties, that often the two causes are supported by quite different kinds of people, and that some individuals are both economic liberals and extreme segregationists. Edward Shils in his analysis of totalitarian ideologies has called attention to the appearance in the same party program of some attitudes that might be considered liberal and others that might be considered conservative: hostility towards private property can be combined with anti-Semitism, inequality and the repression of civil liberties; welfare legislation can be combined with political oligarchy; the elimination of civil liberties can be combined with an increase in equalitarianism. Hence, he finds, what seemed to be a simple unidimensional scheme now turns out to be a complicated multi-dimensional pattern and the two poles of the continuum Right and Left, once considered incompatible and antagonistic, now prove to overlap in many respects. He concludes that the belief that all political philosophies can be classified on a Right-Left continuum is obsolete and that the spurious nature of the polarity of Right and Left has been demonstrated by the recent developments in totalitarian countries.[20]

Actually it was demonstrated long before. Here, as perhaps in other cases, one

19 R. K. Webb, *Harriet Martineau: a Radical Victorian,* London, 1960, p. 363.

20 Edward A. Shils, "Authoritarianism: 'Right' and 'left' ", in Richard Christie and Marie Jahoda, eds., *Studies in the Scope and Method of "The Authoritarian Personality": Continuities in Social Research,* Glencoe, Illinois, 1954, pp. 27-8.

can find in the nineteenth century political phenomena sometimes alleged to be peculiar to the twentieth. The two scales presented here constitute an example of unrelated "liberal" dimensions in the mid-nineteenth century; and I have found evidence pointing to additional examples in later decades, on which I hope to report separately. In this manner, multi-scale analysis does, I believe, change our thinking about the period and make clear things that were not clear before. Not merely does it provide a technique for identifying the dimensions and sorting out which items belong to which, but it also helps to make sense out of these cross-currents and provides a scheme in which they can be intelligibly explained.

5. Party loyalty in the progressive years: the Senate, 1909-1915*

JEROME M. CLUBB† AND
HOWARD W. ALLEN§

The influence of political parties upon the legislative process has long been an object of study by students of American politics, and in recent years particularly, many investigations in this area have involved quantitative analysis of legislative voting behavior. With few exceptions, however, such studies have analyzed legislative voting behavior during the years since 1945; comparable works dealing with more remote time periods are rare. This paper is concerned with the influence of political parties upon the legislative process in the Senate during the Sixty-First, the Sixty-Second, and the Sixty-Third Congresses which were in session from 1909 to 1915. These were the two Taft Congresses and the first Congress of the Wilson administration, and it was during these years that the progressive reform movement had its greatest impact upon politics and government at the national level.[1] Through the use of data processing equipment

* This is a revised draft of a paper read at the annual meeting of the Southern Historical Association, November 19, 1965. The authors wish to express their gratitude to Professor Aage Clausen, Department of Political Science, University of Wisconsin, and to Philip Armstrong of Bowling Green State University for advice and assistance which they generously provided. They also wish to acknowledge indebtedness to the Computer Center, Bowling Green State University and to the Inter-university Consortium for Political Research, The University of Michigan for providing computer facilities necessary to conduct the data processing and analysis for this paper. Reprinted from the *Journal of Politics*, XXIX (August, 1967), pp. 567-84, by permission of the authors and the publisher.

† Jerome M. Clubb, director of historical archives, the Inter-University Consortium for Political Research, and lecturer in history, the University of Michigan, received his Ph.D. from the University of Washington. He is coeditor with Howard W. Allen of a projected 10-volume work on American elections.

§ Howard W. Allen, associate professor, department of history, Southern Illinois University, received his Ph.D. from the University of Washington. He is currently involved in research on voting alignments in the United States Senate, 1909-1935, in collaboration with Jerome M. Clubb and Aage R. Clausen.

1 The party composition of the Senate at the beginning of each of these Congresses was as follows: Sixty-First Congress, sixty-one Republicans and thirty-one Democrats; Sixty-Second Congress, fifty-one Republicans and forty-one Democrats; Sixty-Third Congress, forty-four Republicans, fifty-one Democrats, and one Progressive Republican.

we have analyzed all roll-call votes in the Senate during these Congresses, a total of over eleven hundred. This analysis was designed to assess the comparative level of party unity characteristic of the Senate voting record and to gauge the correspondence between voting behavior and party affiliation.

In analyzing the Senate voting record during these Congresses, two basic devices were employed to assess party unity.[2] While these devices do not involve the use of sophisticated statistical concepts, for purposes of clarity some explanation is perhaps desirable. One of the devices involved the computation of an index of party cohesion for each party for each Senate roll-call vote during the three Congresses. The index of party cohesion employed was originally devised by Stuart Rice in the late 1920's and is simply the difference in percentage terms between the number of members of a party recorded "yea" on a particular vote and the number of party members recorded "nay" on that vote.[3] The second device used to assess party unity involved tabulation of the number of times that each Senator voted with and against the majority of his party. The party position on each roll call was defined as the side of the issue taken by a majority of the recorded members of the party, and in this way a cumulative "party loyalty score" was calculated for each member of the Senate during these Congresses.[4]

These are, of course, relatively simple statistical devices which permit at best diagnosis of only certain general characteristics of the voting record.[5] On the other hand, they provide a useful means to assess average levels of party unity

---

[2] In tabulating roll-call votes Senators who announced themselves—or were announced—as paired for and against a given measure were counted as if they had voted. The lone Progressive Republican in the Sixty-Third Congress—Miles Poindexter of Washington—was tabulated as a Republican. All Senate roll calls during these Congresses were included in the tabulation. Roll-call votes were tabulated from the *Congressional Record* and the *Journal of the Executive Proceedings of the Senate.*

[3] This procedure yields an index number ranging from zero to one hundred. An index number of zero for a particular vote indicates maximum disunity: on such a vote the party was divided with fifty percent of the party members recorded "yea" and fifty percent recorded "nay." An index number of one hundred indicates that the party was unified on the vote in question with all recorded party members voting on the same side. Stuart A. Rice, *Quantitative Methods in Politics* (New York, 1928), 208-209.

[4] If more than fifty percent of the Republicans recorded on a particular vote were recorded "yea" then all Republicans who were recorded "yea" were counted as voting with their party; conversely, all who were recorded "nay" on that vote were counted as voting against their party.

[5] Despite their simplicity and obvious limitations as analytical tools, these devices have been widely and usefully employed by political scientists and other political analysts. For a discussion and criticism of the Rice index of party cohesion, see James G. Grumm, "The Means of Measuring Conflict and Cohesion in the Legislature," *The Southwestern Social Science Quarterly*, XLIV (Mar., 1964), 377-388. For examples of the many recent studies that employ or recommend the use of one or both of these devices see David B. Truman, *The Congressional Party: A Case Study* (New York: John Wiley, 1959); Donald R. Matthews, *U. S. Senators and Their World* (Chapel Hill, North Carolina: University of North Carolina Press, 1960); Malcolm E. Jewell, "Party Voting in American State Legislatures," *American Political Science Review*, XL (Sept., 1955), 773-791; Arend Lijphart, "The Analysis of Bloc Voting in the General Assembly: A Critique and a Proposal," *American Political Science Review*, LVII (Dec., 1963), 902-917. See also the *Congressional Quarterly Almanac* for the years since 1947.

against which individual performance may be compared, and they afford a simple means to compare party unity from one Congress to the next. By classifying roll-call votes in terms of the general legislative issues to which they were relevant it is also possible to identify the types of issue that engendered or disrupted party unity.

The years from 1909 to 1915 were characterized by widespread interest in politics and government, and by considerable political turmoil and division. In these years domestic reform came to be the dominant issue in national politics. During the Taft administration the Republican party was torn by the divisive issues of progressive reform and by the ambitions of rival party leaders. At the beginning of that administration the "Insurgent Revolt" within the party first assumed serious proportions. The Republican party divided in the course of the Taft presidency, the Progressive party was born, and the way was paved for Democratic victories at the polls in 1912. After 1912, the divisive issues of the time presented a more serious challenge to the Democrats, now in a position of power and responsibility, than in the immediately preceding years when theirs had been the minority role.

During this period, the Senate considered and Senators recorded their votes on a wide variety of legislative proposals. Routine items of business such as the government of the District of Columbia, pensions, claims, and the usual appropriations bills were considered by the Senate as in any other years, and some of the roll calls taken were on such matters. But most of the time of the Senate was occupied with proposals of a more controversial nature. While these three Congresses were in session the Senate considered legislative proposals relevant to virtually every goal of the progressive reform movement including regulation of railroads and trusts; tariff, tax, monetary, and banking reform; improvement of the conditions of labor; conservation of natural resources; and a variety of political reforms ranging from the direct election of Senators to woman suffrage. Proposals concerned with immigration restriction, regulation of the liquor traffic, relations with the Philippines and Cuba, and matters more generally relevant to foreign relations were also among those considered by the Senate and upon which Senators recorded their votes. Before the Sixty-Third Congress adjourned in March, 1915, issues generated by war in Europe had begun to distract attention from matters of domestic concern.

Given the political turmoil of the time and the controversial nature of much of the business of the Senate it might be expected that analysis of the voting record would reveal great disunity in both parties. In fact, the measurements of party unity employed in this paper indicate that a rather surprising degree of party unity was characteristic of the cumulative Senate voting record. It is not particularly meaningful, however, to discuss these Congresses in isolation. Without comparative statistics for other Congresses—and ideally, for Congresses both relatively proximate and distant in time—it is impossible to know whether the degree of party unity observed in the Senate during these years was high, low or merely typical. In order to place the progressive Congresses in perspective and more effectively gauge the relative level of party unity, Senate voting records of

TABLE 1
Average Party Unity Scores and Percentage of
"Party Votes" by Congressess

	Congresses						
	54	*55*	*61*	*62*	*63*	*67*	*87*
Democrats:							
Average cohesion score	51	71	78	69	70	71	57
Average percentage of votes with party	76%	85%	91%	85%	86%	85%	78%
Republicans:							
Average cohesion score	57	80	64	59	62	71	62
Average percentage of votes with party	79%	88%	83%	81%	83%	84%	83%
Percentage "party votes"	53%	76%	79%	60%	74%	70%	52%

four additional Congresses have been analyzed using the same procedures as were employed in examining the three Congresses of the progressive period. The Congresses used for comparative purposes were the Fifty-Fourth, the Fifty-Fifth, the Sixty-Seventh, and the Eighty-Seventh. These were respectively, the last Congress of the second Cleveland presidency, the first McKinley Congress, and the first Congresses of the Harding and Kennedy administrations.[6]

In terms of the measurements used, the Republican Senatorial party in the progressive Congresses was both more disunited than the Democratic party and more disunited than at the beginning of either the McKinley or Harding administrations (see Table 1). The decline in Republican unity between the relatively quiet years at the beginning of the McKinley administration and the Taft Congresses is striking. It is also clear that the level of Republican unity was higher, although less pronouncedly so, at the beginning of the Harding administration than during the years from 1909 to 1915. On the other hand, Republicans in the Senate were somewhat more unified during the progressive Congresses than they had been during the turbulent years at the end of the Cleveland presidency, and they were at least as unified as they would be during the Eighty-Seventh Congress.

Variations in Democratic party unity followed a somewhat different pattern across these seven Congresses than was characteristic of the Republicans. The level of Democratic unity during the Sixty-First Congress was the highest of any

---

[6] Selection of these particular Congresses for comparison was in part a product of chance; it happened that usable tabulations of Senate roll calls for three of these Congresses were available from the Inter-university Consortium for Political Research, Ann Arbor, Michigan. Data for the Fifty-Fifth Congress were originally collected by Professor Samuel C. Patterson, data for the Sixty-Seventh by Professor Charles Dollar, and the data for the Eighty-Seventh for the *Congressional Quarterly Almanac*. Neither the original collectors of the data nor the Inter-university Consortium bears any responsibility for the analyses or interpretations presented here.

of the seven Congresses considered, and although Democratic solidarity was lower in the Congresses that immediately followed, it did not drop significantly below the levels of the McKinley and Harding Congresses. The degree of Democratic cohesion observed in all three progressive Congresses is impressive when compared with that of either the last Cleveland or the first Kennedy Congresses.

These measures suggest, then, that Senate Democrats were more successful in maintaining party unity in the face of the issues of the progressive years than were Republicans. The Republican Senatorial party was not the highly unified body that it had been during at least the first two years of the McKinley presidency, nor were Republicans as united as they would be at the beginning of the 1920's when the progressive impulse had waned. On the other hand, neither party was as disunited as at the end of Cleveland's second term in office when nation and Congress felt the impact of depression, silver, Populism and agrarian discontent. Seemingly, the issues of the progressive years did not affect either party as sharply as did the issues of the earlier period. Furthermore, as Table 1 indicates, even though Republican unity had declined from the high levels of the early McKinley years, it remains the case that in the progressive Congress most Senators seldom crossed party lines to record their votes.

There are also further indications of the continuing influence of partisan affiliations in these Congresses. One such indication is the frequency with which legislative proposals were decided by roll-call votes upon which the Senate tended to divide along party lines. The incidence of such roll calls, or "party votes," is also roughly suggestive of the degree to which the two parties differed in their responses to the legislative issues of the time. Most of the Senate roll calls in the progressive Congresses were "party votes": that is, on most of the Senate roll-call votes a majority of the Democrats voted in opposition to a majority of the Republicans (see Table 1).[7] The incidence of "party votes" was significantly higher for all three progressive Congresses than it was either at the end of the Cleveland presidency or at the beginning of the Kennedy administration.[8] Aside from the Sixty-Second Congress, when a condition of near party stalemate prevailed in the Senate, the percentage of "party votes" was at least comparable during the progressive years to that of either the first McKinley or the first Harding Congresses.

Statements of the average level of party unity and the average incidence of "party votes" based upon all roll-call votes, while indicative of the general level

---

[7] Obviously, this procedure has the disadvantage of defining the party position on a roll call as the side of the issue taken by a simple majority of the recorded members of the party. Thus roll-call votes are classified as "party votes" even when one or both parties were seriously divided.

[8] During only one of the five Congresses that were in session from 1955 through 1964—the Eighty-Fourth through the Eighty-Eighth—did the number of "party votes" exceed fifty percent of the total Senate roll calls. The exception was the Eighty-Seventh, the first Kennedy Congress. *Congressional Quarterly Almanac,* Vol. XII (Washington, D. C., 1956), 121; Vol. XIII (1957), 123; Vol. XIV (1958), 123; Vol. XV (1959), 127; Vol. XVI (1960), 139; Vol. XVIII (1962), 762; Vol. XIX (1963), 731; Vol. XX (1964), 741.

of party unity and the general influence of party affiliation, do not reflect variations and complexities characteristic of the voting record. Moreover, these average statistics have the effect of masking important differences in the nature of the divisions within the two parties. In the course of the progressive Congresses there were significant variations in party unity from one issue to the next, and Senators differed rather widely in partisan loyalty.

In order to compare the degree of party unity on the various issues before the Senate between 1909 and 1915, roll calls were arranged in twenty-six categories in terms of the general issues to which they were relevant.[9] The party cohesion scores on roll-call votes in these twenty-six issue categories (see Table 2) indicate a relatively high level of unity as did the average cohesion scores for all roll-call votes. Both parties had high cohesion on the tariff, the corporation tax, postal savings and banking legislation, and on roll calls related to foreign affairs. On these five issues the cohesion scores for the two parties were above average for all roll-call votes in the three Congresses, and roll calls pertinent to these issues constituted about forty percent of all roll-call votes that could be classified by issues. One or the other of the two parties had above average cohesion on another seven issues, and the roll calls on this set of issues amounted to almost twenty-five percent of all roll calls classified. In other words, one of the two parties, or both parties, had high average cohesion scores on about sixty-five percent of the roll-call votes that could be classified in terms of the issues to which they were relevant.

The party cohesion scores on roll calls in the several issue categories also reflect the higher unity enjoyed by the Democratic Senatorial party in these years. This characteristic of the voting record may be seen by comparing the number of issues upon which Democratic cohesion was higher to the number upon which the Republicans were more united. On roll-call votes in thirteen of the twenty-six issue categories—including such major issues as political and tariff legislation, foreign affairs, the income and corporation taxes, Canadian Reciprocity, business regulation and Panama tolls—average Democratic cohesion scores were ten or more points above Republican averages. Conversely, the average level of Democratic cohesion was ten or more points below that of the Republicans only upon legislation pertinent to labor, the District of Columbia, and woman suffrage. Democratic cohesion on roll calls dealing with the District of Columbia and woman suffrage was, in fact, the lowest recorded for either party, but they were clearly exceptions to the general Democratic tendency toward higher party solidarity. Examination of the party cohesion scores presented in Table 2 also gives the distinct impression that Democrats were comparatively more united on

---

[9] One fifth of the roll calls taken in the three Congresses were excluded either because their meaning defied codification or because they dealt with matters of trivial significance for an analysis of partisan influences. Undoubtedly, our classification of some roll calls would be subject to question, but in the main this seems to be a minor problem. The margin of error is probably least in the categories that were voted upon most frequently, and these categories included many important issues of the period, such as the tariff, regulation of business, political reform, labor, foreign affairs, and banking.

TABLE 2
Average Party Cohesion on Selected Issues:
61st, 62nd, and 63rd Congresses

Republican	Average Cohesion Score	Number of Roll Calls	Democrat	Average Cohesion Score	Number of Roll Calls
1. Banking	81	36	1. Foreign Mail Subsidy	98	6
2. Woman Suffrage	75	5	2. Income Tax	96	20
3. Postal Savings	74	13	3. Corporation Tax	94	10
4. Foreign Affairs	72	71	4. Tariff	87	284
5. Corporation Tax	72	10	5. Banking	83	36
6. Tariff	71	284	6. Foreign Affairs	82	71
7. Labor	71	60	7. Canadian Reciprocity	82	34
8. Pensions	67	27	8. Postal Savings	76	13
(Republican Average for All Roll Calls 62)			9. Political Reform	74	82
9. Children's Bureau	61	5	(Democratic Average for All Roll Calls 71)		
10. District of Columbia	60	23	10. Business Regulation	67	135
11. Immigration	58	25	11. Vocational Education	65	5
12. Foreign Mail Subsidy	58	6	12. Panama Tolls	62	11
13. Political Reform	56	82	13. Pensions	59	27
14. Conservation	54	34	14. Prohibition	57	10
15. Vocational Education	53	5	15. Merchant Marine	55	18
16. Army Affairs	52	9	16. Labor	54	60
17. Naval Affairs	51	13	17. Conservation	53	34
18. Canadian Reciprocity	51	34	18. Children's Bureau	52	5
19. Prohibition	50	10	19. Indian Affairs	52	12
20. Income Tax	50	20	20. Agriculture	52	17
21. Business Regulation	47	135	21. Immigration	51	25
22. Agriculture	45	17	22. Claims	49	17
23. Merchant Marine	45	18	23. Army Affairs	48	9
24. Indian Affairs	40	12	24. Naval Affairs	44	13
25. Claims	34	17	25. District of Columbia	27	23
26. Panama Tolls	32	11	26. Woman Suffrage	11	5

more issues of national scope and on more issues that were clearly relevant to progressive reform than were Republicans.

In terms of time expended on debate and number of roll-call votes recorded, the tariff was the most important issue considered by the Senate during these three Congresses. Almost one-fourth of all roll-call votes recorded in the Senate during these Congresses were relevant to tariff proposals, and the Senate devoted more time to tariff debate than to debate on any other single general issue. On tariff roll calls Democrats tended to be more highly unified than were Republicans, but the average cohesion scores for both parties on the tariff were high (see Table 2). That both parties were as united as they were on the tariff is surprising. If Senators were sensitive to the economic interests of their constituents, as has often been assumed, then tariff legislation by its nature should have been marked by low party cohesion. Local and sectional interests ought to have cut sharply across party lines, as they did apparently on such matters as agriculture and Indian affairs. In fact, sectional divisions on tariff votes were few, and the tariff was seemingly a party issue to a degree that other issues were not.[10]

High Democratic solidarity on the tariff might be explained by the regional homogeneity characteristic of the party. Most Democrats who voted on the Payne-Aldrich bill in the Sixty-First Congress were from a single section, the South, for southern Democrats constituted roughly eighty-five percent of the party in that Congress. Democratic victories at the polls in 1910 and again in 1912 worked to reduce the homogeneous character of the party, and when the Sixty-Third Congress convened the South provided only sixty percent of the total Senatorial party. Democratic cohesion on the Underwood Tariff, which was considered in the Sixty-Third Congress, did not decline, but on the contrary rose to near unanimity as northern and western Democrats voted with their southern colleagues on almost every tariff roll call.[11] Democrats were apparently able to construct a tariff position that was acceptable in most of its elements to virtually all members of the party regardless of the section represented.

Democratic unity during the consideration of the Underwood Tariff bill in 1913, it has been suggested, stemmed in part from the skillful leadership of President Woodrow Wilson, the first Democrat in the White House since Grover Cleveland. Democratic cohesion on the Payne-Aldrich tariff in 1909 was somewhat lower than the cohesion index on the Underwood bill of 1913, so it does appear that Democrats were more united in 1913. However, the credit for Democratic solidarity on the tariff in 1913 cannot be attributed solely to factors

---

[10] No doubt, individual Senators did break with their parties on roll calls relevant to specific tariff issues that were of particular interest to their constituencies. However, as the cohesion scores show such deviations from party loyalty were few, and except in the case of a small number of Republican Senators, most members of the Senate supported the party tariff position with high consistency.

[11] The average Democratic cohesion scores on tariff roll calls in the Sixty-First Congress was eighty-one; in the Sixty-Third Congress the party cohesion average on the tariff was ninety-five.

present only in 1913. Clearly Democratic Senators were predisposed to agree on the tariff, as the high cohesion on the Payne-Aldrich bill indicates.

Wilson's leadership, moreover, was not so effective on issues other than the tariff. The Democrats voted together more consistently on only two other items, the income tax, which passed as an amendment to the Underwood Tariff, and the foreign mail subsidy. Democrats were only slightly less cohesive on banking legislation, foreign affairs, and a few other issue groups. But on such important Wilson administration matters as the Panama Canal tolls bill and anti-trust legislation party unity was decidedly lower. Wilson's inability to promote equally high levels of cohesion on non-tariff roll calls is even more evident if the average measurement of party unity across each of the three sessions of the Sixty-Third Congress are compared. During the first session, which was occupied almost entirely with the tariff, Democratic Senators voted together with almost complete consistency. On the other hand, during the next two sessions when matters other than the tariff were under consideration, Democratic unity on roll calls fell sharply. The average degree of Democratic party unity during the second and third sessions of the Sixty-Third Congress was below the party average for both the Sixty-First and Sixty-Second Congresses.[12] In other words, it appears that insofar as voting performance was concerned, the Democratic Senatorial party did not enjoy a new found party unity under the leadership of Woodrow Wilson. Rather, except when the tariff, foreign policy, and a few other issues were under consideration, Democratic Senators, now faced with responsibility, were more disunited on roll calls under Wilson than in either of the two preceding Congresses. It might also be suspected that analysis of the Sixty-Fourth Congress would reveal a further decline of Democratic unity produced by the pressures of continuing power and responsibility.

Just as the degree of party cohesion varied from one general issue to the next, the character of the divisions within the two parties differed, and there were significant changes in individual voting behavior from one Congress to the next. Republican factional alignments were more clearly defined than were those of the Democrats. During the first session of the Sixty-First Congress, Nelson W. Aldrich of Rhode Island successfully engineered an increase in the duties provided by the tariff bill which had been passed by the House of Representatives. Aroused by this alleged violation of the Republican platform of 1908, Senator Robert M. LaFollette of Wisconsin led a small group of Insurgents in an extended floor fight against the tariff position taken by the Republican majority. The disruption of party discipline was not confined to the tariff,

[12]The average Democratic cohesion index for the first session of the Sixty-Third Congress was ninety-two; the combined average for the second and third sessions was sixty-two, a difference of thirty points. The average Democratic cohesion score for the Sixty-First Congress was seventy-eight and for the Sixty-Second Congress, sixty-nine. The average loyalty score, moreover, demonstrated the same characteristic of the data. The "average Democrat" voted with his party ninety-six percent of the time in the first session of the Sixty-Third Congress, but in both the second and third sessions the "average Democrat" voted with his party eighty-two percent of the time. In the Sixty-First and Sixty-Second Congresses respectively the "average Democrat" supported his party ninety-one and eighty-five percent of the time.

TABLE 3
Republican Senators, Sixty-First, Sixty-Second, and
Sixty-Third Congress, by Percentage of Votes
Cast with the Party Majority and by
Geographical Section

	61st Congress		*62nd Congress*		*63rd Congress*	
	90% and above	*below 90%*	*above 80%*	*80% and below*	*85% and above*	*below 85%*
Northeast	18	0	14	0	7	6
East North Central	5	4	5	2	3	3
West North Central	2	13	2	9	2	8
South Atlantic	4	0	3	0	3	0
East South Central	1	0	2	0	1	0
West South Central	0	0	0	0	0	0
Mountain	7	3	8	5	6	2
Pacific Coast	3	2	1	4	0	4
Totals*	40	22	35	20	22	23

* In the Sixty-Second Congress Senator Young did not vote and Senator Frye voted only eight times; neither was included in this Table.

however, and in the months that followed, Insurgents continued to vote against the Republican majority. Few Senators joined ranks with LaFollette, and most Republicans adhered to the party position at a level comparable to that found among most Democrats. Of the sixty-two Republicans who participated in the voting in this Congress, forty voted with the party majority ninety percent of the time or more. Those who did deviate more frequently were few in number, but their rate of deviation was extremely high. In fact, the highest levels of insurgency observed in either party occurred among Republicans in this Congress, and the highest rate of deviation was that of LaFollette who voted with the party majority only twenty-seven percent of the time. He was followed by Bristow of Kansas, Clapp of Minnesota, Dolliver and Cummins of Iowa, and Beveridge of Indiana, who all voted against the party majority over half the time.[13] This was a situation, therefore, in which most Republicans voted together almost consistently while a splinter group seldom voted with the main body of the party. The lower Republican loyalty scores in this Congress, as compared with those of the Democrats, reflect primarily the persistent disloyalty of a small minority rather than general Republican disunity.

The Republican Senators in the Sixty-First Congress who voted most regularly with their party represented every geographical section outside the South, but clearly Northeasterners predominated, as Table 3 indicates.[14] In fact,

[13]Beveridge voted with the Republican majority forty-one percent of the time, Dolliver forty percent, Cummins thirty-four percent, Clapp thirty-two percent, and Bristow thirty percent.

[14]The distinction in Tables 3 and 4 between Senators with high and low loyalty scores is arbitrary, to be sure, but it serves to illustrate the general tendency of Senators in the various geographical sections to support their party. The sectional divisions used in these Tables are those employed by the Bureau of the Census.

every Republican who represented a northeastern state voted with the majority ninety percent or more of the time. Joined with Republicans from the Northeast were most Republicans from the Border and Mountain states, and over half of the Senators from the East North Central and Pacific Coast regions. By contrast, only two of fifteen Republican Senators from the West North Central region fell into this category. Thus the division among Republican Senators in the Sixty-First Congress was sharply sectional: northeastern Republicans supported the party majority most consistently, and Republicans from the states of the Great Plains most frequently opposed their party. Most historians would probably identify the Republican Senators with the highest rates of insurgency in this Congress as progressives and those with lower rates as the opponents of progressivism.

In the following two Congresses Republicans divided along sectional lines similar to those characteristic of the Sixty-First Congress (see Table 3), but deviation from the party majority was by no means as extreme. In these Congresses the Insurgents were again marked by relatively low party loyalty scores, but even the least loyal Republican, Robert LaFollette, voted with the party majority fifty-two percent of the time in the Sixty-Second Congress and sixty-five percent of the time in the Sixty-Third. On the other hand, although Insurgents voted against the party less frequently, other Republicans tended to be somewhat less cohesive than in the first Taft Congress. In that Congress forty Republicans cast ninety percent or more of their votes with the party majority, while twelve did so in the Sixty-Second, and only two in the Sixty-Third. Indeed, in the Sixty-Third Congress the party loyalty scores of some Insurgents—including Cummins, Bristow, and Gronna of North Dakota—were hardly distinguishable from those of such Northeastern "regulars" as Elihu Root, Jacob Gallinger, and Henry Cabot Lodge.[15]

In sum, the sharp Republican factionalism of the Sixty-First Congress became somewhat blurred in the second Taft Congress and was much less apparent in the first Congress of the Wilson administration. Not even the most loyal Republicans in the first Wilson Congress supported the party position, as defined by the majority, as regularly as had loyal Republicans in the first Taft Congress, but no Republican opposed the party as consistently as did the Insurgents in the earlier Congress. In this sense, the Republican party in the Senate had drawn together in the Sixty-Third Congress for Republicans of all persuasions and sections were able to support the party majority with almost equal consistency.

The present analysis, of course, provides no explanation for this change in

---

[15] During the Sixty-Second Congress Clapp voted with the party majority fifty-eight percent of the time, Gronna and Kenyon fifty-nine percent, Poindexter sixty percent, Borah and Dixon sixty-one percent. During the Sixty-Third Congress Cummins and Gronna supported the party majority eighty percent of the time and Bristow eighty-two percent while the equivalent figures for Root, Gallinger and Lodge were eighty-two, eighty-three and eighty-four percent. The party loyalty scores of Clapp, Norris, Poindexter, Kenyon and Borah ranged between seventy and seventy-nine percent. It should be recognized, of course, that Senators with similar party loyalty scores did not necessarily vote with and against the party majority on the same votes.

TABLE 4
Democratic Senators, Sixty-First, Sixty-Second,
and Sixty-Third Congresses, by Percentage of Votes
Cast with the Party Majority and by Geographical Section

	61st Congress		62nd Congress		63rd Congress	
	Above 90%	*90% or below*	*Above 85%*	*85% and below*	*Above 85%*	*85% and below*
Northeast	0	0	0	4	3	2
East North Central	0	1	1	2	4	0
West North Central	2	0	2	1	3	1
South Atlantic	13	2	13	2	11	4
East South Central	7	1	4	4	4	4
West South Central	3	6	4	8	3	5
Mountain	0	2	4	3	6	2
Pacific Coast	0	1	0	1	0	2
Totals*	25	13	28	25	34	20

* Senators Gordon and Thompson each voted less than seven times in the 61st Congress and are not included.

Republican voting behavior, although two rather obvious considerations seem relevant. In the minority, Republicans apparently found it easier to agree in opposition to Democratic proposals than it had been to unite in support of positive legislative action when in the majority. Along the same lines, there is indication that Democratic unity was highest when the party was in the minority and tended to decline when majority control of the Senate was attained. Changes in the composition of the Republican Senatorial party were probably also relevant to changes in voting behavior. Republican defeats in the elections of 1910 and 1912 came primarily in the Northeastern states with the result that this wing of the party was weakened. In effect, the balance of power within the party was shifted, although not in clearly definable sectional terms, with the consequence that Northeastern regulars and Great Plains and Pacific Coast Insurgents alike could support the party majority with almost equal consistency.

Democrats also varied in partisan loyalty in these Congresses, but Democratic divisions were neither as extreme nor as clearly sectional in nature as were Republican divisions of the Taft years. The sectional group that supported the Democratic majority most consistently represented the South Atlantic states. These Democrats provided the core of the party in somewhat the same way as Northeastern Republicans constituted the core of the Republican Senatorial organization in the Taft Congresses. But, as Table 4 indicates, Democratic Senators from virtually all other geographical sections also supported the party with high consistency. The largest regional grouping of relatively disloyal Democrats was composed of Senators from the West South Central states. In all three Congresses the Louisiana Senators frequently voted against the party majority as did one or more Democrats from each of the states of Texas, Oklahoma, Arkansas, and, in the Sixty-Third Congress, Alabama and Mississippi. However, Democrats from this general region opposed the party neither as

TABLE 5
Correlation of Individual Senator's Loyalty
Scores by Congresses

	Republican Loyalty Scores			Democratic Loyalty Scores	
	62nd	63rd		62nd	63rd
61st Congress	.886	.626	61st Congress	.644	.392
62nd Congress	—	.644	62nd Congress	—	.446

consistently nor as frequently as Insurgent Republicans opposed their party. Even so, Democratic sectional divisions, although quite faint, are rather unexpected in that Southerners did not vote with or against the party majority at the same rate. One fringe of the South, the South Atlantic states, consistently supported the party, and the other, the western fringe, provided Democrats with relatively low party loyalty scores.

On the whole, Democratic divisions were also less consistent from one Congress to the next than were Republican divisions. That is to say, individual Democrats tended to vary in partisan loyalty from one Congress to the next while individual Republicans tended more frequently to be either relatively loyal or relatively disloyal in all three Congresses. Correlation of the loyalty scores of individual Democrats and individual Republicans from one Congress to the next clearly reflects this aspect of the voting record. In every instance individual Republican party loyalty rates correlate more highly from Congress to Congress than do Democratic loyalty rates (see Table 5). Thus more Democrats changed in relative partisan loyalty during the three Congresses than Republicans which suggests that factional alignments tended to be more pronounced and more persistent in the Republican Senatorial party.

The pattern of Democratic voting behavior differed from that of the Republicans particularly during the Taft Congresses. Republican Senators varied more widely in degree of partisan loyalty, and the party was divided between a highly cohesive majority and a small but equally cohesive minority. Democrats, by contrast, tended to support their party with more nearly equal consistency, and factional divisions within the Democratic party seemingly were not as sharp. These differences were probably in some degree a product of variations in party strength. Republican factional divisions were most sharp during the Sixty-First Congress when Republicans outnumbered Democrats by almost two to one and waned as the party passed into the minority. Analysis of later Congresses in the Wilson administration might well reveal growing Democratic factionalism as the party continued in power. It is also probable that these differences in party voting behavior are indicative of basic differences in structure and composition between the two parties. It seems likely, for example, that the two parties differed significantly in "style" and organization. The Democratic party, it might be surmised, tended to accept some deviation from the party position as a fact of life. In the Republican party, on the other hand, party discipline was more strict and the occasional Republican dissident was faced with intense pressures for conformity which were sometimes productive of even more dissent. The present analysis, of course, is not designed to cope with issues such as these.

Clearly, then, Senate voting behavior in these Congresses was a complex phenomenon. The parties and individual Senators differed in their responses to the issues of the time, and there were significant shifts in individual and party performance from one Congress to the next. The procedures employed in this paper obviously do not suffice to identify and trace all of these complexities and variations, and certainly these procedures do not explain them. Even so, the general unity of the two parties was surely one of the most salient features of the voting record. On most roll-call votes one or both parties were relatively highly unified; most Senators seldom crossed party lines to record their votes; and most legislative proposals were decided on roll calls that tended to follow party lines. Even on many of the most controversial issues the majority of Senators were able to agree with their party colleagues, despite the wide diversity of the constituencies represented, and the parties were usually able to present a relatively united front to the nation and to their opponents. In the process of achieving agreement, the Republicans were less successful than they had been in the early McKinley years and less successful than were Democrats in the three progressive Congresses. In the Taft Congresses particularly, Republicans were unable to reconcile a dissident minority, but seemingly this difficulty lessened when the burdens of power were removed. It appears necessary to conclude, therefore, that in these years party affiliation significantly influenced the voting behavior of most Senators even on many votes that were relevant to the divisive issues of progressive reform and to other highly controversial issues.

This conclusion provides additional support for the familiar generalization that political parties in the United States have provided a mechanism by which conflict has been reconciled. Even at the height of the progressive movement, during a time of apparent political division and turmoil, the parties performed this function, it seems, with comparatively great effectiveness. This analysis of the voting record also suggests that students of the progressive period may have concentrated upon political conflict and division while neglecting the unity and continuity provided by the party system in Congress at least. Indeed, although the evidence presented here is limited, the present analysis suggests that political parties may have played a more significant role in Congress during the early years of the twentieth century than they have since 1945.

6. Sub-group formation in the Constitutional Convention*

S. SIDNEY ULMER†

I

As John Grumm has recently remarked, "bloc analysis" should play an important role in the study of legislative behavior.[1] For the identification of the sub-groups operating in the legislative arena can shed light on the factors associated with legislative voting choices. Similarly, those working in the area of judicial decision-making have suggested the efficacy of "sub-group analysis" in understanding the voting behavior of Supreme Court justices.[2] And Arend Lijphart has illustrated some of the lessons to be derived from a "bloc analysis" of the United Nations General Assembly.[3]

A related collegial body, as yet untouched by such methods, is the constituent assembly—that body given the responsibility for drawing basic charters or constitutions for government. Such assemblies are like legislatures in that they "make law"; they are like collegial courts in the expectation that their decisions will have some permanence; they are like the United Nations since competing and cooperating interests are reflected inevitably in the voting alignments that produce their decisions. These and other similarities logically

* Reprinted from "Sub-group Formation in the Constitutional Convention," *Midwest Journal of Political Science,* X (August, 1966), pp. 288-303, by permission of the Wayne State University Press.

† The author gratefully acknowledges the support of the Kentucky Research Foundation for the research on which this paper is based. Editors Note: Ulmer is professor of political science and chairman, department of political science, University of Kentucky. He is the editor of *Introductory Readings in Political Behavior.*

[1] John Grumm, "The Systematic Analysis of Blocs In the Study of Legislative Behavior," *Western Political Quarterly,* Vol. 18, No. 2 (June 1965), pp. 350-362.

[2] S. Sidney Ulmer, "Toward a Theory of Sub-Group Formation in the United States Supreme Court," *Journal of Politics,* Vol. 27, No. 1 (February 1965), pp. 133-152.

[3] Arend Lijphart, "The Analysis of Bloc Voting in the General Assembly: A Critique and a Proposal," *American Political Science Review,* Vol. 57, No. 4 (December 1963), pp. 902-917.

suggest that bloc analysis can help us to understand the voting behavior that makes a constitution.

Of course, few constituent assemblies have been of greater significance for American political life than that which framed the 1787 Federal Constitution. The work of that convention has been subjected to over 175 years of analysis. Considerable attention has been given to the various voting alignments that prevailed and to explaining the factors underlying them. Perhaps we now believe that we "know" all that is worth knowing about the activities of that select body of men. Yet, our knowledge of behavior in the Convention has been derived primarily from historical sources using historical methods. Well-worked data, when subjected to modern techniques of analysis or conceptualization, may furnish new insights into an old subject. Indeed, a more methodologically sophisticated approach may enable us to determine whether the facts and interpretations of earlier analysts were the products of the research methods and conceptualizations to which they were wedded.

In this paper, our focus on voting patterns in the Constitutional Convention is for the purpose of answering the following question: What was the number and composition of voting blocs in the Convention and have these groupings been adequately explained? Phrased in this way, our inquiry begs the question of the existence of blocs. But we do not believe that the representatives of the states distributed their votes in a random fashion in respect to (a) issues or (b) other representatives. No significant risk is associated with this initial assumption since, if we are wrong, our methods will so indicate.

II

Previous attempts to explain the Convention suggest that preliminary consideration be given to the economic dimensions of behavior. At least since Aristotle, it has been recognized that man's behavior has an economic dimension. But the precise nature of this "factor"—of the relationship of economic considerations to human behavior—still eludes us. As Lee Benson has pointed out in discussing the Constitutional Movement of 1787, some writers have exhibited a dualism in their thought about the matter.[4] The economic determinists have maintained that behavior is "determined" by economic interests. They, with the modern day Marxists, replace free will with an unreasoning fatalism. A more moderate view is that men are guided and influenced by the sum total of the impressions and inheritances derived from their social environment. From this perspective, behavior may be given an economic interpretation when the environmental influences which motivate it are economic in nature.

Madison's comments in *Federalist Number Ten* leave no doubt of his view that economic interests may influence political decision-making. The apportion-

---

[4] Lee Benson, *Turner and Beard* (New York: Free Press of Glencoe, Illinois, 1960), pp. 95 ff.

ment of taxes on property, he says, would seem ". . . to require the most exact impartiality; yet there is, perhaps, no legislative act in which greater opportunity and temptation are given to a predominant party to trample on the rules of justice."[5] Such statements reflect a decidedly fatalistic theory of political behavior. And his additional comment that "Every shilling with which they over-burden the inferior number, is a shilling saved to their own pockets"[6] is an early conceptionalization of a zero-sum game in which the loss of one interest is the gain of another.

If one focuses only on comments of this genre in Madison's writings, it is not difficult to view him as an economic determinist. Yet Madison, read in the whole, merely subscribed to the view that economic factors are among those which influence behavior in a political context. At the same time he recognized that man may be driven by other forces—that differences and conflicts may flow from other causes. And he did not foreclose the possibility of purer motives for political action.[7]

Charles Beard in his *An Economic Interpretation of the Constitution*[8] does not use Madison's categories. But he mingles interpretative strains with decided emphasis on determinism and the economic basis of group conflict. In spite of this apparent confusion, however, Beard's economic interpretation still deserves consideration by students of the Constitutional Movement of 1787-1789. For the book remains, fifty years after its writing, the most coherent attempt yet made to furnish a systematic theory of the forces that made the constitutional revolution.

Beard's analysis proceeds from a belief system composed of assumptions and observations. He maintained, in general, that social progress comes through the conflict of contending interests in society. The conflict is between those who oppose and those who favor change. But how is the choice of sides to be made? Why should some men favor revolution while others fight to maintain the status quo? Beard resolves this question, as did Madison, in terms of advantage. We must ask, he says, ". . . to whose advantage will changes or the maintenance of old forms accrue?"[9]

As applied to the American experience, Beard concluded that those who stood to profit most from constitutional change in 1787 were men of business and property and holders of public securities. Indeed, he suggests that the behavior of the delegates in the 1787 Convention is explained by their economic interests. This is not to say, he asserts, ". . . that the Constitution was made for the personal benefit of the members of the Convention. . . . The only point here considered is: did they represent distinct groups whose economic interests they

---

[5] *The Federalist* (Modern Library Edition, 1937), p. 57.

[6] *Ibid.*

[7] *E. g.,* Madison's remark that "Enlightened statesmen will not always be at the helm" admits the possibility of enlightenment as a factor influencing behavior. *Ibid.,* p. 57.

[8] Charles Beard, *An Economic Interpretation of the Constitution of the United States* (New York: Macmillan Company, 1962).

[9] *Ibid.,* p. xvii.

understood and felt in concrete, definite form through their own personal experience with identical property rights, or were they working merely under the guidance of abstract principles of political science?"[10]

As to Beard's categorization of the interests represented in the Convention, there is some disagreement. Forrest McDonald asserts that Beard identified two contending groups: real property holders and those who possessed property in the form of personalty.[11] The same interpretation seems apparent in the work of Robert E. Brown.[12] Lee Benson, on the other hand, suggests that Beard differentiated his interest groupings in terms of the amount and kind of property.[13] We do not pause to evaluate the differences among these three historians. Beard himself breaks down his realty and personalty groups into sub-groups and also recognizes exceptions to all his group generalizations. But, whatever his classifications, his methods do not allow him to prove that support for and opposition to the Constitution or the behavior of the delegates in the Convention were "caused" by economic interests.

III

That the states might form certain divisions or groups for "natural" or other reasons occurred to a number of observers prior to Charles Beard. In the early 1780's it was rumored that the states east of the Hudson intended to form a Confederacy. Rufus King, in 1785, expressed the opinion that the eight northern states might "quarrel decisively" with the five southern states over congressional regulation of foreign trade. In a letter to King dated February 11, 1786, General Benjamin Lincoln agreed "that our interests do and will clash, are troubles which will not be questioned. These are the necessary consequences of our great extent, of our difference of climate, productions, views, etc."[14] A year earlier in a letter to John Adams a former member of Congress, Stephen Higginson, wrote: "Experience and observation most clearly evince that in their habits, manners and commercial interests, the Southern and Northern states are not only very dissimilar, but in many instances directly opposed."[15]

Prior to 1787 some southern newspapers had proposed four republics. New Hampshire, Massachusetts, Rhode Island and Connecticut were to form the first; New York, New Jersey, Delaware, Pennsylvania and Maryland the second; Virginia, North Carolina, South Carolina, and Georgia the third. Franklin, Kentucky, and lands lying on the Ohio were to compose the fourth Republic. The argument for this particular division was said to be climate, religion,

---

[10] *Ibid.*, p. 73.

[11] Forrest McDonald, *We the People* (Chicago: University of Chicago Press, 1958), p. 9.

[12] Robert E. Brown, *Charles Beard and the Constitution* (Princeton University Press: Princeton, New Jersey, 1956), p. 111.

[13] *Op. cit.*, p. 123.

[14] Quoted in Charles Warren, *The Making of the Constitution* (Little, Brown & Co.: Boston, Mass., 1929), p. 26.

[15] *Ibid.*, p. 14.

manners and customs.[16] A three divisional arrangement was described by Dr. Benjamin Rush in 1786. In a letter to Dr. Richard Price, he wrote: "Some of our enlightened men who begin to despair of a more complete union of the States in Congress have secretly proposed an Eastern, Middle and Southern Confederacy, to be united by an alliance offensive and defensive. These confederacies, they say, will be united by nature, by interest, and by manners, and consequently they will be safe, agreeable, and durable. The first will include the four New England States and New York. The second will include New Jersey, Pennsylvania, Delaware and Maryland; and the last Virginia, North and South Carolina, and Georgia."[17]

It is well known that in the conflict over the legislature, there was a rough relationship between the positions taken by the state delegations and population in the respective states. From this it may be inferred that the fundamental interests of large or populous states differed from those of the small or sparsely settled states and that such a division was reflected in the behavior of the delegates in the Convention.

The significance of all these comments about "division" lies in the hypotheses they suggest. For if the grouping of state delegations in the Convention represented coincidence of interests among the states in the same grouping and disparity of interests among states in different groups, then the voting behavior of the delegates might have been expected to reflect these "natural divisions." At least that should have occurred if the delegates' votes reflected the interests or characteristics of their states. This is precisely the assumption that Beard made, though his focus was on class interest rather than state interest as such. Nevertheless one of Beard's interpreters, Forrest McDonald, merges state interest and economic class interest in a single category by classifying the states in terms of personalty or realty. This is done by determining the economic interests of a majority of each state's delegation.[18]

The important distinction between Beard's divisions and those suggested by the writers discussed above is that Beard focuses on a single dimension—the economic—while others suggest multi-dimensional differences among the states. While earlier observers did not exclude economic factors, such considerations as custom, habit, views and climate are also mentioned.

IV

In our re-examination, Beard's group approach has been generalized. For we ask, essentially, whether the delegates acting together in the Convention represented states with common characteristics. We need not suggest in advance the lines along which the states should divide in voting on Convention issues. That, after all, is the nub of our inquiry. But it is a question that cannot

---

[16] *Ibid.*, p. 30.

[17] *Ibid.*, p. 27.

[18] *Op. cit.*, pp. 94-95.

legitimately be raised until the divisions themselves are delineated. The first query, therefore, is: Were voting patterns among the state delegations sufficiently different to enable us to talk meaningfully of voting blocs as that term is understood in our literature in 1966? We propose to solve this problem through the use of factor theory as developed by Lewis L. Thurstone and others in their work on the theory of matrices.[19]

Our procedure has been to tally the votes of the state delegations on 421 roll calls in the Convention.[20] From this raw data, agreement-disagreement rates were calculated and the response pattern of each state was correlated with that of every other state. These correlations were then used to derive groupings or blocs of states using the techniques of Elementary Factor Analysis (EFA) developed by Louis McQuitty.[21] EFA produced four sub-groups, as shown in Table 1. The extraction of four factors by the Principal Factor method revealed the same general result. The four principal factors and the correlation of each state with each factor subsequent to varimax rotation are presented in Table 2. These four factors account for a little over 50 percent of the variance in the responses to 421 issues.

Inspection of Table 2 shows that the EFA sub-groups are composed of states that are fairly close to each other across all four factors. Factor one represents most of what is common to EFA group I; factor two reflects that which is most common to EFA group II; factor three and four may be similarly interpreted for EFA groups III and IV. Thus in effect, it is seen that EFA has classified those states with loadings above a certain level on a particular factor as an elementary factor group. If all loadings below point 35 are considered insignificant, then Georgia, South Carolina and North Carolina only load on factor I; New York,

---

19 The general nature of the factor problem is as follows: If N individuals are measured on N attributes or traits, one may hypothesize that these traits are (1) independent or (2) inter-dependent, i. e., overlapping. A factor theorist hypothesizes the latter, i. e., that the traits measured are composed of fewer elementary factors than the number of original measures. The problem is to discover the smaller number of elementary factors in terms of which the original measures may be comprehended. The psychologist uses various types of tests for his initial measures. Test scores are then inter-correlated and this matrix is "factored" to produce the elementary factors. This is referred to as R Technique. A related approach is known as Q Technique, a term referring to the fact that individuals are correlated with individuals with subsequent factor extraction from the resulting matrix. Whereas with R Technique, multiple tests are comprehended in terms of a smaller number of factors, Q Technique may enable us to comprehend the behavior of a number of individuals in terms of a smaller number of groups. For an introduction to factor theory, see: Andrew R. Baggaley, *Intermediate Correlational Methods* (New York: John Wiley and Sons, 1964), pp. 91-168.

20 Roll calls were tabulated by states rather than by individuals. On a given issue, each state was assigned the position taken by a majority of its delegates. This is consistent with the fact that decisions in the Convention were determined by the vote of states rather than the vote of individuals. The source of the roll call data used is E. H. Scott, Editor, *Journal of the Federal Convention kept by James Madison* (Chicago: Scott-Foresman Company, 1898).

21 See: Louis L. McQuitty, "Elementary Factor Analysis," *Psychological Reports,* Vol. 9, 1951, pp. 71-78, and S. Sidney Ulmer, "The Analysis of Behavior Patterns in the United States Supreme Court," *Journal of Politics,* Vol. 22, No. 4 (November 1960), pp. 629-653.

TABLE 1
Voting Blocs in the Constitutional Convention of 1787 Identified by
Elementary Factor Analysis

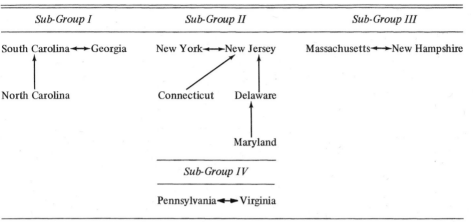

Code: ←→ Highest correlation with each other
——► State at end of arrow has highest correlation with state at point of arrow.

New Jersey and Delaware on factor II; New Hampshire and Massachusetts on factor III; and Virginia, Pennsylvania and North Carolina on factor IV. These groupings may then be equated with the four sub-groups identified by EFA by adding Maryland and Connecticut to group II, and eliminating North Carolina from factor IV. This indicates that while Maryland and Connecticut are closer to the states in group II than to the states in any other grouping, they are in fact marginal group members and might be classified as standing alone. However, EFA places each state in the grouping containing the state with which the candidate state has the highest correlation. Since Maryland correlates highest with Delaware and Connecticut with New Jersey, the two states are most appropriately grouped with Delaware, New York and New Jersey. North

TABLE 2
Varimax Factors (rotated)

States	I	II*	III	IV*
Georgia	.70	.01	.02	.08
South Carolina	.67	−.17	.23	.01
North Carolina	.48	−.08	.08	.39
New York	.30	.74	−.19	.11
New Hampshire	.00	.16	.71	−.04
Massachusetts	−.01	−.14	.65	.08
Virginia	−.06	−.27	−.26	.68
Connecticut	−.07	−.14	−.17	−.69
New Jersey	−.11	.64	−.08	−.32
Maryland	−.21	.15	−.55	−.01
Delaware	−.38	.61	.05	.08
Pennsylvania	−.57	−.19	.11	.39

* Reflected.

Carolina, on the other hand, loads positively on factors I and IV but the loading on I is .483 as compared to .392 on factor IV. Thus North Carolina is appropriately grouped with South Carolina and Georgia.

V

We may now ask how these groupings compare to those suggested by Beard and others. Table 3 summarizes the classification of the states by McDonald and by our factoring techniques. Speculation that the factor groupings constitute a further breakdown of the dichotomous categories used by McDonald is not encouraged by the considerable discrepancies between the two sets of classifications. Since our groupings are not arbitrary but are based on similarity of voting patterns, we must (1) assume that the socio-economic characteristics of the states did not constitute a dominant factor in the determination of voting alliances or (2) reject McDonald's classification of the states as inadequate. Here, we tentatively opt for the latter in order to explore the matter in somewhat greater depth.

TABLE 3
Subjective and Factor Grouping of 12 States in the 1787 Convention

McDonald Classification		Factor Groupings			
Realty States	*Personalty States*	*I*	*II*	*III*	*IV*
N. J.	Mass.	Ga.	N. Y.	N. H.	Va.
Del.	Pa.	S. C.	N. J.	Mass.	Pa.
Md.	N. C.	N. C.	Del.		
N. C.	Ga.		Md.		
S. C.	N. H.		Conn.		
	N. Y.				
	Conn.				

As for the large state-small state dichotomy, that also seems inadequate as an explanation for the overall voting alignments. For the six largest states are found in four different groups with the six smallest being located in four distinct groupings by our analysis. This is not to suggest, of course, that either of the above divisions may not have occurred on certain issues.

The north-south dichotomy suggested by Rufus King and Stephen Higginson, and the proposal of an eastern, middle and southern confederacy gets somewhat closer to the groupings we have identified. Indeed, early suggestions of differences related to geographical considerations and the grouping of states in terms of geographical contiguity were highly prophetic of the voting blocs that actually occurred in the Convention. Southern newspapers referred to groupings of New Hampshire, Massachusetts, Connecticut; New York, New Jersey, Delaware, Pennsylvania, and Maryland; and North Carolina, South Carolina, Georgia, and Virginia. The Rush letter mentions alignments of New York, New Hampshire, Connecticut, Massachusetts; New Jersey, Pennsylvania, Delaware,

Maryland; and Virginia, North Carolina, South Carolina, and Georgia. Comparison with our factor analytic groupings shows that although four blocs are identified as against three suggested by Rush and the newspapers, the newspaper writers misplaced only three and Rush only four of the twelve states grouped. When this is combined with the observation that the factor-analytically derived groupings each includes only states that are geographically contiguous to one another, one is led to suspect that the factors dividing and allying state delegations in the Convention were regional in nature regardless of what their intrinsic content might have been. While the identification of these factors is the next logical step, only a few preliminary probes are made in this paper.

It may be that the states voting together in the Convention were (1) states exhibiting common socio-economic conditions or (2) states with a common bias with respect to certain types of subject matter voted on in the Convention. The first inquiry would not rule out the chance that the personalities of the individual delegates were factors impinging upon individual voting decisions or that the values of the delegates were operative and might, on occasion, have differed from dominant or prevailing values at the local level. What we ask initially is whether certain socio-economic characteristics of the states were associated with voting alignments in the Convention.

To evaluate this inquiry, state by state demographic, economic and social data for the period 1780-1790 were compiled. This was rendered most difficult by the absence of appropriate information on most variables that might readily come to mind. Nevertheless, 17 variables on which the relative rank of the twelve states could be ascertained were identified. The variables used were:

1. percentage of population Negro
2. percentage of Negro population slaves
3. percentage of families holding slaves
4. average number of slaves per family
5. value of slaves per capita in dollars
6. value of slaves per capita for those connected with slave ownership-in dollars
7. total white population
8. number of families
9. density of population
10. number of free population in families
11. percentage increase in population 1780-1790
12. state debt per capita
13. value of corn exported 1789-1790
14. total value of exports 1790-1791
15. value of goods imported (by ad valorem duties) 1789-1790
16. number of post offices in 1790
17. number of papers and periodicals published daily and weekly

Using the ranks of the twelve states on each variable, an intercorrelation matrix was computed. The seventeen variables were then clustered by the procedures of Elementary Factor Analysis into five variable-groupings. Three of these "groupings" consisted of the single variables 9, 11 and 12. The remaining clusters contained variables 1, 2, 3, 4, 5, 6 and variables 7, 8, 10, 13, 14, 15, 16 and 17. Variable 9 can be interpreted as an "urban" factor since density of population only is involved. Variable 11 is a "growth" factor. Variable 12, on the other hand, may be read as a "distress" factor. Of our remaining clusters, that containing variables 1-6 is a "slavery" factor since all six variables involve some aspect of that institution and its importance to the states in which it prevailed. Finally, the last cluster of eight variables is a "population-trade" factor. Since the trade indices are stated in absolute magnitudes, the more populous states would be expected to rank higher on the import-export measurements. South Carolina's "trade," however, was disproportionate to its population.

If there are five distinct dimensions described by our 17 variables, we may ask how each state is characterized on each dimension. Those states similarly situated in socio-economic terms may then be compared with those states similarly situated by their voting responses on 421 Convention issues. We do not propose by such a comparison to prove cause and effect. However, if the same states tend to cluster in voting response and socio-economic characteristics, then the possibility that voting behavior in Philadelphia was influenced by such considerations can not be rejected without further research.

The 12 states may be characterized on each of the five dimensions by their rank orders. In the case of variables 9, 11 and 12, this may be done directly since only one variable is involved in each case. For the two multi-variable clusters, reference factors may be used. The reference variable is that with which the other variables in the same cluster are most highly correlated, and in that sense is representative. The reference variables for the "slavery" and "population-trade" clusters are numbers 2 and 14. We may identify the states in the first five ranks on each variable, i. e., the number of ranks equal to the number of states in our largest voting bloc. These rank orders are presented in Table 4.

TABLE 4
Order of States in Five Ranks on Five Representative Variables

	Variables				
Ranks	2	9	11	12	14
1.	Ga.	Conn.	Mass.	S. C.	Va.
2.	N. C.	Mass.	N. H.	Mass.	Pa.
3.	S. C.	Md.	Ga.	Ga.	S. C.
4.	Md.	Del.	Pa.	N. C.	N. Y.
5.	Va.	N. J.	N. C.	Conn.	Mass.

The grouping of the states on these five variables is remarkably consistent with the groupings derived from our analysis of Convention voting. The first three states on Variable 2 are those states in voting Sub-group I; the first two states on Variable 11 are those in Sub-group III; the first two on Variable 14 are the states constituting Sub-group IV; and the five states on Variable 9 include four of the five states comprising voting Sub-group II. The rank order of the states on the "distress factor" does not coincide with any particular voting bloc though this variable includes in its first five ranks the three states in Sub-group I.

We have shown, then, that the 12 states can be similarly grouped by (1) voting response and (2) socio-economic characteristics. Consequently, it would not be surprising if the voting patterns of the states in Sub-group I were heavily influenced by issues touching on slavery. Likewise we might expect that on issues relating to population and commerce, Virginia and Pennsylvania frequently voted together. The same reasoning would apply to the states high on the "urban" and "growth" factors.

Unfortunately, we cannot evaluate such hypotheses directly. The relationship of ecological data to Convention issues and voting patterns involves some guess work at best. Although such data may reflect interests and interests determine votes, establishing the appropriate nexus is never a simple matter. The problem of issue perception is always present. And Convention issues explicitly defined by debate in terms of geography, slavery, or demographic factors, were too few for statistical analysis. Thus, we shall not be able to claim that the voting differences in the Convention were a consequence of the ecological differences noted. But it is plausible to think that environmental conditions help mold opinions, that opinions shape attitudes, and that attitudes mediate behavior. These data are in conflict with the hypothesis that delegates from dissimilar states voted together out of "statesmanship" or a concern for the "national" interest, at least as far as overall voting response is concerned. The possibility that state delegations occasionally opted for the "public welfare" is not foreclosed, of course.

Our second inquiry concerns the identification of the issues on which each sub-group was unanimous. First we may ask whether the sub-groups identified by tendency of member states to agree with each other were frequently unanimous among themselves. If unanimity occurred with some frequency, as we expect, then we may wish to know the content of the issues that produced it. The assumption underlying these questions is that those issues on which all group members agreed reflect, to a greater extent than issues receiving less than a unanimous vote, the common factors making for group cohesion and solidarity.

Table 5 gives the summary data on in-group unanimity. The table shows that

TABLE 5
Unanimous Agreement within Groups Voting in the 1787
Constitutional Convention

Group	Unanimous in Majority	Dissent	Total	Participation	%
I	180	27	207	371	55.79
II	9	4	13	60	21.66
III	161	16	177	235	75.31
IV	213	50	263	404	65.09

three of the groups were unanimous from 55 to 75 per cent of the time—a remarkable degree of group solidarity. The relatively low figure for sub-group II is a consequence of two factors. First, the lingering absence of the New York representatives from the Convention limited the total opportunities for unanimous voting to 60 times out of a possible 421 instances. Secondly, group II was composed of five states—the largest group. Other studies have suggested that the larger the group, the more difficult unanimity is to attain. When New York is eliminated from consideration and the number of group members is reduced by one, we find group unanimity in 97 of 305 instances or 31.8 per cent of the time. This is still considerably less than the other three blocs. The comparable figure for New York, New Jersey and Maryland is 44.2 percent. Thus, size of group seems a more important factor than the low participation of New York. Yet since this latter figure is also less than those of the other three groupings, it would seem that group II was simply less cohesive than the other three blocs.

It remains to ascertain whether there is a relationship between (a) the voting patterns, (b) the issues and (c) composition of voting blocs. Evidence for an answer may be derived from an analysis of those issues on which each of the four groups presented a solid front. We desire to know (a) the identification of such areas and (b) the extent to which they might be used to support (or conflict with) the four groupings of states previously delineated. Three general categories catch over 70 percent of all issues covered by the instances of unanimity in group voting. Table 6 summarizes the dissent data. The motions

TABLE 6
Percentage Distribution of Unanimous Votes in Dissent

Subject	Grp I	Grp II	Grp III	Grp IV
Legislature	60	100	64	52.5
Executive	30		36	40
Judiciary	10			7.5
N	20	3	11	40

made in the Convention were distributed by subject matter approximately 65 percent to questions concerning the legislature, 29 percent to the executive establishment, and 6 percent to the judiciary. Thus the overall distribution of unanimous group votes in these three categories can be compared for issue bias. Ignoring the distribution for Group II as a result of an inadequate N, the remarkable feature of the data is the almost perfect match of the observed and expected frequencies. The same characteristic marks the majority data as compiled in Table 7. While Sub-group III is somewhat underrepresented in the judicial area and Sub-group IV is under the norm in dissent and over it in majority for legislative questions, the distribution overall suggests that common factors making for group cohesion and solidarity were not seriously affected by such a broad classification of the issue receiving the vote. This does not rule out the possibility that a finer breakdown may show some discrepancies.

TABLE 7
Percentage Distribution of Unanimous Vote in Majority

Subject	Grp I	Grp II	Grp III	Grp IV
Legislature	65	100	62	69
Executive	33		35	26
Judiciary	12		3	5
N	119	7	91	152

Looking at issue subfrequencies, we find that Sub-groups I, III, and IV often cast unanimous group ballots on motions pertaining to legislative power, executive power, representation in the legislature, and selection of the executive. Using the percentage of total motions devoted to each subject to derive quantitative expectations, the Groups may be compared for the extent of deviation and difference among them. Of all votes taken in the Convention approximately 45 percent were devoted to legislative power, and 20 percent to representation; of votes on the executive, approximately 27 percent concerned executive power and 50 percent executive selection. Thus, of unanimous group votes, each bloc should have allocated 45 percent of its legislative votes to legislative power and 20 percent to representation. Of votes on the executive, each bloc should have distributed 50 percent to selection of the executive and 27 percent to executive power. Carrying out the analysis with the binomial test,[22] we find once again that the major feature of the data is the marked closeness of the observed distributions to those expected. Of the twelve sets of relationships tested none showed a statistically significant variation from the expected frequencies. Thus our data suggest that sub-group formation in the Convention was not the result of some political theory concerning a particular branch or sub-branch of the federal system.

VI

We may conclude from this exploratory study that bloc voting existed in the Convention, that the members of the blocs were cohesive in majority and dissent, and that issue variation had little, if any, effect on this cohesion. As to explanation for the voting patterns observed, none of the earlier suggestions concerning large and small states, the economic interests of the delegates, the class interests represented by the state delegations, or the distribution of real property in the states can account entirely for the voting groups revealed. We may note, however, that while the large state-small state dichotomy does not "explain" our four groups, the two largest states—Virginia and Pennsylvania—were found to compose one of the blocs. And while the over-all economic

---

22 This test is appropriate when the populations being analyzed are conceived as consisting of only two classes. A detailed explanation may be found in Sidney Siegel, *Non Parametric Statistics for the Behavioral Sciences* (New York: McGraw-Hill Book Company, Inc., 1956), pp. 36-42.

interests of the states do not coincide with our blocs, the level of investment in the institution of slavery appears as a possible contributing factor in the grouping of particular states.

On the other hand, we have seen that the states in each bloc were geographically contiguous and exhibited certain similar characteristics. Obviously this is inadequate evidence for the view that such characteristics determined the way in which the various delegates perceived their function and consequently determined their votes. A considerably larger number of social dimensions on which the states can be measured needs to be devised. Personality and views of "good government" and the "needs of the country" were undoubtedly contributing factors. But it is important to point out that these views differed and were undoubtedly influenced by the environment from which the respective delegates sprang. There has been a tendency to err in trying to explain Convention behavior by a single factor analysis. The matter is more complex and invites additional efforts to discover quantitative indices to decision-making in the Convention.

BIBLIOGRAPHY

Bibliography

The following is a list of suggestions for further reading which was drawn from a larger, computerized reference file of works cited in the quantitative historical research of the past decade. As such, this list does not presume to be comprehensive. Rather, it is designed to help the reader extend his familiarity with the various dimensions of quantitative history introduced in this volume. To this end, the editors chose for inclusion items that, they believe, have made methodological, theoretical, or substantive contributions to quantitative history and analogous fields in the other social sciences. Several items have been included simply because they serve as bibliographic sources.

I. THEORY AND METHODS

Alker, Hayward R., Jr. *Mathematics and Politics.* New York: Macmillan Co., 1965.

Benson, Lee. *Turner and Beard: American Historical Writing Reconsidered.* Glencoe, Ill.: Free Press, 1960.

Bisco, Ralph L. "Social Science Data Archives: A Review of Developments," *The American Political Science Review,* Vol. LX (March, 1966), pp. 93-109.

Blalock, Hubert M., Jr. *Causal Inferences in Nonexperimental Research.* Chapel Hill: University of North Carolina Press, 1964.

Blalock, Hubert M. and Blalock, Ann B. (eds.). *Methodology in Social Research.* New York: McGraw-Hill Book Co., Inc., 1968.

Borko, Harold (ed.). *Computer Applications in the Behavioral Sciences.* Englewood Cliffs, N.J.: Prentice-Hall., 1962.

Cahnman, Werner J., and Boskoff, Alvin (eds.). *Sociology and History: Theory and Research.* New York: Free Press, 1964.

Challener, Richard D., and Lee, Maurice, Jr. "History and the Social Sciences: The Problem of Communications. Notes on a Conference Held by the Social Science Research Council," *The American Historical Review,* Vol. LXI (January, 1956), pp. 331-38.

Eisenstadt, A. S. "American History and Social Science," *Centennial Review,* Vol. VII (Summer, 1963), pp. 255-72.

Fruchter, Benjamin. *Introduction to Factor Analysis.* Princeton, N.J.: D. Van Nostrand Co., 1954.

Gottschalk, Louis (ed.). *Generalization in the Writing of History: A Report of the Committee on Historical Analysis of the Social Science Research Council.* Chicago: University of Chicago Press, 1963.

Grumm, John G. "The Systematic Analysis of Blocs in the Study of Voting Behavior," *The Western Political Quarterly,* Vol. XVIII (June, 1965), pp. 350-62.

Kerlinger, Fred N. *Foundations of Behavioral Research.* New York: Holt, Rinehart & Winston, Inc., 1964.

Key, V. O., Jr. *A Primer of Statistics for Political Scientists.* New York: Thomas Y. Crowell Co., 1966.

Komarovsky, Mirra (ed.). *Common Frontiers of the Social Sciences.* Glencoe, Ill.: Free Press, 1957.

Koval'chenko, I. D., and Ustinov, V. A. "La vie rurale en Russie au XIXe siècle: Les calculateurs électroniques appliqués aux études historiques," *Annales: Economies, Société Civilisations,* Vol. XX (November-December, 1965), pp. 1128-49.

Labovitz, Sanford. "Some Observations on Measurement and Statistics," *Social Forces,* Vol. XLVI (December, 1967), pp. 151-60.

Lazarsfeld, Paul F. (ed.). *Mathematical Thinking in the Social Sciences.* Glencoe, Ill.: Free Press, 1954.

Lazarsfeld, Paul F., and Rosenberg, Morris (eds.). *The Language of Social Research: A Reader in the Methodology of Social Research.* Glencoe, Ill.: Free Press, 1955.

Lipset, Seymour Martin, and Hofstadter, Richard (eds.). *Sociology and History: Methods.* New York: Basic Books, Inc., 1968.

McGrew, R. E. "History and the Social Sciences," *The Antioch Review,* Vol. XVIII (Fall, 1958), pp. 276-89.

MacRae, Duncan, Jr. "A Method for Identifying Issues and Factions from Legislative Votes," *The American Political Science Review,* Vol. LIX (December, 1965), pp. 909-26.

Merritt, Richard L. *Symbols of American Community, 1735-1775.* New Haven, Conn.: Yale University Press, 1966.

Merritt, Richard L., and Rokkan, Stein (eds.). *Comparing Nations: The Use of Quantitative Data in Cross-National Research.* New Haven, Conn.: Yale University Press, 1966.

Robinson, W. S. "Ecological Correlations and the Behavior of Individuals," *American Sociological Review,* Vol. XV (June, 1950), pp. 351-57.

Rummel, R. J. "Understanding Factor Analysis," *Journal of Conflict Resolution,* Vol. XI (December, 1967), pp. 455-77.

Siegel, Sidney. *Nonparametric Statistics for the Behavioral Sciences.* New York: McGraw-Hill Book Co., Inc., 1956.

_____. "Problems in Analysis of Data.' *American Journal of Mental Deficiency,* Vol. LXIV (September, 1959), pp. 397-409.

Thrupp, Sylvia L. "Comparative Studies in Society and History: A Working Alliance Among Specialists," *International Social Science Journal,* Vol. XVII (1965), pp. 644-54.

Woolf, Harry (ed.). *Quantification: A History of the Meaning of Measurement in the Natural and Social Sciences.* Indianapolis: Bobbs-Merrill Co., Inc., 1961.

II. BUREAUCRATIC HISTORY AND ELITES

Adams, Stuart. "Origins of American Occupational Elites, 1900-1955," *The American Journal of Sociology,* Vol. LXIII (January, 1957), pp. 360-68.

Armstrong, John A. *The Soviet Bureaucratic Elite: A Case Study of the Ukrainian Apparatus.* New York: Frederick A. Praeger, Inc., 1959.

Aron, Raymond. "Social Structure and the Ruling Class," *The British Journal of Sociology,* Vol. I (March and June, 1950), pp. 1-16 and 126-43.

Beck, Carl, and McKechnie, John T. (comps.). *Political Elites: A Select Computerized Bibliography.* Cambridge, Mass.: M.I.T. Press, 1968.

Beck, Carl, and Malloy, James M. *Political Elites: A Mode of Analysis.* Pittsburgh: Archive on Political Elites in Eastern Europe, University of Pittsburgh, n.d.

Benda, Henry J. "Political Elites in Colonial Southeast Asia: An Historical Analysis," *Comparative Studies in Society and History,* Vol. XII (April, 1965), pp. 233-51.

Blau, Peter M. "Formal Organizations: Dimensions of Analysis," *The American Journal of Sociology,* Vol. LXIII (July, 1957), pp. 58-69.

Blau, Peter M., and Scott, W. Richard. *Formal Organizations: A Comparative Approach.* San Francisco: Chandler Publishing Co., 1962.

Edinger, Lewis J., and Searing, Donald D. "Social Background in Elite Analysis: A Methodological Inquiry," *The American Political Science Review,* Vol. LXI (June, 1967), pp. 428-45.

Etzioni, Amitai. *A Comparative Analysis of Complex Organizations: On Power, Involvement and Their Correlates.* New York: Free Press, 1961.

LaPalombara, Joseph (ed.). *Bureaucracy and Political Development.* Princeton, N.J.: Princeton University Press, 1963.

Lasswell, Harold D., and Lerner, Daniel (eds.). *World Revolutionary Elites: Studies in Coercive Ideological Movements.* Cambridge, Mass.: M.I.T. Press, 1965.

Lerner, Daniel; Lasswell, Harold; and Rothwell, C. Easton. *The Comparative Study of Elites: An Introduction and Bibliography.* Stanford, Calif.: Stanford University Press, 1952.

March, James G. (ed.). *Handbook of Organizations.* Chicago: Rand McNally & Co., 1965.

March, James G., and Simon, Herbert A. *Organizations.* New York: John Wiley & Sons, Inc., 1958.

Marsh, Robert M. *The Mandarins: The Circulation of Elites in China, 1600-1900.* Glencoe, Ill.: Free Press, 1961.

Silberman, Bernard S. "Criteria for Recruitment and Success in the Japanese Bureaucracy, 1868-1900: 'Traditional' and 'Modern' Criteria in Bureacratic Development," *Economic Development and Cultural Change,* Vol. XIV (January, 1966), pp. 158-73.

_____. *Ministers of Modernization: Elite Mobility in the Meiji Restoration, 1868-1873.* Tucson: University of Arizona Press, 1964.

Ulmer, S. Sidney "The Analysis of Behavior Patterns on the United States Supreme Court," *The Journal of Politics,* Vol. XXII (November, 1960), pp. 629-53.

III. SOCIAL AND DEMOGRAPHIC HISTORY

Bendix, Reinhard, and Lipset, Seymour Martin (eds.). *Class, Status and Power: Social Stratification in Comparative Perspective.* 2nd ed. New York: Free Press, 1966.
Bogue, Allan G. *From Prairie to Corn Belt: Farming on the Illinois and Iowa Prairies in the Nineteenth Century.* Chicago: University of Chicago Press, 1963.
Briggs, Asa. "Social Structure and Politics in Birmingham and Lyons (1825-1848)," *The British Journal of Sociology,* Vol. I (March, 1950), pp. 67-80.
Cahnman, Werner J. "The Historical Sociology of Cities: A Critical Review," *Social Forces,* Vol. XLV (December, 1966), pp. 155-61.
Curti, Merle E. *The Making of an American Community: A Case Study of Democracy in a Frontier County.* Stanford, Calif.: Stanford University Press, 1959.
Demos, John. "Notes on Life in Plymouth Colony," *William and Mary Quarterly,* Vol. XXII (April, 1965), pp. 264-86.
Donald, David H. *The Politics of Reconstruction, 1863-1867.* Baton Rouge: Louisiana State University Press, 1965.
Glass, D. V., and Eversley, D. E. C. (eds.). *Population in History: Essays in Historical Demography.* Chicago: Aldine Publishing Co., 1965.
Greenstein, Fred I. "New Light on Changing American Values: A Forgotten Body of Survey Data," *Social Forces,* Vol. XLII (May, 1964), pp. 441-50.
Greven, Philip J. "Historical Demography and Colonial America," *William and Mary Quarterly,* Vol. XXIV (July, 1967), pp. 438-54.
Laslett, Peter. "The History of Population and Social Structure," *International Social Science Journal,* Vol. XVII (1965), pp. 582-93.
_____. *The World We Have Lost.* New York: Charles Scribner's Sons, 1965.
McGrew, Roderick E. *Russia and the Cholera, 1823-1832.* Madison: University of Wisconsin Press, 1965.
Rudé, George. *The Crowd in History: A Study of Popular Disturbances in France and England, 1730-1848.* New York: John Wiley & Sons, Inc., 1964.
Stone, Lawrence. *The Crisis of the Aristocracy, 1558-1641.* Oxford: Clarendon Press, 1965.
Thernstrom, Stephan. *Poverty and Progress: Social Mobility in a Nineteenth Century City.* Cambridge, Mass.: Harvard University Press, 1964.
Thompson, E. P. *The Making of the English Working Class.* New York: Vintage Books, 1966.
Tilly, Charles. *The Vendée.* Cambridge, Mass.: Harvard University Press, 1964.
Warner, Sam Bass. *Streetcar Suburbs: The Process of Growth in Boston, 1870-1900.* Cambridge, Mass.: Harvard University Press, 1962.
Wrigley, E. A. (ed.). *An Introduction to English Historical Demography from the Sixteenth to the Nineteenth Century.* New York: Basic Books, Inc., 1966.

Wylie, Lawrence. *Village in the Vaucluse.* Cambridge, Mass.: Harvard University Press, 1957.

_____ (ed.). *Chanzeaux, a Village in Anjou.* Cambridge, Mass.: Harvard University Press, 1966.

Young, James Sterling. *The Washington Community, 1800-1828.* New York: Columbia University Press, 1966.

IV. ECONOMIC AND ECONOMETRIC HISTORY

Bailyn, Bernard, and Bailyn, Lotte. *Massachusetts Shipping, 1697-1714: A Statistical Study.* Cambridge, Mass.: Harvard University Press, 1959.

Basman, R. L. "The Role of the Economic Historian in Predictive Testing of Proffered 'Economic Law,' " *Explorations in Entrepreneurial History,* Vol. II, 2nd Series (Spring-Summer, 1965), pp. 159-86.

Bogue, Allan G., and Bogue, Margaret Beattie. " 'Profits' and the Frontier Land Speculator," *The Journal of Economic History,* Vol. XVII (March, 1957), pp. 1-24.

Conrad, Alfred H., and Meyer, John R. *The Economics of Slavery and Other Studies in Econometric History.* Chicago: Aldine Publishing Co., 1964.

Davis, Lance E. "The New England Textile Mills and the Capital Markets: A Study of Industrial Borrowing, 1840-1860," *The Journal of Economic History,* Vol. XX (March, 1960), pp. 1-30.

Davis, Lance E.; Hughes, Jonathan R. T.; and Reiter, Stanley. "Aspects of Quantitative Research in Economic History," *The Journal of Economic History,* Vol. XX (December, 1960), pp. 539-47.

Engerman, Stanley L. "The Effects of Slavery Upon the Southern Economy: A Review of the Recent Debate," *Explorations in Entrepreneurial History,* Vol. IV, 2nd Series (Winter, 1967), pp. 71-97.

Fogel, Robert W. "A Quantitative Approach to the Study of Railroads in American Economic Growth: A Report of Some Preliminary Findings," *The Journal of Economic History,* Vol. XXII (June, 1962), pp. 163-97.

_____. "Reappraisals in American Economic History—Discussion," *American Economic Review,* Vol. LIV (May, 1964), pp. 377-89.

Goodrich, Carter. "Economic History: One Field or Two?" *The Journal of Economic History,* Vol. XX (December, 1960), pp. 531-38.

Hughes, J. R. T. "Fact and Theory in Economic History," *Explorations in Entrepreneurial History,* Vol. III, 2nd Series (Winter, 1966), pp. 75-100.

Murphy, George G. S. "The 'New' History," *Explorations in Entrepreneurial History,* Vol. II, 2nd Series (Winter, 1965), pp. 132-46.

V. LEGISLATIVE, ELECTORAL, AND PUBLIC OPINION ANALYSIS

Anderson, Lee F.; Watts, Meredith W.; and Wilcox, Allen R. *Legislative Roll-Call Analysis.* Evanston, Ill.: Northwestern University Press, 1966.

Banks, Arthur S., and Textor, Robert B. *A Cross-Polity Survey.* Cambridge, Mass.: M.I.T. Press, 1963.

Belknap, George M. "A Method for Analyzing Legislative Behavior," *Midwest Journal of Political Science,* Vol. II (November, 1958), pp. 377-402.

Benson, Lee. *The Concept of Jacksonian Democracy: New York as a Test Case.* Princeton, N.J.: Princeton University Press, 1961.

Bower, Robert T. "Opinion Research and Historical Interpretation of Elections," *The Public Opinion Quarterly,* Vol. XII (Fall, 1948), pp. 455-64.

Campbell, Angus; Converse, Philip E.; Miller, Warren E.; and Stokes, Donald E. (eds.). *Elections and the Political Order.* New York: John Wiley & Sons, Inc., 1967.

Dreyer, Edward C., and Rosenbaum, Walter A. (eds.). *Political Opinion and Electoral Behavior: Essays and Studies.* Belmont, Calif.: Wadsworth Publishing Co., Inc., 1966.

Farris, Charles D. "A Method for Determining Ideological Groupings in the Congress," *The Journal of Politics,* Vol. XX (May, 1958), pp. 308-38.

Flinn, Thomas A. "Party Responsibility in the States: Some Causal Factors," *The American Political Science Review,* Vol. LVIII (March, 1964), pp. 60-71.

Greenstein, Fred I., and Jackson, Elton F. "A Second Look at the Validity of Roll-Call Analysis," *Midwest Journal of Political Science,* Vol. VII (May, 1963), pp. 156-66.

Grumm, John G. "A Factor Analysis of Legislative Behavior," *Midwest Journal of Political Science,* Vol. VII (November, 1963), pp. 336-56.

_____. "The Means of Measuring Conflict and Cohesion in the Legislature," *The Southwestern Social Science Quarterly,* Vol. XLIV (March, 1964), pp. 377-88.

Harris, Louis. "Some Observations on Election Behavior Research," *The Public Opinion Quarterly,* Vol. XX (Summer, 1956), pp. 379-91.

Hays, Samuel P. "The Politics of Reform in Municipal Government in the Progressive Era," *Pacific Northwest Quarterly,* Vol. LXV (October, 1964), pp. 157-69.

Hyman, Herbert H. *Political Socialization: A Study in the Psychology of Political Behavior.* Glencoe, Ill.: Free Press, 1959.

Key, V. O., Jr. "Partisanship and County Office: The Case of Ohio," *The American Political Science Review,* Vol. XLVII (June, 1953), pp. 525-32.

Lazarsfeld, Paul F. "Public Opinion and the Classical Tradition," *The Public Opinion Quarterly,* Vol. XXI (Spring, 1957), pp. 39-53.

Lipset, Seymour Martin, and Rokkan, Stein (eds.). *Party Systems and Voter Alignments: Cross-National Perspectives.* New York: Free Press, 1967.

MacRae, Duncan, Jr. *Dimensions of Congressional Voting: A Statistical Study of the House of Representatives in the Eighty-first Congress.* Berkeley: University of California Press, 1958.

_____. *Parliament, Parties, and Society in France, 1946-1958.* New York: St. Martin's Press, Inc., 1967.

_____. "The Role of the State Legislator in Massachusetts," *American Sociological Review,* Vol. XIX (April, 1954), pp. 185-94.

MacRae, Duncan, Jr., and Meldrum, James A. "Critical Elections in Illinois, 1888-1958," *The American Political Science Review,* Vol. LIV (September, 1960), pp. 669-83.

Mayhew, David R. *Party Loyalty Among Congressmen: The Difference Between Democrats and Republicans, 1947-1962.* Cambridge, Mass.: Harvard University Press, 1966.

Meller, Norman. "Legislative Behavior Research," *The Western Political Quarterly,* Vol. XIII (March, 1960), pp. 131-53.

_____. " 'Legislative Behavior Research' Revisited: A Review of Five Years' Publications," *The Western Political Quarterly,* Vol. XVIII (December, 1965), pp. 776-93.

Merritt, Richard L. "Public Opinion in Colonial America: Content-Analyzing the Colonial Press," *The Public Opinion Quarterly,* Vol. XXVII (Fall, 1963), pp. 356-76.

Ranney, Austin (ed.). *Essays on the Behavioral Study of Politics.* Urbana: University of Illinois Press, 1962.

Rice, Stuart A. *Quantitative Methods in Politics.* New York: Alfred A. Knopf, Inc., 1928.

Rogin, Michael P. *The Intellectuals and McCarthy: The Radical Spectre.* Cambridge, Mass.: M.I.T. Press, 1967.

Truman, David B. "The State Delegations and the Structure of Party Voting in the United States House of Representatives," *The American Political Science Review,* Vol. L (December, 1956), pp. 1023-45.

Turner, Julius. *Party and Constituency: Pressures on Congress.* Baltimore: The Johns Hopkins Press, 1951.

Wahlke, John C., and Eulau, Heinz. *Legislative Behavior: A Reader in Theory and Research.* Glencoe, Ill.: Free Press, 1959.

Wahlke, John C.; Eulau, Heinz; Buchanan, William; and Ferguson, Leroy C. *The Legislative System: Explorations in Legislative Behavior.* New York: John Wiley & Sons, Inc., 1962.

Index

Index

A

Aguet, Jean-Pierre, 218, 219, 222
Alexander, Thomas B., 7, 112
Allen, Howard W., 115, 370; *see also* Clubb, Jerome M.
American Historical Association, 110, 113, 115, 116, 117, 120
Andrews, C. M., 338
Arendt, Hannah, 119
Aries, Philippe, 310
Arkwright, Sir Richard, 172
Armsen, P., 85
Arnold, Matthew, 112
Aronson, Sidney, 100
Aulard, Alphonse, 193
Aydelotte, William O., 120, 125, 369

B

Bagehot, Walter, 175
Baguenier-Desormaux, H., 193
Bailyn, Bernard, 7
Bailyn, Lotte, 7
Bancroft, George, 336, 372
Barzun, Jacques, 179n.
Basic-nonbasic analysis
  definition of, 275
  and Domesday Book, 275-92
Bateson, Gregory, 206
Bauer, Wilhelm, 64
Beard, Charles, 7, 11, 373, 459, 461, 464
Beauchamp, Alphonse, 191
Beck, Carl, 128
Beer, George L., 336
Bellah, Robert N., 209
Belper, Baron, 173
Bendix, R., 105
Benson, Lee, vii, 4, 11, 112, 113, 115, 119, 126, 397, 458, 460
Bentham, Jeremy, 10
Berelson, Bernard, 30, 31
Bernouilli, Jacques, 73
Bloch, Marc, 199
Bloc analysis, 457
Blum, Leon, 308
Bogue, Allen G., 7
Bois, Paul, 183, 195, 198, 199, 200, 203
Bourniseaux, P. V. J., 191
Bowman, John, 330
Bridenbaugh, Carl, ix

Brinton, Crane, 6, 10, 184
de Broglie, Duc Albert, 129
Brousse, Paul, 308
Brown, Robert E., 460
Bryce, James, 56, 57, 59, 62, 64
Buckle, Henry Thomas, vi, 126
Burke, John, 12
Burnham, Walter, 114, 115

C

Chamber of Deputies (French, 1846-48), 129
  computer print-out of, 140-47
  quantitative analysis of, 130-39
Chambers, William N., 114
Chassin, C. L., 189
Chevalier, Louis, 273, 313
Childs, Harwood L., 24, 42
Chi-square, 143-44
Choudieu, Pierre, 191
Clark, G. Kitson, 6, 416
Cliometrics, 317-19; *see also* Econometric history
Clubb, Jerome M., 370; *see also* Allen, Howard W.
Cobb, Richard, 207
Cobban, Alfred, 208
Cochran, Thomas C., 117, 122
Coefficient of determination, 364-66
Collingwood, R. G. 185
Colquhoun, Patrick, 106
Computer, viii, 81, 394, 420
  analysis, 138f.
  print-out
    example of, 88-97
    2x2 table, 85
  programming, 85-86
  syntax, 85-86
Conrad, Alfred H., 13, 320, 323, 324, 325, 334
Constitutional Convention (American)
  economic interpretation, 458-60
  elementary factor analysis (EFA), 462-70
  natural divisions, 460-61
  sub-group analysis, 457, 464-70
Corn Laws (British), 168, 415, 419, 422, 424, 425, 427, 428, 436, 439
Correlation, coefficient of, 364-65, 394-95, 408f.

Cretineau-Joly, J., 189, 191
Curti, Margaret, 118
Curti, Merle, 116-17

D

Dahl, Robert A., 114, 116
Daniels, George, 112
Dauer, Manning J., 114
David, Paul, 327, 331
Davis, Lance E., 317, 330
Deane, Phyllis, 330
Delumeau, Jean, 7
Demographic data, types of, 295
Demographic procedures
  age structure, 300-305, 310-11
  birth rate, 310-11
  family structure
    age of first marriage, 305
    age of wives, 299
    children per family, 297-98
    interval between marriage and child
      birth, 306-07
    servants per family, 298
    size of households, 296-97, 302-3
  population migration, 312-13
Demography, 10-12, 273-74, 309
Deniau, Abbé, 187
DePillis, Mario S., 179n., 180n.
Desai, Meghnad, 318
Dickerson, Oliver, 336
Disraeli, Benjamin, 168, 176, 177
Domesday Book of England, 275-92; *see
  also* Basic-nonbasic analysis
Dubreuil, Leon, 186, 192, 194, 195, 196
Duverger, Maurice, 119

E

Earl of Derby, 168
Earl of Ellesmere, 177
Easterlin, Richard, 325
Easton, David, 113
Econometric history (cliometrics), 317-19,
  320ff.
Electoral behavior, 369-71
Elites, 127-28
Elton, G. R., v-vi
Engerman, Stanley, 325
Euripides, 356

F

Factor analysis, 396-97, 462-70
Fisher, R. A., 85
Fishlow, Albert, 329, 330, 334
Fogel, Robert W., 7, 20, 116
Ford Foundation, 118
Furst Survey Research Center, 404

G

Gabory, Emile, 184, 186, 192, 195, 197
Gallman, Robert, 330
Gallois, Jean Antoine, 188
Gates, Paul W., 117
Genrō, the, 148-63
  composition of, 149-50
  educational characteristics of, 155-57
  structural characteristics of, 150
Gensonne, Armand, 188
Georve V (England), 165
Gerbner, George, 39
Gerschenkron, Alexander, 321
Gesell, Arnold L., 81
Gini index, 358-59, 364-67
Glass, David V., 274
Godechot, Jacques, 184, 194, 199
Goldstein, Sidney, 106
de la Gorce, Pierre, 192, 194
Gosnell, Harold F., 392
Gottschalk, Louis, x
Greer, Donald, 6, 10-11, 201-2
Greven, Philip J., Jr., 294
Greville, Charles, 177
Grumm, John, 457
Guesde, Jules, 308
Guizot, Francois P. G., 135, 136, 137, 138,
  139
Guttman, Louis (scalogram analysis), 16; *see
  also* Guttman scale
Guttman scale (scalogram analysis), 112,
  417-21, 430

H

Hammond, John L. and Barbara, 102
Handlin, Oscar, 117
Hansard division lists, 415-17
Harper, Lawrence, 336
de Hauranne, Duvergier, 139
Hays, Samuel P., 112, 115, 120, 121, 124
Helbich, Wolfgang J., 29, 39, 40
Herodotus, 273
Hexter, J. H., 19
Higginson, Stephen, 460, 464
Higham, John, 125
Higonett, Trevor B. (with Higonnet, Patrick
  L. R.), 128
Hofstadter, Richard, 119, 125, 180n.
Honigman, John J., 34
House of Commons (British), 6, 10, 16,
  164, 176, 415-42
  and Roebuck motion, 423, 427, 438
House of Lords (British), 164-78
Hughes, Jonathan R. T., 317
Hume, David, 13
Hyman, Herbert, 30, 31, 34, 49

I

Institute for Advanced Study in the Behavioral Sciences, 116, 118
Inter-University Consortium for Political Research, 110, 114, 115
Isard, Walter, 119

J

Jacksonian democracy
  influence of West on, 373-74
  Jackson's personal popularity, 381
  quantitative dimensions of, 373-80
  suffrage qualifications, 380
Janowitz, Morris, 30, 31
Jaurès, Jean, 186, 308

K

Kelvin, Lord, 11
Kendrick, John, 334
Kerr, William T., Jr., 112
Key, V. O., 42, 114, 119, 387, 392, 396
  and theory of critical election, 371, 385-86, 390
Kindahl, James K., 331
King, Rufus, 460, 464
Kling, Merle, 357, 358, 365
Knight, Frank, 11
Kohlmeier, Albert L., 7
Komarovsky, Mirra, 319
Krieger, Leonard, vii
Kuznets, Simon, 330

L

Laboulaye, E. René, 129
Labrousse, Ernest, 179n.
Lampard, Eric E., 209
Lancaster, James L., 29, 36, 39, 40
Landes, David, 273-74
Larevelliere-Lepeaux, 193
Lasswell, Harold D., 128
Lazarsfeld, Paul, ix, 31, 119, 120, 370
Lebergott, Stanley, 330
Lee, Eugene C., 387
Lefebvre, Georges, 186, 191
Legislative behavior, 369-71
Lerner, Daniel, 26, 128
Libby, Orin G., 109
Lijphart, Arend, 457
Lippmann, Walter, 57
Lipset, Seymour M., 105, 361, 367
London Times, 173, 176
Louis-Philippe and the July Monarchy (France), 129-47; *see also* Chamber of Deputies
Lowell, Lawrence, 57
Lowi, Theodore J., 114
Lubell, Samuel, 119
  and election of 1928, 387-88

Lynd, Robert S. and Helen M., 100, 101, 102, 103, 104

M

MacAvoy, Paul, 331
McCormick, Richard P., 6, 14, 111, 112
McDonald, Forrest, 460, 461, 464
McLuhan, Marshall, 45
McQuitty, Louis, 462
MacRae, Duncan, 114, 392, 397, 431
Madison, James, 458
Malin, James C., 117
Malloy, James M., 128
Manchester Examiner, 173
Mantoux, Paul, 325
Map, Walter, 284
Marczewski, Jean, 330
Marx, Karl, 132, 138, 357
Mathematics Social Science Board, 116
Mathiez, Albert, 184
Maxwell, Kenneth R., 29, 39, 40, 42
May, Ernest, 42, 43, 45
Meiji restoration (Japan), 149, 153, 159, 160, 163, 215
Meldrum, James A., 392, 397
Merriam, Charles, 116, 117
Merton, Robert, 40, 119
Meusel, Alfred, 181
Meyer, John R., 14, 320, 323, 324, 334
Michelet, Jules, 186
Michels, Robert, 119
Mill, John Stuart, 176
Miller, S. M., 99
Miller, Warren, 115
Mink, Louis, vi
Momoro, A. F., 185
Mosca, Gaetano, 127
Muret, Theodore, 188, 193
Murphy, George G. S., 321
Mussolini, 309

N

Nagel, Ernest, 27, 28, 37
Nakano Takashi, 210, 212
Namier, Lewis B., 120
National Science Foundation, 115, 123
Navigation Acts (British), 336-41
  and colonial exports, 342-48; *see also* colonial foreign commerce
  and colonial foreign commerce, 350-53; *see also* colonial exports
  and colonial imports, 348-50
  and colonial shipping earnings, 353-55
Nettels, Curtis P., 336
"New" social history, 179-80
Niebuhr, Barthold, 28
North, Douglass, 317, 321, 326

O

Orwell, George, 74
Owsley, Frank L., 7, 11

P

Paret, Peter, 185
Pareto, Vilfredo, 127
Parker, William, 321, 326
Parliament Act of 1911 (British), 178
Parsons, Stanley, 112
Peel, Sir Robert, 167, 168, 169, 176, 415
Perroux, François, 330
Phelps Brown Index, 246
Plato, 357
Pool, Ithiel de So a (with Abelson, Robert), 128
Port, Celestin, 183, 184, 189, 192, 193, 194, 195, 197
Pouthas, Charles, 129, 312
Public opinion
  choosing best indicator for study of, 56-63
  definition of, 23-26, 64, 65
  distribution of, 33-37
  formation of, 37-42
  historical research techniques, 67-70
    area sampling, 73, 75, 76, 77
    depth interviewing, 73
    multiple elements, 72
    purposive sampling, 73-78
    randomization, 73
    specific population sampling, 74
    stratified sampling, 73
  historical study of, 26
  historical survey
    execution of, 71-80
    steps of, 70-71
  impact on government decisions, 42-47
  narrative framework for, 50-52
  operations to measure distribution of, 52-53
  research strategy for historical analysis of, 47-48
  sampling, definition of, 74
  scientific historical study of, 27-30
  simple survey, steps of, 73-74
  social scientists and historical study of, 30-32
  tentative system for historical analysis of, 48-52
  types of indicators, 52-55

Q

Quantification (quantitative analysis), v-xi
  definition of, 4
  limitations of, 5, 15, 17, 18, 20-22
  objections to, 8ff.
    nature of sources, 8-15

Quantification (quantitative analysis)–*Cont.*
  objections to, nature of sources
    qualitative element, 13-14
    taxonomy, 9-12
    unproven conclusions, 15-18
    usefulness of, 18-21
    value of results, 8-9
      interpretation of, 16-17
  value of, 4, 5, 6, 7, 18, 20-22, 130
    application to qualitative problems, 12, 13, 14
    generalization, 4-5, 7-8, 18-19

R

Ranke, Leopold von, 28
Ranney, Austin, 123
Real types
  and computer analysis, 82
  data array, 82
    quartile values, 86
  variables, 82-84
    comparison, 85
    matching, 85
  definition of, 81
  general conclusions, 98
  generation of, 87
  problems of, 98
  selection of, 87, 98
Redlich, Fritz, 321, 333
Reform Act of 1867 (British), 175, 176
Reinhard, Marcel, 208, 311
Reiter, Stanley, 317
Rice, Stuart (Rice Indexing), 119, 370, 444
Richard, Joseph, 191
Riesman, David, 119
Riker, William, 115
Roberts, David, 435
Robinson, James H., vi
Robinson, W. S., 123
du Rocher, Mercier, 189
Rogoff, Natalie, 100, 103
Roper Public Opinion Research Center, 399, 403
Rothwell, C. Easton, 128
Rudè, Georges, 207
Rummel, Rudolph, 361
Russell, J. C., 274
Russell, Lord John, 168
Russett, Bruce M., 319

S

Saigo Takamori, 152
Saionji, Prince, 150
Salisbury ministry (Britain, 1885-86), 172
Satsuma Rebellion of 1877, 152
Savary, J. J. M., 184
Saveth, Edward N., 116

Schafer, Joseph, 112
Schlesinger, Arthur M., Jr., v, 7, 369, 373
Schmidhaeuser, John, 114
Sellers, Charles, 115
Senate (United States, 1909-15)
  party cohesion index, 445f.
    definition of, 444
  party unity analysis, 445f.
    definition of, 444
Shils, Edward, 441
Shover, John L., 371, 385-98
de la Sicotière, L., 195
Siegfried, André, 198, 199
Silberman, Bernard S., 128
Silbey, Joel, 112
Silva, Ruth C., 114
Simulmatics Corporation, The, 402-5
  and data processing, 400-401
    computer simulations, 406-14
    purposes of method, 402
    use of the system, 405-6
  history of, 402-5
Smiles, Samuel, 165
Smith, Robert J., 180
Smyth, Newman, 101, 102
Soboul, Albert, 207
Social mobility
  and blocked-mobility hypothesis, 100, 101, 102, 103, 104
  categories
    hierarchy of income, 241-42
    hierarchy of power, 242-43
    hierarchy of status, 239-43
  causes
    destabilizing factors, 256-58
    factors particular to early modern England, 253-57
    stabilizing factors, 261-62
    universal factors, 253-54
  consequences, 262-71
  data
    approach to, 105-8
    location of, 105-6
  models
    San Gimignano, 238-39
    stepped pyramid, 238
    United Nations, 238-39
  patterns
    changes in group profiles, 242-47
    changes in individual mobility, 247-53
  and "situs" concept, 104-5
  and status degradation, 102-4
Social Science Research Council (SSRC), 115, 116, 118, 119
Spengler, Oswald, vi
Spiethoff, Arthur, 81
Stanford Institute, 118,119
Statistical measures
  Gini index of concentration, 359-67
  Lorenz curve, 359-60

Statistics
  descriptive, 7
  inference, 7
  nature of, 15, 17
Stearns, Peter N., 180
Stone, J. R. N., 330
Stone, Lawrence, 6, 7, 180
Strike activity (France)
  factors operating against, 227-35
  frequency of, 218-19
  goals of, 220-24
  organization of, 219-20, 224-26
Strutt, Edward, 172
Survey Research Center of the University of Michigan, 115

T

Taeuber, Irene B., 209
Taine, Hippolyte, 186
Tawney, R. H., 108
Temin, Peter, 327
Test of significance, 85, 144
Thernstrom, Stephan, 7
Thiers, Adolphe, 134
Thompson, James D., 150
Thrupp, Sylvia L., 7
Thucydides, 32, 33, 35
Thurstone, Lewis L., 462
Tilly, Charles, 7, 180
de Tocqueville, Alexis, 132, 139, 198, 356, 357, 367
Tokugawa period (Japan), 153, 209-16
Toynbee, Arnold, vi, 325
Tuden, Arthur, 150
Turner, Frederick J., 109, 117

U

United Nations, 82

V

Vendée uprising
  analysis of, 196-208
  and French historians, 181-95
Verification, 3-6, 18-20
Victoria, Queen (England), 165
de Villeneuve-Bargemont, Jean P., 132

W

Ware, Norman 102
Warner, Lloyd W., 100, 101, 102
Warner, Sam B., Jr., 7, 11
Weber, Max, 119
Whitney, William, 331
Williamson, Jeffrey, 330

Y

Yamagata Aritomo, 162
Yasukiehi Yasuba, 324
Yoloyama Sadao, 212
Young, G. M., 436

Z

Zevin, Robert B., 327

This book has been set in 10 point Press Roman, leaded 1 and 2 points. Part numbers and titles and reading numbers and titles are 18 point Univers Medium. The size of the type page is 27 by 46½ picas.